FROM AUGUSTUS
TO NERO: THE
FIRST DYNASTY
OF IMPERIAL
ROME

FROM AUGUSTUS
TO NERO: THE
FIRST DYNASTY
OF IMPERIAL
ROME

Edited by
Ronald Mellor

Michigan State University Press
East Lansing, Michigan
1990

FROM AUGUSTUS TO NERO: THE FIRST DYNASTY OF IMPERIAL ROME is a project of
Contemporary Learning Systems of East Lansing, Inc.

Project Director
George A. Colburn, Ph.D.

Supervisory Editor
Jane L. Scheiber

Research Associate
Ralph Gallucci
Lecturer in Classics, Loyola Marymount University

Chief Academic Advisor
D. Brendan Nagle
Associate Professor of History, University of Southern California

Academic Advisory Board

Arther Ferrill
Professor of History
University of Washington

Richard Saller
Associate Professor of History and Classics
University of Chicago

Erich S. Gruen
Gladys Rehard Wood Professor
of History and Classics
University of California at Berkeley

Jo-Ann Shelton
Professor of Classics
University of California at Santa Barbara

Judith P. Hallett
Associate Professor of Classics
University of Maryland

Designer
Tom Gould

Printed in the United States of America.

Michigan State University Press

East Lansing, Michigan 48823-5202

All Michigan State University Press books are produced on paper which meets the requirements of the American National Standard for Information Sciences—Permanence of Paper for printed materials. ANSI 239.48-1984

Library of Congress Cataloging-in-Publication Data
From Augustus to Nero.
    A project of Contemporary Learning Systems of East Lansing, Inc.—t.p. verso. Bibliography: p.383
1. Rome—History—The five Julii, 30 B.C.–A.D. 68.   2. Corruption (in politics)—Rome.
I. Mellor, Ronald. II. Contemporary Learning Systems.
DG281.F76 1989 937′.07 88-42899
ISBN 0-87013-263-6

Contents

Captions

Frontispiece

This idealized statue of a victorious Augustus was found at the Villa of Primaporta thought to belong to his wife Livia. Scenes on the elaborate breastplate depict the Parthians' surrender of captured Roman standards to the emperor's representative, Tiberius, and the Cupid alludes to the divine descent of the Julian family from the goddess Venus. Augustus is barefoot like Greek heroes and gods, and the statue probably dates from after his death in A.D. 14.

   I   Julius Caesar is depicted on a silver denarius minted at Rome early in 44 B.C., the year in which he was assassinated on the Ides (15) of March.

   II A young Octavian is portrayed on a silver denarius issued in 29-27 B.C. after his defeat of Marc Antony, but before he took the title of "Augustus."

   III An idealized portrait of Augustus appears on a large bronze coin issued at Antioch in Syria in 5/4 B.C. The legend KAI AP is Greek for Caesar.

   IV A triumphal arch surmounted by a bronze four-horse chariot containing Octavian appears on the reverse of a silver denarius issued by a south Italian mint about 29-27 B.C. It probably depicts the arch erected in the Roman Forum in 30 B.C. to commemorate Octavian's victory over Marc Antony.

   V   Livia, the wife of Augustus, is depicted on a brass coin issued at Rome by her son Tiberius in A.D. 22-23. She was ill at the time and the legend SALUS AUGUSTA links her recovery to the well-being of the state.

   VI Tiberius is portrayed on a large brass coin issued at Rome. The legend CAESAR DIVI AVG F AVGVST IMP VIII: "Tiberius Caesar Augustus, the son of deified Augustus, proclaimed imperator eight times" provides scholars with a date A.D. 22-23.

   VII The goddess Roma is depicted in armor seated on a breastplate and holding a small figure of Victory in her hand.

   VIII This medal depicts four chariots racing around the central spina (with statues and the central obelisk) in the Circus Maximus. This late-fourth-century brass "contorniate" is not a coin, but a special issue perhaps used for circus prizes or memorials of the games.

   IX The emperor Gaius (Caligula) is portrayed on a brass sestertius issued at Rome in A.D. 39-40. The legend C(aius) CAESAR identifies the emperor and the letters TR(ibunicia) P(otestate) III date the coin to the third year of his reign.

X   Claudius is depicted on a large silver cistophorus (a triple denarius) issued in Asia about A.D. 41-42. The obverse of this Greek-style coin contains an expressive imperial portrait, while the reverse depicts a temple of Roma and Augustus with statues of Roma and Claudius.

XI   The obverse of this Tiberian brass sestertius contains the large letters SC, which indicates that the coinage was issued by the *Senatus consulto*. Though the Julio-Claudian emperors kept all gold and silver coinage under their direct control, senatorial mints continued to issue brass and copper coins.

XII   An instantly recognizable Nero is depicted on a large brass sestertius issued in commemoration of the emperor's restoration of the city after the great fire of A.D. 64.

Preface

This book of readings provides a variety of interpretations about the Julio-Claudian dynasty (31 B.C.–A. D. 68) that gave the Western world a legacy which has endured for twenty centuries. It is a legacy of language, politics, literature, law, philosophy, art, and architecture. The contributions of the early Roman emperors to the legacy are revealed through the writings of the ancients themselves as well as through secondary sources. Also included are a number of original essays by the editor and members of the Academic Advisory Board.

This book was developed by Contemporary Learning Systems of East Lansing, Inc., a company specializing in the development of multi-media educational materials, primarily for adult learners at colleges and universities. Dr. Ronald Mellor, Professor of History at the University of California, Los Angeles, created the concept and structure of the book, selected the readings with the assistance of his advisors, and edited the selections for publication.

We wish to express our appreciation to Professor Brendan Nagle, with whom Professor Mellor consulted extensively on the contents of this book, and to the members of the Academic Advisory Board: Professors Arther Ferrill, Erich S. Gruen, Judith P. Hallett, Richard Saller, and Jo-Ann Shelton.

We are especially grateful to Dr. Jane Cody and Tory Holland for their outstanding assistance in selecting and providing the Julio-Claudian coin illustrations for this volume. We also wish to thank the following: Blake Mellor for his work on the genealogy chart, Judy O'Connor for production editing, Penny Belcher for preparing the manuscript for the press, and Dr. John Ball for coordinating the many aspects of the publishing process.

Roman Empire in the Age of Augustus

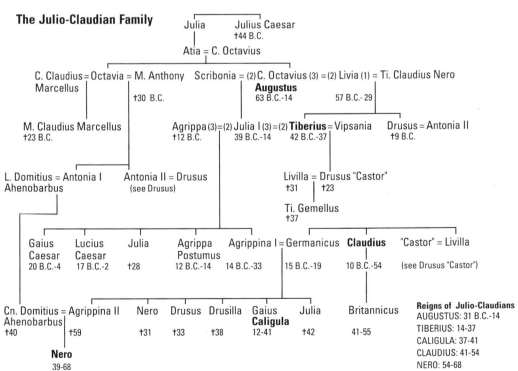

The Julio-Claudian Family

Julia   Julius Caesar
†44 B.C.

Atia = C. Octavius

C. Claudius = Octavia = M. Anthony   Scribonia = (2) C. Octavius (3) = (2) Livia (1) = Ti. Claudius Nero
Marcellus   †30 B.C.   **Augustus**   57 B.C.- 29
                                   63 B.C.-14

M. Claudius Marcellus   Agrippa (3)=(2) Julia I (3) =(2) **Tiberius** = Vipsania   Drusus = Antonia II
†23 B.C.   †12 B.C.   39 B.C.-14   42 B.C.-37   †9 B.C.

L. Domitius = Antonia I   Antonia II = Drusus   Livilla = Drusus "Castor"
Ahenobarbus   (see Drusus)   †31   †23

                                              Ti. Gemellus
                                              †37

Gaius   Lucius   Julia   Agrippa   Agrippa I = Germanicus   **Claudius**   "Castor" = Livilla
Caesar   Caesar   Postumus
20 B.C.-4   17 B.C.-2   †28   12 B.C.-14   14 B.C.-33   15 B.C.-19   10 B.C.-54   (see Drusus "Castor")

Cn. Domitius = Agrippina II   Nero   Drusus   Drusilla   Gaius   Julia   Britannicus
Ahenobarbus   **Caligula**
†40   †59   †31   †33   †38   12-41   †42   41-55

Nero
39-68

Reigns of Julio-Claudians
AUGUSTUS: 31 B.C.-14
TIBERIUS: 14-37
CALIGULA: 37-41
CLAUDIUS: 41-54
NERO: 54-68

Introduction

Just as all roads in Europe once led to Rome, all explorations of western culture lead to the eternal city on the banks of the Tiber. There one finds the origins of the Italian, French, Spanish and much of the English language; there Shakespeare found comedies and historical inspiration to reshape into new masterpieces; there modern legislators found a law code and legal principles that could be adapted to modern conditions; and there Jefferson, Madison and Adams found ideals and political institutions with which to fashion a new constitution for a new nation. This heritage was found in Rome, or through Rome in Athens or Jerusalem; for Greek civilization and Christianity have only come to us filtered through a Roman prism. Thus religion, art, architecture, mythology and philosophy were transmitted and transformed for future generations down to our own. I write these words six thousand miles from Rome in Los Angeles, founded two centuries ago by Spanish missionaries who taught their Indian converts Latin hymns in praise of a deity born under Roman rule. The heritage of Rome remains important after two millennia.

The Greco-Roman synthesis that has so dominated the western cultural and political tradition was formed under the Roman Empire, which brought with it the longest period of peace and prosperity that the Mediterranean world has yet known. In the eighteenth century, Edward Gibbon identified the second century of that Empire as the period "during which the condition of the human race was most happy and prosperous." A century later Theodor Mommsen, who received the 1902 Nobel Prize in literature for his *History of Rome*, said that the Roman Empire "fostered the peace and prosperity of the many nations united under its sway longer and more completely than any other leading power has ever done." Both these great historians, whose ancestors had perhaps been conquered subjects of that same empire, recognized that despite frontier wars and occasional bloody revolts (as in Judaea), the political stability of the Roman Empire had brought enormous benefits to its sixty million subjects.

Just as Rome was not built in a day, the "immense majesty of the Roman peace" (Pliny the Elder) was the product of centuries of struggle. In the eighth century B.C., a collection of villages on some hills beside the Tiber river in central Italy were joined under the name of "Rome." The city was first ruled by kings but, after several centuries, they were expelled and a republic was established. For centuries the hardy citizens of this proud and tenacious city-state struggled against their adversaries in the Italian peninsula, then against Carthage in the western Mediterranean and against Greek cities and kings in the East. By 133 B.C. the city of Rome held parts of three continents under its dominion: culturally diverse Italic peoples and Etruscans, Gauls, Spaniards and Greeks in Europe; Semitic descendants of Carthaginians in North Africa as well as Berber peoples; and a multitude of eastern peoples in Asia Minor. Roman armies, tax collectors and rapacious businessmen dominated the Mediterranean so that booty and taxes flowed into Italy in the form of art, grain, slaves, and money.

But the wealth of Empire brought discord to Rome itself and set into motion forces that would destroy the Republic. Struggles of the landless against the landholders, the Italians against their Roman masters, and factional conflict among the nobility brought continuing discord to Rome in the first century B.C. More than a half-dozen civil wars stretched from 133 to Octavian's defeat of Marc Antony and Cleopatra at Actium in 31 B.C. Though Actium might have merely occasioned a temporary lull, it was in fact a century before hostile soldiers again marched into Rome. And during that century the government, administration, finances, army, and ideology of Rome and its empire were entirely transformed.

Octavian, the adopted son of Julius Caesar, took the name of Augustus and ruled for the next forty-five years. In this golden age of peace and prosperity, Augustus proudly turned Rome itself "from a city of brick to a city of marble" (Suetonius). The Augustan Age was the zenith of Roman poetry and art, and it also saw the final Romanization of Italy. The Italians had been Roman citizens for a half-century, but they had played little role in the political and cultural life of their Roman masters. They had supported Augustus against Antony and he surrounded himself with Italian friends and colleagues: his general Agrippa, his advisor Maecenas, the historian Livy, and the poets Horace from southern Italy and Virgil from the north. There would henceforth be little distinction between Roman and Italian, and Augustus had established a pattern that would be followed by his successors for centuries in Romanizing the Empire.

Augustus had secured power by force of arms, and he skillfully increased his authority through patronage, generosity and propaganda. But his severe illness of 23 B.C. made it clear that his premature death would have brought factional strife and civil war. He then began to legitimate his position in terms of republican precedents, not to protect himself but to ensure continuity after his death. He saw that a return to the old "Republic" would bring a return of political chaos, so he adapted republican institutions to new purposes and the Roman Empire was born. It was indeed an autocracy, though the full extent of the autocracy only gradually became clear during the succeeding century. Some proud senators disdained the new regime which had cost them their *libertas*, and some would continue to oppose it for decades. But that vaunted "liberty," which referred to the senators' political prerogatives, meant little outside the Senate house. Most others welcomed a government which, in the scornful words of the senatorial historian Tacitus, "seduced the people with free food, the army with bonuses, and everyone with the sweetness of peace." After a century of civil war largely provoked by senatorial squabbling, the seduction was a willing one.

Augustus' four successors—Tiberius, Caligula, Claudius and Nero—were his own or his wife Livia's descendants, and historians have called them the Julio-Claudian dynasty. The family ruled from Actium until the suicide in A.D. 68 of Nero, great-grandson of Augustus and great-great-grandson of his old rival Marc Antony. Dynastic intrigue replaced republican politics, and corruption at court overshadowed the corruption of tax collectors or provincial officials. Rivals were eliminated so systematically that, despite the fact that Augustus and Livia had between them nine living grandchildren in A.D. 2, no male descendant survived Nero's death. Writers like Tacitus believed that such behavior portended the decline of the Roman people, and yet the Julio-Claudians established the institutional basis for an Empire that would endure for five centuries at Rome (A.D. 476) and another millennium (A.D. 1453) as the Byzantine Empire at Constantinople. Despite the lurid goings-on at court, the Empire survived and prospered.

This book is a collection of sources and interpretations for that critical period in Roman history. The ancient literary sources provide the tendentious perspective of senators and courtiers on the personalities and actions of the imperial family. They present the familiar view of the Julio-Claudian emperors, corrupted by their mothers, wives, freedmen or by power itself, replacing republican freedoms with despotism. The corruption of power is here graphically depicted in the excerpts from Tacitus' histories and Suetonius' biographies of the Caesars —images of tyranny (Nero) and paranoia (Caligula) that survive to our own day.

But there was more to the Roman Empire than dynastic intrigue. Though no book, nor any single course, can hope to cover the entire range of Roman public and private life, this collection attempts to touch on at least some nonpolitical topics. Ancient writers, however, were generally uninterested in social, economic, or religious history, nor do they document the changes in military or administrative organization. There scholars must use inscriptions, papyri and archaeological evidence to supplement scattered passages from literary sources to provide a coherent picture of the Julio-Claudian age. Thus the chapters on the army, entertainment, religion, women and administration consist largely of recent scholarly interpretations and, in some cases, essays written especially for this volume.

Ancient historians like Tacitus were often moralists, who presented examples of virtue and depravity so that future generations could learn from them. His moral standards were high and his judgments severe. We may be more generous when we judge a Tiberius; his administrative and military skills were admirable, and the few dozen executions of his reign pale against the thousands of the French Revolution, much less the millions killed in the twentieth century. The reign of Claudius also saw the execution of real or imagined conspirators, but we are still entranced by his personal warmth and impressed by his humane legislation and his administrative genius. Even "monsters" like Caligula and Nero seem rather tame after Hitler, Stalin and Pol Pot. And Augustus stands as an extraordinary figure in world history: an ambitious and opportunistic youth who grew to generosity and wisdom so that, through a golden age of peace, political stability and prosperity, he would found an Empire that would endure for centuries. Augustus and his successors all struggled with the problems and temptations of power, and its corrupting effect on the ruler and those around him. This book of readings documents those struggles which, whether successes or failures, have a lasting relevance for us today.

Ronald Mellor
Los Angeles, June 1988

Julius Caesar is depicted on a silver denarius minted at Rome early in 44 B.C., the year in which he was assassinated on the Ides (15) of March.

I

The Rise of The Julio-Claudians

INTRODUCTION
Ronald Mellor

Rome was first ruled by kings and, according to their own patriotic legends, the Romans expelled the last Etruscan king in 509 B.C. and established the Roman Republic. The Romans expanded a small community nestled on the hills alongside the Tiber into the major power in the Mediterranean world. After centuries of tenacious warfare they completed their conquest of Italy and Sicily by 241 B.C.; their conquest of Spain (197), North Africa (146), Greece (146), and sections of present-day Turkey (129) and France (121) followed soon thereafter.

By the first century B.C., however, the vast wealth of empire had brought discord to Rome itself and set in motion the social, economic and political forces that would destroy the Republic. The city was rent by civil strife which only military leaders seemed able to control. Julius Caesar was such a man, but his assassination in 44 B.C. plunged Rome into another decade of civil war until his heir, Octavian, defeated Marc Antony and began more than four decades of rule as the first emperor, Augustus. His own heirs and descendants Tiberius, Caligula, Claudius and Nero sat on the imperial throne for another fifty-five years to complete a century of rule by the Julio-Claudian dynasty.

This chapter surveys the underlying causes of the fall of the Roman Republic and examines the victory of Octavian in the battle of Actium, which ended a century of political and military turmoil. This overview provides a necessary background against which to assess the achievements of Octavian-Augustus in the two following chapters. This chapter also discusses the literary and archaeological sources for the early Roman Empire and includes the treatment of Augustus by the biographer Suetonius, whose lives of the Caesars provides the only continuous source for the Julio-Claudian era.

Augustus and his successors transformed not only the political system, but also the military, economic, religious and administrative elements in the Roman state. They created an empire that was to last for five centuries and to leave its indelible mark on Western civilization to the present day.

From Republic to Empire

Ronald Mellor

Mellor's essay examines the political, social and economic consequences of Rome's conquest of the Mediterranean world which resulted in the civil strife that destroyed the Roman Republic. His brief account of the Civil Wars sketches the problems that the triumphant Octavian-Augustus had to resolve in order to bring peace to Rome and prosperity to the Roman world.

The Roman Republic

Roman tradition attributed the foundation of the city to Romulus and Remus, twin sons of the war god Mars, who were nursed by the she-wolf that became the symbol of the Roman people. Romulus became the first king of Rome, but kings were later seen as tyrants and, according to patriotic legends, in 509 B.C. the Roman people expelled an Etruscan king and established the Roman Republic.

Rome always retained that ancient hostility to monarchy, and republican political institutions were designed to prevent one-man rule. A Senate of elders survived from the monarchy with advisory powers of great authority, but the sovereignty of the Roman people reposed in the popular assembly, which declared war, passed laws and elected annual magistrates. The magistracies were collegial, so that two or more officials simultaneously served in the same post. The early centuries of the Republic were marked by a class struggle between the elite families (*patricians*) and the Roman masses (*plebeians*), but the plebeians were soon protected from arbitrary state power by the institution of tribunes, and were gradually granted full political rights. The constitution adapted itself with remarkable flexibility. Despite this class conflict over civic rights, early Rome was a small agricultural community and the gap between rich and poor was far less than in commercial cities.

Rome's domestic unity and military prowess gradually enabled her to dominate the other peoples of early Italy: the Etruscans in the north, Greek colonies in the south, and a variety of Italic peoples throughout. In 264 B.C., Rome's domination of the peninsula was complete, and

she embarked on a momentous series of wars with the North African merchant city of Carthage for control of Sicily and, ultimately, of the Western Mediterranean. Although the brilliant Carthaginian general Hannibal successfully invaded Italy and occupied parts of the peninsula for more than a decade, Rome emerged triumphant and by 200 B.C. had acquired Sicily, Sardinia, Corsica and Spain as her first overseas provinces.

Rome's legions turned to the East, where they defeated the kings of Macedon and Syria and, within a half-century, became the dominant military power in the entire Mediterranean world. In the fateful year of 146 B.C., Rome razed to the ground the ancient Greek city of Corinth and destroyed her old adversary, Carthage. Later Roman historians saw 146 as the acme of the Roman Republic and the beginning of its decline. That decline was not immediately apparent as Rome extended her sway in the following decades to southern Gaul (France), Greece, Asia Minor (Turkey), Cyprus, Syria, and Cyrene (Lybia). Later Romans defined the decline in moral terms, reflecting on Rome's arrogance and the growing corruption engendered by the vast wealth brought to Italy as booty and tribute. But if these conquests brought to Rome the luxury goods that, in the eyes of a conservative like Cato the Elder, might weaken the character of the Roman people, they also emphasized the growing extremes of wealth and poverty. The social, economic and political changes of the second century B.C. created the forces that would destroy the Roman Republic.

Hannibal's armies ravaged the Italian countryside, and long military service overseas impoverished the yeoman peasantry. The flood of money and slaves allowed senators who controlled the booty to purchase large tracts of land on which more capital intensive enterprises (vines for wine; olive trees for oil; herds of animals) could be staffed by vast gangs of slave labor. Some peasants were forced from their land; others were eager to leave the hard life and poor soil for Rome and other cities where work could be found on construction projects financed by foreign booty. But this urban "proletariat"—a technical Roman term for men who possessed no capital or land—was obviously at the mercy of economic conditions. There was also a growing problem in army recruitment, since the Roman military system required that legionaries own property and the landless could not serve.

Though the Senate was formally an advisory body, it included all present and former magistrates and thus possessed immense authority. That prestige increased immeasurably as a result of its successful management of the wars of conquest, and through much of the second century B.C. the Senate's views were rarely challenged. In the words of Cicero, "The Senate was established by our ancestors as the guardian, president and defender of the state; they willed that the magistrates should be guided by the authority of this order and should act as servants of this great council." Though the popular assembly theoretically possessed supreme power, the Senate developed and implemented all important policy. Since the senators were a landholding elite theoretically prohibited from engaging in commerce, a new class of entrepreneurs arose to bid on government contracts to provision troops, to build bridges, to manage mines and, because Republican Rome had no civil service, to collect taxes. The Romans called them *equites*. As these "equestrians" became aware of their importance to the state, they were increasingly determined to exercise political influence to maximize their profits.

Rome's Italian allies were required to fight whenever called upon, but were still denied Roman citizenship and suffered arbitrary treatment at the hands of Roman magistrates.

Though many allies had been linked to Rome for centuries and served a prominent role in the Roman armies that had conquered the entire Mediterranean world, their commercial rights at Rome were restricted and they were even forbidden to marry Roman citizens. There was mounting anger, which would burst forth in the savage Italian war between Romans and non-Roman Italians in 90 B.C.

All these elements contributed to the social and economic crisis that forms the background to Tiberius and Gaius Gracchus. These brothers served as tribunes, and revived the revolutionary potential of the tribunate—an office once intended to protect the masses from arbitrary treatment but long since co-opted by the Senate. Booty had dried up in the absence of lucrative new conquests, and the unemployed urban proletariat was becoming desperate. The Gracchi proposed distribution of public lands to resettle peasants and improve military recruitment, but large landholders already occupied much of the public land and regarded it as their patrimony. A fierce political struggle developed. Rhetoric became riots, and both Gracchi were killed (Tiberius 133 B.C.; Gaius 121 B.C.) by rampaging mobs led by senators. They were killed perhaps less for their policies than for their personal predominance and high-handed political tactics, which seemed to their opponents to be leading toward tyranny. Blood was shed in civil strife for the first time in centuries, and in the next fifty years a dozen Roman magistrates would be murdered or killed in civil war. An era of political violence began. Later politicians would follow the lead of the Gracchi in appealing to the masses, and the senatorial elite would respond in its turn with resistance and violence.

A generation after the Gracchi, the popular general Marius recruited armies from among the landless to fight in North Africa and Gaul. He provided arms and equipment, trained his troops and provided for their well-being. Rome had taken the first step from an army of peasant farmers to a professional army, but the poor and landless soldiers of this new army owed their loyalty to their commander. They would fight for him in the field and give him political support back in Rome; he would use his political influence to obtain land (which would serve as a pension) for his loyal veterans. The result was inevitable. The first century B.C. became an age of military dynasts who brought Roman troops to Syria, Palestine, Gaul, Britain, Armenia, and Egypt but who also led their armies against their enemies in Italy and even against Rome itself: Marius, Sulla, Pompey, Julius Caesar, Marc Antony, and Caesar Augustus.

The last decades of the Roman Republic were dominated by bitter political battles usually irrelevant to the social, economic and administrative issues requiring attention. The senatorial elite resisted change, and men like Cicero and the younger Cato depicted the demands of the unemployed and the landless as moral depravity and a departure from traditional Roman values. The equestrians and their supporters ruthlessly exploited the Roman provinces while governors were bribed to turn a blind eye to corrupt practices. And the *populares*—nobly born politicians—like the Gracchi who appealed to the masses for support—demanded distributions of free grain and expenditures on building programs and entertainments, but no group proposed a comprehensive reform. A handful of politicians formed political alliances and broke them, manipulated the assemblies and even the state religion, and called on mobs and the armies to attain a fleeting predominance in the sandbox of Roman political life.

But these politicians did not address the most pressing issues:

- This vast empire was administered with institutions developed for a small city-state without a budget or a permanent civil service, and with little efficiency, justice or effective control.
- Extremes of wealth and poverty now made social mobility very difficult, and yet it was necessary to draw administrators for the empire from a wider pool of talent.
- The Italian allies had been granted citizenship and were now "Romans," but they were kept from full participation in the political, social and economic life of Rome.

- Rome's armies remained loyal to their commanders who had recruited them and who took responsibility for their retirement; there was little loyalty to the abstraction of the Senate and the Roman People.

The Civil Wars

Ancient and modern historians have placed the beginning of the "Roman Revolution" in 60 B.C., the year in which Julius Caesar, Pompey the Great, and Marcus Crassus formed a compact—a crude political deal called the "First Triumvirate"—which allowed them to dominate the state. Caesar had the support of the Roman mobs; Pompey was then Rome's greatest general and held the loyalty of the army; and Crassus was the wealthiest man in Rome, representing the economic interests of the equestrians. The Senate was put on the defensive, and the republican Cicero called the Triumvirate "the three-headed monster." It certainly was naked political opportunism intended to satisfy the immediate political and economic needs of each of the triumvirs and his followers. The struggles of this era concerned individual domination and personal loyalty rather than any political program. For ten years, while Caesar as governor of Gaul (present France) campaigned incessantly against Gallic chieftains and thereby developed a superb military machine, Rome was beset by political intrigue and mob violence. It was a pivotal moment in Roman history: republican institutions were powerless in the face of street fighting and wholesale bribery. Pompey, once Rome's greatest general, was detached from Caesar and stood as defender of the Senate and the Republic. Caesar's command in Gaul was expiring, and he saw his enemies in Rome plotting to prosecute him upon his return, so on January 10, 49 B.C., he marched his army across the Rubicon river ("The die is cast") into Italy to begin the Civil Wars. With his legendary political and military decisiveness, Caesar defeated senatorial armies in Greece, Africa and Spain and returned to rule supreme in Rome as Dictator.

Caesar proposed legislation to remedy certain social and economic problems, but his time was limited. Though he was offered the crown by his deputy, Marc Antony, he rejected it and retained the quasi-constitutional office of Dictator. On the eve of his planned military expedition to Parthia, Caesar attended a meeting of the Senate on the Ides of March. There he was struck down by a group of republicans, led by his one-time protégé Brutus, shouting "Liberty! Freedom! Tyranny is Dead!" These were men who thought they were preserving freedom and the Republic, but the Republic was politically bankrupt and existed only in name. They, in fact, were trying to preserve the privileges of a small senatorial clique which had persistently refused to address the real problems of the Roman State. History has been kinder to Caesar than to his murderers. Dante placed Brutus and Cassius together with Judas in the lowest circle of Hell, and Shakespeare had Cassius say of Caesar:

"He doth bestride the narrow world like a Colossus; and we petty men walk under his huge legs, and peep about to find ourselves dishonorable graves."

Gaius Octavius, Caesar's sickly eighteen-year-old grand-nephew who had been studying in Greece, was adopted and named as heir in Caesar's will, taking his name as C. Julius Caesar Octavianus. We call him Octavian. When Brutus and the assassins fled Rome, Marc Antony was best placed to succeed Caesar as master of Rome. He was outgoing, popular with the troops, and had appropriated much of Caesar's wealth (which now rightfully belonged to Octavian) with which to pay them. Octavian, though young and inexperienced, was cool and shrewd—qualities that rarely left him as he dominated the Roman world during the next fifty-eight years. When he arrived from Greece in the weeks after Caesar's death, he began recruiting Caesar's veterans in southern Italy before even reaching Rome. Cicero believed the "divine youth" would ally himself with the Senate against the forces of his natural rival, Marc Antony. Octavian did so for a time and even drove Antony and his army from Italy. But when he saw that the senators planned to use

and discard him, he allied with Antony in a compact called the Second Triumvirate (Lepidus was nominal partner as well) and marched on Rome in November of 43 B.C. The triumvirs proscribed their enemies, and even the great Cicero was cruelly struck down while fleeing to a waiting ship.

Their first task was to deal with Caesar's assassins who had fled to the eastern Mediterranean. After the defeat of Brutus and Cassius at Philippi in northern Greece in 42 B.C., Antony embarked on an extended period of pacification and administrative settlement in the eastern Mediterranean. This was the wealthiest part of Rome's empire, and Antony clearly saw it as a way to gain wealth, increase his personal popularity among the soldiers, and win political support from among Rome's eastern dependent kings. Octavian's task was far less pleasant. He had to find land in Italy on which to resettle the demobilized armies—a process that at first caused deep resentment and even rebellion as land was confiscated. An early poem of Virgil, later a great supporter of the Augustan regime, records the deep bitterness while perhaps a quarter of all Italian land changed hands. And yet, in the course of the decade from 42 to 32 B.C., Octavian won the loyalty of his troops and developed his political base among the leading citizens of the Italian towns, who had for so long been neglected by Roman politicians.

Antony, despite his marriage to Octavian's sister Octavia, conducted a prolonged and highly public affair with the Egyptian queen Cleopatra. The mutual hostility between the triumvirs finally led to a major confrontation in a sea battle near Actium in Greece in 31 B.C. Antony and Cleopatra were defeated and fled to Egypt where, after a final victory by Octavian, they committed suicide in 30 B.C. Antony was a fine general, a shrewd politician, and a jolly and generous man. But he was branded forever as "the triple pillar of the world transform'd into a strumpet's fool." (Shakespeare, Antony and Cleopatra). The victors win the privilege of writing history, and the Augustan Age so entangled Antony's memory in political propaganda and erotic romance that the myths may forever obscure the reality of the man.

In 29 B.C. Gaius Julius Caesar Octavianus returned from his victories over Antony and Cleopatra in the East to celebrate a triple triumph in Rome. His diplomatic arrangements in the East were ratified, his birthday was declared a public holiday, and triumphal arches were erected in his honor. For the first time in more than two centuries, the doors of the Temple of Janus were closed to indicate that Rome was at peace.

Octavian was now the unchallenged master of Rome and her armies, and thus of the entire Mediterranean world. He was thirty-three, the age of Alexander the Great at his death, but his rule would continue for another forty-three years. What was the personality of this man who had such an immense task of reconstruction before him? One image of Octavian is Shakespeare's cold, ruthless opportunist of *Antony and Cleopatra*. He allowed the great Cicero to be murdered by Antony's henchmen in 43 B.C., and he himself ordered Julius Caesar's son by Cleopatra to be killed so that he would have no rivals. But the poets convey another image: the benevolent Father of his Country, the bringer of peace. And the youthful promise and charm of the man had even attracted Cicero. Can these personalities be reconciled? Or has so much propaganda on both sides made it impossible? The emperor's signet ring had a most appropriate emblem: a sphinx. Our uncertainty may be the result of the various masks Octavian-Augustus wished to convey on different occasions: toughness and resolution when his power was in jeopardy; paternal generosity when his authority was absolute. Still, we see throughout his life a strength of purpose, great moral courage, and intelligence—whether in political machinations or strategic planning—that is remarkable among political leaders of any age.

But the defeat of Antony was only a temporary solution, an illusory peace. The problems of the last century had not disappeared. Sulla and Caesar had also defeated rivals, but neither resolved the conflicts consuming the Roman Republic. Octavian recognized and was willing to confront the vast tasks awaiting him:

1. to demobilize large segments of his own and Antony's huge armies, turning their energies against Rome's barbarian enemies, and ensuring the army's future loyalty;

2. to reduce class hostility at Rome;

3. to integrate the Italians (who had supported him against Antony) into the cultural and political lives of the state; and

4. to establish the mechanics of government—the formulation of policy, the provision for the succession, and the staffing of a bureaucracy.

Sources for the Julio-Claudian Age

Ronald Mellor

Mellor's essay surveys the sources available to the scholar and student interested in the early Roman Empire. While Tacitus' histories and Suetonius' biographies of the emperors are the most comprehensive accounts and the ones most often reproduced in this reader, much of interest can be found in the writings of poets and philosophers of the time as well as in other histories, both in Greek and in Latin. Contemporary inscriptions are preserved on stone and bronze, and a wide range of archaeological evidence (especially from Pompeii and Herculaneum) also sheds light on life in the Julio-Claudian age.

More than two thousand years have passed since Caesar Augustus established the first dynasty to rule the Roman Empire, and the surviving sources for the century from Augustus' victory at Actium (31 B.C.) to the death of Nero (A.D. 68) are far from adequate. No reliable treatment by a contemporary historian survives, and from the succeeding generations we have only Suetonius' scandalous *Lives of the XII Caesars* and the incomplete remains of Tacitus' trenchant account of Tiberius, Claudius, and Nero. Together with the later survey by the third century Greek senator Cassius Dio, these accounts serve to establish the chronological framework of political events. They can be fleshed out with nuggets from such diverse sources as the poets Virgil, Horace and Ovid; the Jewish philosopher Philo and the historian Josephus; the Greek geographer Strabo and the Spanish tutor of Nero, Seneca; with fragments of Antony's supporter, the historian Pollio; with the surviving summaries of the later books of Augustus' friend and Claudius' teacher, Livy; with the sincere, but inept, panegyric by Tiberius' loyal follower, the soldier Velleius Paterculus; and with the picture of everyday life found in those Christian books known as the New Testament.

It should be immediately clear that the seemingly coherent account appearing in Roman history textbooks has had to be wrested from recalcitrant, evasive, sycophantic, hostile, biased and, perhaps most frustrating of all, incomplete sources. We call literary sources all the histories, speeches, biographies, poems, epistles, et cetera, that were written and intended for circulation at the time. Scholars have increasingly looked to other sources—inscriptions on stone, records on papyrus, art and architecture, and physical remains brought to light by archaeology. These non-literary sources provide far more information about everyday life than historical texts written in Rome. This is true of all periods of Greek and Roman history, and modern historians of antiquity have consequently become adept at the careful analysis of unpromising sources in order to discover those kernels of truth that help uncover the reality of life in a distant age.

The most vivid account of the Julio-Claudian emperors survives in Suetonius' *Lives of the XII Caesars*. Suetonius, born to a notable equestrian family soon after the fall of Nero, was a civil servant who became imperial librarian. He wrote a series of biographies of illustrious men: poets, grammarians, philosophers, and, of course, emperors. His lives of the Caesars from Julius Caesar to Domitian made a great impact and became the model for later biographers in antiquity and the Middle Ages.

The popular image of Suetonius as a crude scandal-monger obscures his formidable research skills and his wide range of interests. Suetonius collected and sorted numerous anecdotes, including even vulgar stories that might lack the dignity necessary for history. He arranged this material by themes, prefaced by a brief narrative of the emperor's life. Thus he reports an emperor's virtues and vices as well as his victories and defeats, including fascinating details of the personal habits, cultural interests, superstitions and other material more staid writers ignore. Ancient historians usually recast documents and speeches in their own style and impose an intellectual and moralistic framework upon their material. But the more credulous librarian merely reports what he reads. Suetonius reports the letters of Livia and Augustus as he found them in the imperial archives, which is much appreciated by modern historians. He tells his story with little moralizing, though his dry impartiality at times approaches irony. Though he lacks stylistic artistry and his catalogues of detail sometimes remind one of a bureaucratic report—he was a civil servant—he can tell an excellent story; for example, his account of the dramatic accession of Claudius or the melodramatic events of Nero's death. His lives are particularly useful for Caligula and the early years of Claudius, where Tacitus is lost. His prodigious learning provides a great deal of detailed information especially valued by modern historians since, unlike his contemporaries Tacitus and Plutarch, Suetonius did not select his facts to argue a political or moral case. If not a great historian, Suetonius is an essential historical source for the Julio-Claudian age.

The greatest of all Roman historians was the senator Tacitus. His powerful mind, high moral purpose, and trenchant style have combined in a book which is, as Thomas Jefferson said, "a compound of history and morality of which we have no other example." While Jefferson regarded Tacitus as "the first writer in the world without a single exception," John Quincy Adams wrote that he could not imagine a day without reading some Tacitus. Early American democrats savored Tacitus' vivid analysis of the evils of tyrannical government in his *Annals*, which in eighteen books chronicled the Julio-Claudians from the death of Augustus to the death of Nero. The first six books, covering the reign of Tiberius, survive (though there is only a brief fragment of book five), as do books eleven through sixteen, which treat the latter part of Claudius' reign and most of the reign of Nero.

Tacitus was born in the reign of Nero and formed his strong political views in the terrible years of Domitian (A.D. 81-96). It is Domitian whom we find projected back into the monstrous portrait of Tiberius. Some senators supported the tyrant while others publicly opposed the regime and were executed. But Tacitus withdrew into voluntary exile to study and to yearn nostalgically for the *libertas* of the Republic. Thus his writings display bitter resentment mixed with a defensiveness towards the senatorial martyrs. He hardly wrote, as he claimed to do, "without anger or partiality." He attacked the tyrants but found the Stoic opposition too inflexible: he preferred passivity to the dangers of civil war.

Tacitus was not a story-teller; he wrote history to pass moral and political judgments on the past and thereby affect the future. The historian believed that since no autocrat could control the future, his fear of condemnation by future generations was a restraint on his arbitrary exercise of power. Thus Tacitus paints the most compelling psychological portraits of tyranny in historical literature. Amidst the carnage and intrigue, the historian provides models of dignity, liberty and personal courage. Economic and sociological explanations hold no interest for Tacitus, nor do the far-off provinces. He is weak on geography, the provinces, military and legal history. He was writing not a comprehensive history of the Empire, but only of political life and the loss of liberty. His focus is narrow: the imperial court. And yet his subject is broad. He is interested in more than what has been said and done; he wishes to examine the effects of these words and deeds on the minds and characters of the rulers and the ruled. Edward Gibbon, the eighteenth-century author of *The Decline and Fall of the Roman Empire*, regarded Tacitus as the supreme "philosophical historian," and his histories address political and psychological issues that are still with us. In that he has no peer.

The Greek Writers

The bitter critiques of these courtiers are not found in the accounts of Greek-speaking provincials. Authoritarian monarchy was well known to them and was not regarded as inherently evil. And the provincials had hardly lamented the demise of the Republic, with its rapacious governors and marauding armies. So the fragmentary history of Augustus' early years by Nicolaus of Damascus exalts the virtue and wisdom of Augustus and the benefits of Empire. Nicolaus was, to be sure, an advisor to King Herod of Judaea, who owed his survival in power to Augustus, but his themes were echoed by other Greek writers for centuries. Philo of Alexandria, who left us his eyewitness account of the Jewish embassy sent to Caligula, proclaimed that Augustus saved the world by bringing it peace. Strabo wrote in Tiberius' reign of the civilizing mission of Rome, and Augustus' contemporary, the antiquarian Dionysius of Halicarnassus, accepted the new imperial system which allowed peace and freedom in the Greek cities of the eastern Mediterranean. And in the third century, Cassius Dio rose to become consul in Rome and wrote in his native Greek a compendium of Roman history. Though this is a late work necessarily derived from other sources, Dio acknowledges the Greek view that a democratic system can work only on a small scale while empires must be ruled by monarchs.

These Greek writers are sometimes naive, often ill-informed, and usually with biases of their own. But they provide an outside perspective on Roman imperial history and much in their rambling works can be used to understand the Julio-Claudian age.

The Roman Poets

Dozens of other literary texts shed light on the Julio-Claudians and their world. The Augustan Age saw the greatest florescence of Roman poetry, and the greatest luminaries were intimates of the emperor himself, subsidized by his confidant, Maecenas. Virgil, who earlier felt resentment at Octavian's confiscation of family estates, described in the eighth book of his *Aeneid* the shield of Rome's founder, Aeneas, which depicted (far in the supposed future) Augustus leading his troops into victory over Antony at Actium. It was Augustus who ordered at Virgil's death that the unfinished *Aeneid*, the masterpiece of all Latin literature, not be burned as its dying and depressed author had requested.

The poems of Horace record his political odyssey from fighting against Octavian at Philippi in the army of Brutus and Cassius, to his characterization of Cleopatra as a *"fatale monstrum,"* to his exaltation of the new regime in his *"Roman Odes."*

The other great poets of the age were also welcome at court, including the love poet Propertius, who shrewdly lamented his lack of skill for epic poetry that would allow him to sing of Augustus' victories. But tragedy befell one of these court poets: Ovid. His love of poetry, his tongue-in-cheek erotic handbooks, and his great compendium of Greek mythology, *The Metamorphoses*, made his reputation as the most humorous of the Augustan poets, but his taste for frivolity was the cause of his downfall. He is thought to have publicly satirized the behavior of the emperor's daughter, Julia, and Augustus exiled him to Tomi on the Black Sea in present-day Romania. Ovid's pathetic poetic pleas for forgiveness did him no good; he died in exile, an urban sophisticate far from his world. All these contemporaries of Augustus mention him and contemporary events in their poems. In the present day we might judge such subsidized, political poetry to be propaganda, but that would be to misunderstand the spirit of the age. These men were not members of the senatorial elite; in fact, most were from the towns of Italy which were very well treated by Augustus and his new regime. They had lived through the Civil Wars and most believed that they were seeing a new golden age of art, literature and peace. The poets were men who came to believe in the new order, and their poems provided a sincere insight into the Augustan Age.

Other Roman Authors

Writers of the first century A.D. provide varied documentation of the Julio-Claudians. The great historian Livy was welcomed into Augustus' circle despite his republican sympathies, and the emperor himself teasingly called him a "Pompeian." But we have only later summaries of the concluding books of Livy's vast history that went from Romulus in 753 B.C.

down to the death of Drusus in 9 B.C. It is interesting to note Augustus' toleration of dissident historians and even his presence at readings by Cremutius Cordus that heaped praise on Brutus and Cassius. Under Tiberius the same Cremutius was prosecuted and driven to suicide, and his books were burned. Later in the century, under a new dynasty, Pliny the elder would attack the hypocrisy and deceit of the young Octavian and the ambition and crimes of Livia. Seneca satirized the deification of Claudius, while Juvenal lampooned long-dead Sejanus. There were more positive voices, however, even in Rome. Velleius Paterculus began as a modest soldier in Tiberius' legions, and his blind loyalty to Tiberius (and Sejanus) pervades his history of Rome down to A.D. 31. His slavish devotion seems sincere, reflecting the popularity Tiberius enjoyed in Italy, the provinces, and among the army, much more accurately than such senatorial sources as Tacitus. Velleius produced a gullible and stylistically inept work, but he was an eyewitness who treated interesting topics (such as provincialization and colonization) ignored in relentlessly political senatorial histories.

Inscriptions

Historians, biographers, and poets can take us only so far. Such men—and nearly all writers were men in the Julio-Claudian age—have their own interests and constitute a filter. We see it most clearly in a speech by the emperor Claudius which has survived on a bronze plaque at Lyons in France. Tacitus also records the speech, but he improved the style and strengthened the argument. So inscriptions on stone and bronze can provide a more direct view of the emperor's words. The most famous inscription from ancient Rome is the *Res Gestae*, which records Augustus' own account of his achievements. Though copies of this text were set up all around the Empire, the nearly complete text in Greek and Latin only survives on the walls of the temple of Augustus in Ankara, Turkey. It is hardly the "whole truth;" it is a master politician's attempt to rewrite the record

his own way. We must read it with the same skepticism and fascination with which we read memoirs of a Nixon or a Kissinger. Other inscriptions provide details of imperial government and provincial or civic administration, which ancient historians overlooked much as a historian of post-war America may largely disregard the effects of the direct-dial telephone or the social impact of television, the decline of the postal service or the complications of the tax code. Thus we learn from inscriptions much about the deployment of legions, local religious practice, and immigration from the eastern Empire into Rome and Italy. Inscriptions range from official texts of treaties set up on the Capitoline to a humble funeral stone recording the death of a loved one. All can be of use to us in reconstructing the world of the ancient Romans.

Coins and Papyri

Coins provide yet another source for the historian. They were an important official means of propaganda and communication, since even the illiterate in remote regions used Roman coinage and saw the legends or symbols engraved on it. Augustus' diplomatic agreement to have the Parthians return captured Roman legionary standards was presented on coins as a triumph with the legend PARTHIA VICTA (Parthia Conquered), accompanied by a palm tree. The virtues and benefactions of the emperors are repeated from reign to reign: PAX; CONCORDIA; SECURITAS; et cetera. And the coins tell us things that no die-maker had intended: they document Roman trade with India; they date quite precisely archaeological discoveries; and they provide evidence for intentional inflation as, for example, when Nero reduced the proportion of silver in each coin while also slightly shaving its overall weight, so a denarius had about 55 percent the amount of silver as it had a generation before. Rome's durable, and often beautiful, coinage provides insight into the Romans' economic and political life.

Ancient paper, made from the pulp of the papyrus plant native to the Nile valley, survives from antiquity only in the dry sands of Egypt and the Near East. (The single major exception is the Villa of the Papyri at Herculaneum, in which papyri were carbonized in the eruption of Vesuvius in A.D. 79.) Papyrus was used throughout the Empire for books and official records as well as for ordinary letters and notes, but the moisture of two millennia destroyed almost every trace of it in Europe. From Egypt, however, papyri survive in abundance: letters, wills, petitions, military records, tax cases, bills of sale, and even schoolboys' jottings. We must take care in generalizing from this material since the texts are almost always in Greek and the administration of Egypt was unique in the Empire. And yet the papyri are invaluable in providing glimpses of both public and private lives that would otherwise be lost. It is only on a single papyrus that we have Emperor Claudius' judicious letter to the Alexandrians, ordering the Greek community to cease attacking Alexandrian Jews and not to interfere in their religious ceremonies, while telling the Jewish community not to agitate for increased political rights. In the private domain, we have the letter from a young soldier to his mother, insisting that she persuade his father to buy him a white horse since all his friends have one. The tragedies and farces of everyday life in Greco-Roman Egypt stand out in vivid relief in these scraps of papyrus.

The Evidence of Archaeology

Finally, there is the unwritten archaeological record of buildings, walls, roads, and minor artifacts. These range from Roman cities preserved in the sands of North Africa, where the urban plan of Roman colonies is particularly clear, to such great military monuments as Hadrian's Wall, which stretches across the width of northern Britain. Even where monuments cannot be found, aerial photography reveals signs of underground irrigation systems, hidden roads, and patterns of agricultural development. The most spectacular sites are, of course, Pompeii and Herculaneum—thriving towns in southern Italy whose busy lives were cut short on August 25, A.D. 79, by the eruption of Mount Vesuvius. Archaeology has revealed the towns frozen in death: meals left on the table, jewels buried in the yard to be found later, a chained dog asphyxiated, and gladiators who died locked in the stocks. But there's more to Pompeii than its death. The stones reveal the life of a commercial town: the decoration and furniture of private homes; the local banker's accounts; details of the wine and wool trades; the diverse temples and numerous brothels with their examples of sacred and profane art; and the shops, baths, theaters, gymnasium, arena and public piazzas. Through their sudden death, Pompeii and Herculaneum continue to bring to life the lives of ordinary Romans.

There may seem to be much evidence for life in the age of the Julio-Claudians, but compared to more recent periods of history the evidence is skimpy indeed. There are questions which cannot be answered, and perhaps will never be answered, but scholars persist in their examination of the old evidence and their search for new material. There are new papyri to be read, newly discovered inscriptions to be interpreted, and sites to be dug by archaeologists before modern man destroys the remains as the medieval Romans destroyed so much of ancient Rome in building new churches and palaces. There is no easy road to remote antiquity; its investigation demands a long struggle with a variety of difficult materials. Yet does that not make the scholars' triumphs and the students' insights all the more precious?

Life of Augustus

Suetonius

Suetonius' Lives of the XII Caesars is perhaps the most colorful historical source that has come down to us from the ancient world. Suetonius, a scholar and pedant more than a historian, was born about the time that Nero died (A.D. 68). He rose high in the civil service to the post of imperial librarian early in the second century before being dismissed by the emperor Hadrian. He is best known for his scandalous stories, which provide the inspiration and much of the raw material for Robert Graves' famous historical novel, I, Claudius. But his lives also contain invaluable original sources, such as private letters of Augustus and Livia, which he obtained in his official capacity. The more "sophisticated" historians of his time avoided these inelegant documents much as they shunned such banal details as the physical descriptions and personal habits of the emperors. Unlike his contemporary historians, Suetonius did not select his facts to argue a political or moral case, and so his vast collection of disparate information is particularly welcome to modern historians of the period.

The mass of detail in his Life of Augustus shows that he must have completed it when he had access to the imperial archives and before his dismissal from his post. (In fact, he must have copied out a good deal of Augustus' correspondence, since he continued to use it in the lives of Tiberius, Caligula and Claudius.) After a brief summary of the emperor's life, Suetonius arranges his stories by topics: civil wars (9-18), foreign wars (20-23), and other public affairs before he turns (61) to private and familiar concerns. Suetonius can certainly be credulous (as when he relies on Augustus' great rival Marc Antony as a source), but his very lack of discrimination provides a mass of detail that is gratifying to modern historians. Despite the many allegations against Augustus and Livia, Suetonius does not assert that Livia was responsible for the death of Augustus or others of his family, as some other ancient sources allege.

The Youth of Gaius Octavius

5.   Augustus was born [as Gaius Octavius] just before sunrise on September 23, 63 B.C. in the Palatine quarter, where he now has a shrine, built shortly after his death. . . .

7.   . . .Later he took the name of Gaius Caesar from the will of his uncle Julius Caesar, and later the surname Augustus, on the motion of Munatius Plancus. When some expressed the opinion that he ought to be called Romulus as a second founder of the city, Plancus carried the proposal that he should rather be named Augustus, saying that this was not merely a new title but a more honorable one, inasmuch as sacred places consecrated by augural rites are called "august."

8.   At the age of four Augustus lost his father. In his twelfth year he delivered a funeral oration to the assembly in honor of his grandmother Julia. When he came of age four years later, he received military honors at Caesar's African triumph, although he had been too young to take part in the war. When Caesar went to fight the sons of Pompey in Spain, Augustus, though still weak from a severe illness and having suffered a shipwreck, followed over dangerous roads with only a small escort. He thereby greatly endeared himself to Caesar, who soon formed a high opinion of his character.

After recovering the Spanish provinces, Caesar planned expeditions against the Dacians and the Parthians, and sent young Octavius on in advance to Apollonia, where he spent his free time in study. When he learned that his uncle had been assassinated by Brutus and Cassius and that he was his heir, he considered appealing to the nearby legions, but gave up the idea as hasty and premature. He returned to Rome to claim his inheritance in spite of his mother's doubts and his stepfather's strong opposition. Then he recruited armies and thereafter ruled the State, at first with Marc Antony and Marcus Lepidus, then with Antony alone for nearly twelve years, and finally by himself for forty-four years.

The Wars of Augustus

9. After this brief sketch of his life, I will discuss the details, not chronologically, but by subject, to make the account clearer and more intelligible. Augustus waged five civil wars: Mutina, Philippi, Perusia, Sicily, and Actium; Mutina and Actium were against Marc Antony, at Philippi he fought against Brutus and Cassius, at Perugia against Marc Antony's brother Lucius, and in Sicily against Pompey's son, Sextus.

10. The basic reason for all these wars was Augustus' desire to avenge Caesar and keep his laws in force. When he returned from Apollonia he resolved to surprise Brutus and Cassius by taking up arms against them; when they foresaw the danger and fled, he turned to the law and prosecuted them for murder in absentia. . . . To gain greater authority for his program, he announced he would stand for election to replace a plebeian tribune who had died (even though he was a patrician and not yet a senator). Antony, the consul on whose help he had counted, opposed Augustus and wanted a bribe to allow him even ordinary civil rights. The young man then turned to the aristocrats, whom he knew detested Antony, now besieging Decimus Brutus at Mutina, and trying to drive him forcibly from the province given him by Caesar and the Senate. At the advice of some aristocrats, Augustus hired assassins to kill Antony, and, when the plot was discovered, spent money to enroll veterans to protect him and the State. Made propraetor by the Senate, he joined his army with the new consuls Hirtius and Pansa to assist Decimus Brutus, and they successfully completed the campaign in three months. Of the first battle, Antony later wrote that Augustus fled and was not seen again until the next day, when he returned without his cloak and his horse. But all agree that in the second battle he both led and fought well and, when the standard-bearer of his legion was badly wounded, he picked up the standard and carried it in battle.

12. When Augustus learned that Antony had found protection with Lepidus, and that other leaders and armies were coming to terms with them, he quickly abandoned the nobles, claiming some of them called him a "boy," while others openly said he should be praised and dispensed with, so they didn't have to reward him or his veterans.

13. In league with Antony and Lepidus, although sick and barely escaping from his camp to Antony in the first battle, Augustus triumphed in the second battle at Philippi. He was not moderate in victory and sent Brutus's head to Rome to be thrown at the feet of Caesar's statue. . . . When the duties of administration were divided after the victory, Antony undertook to restore order in the East, and Augustus led the veterans back to Italy to settle them on land. But he could neither satisfy the veterans nor the landowners, since the latter complained that they were driven from their homes, and the former that they were not being treated as their services led them to hope.

14. Then Lucius Antonius attempted a revolution, relying on his position as consul and his brother's power. Augustus forced him to take refuge in Perugia, and starved him into surrender. . . .

15. After the fall of that city, he took vengeance on many, answering all requests for pardon with the same phrase, "You must die." Some write that three hundred prisoners of senatorial and equestrian rank were sacrificed on the Ides of March like so many victims at the altar raised to the Deified Julius Caesar. . . .

After the defeat of Pompey in Sicily, Lepidus, whom Augustus had summoned from Africa to help him, became overconfident in his legions and demanded the leadership with terrible threats. Augustus stripped him of his army and sent him into perpetual exile in Circei.

17. Augustus finally broke off his tenuous and often strained alliance with Marc Antony. He ordered the will that Antony left in Rome be published to show that Antony was no longer acting as a Roman citizen: it named his children by Cleopatra among his heirs. Nevertheless, when Antony was declared a public enemy, Augustus sent back to him all his kinsfolk and allies, among them Gaius Sosius and Titus Domitius, who were still consuls at the time. . . . Soon after he won the sea-battle at Actium. . . . He besieged Alexandria, where Antony had taken refuge with Cleopatra, and soon took the city. Although Antony tried to make terms at the eleventh hour, Augustus forced him to commit suicide, and viewed his corpse. He wished to keep Cleopatra alive for his triumph, and even had snake charmers brought to her to suck the poison from her wound, thought to be the bite of an asp. He allowed them both an honorable burial in the same tomb, giving orders that the mausoleum which they had begun should be finished. Young Antony, the elder of Fulvia's two sons, he dragged from the statue of the god Julius, to which he had fled as a suppliant, and slew him. Caesarion, whom Cleopatra bore to Caesar, he put to death. But he spared the other children of Antony and Cleopatra, and later brought them up as if they were his own family.

18. About this time Augustus had the sarcophagus and body of Alexander the Great brought forth from its shrine, and after gazing on it, showed his respect by placing upon it a golden crown and strewing it with flowers. After being asked whether he wished to see the tomb of the Ptolemies as well, he replied, "My wish was to see a king, not corpses." He turned Egypt into a province, and then to make it more fertile and a better source of grain for Rome, he assigned his soldiers to clean out the irrigation canals into which the Nile overflowed, which had silted up with mud. To perpetuate the memory of his victory at Actium, Augustus founded a city called Nicopolis (City of Victory) near Actium, provided for the celebration of games there every five years, and enlarged the ancient temple of Apollo. . . .

21. As general or as commander-in-chief, Augustus subdued northwest Spain, western Gaul, Pannonia, Dalmatia, and all Illyricum, as well as Raetia and the Alpine tribes. He also killed many Dacians and stopped their raids across the Danube, forced the Germans back across the Elbe, except the Suebi and Sigambri, who surrendered and were settled in Gaul along the Rhine. He also pacified other rebellious tribes. But he never made war on any nation without due cause, and felt no desire to expand the Empire or increase his military glory at any cost. . . . He thus gained such a reputation for prowess and moderation that even the Indians and the Scythians [of south Russia], nations known to us only by hearsay, voluntarily sent envoys to plead for his friendship and that of the Roman people. The Parthians also readily yielded to his claims to Armenia, and, at his demand, surrendered the standards which they had taken from Marcus Crassus and Marc Antony; they offered him hostages and when there were rivals for their throne, they accepted his candidate.

22. The temple of Janus, which had only been closed twice [to signify that Rome was everywhere at peace] since the founding of the city, Augustus closed three times having won peace on land and at sea. He entered the city in an ovation, after the war of Philippi, and again after that in Sicily, and celebrated three regular triumphs on successive days for his victories in Dalmatia, at Actium, and at Alexandria.

23. He suffered only two serious defeats, those of Lollius and Varus, both of which were in Germany. Of these, the former was more humiliating than serious, but the latter was nearly fatal: three legions were cut to pieces with their general, his lieutenants, and all the auxiliaries. When the news of this arrived, the emperor ordered a watch be kept by night throughout the city to prevent any outbreak, and he prolonged the terms of the provincial governors so that experienced and familiar men might keep the allies loyal. . . . In fact, it is said he was so greatly affected that for several months he cut neither his beard nor his hair, and would sometimes dash his head against a door, crying: "Quintilius Varus, give me back my legions!" Each year he observed the day of the disaster as one of mourning.

Honors and Offices of Augustus

26. Augustus received offices and honors before the usual age; some were extraordinary ones granted for life. At the age of twenty, he led his legions against Rome as if it were an enemy city, sending envoys to demand the consulship office for him in the name of his army. When the Senate hesitated, his centurion, throwing back his cloak and showing the hilt of his sword, did not hesitate to say in the Senate house, "This will make him consul, if you do not." He held his second consulship nine years later, and a third after a year's interval; the rest up to the eleventh were in successive years. After declining for seventeen years, Augustus asked of his own accord for a twelfth and two years later for a thirteenth, wishing to hold the highest magistracy at the time when he introduced each of his sons Gaius and Lucius to public life upon their coming of age.

27. For ten years Augustus was a member of the triumvirate for bringing order to the State, and though for a while he opposed his colleagues Antony and Lepidus and tried to prevent a proscription, yet when it was begun, he carried it through with greater severity than either of them. For while they could oftentimes be moved by personal influence and entreaties, he alone was most insistent that no one should be spared, even adding to the list his guardian Gaius Toranius, . . . Augustus declared that he had consented to end the proscription only on condition that he was allowed a free hand for the future.

While he was triumvir, Augustus incurred general hatred by many of his acts. For example, when he was addressing the soldiers and a throng of civilians had been admitted to the assembly, noticing that Pinarius, a Roman knight, was taking notes, he ordered that he be stabbed on the spot, thinking him to be a spy. Because the consul-elect Tedius Afer bitterly criticized one of his acts, he uttered such terrible threats that Afer committed suicide. Also, when the praetor Quintus Gallius held some folded writing tablets under his robe as he was paying his respects, Augustus, suspecting he had a sword concealed there, dared not search him on the spot lest he be mistaken, but later had Gallius hustled from the tribunal by some soldiers, tortured as if he were a slave, and though he made no confession, ordered his execution, first tearing out the man's eyes with his own hand. Augustus' own version was that Gallius made a treacherous attack on him at an audience, and was taken to prison; after he was exiled, Gallius died either in a shipwreck or was killed by bandits.

28. He twice thought of restoring the republic; first immediately after the overthrow of Antony, remembering that his rival had often made the charge that it was his fault that it was not restored; and again in the weariness of a lingering illness, when he went so far as to summon the magistrates and the Senate to his house, and submit an account of the general condition of the empire. Reflecting, however, that as he himself would not be free from danger if he should retire, so too it would be hazardous to trust the State to the control of more than one, Augustus continued to keep it in his hands. It is not easy to say whether his intentions or their results were the better. He expressed his good intentions from time to time, and put them on record in the following edict: "May I make the State safe, and reap from that act the fruit that I desire; but only if I may be called the author of the best possible government, and bear with me the hope when I die that the foundations which I have laid for the State will remain unshaken." Augustus realized his hope by making every effort to prevent any dissatisfaction with the new regime.

Accomplishments of Augustus

Since the city was not adorned as the dignity of the empire demanded, and was exposed to flood and fire, he so beautified it that he could justly boast that he had found it built of brick and left it in marble. And he provided as best he could against future disasters.

29. Some of his many public works stand out: The Forum of Augustus with the temple of Mars the Avenger, the temple of Apollo on the Palatine, and the temple of Jupiter the

Thunderer on the Capitol. His reasons for building the forum included the increase in the population and of legal cases, which called for a third forum, since two were no longer adequate. It was opened to the public with some haste, before he completed the temple of Mars . . . which he had vowed to build in the war against Brutus which he undertook to avenge his father. . . .

30. Augustus divided the city into districts and wards, arranging that the former should be under the charge of magistrates selected each year by lot, and the latter under "masters" elected by the inhabitants of the respective neighborhoods. To guard against fires he organized night watchmen, and to control the floods he widened and cleared out the channel of the Tiber, which had for some time been filled with rubbish and impeded by projecting buildings. Further, to make the approach to the city easier from every direction, Augustus personally undertook to rebuild the Flaminian Road all the way to Rimini and assigned other high-ways to others who had been honored with triumphs, asking them to use their prize-money in paving them.

He restored ruined and burned temples, adorning both these and other temples with lavish gifts, depositing in the shrine of Jupiter Capitolinus as a single offering sixteen thousand pounds of gold, besides pearls and other precious stones to the value of fifty million sesterces.

31. After he finally had assumed the office of pontifex maximus upon the death of Lepidus (for he could not bring himself to deprive him of the honor while he lived) Augustus collected whatever prophetic writings of Greek or Latin origin were in circulation anonymously or under the names of authors of little repute, and burned more than two thousand of them, retaining only the Sibylline books and making a choice even among those. He deposited the remaining books in two gilded cases under the pedestal of the statue of Palatine Apollo. Since the calendar, reformed by Julius Caesar, later became confused through negligence, he restored the former system, calling the month Sextilis "August" (though his birthday was in September) because he had won his first consulship and his most

brilliant victories in that month. He increased the number and importance of the priests, their allowances, and privileges, in particular those of the Vestal Virgins.

34. He revised existing laws and enacted new ones on extravagance, adultery, chastity, bribery, and on the encouragement of marriage among the various classes of citizens. Having made somewhat more stringent changes in the last of these than in others, Augustus was unable to carry this law out because of an open revolt against its provisions, until he had abolished or mitigated a part of the penalties, besides increasing the rewards and allowing a three years' exemption from the obligation to marry after the death of a husband or wife. When the knights even then persistently called for its repeal at a public show, he sent for the children of Germanicus and exhibited them, some in his own lap and some in their father's, intimating by his gestures and expression that they should follow that young man's example. Upon discovering that the spirit of the law was being evaded by betrothal to little girls and frequent changes of wives, he shortened the duration of betrothals and set a limit on divorces.

35. Since the number of the senators swelled through low-born and ill-assorted rabble (in fact, the Senate numbered more than a thousand, some of whom were wholly unworthy, and had been admitted after Caesar's death through favor or bribery), Augustus restored it to its former limits and distinction by two enrollments, one according to the members' choice, each man naming one other, and a second made by Agrippa and himself. On the latter occasion, it is thought that he wore a coat of mail under his tunic as he presided and a sword by his side, while ten of his most robust friends among the senators stood by his chair. Cremutius Cordus writes that even then the senators were allowed to approach one by one only after the folds of their robes had been carefully searched. Some he shamed into resigning, but he allowed even these to retain their distinctive dress, as well as the privilege of viewing the games from the orchestra and taking part in the public banquets of the senatorial order. So that those who were chosen and approved might

perform their duties more conscientiously and with less inconvenience, he provided that before taking his seat each member should offer incense and wine at the altar of the god in whose temple the meeting was held; that regular meetings of the Senate should not be held more often than twice a month; and that in the months of September and October only those obliged to attend were drawn by lot, to a number sufficient for the passing of decrees. He also adopted the plan of a privy council *consilium* chosen by lot for terms of six months, with which to discuss in advance matters to come before the entire body. On questions of special importance Augustus called upon the senators to give their opinions, not according to the order established by precedent, but just as he fancied, to induce each man to keep his mind on the alert, as if he were to initiate action rather than give assent to others. . . .

37. To enable more men to take part in the administration of the State, he devised new offices: the charge of public buildings, of the roads, of the aqueducts, of the channel of the Tiber, of the distribution of grain to the people, as well as the prefecture of the city, a board of three for choosing senators, and another for reviewing the corps of the knights whenever it should be necessary. He appointed censors, an office long discontinued. He increased the number of praetors. He also demanded that whenever the consulship was conferred on him, he should have two colleagues instead of one; but this was not granted, since all cried out that it was a sufficient offence to his supreme dignity that he held the office with another and not alone.

38. Augustus was generous in honoring martial prowess: he had regular triumphs voted to over thirty generals, and the triumphal regalia to even more than that number. To encourage senators' sons to gain an earlier acquaintance with public business, he allowed them to wear the broad purple stripe when they took the gown of manhood and to attend meetings of the Senate. . . .

39. With the help of ten senators, Augustus examined each knight on his private life, punishing some whose conduct was scandalous while demoting others; most he merely reprimanded with varying degrees of severity . . . .

40. . . . He revised the lists of the people district by district, and to prevent the commons from leaving work to collect their grain dole, he decided to give out tickets for four months' supply three times a year; at their urgent request he allowed a return to the old custom of receiving a share every month. . . .

Considering it also of great importance to keep the people untainted by any foreign or servile blood, he was reluctant to confer Roman citizenship and limited manumission. When Tiberius requested citizenship for a Greek client of his, Augustus wrote in reply that he would not grant it unless the man appeared in person and convinced him that he had a good reason for the request. When Livia asked it for a Gaul, he refused, offering instead freedom from tribute, and declaring that he would rather suffer a loss of taxes than the debasement of Roman citizenship. . . . He also desired to revive ancient Roman dress, and once when he saw in an assembly a throng of men in dark cloaks, he indignantly quoted Virgil: "Behold the Romans, lords of the world, the nation clad in the toga," and he directed the aediles never again to allow anyone to appear in the Forum except in the toga and without a cloak.

41. He was often generous to all classes. For example, by bringing the royal Egyptian treasures to Rome in his Alexandrian triumph he made ready money so abundant that the rate of interest fell, and the value of real estate rose greatly; after that, whenever there was an excess of funds from the property of those who had been condemned he loaned it without interest for fixed periods to any who could give security for double the amount. He increased the property qualification for senators, requiring one million two hundred thousand sesterces, instead of eight hundred thousand, and made up the amount for those who did not possess it. He gave frequent grants to the people, but usually of different sums: now four hundred, now three hundred, now two hundred and fifty sesterces a man; he did not even exclude young boys, though it was usual for them to receive a share

only after the age of eleven. In times of scarcity, he often distributed grain to each man at a very low price, sometimes for nothing, and doubled the money-tickets.

42. To show he was a prince desiring the public welfare rather than popularity, when the people complained of the scarcity and high price of wine, he sharply rebuked them by saying: "My son-in-law Agrippa has taken good care, by building several aqueducts, that men shall not go thirsty.". . . Once, in a time of great scarcity, he expelled from the city the slaves that were for sale, as well as the schools of gladiators, all foreigners with the exception of physicians and teachers, and a part of the household slaves; and when grain at last became more plentiful he wrote: "I was strongly inclined to do away forever with the grain distributions, since through dependence on them agriculture was neglected; but I did not do so, feeling sure that they would one day be renewed through desire for popular favor." From then on he regulated the practice with concern for farmers' and grain dealers' interests as for those of the populace.

46. After having reorganized Rome, Augustus added to the population of Italy by personally establishing twenty-eight colonies. He furnished many cities with public buildings and revenues, and even gave them some equality with the city of Rome. . . .

47. The stronger provinces, which could not be safely governed by annual magistrates, he took to himself; the others he assigned to proconsular governors selected by lot. . . . Certain of the cities which had treaties with Rome, but were on the road to ruin through their lawlessness, he deprived of their independence; he relieved others overwhelmed with debt, rebuilt some destroyed by earthquakes, and gave Latin rights or full citizenship to those rendering services to the Roman people. I believe there is no province, excepting only Africa and Sardinia, which he did not visit; he was planning to cross to these from Sicily after his defeat of Sextus Pompeius, but was prevented by a series of violent storms. . . .

48. He usually restored conquered kingdoms to their defeated dynasties, united the allied kings by mutual ties, and was eager to encourage intermarriages or friendships among them. He never failed to treat all with consideration as integral parts of the empire, regularly appointing a guardian for those too young to rule or whose minds were affected, until they grew up or recovered; and he brought up the children of many, educating them with his own.

49. Of his military forces he assigned the legions and auxiliaries to various provinces, stationed a fleet at Misenum and another at Ravenna, to defend the western and eastern Mediterranean, and employed the remainder partly as city police and partly as palace guard. . . . However, he never allowed more than three cohorts to remain in the city and even those were without a permanent camp. The rest he regularly sent to winter or summer quarters in towns near Rome. Furthermore, he restricted all soldiery everywhere to a fixed scale of pay and allowances, designating the duration of their service and the rewards on its completion according to each man's rank, in order to keep them from being tempted to revolt after their discharge either by age or poverty. To have sufficient funds available for maintaining the soldiers and paying their pensions, he established a military treasury, supported by new taxes.

To improve communications with the provinces, at first Augustus stationed young men as runners at short intervals along the military roads, and later a chariot service. The latter seemed the more convenient arrangement, since the same men who brought the dispatches from any place could, if necessary, be questioned as well.

50. In passports, dispatches, and private letters he first used as his seal a sphinx, later an image of Alexander the Great, and finally his own, carved by the hand of Dioscurides; and this his successors continued to use as their seal. He always attached to all letters the exact hour, not only of the day, but even of the night, to indicate precisely when they were written.

51. There is ample evidence of his clemency and moderation. Though a full list of his pardoned opponents is unnecessary, I offer that he punished two plebeians, Junius Novatus and Cassius Patavinus, with merely a fine and a mild form of banishment respectively, although the

first circulated a most scathing letter about him under the name of the young Agrippa, while the latter openly declared at a large dinner party that he lacked neither the will nor the courage to kill the emperor.

52. Although it had been usual to vote temples to proconsuls, Augustus only accepted one in a province when jointly dedicated to him and the goddess Roma. In Rome itself he emphatically refused the dedication of a temple, even melting down the silver statues formerly set up in his honor. With the money from them he dedicated golden tripods to Apollo of the Palatine.

When the people did their best to force the dictatorship upon him, he knelt down, threw off his toga from his shoulders, and with bare breast begged them not to insist.

53. He always felt insulted at the title of "Lord." When he heard the words "O just and gracious Lord!" uttered in a comedy and all the people sprang to their feet and applauded as if it was said of him, he at once checked this gross flattery by an angry look, and on the following day issued a stern reprimand. After that he would not allow anyone, even his family, to use "lord" either in jest or earnest, and forbade them to use such flattering terms in talking about him. . . . On the day of a meeting of the Senate he always greeted the members in their seats, calling each man by name without a prompter; and when he left the Senate, he took leave of them in the same manner, while they remained seated. He exchanged social calls with many, and attended all their celebrations, until he was well on in years and was once jostled by the crowd at an engagement party. When Gallus Cerrinius, a senator with whom he was not at all intimate, suddenly became blind and resolved to end his life by starvation, Augustus called on him and by his consoling words convinced the senator to live.

54. As he was speaking in the Senate someone said to Augustus: "I don't understand," and another: "I would contradict you if I had a chance." Several times when rushing from the Senate in anger at the excessive bickering of the disputants, some shouted after Augustus: "Senators ought to have the right of speaking their mind on public affairs.". . . Yet no one suffered from freedom of speech or insolence.

55. Augustus did not dread the lampoons against him scattered in the Senate house, but took great pains to refute them; without trying to discover the authors, he merely proposed that thereafter such published notes or verses defamatory of anyone under a false name should be called to account.

57. It may readily be imagined how much he was beloved because of this admirable conduct. I say nothing of senatorial decrees which seem to have been dictated by necessity. The Roman knights willingly celebrated his birthday, and always for two successive days. Men of every class, in fulfillment of a vow for his welfare, each year threw a small coin into the Lacus Curtius, and also brought a gift to the Capitol on New Year's Day, even when he was away from Rome. With this sum he bought and dedicated in each of the city wards costly statues of the gods, . . . When his house on the Palatine was destroyed by fire, the veterans, minor officials, the tribes, and even individuals gladly contributed money for its restoration, each according to his means; but he merely took a little from each pile as a matter of form, not more than a denarius from any of them. On his return from a province they received him not only with prayers and good wishes, but with songs. It was the rule, too, that punishments should be cancelled whenever he entered the city.

58. The whole body of citizens, on sudden unanimous impulse, proffered him the title of Father of his Country: first the commons, by a deputation sent to Antium, and then, because he declined it, again at Rome. The second occurred as he entered the theatre, which the people attended in throngs, all wearing laurel wreaths; the senators afterwards in the Senate, not by decree or by acclamation, but through Valerius Messala. He, speaking for the whole body, said: "Good fortune and divine favor attend you and your family, Caesar Augustus; for thus we feel that we are praying for prosperity for our country and happiness for our city. The Senate and Roman People hail you as 'Father of thy Country.' " Then Augustus, with tears in his eyes, replied as follows (and I have given his

exact words, as I did those of Messala): "Having attained my highest hopes, Fathers of the Senate, what more have I to ask of the immortal gods than that I may retain your unanimous approval to the very end of my life."

59. In honor of his physician, Antonius Musa, through whose care he recovered from a dangerous illness, a sum of money was raised and Musa's statue set up beside that of Aesculapius, the god of medicine. . . .

Personality and Private Life of Augustus

61. Now that I have shown how he conducted himself in civil and military positions, and in ruling the State in all parts of the world in peace and in war, I shall next give an account of his private and domestic life, describing his character and his fortune at home from his youth until the last day of his life.

He lost his mother during his first consulship and his sister Octavia in his fifty-fourth year. To both he showed marked devotion during their lifetimes, and also paid them highest honors after their death.

62. . . . when Augustus became reconciled with Antony after their first quarrel, and their troops begged that the rivals be further united by some tie of kinship, he married Antony's stepdaughter Claudia, daughter of Fulvia by Publius Clodius, although she was barely of marriageable age. Because of a falling out with his mother-in-law, Fulvia, he divorced her before the union was consummated. He then married Scribonia, who had been previously wed to two ex-consuls and was a mother by one of them. He divorced her also, "unable to put up with her nagging," as he himself wrote, and at once took Livia Drusilla from her husband Tiberius Nero, although she was with child at the time; he loved and esteemed her to the end without a rival.

63. He had a daughter Julia by Scribonia, but he was disappointed to have no children by Livia, save one premature baby which died. . . . He gave Julia in marriage first to Marcellus, son of his sister Octavia and hardly more than

a boy; then, after Marcellus' death, to Marcus Agrippa. . . .

64. From Agrippa and Julia he had three grandsons, Gaius, Lucius, and Agrippa, and two granddaughters, Julia and Agrippina. He married Agrippina to Germanicus, his sister's [and Livia's] grandson. He adopted Gaius and Lucius and raised them in the palace where he initiated them into administrative life while they were still young, sending them to the provinces and the armies as consuls elect. . . . He personally taught his grandsons reading, swimming, and other elements of education, taking special pains to train them to imitate his own handwriting; he never dined in their company unless they sat beside him, or made a journey unless they preceded his carriage or rode close by it on either side.

65. At the height of his happiness and his confidence in his family and its training, Fortune proved fickle. He found the two Julias, his daughter and granddaughter, guilty of every form of vice, and banished them. He lost Gaius and Lucius within the span of eighteen months, the former died in Lycia and the latter at Marseilles. He then publicly adopted his third grandson Agrippa Postumus and at the same time his stepson Tiberius, but soon disowned Agrippa because of his brutal behavior, sending him off to Sorrento in disgrace. He bore the death of his kin with far more resignation than their misconduct. He was not greatly broken by the fate of Gaius and Lucius, but he informed the Senate of his daughter's fall through a letter read in his absence, and in his shame remained in seclusion for a long time, and even thought of putting her to death. At all events, when one of her confidantes, a freedwoman called Phoebe, hanged herself at about that same time, he said: "I would rather have been Phoebe's father." After Julia was banished, he denied her the use of wine and every form of luxury, and would not allow any man, slave or free, to come near her without his permission, and then not without being informed of his stature, complexion, and even of any marks or scars upon his body. It was not until five years later that he moved her from the island to the mainland and treated her somewhat less harshly. But he could not be

persuaded to recall her altogether. When the Roman people several times interceded for her and urgently pressed their suit, Augustus, in open assembly, called upon the gods to curse them with like daughters and wives. He would not allow the child born to his granddaughter Julia after her sentence to be recognized or reared. As Agrippa grew no more manageable, but grew madder from day to day, he transferred him to an island and set a guard of soldiers over him. He also provided by a decree of the Senate that he should be confined there for all time, and at every mention of him and of the Julias, Augustus sighed deeply and quoted from Homer in Greek: "Would that I had never wed and had died without offspring." He only alluded to them as his three boils and his three ulcers.

66. He did not readily make friends, but clung to those he had with great constancy, not only suitably rewarding their virtues but even condoning their faults, provided they were not too great. In fact one cannot readily name any of his numerous friends who fell into disgrace, except Salvidienus Rufus, whom he had advanced to a consul's rank, and Cornelius Gallus, whom he had raised to the prefecture of Egypt, both from the lowest estate. The former he handed over to the Senate that it might condemn him to death, because he was plotting revolution; the latter he denied access to the palace because of his ungrateful and envious spirit. But when Gallus too was forced to undergo death through the declarations of his accusers and the decrees of the Senate, though commending their loyalty and their indignation on his account, Augustus shed tears and bewailed his lot, because he alone could be angry with his friends without dire consequences. But these were exceptions; all the rest continued to enjoy power and wealth to the end of their lives, holding leading places in their classes, despite occasional differences. For example, Augustus sometimes found Agrippa impatient and Maecenas indiscreet. When Agrippa felt Augustus was cool to him and preferred Marcellus, he resigned his offices and went off to Mytilene, while Maecenas betrayed to his wife Terentia the secret of the discovery of the conspiracy of Murena. . . .

68. In early youth Augustus was accused of various shameless acts. Sextus Pompey taunted him with effeminacy; Mark Antony with having earned adoption by his uncle through unnatural relations . . . .

69. Not even his friends could deny that he often committed adultery, although they excused it as done for politics, not for passion, so that he could keep track of his opponents' plans through the women of their households. . . . Mark Antony charged that Scribonia was divorced because she said too much when Augustus had other women. . . . Antony writes to Augustus himself in the following familiar terms, before they had broken privately or publicly: "What has made such a change in you? Because I lie with the queen? She is my wife. I am not just beginning this; didn't it begin nine years ago? What of you—do you lie only with Livia? Good luck to you if when you read this letter you have not been with Tertulla or Terentilla or Rufilla or Salvia Titisenia, or all of them. Does it matter with whom you take your pleasure?"

71. [While the charges of homosexuality seem unlikely, . . .] Augustus could not refute the charge of lustfulness and they say that even in his later years he was fond of deflowering maidens, who were brought together for him from all quarters, even by his own wife. . . .

72. In the other details of his life it is generally agreed that he was most temperate and without even the suspicion of any fault. He lived at first near the Forum Romanum; afterwards, on the Palatine, but in a modest dwelling which was remarkable neither for size nor elegance, having but short colonnades with columns of Alban stone, and rooms without any marble decorations or handsome pavements. For more than forty years too he used the same bedroom in winter and summer; although he found the city unfavorable to his health in the winter, yet continued to winter there. If ever he planned to do anything in private or without interruption, he had a retreat at the top of the house, which he called his "little workshop." In this he used to take refuge, or else in the villa of one of his freedmen in the suburbs; but whenever he was not well, he slept at Maecenas's house. For

vacations he went mostly to places by the sea and the islands of Campania, or to the towns near Rome, such as Lanuvium, Praeneste or Tibur, where he very often held court in the colonnades of the Temple of Hercules. He disliked large and sumptuous country palaces, actually razing to the ground one which his granddaughter Julia built on a lavish scale. His own villas, which were modest enough, he decorated not so much with handsome statues and pictures as with terraces, groves, and objects noteworthy for their antiquity and rarity; for example, at Capri the monstrous bones of huge sea monsters and wild beasts, called the "bones of the giants," and the weapons of ancient heroes.

76. He was a light eater and as a rule ate plain food. He particularly liked coarse bread, small fish, handmade moist cheese, and green figs of the second crop; and he would eat even before dinner, wherever and whenever he felt hungry. . . .

77. He was by nature abstemious. Cornelius Nepos writes that in camp before the battle of Mutina it was his habit to drink not more than three times at dinner. Afterwards, when he indulged most freely he never exceeded a pint; or if he did, he used to throw it up. He liked Raetian wine best, but rarely drank before dinner. Instead he would take a bit of bread soaked in cold water, a slice of cucumber, a sprig of lettuce, or a fresh or dried sour apple.

79. He was unusually handsome and exceedingly graceful at all periods of his life, though he paid no attention to personal appearance. He cared so little about his hair, that he would have several barbers working in a hurry, also shaving or clipping his beard while at the very same time he would be reading or writing. His expression, whether in conversation or when he was silent, was so calm and mild, that a leading Gaul admitted to his countrymen that it had softened his heart, and kept him from carrying out his plan to push the emperor over a cliff, when he had been allowed to approach him under the pretence of a conference, as he was crossing the Alps. He had clear, bright eyes, in which he liked to have it thought that there was a kind of divine power. . . . His teeth were wide apart, small, and ill-kept; his hair was slightly curly and inclining to golden; his eyebrows met. His ears were of moderate size, and his nose projected a little at the top and then bent slightly inward. His complexion was between dark and fair. He was short of stature (although Julius Marathus, his freedman and keeper of his records, says that he was five feet and seven inches in height), but this was concealed by the fine proportion and symmetry of his figure, and was noticeable only by comparison with some taller person standing beside him.

81. In the course of his life he suffered from several severe and dangerous illnesses, especially after the subjugation of Spain, when he so suffered from abscesses of the liver, that he submitted to a hazardous course of treatment: since hot fomentations gave him no relief, his physician Antonius Musa prescribed cold ones. . . .

84. From early youth he diligently studied oratory and literature. Though busy during the war at Mutina, he is said to have read, written and declaimed every day. In fact he never afterwards spoke in the Senate, or to the people or the soldiers, except with a prepared address, although he was quite capable of extempore speaking. Moreover, to avoid the danger of forgetting what he was to say, or wasting time in committing it to memory, he adopted the practice of reading everything from a manuscript. Even his important conversations with individuals and with his own wife Livia, he always wrote out and read from a note-book, for fear of saying too much or too little if he spoke offhand. . . .

85. He wrote numerous works of various kinds in prose, some of which he read to a group of his intimate friends, as others did in a lecture-room; for example, his "Reply to Brutus on Cato," "Exhortations to Philosophy" and some volumes of an autobiography, . . . Though he began a tragedy with much enthusiasm, he destroyed it because his style did not satisfy him, and when some of his friends asked him what had become of *Ajax*, he answered that "my *Ajax* had not fallen on his sword, but on my eraser."

88. He does not strictly follow the rules of spelling laid down by the grammarians, but

prefers to spell exactly as we pronounce. Of course his frequent transposition or omission of syllables as well as of letters are slips common to all mankind. I should not have noted this, did it not seem to me surprising that some have written that he fired a provincial governor, as an uncultivated and ignorant fellow, because Augustus noticed that he had written "ixi" for "ipsi." Whenever he wrote in code, he wrote B for A, C for B, and the rest of the letters on the same principle, using AA for X.

89. He was equally interested in Greek studies, and in these too he excelled greatly. . . . Yet he never acquired the ability to speak Greek fluently or to compose anything in it; for if he had occasion to use the language, he wrote what he had to say in Latin and gave it to someone else to translate. . . . In reading the writers of both tongues there was nothing for which he looked so carefully as precepts and examples instructive to the public or to individuals; these he would often copy word for word, and send to members of his household, or to his generals and provincial governors, whenever any of them required admonition. . . . He encouraged intellectuals of his own age, listening with courtesy and patience to their readings, not only of poetry and history, but of speeches and dialogues as well. But he took offence at being made the subject of any composition except by the most eminent writers. . . .

90. This is what we are told of his attitude towards matters of religion: He was afraid of thunder and lightning, for he always carried a seal-skin about with him everywhere as a protection, and at any sign of a violent storm took refuge in an underground vault, for he was once badly frightened by a narrow escape from lightning.

91. He took seriously his own dreams or those which others dreamed about him. At the battle of Philippi, though he had made up his mind not to leave his tent because of illness, he did so after all when warned by a friend's dream; he was fortunate since his camp was taken and when the enemy rushed in, his bed was stabbed through and through and torn to pieces, in the belief that he was still lying there ill. . . .

94. At this point, it might be appropriate to mention the omens which occurred around the time of his birth, and afterwards, from which it was possible to anticipate his future greatness and uninterrupted good fortune. . . . The day Augustus was born the Senate debated the conspiracy of Catiline, and his father Octavius came late because of his wife's confinement; then the astrologer Publius Nigidius, as everyone knows, learning the reason for his tardiness and being informed also of the hour of the birth, declared that the ruler of the world had been born. Later, when Octavius was leading an army through remote parts of Thrace, and he consulted the priests of Dionysus about his son and they made the same prediction; for a pillar of flame sprang forth from the wine that was poured over the altar, that it rose above the temple roof and mounted to the very sky, and such an omen had befallen no one save Alexander the Great, when he offered sacrifice at the same altar. Moreover, the very next night Octavius dreamed that his son appeared to him in a guise more majestic than that of mortal man, with the thunderbolt, scepter, and insignia of Jupiter Optimus Maximus, wearing a radiant crown and mounted upon a laurel-wreathed chariot drawn by twelve horses of surpassing whiteness. . . . And when Marcus Cicero escorted Julius Caesar to the Capitol, he happened to tell his friends a dream of the night before; that a boy of noble countenance was let down from heaven on a golden chain and, at the door of the temple, was given a whip by Jupiter. Just then seeing the boy Augustus, who had been brought to the ceremony by his uncle Caesar but was still unknown to most of those present, Cicero declared that he was the very boy he had seen in his dream . . . .

95. When Augustus returned to Rome after Caesar's death, though the heaven was clear and cloudless, a circle like a rainbow suddenly formed around the sun's disc, and straightway the tomb of Caesar's daughter Julia was struck by lightning. Again, as he was taking the auspices in his first consulship, twelve vultures appeared to him, as to Romulus, and when he slew the victims, the livers within all of them were found to be doubled inward at the lower end, which all

those who were skilled in such matters unanimously declared to be an omen of a great and happy future.

Death and Deification of Augustus

97. His death, too, of which I shall speak next, and his deification after death, were known in advance by unmistakable signs. . . .

98. After skirting the coast of Campania and the neighboring islands, he spent four days at his villa in Capri, where he rested and relaxed. He next crossed over to Naples, although his bowels were still weak from intermittent attacks. In spite of this he witnessed a gymnastic contest which had been established in his honor, and then started with Tiberius for his destination. But as he was returning, his illness increased and he took to his bed at Nola, calling back Tiberius, who was on his way to Illyricum, and keeping him for a long private conversation, after which he gave attention to no business of importance.

99. On the last day of his life he asked every now and then whether there was any unrest on his account; then calling for a mirror, he had his hair combed and his falling jaws set straight. After that, calling in his friends and asking whether they thought he had played his part well in the comedy of life he added the curtain line from a Greek comedy:

Since I've played my part well, all clap your hands And send me from the stage with your applause.

Then he sent them all off, and while he was asking some newcomers from the city about the daughter of Drusus, who was ill, he suddenly passed away as he was kissing Livia, uttering these last words: "Live mindful of our marriage, Livia, and farewell," thus blessed with an easy death and such a one as he had always longed for. For almost always on hearing that anyone had died swiftly and painlessly, he prayed that he and his might have a like euthanasia, for that was the term he was wont to use. He gave but one single sign of wandering before he breathed his last, calling out in sudden terror that forty young men were carrying him off. And even this was rather a premonition than a delusion, since it was that very number of soldiers of the praetorian guard that carried him forth to lie in state.

100. He died in the same room as his father Octavius, on August 19, A.D. 14 about three o'clock in the afternoon, just thirty-five days before his seventy-sixth birthday. His body was carried by the senators of the municipalities and colonies from Nola all the way to Bovillae, in the night time because of the hot weather, being placed by day in the basilica of the town at which they arrived or in its principal temple. At Bovillae the members of the equestrian order met it and bore it to the city, where they placed it in the vestibule of his house.

In their desire to give him a splendid funeral and honor his memory, the senators vied with one another among many suggestions. Some proposed that his cortege pass through the triumphal gate, preceded by the statue of Victory which stands in the Senate, while a dirge was sung by children of both sexes belonging to the leading families; . . . one proposed that all the period from the day of his birth until his demise be called the Augustan Age, and so entered in the Calendar. But though a limit was set to the honors paid him, his eulogy was twice delivered: before the temple of the Deified Julius by Tiberius, and from the old rostra by Drusus, son of Tiberius; and he was carried on the shoulders of senators to the Campus Martius and there cremated. There was even an ex-praetor who took oath that he had seen the form of the Emperor, after he had been reduced to ashes, on its way to heaven. His remains were gathered up by the leading men of the equestrian order, barefooted and in tunics, and placed in the Mausoleum. This structure he had built in his sixth consulship between the Via Flaminia and the bank of the Tiber, and had given public access to the groves and walks by which it was surrounded.

101. He had made a will in the previous year, in two note-books, written in part in his own hand and in part in that of his freedmen Polybius and Hilarion. These the Vestal Virgins, with whom they had been deposited, now produced, together with three rolls, which were sealed in the same way. All these were

opened and read in the Senate. He appointed as his chief heirs Tiberius, to receive two-thirds of the estate, and Livia, one-third; these he also bade assume his name. His heirs in the second degree were Drusus, son of Tiberius, for one-third, and for the rest Germanicus and his three male children. In the third grade he mentioned many of his relatives and friends.

He left to the Roman people forty million sesterces; to the tribes three and a half million; to the soldiers of the praetorian guard a thousand each; to the city cohorts five hundred; and to the legionaries three hundred. This sum he ordered to be paid at once, for he had always kept the amount at hand and ready for the purpose. He gave other legacies to various individuals, some amounting to as much as twenty thousand sesterces, and provided for the payment of these a year later, giving as his excuse for the delay "the small amount of my property. Not more than a hundred and fifty millions will come to my heirs; for though I have received fourteen hundred millions during the last twenty years in the wills of my friends, I have spent of it, as well as of my two paternal estates and other inheritances, to the benefit of the State." He gave orders that his daughter and his granddaughter Julia should not be put in his Mausoleum, if anything befell them. In one of the three rolls he included directions for his funeral; in the second, an account of what he had accomplished, which he desired to have cut upon bronze tablets and set up at the entrance to the Mausoleum; in the third, a summary of the condition of the whole empire: how many soldiers there were in active service in all parts of it, how much money there was in the public treasury and in the privy-purse, and what revenues were due.

A young Octavian is portrayed on a silver denarius issued in 29-27 B.C., after his defeat of Marc Antony, but before he took the title of "Augustus."

II

Augustus: "The Republic Restored"

INTRODUCTION
Ronald Mellor

After decades of civil war, Rome accepted Augustus' monarchical regime disguised under the traditional terminology of the Roman Republic. The public image of the benevolent Augustus was intended to erase the memory of the cold, manipulative Octavian who had so singlemindedly struggled against Antony for supreme power. The Augustan political program was couched in terms of economic revival and moral regeneration, with a strong emphasis on continuity with the glorious Roman past.

Octavian had taken Caesar's name and he also took as a name "Imperator"—the honorific title once conferred on a triumphant Roman general, which became a permanent name of the Roman "emperors" (a term that is, of course, derived from it). And the familiar title "Princeps" (which became "prince" in English) designated Augustus as the leading man of the state. But Rome's ruler now looked to create new trappings of power. He would avoid the overt military dictatorship of Sulla and Julius Caesar, however popular that might be with the commoners. And he would surely avoid any hint of eastern kingship, for which his propagandists had so castigated Antony.

In January of 27 B.C., the Senate and Roman people played their part in the political drama that Octavian produced. The emperor claimed in his autobiography that he transferred all his powers to the Senate and the Roman people. The Republic was said to be restored: Res Publica Restituta. There is no need to think that all the "popular protests" that followed were orchestrated; the people well knew that only Octavian could prevent the recurrence of civil war. And so the constitutional settlement was reached. Octavian was granted the name of Augustus—which carried a felicitous resonance in Latin, recalling both auctoritas and religious awe. Augustus was granted wide powers—each with a precedent in the Republic, but together quite unprecedented. The power of the princeps far exceeded the standards of the Republic, but it also brought with it the cessation of the bitter personal rivalries among the aristocrats that had so often brought violence to the streets of Rome.

He would hold imperium both in Rome and in the provinces—as Pompey had done in 52 B.C. His proconsulship, which would last for ten years as had Julius Caesar's in Gaul, would cover

Syria, Gaul, and Spain, where twenty of the twenty-six legions were stationed. These offices both legitimized and veiled his position: the magistracies were to cloak, not to bestow, power. The political theorist Machiavelli, writing in 1513, warns princes against relying on the trappings of power, but Augustus needed no such caution. The historian Tacitus, living a century after Augustus, accurately said that Augustus used old titles to mean new things.

The settlement of 27 B.C. did not solve the problems facing the emperor; at most it bought time and support. But within a few years the "Republicans" were again grumbling. The emperor's continuing tenure as one of the two consuls cut in half the number of nobles who could attain the highest office in the state. Since many had consular ancestors and since Roman pride rested on emulating the achievements of one's forebears, dissatisfaction spread among the elite. When Augustus became quite ill, that discontent grew more dangerous.

In 23 B.C. Augustus responded to this unhappiness by changing the formal basis of his power. He resigned his eleventh consulship and in the last thirty-seven years of his reign he assumed it only on two other occasions, and then to preside over celebrations as his grandsons came of age. He took, however, the "tribunician power" adapted from the popular republican office of tribune of the people. He could summon meetings of the Senate and assemblies, propose legislation, and veto laws as well as the actions of other magistrates. In addition, his proconsular imperium was now called "maius" (greater), which meant that it would override that of any other magistrate. It was by the tribunician power that future emperors would identify their regnal years on their coinage—it became the title of the ruler and his successor.

Augustus gradually took other titles and powers as well. He revised the roll of the Senate three times—an opportunity for punishing the recalcitrant and for rewarding his supporters. He also took direct control of the vital grain supply and, with the death of his one-time ally Lepidus in 12 B.C., he took Julius Caesar's old office of Pontifex Maximus. And in 2 B.C., he was formally called Father of the Country—Pater Patriae.

Augustus and his successors avoided the title of rex ("king"), since the legends of the past Etruscan tyrants had given that word a negative force in Latin. The Greeks, however, understood the reality of power and would call the Roman emperors with their word for king—basileus—and Tacitus said that the emperor took over the functions of the Senate, the magistrates and the laws. But this chapter will show how carefully Augustus himself cloaked his extraordinary power in more traditional titles, and it will also examine the impression he made on some of the greatest writers of his time.

The Death of Augustus

Tacitus

Cornelius Tacitus (A.D. 55–117) was the greatest historian of ancient Rome. His family were members of the provincial elite (probably from Gaul), and young Tacitus married the daughter of an important Roman general and attained high office and senatorial rank. During Domitian's reign of terror, he withdrew from public life and began his historical research; he continued to write after the fall of Domitian (A.D. 96) when he was consul and later governor of Asia. Yet his writings show a melancholic conservative who looked longingly at the long-gone era of senatorial predominance which had disappeared more than a century before his birth and which he knew could never return. Despite his protestations that he wrote "without prejudice or partisanship," his hatred of imperial tyranny is evident on every page of his history.

Ancient historians did not wish to produce the sort of objective scholarship that is the aim of modern academic historians; they wrote with passionate political commitment. Tacitus had had an excellent rhetorical education, and he deploys poetic and dramatic devices with passion, moral authority, a sense of drama and an epigrammatic wit that make his histories unique. Though his work may be partisan, he has created a picture of the imperial court so powerful that after 2,000 years we see the Roman court through his cynical and outraged eyes.

The Annals is a history of the period from Tiberius to Nero (A.D. 14–68), and Tacitus' brief treatment of Augustus forms a prologue to that work. Though later in the work he seems to admire Augustus and compares him favorably to his successors, these first pages drip with sarcasm and innuendo against Augustus, Livia and Tiberius. Tacitus often reports a pernicious rumor, only to deny that there is any evidence to support it. Thus he says that some suspected Livia of the death of Augustus, but he merely allows the unsupported accusation to linger in the reader's memory. And the accession of Tiberius is presented as sinister and conspiratorial, though Suetonius quotes letters to show that Augustus was quite contented with Tiberius as his successor. Even in these first pages, Tacitus conveys his bleak vision of tyranny and corruption.

When Rome was first a city, its rulers were kings. Then Lucius Junius Brutus created the consulate and free Republican institutions in general. Dictatorships were assumed in emergencies. A Council of Ten did not last more than two years; and then there was a short-lived arrangement by which senior army officers—the commanders of contingents provided by the tribes—possessed consular authority. Subsequently Cinna and Sulla set up autocracies, but they too were brief. Soon Pompey and Crassus acquired predominant positions, but rapidly lost them to Caesar. Next, the military strength which Lepidus and Antony had built up was absorbed by Augustus. He found the whole state exhausted by internal dissensions, and established over it a personal régime known as the Principate.[1]

Famous writers have recorded Rome's early glories and disasters. The Augustan Age, too, had its distinguished historians. But then the rising tide of flattery exercised a deterrent effect. The reigns of Tiberius, Gaius, Claudius, and

---

1 Tacitus refers to the following events: 753 B.C. legendary date of the foundation of Rome; 510 kings supposedly expelled by Lucius Junius Brutus; 451–49 constitution suspended in favour of two successive annual Councils of Ten to prepare codes of laws; 444–367 (at intervals)

Nero were described during their lifetimes in fictitious terms, for fear of the consequences; whereas the accounts written after their deaths were influenced by still raging animosities. So I have decided to say a little about Augustus, with special attention to his last period, and then go on to the reign of Tiberius and what followed. I shall write without indignation or partisanship: in my case the customary incentives to these are lacking.

The violent deaths of Brutus and Cassius left no Republican forces in the field. Defeat came to Sextus Pompeius in Sicily, Lepidus was dropped, Antony killed. So even the Caesarian party had no leader left except the 'Caesar' himself, Octavian. He gave up the title of Triumvir, emphasizing instead his position as consul; and the powers of a tribune, he proclaimed, were good enough for him—powers for the protection of ordinary people.

He seduced the army with bonuses, and his cheap food policy was successful bait for civilians. Indeed, he attracted everybody's goodwill by the enjoyable gift of peace. Then he gradually pushed ahead and absorbed the functions of the Senate, the officials, and even the law. Opposition did not exist. War or judicial murder had disposed of all men of spirit. Upperclass survivors found that slavish obedience was the way to succeed, both politically and financially. They had profited from the revolution, and so now they liked the security of the existing arrangement better than the dangerous uncertainties of the old régime. Besides, the new order was popular in the provinces. There, government by senate and people was looked upon sceptically as a matter of sparring dignitaries and extortionate officials. The legal system had provided no remedy against these, since it was wholly incapacitated by violence, favouritism, and—most of all—bribery.

To safeguard his domination Augustus made his sister's son Marcellus a priest and a curule aedile—in spite of his extreme youth—and singled out Marcus Agrippa, a commoner but a first-rate soldier who had helped to win his victories, by the award of two consecutive consulships; after the death of Marcellus, Agrippa was chosen by Augustus as his son-in-law. Next the emperor had his stepsons Tiberius and Nero Drusus hailed publicly as victorious generals. When he did this, however, there was no lack of heirs of his own blood: there were Agrippa's sons Gaius Caesar and Lucius Caesar. Augustus had adopted them into the imperial family. He had also, despite pretended reluctance, been passionately eager that, even as minors, they should be entitled Princes of Youth and have consulships reserved for them. After Agrippa had died, first Lucius Caesar and then Gaius Caesar met with premature natural deaths—unless their stepmother Livia had a secret hand in them. Lucius died on his way to the armies in Spain, Gaius while returning from Armenia incapacitated by a wound.

Nero Drusus was long dead. Tiberius was the only surviving stepson; and everything pointed in his direction. He was adopted as the emperor's son and as partner in his powers (with civil and military authority and the powers of a tribune) and displayed to all the armies. No longer was this due to his mother's secret machinations, as previously. This time she requested it openly. Livia had the aged Augustus firmly under control—so much that he exiled his only surviving grandson to the island of Planasia. That was the young, physically tough, indeed brutish, Agrippa Postumus. Though devoid of every good quality, he had been involved in no scandal. Nevertheless, it was not he but Germanicus, the son of Nero Drusus, whom the emperor placed in command of the

---

commanders of tribal contingents granted consular powers; 87–4 four consulates of Lucius Cornelius Cinna; 82–79 Sulla's dictatorship; 60/59–3 informal 'First Triumvirate' of Pompey, Marcus Licinius Crassus, and Julius Caesar; 49–4 Julius Caesar's dictatorships; 43 'Second Triumvirate' of Antony, Octavian (the future Augustus), and Marcus Aemilius Lepidus (III); 43 deaths of Brutus and Cassius; 36 Sextus Pompeius defeated and Lepidus dropped; 30 suicide of Antony.

eight divisions on the Rhine—and, although Tiberius had a grown son of his own, he ordered him to adopt Germanicus. For Augustus wanted to have another iron in the fire.

At this time there was no longer any fighting—except a war against the Germans; and that was designed less to extend the empire's frontiers, or achieve any lucrative purpose, than to avenge the disgrace of the army lost with Publius Quinctilius Varus. In the capital the situation was calm. The titles of officials remained the same. Actium had been won before the younger men were born. Even most of the older generation had come into a world of civil wars. Practically no one had ever seen truly Republican government. The country had been transformed, and there was nothing left of the fine old Roman character. Political equality was a thing of the past; all eyes watched for imperial commands.

Nobody had any immediate worries as long as Augustus retained his physical powers, and kept himself going, and his House, and the peace of the empire. But when old age incapacitated him, his approaching end brought hopes of change. A few people started idly talking of the blessings of freedom. Some, more numerous, feared civil war; others wanted it. The great majority, however, exchanged critical gossip about candidates for the succession. First, Agrippa Postumus—a savage without either the years or the training needed for imperial responsibilities. Tiberius, on the other hand, had the seniority and the military reputation. But he also possessed the ancient, ingrained arrogance of the Claudian family; and signs of a cruel disposition kept breaking out, repress them as he might. Besides, it was argued, he had been brought up from earliest youth in an imperial household, had accumulated early consulships and Triumphs, and even during the years at Rhodes[2]—which looked like banishment but were called retirement—his thoughts had been solely occupied with resentment, deception, and secret sensuality. And then there was that feminine bully, his mother. 'So we have got to be

slaves to a woman,' people were saying, 'and to the two half-grown boys Germanicus and Drusus. First they will be a burden to the State—then they will tear it in two!'

Amid this sort of conversation the health of Augustus deteriorated. Some suspected his wife of foul play. For rumour had it that a few months earlier, with the knowledge of his immediate circle but accompanied only by Paullus Fabius Maximus, he had gone to Planasia to visit Agrippa Postumus; and that there had been such a tearful display of affection on both sides that the young man seemed very likely to be received back into the home of his grandfather. Maximus, it was further said, had told his wife, Marcia, of this, and she had warned Livia—but the emperor had discovered the leakage, and when Maximus died shortly afterwards (perhaps by his own hand) his widow had been heard at the funeral moaning and blaming herself for her husband's death. Whatever the true facts about this, Tiberius was recalled from his post in Illyricum (immediately after his arrival there) by an urgent letter from his mother. When he arrived at Nola, it is unknown whether he found Augustus alive or dead. For the house and neighbouring streets were carefully sealed by Livia's guards. At intervals, hopeful reports were published—until the steps demanded by the situation had been taken. Then two pieces of news became known simultaneously: Augustus was dead, and Tiberius was in control.

The new reign's first crime was the assassination of Agrippa Postumus. He was killed by a staff-officer—who found it a hard task, though he was a persevering murderer and the victim taken by surprise unarmed. Tiberius said nothing about the matter in the Senate. He pretended that the orders came from Augustus, who was alleged to have instructed the colonel in charge to kill Agrippa Postumus as soon as Augustus himself was dead. It is true that Augustus' scathing criticisms of the young man's behaviour were undoubtedly what had prompted the Senate to decree his banishment. But the emperor had never been callous enough to kill any of his

---

2 Tiberius spent the years 6 B.C.–A.D. 2 on the island of Rhodes.

relations, and that he should murder his own grandchild to remove the worries of a stepson seemed incredible. It would be nearer the truth to suppose that Tiberius because he was afraid, and Livia through stepmotherly malevolence, loathed and distrusted the young Agrippa Postumus and got rid of him at the first opportunity. But when the staff-officer reported in military fashion that he had carried out his order, Tiberius answered that he had given no orders and that what had been done would have to be accounted for in the senate.

This came to the notice of Tiberius' confidant, Gaius Sallustius Crispus. It was he who had sent instructions to the colonel, and he was afraid that the responsibility might be shifted to himself—in which case either telling the truth or lying would be equally risky. So he warned Livia that palace secrets, and the advice of friends, and services performed by the army, were best undivulged; and Tiberius must not weaken the throne by referring everything to the senate. The whole point of autocracy, Crispus observed, is that the accounts will not come right unless the ruler is their only auditor.

Meanwhile at Rome consuls, senate, knights, precipitately became servile. The more distinguished men were, the greater their urgency and insincerity. They must show neither satisfaction at the death of one emperor, nor gloom at the accession of another: so their features were carefully arranged in a blend of tears and smiles, mourning and flattery. The first to swear allegiance to Tiberius Caesar were the consuls Sextus Pompeius and Sextus Appuleius; then in their presence the commander of the Guard, Lucius Seius Strabo, and the controller of the corn-supply, Gaius Turranius, next the senate, army, and public. For Tiberius made a habit of always allowing the consuls the initiative, as though the Republic still existed and he himself were uncertain whether to take charge or not. Even the edict with which he summoned the senate to its House was merely issued by virtue of the tribune's power which he had received under Augustus. His edict was brief, and very unpretentious. In it he proposed to arrange his father's last honours, and stay by the

side of his body. This, he said, was the only State business which he was assuming.

Nevertheless, when Augustus died Tiberius had given the watchword to the Guard as its commander. He already had the trappings of a court, too, such as personal bodyguards and men-at-arms. When he went to the Forum, or into the senate, he had soldiers to escort him. He sent letters to the armies as though he were already emperor. He only showed signs of hesitation when he addressed the senate. This was chiefly because of Germanicus, who was extremely popular and disposed of a large Roman force and hordes of auxiliary troops. Tiberius was afraid Germanicus might prefer the throne to the prospect of it. Besides, in deference to public opinion, Tiberius wanted to seem the person chosen and called by the State—instead of one who had wormed his way in by an old man's adoption, and intrigues of the old man's wife. Afterwards it was understood that Tiberius had pretended to be hesitant for another reason too, in order to detect what leading men were thinking. Every word, every look he twisted into some criminal significance—and stored them up in his memory.

At the senate's first meeting he allowed no business to be discussed except the funeral of Augustus. But first the emperor's will was brought in by the priestesses of Vesta. Tiberius and Livia were his heirs, and Livia was adopted into the Julian family with the name of 'Augusta.' Grandchildren and great-grandchildren had been named as heirs in the second degree. In the third degree came the most prominent men in the State; Augustus had detested a good many of them, but their inclusion bragged to posterity that he had been their friend. His legacies were in keeping with the standards of ordinary citizens, except that he left 43,500,000 sesterces to the nation and people of Rome, a thousand to every Guardsman, five hundred each to the troops of the capital, three hundred to every citizen soldier, whether he belonged to a regular brigade or to an auxiliary battalion.

A discussion of the funeral followed. The proposals regarded as most noteworthy were those of Gaius Asinius Gallus and Lucius Arruntius. What Gallus wanted was that the procession should pass through a triumphal arch. Arruntius proposed that the body should be preceded by placards showing the titles of every law Augustus had passed and the names of every people he had conquered. Marcus Valerius Messalla Messallinus also suggested that the oath of allegiance to Tiberius should be repeated every year. When Tiberius asked him to confirm that he, Tiberius, had not prompted this proposal, Messalla answered that it was his own idea—and that in matters of public importance he intended to use his own judgement and no one else's, even at the risk of causing offence. This show of independence was the only sort of flattery left.

Members clamoured that the body of Augustus should be carried to the pyre on the shoulders of senators. Tiberius, with condescending leniency, excused them. He also published an edict requesting the populace not to repeat the disturbances—due to over-enthusiasm—at the funeral of Julius Caesar, by pressing for Augustus to be cremated in the Forum instead of the Field of Mars, his appointed place of rest. On the day of the funeral the troops were out, apparently for protective purposes. This caused much jeering from people who had witnessed, or heard from their parents, about that day (when the nation's enslavement was still rudimentary) of the ill-starred attempt to recover Republican freedom by murdering the dictator Caesar—a fearful crime? or a conspicuously glorious achievement? Now, they said, this aged autocrat Augustus seems to need a military guard to ensure his undisturbed burial, in spite of his lengthy domination and the foresight with which his heirs, too, have been allocated resources for the suppression of the old order.

Then there was much discussion of Augustus himself. Most people were struck by meaningless points such as the coincidence between the dates of his first public office and his death, and the fact that he died in the same house and room at Nola as his father, Gaius Octavius. There was also talk about his numerous consulships—which equalled the combined totals of Marcus Valerius Corvus and Gaius Marius—of his tribune's power con-

tinuous for thirty-seven years, of the twenty-one times he was hailed as victor, and of his other honours, traditional or novel, single or repeated. Intelligent people praised or criticized him in varying terms. One opinion was as follows. Filial duty and a national emergency, in which there was no place for law-abiding conduct, had driven him to civil war—and this can be neither initiated nor maintained by decent methods. He had made many concessions to Antony and to Lepidus for the sake of vengeance on his father's murderers. When Lepidus grew old and lazy, and Antony's self-indulgence got the better of him, the only possible cure for the distracted country had been government by one man. However, Augustus had put the State in order not by making himself king or dictator but by creating the Principate. The empire's frontiers were on the ocean, or distant rivers. Armies, provinces, fleets, the whole system were interrelated. Roman citizens were protected by the law. Provincials were decently treated. Rome itself had been lavishly beautified. Force had been sparingly used—merely to preserve peace for the majority.

The opposite view went like this. Filial duty and national crisis had been merely pretexts. In actual fact, the motive of Octavian, the future Augustus, was lust for power. Inspired by that, he had mobilized ex-army settlers by gifts of money, raised an army—while he was only a half-grown boy without any official status—won over a consul's brigades by bribery, pretended to support Sextus Pompeius, and by senatorial decree usurped the status and rank of a praetor. Soon both consuls, Gaius Vibius Pansa and Aulus Hirtius, had met their deaths—by enemy action; or perhaps in the one case by the deliberate poisoning of his wound, and in the other at the hand of his own troops, instigated by Octavian. In any case it was he who took over both their armies. Then he had forced the reluctant senate to make him consul. But the forces given him to deal with Antony he used against the State. His judicial murders and land distributions were distasteful even to those who carried them out. True, Cassius and Brutus died because he had inherited a feud against them; nevertheless, personal enmities ought to be sacrificed to the public interest. Next he had cheated Sextus Pompeius by a spurious peace treaty, Lepidus by spurious friendship. Then Antony, enticed by the treaties of Tarentum and Brundusium and his marriage with Octavian's sister, had paid the penalty of that delusive relationship with his life. After that, there had certainly been peace, but it was a bloodstained peace. For there followed the disasters of Marcus Lollius and Publius Quinctilius Varus; and there were the assassinations, for example, of Aulus Terentius Varro Murena, Marcus Egnatius Rufus and Iullus Antonius.[3]

And gossip did not spare his personal affairs—how he had abducted the wife of Tiberius Claudius Nero, and asked the priests the farcical question whether it was in order for her to marry while pregnant. Then there was the debauchery of his friend Publius Vedius Pollio. But Livia was a real catastrophe, to the nation, as a mother and to the house of the Caesars as a stepmother.

Besides, critics continued, Augustus seemed to have superseded the worship of the gods when he wanted to have himself venerated in temples, with god-like images, by priests and ministers. His appointment of Tiberius as his successor was due neither to personal affection nor to regard for the national interests. Thoroughly aware of Tiberius' cruelty and arrogance, he intended to heighten his own glory by the contrast with one so inferior. For a few years earlier, when Augustus had been asking the senate to re-award tribune's powers to Tiberius, the emperor had actually let drop in a complimentary oration certain remarks about Tiberius' deportment, style of dressing, and habits. Ostensibly these were excuses; in fact they were criticisms.

After an appropriate funeral, Augustus was declared a god and decreed a temple.

---

3 Tacitus refers to the following events: 23 B.C. execution of Aulus Terentius Varro Murena for alleged conspiracy; 19 execution of Marcus Egnatius Rufus for alleged conspiracy; 16 defeat of Marcus Lollius in Germany; 2 Antony's son Iullus Antonius forced to suicide; A.D. 4 Augustus adopts Tiberius; 9 Publius Quinctilius Varus defeated and killed by Arminius in Germany.

The *Res Gestae* (Achievements of Augustus)

Augustus Caesar

This inscription provides Augustus' own record of what he wished to be remembered about his reign. Suetonius reports that it was originally set up on bronze tablets outside the emperor's mausoleum, but it has been reconstructed from Latin and Greek copies set up in Ankara, Turkey. It follows the example of eastern kings, who erected monumental inscriptions recording their achievements (Res Gestae). Augustus divides his accomplishments into three general categories: honors and offices that were granted to him (1–14); his expenditures for the public good, including building programs, benefactions and games (15–24); and his achievements in war and peace (25–34). This political document emphasizes the republican titles and offices Augustus held, and it never mentions by name such opponents as Marc Antony. While it does conceal the fact of his predominance, it cloaks it in a more traditional garb. Though it remains one of the most important documents for the study of Roman imperial history, it must be read with caution as a work of political propaganda which contains many distortions.

Below is a copy of the accomplishments of the deified Augustus by which he brought the whole world under the empire of the Roman people, and of the moneys expended by him on the state and the Roman people, as inscribed on two bronze pillars set up in Rome.

1. At the age of nineteen, on my own initiative and at my own expense, I raised an army by means of which I liberated the Republic, which was oppressed by the tyranny of a faction. For which reason the senate, with honorific decrees, made me a member of its order in the consulship of Gaius Pansa and Aulus Hirtius, giving me at the same time consular rank in voting, and granted me the *imperium*. It ordered me as propraetor, together with the consuls, to see to it that the state suffered no harm. Moreover, in the same year, when both consuls had fallen in the war, the people elected me consul and a triumvir for the settlement of the commonwealth.

2. Those who assassinated my father I drove into exile, avenging their crime by due process of law; and afterwards when they waged war against the state, I conquered them twice on the battlefield.

3. I waged many wars throughout the whole world by land and by sea, both civil and foreign, and when victorious I spared all citizens who sought pardon. Foreign peoples who could safely be pardoned I preferred to spare rather than to extirpate. About 500,000 Roman citizens were under military oath to me. Of these, when their terms of service were ended, I settled in colonies or sent back to their own municipalities a little more than 300,000, and to all of these I allotted lands or granted money as rewards for military service. I captured 600 ships, exclusive of those which were of smaller class than triremes.

4. Twice I celebrated ovations, three times curule triumphs, and I was acclaimed *imperator* twenty-one times. When the senate decreed additional triumphs to me, I declined them on four occasions. I deposited in the Capitol laurel wreaths adorning my *fasces*, after fulfilling the vows which I had made in each war. For successes achieved on land and on sea by me or through my legates under my auspices the senate decreed fifty-five times that thanksgiving be offered to the immortal gods. Moreover, the number of days on which, by decree of the senate, such thanksgiving was offered was 890. In my triumphs there were led before my chariot nine kings or children of kings. At the time I wrote this document, I had been consul thirteen times, and I was in the thirty-seventh year of my tribunician power.

5. The dictatorship offered to me in the consulship of Marcus Marcellus and Lucius Arruntius by the people and by the senate, both in my

absence and in my presence, I refused to accept. In the midst of a critical scarcity of grain I did not decline the supervision of the grain supply, which I so administered that within a few days I freed the whole people from imminent panic and danger by my expenditures and efforts. The consulship, too, which was offered to me at that time as an annual office for life, I refused to accept.

6. In the consulship of Marcus Vinicius and Quintus Lucretius, and again in that of Publius Lentulus and Gnaeus Lentulus, and a third time in that of Paullus Fabius Maximus and Quintus Tubero, though the Roman senate and people unitedly agreed that I should be elected sole guardian of the laws and morals with supreme authority, I refused to accept any office offered me which was contrary to the traditions of our ancestors. The measures which the senate desired at that time to be taken by me I carried out by virtue of the tribunician power. In this power I five times voluntarily requested and was given a colleague by the senate.

7. I was a member of the triumvirate for the settlement of the commonwealth for ten consecutive years. I have been ranking senator for forty years, up to the day on which I wrote this document. I have been *pontifex maximus*, augur, member of the college of fifteen for performing sacrifices, member of the college of seven for conducting religious banquets, member of the Arval Brotherhood, one of the Titii sodales, and a fetial.

8. In my fifth consulship I increased the number of patricians, by order of the people and the senate. Three times I revised the roll of senators. And in my sixth consulship, with Marcus Agrippa as my colleague, I conducted a census of the people. I performed the *lustrum* after an interval of forty-two years. At this *lustrum* 4,063,000 Roman citizens were recorded. Then a second time, acting alone, by virtue of the consular power, I completed the taking of the census in the consulship of Gaius Censorinus and Gaius Asinius. At this *lustrum* 4,233,000 Roman citizens were recorded. And a third time I completed the taking of the census in the consulship of Sextus Pompeius and Sextus Appuleius, by virtue of the consular power and with my son

Tiberius Caesar as my colleague. At this *lustrum* 4,937,000 Roman citizens were recorded. By new legislation which I sponsored I restored many traditions of our ancestors which were falling into desuetude in our generation; and I myself handed down precedents in many spheres for posterity to imitate.

9. The senate decreed that vows for my health should be offered up every fifth year by the consuls and priests. In fulfillment of these vows, games were often celebrated during my lifetime, sometimes by the four most distinguished colleges of priests, sometimes by the consuls. Moreover, the whole citizen body, with one accord, both individually and as members of municipalities, prayed continuously for my health at all the shrines.

10. My name was inserted, by decree of the senate, in the hymn of the Salian priests. And it was enacted by law that I should be sacrosanct in perpetuity and that I should possess the tribunician power as long as I live. I declined to become *pontifex maximus* in place of a colleague while he was still alive, when the people offered me that priesthood, which my father had held. A few years later, in the consulship of Publius Sulpicius and Gaius Valgius, I accepted this priesthood, when death removed the man who had taken possession of it at a time of civil disturbance; and from all Italy a multitude flocked to my election such as had never previously been recorded at Rome.

11. To commemorate my return from Syria, the senate consecrated an altar to Fortune the Home-bringer before the temple of Honor and Virtue at the Porta Capena, on which altar it decreed that the pontiffs and Vestal Virgins should make a yearly sacrifice on the anniversary of the day in the consulship of Quintus Lucretius and Marcus Vinicius on which I returned to the city from Syria, and it designated that day *Augustalia* from my name.

12. On this occasion, by decree of the senate, a portion of the praetors and tribunes of the plebs, together with the consul Quintus Lucretius and the leading men, was sent to Campania to meet me, an honor which up to this time has been decreed to no one but myself. When I returned to Rome from Spain and Gaul in the consulship

of Tiberius Nero and Publius Quintilius, after successfully settling the affairs of those provinces, the senate, to commemorate my return, ordered an altar of the Augustan Peace to be consecrated in the Campus Martius, on which it decreed that the magistrates, priests, and Vestal Virgins should make an annual sacrifice.

13. The temple of Janus Quirinus, which our ancestors desired to be closed whenever peace with victory was secured by sea and by land throughout the entire empire of the Roman people, and which before I was born is recorded to have been closed only twice since the founding of the city, was during my principate three times ordered by the senate to be closed.

14. My sons Gaius and Lucius Caesar, whom fortune took from me in their youth, were, in my honor, made consuls designate by the Roman senate and people when they were fifteen years old, with permission to enter that magistracy after a period of five years. The senate further decreed that from the day on which they were introduced into the Forum they should attend its debates. Moreover, the whole body of Roman *equites* presented each of them with silver shields and spears and saluted each as *princeps iuventutis*.

15. To the Roman plebs I paid 300 sesterces apiece in accordance with the will of my father; and in my fifth consulship I gave each 400 sesterces in my own name out of the spoils of war; and a second time in my tenth consulship I paid out of my own patrimony a largess of 400 sesterces to every individual; in my eleventh consulship I made twelve distributions of food out of grain purchased at my own expense; and in the twelfth year of my tribunician power for the third time I gave 400 sesterces to every individual. These largesses of mine reached never less than 250,000 persons. In the eighteenth year of my tribunician power and my twelfth consulship I gave sixty *denarii* to each of 320,000 persons of the urban plebs. And in my fifth consulship I gave out of the spoils of war 1,000 sesterces apiece to my soldiers settled in colonies. This largess on the occasion of my triumph was received by about 120,000 persons in the colonies. In my thirteenth consulship I gave sixty denarii apiece to those of the plebs

who at that time were receiving public grain; the number involved was a little more than 200,000 persons.

16. I reimbursed municipalities for the lands which I assigned to my soldiers in my fourth consulship, and afterwards in the consulship of Marcus Crassus and Gnaeus Lentulus the augur. The sums involved were about 600,000,000 sesterces which I paid for Italian estates, and about 260,000,000 sesterces which I paid for provincial lands. I was the first and only one to take such action of all those who up to my time established colonies of soldiers in Italy or in the provinces. And afterwards, in the consulship of Tiberius Nero and Gnaeus Piso, and likewise of Gaius Antistius and Decimus Laelius, and of Gaius Calvisius and Lucius Passienus, and of Lucius Lentulus and Marcus Messalla, and of Lucius Caninius and Quintus Fabricius, I granted bonuses in cash to the soldiers whom after the completion of their terms of service I sent back to their municipalities; and for this purpose I expended about 400,000,000 sesterces.

17. Four times I came to the assistance of the treasury with my own money, transferring to those in charge of the treasury 150,000,000 sesterces. And in the consulship of Marcus Lepidus and Lucius Arruntius I transferred out of my own patrimony 170,000,000 sesterces to the soldiers' bonus fund, which was established on my advice for the purpose of providing bonuses for soldiers who had completed twenty or more years of service.

18. From the year in which Gnaeus Lentulus and Publius Lentulus were consuls, whenever the provincial taxes fell short, in the case sometimes of 100,000 persons and sometimes of many more, I made up their tribute in grain and in money from my own grain stores and my own patrimony.

19. I built the following structures: the senate house and the Chalcidicum adjoining it; the temple of Apollo on the Palatine with its porticoes; the temple of the deified Julius; the Lupercal; the portico at the Circus Flaminius, which I allowed to be called Octavia after the name of the man who had built an earlier portico on the same site; the state box at the Circus Maximus; the temples of Jupiter the Smiter and

Jupiter the Thunderer on the Capitoline; the temple of Quirinus; the temples of Minerva and Queen Juno and of Jupiter Freedom on the Aventine; the temple of the Lares at the head of the Sacred Way; the temple of the Penates on the Velia; the temple of Youth and the temple of the Great Mother on the Palatine.

20. I repaired the Capitol and the theater of Pompey with enormous expenditures on both works, without having my name inscribed on them. I repaired the conduits of the aqueducts which were falling into ruin in many places because of age, and I doubled the capacity of the aqueduct called Marcia by admitting a new spring into its conduit. I completed the Julian Forum and the basilica which was between the temple of Castor and the temple of Saturn, works begun and far advanced by my father, and when the same basilica was destroyed by fire, I enlarged its site and began rebuilding the structure, which is to be inscribed with the names of my sons; and in case it should not be completed while I am still alive, I left instructions that the work be completed by my heirs. In my sixth consulship I repaired eighty-two temples of the gods in the city, in accordance with a resolution of the senate, neglecting none which at that time required repair. In my seventh consulship I reconstructed the Flaminian Way from the city as far as Ariminum, and also all the bridges except the Mulvian and the Minucian.

21. On my own private land I built the temple of Mars Ultor and the Augustan Forum from spoils of war. On ground bought for the most part from private owners I built the theater adjoining the temple of Apollo which was to be inscribed with the name of my son-in-law Marcus Marcellus. In the Capitol, in the temple of the deified Julius, in the temple of Apollo, in the temple of Vesta, and in the temple of Mars Ultor I consecrated gifts from spoils of war which cost me about 100,000,000 sesterces. In my fifth consulship I remitted to the municipalities and colonies of Italy 35,000 pounds of crown gold which they were collecting in honor of my triumphs; and afterwards, whenever I was acclaimed *imperator*, I did not accept the crown gold, though the municipalities and colonies decreed it with the same enthusiasm as before.

22. I gave a gladiatorial show three times in my own name, and five times in the names of my sons or grandsons; at these shows about 10,000 fought. Twice I presented to the people in my own name an exhibition of athletes invited from all parts of the world, and a third time in the name of my grandson. I presented games in my own name four times, and in addition twenty-three times in the place of other magistrates. On behalf of the college of fifteen, as master of that college, with Marcus Agrippa as my colleague, I celebrated the Secular Games in the consulship of Gaius Furnius and Gaius Silanus. In my thirteenth consulship I was the first to celebrate the Games of Mars, which subsequently the consuls, in accordance with a decree of the senate and a law, have regularly celebrated in the succeeding years. Twenty-six times I provided for the people, in my own name or in the names of my sons or grandsons, hunting spectacles of African wild beasts in the circus or in the Forum or in the amphitheaters; in these exhibitions about 3,500 animals were killed.

23. I presented to the people an exhibition of a naval battle across the Tiber where the grove of the Caesars now is, having had the site excavated 1,800 feet in length and 1,200 feet in width. In this exhibition thirty beaked ships, triremes or biremes, and in addition a great number of smaller vessels engaged in combat. On board these fleets, exclusive of rowers, there were about 3,000 combatants.

24. When I was victorious I replaced in the temples of all the communities of the province of Asia the ornaments which my opponent in the war had seized for his private use after despoiling the temples. About eighty silver statues of myself, represented on foot, on horseback, or in a chariot, stood in the city; these I myself removed, and out of the money therefrom I set up golden offerings in the temple of Apollo in my own name and in the names of those who had honored me with the statues.

25. I brought peace to the sea by suppressing the pirates. In that way I turned over to their masters for punishment nearly 30,000 slaves who had run away from their owners and taken up arms against the state. The whole of Italy

voluntarily took an oath of allegiance to me and demanded me as its leader in the war in which I was victorious at Actium. The same oath was taken by the provinces of the Gauls, the Spains, Africa, Sicily, and Sardinia. More than 700 senators served at that time under my standards; of that number eighty-three attained the consulship and about 170 obtained priesthoods, either before that date or subsequently, up to the day on which this document was written.

26. I extended the frontiers of all the provinces of the Roman people on whose boundaries were peoples not subject to our empire. I restored peace to the Gallic and Spanish provinces and likewise to Germany, that is to the entire region bounded by the Ocean from Gades to the mouth of the Elbe river. I caused peace to be restored in the Alps, from the region nearest to the Adriatic Sea as far as the Tuscan Sea, without undeservedly making war against any people. My fleet sailed the Ocean from the mouth of the Rhine eastward as far as the territory of the Cimbrians, to which no Roman previously had penetrated either by land or by sea. The Cimbrians, the Charydes, the Semnones, and other German peoples of the same region through their envoys sought my friendship and that of the Roman people. At my command and under my auspices two armies were led almost at the same time into Ethiopia and into Arabia which is called Felix; and very large forces of the enemy belonging to both peoples were killed in battle, and many towns were captured. In Ethiopia a penetration was made as far as the town of Napata, which is next to Meroe; in Arabia the army advanced into the territory of the Sabaeans to the town of Mariba.

27. I added Egypt to the empire of the Roman people. Although I might have made Greater Armenia into a province when its king Artaxes was assassinated, I preferred, following the precedent of our ancestors, to hand over this kingdom, acting through Tiberius Nero, who was then my stepson, to Tigranes, son of King Artavasdes and grandson of King Tigranes. And afterwards, when this same people revolted and rebelled, after I subdued it through my son Gaius, I handed it over to the rule of King Ariobarzanes, son of Artabazus, king of the Medes, and after his death to his son Artavasdes. When the latter was killed, I dispatched to that kingdom Tigranes, a scion of the royal family of Armenia. I recovered all the provinces extending beyond the Adriatic Sea eastward, and also Cyrenae, which were for the most part already in the possession of kings, as I had previously recovered Sicily and Sardinia, which had been seized in the slave war.

28. I established colonies of soldiers in Africa, Sicily, Macedonia, in both Spanish provinces, in Achaea, Asia, Syria, Narbonese Gaul, and Pisidia. Italy, moreover, has twenty-eight colonies established by me, which in my lifetime have grown to be famous and populous.

29. A number of military standards lost by other generals I recovered, after conquering the enemy, from Spain, Gaul, and the Dalmatians. The Parthians I compelled to restore to me the spoils and standards of three Roman armies and to seek the friendship of the Roman people as suppliants. The standards, moreover, I deposited in the inner shrine of the temple of Mars Ultor.

30. Through Tiberius Nero, who was then my stepson and legate, I conquered and subjected to the empire of the Roman people the Pannonian tribes, to which before my principate no army of the Roman people had ever penetrated; and I extended the frontier of Illyricum to the bank of the Danube River. An army of the Dacians which had crossed to our side of the river was conquered and destroyed under my auspices, and later on, my army crossed the Danube and compelled the Dacian tribes to submit to the orders of the Roman people.

31. Royal embassies from India, never previously seen before any Roman general, were often sent to me. Our friendship was sought through ambassadors by the Bastarnians and Scythians and by the kings of the Sarmatians, who live on both sides of the Don River, and by the kings of the Albanians and of the Iberians and of the Medes.

32. The following kings fled to me as suppliants: Tiridates and afterwards Phraates, son of King Phraates, kings of the Parthians;

Artavasdes, king of the Medes; Artaxares, king of the Adiabenians; Dumnobellaunus and Tincommius, kings of the Britons; Maelo, king of the Sugumbrians, and Segimerus [?], king of the Marcomannian Suebians. Phraates, son of Orodes, king of the Parthians, sent to me in Italy all his sons and grandsons, not because he was conquered in war, but seeking our friendship through pledge of his children. Under my principate numerous other peoples, with whom previously there had existed no exchange of embassies and friendship, experienced the good faith of the Roman people.

33. The peoples of the Parthians and of the Medes, through ambassadors who were the leading men of these peoples, received from me the kings for whom they asked: the Parthians, Vonones, son of King Phraates, grandson of King Orodes; the Medes, Ariobarzanes, son of King Artavasdes, grandson of King Ariobarzanes.

34. In my sixth and seventh consulships, after I had put an end to the civil wars, having attained supreme power by universal consent, I transferred the state from my own power to the control of the Roman senate and people. For this service of mine I received the title of Augustus by decree of the senate, and the doorposts of my house were publicly decked with laurels, the civic crown was affixed over my doorway, and a golden shield was set up in the Julian senate house, which, as the inscription on this shield testifies, the Roman senate and people gave me in recognition of my valor, clemency, justice, and devotion. After that time I excelled all in authority, but I possessed no more power than the others who were my colleagues in each magistracy.

35. When I held my thirteenth consulship, the senate, the equestrian order, and the entire Roman people gave me the title of "father of the country" and decreed that this title should be inscribed in the vestibule of my house, in the Julian senate house, and in the Augustan Forum on the pedestal of the chariot which was set up in my honor by decree of the senate. At the time I wrote this document I was in my seventy-sixth year.

The Augustan Settlement

Dio Cassius

Dio Cassius was a native Greek who held high administrative office at Rome in the early third century A.D. Though his account of the reign of Augustus is the most extensive that has survived, his position at court made him somewhat sympathetic to the emperors (though not always to Augustus), and he has included anachronisms which would be appropriate to his own time but not to the Augustan era. Yet his treatment of Augustus' manipulation of the Senate in 27 B.C., when the Republic was "restored," is instructive, since historical perspective and his Greek origins allowed him to see Augustus as the monarch he was.

[In 27 B.C. Caesar Augustus resigned his offices and, as he claimed in his *Res Gestae*, "restored the state to the Senate and the Roman people."]

11. While Caesar was reading this address, varied feelings took possession of the senators. A few of them knew his real intention and consequently kept applauding him enthusiastically; of the rest, some were suspicious of his words, while others believed them, and therefore both classes marvelled equally, the one at this cunning and the other at this decision, and both were displeased, the former at his scheming and the latter at his change of mind. For already there were some who abhorred the democratic constitution as a breeder of strife, were pleased at the change in government, and took delight in Caesar. Consequently, though they were variously affected by his announcement, their views were the same. For, on the one hand, those who believed he had spoken the truth

could not show their pleasure—those who wished to do so being restrained by their fear and the others by their hopes—and those, on the other hand, who did not believe it did not dare accuse him and expose his insincerity, some because they were afraid and others because they did not care to do so. Hence all the doubters either were compelled to believe him or else pretended that they did. As for praising him, some had not the courage and others were unwilling; on the contrary, both while he was reading and afterwards, they kept shouting out, begging for a monarchical government and urging every argument in its favour, until they forced him, as it was made to appear, to assume autocratic power. His very first act was to secure a decree granting to the men who should compose his bodyguard double the pay that was given to the rest of the soldiers, so that he might be strictly guarded. When this was done, he was eager to establish the monarchy in very truth.

12. In this way he had his supremacy ratified by the senate and by the people as well. But as he wished even so to be thought democratic, while he accepted all the care and oversight of the public business, on the ground that it required some attention on his part, yet he declared he would not personally govern all the provinces, and that in the case of such provinces as he should govern he would not do so indefinitely; and he did, in fact, restore to the senate the weaker provinces, on the ground that they were peaceful and free from war, while he retained the more powerful, alleging that they were insecure and precarious and either had enemies on their borders or were able on their own account to begin a serious revolt. His professed motive in this was that the senate might fearlessly enjoy the finest portion of the empire, while he himself had the hardships and the dangers; but his real purpose was that by this arrangement the senators should be unarmed and unprepared for battle, while he alone had arms and maintained soldiers. . . .

16. These regulations were established at that time, to speak generally; for in reality, Caesar himself was destined to have absolute control of all matters for all time, because he was not only master of the funds (nominally, to be sure, he had separated the public funds from his own, but as a matter of fact, he always spent the former also as he saw fit), but also commanded the soldiers. At all events, when his ten-year period came to an end, there was voted to him another five years, then five more, after that ten, and again another ten, and then ten for the fifth time, so that by the succession of ten-year periods he continued to be sole ruler for life. And it is for this reason that the subsequent emperors, though no longer appointed for a specified period, but for their whole life once for all, nevertheless always held a celebration every ten years, as if then renewing their sovereignty once more; and this is done even at the present day. . . .

. . . The name Augustus was at length bestowed upon him by the senate and by the people. For when they wished to call him by some distinctive title, and men were proposing one title and another and urging its selection, Caesar was exceedingly desirous of being called Romulus, but when he perceived that this caused him to be suspected of desiring the kingship, he desisted from his efforts to obtain it, and took the title of "Augustus," signifying that he was more than human; for all the most precious and sacred objects are termed *augusta*. Therefore they addressed him also in Greek as *Sebastos*, meaning an *august* personage, from the passive of the verb *sebazo*, "to revere."

In this way the power of both people and senate passed entirely into the hands of Augustus, and from this time there was, strictly speaking, a monarchy; for monarchy would be the truest name for it, no matter if two or three men did later hold the power at the same time. The name of monarchy, to be sure, the Romans so detested that they called their emperors neither dictators nor kings nor anything of the sort; yet since the final authority for the government devolves upon them, they must needs be kings. The offices established by the laws, it is true, are maintained even now, except that of censor; but the entire direction and administration is absolutely in accordance with the wishes of the one in power at the time. And yet, in order to preserve the appearance of having this power by virtue of the laws and not because of their own domination, the emperors have taken to themselves all the functions, including the titles, of the offices which under the republic and by the free gift of the people were powerful, with the single exception of the dictatorship. Thus, they very often became consuls, and they are always styled proconsuls whenever they are outside the pomerium. The name of *"imperator"* is held by them all for life, not only by those who have won victories in battle, but also by those who have not, in token of their independent authority, and this has displaced the titles "king" and "dictator." These last titles they have never assumed since the time they first fell out of use in the conduct of the government, but the functions of those offices are secured to them under the appellation of *"imperator."* By virtue of the titles named they secure the right to make levies, to collect funds, declare war, make peace, rule foreigners and citizens alike everywhere and always—even to the extent of being able to put to death both knights and senators inside the pomerium—and all the other privileges once granted to the consuls and other officials possessing independent authority; and by virtue of holding the censorship they investigate our lives and morals as well as take the census, enrolling some in the equestrian and senatorial classes and erasing the names of others from these classes, according to their will. By virtue of being consecrated in all the priesthoods and of their right to bestow most of these positions upon others, as well as from the fact that, even if two or three persons hold the imperial office at the same time, one of them is high priest, they hold in their own hands supreme authority over all matters both profane and sacred. . . .

17.11 These are the institutions which they have taken over from the republic, essentially in the form in which they severally existed then, and also making use of these same names, their purpose being to create the impression that they possess no power that has not been granted them. And further, they have acquired also another prerogative which was given to none of the ancient Romans outright and unreservedly, and the possession of this alone would enable them to exercise the powers above named and the others besides. For they have been released from the laws, as the very words in Latin declare; that is, they are free from all compulsion of the laws and are bound by none of the written ordinances. Thus by virtue of these democratic names they have clothed themselves with all the powers of the government, to such an extent that they actually possess all the prerogatives of kings except their paltry title. . . .

Such is the number and nature of the appellations which those who possess the imperial power employ in accordance with the laws and with what has now become tradition. At present all of them are, as a rule, bestowed upon the emperors at one and the same time, with the exception of the title of censor; but to the earlier emperors they were voted separately at different times. . . .

19. In this way the government was changed at that time for the better and in the interest of greater security; for it was no doubt quite impossible for the people to be saved under a republic. Nevertheless, the events occurring after this time cannot be recorded in the same manner as those of previous times. Formerly, as we know, all matters were reported to the senate and to the people, even if they happened at a distance; hence all learned of them and many recorded them, and consequently the truth regarding them, no matter to what extent fear or favour, friendship or enmity, coloured the reports of certain writers, was always to a certain extent to be found in the works of the other writers who wrote of the same events and in the public records. But after this time most things that happened began to be kept secret and concealed, and even though some things are perchance made public, they are distrusted just because they can not be verified; for it is suspected that everything is said and done with reference to the wishes of the men in power at the time and of their associates. As a result, much that never occurs is noised abroad, and much that happens beyond a doubt is unknown, and in the case of nearly every event a version gains currency that is different from the way it really happened. Furthermore, the very magnitude of the empire and the multitude of things that occur render accuracy in regard to them most difficult. In Rome, for example, much is going

on and much in the subject territory, while, as regards our enemies, there is something happening all the time, in fact, every day, and concerning these things no one except the participants can easily have correct information, and most people do not even hear of them at all. . . .

20.4 Augustus attended to all the business of the empire with more zeal than before, as if he had received it as a free gift from all the Romans, and in particular he enacted many laws.

21. I need not enumerate them all accurately one by one, but only those which have a bearing upon my history; and I shall follow this same course also in the case of later events, in order not to become wearisome by introducing all that kind of detail that even the men who devote themselves to such studies do not know to a nicety. He did not, however, enact all these laws on his sole responsibility, but some of them he brought before the public assembly in advance, in order that, if any features caused displeasure, he might learn it in time and correct them; for he encouraged everybody whatsoever to give him advice, in case any one thought of any possible improvement in them, and he accorded them complete liberty of speech, and actually changed some provisions of the proposed laws. Most important of all, he took as advisers for periods of six months the consuls (or the other consul, when he himself also held the office), one of each of the other kinds of officials, and fifteen men chosen by lot from the remainder of the senatorial body, with the result that all legislation proposed by the emperors is usually communicated after a fashion through this body to all the other senators; for although he brought certain matters before the whole senate, yet he generally followed this plan, considering it better to take under preliminary advisement most matters and the most important ones in consultation with a few; and sometimes he even sat with these men in the trial of cases. The senate as a body, it is true, continued to sit in judgment as before, and in certain cases transacted business with embassies and heralds, from both peoples and kings; and the people and the plebs, moreover, continued to meet for the elections; but nothing was done that did not please Caesar. It was he, at any rate, who selected and placed in nomination some of the men who were to hold office, and though in the case of others he adhered to the ancient custom and left them under the control of the people and the plebs, yet he took care that none should be appointed who were unfit or as the result of partisan cliques or bribery.

22. It was in this way, broadly speaking, that he administered the empire. . . .

30. When Augustus was consul for the eleventh time, he felt so ill once more as to have no hope of recovery; at any rate, he arranged everything as if he were about to die, and gathered about him the magistrates and the foremost senators and knights. He did not, to be sure, appoint a successor, though all were expecting that Marcellus would be preferred for this position, but after talking with them awhile about the public affairs, he gave Piso the list of the forces and of the public revenues written in a book, and handed his ring to Agrippa. And although he lost the power of attending even to the most urgent matters, yet a certain Antonius Musa restored him to health by means of cold baths and cold potions. For this, Musa received a great deal of money from both Augustus and the senate, as well as the right to wear gold rings (for he was a freedman), and he was granted exemption from taxes, both for himself and for the members of his profession, not only those living at the time but also those of future generations. But it was fated that he who had taken to himself the functions of Fortune or Destiny should speedily be caught in her toils; for though Augustus had been saved in this manner, yet when Marcellus fell ill not long afterward and was treated in the same way by Musa, he died. Augustus gave him a public burial after the customary eulogies, placing him in the tomb which he was building, and as a memorial to him finished the theatre whose foundations had already been laid by the former Caesar and which was now called the theatre of Marcellus. And he ordered also that a golden image of the deceased, a golden crown, and a curule chair should be carried into the theatre at the Ludi Romani and should be placed in the midst of the officials having charge of the games.

31. This he did later; at the time, after being restored to health, he brought his will into the senate and desired to read it, by way of showing people that he had left no successor to his realm; but he did not read it, for none would permit it. Absolutely everybody, however, was astonished at him because, although he loved Marcellus both as son-in-law and nephew, and in addition to other honours shown him had to such an extent helped him make a brilliant success of the festival which he gave as aedile that he had sheltered the Forum during the whole summer by means of curtains stretched overhead and had exhibited on the stage a dancer who was a knight, and also a woman of high birth, nevertheless he had not entrusted to him the monarchy, but actually had preferred Agrippa before him. Thus it would appear that he was not yet confident of the youth's judgment, and that he either wished the people to regain their liberty or for Agrippa to receive the leadership from them. For he well understood that Agrippa was exceedingly beloved by them and he preferred not to seem to be committing the supreme power to him on his own responsibility.

32. When he recovered, therefore, and learned that Marcellus because of this was not friendly toward Agrippa, he immediately sent the latter to Syria, so that no occasion for scoffing or for skirmishing might arise between them by their being together. And Agrippa straightway set out from the city, but did not reach Syria; instead, acting with even more than his usual moderation, he sent his lieutenants thither, and tarried himself in Lesbos.

33.4 Livia, now, was accused of having caused the death of Marcellus, because he had been preferred before her sons; but the justice of this suspicion became a matter of controversy by reason of the character both of that year and of the year following, which proved so unhealthful that great numbers perished during them. And, just as it usually happens that some sign occurs before such events, so on this occasion a wolf was caught in the city, fire and storm damaged many buildings, and the Tiber, rising, carried away the wooden bridge and made the city navigable for boats during three days.

The Shield of Aeneas

Virgil *Aeneid* VIII 675 ff.

Virgil, the greatest of all the Roman poets, was born near Mantua in northern Italy. Though he lost his family farm in Octavian's confiscations after Philippi, he was later brought into Octavian's circle and was handsomely rewarded. His Aeneid was a great patriotic epic modeled on Homer's Iliad and Odyssey, in that it contained both the voyage of Aeneas from Troy and his conquest and settlement in Italy. The establishment of the Roman people in Italy required of the hero many sacrifices, not least the love of queen Dido, and there are evident parallels to Augustus' task of restoring the Roman state after decades of civil wars. Virgil had not completed the poem when he died while returning from Greece in 19 B.C., and Augustus personally countermanded the poet's request that the manuscript be burned. The following passage describes the bronze shield of Aeneas on which the gods have depicted scenes from future Roman history. There Augustus leads the Senate and Italian people into battle against Antony and Cleopatra at the battle of Actium.

Across the center of the shield were shown
the ships of brass, the strife of Actium:
you might have seen all of Leucata's bay
teeming with war's array, waves glittering
with gold. On his high stern Augustus Caesar

is leading the Italians to battle,
together with the senate and the people,
the household gods and Great Gods; his bright brows
pour out a twin flame, and upon his head
his father's Julian star is glittering.
Elsewhere Agrippa towers on the stern;
with kindly winds and gods he leads his squadron;
around his temples, glowing bright, he wears
the naval crown, magnificent device,
with its ships' beaks. And facing them, just come
from conquering the peoples of the dawn,
from the red shores of the Erythraean Sea—
together with barbaric riches, varied
arms—is Astonius. He brings with him
Egypt and every power of the East
and farthest Bactria; and—shamefully—
behind him follows his Egyptian wife.
The squadrons close headlong; and all the waters
foam, torn by drawn-back oars and by the prows
with triple prongs. They seek the open seas;
you could believe the Cyclades, uprooted,
now swam upon the waters or steep mountains
had clashed with mountains as the crewmen thrust
in their great galleys at the towering sterns.
Torches of hemp and flying darts of steel
are flung by hand, and Neptune's fields are red
with strange bloodshed. Among all this the queen
calls to her squadrons with their native sistrum;
she has not yet looked back at the twin serpents
that swim behind her. Every kind of monster
god—and the barking god, Anubis, too—
stands ready to cast shafts against Minerva
and Venus and at Neptune. In the middle
of all the struggle, Mars, engraved in steel,
rages beside fierce Furies from the sky;
and Discord, joyous, strides in her rent robe;
Bellona follows with a bloodstained whip.
But Actian Apollo, overhead,
had seen these things; he stretched his bow; and all
of Egypt and of India, and all
the Arabs and Sabaeans, turned their backs
and fled before this terror. The queen herself
was seen to woo the winds, to spread her sails,
and now, yes now, let fall the slackened ropes.
The Lord of Fire had fashioned her within
the slaughter, driven on by wave and west wind,
pale with approaching death; but facing this,
he set the Nile, his giant body mourning,
opening wide his folds and all his robes,

inviting the defeated to his blue-gray
breast and his sheltering streams. But entering
the walls of Rome in triple triumph, Caesar
was dedicating his immortal gift
to the Italian gods: three hundred shrines
throughout the city. And the streets reechoed
with gladness, games, applause; in all the temples
were bands of matrons, and in all were altars;
and there, before these altars, slaughtered steers
were scattered on the ground. Caesar himself
is seated at bright Phoebus' snow-white porch,
and he reviews the spoils of nations and
he fastens them upon the proud doorposts.
The conquered nations march in long procession,
as varied in their armor and their dress
as in their languages. . . .
Aeneas marvels at his mother's gift,
the scenes on Vulcan's shield; and he is glad
for all these images, though he does not
know what they mean. Upon his shoulder he
lifts up the fame and fate of his sons' sons.

The Cleopatra Ode

Horace Odes I 37

Horace was a native of southern Italy who fought at Philippi in the army of Brutus. But Virgil introduced him into the circle of Augustus, who gave him property to allow him the leisure to write. His lyric poems praise love, wine and the simple life of the countryside, but some poems praise Augustus and his restoration of traditional Roman values. This poem celebrates Augustus' triumph over Antony and Cleopatra at Actium, and in it Horace acknowledges the nobility of the Egyptian queen who preferred suicide to the debasement of decorating Augustus' triumphal procession.

Friends, now is the time to drink,
now tread the earth with our dancing,
now set Salian delicacies
before the Gods' couches.

Heretofore it had been a sin
to produce Caecuban from ancient racks,
while a crazy queen was plotting,
with her polluted train

of evil debauchees, to demolish
the Capitol and topple the Empire—
a hopeful derangement drunk
with its luck. But the escape

from the flames of scarcely one ship
dampened her fury, and Caesar
dragged back to fearful reality
her mind swimming in Mareotic:

his galleys harried her fleeing from
Italy (just as the hawk the mild dove,
or the quick hunter the hare across
(Thessaly's plains of snow), in order

to put the curs'd monster in chains. Yet she,
seeking to die more nobly, showed
no womanish fear of the sword nor retired
with her fleet to uncharted shores.

Her face serene, she courageously viewed
her fallen palace. With fortitude
she handled fierce snakes, her corporeal
frame drank in their venom:

resolved for death, she was brave indeed.
She was no docile woman but truly scorned
to be taken away in her enemy's ships,
deposed, to an overweening Triumph.

Paean to Augustus

Ovid *Metamorphoses*

Ovid was the third of the great Augustan poets and, like Virgil and Horace, he was Italian rather than Roman in origin. But Ovid was a far less serious poet who, as he himself said, had a comic Muse. There were not only short love poems, but his great Art of Love and its sequel, Remedy for Love, were parodies of ancient didactic poems that taught everything from farming to fishing. His masterpiece is the urbane and witty Metamorphoses, which is the most comprehensive treatment of ancient mythology in Latin. The stories of transformation in that poem have had a lasting influence through the Middle Ages and Renaissance down to My Fair Lady (Ovid's Pygmalion tale). Late in the reign of Augustus, Ovid was involved in some mysterious scandal (perhaps concerning the emperor's errant daughter, Julia) which caused his banishment to Tomis (present-day Romania) on the Black Sea.

The excerpt below is the formal praise of Augustus at the end of the final book of the Metamorphoses.

.... 'This man for whom you are distressed, my Venus, has finished his allotted span, and completed the number of years he was fated to spend on earth. But he will enter heaven as a god, and be worshipped on earth in temples: for you will bring this about, you and his son who, inheriting his name, will bear alone the burden set upon his shoulders. Yet, in his heroic quest for vengeance for his murdered father, he will have us on his side in war. The walls of Mutina, besieged by an army under his auspices, will be defeated, and will sue for peace. Pharsalia will feel his power, Macedonian Philippi will be soaked in blood a second time. The great name of Pompey will be vanquished on the Sicilian seas, and the Egyptian consort of a Roman general, trusting in that marriage bond to her cost, will be brought low. Her threats to make my Capitol the slave of her Canopus will prove an empty boast. Why should I go through the tale of barbarian lands and races, lying on the shores of ocean, in the east and in the west? All habitable lands on earth will be his, and even the sea will be his slave.

'When the blessing of peace has been bestowed upon the earth, he will turn his attention to the rights of the citizens, and will pass laws, eminently just. . . .'

Jupiter controls the palaces of heaven, and the kingdoms of the threefold universe. The earth is under Augustus' sway. Each is a father and a ruler. I pray you, gods who accompanied Aeneas, to whom fire and sword gave way, gods of our own land, and you, Romulus, founder of our city, Mars, the father of unconquered Romulus, and Vesta too, worshipped among Caesar's household gods, and with her you, O Phoebus, who have your home with us, and Jupiter on high, who dwell on the Tarpeian citadel, and all the rest whom it is right and proper for a poet to invoke: may that day be slow to come, postponed beyond our generation, on which Augustus, leaving the world he rules, will make his way to heaven and there grant the prayers which he is no longer present to receive . . . .'

The Republic Restored

Donald Earl

In this essay Professor Donald Earl of Hull University describes the problems faced by Octavian after the defeat of Antony at Actium in 31 B.C. and his successful attempt to demobilize the enormous armies and purge the Senate of his enemies. Earl examines carefully the constitutional settlements of 27 and 23 B.C. through which Augustus regularized his position while retaining institutions and titles familiar from the Republic. He regards as valid Augustus' claims to have restored the Republic—though not in the modern sense of "republic," nor in the sense used by senators in the first century B.C. The power of Augustus was welcome to the Roman masses: he brought peace and security to the Roman state and its people.

. . . 'In my sixth and seventh consulships, after I had extinguished the civil wars, having acquired by general consent supreme and absolute power, I transferred the *respublica* from my own control to the disposal of the Senate and the Roman People.' Thus Augustus himself in the *Res Gestae* described the new settlement. It is a sentence of consummate political art. Octavian's supreme power over the whole state

and the whole empire before 27 B.C. is not disguised but openly paraded. The document was not written until A.D. 14, not published until Augustus' death. Emphasis of the supremacy of his position over forty-one years before made its renunciation the more magnanimous. But as the foundation for this position Augustus could claim no legal enactment. He had to pass beyond the forms of the constitution to the universal consent of public opinion. Completely lacking is any detailed account of the exact form of the transference of power, although a long sentence follows which lists various honours conferred on Augustus by the Senate. . . .

It remained to order the position and powers of Octavian himself. On January 13, 27 B.C., when consul for the seventh time with Agrippa again as his colleague, he appeared before the Senate and resigned all his powers and all his provinces to the disposal of the Senate and the Roman People. The senators vociferously urged him not to abandon the *respublica* which he had saved. At length Octavian, with ostensible reluctance, consented to assume the command of a large *provincia* consisting of Spain, Gaul and Syria for a period of ten years. Three days later the Senate met again to vote exceptional honours to the saviour of the state. A wreath of laurel was to be placed on Octavian's doorposts and oak on his lintel because he had saved the lives of Roman citizens. A golden shield, inscribed with his virtues . . . was set up in the Senate House. New or later copies were widely disseminated in Italy and the provinces. To make the new dispensation Octavian took a new name. On the proposal of the pliant L. Munatius Plancus he became, by decree of the Senate, Augustus. The month Sextilis was also so renamed, just as Quinctilis had earlier become July in honour of Julius Caesar.

Thus Augustus 'restored the Republic.' It was not the sudden or spontaneous gesture that propaganda pretended. Every action and reaction had been carefully weighed and provided for, the leading men of his faction consulted. How much of Agrippa was in the settlement is unknown. The ancient sources, piously based on propaganda, concentrate on the magnanimity of Augustus. We do know that Augustus was eager for the name of Romulus but this would not have been a wise choice. By the convolutions of centuries of legend and propaganda the first founder of Rome had become an equivocal figure. He had killed his brother and, so one version ran, had himself been killed by Roman senators for aspiring to tyranny, hardly a good omen for Rome's second founder. Who

dissuaded Augustus we do not know, the practical and utilitarian Agrippa or the subtle and agile Maecenas. The name finally decided on was a brilliant choice. Suetonius summarized what it conveyed to Romans: 'Sacred places and all those in which anything is ritually consecrated are called august. . . as Ennius also tells us when he writes, 'when by august ritual glorious Rome had been founded.''' A sacerdotal term implying formal consecration by due observance of augural ritual, the name of Augustus was ideally suited to proclaim the reestablishment of legitimate government under the favour of the gods.

But in what sense was the Republic restored? Augustus' settlement had been variously seen as a blatant fraud and as a genuine attempt to share power with the Senate, to establish a dyarchy. It was, in fact, neither. The real power of Augustus no law of the Roman People, no decree of the Senate, no settlement however far-reaching and comprehensive could affect either by addition or by diminution. The Roman world was his by right of conquest and his power was personal, resting on the enrollment of the population of Rome, of Italy, of the provinces in his private *clientela*. The oath of allegiance before Actium, not the settlement of 27 B.C., was the foundation charter of the Augustan Principate. Yet the restoration of the Republic was not an idle or unnecessary act, nor was it a hollow pretence. Neither the modern connotations of the word Republic nor the special definition imposed on the Latin term *respublica* by the nobility of the Late Republic are helpful. *Respublica* did not denote first and foremost a specific structure of government or distribution of power. Nor did it necessarily imply the freedom of the leading men to scramble for office and power, to govern the Roman world in their own interest and for their own profit. At Rome, naturally, it implied the continued existence of the traditional organs of government, the magistrates, the Senate and the assemblies of the Roman People. But elsewhere different criteria applied. *Respublica* was less an intellectual concept, less a description of a specific form of government than an emotion and a pledge of a purpose of government. The restoration of the

Republic, *respublica restituta*, stood for the re-establishment of legitimate government, the restoration of the rule of law, the reaffirmation of the rights and liberties of the citizens. Augustus' restoration of the Republic was not fraudulent because he did not claim to have restored a particular form of government or a specific distribution of power. His claim was that the lawless anarchy of the Triumviral period was ended, that military usurpation and the rule of force had given place to legitimate government and the rule of law.

Not the rule of law only. The inseparability of law and order is a very English concept: the sole guarantee of ordered social life is an effectively enforced system of law, which, as social structure increases in complexity, itself becomes ever more complex and pervasive. It is not the only possible system. In China, for instance, the effective guarantee of order in the Confucian system was not law but social conformity enforced by a clearly defined hierarchy of moral authority. At Rome both systems operated. Over against law stood custom and habit; the health and stability of society was assured by good laws and good habits together. To legislate men into virtue may seem to us a useless occupation but not so to the Romans. The more a society lost its moral bearings, the less assured became its discipline; the less assured its discipline, the more certain the collapse of internal stability and with the collapse of internal stability went loss of empire. Thus the Romans explained the failure of the Republic. A long and ineffective tale of laws in the last two centuries of the Republic condemned and forbade every conceivable form of vice and luxury. If men were not moral by nature, they could be coerced into morality by law, for if the individual citizen were corrupt then the whole empire was in danger. The restoration of the Republic included, therefore, not merely the regularization of Augustus' position and the reaffirmation of the rule of law. It involved also the consolidation of the traditional morality. The poet Horace summarized the Roman attitude when he addressed Augustus as the man who 'alone bears the weight of all public affairs, guards the state of Italy in war, adorns her with morals, reforms her with laws'.

Care for morality was as important as administrative ability, military quality or legislative activity.

In 19, 18 and 11 B.C. Augustus was pressed by the Senate and the People to accept a general oversight of morals and laws with supreme power. He seems to have accepted censorial power for a period of five years; then in 18 B.C. he presented in person to the Roman People a body of legislation designed to stabilize and encourage marriage and childbirth. An abortive attempt appears to have been made ten years earlier as part of the original restoration of the Republic, but the laws, if they were ever formally promulgated, were withdrawn in the face of protest and opposition. Now came the *lex Iulia de adulteriis coercendis* and the *lex Iulia de maritandis ordinibus*. The former for the first time made adultery a public crime, the latter liberalized the Roman law of marriage by recognizing the validity of unions between free-born citizens and men and women freed from slavery, although senators were expressly forbidden to marry freedwomen. The law assumed that marriage and parenthood were the natural state of men between the ages of twenty-five and sixty and of women between the ages of twenty and fifty. It therefore imposed disabilities on those who abstained from marriage or childbirth. On the other hand, husbands and fathers who entered public life were rewarded by more rapid promotion. The number of a man's children gave him precedence when he stood for office and he could stand as many years before the legal minimum age as he had children. In A.D. 9 the law was modified by the *lex Papia Poppaea*, which increased the distinction between the merely and, possibly, unwillingly childless and those who contumaciously refused even to marry. It also allowed women who had been divorced or widowed a longer period in which to remarry before they incurred the legal penalties.

How successful this legislation was in its ostensible object it is impossible to determine. It was maliciously observed that neither of the consuls who carried the *lex Papia Poppaea* was married or a father. But practical effect was, perhaps, not the most important purpose. Just as the constitutional arrangements of 27 B.C. and subsequent settlements regularized and legitimized Augustus' position without affecting his real power, so the moral legislation proclaimed a return to traditional moral standards, the flagrant abandonment of which among the nobles of the Late Republic had been held to have been the cause of the Republic's ruin. It was an essential part of the restoration of the *respublica*.

For what Augustus' restored Republic meant to contemporaries we have the impressive testimony of the poets Virgil and Horace. At one level Virgil's *Aeneid* expounds the ideal of the new order which had replaced the self-seeking chaos that had gone before. The nobles of the Late Republic by pursuing glory at the expense of the state had destroyed the *respublica*. All that they had meant by glory Virgil showed to be false and disruptive. True glory attended the foundation of a secure society, based not on war but on the rule of law and extending its civilizing influence over the whole world . . . . Horace agreed with Virgil that there was no room in the new order for the pursuit of that glory which had ruined the Republic. . . . Again and again Horace insisted that it was Augustus who had saved the Roman world from ruin and that it was Augustus alone who prevented the return of hypocrites—and they were right. . . . The propaganda of Augustus succeeded precisely because, unlike the polemic of the factional strife of the last age of the Republic, it was founded ultimately on real issues. Before Actium the unity of Italy was a real aspiration and the division of the empire into East and West aroused real fear. After the restoration of the Republic order, security and the *Pax Augusta* answered men's prayers. For them liberty and the Republic, as they had lately existed, were well lost. The Roman People understood; they wanted Augustus to assume more power, not less, and to assume it more openly.

The regularization and self-legitimization of absolute power won by conquest is a delicate business. In the middle of the year 27 B.C. Augustus left Rome to attend the war in Spain, still not completely conquered after two centuries. He was absent for three years, returning about the middle of the year 24 exhausted and ill. In his absence he had been elected consul year after year. This series of consulships was certainly an integral part of the settlement of 27 B.C., but we do not know that it was publicly announced at the time. Not only did Augustus thus annually remove one of the consulships from competition; there were no suffects and his colleague in each year was a loyal adherent attached to his cause by past service, interest or marriage. Augustus had, therefore, placed himself in a position which could scarcely be called Republican. Moreover, his possession of the consulship nullified the ostensible purpose of the settlement of 27 B.C., a return to legitimate government in which Augustus resigned his powers to the Senate and the People and received in return a defined sphere of duty. . . . Matters were not improved by the ostentatious parade of Augustus' nephew M. Marcellus as his heir.

Augustus had dangerously exposed the reality behind the settlement of 27 B.C. In 23 B.C. came the reckoning. That year, it has been said, might well have been the last, and was certainly the most critical in all the long Principate of Augustus. . . . A conspiracy was discovered, its author the mysterious Fannius Caepio. Varro Murena was implicated. The conspirators were condemned in absence, captured and killed. . . . The conspiracy and executions of Fannius and Murena cast a glaring and unwelcome light on the real nature of Augustus' new Republic. . . . The strain proved too much for Augustus' health. Never robust, it had been undermined in Spain and had grown steadily worse. Now he was close to death. He handed his signet ring to Agrippa, certain state papers to Cn. Calpurnius Piso, whom he had appointed (there was no question of an election) to the consulate vacant on Murena's death, but gave no indication of his intentions for the empire.

Augustus, however, recovered, saved by a drastic regimen of cold baths prescribed by his doctor Antonius Musa. On July 1 he resigned the consulship. In his place there was appointed L. Sestius, an open admirer of Marcus Brutus. . . . Sestius attests the readiness of old Republicans to support the new order and of

Augustus to use them for his own purposes. In twenty years Augustus had held eleven consulships, the last nine of them in succession. In the remaining thirty-six years of his reign he held the office only twice, in 5 and 2 B.C. To compensate for the loss of the powers of the supreme magistracy, the power he exercised in his *provincia* was modified in two ways: it was not to lapse when he entered the city of Rome, as did the *imperium* of an ordinary proconsul, and it was to be superior to that of all other proconsuls. In this way Augustus was placed with regard to the provinces in much the same position as he had had as consul. If anything his position was strengthened, for he could now exercise control over the other provincial governors by virtue of powers expressly granted and formally defined, instead of relying on the vague, undefined and challengeable powers of the consulship. But in Rome and Italy Augustus now lacked legal standing. A proconsul possessed his *imperium* until he entered the city of Rome, when it automatically lapsed, but without special authorization from the Senate or the People he could exercise it only in the sphere of duty, the *provincia*, assigned him by the Senate. To provide Augustus with a modest position in Rome the Senate and, no doubt, the Roman People voted that he should possess tribunician power for life. . . .

It was a modest position indeed. The plebeian tribunate lacked the trappings of power that attended the consul, occupied a humble and inessential place in the career of office and enjoyed a very low priority in summoning and consulting the Senate. True, the negative powers of the tribune were enormous. One tribune could by his veto paralyze the whole machinery of state. There is no evidence that Augustus used it. Nor did he much employ the milder positive powers. . . . Of the actual powers of the tribunate Augustus had no need. Formal veto was unnecessary where mere hint of displeasure would suffice. Personal action or intervention was not called for when there were members of the government in high office to act for him. If it were called for in an exceptional crisis, then Augustus would act by virtue of his immense extra-constitutional powers.

The attraction of the tribunate lay elsewhere. It was essentially a civilian office. A tribune could not command armies and his competence was restricted to the city of Rome. Created in the early years of the Republic to protect the Plebeians from Patrician oppression, the traditional function of the office was the defence of the liberties of the citizens. In the factional struggles of the last century, Republican propaganda had made great play with the liberties of the People and the rights of the tribunes. In every sense it was a popular office. To the whole of this popular tradition, from the early defenders of the Plebeians to more recent heroes such as the Gracchi, Augustus now laid formal claim. The events of the early months of the year 23 B.C. had shown the difficulty of satisfying the politicians. Against them Augustus appealed to his faithful clients, the common people of Rome, whom he pledged himself, by his assumption of tribunician power, not to desert.

The People responded. The winter of 23–22 B.C. brought floods, famine and plague. The People rioted and pressed Augustus to assume a dictatorship, an annual and perpetual consulship or the censorship. The offers were declined, but Augustus did assume control of the corn supply and had censors elected. . . . At the elections for 19 B.C. the People once more insisted on reserving one consulship for Augustus. By the summer of 19 the situation was so serious that the Senate passed its 'last decree' calling on the one consul in office and the other magistrates to see that the State took no harm and the consul begged Augustus to return. He arrived on October 12 to the Senate's great relief. A special delegation of senators went to Campania to meet him and the Senate decreed the erection of an altar to Fortuna Redux.

Augustus and the Roman People had taught dissident politicians a sharp lesson. Spontaneous demonstrations of popular enthusiasm for any regime are rightly suspect in any age, but the agitation would scarcely have been so sustained had it not been founded on genuine popular sentiment. Augustus' propaganda—the defence of Rome and Italy against the corrupt forces of the East, the victory at Actium and the clemency which followed it, the restoration of the Republic—had been highly successful. To the ordinary Roman Augustus was indeed the great leader of his country. More than that, the ordinary Roman had grasped the essential truth that only the person and power of Augustus stood between Rome and the return of factional strife. The Roman People wanted order and security, not the anarchy of the Late Republic. Beside that constitutional niceties were irrelevant luxuries.

Augustus could now recover the ground he had lost in 23 B.C. Exactly what form the arrangements of 19 and 18 B.C. took is difficult to determine. Augustus makes no mention of them in the *Res Gestae*, but there is much of importance which that document omits. It would appear that his *imperium*, now merely proconsular, was upgraded to make it equal to that of the consuls. Certainly we find Augustus once more exercising powers and performing functions normally reserved to holders of full consular power. He commanded troops, the praetorian cohorts in Italian towns and the three urban cohorts and the *Vigiles* in Rome itself. He raised soldiers by conscription in Rome and Italy. He exercised a criminal and civil jurisdiction and a power of summary punishment, as when he relegated by edict the poet Ovid to Tomis. In the latter part of his reign he received, concurrently with the consuls, formal declarations of candidature for the consular and praetorian elections. In 8 B.C. and A.D. 14 he conducted censuses in Italy by virtue of consular power. Most significantly, he appointed Prefects of the City to govern Rome when he was absent and delegated *imperium* within the city to them. Thus Augustus' legal power was again released from the territorial limitations imposed on it in 23 B.C. and from late in the year 19 B.C. he exercised it not merely in his own and, when necessary, in the senatorial provinces, but also in Rome and Italy.

Thus Augustus arrived at a final regularization of his constitutional position. Behind all the constitutional shifts, however, lay a sharp and urgent problem: how was he to ensure his personal survival? The nobles who had joined him against Antony did so for their own interest and their own power. Their chance and Augustus' danger came with the defeat of Antony. Then they might have decided to restore their notion of the Republic by removing Augustus. After Actium, despite the purge of the Senate, the political class at Rome included men of many sympathies, not all of them devoted to the new order and the preservation of its founder. The events of the decade after Actium, therefore, constitute the education of this class in political responsibility by Augustus and the leading men of his party, chief among them Agrippa. Those who remained unconvinced had to learn what the ordinary Roman already knew: that Augustus alone was the guarantee of peace, order and prosperity, that the insane pursuit of personal power and personal position which had ruined the Republic was an anachronism. Augustus and his closest associates had a lesson to learn too: how best to deploy the immense power he had acquired.

In this respect the various constitutional adjustments were in the last resort irrelevant to the realities of Augustus' position. The power of the leading men of the Republican oligarchy, the *principes*, had rested on the system of clientship which pervaded the society of Rome and Italy, the provinces and the client kingdoms. When Augustus emerged as sole Princeps he gathered to himself all the privileges and prerogatives shared and competed for by the many *principes* of the Republic. All the inhabitants of the Roman world were his clients. The army and the Roman People were the twin pillars of his power and his hold over them was personal and beyond the constitution. Not merely clientship became the monopoly of one man, but all glory, dignity and that particular form of prestige which had attached to the leading men of the Republic, *auctoritas*. The term denoted the moral influence and authority, not sanctioned by law, possessed by a man who was an instigator and originator of public policy. . . . After Actium it belonged to Augustus alone. This, too, the constitutional adjustments could not touch. As he himself wrote in the *Res Gestae*, 'After that time (28–27 B.C.) I was superior to all in *auctoritas*, but I had no more legal power than the other men who were my colleagues in each magistracy.'

Peace and the Princeps

Sir Ronald Syme

Nineteen centuries after the reign of Augustus, the Fascist leader Mussolini was to draw heavily on the Roman emperor's propaganda to legitimize his own regime. In the 1930s the Duce (derived from the Latin dux) sponsored excavations of the Forum of Augustus, lavish editions of the works of the Augustan poets, and the reconstruction of the Altar of Augustan Peace. The culmination was the vast exhibition mounted in Rome in 1937 to celebrate the bimillennium of Augustus' birth in 63 B.C. Against this background of the rise of authoritarian regimes in Europe of the 1930s, Sir Ronald Syme of Oxford University produced in The Roman Revolution the most comprehensive account of Augustus' rise to power and one of the great historical works of the twentieth century. His trenchant account of the policies and personalities of the new regime is reminiscent, both in its biting style and in its political stance, of the Roman historian Tacitus. In this chapter Syme argues that Augustus attained power through a violent revolution and his domination of the state was absolute and unconstitutional. And yet, despite his personal rule, Augustus created a government for the Empire and had politically regenerated the Roman people.

When a party has triumphed in violence and seized control of the State, it would be plain folly to regard the new government as a collection of amiable and virtuous characters. Revolution demands and produces sterner qualities. About the chief persons in the government of the New State, namely the Princeps himself and his allies, Agrippa, Maecenas and Livia, history and scandal have preserved a sufficient testimony to unmask the realities of their rule. The halo of their resplendent fortune may dazzle, but it cannot blind, the critical eye. Otherwise there can be no history of these times deserving the name, but only adulation and a pragmatic justification of success.

One man only of all whom the Revolution had brought to power deserved any public repute, and that was Agrippa, so some held. Candid or malignant informants reveal the most eminent personages in the national government as a sinister crew, worthy heirs to the terrible marshals of the Triumvirs. . . .

The rule of law had perished long ago, with might substituted for right. The contest for power in the Free State was splendid and terrible. . . . The *nobiles*, by their ambition and their feuds, had not merely destroyed their spurious Republic: they had ruined the Roman People.

There is something more important than political liberty; and political rights are a means, not an end in themselves. That end is security of life and property: it could not be guaranteed by the constitution of Republican Rome. Worn and broken by civil war and disorder, the Roman People was ready to surrender the ruinous privilege of freedom and submit to strict government. . . .

So order came to Rome. . . . The New State might be called monarchy, or by any other name. That did not matter. Personal rights and private status need not depend upon the form of government. And even though hereditary succession was sternly banished from the theory of the Principate, every effort was made to apply it in practice, for fear of something worse: sober men might well ponder on the apparent ridicule and solid advantages of hereditary monarchy.

Under the new order, the Commonwealth was no longer to be a playground for politicians, but in truth a *res publica*. Selfish ambition and personal loyalties must give way before civic duty and national patriotism. With the Principate, it was not merely Augustus and his party that prevailed—it meant the victory of the nonpolitical classes. They could be safe and happy at last. . . . No longer was the proletariat of Italy pressed into the legions to shed its blood for ambitious generals or spurious principles, no longer were the peaceful men of property to be driven into taking sides in a quarrel not their own or mulcted of their lands for the benefit of the legions. That was over. The Republic was something that a prudent man might admire but not imitate. . . .

Even among the *nobiles* there can have been few genuine Republicans in the time of Augustus; and many of the *nobiles* were inextricably bound up with the New State, being indebted to it for their preservation and standing. As more and more sons of Roman knights passed by patronage into the ranks of the governing class, the conviction not merely of the inevitability but also of the benefits of the system must have become more widely diffused in the Senate. Yet while this process was going on, the Republic itself became the object of a sentimental cult, most fervently practised among the members of the class that owed everything to the Empire. The senator Helvidius Priscus, the son of a centurion, may have been sincere in his principles: but the Roman knight who filled his house with the statues of Republican heroes was a snob as well as a careerist.

The Republican profession was not so much political as social and moral: it was more often a harmless act of homage to the great past of Rome than a manifestation of active discontent with the present state of affairs. It need not be taken as seriously as it was by suspicious emperors or by artful and unscrupulous prosecutors. While the Republic still maintained for a season its formal and legal existence, there had been deception enough in the assertion of Republicanism. With monarchy now firmly based in habit and theory as well as in fact, the very absence of any alternative form of rule was an encouragement to the more irresponsible type of serious-minded person. No danger that they would be challenged to put their ideals into practice.

The Republic, with its full record of great wars abroad and political dissensions at home, was a splendid subject for history. Well might Tacitus look back with melancholy and complain that his own theme was dull and narrow.

But the historian who had experienced one civil war in his own lifetime, and the threat of another, did not allow his judgement entirely to be blinded by literary and sentimental conventions. Like Sallustius and Pollio, he had no illusions about the Republic. The root of the trouble lay in the nature of man, turbid and restless, with noble qualities as well as evil—the strife for liberty, glory or domination. Empire, wealth and individual ambition had ruined the Republic long ago. Marius and Sulla overthrew *libertas* by force of arms and established *dominatio*. Pompeius was no better. After that, only a contest for supreme power. Tacitus does not even admit a restoration of the Free State if Brutus and Cassius had prevailed at Philippi. Such was the conventional and vulgar opinion. Tacitus himself would have thought it impossible after a civil war. . . .

There could be great men still, even under bad emperors, if they abated their ambition, remembered their duty as Romans to the Roman People and quietly practised the higher patriotism. It was not glorious: but glory was ruinous. A surer fame was theirs than the futile and ostentatious opposition of certain candidates for martyrdom, who might be admired for Republican independence of spirit but not for political wisdom. Neither Tacitus nor Trajan had been a party to this folly; the brief unhappy Principate of Nerva was a cogent argument for firm control of the State. Like the vain pomp of eastern kings, the fanaticism of the doctrinaire was distasteful to the Romans. . . .

His rule was personal, if ever rule was, and his position became ever more monarchic. Yet with all this, Augustus was not indispensable— that was the greatest triumph of all. Had he died in the early years of the Principate, his party would have survived, led by Agrippa, or by a group of the marshals. But Augustus lived on, a progressive miracle of duration. As the years passed, he emancipated himself more and more from the control of his earlier partisans; the *nobiles* returned to prominence and the Caesarian party itself was transformed and transcended. A government was created.

['The legions, the provinces, the fleets, the whole administration had been centralized.'] So

Tacitus described the Empire and its armed forces. The phrase might fittingly be applied to the whole fabric of the Roman State. It was firm, well-articulated and flexible. By appeal to the old, Augustus justified the new; by emphasizing continuity with the past, he encouraged the hope of development in the future. The New State established as the consolidation of the Revolution was neither exclusive nor immobile. While each class in society had its peculiar functions, there was no sharp division between classes. Service to Rome won recognition and promotion for senator, for knight or for soldier, for Roman or for provincial. The rewards were not so splendid as in the wars of the Revolution; but the rhythm, though abated, was steady and continuous.

It had been Augustus' most fervent prayer that he might lay the foundations of the new order deep and secure. He had done more than that. The Roman State, based firmly on a united Italy and a coherent Empire, was completely renovated, with new institutions, new ideas and even a new literature that was already classical. The doom of Empire had borne heavily on Rome, with threatened ruin. But now the reinvigorated Roman People, robust and cheerful, could bear the burden with pride as well as with security.

Augustus had also prayed for a successor in the post of honour and duty. His dearest hopes, his most pertinacious designs, had been thwarted. But peace and the Principate endured. A successor had been found, trained in his own school, a Roman aristocrat from among the *principes*, by general consent capable of Empire. It might have been better for Tiberius and for Rome if Augustus had died earlier: the duration of his life, by accustoming men's minds to the Principate as something permanent and enhancing his own prestige beyond that of a mortal man, while it consolidated his own regime and the new system of government, none the less made the task of his successor more delicate and more arduous.

The last decade of Augustus' life was clouded by domestic scandals and by disasters on the frontiers of empire. Yet for all that, when the end came it found him serene and cheerful. On his death-bed he was not plagued by remorse for his sins or by anxiety for the Empire. He quietly asked his friends whether he had played well his part in the comedy of life. There could be one answer or none. Whatever his deserts, his fame was secure and he had made provision for his own immortality.

During the Spanish wars, when stricken by an illness that might easily have been the end of a frail life, Augustus composed his *Autobiography*. Other generals before him, like Sulla and Caesar, had published the narrative of their *res gestae* or recounted their life, deeds and destiny for glory or for politics: none can have fabricated history with such calm audacity. Other generals had their memorial in the trophies, temples or theatres they had erected; their mailed statues and the brief inscribed record of their public services adorned Augustus' Forum of Mars Ultor. This was the recompense due to 'boni duces' after death. Sulla had been 'Felix,' Pompeius had seized the title of 'Magnus.' Augustus, in glory and fortune the greatest of *duces* and *principes*, intended to outshine them all. At the very moment when he was engaged upon the ostensible restoration of the Republic, he constructed in the Campus Martius a huge and dynastic monument, his own Mausoleum. He may already, in the ambition to perpetuate his glory, have composed the first draft of the inscription that was to stand outside his monument, the *Res Gestae*, or at the least, it may be conjectured that some such document was included in the state papers which the Princeps, near to death, handed over to the consul Piso in 23 B.C. But earlier versions may more easily be surmised than detected. The *Res Gestae* in their final form were composed early in A.D. 13, along with the last will and testament, to be edited and published by Tiberius.

This precious document, surviving in provincial copies, bears the hall-mark of official truth: it reveals the way in which Augustus wished posterity to interpret the incidents of his career, the achievements and character of his rule. The record is no less instructive for what it omits than for what it says. The adversaries of the Princeps in war and the victims of his public or private treacheries are not mentioned by name but are consigned to contemptuous oblivion. Antonius is masked and traduced as a faction, the Liberators as enemies of the Fatherland, Sex. Pompeius as a pirate. Perusia and the proscriptions are forgotten, the *coup d'état* of 32 B.C. appears as a spontaneous uprising of all Italy, Philippi is transformed into the victory of Caesar's heir and avenger alone. Agrippa indeed occurs twice, but much more as a date than as an agent. Other allies of the Princeps are omitted, save for Tiberius, whose conquest of Illyricum under the auspices of Augustus is suitably commemorated.

Most masterly of all is the formulation of the chapter that describes the constitutional position of the Princeps—and most misleading. His powers are defined as legal and magisterial; and he excels any colleague he might have, not in *potestas*, but only in *auctoritas*. Which is true as far as it goes—not very far. *Auctoritas*, however, does betray the truth, for *auctoritas* is also *potentia*. There is no word in this passage of the *tribunicia potestas* which, though elsewhere modestly referred to as a means of passing legislation, betrays its formidable nature and cardinal role in the imperial system—'summi fastigii vocabulum.' Again, there is nowhere in the whole document even a hint of the *imperium proconsulare* in virtue of which Augustus controlled, directly or indirectly, all provinces and all armies. Yet these powers were the twin pillars of his rule, firm and erect behind the flimsy and fraudulent Republic. In the employment of the tribunes' powers and of imperium the Princeps acknowledges his ancestry, recalling the dynasts Pompeius and Caesar. People and Army were the source and basis of his domination.

Such were the *Res Gestae Divi Augusti*. It would be imprudent to use the document as a sure guide for history, petulant and pointless to complain of omission and misrepresentation. No less vain the attempt to discover ultimate derivation and exact definition as a literary form. While the Princeps lived, he might, like other rulers, be openly worshipped as a deity in the provinces or receive in Rome and Italy honours like those accorded to gods by grateful humanity: to Romans he was no more than the head of the Roman State. Yet one thing was certain. When he was dead, Augustus would receive the honours of the Founder who was also Aeneas and Romulus, and, like *Divus Julius*, he would be enrolled by vote of the Roman Senate among the gods of Rome for his great merits— and for reasons of high politics. None the less, it will not help to describe the *Res Gestae* as the title-deeds of his divinity. If explained they must be, it is not with reference to the religions and kings of the Hellenistic East but from Rome and Roman practice, as a combination between the *elogium* of a Roman general and the statement of accounts of a Roman magistrate.

Like Augustus, his *Res Gestae* are unique, defying verbal definition and explaining themselves. From the beginning, from his youthful emergence as a revolutionary leader in public sedition and armed violence, the heir of Caesar had endured to the end. He died on the anniversary of the day when he assumed his first consulate after the march on Rome. Since then, fifty-six years had elapsed. Throughout, in act and policy, he remained true to himself and to the career that began when he raised a private army and 'liberated the State from the domination of a faction.' Dux had become Princeps and had converted a party into a government. For power he had sacrificed everything; he had achieved the height of all mortal ambition and in his ambition he had saved and regenerated the Roman People.

Augustus and the Succession

Ralph Gallucci

In this essay Professor Ralph Gallucci of Loyola Marymount University traces Augustus' efforts to ensure that power would pass to a successor without a reversion to the terrible civil wars that had wracked the Roman world between 49 and 31 B.C. Augustus' primary goal was to preserve the stability of the Empire, but his unexpectedly long life (after a sickly youth) and the early deaths of his sons-in-law and grandsons made the emperor's search for a successor a painful process that lasted more than thirty years.

The constitutional settlements of 27 and 23 B.C. regularized the political position of Augustus and established the constitutional framework of the Principate. Augustus clearly intended to retain the office of princeps until his death, and he did not really want to restore the old Republic with all its problems. Though there was no constitutional provision for the inheritance of his offices and powers, Augustus sought to establish a dynastic line of succession from within the Julian clan, preferably of his own bloodline.

Many scholars believe that as early as 25 B.C. Augustus had already selected his nephew, Marcellus, as his successor. Augustus arranged for the marriage of Marcellus and Julia and accelerated his assumption of the magistracies.

It is far from certain, however, that Augustus had in fact decided that Marcellus was to succeed him. Augustus never adopted his son-in-law as he would later adopt Gaius and Lucius, Tiberius and Agrippa Postumus. Nor had he arranged for Marcellus to be his heir, as Caesar had done for him. On his sickbed in 23 B.C., Augustus gave his signet ring to his friend and colleague, Agrippa. This is not to say that Augustus did not want to have someone of the Julian clan succeed him, but he may have thought that Marcellus was not yet able to maintain the principate. Agrippa would certainly have had a better chance of doing so and, since he was married to Augustus' niece Marcella, his children would carry the blood of the Julians.

After Augustus recovered his health, he gave Agrippa imperium over the East and Agrippa left shortly thereafter. One can read in the works of both ancient and modern writers that Augustus either sent Agrippa away to appease Marcellus, who felt slighted that Augustus had given Agrippa his signet ring, or that Agrippa, knowing that Marcellus was to be Augustus' successor, felt slighted and asked to be sent to the East. Neither explanation is really plausible; both suppose that Marcellus was Augustus' designated successor. Augustus on his recovery offered to show the Senate his will—he had selected no heir. Our ancient sources are merely reporting gossip current in Rome in 23 B.C. Further, one does not give a potential enemy control of the East. Throughout Augustus' rule, Agrippa, Tiberius, Drusus, and Germanicus were all away for long periods of time to tend the affairs of the empire. We must also remember that Augustus was only in his thirties with a wife of child-bearing age. It is not unlikely that Augustus still had hopes of producing with Livia an heir of his own. Augustus wanted the principate to continue, but he would wait until Marcellus and Julia or Marcella and Agrippa had male issue or until Livia was no longer fertile before deciding on a successor. Until then, each member of his family would continue to help in the administration of the empire: Agrippa would go to the East with imperium, Marcellus would remain in Rome to be consul, Tiberius and his brother Drusus, like Marcellus, would hold the important magistracies to prepare them for the consulship.

Shortly after Agrippa left Rome, Marcellus died. Agrippa returned in 21 B.C. and, after divorcing Marcella, married the widowed Julia. A son, Gaius, was born in 20 B.C. This grandson carried the blood of Augustus. In 18 B.C.

Agrippa received imperium over the senatorial provinces as well as a grant of the tribunician power for five years. These grants were undoubtedly given to secure the position of Agrippa and his sons should Augustus die. A second son, Lucius, was born in 17 B.C., and in the same year Augustus adopted both boys. By then it may have been clear that he would have no issue with Livia. In any case, there is no doubt that he expected them to succeed him. One source records a letter from Augustus to Gaius in which the emperor says that he expected them to succeed him; and to this end, according to Suetonius, Augustus directed their schooling and took them everywhere with him so that they might learn how to rule.

After 17 B.C. Augustus promoted the glorification of his family and adopted sons, preparing the people and the empire for their succession. The adoption of his two grandsons was celebrated on Roman coinage, and in the following years annual games and festivals were held in their name. There were statues of them throughout the empire, but even more there was a new emphasis on the divine descent of the Julian clan: Julius Caesar, Romulus, Aeneas and his mother, Venus. Prime examples of this are the Ara Pacis started in 13 B.C. to commemorate Augustus' return from Spain and the iconography and obvious symbolism in the Augustan forum.

In 12 B.C. the premature death of Agrippa at age fifty, however, forced Augustus to rely on Tiberius and Drusus as he once had on Agrippa. To secure their loyalty and protect the succession, he arranged the marriage of Tiberius and his daughter, Julia, in 11 B.C., and in the same year Drusus married Antonia, Augustus' niece. In 6 B.C. Tiberius was granted tribunician power for five years. Tiberius, wishing to retire from political life, left the same year for self-imposed exile on Rhodes, where he remained for seven years. Some writers have said he left because he felt slighted by Augustus: he had been forced to divorce his first wife, Vipsania, whom he loved, and he had served Augustus loyally throughout the empire as an administrator and general, and yet he was passed over as Augustus' successor in favor of

his stepsons. Tiberius was a better man and perhaps he wanted to be Augustus' heir, but there is no reason to believe that Augustus had ever given Tiberius any hope that he would be the next princeps. Augustus intended Tiberius to be his co-administrator and the protector of his adopted sons until Gaius and Lucius were old enough to assume greater responsibilities. This occurred in 5 B.C.

In that year Augustus assumed the consulship once again to introduce Gaius to adult society by bestowing on him the *toga virilis*—the toga of manhood. Gaius was designated to hold the office of consul in A.D. 1. Augustus held the consulship again in 2 B.C. and conferred the toga virilis upon Lucius with the same honors that had been granted his brother. In 1 B.C., at the age of nineteen, Gaius received proconsular imperium to deal with Armenia and Parthia.

The deaths first of Lucius in A.D. 2 en route to Spain and then of Gaius in A.D. 4 derailed Augustus' plans for a member of the Julian clan to succeed him and forced him to make new plans. In A.D. 4 Augustus adopted Tiberius and gave him tribunician power and imperium. Augustus, however, also adopted Agrippa Postumus and forced Tiberius to adopt Germanicus, the son of his brother Drusus. In addition, Germanicus married Agrippina, the daughter of Agrippa and Julia. Through Germanicus, Augustus had again attempted to secure succession in the next generation with someone of his blood. He adopted Tiberius out of necessity; he added to his adoption papers the words: "I do this for reasons of state."

By A.D. 7 the succession seemed clearly defined: Augustus had banished Postumus; Tiberius would succeed Augustus; and Germanicus would be Tiberius' designated successor. During these years Germanicus held various magistracies. By A.D. 12 he had already held the consulship. In A.D. 13 the tribunician power of Tiberius was renewed, together with a grant of imperium. When Augustus died in A.D. 14, the transition went smoothly. By virtue of his imperium Tiberius controlled the Army, and by virtue of his tribunician power he summoned the Senate, which dutifully renewed his imperium. Still, Augustus had not explicitly stated in his will that Tiberius was to be the next princeps; even in death Augustus tried to keep the facade of the old Republic alive, leaving to the Senate the pro forma vote. The system Augustus had created carried over and the principle of heredity, fictive or real, now became the norm for the next two centuries.

An idealized portrait of Augustus appears on a large bronze coin issued at Antioch in Syria in 54 B.C. The legend KAI AP is Greek for Caesar.

III

Augustus: The New Regime

INTRODUCTION
Ronald Mellor

The true test of a ruler is not how he acquires power, but how he exercises it. Augustus had succeeded in achieving supreme power and he effectively disguised the more brutal aspects of his rule, but the great task remained: to administer an empire of fifty million people. Armies had to be recruited, trained, paid and safely pensioned off; taxes had to be collected; provinces had to be well-governed; and the future had to be secured lest civil war break out again.

This unit provides an overview of the extraordinary achievements of Augustus, as well as some ancient and modern judgments on the founder of the Roman Empire. He was a man who not only desired power but wielded it effectively. He began the development of an administrative apparatus for the Empire and the professionalization of the army. The Res Gestae reflects the emperor's pride in restoring financial stability after the depredations of decades of civil war. The Italians were given access to important administrative and political posts, and the leading writers of the Augustan golden age were from Italian rather than Roman families. Even Tacitus agreed that the provincials lived better under the new regime than under the corrupt governors and greedy tax-collectors of the Republic.

Perhaps less successful were Augustus' attempts at social reform and religious revival. He wished to restore the mos maiorum—the traditional morality of earlier Romans. But neither his own life nor that of his family provided a secure platform from which to attack adultery, divorce and childlessness. His dramatic reforms certainly ruffled feathers, but they do not seem to have had a lasting impact. And his rebuilding of neglected temples was finally ineffective in a state that was at the point of transition to new forms of cult and new moral codes.

Augustus' most difficult struggle was to choose and train his successor and thus ensure the survival of the imperial system that he had created and nurtured. This sickly young man grew more robust with age and he outlived his chosen successors, Marcellus and Agrippa, and his grandsons, Gaius and Lucius Caesar. Finally, after much anger and sorrow, he handed the Empire on to his gloomy stepson, Tiberius. It cost the emperor much to ensure the continued rule of his family but, even if his immediate successors violated the Augustan constitution and did much harm to the senatorial elite, the provinces continued to prosper and the Roman Empire remained vigorous.

Augustus: The New Regime

Ronald Mellor

This essay, written especially for this volume, examines Augustus' establishment of a bureaucratic system to administer his vast empire. His financial policies provided ample funds to ensure payment of the troops and provisioning of the capital—both necessary for the survival of the dynasty. Augustus was also successful in integrating the Italians into the political and administrative workings of the state, though his social reforms were less enduring. The essay concludes with a positive assessment of the achievements of Augustus.

The Roman Republic had developed neither a civil service nor a permanent administrative apparatus. Political leaders (consuls or dictators) were expected to provide their staffs from their own households and to complete the necessary paperwork with little or no state support. The collection of taxes and provisioning of the armies were contracted out to often corrupt private entrepreneurs.

Augustus began the process of creating a genuine governmental system for the Empire. He saw the necessity for greater continuity of policy as well as the need to develop careers for skilled administrators. The emperor had a *consilium*, made up of the consuls, representatives of other magistracies, and fifteen senators who would rotate twice a year. The *consilium* set the legislative agenda, advised the emperor, and exposed him to a group of ordinary senators whom he might later tap for high office. Though there is little doubt that many important decisions (especially personnel decisions) were made with a smaller group of advisors, including Augustus' wife, Livia, the *consilium* was a useful mechanism to channel imperial opinion to the aristocracy and to keep Augustus apprised of its concerns.

If the first emperor was concerned with the opinions and feelings of the Senate, it was not because he regarded that venerable institution as a partner in power, but rather because he needed the individual senators to formulate policy, to lead armies and to govern provinces. It was a division of labor, not a division of power. When Augustus reviewed the roll of the Senate, he purged some members and added names of his supporters, especially new blood from Italy and the colonies. When he found efficient administrators, he would keep them in their posts (such as governorships) for several years. Augustus sometimes even provided the minimum property qualification of one million sesterces (at a time when an ordinary Roman soldier had an annual salary of less than one *thousand* sesterces), so that promising candidates could qualify for the Senate or so that a distinguished but impecunious family could continue there.

An Empire that stretched the length of the Mediterranean, however, needed more administrators than the Senate could provide. The emperor therefore drew upon the *Equites*—a term that now referred to those with a minimum property of 400,000 sesterces—for a wide range of administrative tasks. They served in many financial posts, both in Rome and in administering the emperor's domains abroad. The equites (sometimes called the equestrian order) also served as governors in some of the smaller provinces—Pontius Pilate was an equestrian. But the highest positions in the equestrian career were the prefectureships, so sensitive that Augustus preferred not to entrust them to a senator who might become a possible rival. Some of these (praetorian prefect, prefect of the vigiles) involved the command of troops in Rome itself; others, such as the prefect of the grain supply, were equally sensitive. The province of Egypt, taken from its last queen, Cleopatra, remained the personal property of the emperor, which he ruled through an equestrian prefect. After his experience with Antony, Augustus was so concerned that Egypt might become the springboard of a rebellion that he executed one untrustworthy prefect, his friend the poet Gallus, and forebade senators from even entering Egypt without imperial permission.

The everyday business of administration continued to follow the household model in which Augustus' slaves and freedmen, many of whom had extraordinary financial skills, were responsible for a range of public duties. One can well imagine the tasks of keeping records, writing official and private correspondence, answering petitions, drawing up official documents—both in Rome and in the provincial capitals. Under Claudius, these freedmen would assume high office in the imperial palace and preside over important secretariats.

The provincial view of Augustus' power is evident at the beginning of Luke's biblical account of the Nativity. "In those days a decree went out from Caesar Augustus that the whole world should be counted." Despite doubts about the historicity of this universal census, this account by a provincial demonstrates that it was not regarded as inherently improbable that poor villagers living hundreds of miles from Rome and knowing no Latin would be expected to obey an imperial command—even in a state racked by civil war only twenty-five years earlier.

The Army

After the battle of Actium in 31 B.C., the sixty legions of Octavian and Antony were trimmed to twenty-eight legions of about 160,000 men. Augustus' earlier attempts, following the defeat of Brutus in 42 B.C., to give discharged veterans land that he had confiscated in Italy had caused bitterness and even civil insurrection. Now, with 100,000 men to demobilize, Augustus (as he boasted in his autobiography) purchased land for some with the vast wealth of Egypt, and settled others in numerous new colonies in Italy, North Africa and Asia. Nimes, Barcelona, Tangier and Beirut had such Augustan foundations.

Augustus was also determined to ensure the army's continued loyalty to the central government, so that no future Sulla or Julius

Caesar might threaten the regime. He established a military treasury with a large initial grant, and thereafter the military treasury received a 5 percent inheritance tax and a 1 percent sales tax. After twenty years of loyal service, the legionary could expect a grant to purchase land that would support him in retirement. The organization of Rome's new professional army will be examined later in this book. But we should note here that Augustus established the elite Praetorian Guard to protect Italy and Rome itself, though its role as a palace guard which created and destroyed emperors was still in the future. The emperor similarly created the Vigiles and Urban Cohorts to provide the city with fire protection and to ensure public order.

Finance

The problem of financing the imperial government demanded early resolution. The Civil Wars had depleted the treasury, and the corrupt republican system of tax-farming was not the most efficient means of collecting taxes. The Republic had had no formal budget, and funds were spent as they arrived in Rome. Augustus had to face enormous demands on the state treasury: free grain to the Roman plebs, who numbered perhaps 200,000; the cost of a standing army; repairs to buildings and roads damaged or neglected during the Civil Wars; festivals and games to keep the people amused.

Augustus established several different treasuries in addition to the official state treasury. We have already mentioned the military treasury. There was also a fiscus (literally, money basket, or treasury; the root of "fiscal") for each province. In addition, the emperor's private purse, *patrimonium*, contained the vast wealth of Egypt, revenues from imperial lands, and gifts and legacies (which alone came to 1.4 billion sesterces—enough to pay the entire Roman army for ten years!). To keep these treasuries solvent, Augustus transformed and regularized taxation, imposing a head tax, land tax, and sales and inheritance taxes, as well as various duties. The use of specific figures in the emperor's autobiography shows that careful records were kept, and for the first time budgeting was introduced into Roman government.

Augustus also instituted central control over coinage, not only for obvious economic reasons, but also because coins provided the most effective medium of widespread communication and propaganda throughout the Empire. The triumph of Actium or the functional conquest of Parthia were equally proclaimed in words and images on coins that would be seen by tens of millions of people. These issues provide scholars with immediate evidence of the program that the emperor wished to convey to his subjects.

Italy and the Provinces

Augustus proudly proclaimed in his autobiography that all Italy had voluntarily sworn an oath of allegiance to him in his war with Antony. This was not merely political rhetoric; the fact is that Italy was overwhelmingly sympathetic to him and, like his great-uncle Julius Caesar, he was committed to the integration of Italians into the social and political elite of Rome. When he came to power, Greek was still spoken in the south, Italic languages were widely spoken and Etruscan had only recently died out as a living language. The emphasis of Augustus was on the cultural and social unification of Italy. The court poets Horace, Virgil and Propertius were all from the Italian countryside, and the great historian Livy was from Padua. Augustus' closest advisor, Maecenas, was descended from an Etruscan family. The economic boom of this era enriched towns throughout Italy as well as Rome, and it was Augustus who truly achieved the cultural, political and economic unification of Italy.

The provinces received better administration than they ever did from the rapacious governors of the Republic, as even Tacitus was forced to admit. Augustus retained considerable flexibility, ruling in Egypt as successor of the Pharaohs while employing elsewhere client kings such as Herod of Judea. The cities of Asia and Gaul formed *concilia* to worship the emperor and to petition the provincial governor. After the defeat of Antony, Augustus pacified Spain, and he expanded Roman domination in the Alps and the Balkans by establishing new provinces such as Raetia (Bavaria and eastern Switzerland) and Moesia (southern Rumania and parts of Yugoslavia) or adding newly conquered areas like Noricum (Austria) to existing military commands. His stepson Drusus successfully marched across Germany to the Elbe before his death in 9 B.C., but less than twenty years later those conquests were lost when Varus led three legions into an ambush and saw them annihilated. That disaster—the worse Roman defeat since Hannibal two centuries before—caused Augustus to retreat to a policy of caution and consolidation.

Citizenship

Early in the Republic the Romans had extended full or partial citizenship to other favored peoples in Italy, and many historians now believe that Romulus' abduction of the Sabine women was a legend representing the incorporation of the nearby Sabine people into the Roman state. After the Social War (90–88 B.C.), all Italy south of the Arno received citizenship, and Julius Caesar extended it throughout the cities in the Po valley in northern Italy. The Romans were exceptional among ancient peoples in extending citizenship so widely that eventually even Gauls and Greeks, Jews and Egyptians might hold Roman citizenship.

There was a tradition in antiquity wherein great conquerors founded new cities. Alexander, Pompey and Julius Caesar had all done so, and Augustus followed in their path. He established more than forty colonies, usually with demobilized veterans who retained their Roman citizenship. Augustus was, of course, patron of these foundations, but he was also in a certain sense the patron of all Roman citizens, who numbered about five million by the end of his reign.

Social Reform

Roman moralists viewed the last century of the Republic as an age of personal and political corruption. The historian and politician Sallust saw the destruction of Carthage in 146 B.C. as the point at which the Roman elite abandoned the customs (*mores*) of their ancestors and became unrestrained in their pursuit of personal pleasure. The close families of earlier times were weakened as divorce became more common. Some contemporary commentators attributed the prevalence of divorce and adultery to the growing independence—financial and otherwise—of women, but we see many prominent men indulging themselves with young wives or seeking short-term political advantage through marriage. Both paths must often have led to infidelity and divorce. Caesar married three times, Sulla five times, and even social conservatives like Cicero and Cato treated marriage with less than antique reverence. Even bachelorhood became popular, since unmarried men not only had greater sexual freedom but they remained open for the opportunity of a brilliant marriage as well as for flattery by the "legacy-hunters" whom the poet Horace satirized.

These attitudes produced a marked decline in the birth rate among the elite which, together with the Civil Wars and proscriptions, was leading to the disappearance of old and distinguished families. Augustus believed that he needed these families to propagate Roman values and to assist in the administration of his vast Empire. (As it developed, Italians without noble antecedents were able to take on the task, but the emperor could not yet know how successful his policies would be in this regard.) Furthermore, the declining birth rate among Roman citizens would affect recruiting for the legions. Thus Augustus proposed a series of laws to encourage stable marriages and large families.

The Julian laws of 18 B.C. and the *Lex Papia Poppaea* of A.D. 9 prohibited long engagements and encouraged all bachelors, spinsters and widows to marry. Penalties included restrictions on the right to receive legacies and to hold office. Married couples without children were likewise disadvantaged, while those with three or more children were granted social and political privileges. But these laws could hardly be rigorously enforced, since Augustus had only one child, his intimate Maecenas had none, and the court poets Horace and Virgil, as well as the consuls Papius and Plautius who gave their names to the law, were bachelors. Adultery was made a criminal offense, with a special court established for prosecutions. It is evident that the sexual promiscuity of his daughter, Julia, must have caused the emperor considerable embarrassment. Although these laws remained nominally in force until the triumph of Christianity, they were never effective, and the Romans seem to have strongly resisted state interference with marriage and private life.

Religious Policy

As part of his policy of renewal, Augustus revived long-neglected religious ceremonies and rebuilt, according to his own testimony, eighty-two temples that had fallen into ruins. He built the great temple of Mars the Avenger in the new Forum of Augustus to celebrate the victory over Brutus and Cassius at Philippi, through which he avenged the murder of his great-uncle, Julius Caesar. And in 17 B.C. the Secular Games were celebrated with festivals and poetry to commemorate the foundation of Rome. On the Altar of Augustan Peace, the reliefs depict Aeneas and the goddess Roma as well as the entire imperial family in procession. The emperor became High Priest (*Pontifex Maximus*) in 12 B.C., but all through his reign he used traditional religion as part of his political program of renewal.

Perhaps the most striking religious innovation was the deification of Augustus in the Greek cities of the East. He was worshipped together with the goddess Roma, and their cult also appeared in the Gallic capital at Lyons. Even though there were dedications to Roma and Augustus in the cities of Italy, the cult was not permitted at Rome itself. Caesar had been deified after his death—*Divus Julius*—allowing Augustus to be called the son of the deified one. That pattern of deification after death was followed at Rome for centuries, and it will be examined in greater detail in later readings.

Succession

His serious illness in 23 B.C. had brought home to the emperor the need for making clear arrangements for the succession. Though he ostensibly owed his position to the Senate and the Roman people, his death might provoke another series of civil wars, which Rome could ill afford. During his illness Augustus gave his signet ring to his faithful general Agrippa, but he certainly viewed his heir to be his nephew Marcellus, who had married the emperor's only child, Julia, in 25 B.C. Marcellus was honored by Augustus and popular with the masses, but he suddenly died late in 23 B.C. at the age of twenty. Faithful Agrippa was recalled from the East to marry Julia, and their two sons, Gaius and Lucius, were groomed for the imperial throne and later adopted by Augustus. On the death of Agrippa in 12 B.C., Livia's son Tiberius was made to divorce his wife and marry Julia and serve as guardian of the boys. In the most painful period of Augustus' reign, Tiberius was outraged at Julia's infidelities and withdrew to the island of Rhodes for almost a decade. But Julia was herself banished and Tiberius recalled in A.D. 2, and, after the inopportune death of the boys, he was adopted as Augustus' son and heir and later actually became the co-regent.

Thus, step by step, Augustus established the hereditary principle that his successors would follow for the first century of the Empire. But succession was rarely an easy matter for the Julio-Claudians, and the combination of heredity and adoption led to confusion and even murder as the struggles for power once fought on the battlefield were now waged in the bedchambers of the imperial palace.

The Achievements of Augustus

We have seen that Augustus faced an immense task on his return to Rome in 29 B.C. The Roman Republic, ravaged by two decades of civil wars, was in tatters, with the social and economic web of the state in disarray. Augustus had brought social reconstruction without a revival of the partisan political struggles of the 60s and 50s B.C. Grain distributions kept the urban proletariat contented, the troops had been successfully settled in colonies, and the new professional army provided a path of social mobility. Italy was now fully integrated into the Roman state; in only a half century an Italian Vespasian would sit on the imperial throne.

The economic reconstruction of Rome and the Empire had begun. Augustus justly boasted that he had found Rome a city of brick and left it a city of marble. But cities throughout Italy and Roman colonies around the Mediterranean were embellished with civic amenities as well—for example, the aqueducts (such as the Pont du Gard in Provence), which carried fresh water to the cities. The government promoted commerce through urbanization, the improvement of port facilities, roadbuilding, and the protection of the seas from piracy.

The general revival was trumpeted in poetry and art: pride in Rome's past and the restoration of traditional temples. Of course, much of this was politically inspired, but it may have been no less sincere. Peace and prosperity must have improved the morale of the Romans, and Augustus' administrative reforms (including restraints on tax collectors) made the lot of the provincials far happier than ever before.

Augustus' greatest benefaction was peace. The image of Rome's armies bringing war and chaos is true enough for the periphery of the Empire. When the British leader Calgacus urges his army on against Roman rule, Tacitus has him say: "They bring destruction and they call it peace." But most of the Mediterranean peoples were to experience in the two centuries after Augustus the most lasting peace they had ever known, or have ever known since: the *Pax Romana*. In that world commercial and cultural interchange flourished, and Greek ideas and eastern religions (including Christianity) were able to spread throughout the Mediterranean.

The historian Tacitus said sarcastically that Augustus had seduced the troops with gifts, the people with grain, and all with the sweetness of peace. For Tacitus, the loss of liberty was too great a price to pay for relief from civil war. But we might question that vaunted liberty of the Roman Republic—freedom for a few hundred senators to divide the offices and spoils while the proletariat starved and the provincials were abused by this elite. The Republic was a facade to conceal the self-interest of political factions and military leaders; no genuine *res publica*, no political structure devoted to the common good. After a century of civil strife and decades of open civil war, Augustus had brought peace. That peace, for all but a few, was worth far more than the corrupt institutions of a counterfeit Republic.

On his deathbed, Augustus asked whether he had played his part well in the *mimum vitae*—the comedy of life. And he added an actor's line from a Greek comedy requesting the audience's applause. He certainly had played many roles and nearly all of them well. Greek cities had called Augustus a god in his lifetime and had bestowed upon him the traditional title of "Savior," and on his death he was deified in Rome. And, we may ask, why not? In an age in which benefactors were granted divine honors, did not Augustus, the bringer of civil peace, deserve those honors above all others? He had truly, not merely rhetorically, been the Savior of the Roman state.

Later Roman Judgments on Augustus

Velleius Paterculus

Velleius Paterculus served as a soldier under Tiberius in Germany and Pannonia, and was fanatically devoted to the imperial family. He reached the praetorship under Tiberius and his sons reached the consulship under Nero. His brief Compendium of Roman History *quickly skims over the early centuries and concentrates on the reigns of Augustus and his hero, Tiberius. Velleius was not a skillful stylist, but his work remains a useful source for Augustus and Tiberius. He here provides a glowing panegyric of Augustus.*

As for Caesar's return to Italy and to Rome—the procession which met him, the enthusiasm of his reception by men of all classes, ages, and ranks, and the magnificence of his triumphs and of the spectacles which he gave—all this it would be impossible adequately to describe even within the compass of a formal history, to say nothing of a work so circumscribed as this. There is nothing that man can desire from the gods, nothing that the gods can grant to a man, nothing that wish can conceive or good fortune bring to pass, which Augustus on his return to the city did not bestow upon the republic, the Roman people, and the world. The civil wars were ended after twenty years, foreign wars suppressed, peace restored, the frenzy of arms everywhere lulled to rest; validity was restored to the laws, authority to the courts, and dignity to the Senate; the power of the magistrates was reduced to its former limits, with the sole exception that two were added to the eight existing praetors. The old traditional form of the republic was restored. Agriculture returned to the fields, respect to religion, to mankind freedom from anxiety, and to each citizen his property rights were now assured; old laws were usefully emended, and new laws passed for the general good; the revision of the Senate, while not too drastic, was not lacking in severity. The chief men of the state who had won triumphs and had held high office were at the invitation of Augustus induced to adorn the city. In the case of the consulship only, Caesar was not able to have his way, but was obliged to hold that office consecutively until the eleventh time in spite of his frequent efforts to prevent it; but the dictatorship which the people persistently offered him, he as stubbornly refused. To tell of the wars waged under his command, of the pacification of the world by his victories, of his many works at home and outside of Italy would weary a writer intending to devote his whole life to this one task. As for myself, remembering the proposed scope of my work, I have confined myself to setting before the eyes and minds of my readers a general picture of his principate.

Pliny the Elder

Pliny the Elder was a man of great learning of the first century A.D. whose huge Natural History reflects his wide interests in everything from politics to painting, geography to anthropology. He was commander of the Roman fleet in southern Italy, and died while rescuing survivors from the eruption of Vesuvius in A.D. 79 and overindulging his curiosity about the catastrophe. Pliny provides an early account (a generation before Tacitus and Suetonius) of the difficulties of Augustus, raising the possibility that a plot by Julia against him caused her banishment. Pliny's dark portrayal of Augustus' problems contrasts sharply with the bright view presented in the previous document.

Also in the case of his late Majesty Augustus, whom the whole of mankind enrolls in the list of happy men, if all the facts were carefully weighed, great revolutions of man's lot could be discovered: his failure with his uncle in regard to the office of Master of the Horse, when the candidate opposing him, Lepidus, was preferred; the hatred caused by the proscription; his association in the triumvirate with the wickedest citizens, and that not with an equal share of power but with Antony predominant; his flight in the battle of Philippi when he was suffering from disease, and his three days' hiding in a marsh, in spite of his illness and his swollen dropsical condition (as stated by Agrippa and Maecenas); his shipwreck off Sicily, and there also another period of hiding in a cave; his entreaties to Proculeius to kill him, in the naval rout when a detachment of the enemy was already pressing close at hand; the anxiety of the struggle at Perugia, the alarm of the Battle of Actium, his fall from a tower in the Pannonian Wars; and all the mutinies in his troops, all his critical illnesses, his suspicion of Marcellus' ambitions, the disgrace of Agrippa's banishment, the many plots against his life, the charge of causing the death of his children; and his sorrows that were not due solely to bereavement, his daughter's adultery and the disclosure of her plots against her father's life, the insolent withdrawal of his stepson Nero, another adultery, that of his grand-daughter; then the long series of misfortunes—lack of army funds, rebellion of Illyria, enlistment of slaves, shortage of man-power, plague at Rome, famine in Italy, resolve on suicide and death more than half achieved by four days' starvation; next the disaster of Varus and the foul slur upon his dignity; the disowning of Postumius Agrippa after his adoption as heir, and the sense of loss that followed his banishment; then his suspicion in regard to Fabius and the betrayal of secrets; afterwards the intrigues of his wife and Tiberius that tormented his latest days. In fine, this god—whether deified more by his own action or by his merits I know not—departed from life leaving his enemy's son his heir.

Philo of Alexandria

The philosopher Philo became the leader of the Jewish community in Alexandria, which he represented on an embassy to the emperor Caligula in A.D. 39. He recounts that episode in his essay Embassy to Gaius, *which also extolls the benevolence of Augustus in contrast to Caligula, who wished to be worshipped in the Temple at Jerusalem.*

Then again: What about the Emperor whose every virtue outshone human nature, who through the greatness of his imperial rule and of his valor alike became the first to bear the name 'Augustus,' who did not receive the title by inheritance from his family as part of a legacy, but was himself the source of the reverence paid to his successors also? What about the man who pitted himself against the general confusion and chaos as soon as he took charge of public affairs? For islands were struggling for supremacy against the continents and continents against islands, with the Romans of the greatest distinction in public life as their generals and leaders. Again, large parts of the world were battling for the mastery of the empire. Asia against Europe and Europe against Asia; European and Asian nations from ends of the earth had risen up and were engaged in grim warfare, fighting with armies and fleets on every land and sea, so that almost the whole human race would have been destroyed in internecine conflicts and disappeared completely, had it not been for one man, one *princeps*, Augustus, who deserves the title of 'Averter of Evil.' This is the Caesar who lulled the storms which were crashing everywhere, who healed the sickness common to Greeks and barbarians alike, which descended from the South and East and swept across to the West and North, sowing misery in the lands and seas between. This is he who not merely loosened but broke the fetters which had confined and oppressed the world. This is he who ended both the wars which were before everyone's eyes and those which were going on out of sight as a result of the attacks of pirates. This is he who cleared the sea of pirate-ships and filled it with merchant-ships. This is he who set every city again at liberty, who reduced disorder to order, who civilized all the unfriendly, savage tribes and brought them into harmony with each other, who enlarged Greece with many other Greek lands,

and who Hellenized the most important parts of the barbarian world. This is he who safeguarded peace, gave each man his due, distributed his favours widely without stint, and never in his whole life kept any blessing or advantage back.

During the forty-three years of this wonderful benefactor's rule over Egypt, the Alexandrians neglected him and did not make a single dedication on his behalf in the synagogues—neither a statue nor a wooden image nor a painting. Yet if new and exceptional honors should have been voted to anyone, it was appropriate in his case. This was not merely because he founded and originated the Augustan dynasty, nor because he was the first and greatest universal benefactor, who ended the rule of many by handing the ship of state over to a single helmsman, namely himself, with his remarkable grasp of the science of government, to steer. (The saying 'the rule of many is not good' is very true, since a multitude of votes causes manifold evils.) It was because the whole world voted him honors equal to those of the Olympians. Temples, gateways, vestibules, and colonnades bear witness to this, so that the imposing buildings erected in any city, new or old, are surpassed by the beauty and size of the temples of Caesar, especially in our own Alexandria. There is no other precinct like our so-called 'Augusteum,' the temple of Caesar, the protector of sailors. It is situated high up, opposite the sheltered harbours, and is very large and conspicuous; it is filled with dedications on a unique scale, and objects of gold and silver. The extensive precinct is furnished with colonnades, libraries, banqueting-halls, groves, gateways, open spaces, unroofed enclosures, and everything that makes for lavish decoration. It gives hope of safety to sailors when they set out to sea and when they return.

Seneca

The philosopher Seneca was the tutor and close advisor of the emperor Nero and was considered to be responsible for the moderation of Nero's early years in power. His speech On Mercy, *excerpted below, was given before Nero soon after his accession to the throne. Seneca does not disguise the notorious cruelty of the young Octavian, but he praises the mature Augustus for having wearied of it.*

By an example from your own family I wish to remind you how true this is. The deified Augustus was a mild prince if one should undertake to judge him from the time of his principate; but when he shared the state with others, he wielded the sword. When he was at your present age, having just passed his eighteenth year, he had already buried his dagger in the bosom of friends; he had already in stealth aimed a blow at the side of the consul, Mark Antony; he had already been a partner in proscription. But when he had passed his fortieth year and was staying in Gaul, the information was brought to him that Lucius Cinna, a dull-witted man, was concocting a plot against him. He was told where and when and how he meant to attack him: one of the accomplices gave the information. Augustus resolved to revenge himself upon the fellow, and ordered a council of his friends to be called. He spent a restless night, reflecting that it was a young man of noble birth, blameless but for this act, the grandson of Gnaeus Pompeius, who was to be condemned. He could not now bear to kill one man, he to whom Mark Antony had dictated the edict of proscription while they dined. He moaned, and now and then would burst forth into fitful and inconsistent speech: 'What then? shall I let my murderer walk about in unconcern while I am filled with fear? . . . What end will there be of punishments, and of bloodshed? I am the obvious victim for whom young men of noble birth should whet their swords. If so many must perish in order that I may not, my life is not worth the price.' At length Livia, his wife, broke in and said: 'Will you take a woman's advice? Follow the practice of physicians, who when the usual remedies do not work try just the opposite. So far you have accomplished nothing by severity. Salvidienus

was followed by Lepidus, Lepidus by Murena, Murena by Caepio, Caepio by Egnatius, to say nothing of the others whose monstrous daring makes one ashamed. Try now how mercy will work: pardon Lucius Cinna. . . . ' [*Augustus summons Cinna and tries to discover his reasons*]

'What is your purpose in this? Is it that you yourself may become the prince? On my word, the Roman people are hard put to it if nothing stands in the way of your ruling except me. You cannot guard your own house; just lately the influence of a mere freedman defeated you in a private suit; plainly, nothing can be easier for you than to take action against Caesar! Tell me, if I alone block your hopes, will Paulus and Fabius Maximus and the Cossi and the Servilii and the great line of nobles, who are not the representatives of empty names, but add distinction to their pedigree—will these put up with you?'

Not to fill up a great part of my book in repeating all his words—for he is known to have talked more than two hours, lengthening out this ordeal with which alone he intended to be content—at last he said: 'Cinna, a second time I grant you your life; the first time you were an open enemy, now, a plotter and a parricide. From this day let there be a beginning of friendship between us; let us put to the test which one of us acts in better faith—I in granting you your life, or you in owing it to me.' Later he, unsolicited, bestowed upon him the consulship, chiding him because he did not boldly stand for the office. He found Cinna most friendly and loyal, and became his sole heir. No one plotted against him further.

Your great-great-grandfather spared the vanquished; for if he had not spared them, whom would he have had to rule? Sallustius and a Cocceius and a Deillius and the whole inner circle of his court he recruited from the camp of his opponents; and now it was his own mercifulness that gave him a Domitius, a Messala, an Asinius, a Cicero, and all the flower of the state. What a long time was granted even Lepidus to die! For many years he suffered him to retain the insignia of a ruler, and only after the other's death did he permit the office of chief pontiff to be transferred to himself; for he preferred to have it called an honour rather than a spoil. This mercifulness led him on to safety and security, this made him popular and beloved, although the necks of the Roman people had not yet been humbled when he laid hand upon them; and today this preserves for him a reputation which is scarcely within the power of rulers even while they live. A god we believe him to be, but not because we are bidden; that Augustus was a good prince, that he well deserved the name of father, this we confess for no other reason than because he did not avenge with cruelty even the personal insults which usually sting a prince more than wrongs, because when he was the victim of lampoons he smiled, because he seemed to suffer punishment when he was exacting it, because he was so far from killing the various men whom he had convicted of intriguing with his daughter that he banished them for their greater safety, and gave them their credentials. Not merely to grant deliverance, but to guarantee it, when you know that there will be many to take up your quarrel and do you the favour of shedding an enemy's blood—this is really to forgive.

Such was Augustus when he was old, or just upon the verge of old age. In youth he was hot-headed, flared up with anger, and did many things which he looked back upon with regret. To compare the mildness of the deified Augustus with yours no one will dare, even if the years of youth shall be brought into competition with an old age that was more than ripe. Granted that he was restrained and merciful—yes, to be sure, but it was after Actium's waters had been stained with Roman blood, after his own and an enemy's fleet had been wrecked off Sicily, after the holocaust of Perusia and the proscriptions. I, surely, do not call weariness of cruelty mercy.

War and Peace in the Age of Augustus

Erich S. Gruen

Professor Erich Gruen of the University of California at Berkeley argues that the concept of Pax *(Peace) in Augustan poetry and propaganda has been overemphasized as well as misinterpreted. The Romans had no particular devotion to peace per se; they were a martial people and peace was an indication of victory under arms. The appearance of* Pax *is therefore a celebration of Augustus' military victories.*

Civil tension, strife and war had gripped Rome for nearly two decades since the crossing of the Rubicon. Actium called a halt. Octavian could claim to have terminated the slaughter of Roman by Roman—though he had himself contributed substantially to it. Actium ushered in a new era. A time of tranquility and prosperity could be anticipated. Virgil had forecast a golden age some years earlier, as had Horace in some of his loftier verses. The coming of peace would seem a most appropriate characterization of the period. And Pax Augusta (Augustan Peace) has indeed become a standard designation for the Augustan achievement.

But a question arises. Does that designation faithfully represent the ideology of the age of Augustus? Familiar facts incline to such a conclusion. Augustus closed the gates of the temple of Janus, thus signifying that no war troubled the empire. The saecular games of 17 officially announced the dawn of a new age. The Ara Pacis (Altar of Peace) of 13 symbolized it in monumental form. As Jupiter predicted in the first book of the *Aeneid*, wars will be put aside and harsh times will soften. Horace proclaims the return of ancient virtues, including *Pax*. Janus' doors are shut, faithful guardian of peace in a world now free of wars. Ovid in the *Fasti* pays eloquent homage to the Ara Pacis and prays both for eternal peace and for a gentle ruler. A century later Tacitus applied the phraseology with characteristically caustic overtones: Augustus gave us laws under which we enjoy *pax et princeps*—whereby our bondage has become the more bitter. In the formulation of Lucan, "such a peace brings a master." For good or ill, Augustus and peace

appear inseparable. The *princeps* projected an image of author and guarantor of *pax*.

Or did he? The matter can benefit from closer scrutiny. What would be the advantage for Augustus, politically or psychologically, of projecting such an image? He was in process of fashioning a new regime, but took care to assert and emphasize its continuities with the past. *Pax* would hardly qualify as a strong link to that past. It had rarely been in evidence through the long centuries of the Roman Republic. Nor had it been an object of devotion. Fame and glory went to the conqueror, not to the peace-maker. Roman leaders scrambled for triumphs, laurels, and prestige. *Victoria* holds prominence as a symbol almost from the start, a repeated figure on the coinage of the Republic. By contrast, *Pax* seldom puts in an appearance as slogan or goal while Roman arms marched to conquest and brought the Mediterranean world under their control. It became more desirable, significantly enough, when civil war wracked the empire. The end of the Republic gave greater urgency to the concept and increased exposure to the term. . . . But even with regard to civil peace, it soon passed out of vogue, giving way to the more common *concordia* (domestic concord). The principal resonances of *Pax* did not recall the Republic. As propaganda to remind Romans of the glories of yesteryear, it would be largely ineffective and inappropriate.

The ideology of war had had fuller development. Militarism and conquest had been a way of life for many generations before the age of Augustus. . . . Military power generated Rome's supremacy, a fact to which Cicero points with pride: the whole world now submits to her *imperium.* The dominion, of course, is salutary: nature herself guarantees that the strong will govern the weak to their own best advantage. But the achievement of mastery can be an end in itself, in no need of justification or rationalization. . . . As Cicero declared unhesitatingly, "our ancestors took up arms not only to gain freedom but to rule." *Pax*, when applied to the peoples under Roman sway, referred to those who had been subdued and pacified. Such is the ideological background against which the Principate must be viewed: conquest, power, extension of Roman authority and control over the nations of the world—in short, empire.

What profit then would accrue to Augustus from representation as peacemaker and guardian of tranquility? In fact, there were wars aplenty in the Augustan age, ordered, directed, or sanctioned by the *princeps*. Fighting took place in Spain and Gaul, in the Alps, on the Rhine and the Danube. . . . New provinces fell into Roman hands: Egypt, Noricum, Raetia, Pannonia, and Moesia. There were campaigns in Arabia and Ethiopia, and a thrust to the Elbe in Germany. These advances constituted memorable achievements and, in many cases, brought enduring imperial acquisitions. Would Augustus softpedal such accomplishments, subordinate martial deeds to serenity, and disguise conquest as peace?

The answer is surely that he did nothing of the kind. *Pax Augusta* is not the product of an Augustan propaganda machine. The *princeps* wrapped himself in the mantle of Republican heroes, repeated and elaborated upon Republican slogans in order to enhance his own credentials. Peace had never been a prominent ideal in the Republic nor a distinctive mark of successful statesmanship. Roman experience had found peace a respite between wars, a temporary shoring up of resources before renewed displays of power, rather than a state of lasting serenity.

The Republican connotations emerge plainly in Augustus' own words. The *Res Gestae*, composed perhaps over an extended period of time but given its finishing touches near the end of his life, affords our most direct view of how the *princeps* represented his accomplishments to the public. And that document is studded with prideful references to martial prowess and the plaudits of victory.

The work opens with Octavian's enlistment of a private army at personal expense. The object was to revenge himself upon the assassins of Caesar while he rescued the *libertas* of the state from the domination of a faction. That beginning sets a tone for the whole: Augustus identifies his individual objectives with the interests of the state.

Victorious achievements predominate. They are even quantifiable: two *ovationes*, three triumphs, twenty-one salutations as *imperator*, fifty-five thanksgivings, nine kings or princes led in triumph. The *princeps* annexed Egypt, advanced into Ethiopia and Arabia, recovered all the eastern provinces, regained the captured standards of Roman armies from Spaniards, Gauls, Dalmations, and Parthians, defeated Pannonians and Dacians, and extended Illyria's frontiers to the Danube. The limits of every province were expanded against peoples who failed to acknowledge Roman authority. Conquests carried material benefits as well. Gifts for plebs and soldiers derived from war booty. And the proceeds of victory financed both the temple of Mars Ultor and the grand Forum Augustum.

Allusions to *Pax* are subdued and secondary. Augustus does register the fact that the Senate decreed erection of the Ara Pacis to commemorate his return from Spain and Gaul in 13. The event, however, receives no special prominence in the text. Certainly no more so than the altar of Fortuna Redux (Good Fortune of the Safe Return) consecrated by the Senate to celebrate Augustus' successful return from Syria in 19. That hardly implies that *Pax* had become the watchword of the regime—any more than *fortuna redux* had.

More significant, at least on common interpretation, is the closing of the temple of Janus. Janus' gates swung open to symbolize the marching out of Roman forces to war. Augustus boasted in the *Res Gestae* that, whereas only twice before in all of Roman history were the doors to the temple closed, marking peace on land and sea everywhere in the empire, the Senate voted for closure three times during his Principate. What is the import of this action? It is almost always taken as centerpiece of the Augustan propaganda: the princeps put an end to war everywhere in the Roman dominions. But the matter needs closer attention—and reconsideration. First, Augustus does not so much celebrate peace as the means of its accomplishment: *parta victoriis Pax* (peace born of victories). He pronounced no pacifist's creed but declared a warrior's achievement. Second and more important is a fact easily overlooked as too obvious: the fact that Augustus closed the temple of Janus not once but three times. It follows inescapably that the doors stood open between closings—and indeed remained so through most of the Augustan Principate. What Augustus' boast emphatically does *not* do is to claim that he brought permanent peace. This is *Pax* as the Republic had known *Pax*: a temporary breathing spell between wars. The *princeps* takes pride in thrice having brought foes to submission so that no conflict troubled the empire—for a time. But wars would recur, the power of Rome to be tested repeatedly. That expectation is implicit in Augustus' boast, and detracts not at all from his sense of achievement. Perpetual peace was unrealistic—perhaps even undesirable.

The *Res Gestae* places emphasis not on peace but on pacification. Augustus has recourse to the verbs *pacare* and *pacificare*. He subdued the sea by clearing it of pirates. He pacified Gaul, Spain, and Germany from Gades to the Elbe. And he imposed peace on the Alpine regions from the Adriatic to the Tuscan Sea. In each case peace derives from force of arms. And its maintenance required continued use of force, or the threat of force. Both concept and phraseology reproduce features familiar from Republican formulations. The *princeps* does not here engage in concealment, disguise, or euphemism. Once only in the *Res Gestae*, with regard to the Alpine tribes, does Augustus trouble to state that he had brought them to submission without waging an unjust war. Elsewhere he eschews apologies, justifications, or explanations. The legitimacy of Roman conquest and expansion is simply taken for granted.

Augustus' personal record of his achievements sets military might in the forefront. The demonstration of Roman power enforces acquiescence upon the most far-flung peoples and nations of the world. The scramble to seek Rome's friendship and to offer obeisance receives repeated mention in the *Res Gestae*. Augustus' fleet sailed from the mouth of the Rhine to regions never traversed by a Roman, and there received homage from . . . remote German tribes. Parthians were compelled to seek Roman friendship. The *princeps* arranged the succession of Armenia. Legates from distant lands curried his favor; . . . even a number of delegations from Indian rulers not hitherto seen in the company of a Roman general. Kings and princes fled as refugees and suppliants to him, from the Parthians, Medes, Adiabeni, Britons, Sugambri, Marcomanni, and Suebi, to seek restitution or backing for their royal aspirations. The roll call of nations impressively underscores the majesty of the empire and of Augustus' contributions to its dominance. The *Res Gestae*, in short, registers the authority of Rome everywhere in the known world and the martial virtue that subdued or overawed the most distant nations, a virtue embodied in the person of the *princeps*.

When one turns to the literary figures of the Augustan age, similar portrayals take shape. We may pardonably forbear entering the tangled thicket of interpretation that seeks to determine how far the Augustan writers mouthed the precepts of the *princeps* or served as subsidized spokesmen for the regime. The question is complex, ambiguous, and perhaps ultimately unanswerable. But it is not essential for our purposes to determine whether the poets conveyed official propaganda or acted as purely free agents, whether they were advocates or critics of the government. We operate instead on a different premise: when certain concepts reappear with consistency in Augustan literature, this reflects at least the prevailing atmosphere of public discussion.

Virgil supplies suitable verses. Augustus' victory at Actium called forth praise in the

Georgics. Virgil sees the *princeps* as heir to Rome's hardiest warriors of the past: Decius, Camillus, Scipio, Marius. Octavian eclipses them all: *maxime Caesar.* He is victor in the furthest bounds of the East; even India is rendered helpless and kept at a safe distance from Rome. Whether those lines constitute genuine flattery or subtle irony need not be decided here. The expressed sentiments, in any case, parallel those found in the *Res Gestae.* The same holds for some striking verses at the end of the *Georgics.* The poet depicts Octavian as mighty conqueror, thundering on the banks of the Euphrates and imposing laws upon compliant peoples. This image of arbiter over foreign nations quietly submissive to the conqueror corresponds closely to assertions in the *Res Gestae.*

Familiar lines in the *Aeneid's* sixth book carry on the theme. Anchises foresees a time when Caesar Augustus will recreate a golden age in Latium. But that golden age is characterized as an era when Roman power extends beyond the furthest reaches of imagination, when peoples everywhere, whether on the Caspian Sea, the Nile or the Maeotian land, shrink in terror at Augustus' approach. On the face of it, those lines might indicate eager approval of imperial expansion. A more cautious conclusion is preferable: Virgil recognized imperial rule as a prime slogan of the regime.

Pax, of course, is not absent from the great epic. Jupiter in Book I promises Venus that a time will come, in the age of Augustus, when the gates of war are shut. . . . But those verses follow directly upon the god's proclamation that the imperial holdings of Rome will know no limits. Peace thus depends on victory, conquest, and subjugation. . . . It is most appropriate that the shield of Aeneas, on which Vulcan fashioned highlights of the history of Rome, should have as its climactic scene Augustus' triple triumph of 29. The *princeps* is depicted as sitting in proud splendor while long rows of conquered peoples from Africa to the Euphrates pass in array before him. One will not infer that the poet rejoiced in such a scene. But he conveys the symbols that dominated Augustan Rome.

Comparable representations find place in the songs of Horace. The poet decried civil strife in the 30s for it kept Rome from her real business—that of expansionistic wars. Why spill Roman blood when weapons should be directed toward Britons and Parthians? After Actium Horace takes for granted that there will be offensive thrusts against Parthians, Gauls, Scythians, Arabs, and Britons. Augustus will rule all the world as agent and representative of Jupiter. . . . And prophecy issues forth from Juno in the third Roman Ode: the power of Rome will extend to universal dominion . . . . The parallels with the *Res Gestae* impose themselves. Peace is obtained through war—and manifested through the obeisance paid by defeated or dependent peoples. The poet does not depict a world of contented concord. . . .

One may discover similar allusions even in that most unwarlike of poets, Propertius. His poems of the 20s . . . also provide a glimpse of the regime's public posture. The poet disclaims competence to sing of Augustus' martial feats, the victories abroad, and the succession of kings held fast by golden fetters and led in triumph. . . . Like Horace, Propertius takes for granted the mounting of major campaigns whose success is assured and which will penetrate Bactria, India, and Britain, rendering the Parthians timid and subservient. Irony may be discerned here, perhaps a mock-heroic character invested in the poems. But they give access to the image projected by Augustus. Rome dictates governance to the conquered.

A few years later, corresponding features recur in the verses of Ovid. The closing lines of the *Metamorphoses* make a point of stressing Augustus' rulership over the universe. The poet, to be sure, speaks of the coming of peace, the imposition of law and order, the administration of civil justice. But, as in the other passages scrutinized, the blissfulness stems from bloodstained victories and the subjugation of barbarian peoples. Emphasis is placed upon Roman power and widespread sway over subdued lands. . . .

Public manifestations of the regime deliver the same message. Coins, inscriptions, and monuments converge in transmitting the picture of Roman might and imperial dominance. . . .

The major public monuments of the Augustan Principate reinforce the image of conqueror, master, and guarantor of security through force. Octavian signalled his inclinations in 29 by installing a statue of Victory in the Curia Julia. A triumphal arch commemorated his successes abroad. Two years later the Senate appropriately voted Augustus the privilege of placing laurel trees before his residence and setting an oak crown above them—a gesture that symbolized his role both as perpetual victor over enemies and as savior of citizens. Those acts set the proper tone.

The Forum Augustum gives clearest insight into the public representation of the regime. That ambitious building project with the explicit stamp of the *princeps*' approval conveyed his message as plainly as one could wish. Its most prominent feature was the imposing temple of Mars Ultor vowed by Augustus after Philippi but not completed until 2. The martial virtues as emblematic of his ascendancy were not soft-pedaled, even at that late a date. The temple of Mars would be the meeting place of the Senate for all declarations of war or awards of triumphs, and the symbolic starting point for every general to lead his troops abroad. The Forum Augustum served as repository for weapons of all sorts and for arms seized as booty from the defeated foes of Rome. Augustus lodged statues of the great men of Rome's past in niches along the forum, with inscriptions attesting to their military achievements and triumphal honors. Opposite that array of heroes stood the figures of Aeneas and all the representatives of the Julian line. The *princeps* thus linked himself to a gallery of Republican [military leaders]: he was in the line of Camillus, Ap. Claudius Caecus, Duillius, Fabius Maximus, Aemilius Paullus, even Marius and Sulla. There can be no doubt that in this setting Augustus sought to project himself as heir to the grandest martial traditions of the state.

The striking statue of Augustus at Prima Porta leaves similar impressions. The *princeps* wears an elaborately engraved cuirass, thus as commander, and apparently in a pose of [addressing] his soldiers. The centerpiece of the breastplate displays the transfer of captured standards by the Parthians to Rome, emblematic of Roman supremacy in the East. Two submissive and dejected female barbarians appear in the middle zone of the cuirass, representations, it seems, of Celtic peoples humbled by Rome. . . . The triumphal symbolism dominates. It would be incautious, of course, to insist upon a single-minded version of the statue's imagery. Caelus at the top of the cuirass holds the mantle of heaven above Sol who drives his horses across the sky, perhaps as dawning of a new age. And a mother earth figure reclines at the bottom, with cornucopiae and babies, projecting prosperity and the bountifulness of the land. The principal features of the work, however, demand the conclusion that this new and prosperous age depends upon armed force and constitutes the fruits of victory. . . . An association with military success and achievement is inescapable. The Prima Porta figure signifies conquest of the empire and world-wide rule assured by the continual vigilance of the *princeps*.

The Ara Pacis itself, of course, demands consideration. That impressive monument has justifiably stimulated an endless stream of literature. That it carried symbolic importance for Augustus is obvious. But that importance can be overstated or misconceived. The very fact of the altar's survival has accorded it a stature out of proportion to its role in the larger context of Augustan policy and image. The existence of the Ara Pacis does not itself imply that peace held central place in the public presentation of the government. A more circumspect approach will be salutary.

One might note first of all that *Pax* herself, as a representational figure, does not appear anywhere on the monument. Nor is the Ara Pacis depicted on any Augustan coins. This casts serious doubt upon any inference that peace or her monument served as chief emblem of Augustus' Principate. Of course, the friezes of the altar portray a solemn and serene religious procession. But that itself need not have direct reference to peace as a principle or a goal. The panel of Aeneas on the west side of the altar has him performing sacrifice to the Di Penates, a scene that evidently celebrates his homecoming, just as the altar itself was erected to commemorate Augustus' homecoming from Gaul and Spain. But that panel is balanced by another, featuring the partially preserved Mars, father of the twins Romulus and Remus, and preeminent god of war. A similar balance occurs on the eastern panels of the altar. One presents a female deity, a figure with the attributes of fertility and prosperity, calling attention to the blessings of a tranquil time. But its counterpart is the very fragmentary panel of the goddess Roma resting, as often, on a pile of arms. The imagery takes on meaning in combination. The accomplishment of peace is inseparable from success in war. It is fitting that the Ara Pacis was built at the Campus Martius. . . .

The importance of the Ara Pacis cannot be gainsaid. But it has to be understood in context. The recent discovery that close connection held between the altar and the Egyptian obelisk that stood as the pointer of the colossal sundial of Augustus provides welcome reassurance. The shadow of the obelisk pointed squarely at the center of the Ara Pacis on the 23rd of September, the birthday of Augustus himself. That association has revealing import. The obelisk was set up to memorialize Augustus' subordination of Egypt to the control of the Roman empire. The linkage of peace with military authority and imperial expansion here receives dramatic display.

The thrust of Augustus' propaganda leaves a clear impression. Stress falls on martial might and the power of Rome. The idea that Augustus somehow concealed force under the guise of tranquility is refuted by the *princeps* himself, by the poets and intellectuals, by the numismatic slogans, the epigraphical testimony, and the public monuments. The regime prided itself upon universal rule—and the pacification of the enemy.

Modes of Propaganda

Chester Starr

Professor Chester Starr of the University of Michigan examines Augustus' need to win sympathy for his political program in all levels of society. While poetry might affect a small sophisticated elite in the capital, it would hardly affect the illiterate masses across the vast Empire. Thus the emperor turned to coins, which reached the furthest corners of the Empire. These coins usually depicted the emperor on the obverse and some emblem of political importance on the reverse: a crocodile with the legend "Egypt captured" issued after the defeat of Cleopatra would be understood by the literate and illiterate alike. In a society without modern means of communication, coinage constituted the only mass media that could carry the emperor's message throughout the Roman world.

The depth and character of the Augustan program had far-reaching effects on Augustus' attitude toward the thought of his age. All physical defiance of his sway had failed, and Augustus kept under arms a sufficient force to make any subsequent opposition of this nature a most foolhardy gamble. For his system of government to succeed—especially for his program of rejuvenation to bear ripe fruit—he had permanently to gain not men's bodies but men's minds. The efforts which Augustus made to this end show that he drew the proper conclusions and that he realized the difficulty of his task.

Genuine success rested primarily upon untiring attention to the details of government. His acts, however, might be reinforced in two complementary directions: he could implant his program in public opinion, and he could prevent the vocal or physical expression of discontent. Augustus shrewdly utilized a host of means to bend the thought of his contemporaries and of posterity—for always he had in mind the judgment which later generations would pass on his work. Upon the Augustan foundations his successors built a mighty structure of propaganda and control, the development of which is a mark of the unfolding of their absolutism.

Augustus thus shaped a great appeal to public opinion and extended it far beyond the mere security of his personal position, though that aspect was never forgotten. His message was addressed to all levels of society, from slaves, freedmen, and provincials to the upper classes of Rome and Italy, but was aimed particularly at the latter. To present his ideas to these groups Augustus utilized physical objects—coins, sculpture, inscriptions, and architecture—and words, both his own in edict and speech and those of the authors of the era. Beyond these vehicles lay also his personal example, his deft interweaving of himself into the patriotic and religious institutions of Rome and the Empire, and other subtle devices.

In the Roman world coins were a means of exchange and payment, particularly of the troops; by the Late Republic they had also become a potent vehicle for the explanation of state policy to the public. In the Empire the legends and types of coins came to change as frequently as those of modern stamps, as varying aspects of state policy came to the fore or dropped back. Coins could be charged with great symbolic value by combinations of very simple motifs such as the representation of Concord, Peace, and other virtues, Greco-Roman deities (each aiding man in a special sphere), military standards, harvest tools, and the like. Though much of this significance is undoubtedly lost to us, the essential messages had to be put very directly, and so we can detect at least the main lines of official policy as reflected on the coins.

The republican coinage had been theoretically carried out by junior officials under the control of the Senate. In the late second and the first century B.C. the types had been chosen largely by the mintmasters to celebrate current events or the glorious deeds of their own ancestors. This coinage, ever more factional, led on to nearly independent issues by the great warlords in the provinces; Caesar, the greatest of these, gained mastery of Rome and was the first to place the head of a living person (himself) on Roman coins in his last years when he was claiming divine honors. In the civil wars after his death the triumvirs, as well as Brutus and Cassius, struck with their own heads, but Augustus proceeded even further in bending the state coinage to his own purposes. . . .

The types represented on the coins of the Augustan mints do not furnish as complete a statement of policy as do those of later rulers, but they do indicate the general road down which Augustus tried to steer public opinion. The military and diplomatic triumphs of the reign are quite frankly emphasized—Actium, the conquest of Egypt, the recovery of the Roman standards lost to Parthia in the defeat of Crassus and two later generals, the domination of Armenia, and to a lesser extent the victories on the northern frontier. Augustan peace is clearly not a craven matter; Augustus was directing the bulk of his coinage not at the provinces but at the citizen body of Rome and Italy.

More important than peace, according to the coins, was internal security, and this arose from the moderation of Augustus; a common motif is the shield of virtue, often held by a flying Victory, which had been given him by the Senate in 27 B.C. His salvation of the Roman citizen body by ending the civil wars is also emphasized. The Senate presented to him, likewise in 27, an oak crown, the usual trophy for a soldier who had saved a fellow soldier, and this wreath appears frequently on the coins, encircling the words "for saving citizens." The type, which emphasized clearly to the subjects that their security depended on their rulers, became standard under later emperors.

Even the briefest examination of the Augustan coinage reveals both the pride which Augustus felt in his achievements and also his effort to convince the Roman world that he was all-important to its continuation. Vows taken by the Senate and the people for his safe return to Rome after his various trips or for his health in time of sickness are carefully commemorated. Except for the few republican-type coins before 12 B.C., his head always appears on the obverse of gold and silver coins and on the copper *as*, which was used particularly in paying troops. The legend conveys his legal powers in considerable detail. Frequently the reverse is given over to such types as a globe (for universal domination), the rudder of Fortune, the cornucopiae of prosperity, the Capricorn of his birthday, statues and arches erected to him, and the like. . . .

In the later years of his reign the variety of Augustan coinage decreased. The Lyons mint emphasized year after year a few major themes, first Augustus the victorious and then, from 2 B.C., the continuation of his dynasty. A long series celebrates his grandsons Gaius and Lucius even after their death; then another belatedly notes the final selection of his stepson Tiberius as his heir. The monotonous repetition of these themes is in a sense a testimony to Augustus' security of position; in another respect it may also serve as evidence of his weariness, of the fact that he and his world no longer felt the fresh appeal of his program.

The imperial coinage reflects most directly the ideas of Augustus, but the ordinary subject in the provinces saw chiefly the copper or, in some cases, silver issues of his local city or province. The tone of these countless issues followed, though at considerable distance, the Augustan picture of the reformed constitution and the security of the new system, and alluded discreetly to the local bearing of the new order. . . .

To sum up the program of the Augustan coinage generally, the *princeps* was not reluctant to emphasize his own military accomplishments or his virtues, which were evidently to be taken as a guarantee and source of felicity to the Roman world. The appeal of the imperial coinage was primarily to Roman and Italian circles; to find any great emphasis on the themes of peace and prosperity or local sentiments one must turn to local coinages, especially of the Eastern cities.

The tone of the coinage is a positive one. Augustus might roam his palace begging Varus to return the legions destroyed in the German disaster of A.D. 9, but the coins of Alexandria in 10 and 11 tell the subjects only of the "victory" secured by Tiberius on the Rhenish frontier during those two years.

Augustus' Conception of Himself

Meyer Reinhold

Professor Meyer Reinhold of Boston University has chosen to pursue a psychohistorical examination of Augustus. He suggests that young Octavius had a low level of self-esteem and thus sought power while he could not tolerate competition. Reinhold sees Augustus' protestation that he is a "servant of the state" to be a rationalization of his own emotional need to cling to power. Though some scholars are skeptical of the value of psychohistory in the study of antiquity because our evidence is relatively skimpy, Reinhold believes that there is sufficient material on Augustus' personality to allow a modern scholar to explain his political behavior.

It is a received commonplace that the personality of Augustus, who was at the center of Roman political power for almost sixty years, and bestrode the Mediterranean world as sole arbiter for about fifty (the longest hold on power in Rome's long history) is an enigma. . . . In quest of definition of the psychic texture, the inner life and motives of the first *princeps*, whose acts and times are among the most extensively documented in antiquity, one may regret the loss of Plutarch's life of Augustus and of the autobiography of the founder of the Roman Empire. True, we have . . . Augustus' [own words] preserved in scattered quotations and in letters, and in the "queen of Latin inscriptions," the *Res Gestae Divi Augusti* (Achievements of the Deified Augustus), that extraordinary summation of his career. But this "obituary notice" of himself compels caution because of its selectivity and calculated aim to bequeath at the end of his life a posthumous image of his place in history.

Despite Augustus' longevity, the dynamically transitional character of his times, our awareness of his consummate skill as myth maker for his age and posterity, his artful use of propaganda and symbols, the numerous crises and blows of fortune he encountered, it is now possible to reexamine the evidence and elicit insights into his inner world, his conception of himself and his role—thanks, in part, to the tools at hand from the avalanche of fundamental studies in the past half century in humanistic psychology, the nature of power and leadership, the personality of power-seekers and power-wielders, and the typology of political personalities. Equally important, we may in conjunction bring to bear on Augustus' words and deeds our increasingly refined knowledge of the Roman ethos, of the motives of Romans of his social stratum, and of Roman political, social, and economic institutions.

The data we possess about Augustus' earliest years, before he emerged in the political arena at the age of eighteen as Caesar's heir, are sparse, but telling. They afford us glimpses into events and circumstances that affected the emotional life of the intensely ambitious young man he was: his birth in 63 B.C. in the small Italian town of Velitrae . . . into the family of the Octavii, of plebeian, but equestrian stock; the sudden death of his father Gaius Octavius (who married the heiress Atia, niece of Julius Caesar) when the boy was only four years old; the *ignobilitas* of the family; his upbringing at Rome in the house of his grandmother Julia (Caesar's sister) until she died in 50 B.C. when he was twelve; finally his transfer to the home of his remarried mother and his stepfather, Lucius Marcius Philippus.

It is speculative, of course, to try to assess the degree of psychic damage caused by this series of personal dislocations at such an impressionable age, but we may confidently record that he was ashamed of his father's familial background and of the relatively humble rank of the Octavii within the highly stratified status-conscious Roman social and political hierarchy. Stories were allowed to circulate later—not without his own connivance—that he was sired on Atia by the god Apollo, and there was even attributed to himself the statement, "Some think I was the son of Octavius; some suspect that I was born from someone else." It was therefore balm to his ego esteem when at the age of fourteen he received marks of favor from his patrician great-uncle the glamorous Julius Caesar (who lacked a legitimate male heir), and when he was adopted by Caesar's will at the age of eighteen. . . .

Ministering strongly to Augustus' self-doubts was his chronic sickly nature. His illnesses and disabilities are extensively documented from age seventeen to seventy-six. Hypochondriacal and a lifelong valetudinarian, he was constantly solicitous about his health, with a strong will to overcome his weaknesses; he exercised great care in his living habits, disciplining his eating, drinking, sleep, and rest periods . . . . Augustus' physical appearance, moreover, was unprepossessing. He was short (under 5'7", according to his freedman secretary, Julius Marathus), and as a result wore somewhat high-soled shoes to make him appear taller than he actually was. His teeth were wide apart and poorly kept, and his body had numerous calluses from chronic itching and use of the strigil. Eschewing the traditional Roman preference for realistic portraits, Augustus wished always to be depicted in idealized form; the approximately 150 known portraits of him in sculpture, based on authorized official prototypes, consistently show him as a handsome person, and this style was maintained even in portraits made in his old age.

Yet there is little doubt that Augustus fully recognized his own limitations, not only in health but in spheres that brought fame and glory to many other Romans: He was neither a great general, nor orator, nor intellectual, nor political theorist, nor writer. No wonder that his attitude to his adoptive father Julius Caesar as role model was ambiguous. Though he owed the launching of his career to Caesar's adoption of him (Cicero: "a boy . . . who owes all to a name"), diligently performed his duty as *ultor Caesaris* ("avenger of Caesar"), and eagerly inherited his wealth, *clientela* and veterans, he studiously maintained a conscious distance from the memory of Caesar. This negative reaction to his famous adoptive father was due not merely

to personality differences but to compelling ideological and tactical considerations: Caesar's liaison with Cleopatra, his monarchical aspirations, supranational cosmopolitanism, and notorious trampling on due process. True, the name "Caesar" and the patronymic *divi filius* ("son of a deified person") were both used by Augustus in his official titulature as glamorous, potent, authoritative, but little was said in the Augustan Age of the acts and memory of Caesar himself.

It was rather with Alexander the Great that Augustus consciously and calculatedly associated himself, both as universal conqueror and ruler, and champion of western civilization over the East. After the deaths of Cleopatra and Antony in 30 B.C., Augustus visited the tomb of Alexander in Alexandria, touched his mummy (presumably to absorb its "power"), placed a crown on the body and strewed it with flowers. Indeed, Augustus' seal ring from 30–23 B.C. bore a portrait of Alexander. Moreover, in the high enthusiasm created by his victories in the East, Augustus' *imitatio Alexandri* spawned ambitious, romantic plans for massive expansion on all frontiers to achieve a dream of universal empire . . . . It is characteristic of Augustus' ego needs that he was determined to surpass Alexander. When he soon abandoned his grandiose dreams of world conquest, he faulted Alexander for not deeming the administration of the existing empire of greater import than winning it. . . .

Augustus' need to present himself as excelling Alexander stems from his conception of himself as an extraordinary and unique person, a man of paramount virtues and achievements, a leader unparalleled in the annals of Rome, indeed in world history. He resented being called *"puer"* (boy) in his younger upward-striving days, but in later years he boasted that he was the youngest in world history to rise to power. It is true that it was through Caesar's favor that he was early brought into the entourage of the great dictator, and even elected *pontifex* at the age of fifteen. But after Caesar's death he mounted his own drive for power: at nineteen he mobilized an army (of Caesar's veterans, of course), was co-opted into the Senate, and unprecedentedly elected consul; at twenty he was one of the triumvirs for reorganizing the state (with Antony and Lepidus). Unprecedented as these early conquests were, Augustus took pains throughout the *Res Gestae* to parade the many unparalleled "firsts" and "mosts" in his career, including honors, victories, offices, in his private expenditures for public purposes, in census statistics, in his building program, shows and spectacles provided for Rome, and in expansion of Roman territory. Typical are such boasts as "an honor which hitherto had been decreed to no one besides myself" (Ch. 12); "I was the first and only one to have done [this]. . . in the memory of my generation" (Ch. 16); [Envoys from India came to him] "previously not seen in the presence of any Roman general" (Ch. 3); [At his election to *pontifex maximus*] "a great multitude flocked from all of Italy such as never before had been recorded at Rome" (Ch. 10). The most self-revealing phrase is *prius quam nascerer* ("before I was born"), in reference to the fact that in all Roman history only twice before was the Temple of Janus closed—to signify peace in the entire empire—but in his Principate it was closed three times (Ch. 13).

One may readily grant him his pride in his achievements and his awareness of the mark he made in history. But Augustus' need to demonstrate his uniqueness with such overkill is, one may posit, a reflection of deep-rooted incapability to abide competition with his contemporaries. Indeed, not once in his long political career did he subject himself to the normal competitive electoral chance, neither as consul (thirteen times), nor when he became a triumvir (for ten years), nor even as *pontifex maximus*. The extraordinary powers he obtained from 23 B.C. to the end of his life— the *imperium proconsulare maius* (superior proconsular power) and the *tribunicia potestas* (tribunician power) were overriding supramagisterial innovations that removed him from the indignity of the electoral process, and assured him unique superiority and priority in decision-making without competition in both the military and civil spheres. . . .

For about sixty years Augustus was indeed "the first servant of the State," to which he rendered "constant unwavering laborious service." He rarely took a vacation from matters of state; he was one of the master toilers in world history. From Stoic teaching of the "assigned post" and Roman military language he formulated the political concept of his mission as *statio principis* ("the ruler's post"), his legacy to all future emperors. Whether we view him as fulfilling strong ego needs or as proceeding out of principled sense of public duty, Augustus was a devoted, untiring public servant with an enormous capacity for work. Painstaking, meticulous, omnipresent, he was constantly involved in decision-making, legislation, and administration, even in the smallest details, in all spheres: military, political, religious, economic, social, cultural. Dio Cassius put the following words into Augustus' mouth:

I have devoted myself unstintingly to you in all circumstances . . . . From all this I have derived no gain for myself.

. . . Augustus made gestures of refusal of power, but it is clear that he never seriously contemplated resigning power and retiring to private life. In the *Res Gestae* (Ch. 6), he asserts that he "accepted no office contrary to the ancestral tradition." In 22 B.C., after he stepped down from the consulship (his eleventh, held nine years in a row), the urban plebs in a season of great distress in Rome took to the streets to urge the Senate to appoint him dictator for life. He thereupon made a dramatic appearance before the people: he went down on his knees before them, and bared his breast, in token of readiness to die rather than accept such an office. Augustus acted here in all sincerity regarding the dictatorship, which had been fatal to Caesar, even though we know that the gesture of refusal of power was a traditional [sign of virtue]. The year before, in 23 B.C., when he was almost fatally ill, he is said to have contemplated resigning his authority. "But reconsidering that as a private person he would not be without danger, and that the State would thus be entrusted rashly to the judgement of the masses, he continued to maintain his hold on power." Seneca writes that Augustus constantly prayed for a rest and vacation from affairs of state, and for the enjoyment of leisure, and he cites a letter sent by Augustus to the Senate in which he expressed his expectation that if he retired he would not be diminished in high status, and that his fame would remain unimpaired. . . .

But Augustus never seriously contemplated stepping down from his supreme status to a lower one. . . . Augustus' inability to dissociate himself from his hold on power, originating in his ego needs, was in time rationalized as society's need for himself as indispensable agent of the stability of the exemplary state he had created. In an edict he once proclaimed, in memorable words:

May it be granted to me to see the state firm in its place, safe and sound, and to reap the reward I aspire to from this, namely, that I be known as the author of the best type of government, and that when I die I may take with me the hope that the foundations of the government I have laid will remain in their original form.

Augustus' conception of himself as "first servant of the state," as wholly dedicated to society's needs, is reflected in his enormous expenditures for public purposes out of his own vast private fortune, especially on distributions of food, on games and spectacles, public buildings and public works, largesses to the people of Rome, and donations and bonuses to the soldiers. Moreover, since considerable sums of money tended to concentrate in his hands through legacies, he served as a sort of economic conduit for channeling the private wealth of others into public uses. In his will he declared that he had little of his own wealth left at the end of his life, having spent most of it . . . [on the state]. There is no reason to doubt this. "In private life poor, in public life rich," wrote Dio Cassius of him.

In keeping with his dedication to public interests, throughout his regime Augustus maintained a relatively frugal life style: his pleasures, food, and dress were simple and without ostentation, and he muted ceremonial gestures and did not give in to the pageantry of power. His personal home on the Palatine was not a "palace," even though hardly as small as conventionally described; we now know that his property on the Palatine was indeed vast in extent. In contrast with the luxurious estates of many of his contemporaries, his villas were modest retreats.

Despite his need for uninhibited power and constant approbation throughout his life, Augustus conceived of himself as cautious and low-keyed. His aversion to eccentricity and flamboyance in himself and others, and his calculating nature are revealed by his obsession with the Greek *topos*, ... "Make haste slowly," which he used over and over again; and he was prone also to quote Euripides that "A cautious general is better than a rash one." Caution and prudence were also Augustus' guidelines as a speaker; he never spoke extemporaneously. It was his practice to read everything from a carefully prepared speech, whether before the Senate of the people or soldiers. In important private conversations (even, it is said with his wife Livia!) he spoke with a written text before him, "so that he might not say more or less. . . . "

Augustus' characteristic restraint and moderation are also revealed by his response to the outpouring of divine honors to him throughout the empire, especially in the eastern provinces. Augustus studiously adhered to the Roman tradition that forbade public worship of a living person. Private worship of himself as a god burgeoned, and formal cults of Augustus were established in many places [But] in Augustus' own conception of himself, there was never any question that distance between himself and the gods should be maintained, and that his proper role was that of mortal mediator between the divine and human spheres. It is noteworthy that in the *Res Gestae* he makes no claim to divine honors. Tiberius followed consciously the model of Augustus in rejecting divine honors. . . .

Indeed Augustus recognized that his temperament was pre-eminently civilian, despite his quest for military éclat. His forte was that of mediator, between gods and men, past and future, Rome and Italy with the rest of the empire. We should concede to him that, for all his passion for power, his determination to claw his way to the top of the Roman social and political hierarchy in order to compensate for his damaged self-esteem and sickly nature, and his yearning for fame and glory, Augustus was not cunningly dishonest, deceitful, or hypocritical, as some have depicted him, but rather basically sincere in his aims and methods. It is doubtful whether he distinguished between the young ruthless power-hungry Octavian and the benevolent statesman Augustus. His personal ego needs were inextricably fused with the work he did in tidying up the Mediterranean world, and moderating and holding in balance the great tensions of the times.

Augustus would have conceded that without the favor of Julius Caesar and the legacy of his name his own ambitions would have come to naught; and he surely understood that *fortuna* (luck), that his many loyal helpers, and his control over vast resources of wealth all contributed greatly to his success. Though "the assemblage of qualities and capacities that made up his personality are not such as to strike the imagination of the world," he remains one of the *grands hommes politiques* in world history. Yet we may still applaud [the historian] Mommsen's verdict that . . ."Augustus adroitly played the role of the great man without himself being great."

Augustus in the View of History

David Stockton

David Stockton of Braesnose College, Oxford, believes that there is some justification for Augustus' claim that he had restored the Republic. The emperor's constitutional arrangements were not merely a smokescreen; Augustus did not exercise arbitrary rule, but rather governed under a system of law. It would be an anachronism to project a modern tyrannical police state back to Augustus' reign.

And so to Augustus we come at last. He was born in September 63 B.C., the year of Cicero's famous consulship, *consule Tullio*. The childless Julius Caesar, his grandmother's brother, discerned and encouraged his precocious promise, and after his assassination in March 44 B.C., Caesar's will disclosed that he was to be Caesar's adopted son. Thus, at the age of eighteen, when young men nowadays are beginning their freshman year at college, Gaius Octavius became Gaius Julius Caesar Octavianus, and at once threw himself headlong into the maelstrom of war and intrigue that swirled all over the Mediterranean world. Thirteen years later he eliminated the last and most formidable and durable of his rivals at Actium and, like his adoptive father before him, now bestrode that world like a colossus. But this new colossus did not have feet of clay. Julius himself survived barely six months after his return to Rome from his final victory in Spain before he lay dead at the pedestal of the statue of his great rival Pompey, bleeding from many wounds. His assassins were a very mixed collection of Republicans and Pompeians and prominent adherents of the dictator himself: men who could look to stand high in his favor, united only by a common fear or distaste of Julius' despotic and quasi-monarchic authority, which they all wanted to end. But Augustus survived his final victory at Actium by forty-four years, and when he died in his own bed at the age of seventy-six he bequeathed to Rome and the Empire not civil war and uncertainty, but that stable and long-lasting system of government that we call "the Principate."

For three years or so after his victory at Actium, Octavian's rule, like that of Julius, was essentially of a personal nature. But he was careful not to seek to formalize his autocracy, and (as the event showed and probably as many of those close to him knew or suspected) he was using this time to think out his long-term position while at the same time briskly tidying up the many loose ends in preparation for his "first constitutional settlement" of 28/27 B.C., when he formally surrendered his extraordinary power and restored the state to the discretion of the Senate and people of Rome. As he himself expressed it in his *Res Gestae*, the long inscription recording his services to Rome which he composed himself and directed to be set up outside his mausoleum in the Campus Martius where the population of the capital could read it after his death: ["In my 6th, 7th consulship, after I had put an end to civil war, having acquired by universal consent the control of all affairs, I transferred government from my own authority to the Senate and Roman people."] Thus the final form of his constitutional position was essentially laid down. He was to have no authoritarian power, no perpetual dictatorship such as Julius had had himself voted early in 44 B.C., or anything like it. From Senate and people he received back the charge of the imperial provinces where the overwhelming bulk of the legions were stationed, and whose actual governors and military commanders were his own chosen legates and directly subordinate to his authority. At Rome itself he relied on continuing tenure of one of the two consulships for his formal power, while his enormous informal influence and prestige and patronage, his *auctoritas* as the Romans termed it, could be counted on to plug any gaps and oil the wheels of government. Four years later, in 23 B.C., he gave up the annual tenure of the consulship, and in place of it received the tribunician power for life, while his *imperium* as a provincial governor and military commander was specifically declared superior (*maius*) to that of all other governors: a change probably provoked by his own experience of the working of the 28/27 B.C. settlement and by certain uneasy stirrings in a section of the ruling aristocracy, but a change which still preserved the philosophy of that first settlement.

The self-consciously sophisticated and worldly-wise smile knowingly and purport to penetrate a clumsily-laid smoke-screen to get at the truth which lay behind it: Augustus (to use the auspicious name which he was granted in January 27 B.C., and by which he was known thereafter) was simply concerned to run up a fairly crude facade of constitutionalism behind which he continued to govern as an autocrat. That is not a view which I share. I find it difficult to believe that Augustus, surely one of the ablest masters of politics and diplomacy known to history, would have taken the very great trouble, which he evidently did take, simply in order to try to pull off a pretty obvious confidence-trick, or that the people who were supposed to be taken in by it should have been so gullible. When Julius Caesar was struck down, it was the reality and not the appearance of autocracy that his assassins were seeking at great peril to themselves to destroy. Less than twenty years later the Roman governing-class had not become so ingenuous as to mistake appearance for reality. That from 31 and 27 and 23 B.C. onwards Augustus was the effective ruler of the Roman world was as clear to them as it is to us. The form which that rule took was of vital importance. To restore the Republic in any literal sense of re-establishing the system that had existed fifty or a hundred years earlier would have been an act of folly, as damaging to the inhabitants of Italy and the Empire as to any personal aspirations of Augustus himself, and few if any modern historians of Rome would regard the attempt to do so as anything but seriously misguided; the work of a man who was blind to practical realities. To establish an open autocracy or monarchy would

not only have run dangerously across the grain of the deep-seated prejudices of a governing-class which Augustus no more than Julius Caesar could afford to think of doing without (such classes, whatever their shortcomings, can not be disposed of and replaced speedily), but would have been to fly in the face of five hundred years of Roman history and throw away much that was of hard-won practical value and much that was of enormous psychological importance. Augustus preferred a middle way, and it was not for nothing that his watchword was to "make haste slowly." Luckily, time turned out to be on his side: Rome, they say, was not built in a day—and Augustus had over forty years for the task.

In so far as in a very important sense *res publica* connoted constitutional government, the rule of law, the establishment and operation of universally recognized rules, as opposed to what the Romans called *regnum* (absolute and arbitrary rule), there was more justice in the claim that Augustus restored the Republic than has often been allowed, and not merely in contrast with the abnormal circumstances of the preceding twenty years of dynastic power-politics and the predominance of those with the biggest battalions. In defining his powers Augustus necessarily delimited them, and made it clear in what areas he would claim to exercise open authority and in virtue of what legal prerogatives and in general conformity with what precedents. By the same token he advertised in what areas he would not seek or claim to exercise open authority. In a nutshell, there were going to be rules, and the rules themselves were not new: Augustus was equipped not with any extraordinary powers but rather with an extraordinary set of traditional powers. Whatever his motives may be supposed to have been (and the motives even of modern politicians, let alone ancient ones, are always difficult and often impossible to fathom with confidence—indeed, many of us can never be quite sure about our own), the plain fact remains that for Augustus, his constitutional powers and prerogatives were not a matter of superficial concern as compared with the stark reality of force. That much is evident from the time and trouble which he spent on them, and at bottom it is not hard to see why.

None of the foregoing should be taken to imply that the sheer *potentia* of Augustus, his immense patronage, his control of the army, his enormous wealth, in general his powerful influence or *auctoritas* stemming from all these, was not the ultimate guarantee of the security and stability of his new order. Had any rival been able to use the army against him, his constitutional powers would have been of as little use to him as those of the governments of the late Republic had been to them when faced with the military challenge of a Sulla or a Caesar at the head of veteran legions loyal to their commanders. But rule in a stable and civilized society is much more than the possession of the biggest club to hit other people on the head with. Nobody takes it amiss nowadays that the Presidents of the United States and of France, and the Prime Minister of the United Kingdom can count on the loyalty and obedience of the military and police forces of their countries. It would be a sorry state of affairs if they could not, for any country of which that is not true lives in a condition of weakness and uncertainty, or in the grip of some covert group or junta which uses the nominal government as a screen for its own dominance. What worries most of us is the spectacle of a government which relies on army and police to hold down a populace which otherwise would not tolerate it. There is no shred of evidence that that was true of Augustus' government, so that glib and anachronistic comparisons with a modern Batista or Franco (to name but two) will not do. Quite the contrary, since there is every reason to believe that, leaving aside a handful of ambitious men whose notions of what constituted *libertas* were anything but democratic or egalitarian, the overwhelming majority of the inhabitants of Italy and the provinces welcomed the peace and stability and material prosperity and administrative efficiency which came with the principate of Augustus. Rather than focus our attention too fixedly on the admittedly important question of how Augustus managed to take the army out of politics, we should also give close attention to the actual use which he made of his secure

authority, for it may legitimately be questioned whether his security would have been very long-lived had he not paid close and constant attention to the wider basis on which it rested. Military dynasts had appeared on the Roman scene before, one moment all-powerful and the next only a memory. Making every allowance for the widespread weariness and longing for peace and quiet, which had become more deeply felt as the years of violence and instability went by, and for the deaths of many possibly formidable opponents, there could be no certainty that Augustus would be the last of the series and prove exempt from the mutability of fortune which had stopped his predecessors in their tracks. If he was going to stay, it was not a foregone conclusion, but one which he would have to work hard for.

There are those who regard questions about "what might have happened if only" as not to be asked, or not worth asking, by the serious-minded historian. But Mommsen did not hesitate to condemn "the flatness of that sort of historical inquiry which thinks it proper to take no account of what never happened." Had Augustus not completed the task he set himself, the world would have been a very different place. The Roman Empire might have split into fragments, or at least that fateful division between East and West, which came about from the fourth century A.D. onwards, could well have occurred much earlier. The issue at Actium was not only between Italy and Greece, but between the Republican tradition and autocracy. The natural successor of the Hellenistic monarchies was the autocracy of Byzantium. But the victorious Augustus did not make himself a king; he was known as "*princeps*," the first man in the state. In effect, he invented constitutional monarchy, the rule of one man, but a man whose powers were defined by law, limited by law, exercised within conventional legal limits. For all its many shortcomings, the Principate was far superior to the autocracies and anarchies which proceeded and followed it, and the sophisticated and cynical seductions, even of a Tacitus, should not be permitted to blind us to that truth. It was Augustus' achievement that freedom under the law, one of the ideals of classical Greece and Republican Rome, was still an ideal of the Roman Empire. It grew gradually more remote, but it remained an ideal to be passed on to later ages. To give just one example: when the Emperor Claudius wanted to marry within the degrees forbidden by law, he did not assume that as Emperor he was above the law, but had the law changed so that not just he, but anybody, could legally marry a niece. The point may seem a very slight one, but on reflection it will be seen to be a vital one.

Without the united Empire which Augustus ensured, the Romanization of western Europe might well never have come about, with all its momentous consequences. But western Europe in fact got the best of both worlds, an Italian civilization enriched by Greek literature and art and science and philosophy, and both in Europe and in the Americas we are all of us today the beneficiaries. Without that Empire in which to spread and fructify, the story of Christianity would not be the one which we know. There might well be no story to tell, but only a footnote to write. But Augustus won and Augustus survived, and he created a system so tough and durable that it could survive the rule of an aging, embittered, and suspicious Tiberius; of a paranoiac like Caligula; a bumbling eccentric like Claudius; and, a retarded adolescent like Nero, to emerge essentially intact into the sunlit uplands beyond. To few men, if indeed to any other man at all, has it been given to build so solid and lasting an edifice. Even after the western provinces had been overrun by the barbarians, the church survived. And, with its capital at Byzantium, the eastern Empire hung on for another thousand years, preserving the treasures of the classical world for transmission to modern Europe, gradually civilizing—as far as it could—Bulgarians and Russians. It was not until A.D. 1453 that this last direct link with Augustus, and through Augustus with Homer, Thucydides, Plato and Aristotle, Cicero and Virgil, was finally snapped, when the last Roman Emperor fell sword in hand at the gate of Saint Romanus. By now, happily, western Europe was beginning to be grown up enough to carry on on its own. Just over thirty years after the fall of Constantinople, Richard III of England died on Bosworth field, and the Middle Ages were over. And, within forty years of the destruction of the eastern Roman Empire, Christopher Columbus was being rowed ashore at the end of his long voyage to the West. The legacy of Greece and Rome and Judaea was being transported to a New World.

A triumphal arch surmounted with a
bronze four-horse chariot containing
Octavian appears on the reverse of a
silver denarius issued by a south Italian
mint about 29–27 B.C. It probably
depicts the arch erected in the Roman
Forum in 30 B.C. to commemorate
Octavian's victory over Marc Antony.

The Armies And The Provinces

INTRODUCTION
Ronald Mellor

Through the second century B.C., *the Roman legions were recruited from among the propertied classes—often by voluntary enlistment or, in times of emergency, by conscription. But Roman imperialism outside Italy made military service with long tours of duty far from home less attractive, and the influx of cheap slaves in the second century drove many yeoman farmers from their lands and thus made them ineligible for service. During the first century* B.C. *the great military leaders drew their armies from among the landless proletariat, who craved booty, adventure and improvement in their status. These were the men who fought for Pompey in Asia and Caesar in Gaul, but they also fought each other in the civil wars that brought down the Roman Republic. They were paid by their commanders and rewarded with grants from booty, and they expected their commanders to procure grants of land to sustain them in retirement.*

After Actium, Octavian was left with the remains of his own and Antony's sixty legions. He had to discharge veterans and ensure loyalty while reorganizing the army. He purchased land and established colonies around the Mediterranean for 100,000 demobilized men, and he organized the rest into 28 legions with a nominal strength of 6,000 soldiers each. But Octavian-Augustus had to transform a fighting force into a peacetime army. With little prospect of booty (unless they were to support a rival for the imperial throne), it was essential to bind the loyalty of the troops with regular pay, promotions, and pensions. Thus Augustus and his successors were able to ensure the support of the legions for the Julio-Claudian dynasty for a hundred years.

Augustus established a military treasury with an enormous initial grant of 42 million denarii— a year's pay for the entire army of 180,000 men—and he ensured its solvency by earmarking sales and inheritance taxes for this purpose. Each ordinary soldier was annually paid 225 denarii, and we know that a year's supply of grain cost about 60 denarii. It was a living wage, and there were prospects for special grants like the 75 denarii each provided in Augustus' will—four months pay! Promotion could bring enormous increases in salary and, proportionally, in any imperial grants. Each of the sixty centuries in a legion contained one hundred legionaries who were led by a centurion. The centurions, non-commissioned officers who were promoted from the ranks, each received a salary of 3,750 denarii. A senior group of centurions received 7,500 denarii each, while the primus pilus, *the ranking centurion in a legion, received 15,000 denarii—over 65 times the pay of an ordinary legionary. After about twenty years' service, the imperial soldier would receive a grant (in land or cash) equal to about fourteen year's pay, which would serve to sustain him and his family in retirement.*

The legionaries were all Roman citizens and constituted the Empire's infantry. But conquered peoples also provided auxiliary troops to support the legions in the field, and they often supplied skills that the Roman lacked. Horsemen from Gaul and Thrace, slingers from Majorca, archers from Lebanon all served (at about half a legionary's salary) in the service of Rome. This polyglot group were expected to learn Latin and were important for the spread of Latin. Upon discharge each auxiliary was granted Roman citizenship for himself and his family. Tacitus tells us that in A.D. 14 the auxiliaries equalled in number the legionaries: about 180,000 each. Even now it does not seem an enormous force to secure the frontiers and ensure internal security in an Empire of some 50 million souls.

The navy always had less prestige than the army. In the earliest days, the sailors were slaves or freedmen, but under the Julio-Claudians they attained the status of auxiliaries. There were no naval wars in this period; the ships served in convoy duty or in campaigns against pirates. The great Italian fleets were based at Misenum on the Bay of Naples and at Ravenna, but there were other fleets on the Rhine and Danube, in the Black Sea and the English Channel, as well as at Alexandria.

Republican generals had kept a body guard (cohors praetoria) which Augustus developed into a special corps to ensure internal security in Italy, where legions were not normally stationed. These praetorians were paid 750 denarii—more than three times the pay of an ordinary legionary—and they also received special grants from the emperor. The praetorian guard became an elite detachment for the protection of the emperor and the imperial family, and Tiberius' retirement to Capri enabled his prefect Sejanus to control access to the emperor. The guard and its prefects eventually became a two-edged sword: protecting Tiberius and later murdering Caligula. In our contemporary political jargon, a "praetorian guard" not only protects a president but limits access to him and thereby controls whom he sees, what he reads and what he thinks.

Rome's dominion in the Julio-Claudian era extended over parts of the three continents that encircle the Mediterranean, from the Atlantic coast of Africa across to Egypt, Palestine and Syria and back through the Balkans to central and western Europe on the Atlantic coast of Gaul and Spain. Mauretania in westernmost Africa (present Morocco) was a client kingdom until Caligula provoked a rebellion through his murder of its king. It was reconquered by Claudius, who turned it into two provinces secured with colonies of Roman veterans. The great province of Africa, which incorporated present Tunisia as well as sections of Algeria and Libya, had been a breadbasket of Rome since it became a province upon the defeat of Carthage, and the great tracts of excellent farmland increasingly became the domain of the imperial family. Though there was sporadic skirmishing on the southern frontiers, the province was generally peaceful and was ruled by a senatorial proconsul for whom this post (along with the proconsulship of Asia) might be regarded as the peak of his career. Cyrene (present Libya) was linked with Crete under a single senatorial governor.

The defeat of Antony and Cleopatra brought about the annexation of Egypt, and its importance as a breadbasket for Italy led Augustus to retain it as something close to a personal domain: there he succeeded to the honors and prerogatives of the Pharaohs. The governor was an *equestrian prefect responsible directly to the emperor. The first prefect was the poet Cornelius Gallus, who was a personal friend of Augustus. Though the circumstances surrounding his execution for treason are unclear, the episode shows the special care taken by the emperor lest the wealth of Egypt be used (as it was by Antony) to establish a rival for the imperial throne. The emperor did not allow senators or even members of the imperial family to enter Egypt without explicit permission—Germanicus was rebuked by Tiberius for doing so. The prefect had two or three legions and a river patrol was maintained on the Nile to protect against incursions from the south. The greatest disturbances in the first century A.D. were the disputes between the Greek and Jewish communities in Alexandria which were inflamed by Caligula and quieted by Claudius.*

The small and large kingdoms in the eastern Mediterranean had caused Rome difficulties for the last century of the Roman Republic and would continue to do so through the Julio-Claudian era, though Augustus allowed some kings to retain their territories while they supported Roman armies and diplomatic aims. Rome had inherited the province of Asia (western Turkey) from the kings of Pergamum in 133 B.C.—its first territory on the Asian continent—and it had to fight to maintain it against rebellion and invasion. Sulla (88), Pompey (66) and Julius Caesar (47) all fought to restore Roman interests in Asia Minor, and further east, Crassus' army was destroyed by Parthia (53), which defeat Caesar, Antony and Augustus dreamed of avenging. Augustus took over from Antony a patchwork of small client kingdoms and provinces and, though he realized that the client kings took on military burdens and allowed Rome to deploy her forces elsewhere, throughout his reign he gradually transformed the weaker kingdoms into provinces.

Judaea was left in the hands of Antony's client Herod, who offended his orthodox subjects by promoting hellenization. On his death in 4 B.C. the kingdom was divided between his three sons, and one part (also, confusingly, called Judaea) soon became a small Roman province ruled by an equestrian procurator. Caligula restored the kingdom to his friend Herod Agrippa, but after Herod's death Claudius restored Judaea to provincial status. To the north, the imperial province of Syria constituted the principal Roman garrison in the East. An imperial legate served as governor and commander of four legions, which could be directed at Parthia, Armenia, Asia Minor or Judaea.

Armenia sometimes served as a Roman client, sometimes as a genuinely neutral buffer kingdom between Rome and her great enemy to the East, Parthia. And other client kingdoms in Asia gradually were transformed into Roman provinces: Galatia and Pontus under Augustus, Cappadocia and Commagene under Tiberius, and Lycia under Claudius. The jewel in the Roman imperial crown in the East was the great senatorial province of Asia, which included the rich Greek cities along the Aegean coast. The proconsulship of Asia was regarded as the highest honor a senator could receive.

Augustus separated Achaea (the Peloponnesus and central Greece) from Macedonia to form two senatorial provinces, while he administered the new Danubian provinces through imperial legates: Illyricum, Moesia, Rhaetia, Noricum and Pannonia. These provinces, which stretched from present Switzerland through Austria, Yugoslavia, Hungary and Bulgaria, remained unsettled until the great Pannonian rebellion of A.D. 6; Roman forces were stretched thin, and it took Tiberius three years and an army of 100,000 to restore order in the Balkans.

The Rhine had been the frontier between the Romans and the Germans until 12 B.C., when Drusus led Roman troops as far as the Elbe in central Germany. Augustus seems to have had great ambitions and, after the accidental death of Drusus, his brother Tiberius continued the pacification of Germany until he was summoned to deal with the Pannonian revolt in A.D. *6. Before he was able to return, Varus and three legions were destroyed in an ambush—the greatest Roman military disaster for centuries. Tiberius and Germanicus reorganized Roman forces to defend the Rhine, which remained Rome's frontier for centuries and still divides Germanic from Romance Europe.*

Southern France became the province of Gallia Narbonensis in the second century B.C., and the extensive Roman remains in present-day Provence attest to the high level of Roman urbanization in that senatorial province. But the rebellious tribes who lived in the Alpine passes required subjugation, and the Trophy of Augustus, which survives high above Monaco, names dozens of peoples subdued by Augustus. Though the rest of Gaul had been conquered by Julius Caesar, Augustus had to carry on the task of organization. Gaul itself was peaceful through the Julio-Claudian era and so the imperial legate who governed the province kept the substantial legionary forces stationed along the Rhine.

Rome's first Spanish province had been taken from Carthage in 205 B.C., but the peoples of northwest Spain remained savage and unpacified until the Augustan age. The peaceful and urbanized south became the senatorial province of Baetica, while three legions remained stationed in Lusitania (Portugal) and Tarraconensis, which were governed by imperial legates. Finally, Claudius invaded the island of Britain with four legions in 43 B.C., and it remained a province until the Roman withdrawal in A.D. 410. Britain provided little wealth, but British auxiliaries were used to support Roman legions in other provinces.

Augustus employed a range of administrative models to govern his sprawling Empire. He retained imperium (military command) in those provinces which contained the bulk of the imperial armies and ruled them through a personal legate, while senatorial governors administered the more peaceful provinces. Some small provinces were governed by equestrian procurators (like Pontius Pilate in Judaea), and Egypt was kept under the scrutiny of an equestrian prefect. And client kings took on the burdens of supporting Rome and allowed the emperor to deploy his forces elsewhere.

A popular view of Rome remains that of a militaristic state which enslaved all who opposed its domination. The historian Tacitus quotes a fiery British tribal leader: "They bring devastation, and they call it peace." And there were peoples on the periphery of Empire—Germans, Jews, Britons—who suffered the full force of Roman armed might. But there were tens of millions of others for whom the Pax Romana was just that—a time more peaceful and more prosperous than any within memory. There were rapacious tax collectors, but they were sometimes punished by higher authority. Many emperors were far more concerned with the well-being of their subjects than Romans had been in the Republic: roads, aqueducts, baths and the foundation of new cities brought the benefits of Roman civilization to three continents. Rome's armies secured the frontiers and suppressed banditry and piracy so that, depite the bizarre behavior of a Caligula or a Nero, Rome's provincial subjects derived the benefits of a (generally) benevolent Empire.

Mutiny

Tacitus

Tacitus here recounts the story of the mutiny that took place among the northern armies on the death of Augustus in A.D. 14. Here a soldier on the Danube bemoans their harsh treatment by their centurions and neglect by Rome: their pay of 225 denarii should be raised to 350—one per day—and they should be retired after sixteen years. After a fortuitous lunar eclipse, Tiberius' son Drusus was able to intimidate the frightened soldiers and quell this rebellion.

While these events were taking place at Rome, mutiny broke out in the regular army in Pannonia. There were no fresh motives for this, except that the change of emperors offered hopes of rioting with impunity and collecting the profits afforded by civil wars. Three brigades were stationed together in a summer camp with Quintus Junius Blaesus in command. When he heard of the death of Augustus and accession of Tiberius, he suspended normal duty for public mourning (or rejoicing). This was when insubordination and altercation began.

Before long, easy living and idleness were all the troops wanted; the idea of work and discipline became distasteful. There was a man called Percennius in the camp. Having become a private soldier after being a professional applause-leader in the theatre, he was insolent of tongue, and experienced in exciting crowds to cheer actors. The soldiers, simple men, were worried—now that Augustus was dead—about their future terms of service. Percennius gradually worked on them. After dark or in the evening twilight, when the better elements had dispersed to their tents and the riff-raff collected, they talked with him.

Finally Percennius had acquired a team of helpers ready for mutiny. Then he made something like a public speech. 'Why,' he asked, 'obey, like slaves, a few commanders of companies, fewer still of battalions? You will never be brave enough to demand better conditions if you are not prepared to petition—or threaten—an emperor who is new and still faltering. Inactivity has done quite enough harm in all these years. Old men, mutilated by wounds, are serving their thirtieth or fortieth year. And even after your official discharge your service is not finished; for you stay on with the colours as a reserve, still under canvas—the same drudgery under another name! And if you manage to survive all these hazards, even then you are dragged off to a remote country and 'settled' in some waterlogged swamp or untilled mountainside. Truly the army is a harsh, unrewarding profession! Body and soul are reckoned at two and a half sesterces a day—and with this you have to find clothes, weapons, tents, and bribes for brutal company-commanders if you want to avoid chores.

'Heaven knows, lashes and wounds are always with us! So are hard winters and hardworking summers, grim war and unprofitable peace. There will never be improvement until service is based on a contract-pay, four sesterces a day; duration of service, sixteen years with no subsequent recall; a gratuity to be paid in cash before leaving the camp. Guardsmen receive eight sesterces a day, and after sixteen years they go home. Yet obviously their service is no more dangerous than yours. I am not saying a word against sentry-duty in the capital. Still, here are we among tribes of savages, with the enemy actually visible from our quarters!'

Percennius had an enthusiastic reception. As one point or another struck home, his hearers indignantly showed their lash-marks, their white hair, their clothes so tattered that their bodies showed through. Finally, in frenzied excitement, they clamoured that the three brigades should be merged into one. But jealousy wrecked this suggestion, because everyone wanted it to take his own brigade's name. So the proposal was altered, and instead the three Eagles, and the standards of the battalions, were put side by side. Turf was piled up, and a platform erected so as to make the place as conspicuous as possible. As they were hurrying ahead with this, Blaesus came up and began to revile them. Seizing hold of one man after another, he cried: 'Dye your hands in my blood instead! It would be less criminal to kill your general than to rebel against the emperor. As long as I live I shall keep my troops loyal— if I die, my death will help to bring them to their senses. . . .'

Now the mutiny gained momentum. More and more leaders came forward.

The natural inscrutability of Tiberius was always particularly impenetrable in a crisis. However, this news impelled him to send to the scene his son Drusus with a distinguished staff and two battalions of the Guard. Drusus was given no definite instructions—he was to act as the circumstances required. The Guard battalions were strengthened beyond their usual numbers by picked drafts, and were further augmented by a substantial part of the horse Guards and also by the best of the Germans who at that time guarded the emperor's person. With them went a man whose influence over Tiberius was very great, Lucius Aelius Sejanus, joint commander of the Guard with his father, Lucius Seius Strabo. He was to be the prince's adviser, and not to let the rest of the party forget what they stood to gain—or lose.

As Drusus approached, the soldiers met him. Ostensibly this was a mark of respect. But there were none of the customary demonstrations of pleasure and glittering full-dress decorations. The men were disgustingly dirty, and their expressions, intended merely to display dejection, looked virtually treasonable. As soon as Drusus had passed inside the outworks, they picketed the gates, and set armed detachments at key points of the camp. Everyone else crowded round the dais in a gigantic mob. Drusus mounted it with a gesture calling for silence. The mutineers, looking round at the great crowd, set up a truculent roar. But the next instant, as they caught sight of the Caesar, their nerve faltered. Violent yells alternated with confused mutterings, and then silence. They were terrifying and terrified in turn, as their feelings shifted. When Drusus finally got the better of the noise, he read out a letter from his father. It stated that the heroic Roman soldiers, his comrades in so many campaigns, were particularly near his heart, and that as soon as the shock of his bereavement was over, he would refer their claims to the senate. Meanwhile he had sent his son to grant without delay any concessions that could be awarded immediately. The remaining points must be saved up for the senate, which was as capable, they must understand, of generosity as of severity.

The answer came from the crowd that the company-commander Julius Clemens was briefed to put forward their demands. He started by proposing a sixteen-year term of service, with gratuities at its completion, pay of four sesterces a day, and no recalls after release. Drusus urged that the senate and emperor must have their say. This caused uproar. 'Why have you come,' they shouted, 'if you are not going to raise salaries, improve terms of service, or help us at all? Anyone, on the other hand, is allowed to murder and flog! It used to be Tiberius who blocked the regular army's grievances by citing Augustus. Now Drusus has revived the same old trick. It looks as though our visitors will always be young men with fathers. How curious it is that the only army matters which the emperor refers to the senate are reforms in service conditions! If he does this, he ought also to consult them when death penalties or battles are in store. Clearly when rewards are concerned, he is not his own master— whereas no one controls punishments. . . .'

At daybreak Drusus called a meeting. Though not a practised orator, he spoke with natural dignity. He censured their former behaviour, and expressed approval of their new attitude. Intimidation and menaces, he said, made no impression on him. If, however, he found that discipline had prevailed and they were pleading for pardon, he would write to his father recommending a merciful hearing for their pleas. They begged him to do this. So the younger Blaesus was again sent to Tiberius, accompanied by a Roman knight on Drusus' staff, Lucius Aponius, and a senior company-commander, Catonius Justus. There was now a division of opinion. One proposal was that the return of this delegation should be awaited, and that meanwhile the soldiers should be treated gently and humoured. Others favoured a more forceful solution, arguing that the masses only dealt in extremes and would terrorize unless they were terrorized—once intimidated, they could be disregarded with impunity: now, when superstition had a hold of them, was the time for the general to intensify their panic by striking down the leaders of the mutiny. Drusus had a natural preference for severe measures. Summoning Vibulenus and Percennius, he ordered them to be executed. Report has it that they were buried inside the general's tent. According to another account, however, the bodies were thrown outside the lines to be exhibited. Then all the chief instigators of the mutiny were hunted up. Some were killed by company-commanders or Guardsmen as they wandered blindly about outside the camp. Others were given up by their own units as a proof of loyalty.

The Roman Army

Josephus

The Jewish general Josephus led rebel forces in Galilee until he was captured by the Roman commander Vespasian in A.D. 67. He lived for many years in Rome and tried to explain Jewish history and the great rebellion to Greeks and Romans through his Jewish Antiquities *and* Jewish War, *both published in Greek. This passage describes the progress of a Roman army on the march.*

If one goes on to study the organization of their army as a whole, it will be seen that this vast empire of theirs has come to them as the prize of valor, and not as a gift of fortune. For they do not wait for the outbreak of war, nor do they sit with folded hands in peacetime only to put them in motion in the hour of need. On the contrary, as though they had been born with weapons in hand, they never have a truce from training, never wait for the emergencies to arise. Moreover, their peacetime maneuvers are not less strenuous than veritable warfare; each soldier daily throws all his energy into his drill, as though he were in action. Hence that perfect ease with which they sustain the shock of battle. . . .

The Romans never lay themselves open to a surprise attack; for, whatever hostile territory they may invade, they engage in no battle until they have fortified their camp. Thus an improvised city, as it were, springs up, with its market place, its artisan quarter, its judgment seats, where officers adjudicate any differences which may arise. The outer wall and all the installations within are completed more quickly than thought, so numerous and skilled are the workmen. . . .

Once entrenched, the soldiers take up their quarters in their tents by companies, quietly and in good order. All their fatigue duties are performed with the same discipline, the same regard for security: the procuring of wood, of food supplies, and water, as required—each company having its allotted task. The hour for supper and breakfast is not left to individual discretion; all take their meals together. The hours for sleep, sentinel duty, and rising are announced by the sound of trumpets; nothing is done without a word of command. At daybreak the rank and file report to their respective centurions, the centurions go to salute the tribunes, the tribunes with all the officers then wait on the commander-in-chief, and he gives them according to custom the watchword and other orders to be communicated to the lower ranks. The same precision is maintained on the battlefield; the troops wheel smartly round in the requisite direction, and, whether advancing to the attack or retreating, all move as a unit.

When the camp is to be broken up, the trumpet sounds a first call; at that none remain idle; instantly, at this signal, they strike the tents and make all ready for departure. The trumpets sound a second call to prepare the march; at once they pile their baggage on the mules and other beasts of burden, and stand ready to start. . . . They then set fire to the encampment, both because they can easily construct another. . . and to prevent the enemy from ever making use of it. A third time the trumpets give a similar signal for departure, to hasten the movements of stragglers, whatever the reason for their delay, and to ensure that none is out of his place in the ranks. Then the herald, standing on the right of the commander, inquires in their native tongue whether they are ready for war. Three times they loudly and lustily shout in reply, "We are ready," some even anticipating the question; and worked up to a kind of martial frenzy, they raise their right arms in the air along with the shout. . . .

The infantry are armed with cuirasses and helmets and carry a sword on either side; that on the left is far the longer of the two, the dagger on the right being no longer than a span. The picked infantry, forming the general's guard, carry a spear and round shield, the regiments of the line a javelin and oblong shield; the equipment of the latter includes, further, a saw, a basket, a pick, and an axe, not to mention a strap, a bill-hook, a chain, and three days' rations, so that an infantry man is almost as heavily laden as a pack mule.

The cavalry carry a large sword on their right side, a long pike in the hand, a buckler resting obliquely on the horse's flank, and in a quiver slung beside them three or more darts with broad points and as long as spears; their helmets and cuirasses are the same as those worn by all the infantry. The select cavalry, forming the general's escort, are armed in precisely the same manner as the ordinary troopers. The legion which is to lead the column is always selected by lot. . . .

By their military exercises the Romans instill into their soldiers fortitude not only of body but also of soul; fear, too, plays its part in their training. For they have laws which punish with death not merely desertion but even a slight neglect of duty; and their generals are held in even greater awe than the laws. For the high honors with which they reward the brave prevent the offenders whom they punish from regarding themselves as treated cruelly.

This perfect discipline with regard to their generals makes the army an ornament of peacetime, and in battle welds the whole into a single body; so compact are their ranks, so alert their movements in wheeling, so quick their ears for orders, their eyes for signals, their hands for tasks. Prompt as they consequently ever are in action, none are slower than they in succumbing to suffering, and never have they been known in any predicament to be beaten by numbers, by ruses, by difficulties of terrain, or even by fortune; for victory is more certain for them than fortune. When counsel thus precedes active operation, where the leaders' plan of campaign is followed up by so efficient an army, no wonder that the Empire has extended its boundaries on the east to the Euphrates, on the west to the Ocean, on the south to the most fertile tracts of Africa, and on the north to the Danube and the Rhine.

The Empire and the Army

Donald Earl

Professor Donald Earl of Hull University points out the reluctance of the republican Senate to assume direct responsibility for the efficient government of overseas provinces; they allowed the governors and tax-collectors the freedom to fleece the provincials almost at will. Though Augustus theoretically governed some provinces through his legates and allowed the Senate to govern the others, this was a convenient fiction and the emperor was himself responsible for the well-being of all provincials. He supervised tax-collecting, regulated provincial administration and provided troops to ensure local security. Augustus founded colonies of legionary veterans all across the Empire to promote Romanization and urbanization in backward areas of the West while ensuring control of the occupied areas. He professionalized the army with regular pay, bonuses and a bounty on retirement (which served as a pension), which bought loyalty to the imperial throne and the Julio-Claudians. It was only with the fall of the dynasty at the suicide of Nero that the first full-scale civil wars broke out, a century after Actium.

By conquest, bequest and default the Roman Republic acquired an overseas empire, but resolutely refused to provide proper civil administration for the provinces. The most that was done was to establish a military presence (the main function of a Republican provincial governor was military, to command the legions stationed in his province) and to arrange for the collection of taxes. This meant that the provincials, if they caused no trouble, enjoyed a quite remarkable amount of freedom. It also meant that, especially in the East, they suffered greatly from the lack of proper government when Rome, in assuming control of a country, destroyed the existing central authority without replacing it by her own. The Senate, indeed, was extremely reluctant to assume direct responsibility for territory overseas, which not infrequently embroiled Rome in quite unnecessary warfare as in Greece in the first half of the second century B.C. When annexation became unavoidable, the Senate's preference was to reduce Rome's commitment to the minimum. Thus, for instance, Italy's northern frontier was exposed to continual raids from the Gauls in Europe. Moreover, the vital road from Italy to the Roman provinces in Spain required protection. Yet as late as 125 to 120 B.C. a major war fought in Transalpine Gaul did not lead to annexation. It was years later, when the danger from the north had become quite inescapable, that a colony was established at Narbo Martius (Narbonne) and even this foundation was opposed by the majority of the Senate. It was not until the Germans had come down on Gaul and northern Italy, before Marius' final victory, and successive Roman armies had suffered shattering defeat, that the Senate accepted that to leave this vital area to the protection of two or three isolated Roman garrisons, helped only by Massilia, was highly dangerous and the province of Transalpine Gaul was established.

. . . Even the province Asia, which was, according to Cicero in 66 B.C., by far the most profitable of lands (the other Roman provinces produced merely enough to pay for themselves) was probably treated much the same as Cyrene when it was first accepted by Rome as a bequest from Attalus III. It was not until a decade later, in 123 B.C., that C. Gracchus arranged for the efficient collection of its revenues. It was Pompey who carried this attitude to its final conclusion. He claimed to have found Asia a frontier province and left it the centre of the empire. His claim was founded on the buffer of client states on the eastern boundaries of the Roman provinces. They represent his great contribution to Roman imperial theory, for he made them pay tribute to Rome. It was the perfect solution: taxation with no responsibility for government and administration.

. . . Behind the business man and the tax collector, who bulk large in modern accounts of the misgovernment of the empire, lay the vast wealth of the leading members of the Senate, the ultimate recipients of the profits of the provinces whether they were extorted by the tax collectors or exacted by the governors. As Professor Ernst Badian has written, not over harshly, no administration in history has ever devoted itself so whole-heartedly to fleecing its subjects for the private benefit of its ruling class as Rome of the last age of the Republic. And in return Rome gave her subjects neither adequate government nor tolerable peace. Triumph hunting, no less than the pursuit of wealth, was a favourite occupation of the Roman nobility. From the second century B.C. onward we hear again and again of wars unnecessarily begun and unnecessarily prolonged to serve the insatiable appetite of the Roman noble for prestige and military glory. In Caesar, as usual, the characteristics of his class reached their consummation. He deliberately began a major foreign war in Gaul, prosecuted it with unsurpassed brutality and treachery, followed it by a march on Rome and civil war—all for his own personal glory and profit.

After the victory at Actium the whole Roman world was Augustus' personal possession, all its inhabitants his own personal clients. But this power, private and personal, lying beyond the constitution, had to be made regular and legitimate. Systems of administration had to be evolved to mediate it and make it effective. The settlement of 27 B.C. had been largely concerned with the provinces. Augustus took a large *provincia*: Spain, Gaul and Syria. The Senate continued to administer the rest: Africa, Illyricum, Macedonia with Achaea, Asia, Bithynia-Pontus, Crete and Cyrene, Sardinia and Corsica, Sicily . . . Augustus commanded a large army, twenty legions or more. . . . Moreover, Spain, Gaul and Syria were precisely those areas in which serious and continued warfare was intended or apprehended. . . . The senatorial provinces continued to be governed, as before, by proconsuls, who might be ex-consuls or ex-praetors, holding office for one year only. . . .

Augustus divided his vast *provincia* into regions to be administered by legates drawing their power and authority from him. The division varied according to the needs of each particular territory and the necessities of a particular time. It was a very flexible arrangement, well suited to the large, imperfectly conquered and inadequately organized areas which constituted much of his portion. It also enhanced his own safety. For Augustus began the process which eventually, to ensure that no provincial governor could challenge the emperor's power, fragmented the Roman empire into almost a hundred provinces, each too small for adequate administration and serious defence. Spain, for instance, which in the Late Republic had been under a single governor of consular rank, was now governed by two or three legates, inferior in standing and power and subject to Augustus himself. As in the senatorial provinces, so in Augustus' portion the distinction between consular and praetorian governorships emerged slowly and gradually as, equally slowly and gradually, his arrangements for his *provincia* crystallized into a number of distinct commands or separate provinces. Some of Augustus' governors were not senators at all, but drawn from the Equestrian Order. To give provincial governorships to non-senators, to divorce, in effect, the governing of the provinces from the magistracies of the Roman People, was one of Augustus' most radical innovations.

Yet the distinction of senatorial and imperial provinces was one of convenience merely. It does not disclose opposing centres of power and authority. It is easy but erroneous to suppose that, since the name remained the same, the Augustan Senate retained all the habits and attitudes of the Senate of the Late Republic. It was, on the contrary, a very different body in composition and function. The emperor Tiberius' troubled relations with the Senate arose largely from his refusal to realize this. To expect a body of experienced and able administrators to return to the Republican practice of initiating policy was unrealistic folly and a failure to accept what was properly the emperor's responsibility. Augustus had a keen appreciation of the Senate's function and an ideal of the standards to be expected in public life. . . . It became a valuable and trusted organ of Augustus' government. . . .

Both Augustus and the Senate made regulations affecting all the provinces. Not infrequently they acted together. But if the Senate decreed a law, for instance, this law was valid throughout the empire. Changes in private and public law made by the Senate affected all provinces, imperial and senatorial alike. The text exists, in fact, of a decree of the Senate issued in 4 B.C. on the procedure to be followed in cases of maladministration by provincial governors. It refers to all provinces. The division of the empire between Augustus and the Senate had therefore only one practical consequence: there were now two types of provincial governorship, differing in method of appointment and length of tenure, in other words a mere administrative convenience.

The ultimate guarantee of the well-being of the provincials was Augustus himself. It was not merely that for the provincials as for the Italians his presence and power stood against the return of civil war and the disintegration of the empire. Wealthy beyond any man and supreme in honour and prestige he had no incentive to rob and exploit the provinces. His immense power, lying beyond the governors, the Senate and the courts, was always there to be stimulated by initiative or pressure from below. And he provided as far as was possible (against human greed or folly it is impossible to provide) sound and just administration. Above all, he broke the unholy alliance of the senatorial nobility and the companies of tax collectors which had bled the provinces under the Republic. To secure fair and just taxation Augustus undertook surveys of the resources of the various provinces. Gaul, for instance, was subject to such censuses in 27 and 12 B.C. and in A.D. 14, just after Augustus' death. On the basis of such returns taxes were collected. The chief direct taxes levied on provincials were a land tax and a property tax, which in backward areas became a poll tax (i.e. a per capita tax). The land tax was paid not merely by natives but also by Roman citizens resident in the provinces. A very few communities were granted the exemption enjoyed by the whole of Italy. Other towns were exempted from the property tax. Augustus could and did grant such exemptions to individuals and communities for honour and reward. The indirect taxes were harbour and customs dues of up to five per cent, a tax on the manumission and sale of slaves, which was also levied in Italy, and a requisition of grain for the governor and his staff. Death duties were paid only by Roman citizens in the provinces.

In the imperial provinces the direct taxes were collected by a procurator of Equestrian rank whose appointment was quite separate from that of the governor and his staff. The indirect taxes were still farmed to independent contractors, *publicani*, but they were now closely supervised. In the senatorial provinces all financial affairs were in the hands of the quaestor, who could employ *publicani* if necessary. In any senatorial province in which Augustus personally owned property there was a procurator, who would, no doubt, let his eye range beyond the boundaries of his immediate and official assignment. Legislation and administrative arrangements, however efficient, do not produce virtue and abuses continued to occur. But now the opportunities were less and retribution more swift and sure. The ultimate deterrent was Augustus' own displeasure and the abrupt end of career or life. Unrest in the provinces struck at Augustus himself. It was from him that all honour and office now flowed. The owner of the Roman world could dispose as he pleased.

The proper administration of the provinces was essential to Rome. She existed on the provincial revenues. Moreover, maladministration producing refusal of the provincials to co-operate would provoke either the necessity for armed intervention or the collapse of Roman control. For as in the Republic so under Augustus, Roman provincial administration relied on the co-operation of the provincials themselves. The Romans made no attempt to dictate or arrange the forms of local government. The administrative system which was imposed was for the province as a whole. It accepted the existing communities whether cities or, in the more primitive areas, tribes as the units through which it worked. The Roman empire has been described, rightly, as a vast experiment in local self-government. If there was no attempt to impose particular forms of local government, still less is there any sign of the deliberate propagation of Roman civilization and culture among the provincials. The attitude of Augustus to the spread of Roman citizenship is indicative. It is, unfortunately, often impossible to distinguish Augustus' work in this sphere from that of Julius Caesar, but the fundamental principle is clear enough. Although the age of Caesar and Augustus saw the first large scale extension of the Roman citizenship in the provinces, it was limited to those areas in which there already existed a considerable body of Italian immigrants. These might be legionary veterans settled in a colony after discharge from the army or, much more rarely, Roman civilians similarly established in formal settlements. There was also much casual emigration from Italy of farmers, merchants and business men. Roman business men domiciled in provincial towns grouped themselves together for the administration of their own affairs. Such groups, too, formed a nucleus which could lead to an eventual grant of citizenship to the whole town. The grant of Roman citizenship or of the lesser status known as the Latin Right came only at the end of a long process of self-Romanization by the provincial communities. It was a passive recognition of a state of affairs which had arisen naturally, not an active instrument of government policy. The grant of any form of Roman civic rights to the purely native communities in the provinces is almost unknown.

The view that Augustus retreated sharply from the lavish liberality with which Caesar extended Roman citizenship in the provinces is difficult to support. The differences between the practices of the two men are to be explained not by any deliberate divergence of policy but by the different situations in which they found themselves and the different conditions with which they had to deal. Caesar was a pioneer. Before him only one Roman colony had been founded outside Italy, that at Narbo. For him colonial foundation was an instrument of power, to bind

to himself in a revolutionary age the legionary soldiers and the civilian poor. Similarly generous grants of rights and privileges assured him the support of communities in the provinces, whose decisive importance for the game of power politics at Rome had been demonstrated in the first century B.C. Caesar's attitude was essentially that of the other monarchic faction leaders of the Late Republic, notably Pompey. The provinces were there to be used to influence the balance of power at Rome: any method which would ensure their support was to be employed. Augustus after Actium was concerned not with revolution but with stability and order, for the good of Rome and his own power. Thus Antony to secure the island's allegiance had given full Roman citizenship to the whole of Sicily, which still remained in part Greek rather than Roman in population and culture. Augustus rescinded the wholesale grant and replaced it by a gradual extension of citizenship to individual communities, assisting the process by the foundation of colonies.

Colonies of legionary veterans were founded by Augustus all over the Roman empire in very large numbers. The purpose of these foundations was simple, straightforward and traditional: to provide a livelihood for discharged soldiers and to form centres of Roman power for the control of occupied territory. It had been the practice in the Republic to settle in a conquered country a proportion, at least, of the army which had conquered it. This had been the way in which Rome had controlled Italy and its export to the empire overseas, when this was acquired, was a natural development. If a colony induced the surrounding natives to adopt Roman customs or to learn Latin, this was to Rome's benefit. But it was not the primary purpose of the colony, merely an accidental by-product. The purpose of all such colonies, with the exception of a few purely civilian foundations, was military. Augustus followed closely traditional practice. What makes his colonial foundations particularly important is the largeness of scale. The influence of these colonies on the neighbouring natives differed sharply in the West from that which they exerted in the East. It is only in the western provinces that we can speak properly of Romanization. When Roman power expanded into Europe it met comparatively primitive culture and comparatively backward, mostly tribal, social structure. It was, on the whole, the Roman veteran colonies which determined the pattern of urbanization for western Europe and to this the Augustan foundations made a large contribution. In this part of the empire the spread of Roman customs and the Latin language was rapid, for they were filling, as it were, a vacuum. . . .

For a government so militaristic and aggressive as that of the Roman Republic, the military system remained curiously haphazard and amateur. At formation level, in the legion and below, organization and performance were alike good. But just as there was no general conception of the principles of the constitution or of provincial administration so military policy remained a series of particular reactions to particular situations. The basic concept was that of a citizen army, recruited annually by conscription for a single short campaign, in which service was a positive right not a burdensome duty and which could be commanded by whoever filled the chief elective offices of state for that year. The acquisition of an overseas empire destroyed the validity of this approach. It became necessary for armies to be stationed permanently in the provinces. These frontier armies became standing forces and in the Late Republic a permanent military establishment was stationed exactly in those areas in which Augustus afterwards concentrated his troops, Spain, Gaul, Macedonia and Syria. But these armies remained small, scarcely adequate for defence under normal conditions and quite incapable of withstanding a determined invasion. Nor were they integrated into a general strategy of frontier defence. That simply did not exist, as the northern frontier of Italy amply demonstrates. Emergencies of defence or campaigns of conquest or retaliation were still met by a development of the citizen army of early Rome. A force, often a very large one, was raised for the specific crisis and demobilized when the crisis had passed. It was these emergency armies which had destroyed the Republic. For the ruling oligarchy, instead of establishing proper control over them and making proper provision for their demobilization, preferred to use them as instruments of their own political ambitions. They became client armies and their patrons sought to use them exactly as they had used their civilian clients. But the capacity of a civilian client for mischief through rioting or the ballot box was necessarily limited. When the clients were soldiers to deploy one's own or to attempt to erode one's opponent's *clientela* led straight to civil war.

Augustus rose to power through civil war and proscription by the relentless manipulation of the client army. After Actium the first and most urgent of his preoccupations was to control the armies, to prevent himself suffering the fate of the Marian party against Sulla, of Pompey against Caesar, of Brutus and Cassius against Antony, of Antony against himself. It was not a subject patient of legislation. To march beyond the boundaries of your province with your army and without express authorization by the Senate and the Roman People had long been illegal under the Republic. It was no defence against a man determined or desperate enough and backed by an army of faithful clients. Augustus' solution was simple in conception, complex in execution and, typically, hardly innovatory: the client armies would remain, but they would all be clients of a single patron, himself. If he retained the allegiance of the soldiers, then the ambitious and armed proconsuls would be powerless. Not that this solution emerged from conscious debate and careful weighing of alternatives. It was simply that Augustus' position after Actium was maintained and enhanced. He had become after the defeat of Antony the owner of the whole Roman world. That the vast majority of its inhabitants, civil and military, were his own personal and private clients was the essential basis of his power and position. His treatment of the army, like his restoration of the Republic and his provincial arrangements, was but to institutionalize and make permanent and public this fundamental fact. But it limited or modified his ultimate power no more than his acceptance of certain formal powers in the settlements of 27 and 23 B.C. or his alleged division of the provinces with the Senate.

The civil wars of the Late Republic had revealed the essential truth about the client armies: that their allegiance, like that of civilian clients, went where they saw or could be persuaded that the greatest benefits lay. If their demands were not met or if they received a better offer, transference of allegiance was easy and rapid. This characteristic Augustus knew well: he had exploited it against Antony. The principal material benefits were two: pay during service and the provision of a gratuity in land or money after discharge. Augustus' vast personal wealth (his private income alone was greater than all the public revenues of the Roman state and he recorded in the *Res Gestae* that he four times bailed out the treasury from his own pocket) enabled him to keep both benefits firmly in his own hands. The mere fact that no individual, not even the Roman treasury, could in any way approach Augustus' own fortune made the soldiers less likely to look elsewhere for benefits. The great demobilization after Actium and the way the discharged troops were settled formed a proclamation to the armies no less than to the civilian populations of Italy and the provinces. For it demonstrated to the soldiers not only to whom they must look for their benefits but also that Augustus had the resources to provide them. Succeeding years made it clear that the resettlement of his veterans was to be Augustus' permanent care and the lesson was reinforced by extraordinary donations to the troops and the veteran colonists.

Augustus made only one major innovation, but that affected the nature of the whole army. He abolished the emergency army which had fought most of the wars of the Late Republic and which had afforded large opportunities for ambitious generals. Instead the frontier force was enlarged to a permanent wartime establishment. The size of the army retained after the demobilization after Actium, twenty-eight legions, was the product of a complex set of calculations. The safety of Augustus himself demanded that the army should be no larger than absolute military necessity dictated. At the same time the safety of Rome and the empire had to be provided for. Economic resources entered the calculation; so did the available supply of volunteers and the foreseeable amount of work for the army, for an idle army is a dangerous one. Augustus succeeded in preventing armed usurpation. But twenty-eight legions dispersed on the frontiers placed a heavy burden on Rome's economic resources and, as the aftermath of the Varian disaster showed, on the sources of recruitment. Much better would have been a smaller frontier force backed by a central mobile reserve in Italy. But that the safety of Augustus would not allow.

As it happened, Augustus' system just worked, although even he was slow to learn the limitations it imposed. Pay, bonuses and gratuities after service were the essentials in securing the loyalty of the legions. The dispersal of the armies to the frontiers was a valuable precaution. We must not forget also the simple passage of time. In many respects the most important thing that Augustus did was a sheer accident of nature: he lived until A.D. 14. Thus a whole generation had grown up which knew only his dispensation. Use and the passage of time assured the stability of the system; it changed the nature of the Senate and of the whole administration, and it changed too the nature of the army. The purpose of the grand demobilization after Actium was not merely to reduce in size an army too big for Rome's needs and resources and the safety of Augustus; it also removed from service those soldiers who had learned their concept of loyalty in the treacheries of civil war. In the Augustan army as established thereafter the annual rate of retirement was, on average, about 9,000 men and the normal length of service sixteen years. Thus by 15 B.C. the whole army consisted of men recruited by Augustus as Princeps. They had known no other terms and conditions of service. In 13 B.C., in addition to the formal fixing of the term of service at sixteen years, the resettlement of veterans on land, Italian and provincial, which Augustus bought with his own funds, was given up and instead a cash bounty was paid. In A.D. 6 the provision of this bounty became at last a function of the state instead of the personal gift of Augustus as a private patron. In that year he established the military treasury, the *aerarium militare*, with an initial gift of 170,000,000 sesterces from his own fortune and provided for its future by the institution of two new taxes, a sales tax and death duties.

The first veterans to receive the cash bounty under the arrangements of 13 B.C. would be those who had formed the first intake into the army after the great demobilization of the years 30 and 29 B.C. The first veterans to be provided for from the *aerarium militare* would be the first army intake born since Actium. Double coincidence is possible, but it seems likely that these two developments mark two deliberate stages in Augustus' growing confidence in the loyalty of his soldiers. To secure this loyalty he had had to make himself personally responsible for all aspects of military service. No longer, as under the Republic, were individual generals to decide when their soldiers should be discharged or what provision should be made for them after discharge. Everything was to come from Augustus and to be seen to come from him and to be in the gift of no one else. There was to be one patron and one only. In A.D. 6 this patronage was made institutional. The junior officers, centurions and military tribunes were probably easier to deal with than the common soldiers or the army commanders, for if any vestige of higher loyalty survived it remained with them. Sergeants-major and subalterns are in any army the staunchest defenders of tradition. When Sulla marched on Rome all his military tribunes save one deserted him. To the centurions especially Augustus had opened whole new fields of opportunity by his organization of the Equestrian career both civil and military,

but for the senior officers and commanders no general rules could apply, and careful selection was the only method. Many anomalies in the careers of prominent men, especially in the earlier years of Augustus' Principate, are doubtless to be explained by the operation of the loyalty test. The major military operations were conducted either by men like Agrippa whose allegiance had been tried in the years of civil war or by members of Augustus' own family, especially by Drusus and Tiberius.

Augustus succeeded in his chief purpose. Domestic conspiracy, not the armed proconsul, was his major danger. He handed on to his successor an army whose loyalties lay firmly with the emperor. So long as the emperor could claim to be even by the most tenuous links of adoption the heir of Caesar, the army knew whom to obey, were he a Caligula, a Claudius or a Nero, and obeyed readily. It was only when the dynastic link was broken, as it was with the suicide of Nero, that the Roman world exploded once more into civil war. The army, without a focus for its loyalty, was an easy prey for the ambitions of unscrupulous men. At the same time the soldiers realized the ultimate right and power of a client—to appoint his own patron. The Year of the Four Emperors revealed not the failure of the Augustan approach, but its essential soundness. Subsequent events confirmed it: the history of the first four centuries of the Roman imperial system, as dynasty succeeded dynasty, demonstrates clearly despite the military anarchy of the third century A.D., the adherence of the army to the hereditary principle, the strength of the bond between the emperor and his military clients and the importance of that bond for the stability and peace of the Roman empire.

The Julio-Claudian System

Edward Luttwak

Edward Luttwak is a defense analyst who has worked both in government and in academia. In his provocative book, The Grand Strategy of the Roman Empire *(1976), he applies the methods of "strategic thinking" to the Roman Empire. He finds that the deployment of the Roman armies relied on the concept of "economy of force." The Julio-Claudians did not attempt to provide fixed defenses along a perimeter of 4,000 miles, but they concentrated their forces at certain fixed points. In the East they relied on client kings such as Herod of Judaea for local security and maintained only a few legions in Syria for the entire region. Through such an "economy of force" an army of only 150,000 Roman legionaries and an equal number of foreign auxiliaries was able to garrison and defend an Empire of over 50 million people. It was a system well suited to further expansion, as Claudius showed Britain.*

The System in Outline

The most striking feature of the Julio-Claudian system of imperial security was its economy of force. At the death of Augustus, in A.D. 14, the territories subject to direct or indirect imperial control comprised the coastal lands of the entire Mediterranean basin, the whole of the Iberian peninsula, continental Europe inland to the Rhine and Danube, Anatolia, and, more loosely, the Bosporan Kingdom on the northern shores of the Black Sea. Control over this vast territory was effectively ensured by a small army, whose size was originally determined at the beginning of the principate and only slightly increased thereafter.

Twenty-five legions remained after the destruction of Varus and his three legions in A.D. 9 and throughout the rule of Tiberius (A.D. 14–37). Eight new legions were raised between the accession of Gaius-Caligula in A.D. 37 and the civil war of A.D. 69–70, but four were cashiered, so that under Vespasian there were twenty-nine legions on the establishment, only one more than the original number set by Augustus.

There is some small margin of uncertainty on the exact manpower strength of the legions, but the authorities agree that each consisted of about 6,000 men, including 5,120 or 5,280 foot soldiers, a cavalry contingent of 120 men, and sundry headquarters' troops. On this basis, the upper limit on the number of legionary troops would be about 168,000 men until A.D. 9, 150,000 thereafter, and no more than 174,000 after A.D. 70.

In addition to the legions of heavy infantry, then still manned mostly by long-service citizen volunteers, there were the *auxilia*, generally manned by non-citizens during this period. Organized into cavalry "wings" (*alae*), light infantry cohorts, or mixed cavalry/infantry units (*cohortes equitatae*), the *auxilia* were functionally complementary to the legionary forces.

There is no satisfactory evidence on the total size of the auxiliary forces for the empire as a whole, but the authorities accept the general validity of a statement in Tacitus according to which, in the year A.D. 23, the aggregate number of the auxiliary forces was roughly the same as that of the "Roman," or legionary, forces.

For our purposes, it suffices to know that the total number of auxiliary troops did not greatly exceed that of the legionary forces—a possibility nowhere suggested in the literature. Accepting the 1:1 ratio as a valid approximation, the total number of Roman troops would thus be on the order of 300,000 for A.D. 23, with a theoretical maximum of roughly 350,000 for the balance of the period until A.D. 70.

Since Augustus claimed to have personally paid off 300,000 men on retirement with either lands or money, it would seem that the total number of men in the ground forces was not particularly large by the standards of the time. However, the well-known difficulties of citizen-recruitment, already acute at this time, reflected a true demographic problem—Pliny's "shortage of youths" (*inventutis penuria*): the total male population of military age in Italy probably numbered less than a million.

It was easier to pay for the army than to recruit its members. Annual pay and upkeep for a trained legionary soldier in the ranks came to 225 *denarii* per year; the overall cost of retirement grants, set at 3,000 *denarii* in A.D. 5, was a burden not much smaller than pay and upkeep, and there were also occasional donatives. Nevertheless, it has been suggested that the total cost of the army on an annual basis did not amount to more than half of the imperial revenue during the early principate.

In view of this, there is no reason to believe that the reorganization of the army after the Battle of Actium was dictated by financial or even manpower constraints. It appears more likely that the number of legions was set at twenty-eight, from a total of sixty or so (some only fragments) deployed by both sides during the Civil War, on the basis of a rational scheme of deployment, in which it was the desired level of forces that set the costs, rather than the other way around.

In a famous passage of the *Annals* Tacitus provides the only comprehensive survey of the deployment of the legions extant in the narrative sources. Its accuracy is generally accepted by the authorities. According to Tacitus, in A.D. 23, ninth year of the principate of Tiberius, there were eight legions on the Rhine, three in Spain, two in the province of Africa, two in Egypt, four in Syria, two in Moesia and two in Pannonia (for a total of four along the Danube), and finally two in Dalmatia, for a total of twenty-five. And then there were the *auxilia*, of which Tacitus refrains from giving a detailed breakdown.

From this account one may gather the impression that the legionary forces, and the auxiliary troops with them, were distributed to form a thin perimeter. The consequent lack of a strategic reserve, held uncommitted in the deep rear, is regularly remarked on and

criticized. It is true that the forces in Italy, nine praetorian cohorts and four urban cohorts, did not amount to much; the latter were primarily a police force and the former could provide no more than a strong escort for the rulers of Rome when they set out to campaign in person. On the other hand, Tacitus describes the two Dalmatian legions as a strategic reserve, which could cover *in situ* the northeastern invasion axes into Italy while also being available for redeployment elsewhere, since Dalmatia was not a frontier province.

In fact, the impression of a perimeter deployment is misleading. For one thing, as it has been pointed out, a key factor in the distribution of the legions was the need of internal, rather than external, security. Hence the three legions in Spain, which was not frontier territory but was in the final stages of a secular pacification effort, and the two legions of Dalmatia, in the rear of the forces holding Pannonia. As Tacitus points out, Dalmatia was a convenient location for a strategic reserve, but the province had also been the scene of the dangerous Pannonian revolt in A.D. 6–9, "the most serious of all our foreign wars since the Carthaginian ones," according to Suetonius.

Similarly, the two legions in Egypt were obviously not required to ward off external threats, i.e., nomadic incursions. To counter or deter such elusive enemies, auxiliary units, especially if mounted, were much more effective than the solid mass of the legions. The latter, on the other hand, were very suitable for the task of maintaining internal security.

There was as yet no demarcated imperial frontier and no system of fixed frontier defenses, nor were the legions housed in permanent stone fortresses as they were to be in the future. Instead, the troops slept in leather tents or in winter quarters built of wood, in camps whose perimeter defenses were no more elaborate than those of the marching camps that legionary forces on the move would build each afternoon at the conclusion of the day's march. Nor were such legionary camps cited as tactical strong points. Indeed, they were not defensive positions at all.

Deployed astride major routes leading both to unconquered lands ahead and to the sometimes unsettled provinces in the rear, the legions were not there to defend the adjacent ground, but rather to serve as mobile striking forces. For practical purposes, their deployment was that of a field army, distributed, it is true, in high-threat sectors, but not tied down to territorial defense. Uninvolved in major wars of conquest between A.D. 6 and A.D. 43 (Britain), the salient function of the army was necessarily defensive, i.e., providing security against the sudden emergence of unforeseen threats.

These threats were primarily internal. Aside from the sporadic transborder incursions of Germans, Dacians, and later, Sarmations, and the conflict with Parthia over the Armenian investiture, Rome's major security problems were the result of native revolts within the empire. Characteristically, a delay, sometimes of generations, would intervene between the initial conquest and the outbreak of revolt: while the native power structure and "nativistic atmosphere" were still largely intact (and with Rome itself having introduced concepts of leadership and cohesion through the local recruitment of auxiliary forces), the resistance to the full impact of imperial taxation and conscription was often violent, sometimes more so than resistance to the initial conquest had been. Thus the revolt in Illyricum of A.D. 6–9 and the intermittent revolt of Tacfarinas in Africa between A.D. 14 and 24; there were also more localized uprisings, such as that of Florus and Sacrovir in Gaul, of A.D. 21 and, as a borderline case, the Jewish War.

Since northwest Germany had been counted as conquered, and P. Quinctilius Varus, "a leading lawyer without any military qualities," was there to organize a province rather than conquer one, the Varian disaster of A.D. 9 must also be counted as an "internal" war. Throughout this period, the control of internal insurgency presented a far more difficult problem than the maintenance of external security vis-a-vis Parthia—whose power was the only "systemic" threat to Rome, and then only on a regional scale.

The colonies were a second instrument of strategic control. Julius Caesar had routinely settled his veterans outside Italy, and Augustus founded twenty-eight colonies for the veterans discharged from the legions. Not primarily intended as agencies of Romanization, the colonies were islands of direct Roman control in an empire still in part hegemonic; as such, they were especially important in areas like Anatolia, where legions were not ordinarily deployed. Whether located in provincial or client-state territory, the colonies provided secure observation and control bases. Their citizens were, in effect, a ready-made militia of ex-soldiers and soldiers' sons who could defend their home towns in the event of attack and hold out until imperial forces could arrive on the scene.

Neither the legions and *auxilia* deployed in their widely spaced bases nor the colonies outside Italy, scattered as they were, could provide anything resembling an all-round perimeter defense. There were no guards and patrols to prevent infiltration of the 4,000 miles of the imperial perimeter on land; there were no contingents of widely distributed mobile forces ready to intercept raiding parties or contend with localized attacks; there was no perimeter defense. In other words, there was no *limes*, in its later sense of a fortified and guarded border. At this time the word still retained its former (but not, apparently, original) meaning of an access road *perpendicular* to the border of secured imperial territory; *limes* thus described a route of penetration cut through hostile territory rather than a "horizontal" frontier, and certainly not a fortified defensive perimeter.

It is the *absence* of a perimeter defense that is the key to the entire system of Roman imperial security of this period. There were neither border defenses nor local forces to guard imperial territories against the "low-intensity" threats of petty infiltration, transborder incursion, or localized attack. As we shall see, such protection was provided, but by indirect and nonmilitary means. By virtually eliminating the burden of maintaining continuous frontier defenses, the net, "disposable" military power generated by the imperial forces was maximized. Hence, the total military power that others could perceive as being available to Rome for offensive use—and that could therefore be put to political advantage by diplomatic means— was also maximized. Thus the empire's potential military power could be converted into actual political control at a high rate of exchange.

The diplomatic instruments that achieved this conversion were the client states and client tribes, whose obedience reflected both their perceptions of Roman military power and their fear of retaliation. Since clients would take care to prevent attacks against provincial territory, their obedience lessened the need to provide local security at the periphery of empire against low-intensity threats, thus increasing the empire's net disposable military power . . . and so completing the cycle. . . .

The Client States

In A.D. 14, when Tiberius succeeded Augustus to the principate, a substantial part of imperial territory was constituted by client states, which were definitely *of* the empire even if perhaps not fully within it. . . .

Roman notions of foreign client policies and the Roman view of the relationship between empire and client were rooted in the traditional pattern of patron-client relationships in Roman municipal life. The essential transaction of these unequal relationships was the exchange of rewards (*beneficia*)—accorded by the patron—for services (*officia*) performed by the client. Discrete gradations of the inequality between empire and client were recognized, though with the continuing increase in Roman power a divergence often developed between the formal and the actual relationship. By the later stages of the process, a client king whose formal status was that of a "friend of the Roman people" (*amicus populi Romani*)—a title suggesting recognition for services rendered "with a lively sense of favors still to come," but with no connotation of subservience—was generally no more than a vehicle of Roman control. This applied not only to foreign and security policies but also to dynastic and domestic matters. In fact, no clear areas

of authority were left as the client ruler's prerogative.

The conventional characterization of the client kingdoms as "buffer states" does not correctly define their complex role in the system of imperial security. Only Armenia was a true buffer state, serving as a physical neutral zone between the greater powers of Rome and Parthia, and providing them with a device that would serve to avoid conflict as long as they desired to avoid conflict. . . . The security *officia* provided by the client states amounted to much more than the passivity of a true buffer state. There were positive acts (including the provision of local troops to serve as auxiliaries for the Roman army and for purely Roman purposes), but the most important function of the client states in the system of imperial security was not formally recognized as an *officium* at all: by virtue of their very existence, the client states absorbed the burden of providing peripheral security against border infiltration and other low-intensity threats. . . .

Partly because of the very nature of the threats faced by Rome, the value of the client states in the security system as a whole far exceeded their actual military effort, because their contribution was not merely additive to Roman military power, but complementary. Efficient client states could provide for their own internal security and for their own perimeter defense against low-intensity threats, absolving the empire from that responsibility. Thus, no legions had to be committed to Judea while Herod's regime lasted. By contrast, after Herod that turbulent province required the presence of at least one legion and sometimes more: three legions from A.D. 67 until the Jewish revolt was finally suppressed three years later, . . . two legions following the outbreak . . . of Bar-Kokba's revolt of A.D. 132, and . . . thereafter.

The provision of internal security was of course the most obvious function of client states, and the one most commonly recognized. In addition, however, efficient client states would also shield adjacent provincial territories from low-intensity threats emanating from their own territory or from the far side of the client state periphery. Often approximated but not always achieved even by the most successful client states, this level of efficiency required a delicate balance between strength and weakness, such as that supposedly achieved by Deiotarus, client king of Galatia (d. 25 B.C.), who was described in Cicero's special pleading as strong enough to guard his borders but not strong enough to threaten Roman interests.

More commonly perhaps, the client states could *not* ensure high standards of internal and perimeter security comparable to those of provincial territory. Sometimes there were major disorders that threatened adjacent provincial lands or important strategic routes and therefore required the direct intervention of imperial forces. . . . If direct Roman intervention did become necessary, its goal could be limited to the essential minimum of protecting local Roman assets and keeping the client ruler in control of people, in contrast to the much greater military effort ordinarily required for suppressing insurgencies fully and bringing the affected areas up to provincial standards of tranquility. In other words, the direct intervention of Rome in the affairs of a client state would not mean that every rebel band would have to be pursued into deep forest or remote desert as the Roman system of deterrence and Roman prestige required in provincial territory.

Thus, where client forces were inadequate, the locals could at least *absorb* the resultant insecurity, and the Romans were content to let them do so. To censure Rome for such attitudes, as Mommsen did in commenting that the client states enjoyed neither "peace nor independence," reveals a lack of historical perspective. As we shall see, it was only much later that the systemic goals of the empire changed, requiring a change in the fundamental strategy toward provision of high standards of security even at the peripheries of empire.

The Strategic Deployment of Forces

Until Domitian forbade the practice, the large-unit structure of the Roman army, organized as it was around legions of roughly 6,000 men, was accentuated still further by the habit of deploying the forces in multi-legion camps like Mogontiacum (Mainz), Vetera (Xanten), and Oppidum Obiorum (Cologne) on the Rhine frontier. Since the *auxilia* were with the legions, the forces of the Roman army were concentrated on a few points around the periphery of the empire, leaving little or nothing for the interior and with a very uneven distribution on the perimeter itself.

Thus, in A.D. 6, out of a total of twenty-eight legions, four were in Spain, five on the Rhine or beyond, two in Raetia, five in Illyricum, three in Moesia, and nine in the whole of North Africa, Egypt, and Syria. After the ambush of Varus's legion in A.D. 9, the Spanish garrison was reduced to three legions, the German increased to eight, the Raetian eliminated, the Illyrian left unchanged, and the Moesian reduced to two. One legion remained in North Africa, two in Egypt, and four in Syria. This distribution was maintained until the invasion of Britain in A.D. 43.

Clearly, then, the uneven development of client states in East and West had military implications: in the East, where client states were highly developed (and where the Armenian settlement of 20 B.C. left a deep buffer zone between Rome and Parthia), Roman security was ensured by a few mediocre legions, powerfully supplemented by the obedience of clients aware of the much greater potential of Roman forces elsewhere. In the West, on the other hand, the day-to-day security of the imperial periphery could only be ensured by immediate and visible legionary presence. What the sophisticated populations and leaders of the civilized East could readily visualize, Germans and Dacians had to see with their own eyes.

By absorbing the burden of providing internal and perimeter security, the client states of the East allowed the Romans to keep their striking power concentrated—and it was, of course, this same concentrated strength that generated the powerful "armed suasion" that kept the client states in subjection in the first place. Small though it was, the four-legion garrison in Syria had this quality of concentrated strength which, paradoxically, would have been dissipated by the attempt at *military* control of vast territories of Asia Minor. Moreover, with Parthia to the east still the only great power on Rome's horizon, a dispersion of strength would have entailed grave dangers. It is in this light that the deployment policy of the period must be seen. Both the lack of central reserves and the chosen deployment of the legions on the perimeter must be viewed in the perspective of a security structure that was still anchored on the complex, fragile, but supremely efficient client system. There *was* a strategic reserve, but it was deployed on the line. Located near zones of expected threat or opportunity (i.e., opportunity for conquest), the legions were not actually committed to the territorial defense of their segment of the perimeter, as was later the case. If a threat materialized in any one sector, forces could ordinarily be withdrawn from the others; there was no real danger that Germans, Dacians, and Parthians would coordinate their attacks on the empire.

Under these political circumstances, the defense strategy of the empire had to cope with two kinds of threats: "endemic" threats, which were more or less stable in intensity over prolonged periods of time (such as the German threat between A.D. 9 and the crisis of A.D. 69–70), and "sporadic" threats, which were inherently unpredictable (such as native revolts). It would therefore have been wasteful to retain substantial forces in a central strategic reserve. Such a reserve is preferable to the use of *ad hoc* forces drawn from the line only if it can be redeployed in time to reinforce sectors under attack, and quick redeployment could rarely be accomplished in the Roman Empire. Where the threat was endemic and stable, it was not the availability of a reserve that was needed, but permanently deployed forces; where the threat was sporadic and unpredictable, reserves could hardly ever hope to arrive on the scene in good time, and the damage done was likely to be inflicted very early, in any case. It was much more efficient to keep all forces on the perimeter, where their presence was continuously useful either militarily or diplomatically, and not in an interior reserve.

The peculiar geography of the empire—a hollow ring around the Mediterranean—

deprived the Romans of the defender's usual advantage, shorter inner lines of communication, except when sea transport was feasible. In the absence of early warning of emerging threats, Roman forces could only march at three miles an hour toward an enemy whose offensive was already under way. This meant that a strategic reserve could not make a great deal of difference, for it would not matter much if enemy incursions within imperial territory lasted one month rather than two; with or without a centralized reserve, the Roman response could rarely be rapid enough to reinforce a sector while it was still successfully containing enemy attacks.

The system did, however, entail additional risks. For one thing, there was always the possibility that major threats—even if uncoordinated—would materialize simultaneously on different segments of the perimeter. Moreover, there was one danger that was more than a contingency: when legions were withdrawn from one sector to meet a threat on another (or to build a concentration of offensive forces), unsubdued provincial populations and enemies beyond the border were liable to take the opportunity to rebel against Roman rule or to raid imperial territory. This was more than a contingency since there was obviously a causal relationship between the removal of Roman troops from a given sector and the emergence of threats previously latent. And there was the further risk of a chain reaction, such as that which materialized in A.D. 6. In that year, the Pannonian revolt broke out when Illyricum was stripped of its legions to augment the forces being concentrated for the two-pronged offensive against Maroboduus and for the strategic encirclement of Bohemia. Tiberius, in charge of five legions, had actually crossed the Danube on his northwest line of advance from Carnuntum, when the revolt broke out to his rear. The small Roman force left in the base of Siscia (now Sisak, in Croatia) was besieged by the rebels, who seem to have gained control of most of the province. The provincial legate of Moesia, A. Caecina Severus, who was bringing his forces north to join Tiberius for the planned offensive against Maroboduus, instead set out to quell the revolt. But the Danubian frontier of his own province had now been stripped of its two legions, and Dacian raiders crossed the river and penetrated Moesia. Just as Tiberius was forced to cancel the invasion of Bohemia in order to return to fight in Illyricum, so Severus was forced to cut short his own rescue effort in order to return to Moesia. In the end, it took three years and all the forces the Romans could muster to subdue Illyricum.

Viewed in the context of the sporadic and widely separated threats the Romans had to face, the chain reaction brought about by the planned offensive against Maroboduus was only an exception, even if a very important one. The normal experience of the early principate was the successful maintenance of imperial security on a very narrow and very economical base of military power.

Conclusion

Under the republic, the Romans generally solved the security problems of their growing empire by further expansion, but this expansion was mostly hegemonic rather than territorial. The usual outcome of Roman wars and Roman victories was a minimum of territorial aggrandizement and an altogether more far-reaching extension of Rome's diplomatic control by means of the client system. In the late republic, however, new policies were formed by new forces in Roman political life, and the rhythm of territorial expansion accelerated perceptibly, reaching a climax under Augustus.

Augustus obviously did not practice in his own lifetime what he preached in his famous posthumous injunction against further conquest recorded by Tacitus (and to which Tacitus strongly objected). Under his direction, wars of conquest were fought in all directions, resulting in the annexation of vast territories: the future provinces of Moesia, Pannonia, Noricum, and Raetia, as well as the Alpes Cottiae and Maritimae. These last annexations were long overdue security measures against the depredation of the Salassi upon transalpine traffic, but the security motive was less compelling elsewhere. The annexation of manageable and efficient client states was not, however, Augustan policy, except as a last resort: Judea was annexed in A.D. 6, but only because no adequate successor to Herod was to be found in his family—and Judea was not a province to be lightly entrusted to one of the entrepreneurial client princes of Asia Minor.

Due to the system's economy of force, the Augustan military establishment was sufficient not only to defend the empire but also to sustain expansion; at any one moment large troop concentrations could be assembled for wars of conquest by drawing down the forces ordinarily deployed on the line, albeit at some risk. In A.D. 6, for example, out of a total legionary establishment of only twenty-eight legions, no fewer than twelve could be concentrated for the offensive into Bohemia that was to take Roman power to the Elbe. Admittedly, this proportion proved to be too high and entailed grave risks, but the system was undoubtedly highly elastic.

The accepted view is that Augustus' goal, even before the great crises of A.D. 6–9 in Illyricum and Germany, was limited to the establishment of a "scientific" frontier on the Elbe—a "Hamburg–Prague–Vienna" line. More recently, it has been argued convincingly that Augustus had set himself no such limit, being still in full pursuit of the Alexandrian—and Roman—dream of world conquest. It has also been pointed out that Roman geographic (and demographic) knowledge was still so undeveloped that even the conquest of China could seem feasible.

In any case, the system was well-suited to the support of further expansion, and it was so employed by Claudius in the conquest of Britain. As long as there were peoples and cultures susceptible to the "armed suasion" radiated by Rome's military power, and thus turned into dependable clients who would themselves absorb the security burdens resulting from past expansions, further expansion remained possible.

The Praetorian Guard

Michael Grant

Michael Grant was formerly Professor of Humanity at the University of St. Andrews and President of the Queen's University, Belfast. He has written on nearly all aspects of ancient history and civilization. In this essay he traces the origins of the praetorians to the bodyguards of the warlords of the Republic. Augustus organized nine praetorian cohorts of 500 men each, of which three were stationed in Rome, where they served as escorts, messengers, and intelligence agents. Their commander was a prefect of the equestrian class, lest a potential senatorial rival use the guard to seize the throne. But the prefects and the guard eventually assumed the power to make and destroy emperors.

These military powers in the home country were very necessary to Augustus. But he needed them not so much in order to command the fleets as to protect the safety of his own person. Plotting, as we have seen, was inevitable; and plots, or alleged plots, duly materialized. For this reason Agrippa, in a speech attributed to him by Dio, takes it for granted that the *Imperator* should be carefully guarded, and Augustus' wife Livia urges that this essential precaution should never at any time be neglected. When Augustus in association with Agrippa was conducting that very unpopular operation, a revision of the senate (28 B.C.), it was said that beneath his toga he wore mailed armour and carried a sword, that he had ten of the toughest and loyalest senators standing round his chair, and that the other senators were only allowed to approach him one by one, and even then not until they had been thoroughly searched.

Obviously the warlords of the later Republic had relied heavily upon bodyguards. Sertorius, in Spain, had employed Spaniards for this purpose; and the custom of employing foreigners of more or less barbarian character as personal guards (sometimes on horseback) had persisted. This was partly because of the physical strength of these men. But it was also because their imperfect acquaintance with the Latin language, and presumed lack of interest in Roman politics, meant they were less likely to be suborned into murdering the man they were supposed to protect. Caesar, who fought three campaigns in Spain, followed the example of Sertorius and enrolled a Spanish guard. Later on, however, he disbanded it. This was imprudent, according to his friends, who unsuccessfully urged him to reverse his decision. After he was dead, Octavian returned to the practice his great-uncle had abandoned, and employed a bodyguard from the Spanish town of Calagurris (Calahorra). After Actium, however, he replaced it by a guard of Germans, a race who honoured above all else the bond of personal fidelity to their selected master. Inscriptions relating to its members, known as *corporis custodes*, have survived. They were slaves and freedmen, and constituted a private body, not forming part of the Roman army.

But this German bodyguard was only supplementary to Augustus's principal guard, the praetorians, who were Roman citizens and belonged to the army. This praetorian guard had certain Republican roots. At first, it is true, the escorts with which earlier leaders had been accustomed to surround themselves, both on active service and in their civilian lives, had consisted not of army personnel, but of their own friends. However one of the two Scipios, it is not clear which, was said to have employed a military guard. But it seems to have been Marius who first made use of a regular military escort, when he was accompanied in Numidia by a 'bodyguard of cavalry formed of the bravest soldiers rather than of his most intimate friends' (106 B.C.). Such guard units, whether of cavalry or infantry, came to be known as praetorian cohorts (*cohortes praetoriae*). This was because in early times

Roman generals had often held the office of praetor, which was originally, before the consulship outranked it, the chief elective office of the state.

The task of the guardsmen was to intervene in order to prevent or crush mutinies, but above all to protect the person of the commander. Thus Julius Caesar, despite the impressive gesture he made by disbanding his Spanish guard, took two thousand soldiers with him when he went to dine with Cicero in his house at Cumae (Cuma) in Campania, to his host's understandable dismay. And then, when he left Cicero and rode past a neighbouring dignitary's house, he ordered the whole of this guard to parade under arms on either side of him. After Caesar's death, Antony maintained a very substantial military force for his personal protection, including numerous centurions—and he accused Octavian of tampering with its loyalty. This bodyguard was said to have been six thousand strong, and the figure is not impossible when we bear in mind that later on, when for a time the two men were ostensibly reconciled, Octavian sent him a gift of two thousand picked men, splendidly equipped with full armour, to serve as praetorian guardsmen. In due course Antony organized his guard into a number of cohorts. This is demonstrated by an inscription on his coinage. For when, shortly before Actium, he decided to issue a series of coins celebrating the units under his command, the praetorian cohorts are commemorated in the plural (CHORTIVM PRAETORIARVM).

When Actium had been lost and won Octavian organized his own praetorian guard into no less than nine cohorts. Each contained five hundred infantrymen, divided into three maniples and six centuries of eighty men each. There was also a praetorian cavalry section of ninety men (*equites praetoriani*), consisting of three squadrons.

The victorious *Imperator* thought it best not to station more than three of the praetorian cohorts in Rome; and even for those three no permanent camp was yet established. The other six were allotted both summer and winter quarters outside the capital and around various Italian towns. This was partly because he felt that the concentration of all nine cohorts in Rome would have constituted a danger rather than a protection to his life—and would have tempted other potential leaders to seduce its loyalty. Moreover, bearing in mind that the whole idea of keeping troops in the homeland was un-Republican, he was eager not to give the impression of ruling by force of arms, and so large a convergence of troops round himself might have seemed to imply this. For the praetorians, thus highly organized, already looked less like the praetorian guards of Republican generals than some guard surrounding a Greek monarch. Furthermore, in Republican times, although unofficial armed gangs had been all too painfully familiar, armed men under official military command had not normally been present at the capital at all except on the occasion of an external attack or a Triumph. Since this was now going to be changed, the change was better not made too obtrusively.

The primary duty of the praetorians was to guard the emperor, whether at Rome or elsewhere. In the city they provided him with an escort to the forum and senate, and a cohort stood on duty at the palace every day and night, changing guard between the afternoon siesta and the evening meal. While on duty in Rome the praetorians showed deference to Republican opinion by replacing their military uniforms by togas, under which their weapons were ordinarily kept concealed. When they escorted the emperor to a sacrifice or a festival, they normally went unarmed. As time went on, there was a tendency to enlarge their responsibilities to the ruler considerably beyond the protection of his person. For example a praetorian cohort was normally present at performances at the theatre, where demonstrations timed to coincide with his presence often assumed a threatening aspect, and could lead to perilous riots. Moreover when there was serious fighting on the frontiers the praetorians often contributed contingents—especially when the *Imperator* himself was there, or (before long) when there was a member of his family to look after. But they were never, at this period at least, regarded in the light of a central military reserve, for nothing of the kind existed.

The guardsmen were mostly recruited, Tacitus records, not very far from Rome, in the ancient central Italian regions of Latium, Etruria and Umbria. Before long north Italians were added, but inscriptions and other sources suggest that only about 10 per cent of the force were provincials—a considerably smaller proportion than were to be found in the legions: that is to say they were essentially an Italian force, and that is what they remained for a long time to come. 'Italy' as a meaningful term was something fairly new—a product of the first century B.C. in which the Social War had united the country in common Roman citizenship—and Caesar had enlarged it by adding the north Italian lands, teeming with potential recruits. When Virgil, who felt the emotive power of 'Italia' profoundly, tells how at Actium, against the eastern hordes of Antony, the westerner Octavian lead *Italians* into battle, some old-fashioned Romans may still have found the concept unfamiliar or even shocking. But such men belonged to the past, for Augustan thinking and writing included many a paean to the triumph won against her foreign enemies by Italy.

Indeed, as the composition of army and senate alike suggested—in both of which the proportion of non-Roman Italians showed a substantial increase—the principate could, in a sense, be described as the victory of Italy over the capital itself. But this was never openly said. What came to be emphasized instead was the identification between the two—so that there seemed nothing paradoxical about an emperor flattering the praetorians as 'the children of Italy, Rome's true warrior youth.' This declaration that the guardsmen were the truest Italians, and therefore the truest Romans too, had its political dangers. Once they themselves decided to take the idea seriously, they would begin claiming that they were better able than anyone else to judge whom Italy and Rome ought to have as their ruler. However, such political dangers rarely escaped the notice of Augustus: and this particular hazard provided just one more reason why he

preferred to station only one-third of the praetorian cohorts inside Rome itself.

Even so, however, a bodyguard of three praetorian cohorts in the capital, amounting to over fifteen hundred men, was somewhat unwieldy viewed as a force for his personal protection. Within the ranks of the guard, as a result, there developed a special, inner corps of mounted *speculatores*.

Men of this designation were already known before Augustus's time because they had formed a regular component of the legions. Each legion normally included its own sub-unit of ten *speculatores*, acting as scouts, messengers and collectors of military intelligence. For example, a *speculator* spying for GSnaeus Pompeius junior, son of Pompey the Great, was captured by Caesar's troops and put to death. And these legionary *speculatores* still continued to exist during the empire, being especially employed for the carrying of urgent dispatches, and in addition for military police functions of various kinds. When their missions brought them to Rome, they were quartered, like other visiting or 'foreign' soldiers, in the Castra Peregrina ('foreign camp') on the Caelian Hill.

Meanwhile, however, a novel type of *speculatores* had also been developing. Their duties were centred upon the supreme commander himself; for example the itinerant executioners who killed the men proscribed by the triumvirs were described by this term. Antony had formed his *speculatores* into a special cohort, mentioned separately among the units honoured on his coinage (CHORTIS SPECVLATORVM). In his army they were distinct from the praetorian cohorts, since the two types of soldier are commemorated under different names and on different coins. Under the emperors, however, although they proudly call themselves '*speculatores* of Caesar,' the central corps bearing this name belonged to the praetorian guard, and, being mounted, were in effect a special reinforcement of its cavalry squadrons. These arrangements no doubt went back to Augustus himself. He is recorded to have stayed at the country house of one of his *speculatores*, and to have entertained him back. These men were chosen for their impressive physique, and their main task was to save the *Imperator* from assassination—that was why, as we happen to be told, one of them (not on horseback on this occasion) stood so close to his master that by mistake he nearly wounded him with his lance. To preserve the ruler from assassins was likewise the task of Augustus's German bodyguard, and it might seem, therefore, that there was unnecessary duplication. But he felt safer if he had two distinct, indeed rival, groups of men devoted to this same purpose. This was partly because, in the event of an attempt on his life, if either the guardsmen or his *speculatores* happened to prove too slow, or insufficiently loyal, the other group might be able to intervene on his behalf, and ward the peril off.

This corps of mounted *speculatores* of the praetorian guard was also employed, like their legionary counterparts, for the rapid conveyance of messages and dispatches, and the provision of information, secret or otherwise, to the ruler. There is also some reason to suppose that they were used for undercover activities such as espionage, arrests, the guarding of suspects and detainees, and (as under the triumvirate) the executions of condemned men. This was certainly the case in later years, and Augustus's reign saw its share of all these activities. Caesar had already done a great deal to develop military intelligence, and there is no reason to suppose that Augustus fell short of him. As regards the civilian field, although he could rely to some extent on the traditional institution of professional informers, he also had to have spies of his own, and he scarcely needed Maecenas's alleged advice that he should employ 'persons who are to keep eyes and ears open to anything which affects his supremacy'. The extent to which he, like his successors, employed his praetorian *speculatores* to conduct and organize this potentially sinister necessary activity is uncertain. But it is not improbable that this was one of the functions that he required them to perform.

The praetorians were privileged above other soldiers. They always had an exceptionally good chance of catching the right eye and obtaining promotions, for example to legionary centurionates. Moreover, whereas the length of service required of legionaries was at first sixteen

years and then twenty (without including their additional tenure as veterans or *evocati*), the service of praetorians was twelve years and then sixteen. And, in spite of this shorter service, they were paid considerably more than the legionaries. At first their wages were probably 375 *denarii*, while the legionaries were given 225. But then, already before the end of Augustus's reign, they were receiving as many as 750 *denarii*. Their bonuses, too, were the largest in the army. In the early part of the reign they received land settlements like other soldiers. Later, when lands were replaced by cash gratuities, they were allocated 5,000 *denarii*, as against the legionaries' 3,000. In Augustus's will the differential was increased, since he left the legionaries 300 *denarii* each, but the praetorians 1,000. They were treated with this additional generosity in the will because, as the events during the next half-century were to confirm in no uncertain fashion, it was they above all others whose help would be needed to see the new ruler safely into the saddle.

All military camps and headquarters had military amphitheatres in which the soldiers could be kept amused by shows, and in the capital the praetorians were equally well looked after. At the same time, however, there were also certain disqualifications which they shared with their fellow-soldiers. For example, like the legionaries, they were not allowed to get married during their period of service. But after demobilization they were allowed, unlike all other army personnel, to contract a legally valid marriage with a foreign woman, or to legalize unions that had already been informally contracted during their service. To the existence of such informal unions, and families resulting from them, inscriptions bear witness. (They also testify to the guardsmen's possession of slaves, who were kept, like those of the legionaries, outside the camps.) The dispensation legalizing these informal partnerships meant that, after the guardsmen had been discharged, children born from such alliances became Roman citizens. That accounts for the apparently anomalous fact that, unlike legionaries but like auxiliaries, they were issued diplomas when their service came to an end.

This was because their unions needed formal, written sanction.

The praetorian centurions were men in whom great confidence was placed. Many of them came up through the ranks, though they could also have held centurions' posts in other branches of the metropolitan forces before becoming centurions in the guard; this became normal practice later. Once appointed to the guard centurionate, they might rise impressively through its various grades by obtaining other posts, legionary or civilian, between one grade and the next. And thereafter some of them, though not very many, were elevated to senior officer posts, or civilian equestrian offices. There were very few praetorian centurions who were not Italians. They came, for the most part, from the loyal governing classes of the municipalities of Italy. These were places where, in spite of continuing reverence for ancient Roman traditions, the pretensions of the Roman senate of the day might still, even so long after the Social War was over, be regarded with something less than excessive veneration. This meant that their inhabitants' personal loyalty to the ruler, who was so plausibly claiming to restore the antique Republic, was easier to secure; and so the people of these towns became officers of the praetorian guard, upon which his safety so largely depended.

When, shortly after Actium, Augustus first established his praetorian cohorts, their highest officers were military tribunes. One of these, of senatorial rank, commanded each cohort, with other tribunes, mainly of knightly status, in support. The cohort commanders were at first under the direct command of the *Imperator* himself. The odium of stationing troops in Italy seemed less if they came directly under so august a personage, rather than under some general or another whose military power in Italy his equals would have been likely to resent.

However this arrangement soon proved impracticable. Augustus was too busy to direct the activities of the praetorians himself, and the military tribunes were not senior enough to be trusted with such large responsibilities, with obvious political implications. Accordingly, he decided to appoint prefects to take command of the guard, over the heads of the tribunes. There seems to have been no Republican precedent for this; though during Augustus's own earlier absences from Rome, when Maecenas or Agrippa had been left informally in charge of the city, it is conceivable that they were given some control over the praetorians.

The new prefects were not senators but knights. This made it less likely that they would feel a distracting loyalty to some senatorial faction. It was also in keeping with his policy of allocating some of the most important posts not only in the army, but in the whole empire, to this great, influential section of non-senatorial society. Other highly conspicuous posts allotted to knights were the prefectures of Egypt and of the grain supply (*praefectura annonae*). To begin with the praetorian command, though already senior to the prefecture of the grain supply, still ranked below Egypt. But over the ensuing decades it began to outshine even the Egyptian post.

The first praetorian prefects were appointed in 2 B.C. They were two in number—two colleagues holding the office jointly. The initial holders of the office were Quintus Ostorius Scapula (who was later promoted to the prefecture of Egypt) and Publius Salvius Aper. This collegiate arrangement, as Dio makes Maecenas remark, had the advantage that, if one of the pair was sick, there would always be another available. And the same advantage, he might have added, would apply if the loyalty of one of them was suspect.

Occasionally, in the distant future, there were to be more than two prefects at a time. But, as Dio observed, this tended to lead to confusion. The initial avoidance of a sole prefect is easy to understand, since, as subsequent history would abundantly show, such an official might become so powerful that he would bring peril rather than security to his master. For this reason, throughout the whole period of more than three centuries during which the post existed, there were barely a dozen occasions on which a prefect was appointed without a colleague.

However, two of these exceptions came almost immediately, before the reign of Augustus drew to its end. For in spite of all the advantages of having joint prefects, he very quickly felt sure enough of his guard's reliability to appoint a single holder of the office—and then, after his retirement, another. The first was Valerius Ligur, and the second Lucius Seius Strabo. The degree of eminence attained by Ligur is unknown, but Strabo, although like other praetorian prefects he only possessed knightly rank, was extremely well connected. His mother Terentia was apparently the sister-in-law of Maecenas (who had died in 8 B.C.), and his wife belonged to one of the very greatest families of Rome, the Cornelii Lentuli.

Strabo evidently began the enhancement of the prefect's position, which was to reach its climax in the next reign when his son Sejanus had succeeded him. It was obvious enough why prefects were so important. Holding, as they did, the emperor's personal safety in their own hands, and possessing at their disposal an elite body of troops in and near the capital itself, they rapidly and inevitably came to fulfill an essential role in the inmost councils of the *Imperator*, and received his most intimate confidences. Moreover they were in a position to keep an eye on his correspondence with imperial governors and others in the provinces. For his letters to them, and their replies, were carried by the *speculatores*, who formed part of the prefect's command. The other confidential functions of the *speculatores*, such as espionage, detention and execution, were likewise subject to the prefect's direction, and added still further to his power.

The Army in Peacetime

Graham Webster

In this concluding section of his standard book The Roman Imperial Army, *Professor Graham Webster of Birmingham turns his attention to the peaceful accomplishments of Roman legionaries and auxiliaries throughout the Empire: roadbuilding and other engineering projects, agricultural settlement in dangerous areas and the spread of the Latin language and Roman civilization.*

It is doubtful if the Roman administrators ever saw themselves as civilizing influences any more than the colonial officers in modern times in the more backward areas of Africa or Asia. Nevertheless the upper levels at least of Roman society possessed a deep sense of the destiny of Rome and a feeling that their nation had been singled out from the earliest times as the natural ruler of the world. This is implicit in the great history of Livy and the old stories and legends were adapted and shaped to this end. But it was not until the rise of Augustus that Rome's destiny seemed to have been fulfilled. Now could Virgil put into the mouth of Anchises the true role of the new Empire:

Let it be your task, Roman, to control the nations with your power (these shall be your arts) and to impose the way of peace; to spare the vanquished and subdue the proud.

Words which are echoed through the centuries from Aelius Aristides to the late fourth-century poet Claudian.

Roman governors and high-ranking officials, military and civil, spread the Roman way of life, not through any sense of duty, but because this was the only acceptable way, and they would fail to understand people who had the means yet rejected the concept.

There was also a strong practical aspect which helped to emphasize this Roman feeling of rightness, since warlike barbarians, humbled by defeat, donned the toga and became respectable citizens. It was this combination of realities and sense of inevitability, so typically Roman, that led to the successful assimilation of alien peoples within the folds of the Empire. But there were Roman cynics like Tacitus who saw this process merely as enslavement, the free men being seduced by the soft pleasure of civilization.

The most revealing passage concerns the Britons and comes in the *Agricola*:

The following winter (i.e. A.D. 78–79) was spent in introducing new schemes. A scattered and savage people, addicted to war, were to be drawn from their habits into the pleasures of quietude and peace. (Agricola) gave private encouragement and official help towards the building of temples, fora and private houses, praising those who quickly responded and castigating the slothful; the desire to gain honour became more effective than compulsion. He also arranged for the sons of the chiefs to be educated in the liberal arts and expressed a preference for the natural ability of the Britons to the studiousness of the Gauls. A distaste for the Latin tongue gave place to an aspiration to speak it with eloquence, thereafter our national dress became acceptable and the toga was commonly seen. Gradually they were drawn towards the blandishments of vice, colonnades, baths and elegant banquets, but what were regarded as refinements of civilization were in effect their chains of enslavement.

To Rome the only possible way of life was that of the town and the most remarkable aspect of the Empire is the spread of these urban centres, each consciously modelled, however modestly, on Rome itself. The main features were the gridded plan of the streets, the enormous public buildings such as the forum with its market-place and law-courts, the temples and the bathhouses, many of which survive in part or ruin simply because they were of such durable and solid construction. The wonder is that these were successfully imposed on people totally alien to these conceptions—to the Briton it was a revolution indeed. It has even been considered that it was an entirely artificial scheme which disintegrated when faced with serious economic stresses; such a view is no longer valid. In spite of the difficulties, the British way of life was totally transformed within a few generations, but how deeply this change penetrated into the lower strata of society is another matter. The mass of peasants tied to the land may have viewed these splendours from a distance and been touched not by the gentle refinements of the new civilization but by the lash of a rapacious new landowner.

The wealth of the Empire was based on agriculture and trade and they are aspects which leave little record in the pages of contemporary history or in inscriptions. It has been left to scholars in this century like Rostovtzeff, Tenney Frank and Charlesworth to show the extensive, closely knit trade relationships throughout the Empire and beyond. The life-blood of the Empire was its commerce developed by hard-headed entrepreneurs in Rome and fed by a remarkable network of communications by road, sea and river. But this would have been quite impossible but for the *Pax Romana* maintained by the Army. As long as there were no civil wars and the barbarians were kept firmly beyond the frontiers, the great variety of peoples within the Empire could prosper under the rule of Rome in new and unaccustomed ways of life.

But the responsibility of the Army went far beyond the mere guardianship of the frontiers. It was the army staff officers who were responsible for much of the administration and justice in the imperial provinces. Engineers, architects and surveyors would doubtless have been made available for advice and technical assistance where large public buildings were constructed and water and drainage projects undertaken. This would apply especially to those provinces, such as Britain, where these skills were non-existent. There is, however, little direct evidence of army participation in the early period, except on road and bridge building, which are of strategic importance, and such projects as the canal of Drusus which linked the Rhine with the Zuyder Zee. When large-scale emergency schemes were carried out, the Army must have taken part at least in planning and supervision; an example could have been the Car Dyke in Britain which helped to bring the Fens into

cultivation and also to supply a link by water between this area and first Lincoln via the Witham, the Fossdyke and possibly later York via the Trent and Ouse. Unless masons and architects had been specially imported from Gaul, their army equivalents must have been available for the planning of the early *fora* and *thermae* of Roman Britain. The British *fora* form a distinctive pattern unlike those of other provinces. The striking similarity between the plans of most of the British *fora* and the military headquarters building can hardly be a coincidence, and one may be justified in seeing here the hand of the military technician. Only at Verulamium, the only known first-century forum, is there a lack of conformity and closer approach to the Gallic plan. The use of soldiers as miners was by no means exceptional, but guarding and supervision was a common practice, since prison labour was often used and the mines were in wild mountain areas.

The founding of *coloniae* was one means by which it was hoped that Roman ideas would become established in newly conquered areas. This was an eminently sensible and practical way in which the problems of demobilization could be solved. The veteran settlements were designed to convert professional soldiers into respectable citizens instead of their banding together and resorting to brigandage. In some cases the sites chosen were those from which legions had been moved; the veterans might have spent most of their lives there and raised families. This was a technical irregularity which was put right on discharge. The idea of settling there in the old and accustomed haunts would have had a great appeal. When an attempt was made to transplant veterans in Italy at Tarentum and Antium to arrest depopulation, most of them returned to their provinces, 'in which they had served for so long and since they were unable to marry and rear families the homes they had left were childless and without heirs. The settlers now were strangers among strangers; men from totally different maniples; without leaders, with no common cause except that they were all soldiers, put into one place to make up an aggregate rather than a colony.' [Tacitus, *Annals*]

The *colonia* had definite advantages; it not only gave a strategic reserve in newly conquered areas at least for a few years, but the sons of the veterans would turn naturally to the colours and so *coloniae* were valuable centres of recruitment. The setting up of a model city was also intended as an example to the natives, but theory, as is often the case, was not always reflected in practice. The colonists settled by Ostorius Scapula at Camulodunum (Colchester) receive a scathing comment from Tacitus: 'They were acting as if they had been given the whole country, driving the natives from their homes, evicting them from their lands, they called them 'captives' and 'slaves'. These veterans were hardly the model citizens in their model town, exemplars to all aspiring Britons; but the main focus of hatred and anti-Roman feeling was the great temple of Claudius, prematurely deified, which was the *arx aeternae dominationis* (citadel of our eternal tyranny).

One might indeed consider whether the service in the Army could be regarded as a civilizing influence in itself. Many of the recruits to the rank and file were deliberately taken from the barbarous frontier districts, the legionaries being given citizenship on enlistment. They served most of their lives on the frontiers and would rarely have visited any of the large cities. The young recruits were moulded into disciplined soldiers, tied by oath of loyalty to the emperor, forming part of a complex sophisticated organization, and soon adopting the ideas of personal hygiene reflected in the bath-house. The traditional view of soldiers as unruly and licentious is usually true of times of unrest or when they are far from their base. In the frontier forts and fortresses the young barbarians quickly learnt the basic elements of civilization by becoming members of an organized community and becoming exposed to Roman influences at least in the religious and social spheres. There were opportunities for betterment open to the bright young man with ambition and intelligence. If one accepts the Army as a rough but effective way of introducing fresh blood into the ranks of Roman civilization it is, numerically at least, impressive, for it means on an average about 10,000 new citizens a year. If, however, one adds their wives and families, the total can be at least doubled and probably trebled over a hundred years. The Army could well have been responsible for adding three million citizens to the roll. All this helped to dilute the value of citizenship and it is likely that Caracalla's *constitutio Antoniniana* was not such a sweeping extension of the franchise as might appear at first glance.

While a large number of young men were steadily brought from the fringes of the Empire under the influence of Rome it is clear that it was by no means a one-way effect. The steady flow of barbarians into the Army had an equal consequence of diluting the Roman way of life. The old Roman virtues so evident in the early Empire tended gradually to fade, but the most obvious loss is in the arts; while architecture continued to blossom with technical innovation there was a marked coarsening in sculpture and a more obvious decline in literature.

While these effects were only slow and gradual throughout the second century, the process may have been quickened by Severus, who was not readily accepted by the Senate and sought to bind the Army closer to himself and his family. The Army became the road to advancement even into the Senate. Severus, according to Rostovtzeff, 'militarized the principate,' but at the same time encouraged liberal legislation and protection for the lower classes from which the military caste was drawn. While critics may deplore the dimming of ancient glories, it was this egalitarianism with the continuous introduction of so much new blood which enabled the Empire to hold together for so long and adapt itself to the changing conditions of the third and fourth centuries.

Livia, the wife of Augustus, is depicted on a brass coin issued at Rome by her son Tiberius in 22-23 A.D. *She was ill at the time and the legend* SALUS AUGUSTA *links her recovery to the well-being of the state.*

Women and The Family
In Imperial Rome

INTRODUCTION
Ronald Mellor

The history of the first century of the Roman Empire is largely the history of the Julio-Claudian family: events within the imperial household such as marriage, divorce and infidelity had a powerful effect on the political history of the age. Livia stood first in a series of powerful Roman empresses who determined imperial policy; while Livia shocked her contemporaries by receiving ambassadors, her successors even led Roman armies in battle and sat in the Roman Senate. Though the ancient sources usually depict powerful women as motivated primarily by family ambition, there exists little doubt that the Julio-Claudian women played important roles on the wider political stage.

Aristocratic Roman women were nothing new to political life. During the centuries, stories circulated about noblewomen who exercised an influence on Roman public policy. Even if such accounts obviously depict exceptional situations, they also show that women occupied a far more visible place in Roman society than they did in the Greek world. In ancient Athens, a respectable woman would not even appear at dinner with her husband's friends. Athenian women were not only sheltered from public life, but were also emotionally distanced from their spouses; at least the affective bonds between Athenian husbands and their reclusive wives seem to have been less important than those between Roman marital partners. At Rome, the matron (mistress of the household) had always loomed as a powerful figure who usually occupied the emotional center of the household. Strong ties to such women, and the loyalty to the extended family that these ties created, informed Roman social and political life throughout the Roman Republic.

The importance assigned to women in the Roman household, however, contrasted with the limited rights originally accorded them by Roman law. In earliest times the Roman paterfamilias retained control over the life and property of his children and grandchildren. A Roman male could become independent when his father died, whereas a Roman woman always remained in the guardianship of a male relative. After her father's death, a guardian, most often an uncle or a brother, controlled her property and had to approve her will and any inheritance she might receive. Marriage, which was a family decision rather than a personal or emotional one, was usually concluded with manus ("hand," or control), by which a girl was transferred into her husband's family "in the position of a daughter" to obey her father-in-law or husband.

Nevertheless, marital relations, like so much else in Roman life, first began to change as a consequence of the growth of Roman power in the second century B.C.; the changes continued into the early Empire. Increasing wealth made families reluctant to see their daughters take property to another family. Marriage without manus, by which the woman remained in her father's family, thus grew increasingly common until it became the norm in the Julio-Claudian period. Wealthy women were more independent when they remained under the guardianship of their own relatives; furthermore, the power of guardians was diminished by legislation of Augustus, who promoted fertility by allowing a woman who had borne three children total independence from her guardian. Guardianship was further weakened by Claudius, and aristocratic women eventually possessed almost total control over their property.

The aristocrats of the late Republic used marriage (and divorce) as political tools. Roman leaders such as Sulla, Pompey, Caesar and Antony, who modeled so much of their behavior on eastern kings, also used their wives and children much as the Hellenistic monarchs had done. Cornelia, daughter of Scipio (the conqueror of Hannibal) and mother of the Gracchi, even received a proposal of marriage from King Ptolemy of Egypt; Ptolemy's descendant Cleopatra had notorious liaisons with both Julius Caesar and Marc Antony. The behavior of Livia, Julia, and the Agrippinas must be seen in the context of this "sexualized" political environment.

But the behavior and attitudes of Roman women, whether humble or aristocratic, are reported only in male sources. Neither the idealized Roman women described by Pliny, nor the immoral empresses found in Tacitus' Annals, nor the terrible women satirized by the misogynist Juvenal in and of themselves shed much light on the condition of ordinary Roman women. Professor Judith Hallett's essay discusses the problems with these sources and suggests some new lines of inquiry. During the past two decades scholars have been attempting to piece together an unromanticized picture of women and the family in ancient Rome. It is an embryonic scholarly enterprise, but one which holds both promise and excitement.

Letters on the Virtues of Roman Women

Pliny the Younger

The younger Pliny reached the highest office with the Empire about 100 A.D., and his correspondence reveals the attitudes of the Roman elite on many subjects. The following letters reflect Pliny's conventional views on the public and private virtues of upper-class Roman women.

The first letter presents an idealized view of Roman marriage as Arria disguises from her sick husband their young son's death. This heroic lady is most famous for her courage in the face of death when, with her husband Paetus condemned for conspiring against Claudius, she stabbed herself first and handed him the dagger with the words, "It does not hurt, Paetus."

The second letter is to Pliny's young wife's aunt, in which he extols her domestic virtues and her devotion to Pliny himself and his writings. For Pliny, self-abnegation is clearly an important virtue in a Roman wife. His self-satisfied smugness is evident here as it is throughout his correspondence.

The third letter treats the genuinely close tie that existed between a Roman father and his daughter. A friend of Pliny has lost his young daughter, and the writer's distress is no rhetorical exercise but an expression of heartfelt grief.

To Metilius Nepos

I think I have remarked that the more famous words and deeds of men and women are not necessarily their greatest. I was strengthened in this opinion by a conversation I had yesterday with Fannia, granddaughter of the famous Arria who sustained and encouraged her husband by her example at the time of his death. She told me several things about her grandmother which were quite as heroic though less well known, and I think they will make the same impression on you as you read them as they did on me during their telling.

Arria's husband, Caecina Paetus, was ill, so was their son, and it was thought that neither could recover. The son died, a most beautiful boy with an unassuming manner no less remarkable, and dear to his parents for reasons beyond the fact that he was their son. Arria made all the preparations for his funeral and took her place at the ceremony without her husband knowing; in fact whenever she entered his room she pretended that their son was still alive and even rather better, and, when Paetus kept asking how the boy was, she would answer that he had had a good sleep and was willing to take some food. Then when the

tears she had left back for so long could no longer be kept from breaking out, she left the room; not till then did she give way to her grief. Her weeping over, she dried her eyes, composed her face, and returned as if she had left the loss of her child outside the room. It was a glorious deed, I know, to draw a sword, plunge it into her breast, pull it out, and hand it to her husband with the immortal, almost divine, words: 'It does not hurt, Paetus.' But on that well-known occasion she had fame and immortality before her eyes. It was surely even more heroic when she had no hope of any such reward, to stifle her tears, hide her grief, and continue to act the mother after she had lost her son.

At the time of the revolt against Claudius raised by Scribonianus in Illyricum, Paetus had joined his party, and after Scribonianus's death was being brought as a prisoner to Rome. He was about to board ship when Arria begged the soldiers to take her with him. 'This is a senator of consular rank,' she insisted, 'and of course you will allow him a few slaves to serve his meals, dress him and put on his shoes; all of which I can do for him myself.' Her request was refused. She then hired a small fishing smack, and the great ship sailed with her following in her tiny boat.

Again, when she came before Claudius and found the wife of Scribonianus volunteering to give evidence of the revolt, 'Am I to listen to you,' she cried, 'who could go on living after Scribonianus died in your arms?' This proves that her determination to die a glorious death was not a sudden impulse. Indeed, when her son-in-law Thrasea was trying to persuade her not to carry out her resolve, in the course of his argument he asked her whether if he ever had to die she would wish her daughter to die with him. 'If she lives as long and happily with you,' she said, 'as I have with Paetus—yes.' This answer increased the anxiety felt for her by her family and she was watched even more carefully. Perceiving this, 'It is no good,' she said. 'You can make me choose a painful death, but you cannot make it impossible.' With these words she leaped out of her chair and dashed her head against the wall opposite, so that she fell senseless from the violent blow. When she came round, 'I told you,' she said, 'that I should find a hard way to die if you denied me an easy one.'

Surely you think these words greater than the well-known 'It does not hurt, Paetus' which was their culmination? And yet this is widely famous, while the earlier sayings are not known at all. Hence the inference with which I began this letter, that the words and deeds which win fame are not always the greatest.

To Calpurnia Hispulla

You are a model of family affection, and loved your excellent and devoted brother as dearly as he loved you; you love his daughter as if she were your own, and, by filling the place of the father she lost, you are more than an aunt to her. I know then how glad you will be to hear that she has proved herself worthy of her father, her grandfather and you. She is highly intelligent and a careful housewife, and her devotion to me is a sure indication of her virtue. In addition, this love has given her an interest in literature: she keeps copies of my works to read again and again and even learn by heart. She is so anxious when she knows that I am going to plead in court, and so happy when all is over! (She arranges to be kept informed of the sort of reception and applause I receive, and what verdict I win in the case.) If I am giving a reading she sits behind a curtain near by and greedily drinks in every word of appreciation. She has even set my verses to music and sings them, to the accompaniment of her lyre, with no musician to teach her but the best of masters, love.

All this gives me the highest reason to hope that our mutual happiness will last for ever and go on increasing day by day, for she does not love me for my present age nor my person, which will gradually grow old and decay, but for my aspirations to fame; nor would any other feelings be suitable for one brought up by your hands and trained in your precepts, who has seen only what was pure and moral in your company and learned to love me on your recommendation. For you respect my mother like a daughter; and have given me guidance and encouragement since boyhood; you always foretold that I should become the man I am now in the eyes of my wife. Please accept our united thanks for having given her to me and me to her as if chosen for each other.

To Aefulanus Marcellinus

I am writing to you in great distress: our friend Fundanus has lost his younger daughter. I never saw a girl so gay and lovable, so deserving of a longer life or even a life to last for ever. She had not yet reached the age of fourteen, and yet she combined the wisdom of age and dignity of womanhood with the sweetness and modesty of youth and innocence. She would cling to her father's neck, and embrace us, his friends, with modest affection; she loved her nurses, her attendants and her teachers, each one for the service given her; she applied herself intelligently to her books and was moderate and restrained in her play. She bore her last illness with patient resignation and, indeed, with courage; she obeyed her doctor's orders, cheered her sister and father, and by sheer force of will carried on after her physical strength had failed her. This will power remained with her to the end, and neither the length of her illness nor fear of death could break it. So she has left us all the more sad reasons for lamenting our loss. Hers is a truly tragic and untimely end—death itself was not so cruel as the moment of its coming. She was already engaged to marry a distinguished young man, the day for the wedding was fixed, and we had received our invitations. Such joy, and now such sorrow! No words can express my grief when I heard Fundanus giving his own orders (for one heart-rending detail leads to another) for the money he had intended for clothing, pearls and jewels to be spent on incense, ointment and spices. He is indeed a cultivated man and a philosopher who has devoted himself from youth to higher thought and the arts, but at the moment he rejects everything he has so often heard and professed himself: he has cast off all his other virtues and is wholly absorbed by his love for his child. You will forgive and even admire him if you think of what he has lost—a daughter who resembled him in character no less than in face and expression, and was her father's living image in every way.

If then you write anything to him in his very natural sorrow, be careful not to offer any crude form of consolation which might suggest reproof; be gentle and sympathetic. Passage of time will make him readier to accept this; a raw wound shrinks from a healing hand but later permits and even seeks help, and so the mind rejects and repels any consolation in its first pangs of grief, then feels the need of comfort and is calmed if this is kindly offered.

Funeral Eulogy of Turia

Author Unknown

An inscription found in Rome records this loving eulogy to Turia by her husband of forty-one years. She had protected him and interceded on his behalf during the proscriptions of 43 B.C. and, after his pardon, she was praised by Augustus himself. But her husband goes on to praise her generosity in being willing to divorce him so that he could have children by another wife and, more exceptional in a Roman, to angrily reject this suggestion. It is a unique document which, even if atypical, gives us a glimpse of a marriage of mutual love and commitment.

. . . In our day, marriages of such long duration, not dissolved by divorce, but terminated by death alone, are indeed rare. For our union was prolonged in unclouded happiness for forty-one years. Would that it had been my lot to put an end to this our good fortune and that I as the older—which was more just—had yielded to fate.

Why recall your inestimable qualities, your modesty, deference, affability, your amiable disposition, your faithful attendance to the household duties, your enlightened religion, your unassuming elegance, the modest simplicity and refinement of your manners? Need I speak of your attachment to your kindred, your affection for your family—when you respected my mother as you did your own parents and cared for her tomb as you did for that of your own mother and father—you who share countless other virtues with Roman ladies most jealous of their fair name? These qualities which I claim for you are your own, equalled or excelled by but few; for the experience of men teaches us how rare they are.

With common prudence we have preserved all the patrimony which you received from your parents. Intrusting it all to me, you were not troubled with the care of increasing it; thus did we share the task of administering it, that I undertook to protect your fortune, and you to guard mine. On this point, I pass by many things in silence, for fear of attributing to myself a portion of your own deserts. Suffice it for me to indicate your sentiments. . . .

I owe you no less a debt than Caesar Augustus himself, for this my return from exile to my native land. For unless you had prepared the way for my safety, even Caesar's promises of assistance had been of no avail. So I owe no less a debt to your loyal devotion than to the clemency of Caesar.

Why shall I now conjure up the memory of our domestic counsels and plans stored away in the hidden recesses of the heart?—That, aroused by the sudden arrival of messages from you to a realization of the present and imminent perils, I was saved by your counsel? That you suffered me not to be recklessly carried away by a foolish rashness, or that, when bent on more temperate plans, you provided for me a safe retreat, having as sharers in your plans for my safety, when an exile—fraught with danger as they were for you all—your sister and her husband, C. Cluvius. But I should not finish, were I to attempt to touch on all these matters. Suffice it for me, and for your memory, that the retreat provided by you insured my safety.

I should confess, however, that on this occasion I suffered one of the bitterest experiences of my life, in the fate that befell you, much against my will. When the favor and permission of Caesar Augustus, then absent [from Rome], had restored me to my country, still a useful citizen perhaps, M. Lepidus, his colleague, then present in the city, interposed objections. Then prostrating yourself at his feet, he not only did not raise you up—but, dragged along and abused as though a common slave, your body all covered with bruises, yet with unflinching steadfastness of purpose, you recalled to him Caesar's edict [of pardon] and the letter of felicitation on my return, that accompanied it. Braving his taunts and suffering the most brutal treatment, you denounced these cruelties publicly so that he [Lepidus] was branded as the author of all my perils and misfortunes. And his punishment was not long delayed.

Could such courage remain without effect? Your unexampled patience furnished the occasion for Caesar's clemency, and, by guarding my life, he branded the infamous and savage cruelty [of the tyrant Lepidus]. . . .

When all the world was again at peace and the Republic re-established, peaceful and happy days followed. We longed for children, which an envious fate denied us. Had Fortune smiled on us in this, what had been lacking to complete our happiness? But an adverse destiny put an end to our hopes. . . . Disconsolate to see me without children . . . you wished to put an end to my chagrin by proposing to me a divorce, offering to yield the place to another spouse more fertile, with the only intention of searching for and providing for me a spouse worthy of our mutual affection, whose children you assured me you would have treated as your own. . . . Nothing would have been changed, only you would have rendered to me henceforth the services of a devoted sister or mother-in-law.

I will admit that I was so irritated and shocked by such a proposition that I had difficulty in restraining my anger and remaining master of myself. You spoke of divorce before the decree of fate had forced us to separate, and I could not comprehend how you could conceive of any reason why you, still living, should not be my wife, you who during my exile had always remained most faithful and loyal. . . .

Would that our time of life had permitted our union to have endured until I, the older, had passed away—which was more just—and that you might perform for me the last sad rites and that I might have departed, leaving you behind, with a daughter to replace me at your side.

By fate's decree your course was run before mine. You left me the grief, the heart-ache, the longing for you, the sad fate to live alone. . . .

The conclusion of this discourse will be that you have deserved all, and that I remain with the chagrin of not being able to give you all. Your wishes have always been my supreme law; and whatever it will be permitted me to accord them still, in this I shall not fail.

May the gods, the Manes, assure and protect your repose!

Perspectives on Roman Women

Judith P. Hallett

In an original essay written for this volume, Professor Judith P. Hallett of the University of Maryland examines the literary and inscriptional sources for our knowledge of Roman women. The shortcomings of this material, she argues, make it virtually impossible for us to know what Roman women actually thought and felt. Instead she attempts to examine certain Roman male perceptions of the role of women and analyze the historical evidence for these perceptions.

Agrippina, his mother, writes that she delivered Nero, who was emperor just a few years ago, and—during his entire reign as emperor—the enemy of mankind, feet first.

But these little irregularities of the human condition are recognized as assuming different forms in many individuals. Take the instance of Antonia, wife of Drusus, who never spit.

Random and varied information about women prominent in classical Roman society survives in the works of several ancient Roman authors. This information even includes details, such as the tidbits above, which appear in the encyclopedic *Natural History* of Pliny the Elder (A.D. 23–79). Agrippina and Antonia belonged to the eminent Julio-Claudian family, the first dynasty to rule the Roman Empire. Agrippina's son Nero ended the line of the Julio-Claudian emperors in A.D. 68, while Antonia, wife of Drusus, herself gave birth to Nero's immediate predecessor—and Agrippina's last husband—the emperor Claudius.

Nevertheless, the nature of our extant Roman sources does not make it easy to reconstruct a comprehensive picture of how such illustrious women lived, and makes it even more difficult to reconstruct the lives of women from humbler backgrounds. The elder Pliny alludes to the memoirs of Nero's mother, Agrippina. The historian Tacitus, who lived in the generation after Pliny, also mentions these writings, stating in his *Annals* that in these recollections the younger Agrippina "recalled her life and the experiences of her kinfolk for later generations." These memoirs have not, however, survived.

Nor, for that matter, has anything which was written by Roman women themselves, save for a few love poems attributed to one Sulpicia, who lived during the principate of Augustus. As a result, we must rely almost exclusively on male authorities when we try to recover what Roman women did, felt and thought. These sources are still further limited in their usefulness by a number of other shortcomings, whether these sources are "literary" accounts for a specialized audience, in the form of histories, biographies, letters or philosophical essays, or inscriptions intended merely to impart information to the general public. Consideration of these shortcomings warrant our attention next, so that we can be better aware of what can and cannot be recovered about women in classical Rome.

Literary Source Material

The shortcomings of literary source material on Roman women include their focus on male subjects, the elite background of the male authors and audience, and their biased and self-interested representations.

Although some male authors acknowledge the influence exerted by the women of the imperial family, and devote substantial attention to their conduct, even these writers rarely regard such notable women as the primary focus of their texts. Like their contemporary Tacitus, Suetonius and Plutarch frequently detail information about the female relations of Rome's political leaders, but such information tends to occur in anecdotes and episodes centering on the male leaders themselves. Suetonius, for example, relates the rumor that Antonia died prematurely from poisoning. Yet he only does so in passing, in his life of her grandson Caligula, as an example of that emperor's cruel treatment of his family. Nor does Suetonius make any effort to substantiate this rumor. In fact, Suetonius' comments on Antonia's death center on Caligula's reported conduct toward her, such as his failure to grant her any posthumous honor and his casual viewing of her funeral pyre while having a meal in his dining room.

Ordinary Roman women, even those of relatively prominent families, and especially those of lower social classes, are accorded even less notice from our surviving Roman male sources. For as a rule, Roman authors wrote for an audience that was not only largely male, but also elite. Many writers, such as the elder Pliny and Tacitus, themselves came from privileged backgrounds and occupied prestigious positions in the all-male ranks of Roman government and military administration. To be sure, some of the élite authors did occasionally address a literary offering to a woman of their family or a close acquaintance, and have thereby allowed posterity a glimpse of what they judged to be significant in this woman's experiences and endeavors. Nero's tutor, the younger Seneca, is remarkable for leaving us two essays which he wrote to console women unhappy over painful personal losses: one to Seneca's own mother Helvia, who grieved deeply over his exile; the other to a friend, Marcia, who was bereaved of a promising and precious son. In these essays Seneca even affords his readers a few details about the family ties and backgrounds of each woman, and comments at some length on what he would imagine to be her priorities and concerns.

In his concluding words to his mother, for instance, Seneca emphasizes that she had been limited by the old-fashioned strictness of his deceased father in the amount of philosophy she had been permitted to study. Seneca ascribes this restriction to a view that "certain women use learning in the liberal arts not to achieve wisdom but to be groomed for a hedonistic existence;" he here urges Helvia to return to such studies. He insists, though, that until she reaches "that harbor which such studies promise," she recognize her present consolations: her other two sons, one successful

in public life and the other averse to it; her grandchildren; and especially her sister. Now earlier in this essay Seneca had alluded to his mother's considerable wealth, while relating that she had made generous financial gifts to her sons, although they were already rich, and even though she was still under the legal control of her living father (and had not, for that reason, inherited his estate). Yet Seneca does not list his mother's material affluence among her consolations, presumably because he devotes much of this essay to deploring material wealth and defining "true" riches as the blessings of philosophical reflection.

In other words, even those Roman male authors who furnish us with literary representations of actual women whom they knew well and admired employ these representations to reflect and promote their own interests. These, moreover, may not necessarily have been the actual interests of the women they represent. Helvia may well have shared her son's assessment that her relations—and not her financial assets—mattered most in her existence. Still, various details provided in this essay by Seneca himself suggest that Helvia did not wholly embrace his anti-materialistic philosophy: the reference to the curtailment of her own education in this area; the allusion to the monetary gifts she had bestowed upon her sons; Seneca's own need to expound and defend his beliefs when consoling her. Without any testimony from Helvia herself, we can do little more than speculate on her own views. Much the same point, moreover, could be made about Seneca's representation of Marcia's concerns in his essay consoling her. For it not only asserts the worth of his philosophical beliefs in much the same way, but even tries to justify personal circumstances—a mother's loss of her beloved grown son—with which he himself attempted to come to terms when consoling Helvia.

Inscriptions

The shortcomings of inscriptional material—another major source for our knowledge of

Roman women—include the conventionality of female commemoration and the self-serving goals of male commemorators.

The actual behavior and thoughts of other Roman women, like those of Marcia and Helvia, also seem likely to have been at variance with what male sources have chosen to report about them. Furthermore, such misrepresentation appears to have been just as likely in sources of a non-literary nature. Roman funeral inscriptions contain a sizeable body of data about Roman women—pertaining to lowly born as well as to elite individuals. Many of these inscriptions commemorate dead women, or supply details about female survivors of the deceased. But one cannot be sure how accurately these epitaphs reflect these women's sentiments or portray their behavior. Statements identifiable as funerary dedications by a mourning mother, daughter or wife may merely have been conventional utterances, approved but not individually composed by the mourner in question. Resemblances among numerous epitaphs which were dedicated by women of differing social backgrounds, locales and periods alone would imply as much. Scholarly studies of these inscriptions frequently remark that the sentiments expressed in epitaphs dedicated by women tend to be banal and ordinary, referring to the deceased in such general terms as "well-deserving." Similar conclusions have been reached about the sentiments commonly expressed in inscriptions about women who have died. Not only is it unlikely that these deceased women themselves played much of a role in deciding how they were to be remembered after their deaths; it is also highly probable that those who commemorate these women—the overwhelming majority of whom were men—were in these instances resorting to customary, socially acceptable and self-serving assertions about women's proper value and behavior.

Such misrepresentation even occurs in what appears to be the most realistic type of Roman funerary inscription: epitaphs which portray the deceased as speaking about himself or herself in the first person. By seeming to record the actual words of a dead individual, such epitaphs impart to their message an air of sincerity and poignant immediacy: they give the impression of being distinctive and authentic voices from the Roman past. Inscriptions of this sort which commemorate women may sound particularly affecting and genuine. An awkwardly phrased epitaph, written in verse, of a woman called Lesbia serves as a case in point.

Wayfarer, stand and weep, if there is any human feeling in you, When you look upon my buried and sorrowful bones. I whose ways were praised, and whose beauty was shown approval by Anchialus whom troubled affection makes weak. I am Lesbia, who alone have left enduring ways And because when living my life I was obedient in my duties.

Admittedly, this epitaph is no mass-produced effort, serviceable for all manner of Roman female gravestones, but a personalized composition. We can assume as much from the clumsy and repetitive language of these six lines, and from the four lines that follow, which disclose that this Lesbia, as her Greek name also implies, was a slave or former slave who shared her favors with two men, Anchialus and Spurius.

If you want to know my name, I am Lesbia, if you want those of my two lovers, Endearing Anchialus with the amiable man Spurius. But why do I look upon this? My bones are here in a container, Buried. Wayfarer, live while you may and farewell.

Still, despite its first-person style and complimentary words on her two male partners, this inscription is unlikely to have been commissioned, much less written, by this Lesbia before her death. Rather, her lover Anchialus—and perhaps her lover Spurius as well—seems to be paying her tribute. After all, such female conduct is rarely mentioned, much less in a positive light, on Roman funerary texts; it is much more plausible that Lesbia's lover(s) would commemorate her by acknowledging—as she herself would probably not—that she behaved much differently from the chaste, monogamous woman so often honored in other Roman epitaphs.

Significantly, however, the language employed and the qualities noted in this characterization of Lesbia have a great deal in common with the language conventionally used and traits ordinarily cited by men who praise dead female kin as monogamous, chaste and domestically devoted. Consider, for example, a lengthy epitaph of the late first century B.C., in which a well-born matron is touchingly eulogized by her husband of forty-one years. He describes his wife as "devoted to her home, good and chaste" as well as "obedient" and meriting "praises." "Obedience," "approved conduct" and "praiseworthiness" are listed along with "chastity," "woolmaking," and "fidelity" as the memorable attributes of another well-born woman, Murdia, in the funeral homage from her son. While the description of Lesbia in terms more appropriate for loftier and more respectable women seems at odds with the laudatory words of her two lovers, the language used to describe her can be explained as further evidence that one or both commissioned this epitaph, and did so as a self-serving effort. After all, we may argue that Lesbia's resemblance to socially esteemed women was emphasized so as to render her lover(s) more worthy in other men's eyes: if she is portrayed as displaying traits characteristic of well-born matrons, her display of virtue would enhance the image of the male(s) publicly connected with her. Such, moreover, seems the implication of the references to Anchialus as "endearing" as well as "weak from troubled affection," and to Spurius as "amiable." Why else acknowledge both her unions and the attractive qualities of the two men involved?

In sum, the limitations of our literary and inscriptional material on ancient Roman women strongly militate against compiling extensive data on even the most illustrious of their number. In particular, these limitations make the task of determining what any Roman woman actually thought and felt practically impossible. What information we can extract from these sources at most appears to be incidental male impressions of how female conduct intersected with masculine activities. Much of what these male authors report, moreover, may well be colored by individual self-interest, or conventional "prescriptive" notions of how women were ideally supposed to act.

Male Ideals and Assumptions

Instead of trying to recover the "lived reality" of Roman women from our own perspective we might do better to set our sights on recovering some of the varying male ideals, expectations, and assumptions informing Roman women's representations. For one thing, these Roman male ideals, expectations and assumptions are important objects of investigation in and of themselves. It also seems likely that such notions would inform the actual lives of women in a male-controlled social environment such as the patriarchal milieu of classical Rome; so, too, these notions seem to pervade the representations, and perhaps the lives, of women from widely differing social backgrounds—be they lowly born like the lamented Lesbia or exalted in rank like the younger Agrippina. Furthermore, careful readings of our sources—like our prior scrutiny of Seneca's advice on philosophical study to his mother, or of Lesbia's anomalous epitaph—often permit us to detect discrepancies between some of these male ideals and what is more likely to have been the reality in an individual case. And while the major Roman male notions of what should matter in women's lives bear clear resemblances to views held in subsequent Western societies such as our own, these attitudes differ enough in some respects from contemporary beliefs, both conservative and progressive, to deserve special consideration. Among these notions are the importance of blood family ties; the positive public association between women of all ranks and household activity; the idealized concept of marriage as a mutually affectionate partnership; and women's important role in influencing the next generation. Let us look at these four notions, examine how each notion affects the way in which Roman women were perceived to act, and finally see where these notions do and do not seem to coincide with what evidence suggests to have been Roman realities.

The Pull and Priority of Blood Family Ties

One might not expect blood relationships to have much importance in the lives of ancient Roman women, for Roman women of all social backgrounds tended to marry at a relatively early age: by their late teens and (in the case of many from imperial and elite households) often before that. The younger Pliny—nephew and adopted son of the elder—describes the tragic and untimely death of a well-born girl who had not yet reached the age of fourteen. He remarks that she was "already engaged to marry a young man, the day of the wedding was already fixed, and we had already received our invitations;" he himself claims to have grieved to hear the girl's father order the money he had intended to spend on wedding clothes, pearls and jewelry to be spent on funeral incense, ointment and spices. Similarly, Tacitus reports that the emperor Tiberius betrothed Nero's mother, the younger Agrippina, to Gnaeus Domitius in A.D. 28, when she was thirteen. Funeral inscriptions establish that women of the lower classes tended to wed, or, like Lesbia, at least enter into long-term sexual unions with men, at early ages as well. The epitaph of one Crispina identifies her as the nurse of two senators, and as the wife of Albus, with whom she lived for seventeen years. Yet she was only thirty years old when she died. The epitaph of a freeborn fourteen-year-old girl, Fabia Ionis, daughter of Lucius, refers to her as the "dearest female friend" of one M. Claudius Zosimus.

It would seem, moreover, that all Roman women of elite background could expect to marry at least once. Spinsterhood was not a choice, or even a possibility, for any well-born females except for the six Vestal Virgin priestesses. Few well-born Roman women are recorded as having chosen, or even as having much of a say in choosing, their husbands. A girl's parents or, as the case of the younger Agrippina illustrates, elder relatives took charge of such

arrangements, often with an eye to their own economic, political and social advantage rather than to the couple's mutual physical or emotional compatibility.

The younger Pliny, for example, writes his friend Junius Mauricius about his endeavors to find a husband for Junius' niece. While recommending one Minicius Acilianus, Pliny cites his own affection for the girl's late father Aruleius Rusticus, his eagerness to select a young man worthy to father Rusticus' grandchildren, and his view that Acilianus' good looks are a compensation of sorts for a bride's virginity. Yet he says nothing about the bride herself. It is not even clear that he was acquainted with her. Instead, he emphasizes the excellence of the young man's political prospects, and the virtues of his close kin, briefly noting his father's substantial means. Curiously, Pliny singles out a female relation of Acilianus, his mother's mother Serrana Procula, as one of his most outstanding kinfolk, "an example of upstanding conduct even among her upright fellow Paduans." Pliny's lack of interest in this bride-to-be does not indicate an indifference to the character traits of women, merely the low priority assigned to the individual personal qualities of marriageable Roman girls. Pliny's correspondence having to do with his own wife Calpurnia, whom he wed when he was in his forties and she in her teens, documents—as we shall see—that he cherished her precisely for her lack of individual qualities, for her total devotion to him and his ambitions. The personal attributes of the bride and groom do not even seem to have loomed as a factor in Tiberius' politically motivated matchmaking between the younger Agrippina and Gnaeus Domitius either, although one of them attests to their similar, unpleasant character traits. At Nero's birth, Suetonius tells us, Domitius allegedly said that "nothing could have been born from him and his wife unless it was hateful and a danger to the Roman state."

Nevertheless, notwithstanding the disregard for the mutual compatibility of prospective marital partners, Roman society held the institution of marriage in high esteem. The legal status of wife in particular conferred respectability. This is why cohabiting individuals of the lower social orders, such as Lesbia and her lovers, sought to give informal unions respectability by describing the women so involved in the language commonly used for sanctioned female marital conduct in legalized relationships. One woman of the Julio-Claudian family is said to have been eager for marriage as a desirable goal in and of itself, regardless of her prospective husband's identity. Tacitus tells us that the widowed elder Agrippina pleaded with Tiberius to give her a husband, maintaining that there was no other consolation to women of virtue than marriage. His source, he says, is the memoirs of this woman's own daughter, and thus may reflect some female thinking on the matter.

Admittedly, abundant testimony establishes the frequency of divorce among the Roman elite. Each of the Julio-Claudian emperors divorced at least one of his wives. Some, such as Augustus and Nero, themselves married divorcees. In eulogizing the woman to whom he had been wed for forty-one years, the author of the lengthy funerary inscription mentioned earlier comments that long lasting unions such as theirs were rare, and even notes that his wife had offered him a divorce when she proved unable to bear children. Still, it merits emphasis that the dissolution of so many Roman marriages may point to a weakness in individual marital relationships, and in the bond between Roman spouses generally, but not to low regard for the institution of marriage itself. Rather, divorces usually occurred so that one partner could marry someone else, and remarriage was common for the other partner. The Roman propensity for divorce, it can be argued, provides further evidence for the importance accorded marriage.

But marriage, as we have seen, also served a variety of key economic, political and social functions among the Roman elite. While begetting legitimate offspring to perpetuate the family was the most valued of these functions, it was far from the only one. The creation of alliances between families, and the benefits that such alliances brought to these families' quests for public distinction and material gain, loomed no less consequentially. For this reason the importance of Roman marriage did not result in the diminution of married women's ties to, or their identification with, their blood relations. Unlike many modern Western and nonwestern cultures, in which married women shift allegiances and identities primarily to the families of their husbands, classical Roman society accorded as much significance to women in their blood familial roles as in their wifely capacities. The early age of marriage for Roman women, which would tend to separate Roman brides physically from their fathers' households, makes the significance assigned to blood ties somewhat surprising and particularly noteworthy.

The Roman system of naming women itself encouraged women to be viewed as representatives of their blood families even after they had married, and remarried. Customarily a woman received and kept until her death the feminine form of her father's family name, with the result that she continued to be known by the same name as her father and brothers. The daughter of Marcus Antonius, for example, was called Antonia and hence publicly associated with her father and brother Iullus Antonius even after both men had died in public disgrace. During the principate of Augustus, some women began to receive the feminine forms not of their fathers', but of their mothers' fathers', names. Hence Augustus' intimate and son-in-law Agrippa had both a daughter and her daughter named Agrippina after him. Agrippa's wife Julia, daughter of Augustus (who was himself technically a member of the Julian family) was not only called Julia but had a daughter of that name as well. Although women known by the names of maternal grandfathers would not be readily identified with their fathers and paternal blood family, they would still be closely associated with maternal blood kin.

Roman authors also make it clear that married women were still regarded by others, and assumed to have regarded themselves, as daughters, sisters and granddaughters of their male blood relations. Sources indicate, too, that these blood familial roles were accorded considerable cultural significance. Tacitus, for example, tells us that the elder Agrippina initially refused to depart from her husband's side during his German military campaign, although she was herself pregnant and had with her their baby son (the future emperor Caligula). Agrippina stressed her descent from her maternal grandfather, Augustus, and was determined to behave in a manner worthy of him. When Agrippina finally agreed to leave, Tacitus continues, the soldiers felt particular sorrow as they reflected upon both her blood lineage, as daughter of Agrippa and granddaughter of Augustus, and her outstanding conduct as a wife and mother. Tacitus later credits the popular enthusiasm for Agrippina after her husband's death to regard for her as Augustus' "only blood descendant."

In consoling Marcia on the loss of her son, Seneca makes much of Marcia's devotion to her late father, Cremutius Cordus. By terming her love for studies "a virtue inherited from her father," Seneca points up her similarity to her father as well. Further on in this essay, Seneca recalls the grief suffered by Augustus' sister Octavia on the death of her own son Marcellus. Seneca observed that Octavia mourned so deeply for the rest of her life that "she would not even give a thought to her brother, and hated even the good fortune of her brother's greatness which shone around her." By the same token, Seneca's consoling words to his own mother, Helvia, claim that he would count Helvia's father among her great comforts if her father were not now absent. Seneca then urges Helvia to judge her survival for her father's sake more crucial than her sacrifice for the sake of himself, her son. When the younger Pliny writes about the failing health of his friend Fannia, he remarks that she has grown so weak that only "the courage and spirit most worthy of her husband and father survive." In another letter, Pliny maintains that he cherishes Corellia "with the highest reverence": first as sister of Corellius Rufus, then as close friend of his own mother, and lastly because he had strong ties with her husband and son.

The importance accorded to Roman women's ties with their blood kinsmen additionally emerges from sources who assign women major roles in Roman political affairs

as representatives of their blood families. Tacitus' *Annals* features several women, many of them married, whose conduct is said to have affected the public fortunes of their relations. The indictment of Aemilia Lepida, and her brother's futile attempts to defend her, earn substantial attention in Book 3. Tacitus refers to her condemnation with the words "the Aemilii had lost Lepida." Later in the same book Tacitus reports that a Vestal Virgin named Junia Torquata managed to secure from Tiberius a less bleak exile for her brother Junius Silanus, as a concession to the Junian family and to the man's former status as a senator. In Book 16, Tacitus describes how the teenaged Servilia, wife of the exiled Annius Pollio, was summoned before the senate on a charge of consulting magicians. This summons occurred when Servilia's father had been accused of subversive behavior toward the emperor Nero. Tacitus records the father's unsuccessful plea in his daughter's defense—that she was only guilty of too much familial devotion—and notes that both father and daughter were subsequently sentenced to death. In his consolation to Marcia, Seneca extols her for recovering her father's outlawed writings; he contends that the Roman state had endured a great loss until Marcia rescued her father's works from oblivion. In commemorating his esteemed wife, the author of the late first century B.C. funeral inscription cites her and her sister's successful efforts to avenge the deaths of their parents.

As Roman women's influence on *behalf* of their blood relations is represented by diverse sources, so is their influence with them. The younger Pliny attempts to ensure that his self-serving interpretation of why his young wife miscarried is accepted by the girl's grandfather Calpurnius Fabatus; thus he not only writes the old man himself, but even asks Calpurnius' own daughter to explain the accident to the old man. Seneca compares Marcia's power over her father, Cordus, to that of Cordus' accuser Sejanus: here Seneca says that Cordus had to beg with Sejanus if he wished to live, with his daughter if he wished to die. And as both Sejanus and Marcia proved inexorable, Cordus decided to deceive his daughter and commit suicide.

Women's influence with blood relations is portrayed as especially strong with those kinsmen who were their juniors and contemporaries—sons, grandsons and brothers. Seneca does not merely discuss Marcia's influence over her late son in the essay consoling her. He is one of many authors who invoke the deferential behavior shown by two leading political figures of the late second century B.C., the Gracchi, to their imperious mother, Cornelia. In his essay consoling his mother, Seneca points out that one of these sons even fulminated in the senate to one of Cornelia's detractors, "Would you speak ill of my mother, who bore me?" Suetonius' lives of several Caesars represent these men as subject to maternal pressures and eager not to disappoint their mothers' expectations, at various junctures in their political careers. For example, in his life of Julius Caesar, Suetonius reports that Caesar kissed his mother before his election for chief priest with the remark that he would not return home that day if he did not win. In his life of Tiberius, Suetonius acknowledges that Tiberius was sometimes in the habit of needing and exploiting the advice of his mother, Livia, but he did not wish others to think he was ruled by it. The life of Nero relates numerous instances of Nero's efforts to gratify his mother, among them the occasion when he even gave courtroom testimony against one of Agrippina's rivals, his father's sister. Tacitus similarly characterizes the relationship between Tiberius and Livia, and between Nero and the younger Agrippina, asserting that Tiberius retained a deep-rooted deference to his mother as long as she lived. The younger Pliny praises the upstanding ways of one Quadratus, grandson of the wealthy and indulgent Ummidia Quadratilia, and attributes the young man's disciplined self-conduct to his grandmother's insistence that he go away and work whenever she amused herself with games or live entertainment. Suetonius portrays the emperor Claudius as obeying his grandmother Livia as well as his mother, Antonia, in omitting the period of Rome's civil wars from his history of Rome.

Among the sisters depicted by our sources as exerting substantial influence over brothers are Augustus' sister Octavia and Domitia Lepida, sister of Nero's father Domitius Ahenobarbus. In his life of Mark Antony, Plutarch ascribes to Octavia, at the time she was married to Antony, her brother's decision to make peace with her husband. Plutarch also credits Octavia with Augustus' decision to marry his daughter Julia to Agrippa, even though it meant that Agrippa had to divorce Octavia's own daughter first. Suetonius represents Nero's father as teased by Domitia for defrauding charioteers during his praetorship; as a result, he changed the practice of awarding them prize money.

Warranting special emphasis in the importance assigned by Roman society to women's ties with blood kin is the fact that these ties were emotionally charged and highly sentimentalized, whether they involved women in their roles as daughter, sisters or mothers. One need only consider the way in which Seneca depicts various women bereaved of blood kin and seeking consolation from surviving blood relations, or the way in which he portrays various men bereaved of female blood relations in the *Consolation to Polybius*, an essay sympathizing with a male friend who has lost his brother. Seneca heads the list of the many losses endured by Augustus with that of his "dearest sister Octavia," and only then enumerates other deceased relatives, several of whom were Augustus' appointed political heirs. But the strong affect investing these blood bonds is just as apparent in situations which do not involve mourning and bereavement. The matron paid tribute by her husband of over four decades is said to have reared in her home several young female blood relations, even furnishing them with dowries so that they could attain a station worthy of their families. Tacitus relates that young Nero owed his fond feelings among the public to the fact that he was the sole male descendant, through his mother, of the beloved Germanicus; he additionally notes that Nero's mother invoked her role as daughter of Germanicus in challenging Seneca and Burrus, her son's advisers. Blood was not only regarded as all-important, far "thicker than water" in Roman eyes; it provided a basis for the strongest and most deeply felt affective ties. Women clearly acquired much of their social identity as a result of this cultural emphasis on blood relations, and hence were far more likely to be recognized publicly in their roles as daughters, sisters, mothers and grandmothers than are Western women today. They were, moreover, highly valued in these familial roles by both their own male kin and men outside their families.

The Positive, Public Association Between Roman Women and Domestic Activity

In the *Dialogue on Oratory*, Tacitus portrays one of the characters as lamenting the decline of traditional discipline in the education of children. During the Roman republic, this man maintains, "the son of every citizen, the child of a virtuous mother as well, was from the beginning reared not in the cubicle of a hired nurse, but in the lap and bosom of his mother, whose special praise it was to look after her home and devote herself to her children. . . ." Thus we learn that Cornelia, mother of Tiberius and Gaius Gracchus, Aurelia, mother of Julius Caesar, and Atia, mother of Augustus Caesar, took charge of their children's educations and provided sons who led the Roman state. The contrast between these models of domestic dedication and the women of his day is hence represented as both strong and consequential. Seneca, writing to his mother, makes the same point more explicitly, when he contends that many contemporary women devoted to the political futures of their sons do not dispense maternal solicitude in the context of virtuous domesticity and unselfish motives. Such mothers, he says, in the *Consolation to Helvia*, "make use of their sons' powers with female lack of self-control, who, because women are not allowed to achieve political honors themselves, seek power through their sons, who both drain their sons' inheritances and hope to inherit from them, who exhaust their eloquence in lending it

to others." Selfless dedication to care of the home and children was, as these passages indicate, an ideal which not all Roman women may have attained—and of which many were criticized of falling short. But even though a prescriptive rather than a descriptive notion about women, this ideal manifests itself in diverse Roman situations. Its prominence in our sources thus merits interest not only because most women failed to achieve it, but also because such prominence bespeaks a widely held perception that women should be defined and valued in terms of their ties to household responsibilities.

Suetonius relates that Augustus so educated his daughters and granddaughters that they even became familiar with the spinning and weaving of wool, and reports that Augustus customarily wore home-made clothing, woven by his sister, wife, daughter and granddaughters. The activities of spinning and weaving wool were regarded by Roman society as quintessentially feminine. Writing in the late republican period about different types of witticisms, Cicero records an insult to an effeminate man named Egilius which ran, "What about it, my dear Egilia? When are you coming to see me with your distaff and wool?" Such activities, moreover, were associated with women of all social classes, even those with staffs of slaves to perform tasks of this sort. Indeed, these tasks were invested with special social significance, as general symbols for women's devotion to the household.

We may observe the widespread use of woolworking as symbol for valued female behavior most clearly in epitaphs of women from different periods and classes. A funeral inscription of the second century B.C. says that the deceased, one Claudia, "loved her husband with all her heart, bore two sons, was charming in conversation and of gentle movement. She kept up her household, and made wool." The first century B.C. inscription by the husband commemorating his wife of forty-one years, which identifies the late woman as a wealthy aristocrat, nonetheless lists "devotion to woolmaking" among the attributes, such as chastity and obedience, that follow her description as "dedicated to her home." As we have seen, the funerary homage paid by Murdia's son includes "woolmaking" among his mother's key attributes as well. And in a lengthy poem written as a funerary tribute later in the imperial period, a freedwoman is said "to have never let wool drop from her hands without good reason." This comment, though, is made by her patron, who also pays tribute to her breasts, legs and fastidiousness in plucking hairs from her body, and who notes that she and her two young lovers peacefully shared the same household; indeed, this inscription and the epitaph of Lesbia discussed earlier are highly unusual in recognizing the multiple sexual partners of a Roman woman in a laudatory public context.

Devotion to housework, as symbolized by the working of wool, was, like chastity and obedience, publicly proclaimed as praiseworthy female conduct. Even the few sources we have mentioned establish that the association between women and wool-working figured in such prestigious forms of communication as imperial propaganda, commemorative monuments and literature of a serious political and philosophical aim. Western women today may be expected to have household responsibilities, but are not generally celebrated in public contexts (their own obituaries or even the published biographies of their male kinfolk) for undertaking these burdens. References to actual household tasks, such as cooking or ironing or cleaning, are rarely made in positive, public tributes. Roman society, however, stressed this connection between women and housework even in the case of women unlikely to have performed any tasks of this kind.

The Ideal of Marriage as a Mutually Affectionate Partnership

The younger Pliny wrote to the aunt of his young wife Calpurnia to describe Calpurnia's enthusiastic reaction to his own activities and to express the hope that their shared happiness will continue and grow. In eulogizing the woman to whom he was wed for forty-one years, the dedicator of the first century B.C. inscription also stresses the mutuality of their affection for and commitment to each other: the word *communis*, "shared," recurs frequently in the text, describing different aspects of their marriage. Epitaphs of more lowly Romans similarly characterize the marital relationship as a valued partnership. A pair marking the burial site of former slaves, whose separations from their blood kin would cause ties that were formed voluntarily to assume a strong emotional importance, serve as a case in point. The tombstones of the freedwoman Aurelia Philmatium and her husband indicate that she came to live with him at age seven, and hence viewed him as "more than a father." Nonetheless, their bond is characterized as "involving equal devotion on both sides."

This notion of husband and wife as forming a mutually sharing and caring partnership does not, however, signify the equality of the two partners: equality in Roman marriage seems more of an ideal than an achieved or even achievable reality. For one thing, the notion conflicts with what was apparently both an ideal and the reality of wifely deference and subordination. The Roman practice of marrying women at a relatively early age—to men several years their senior and of substantially greater worldly experience and formal education—would by itself have discouraged the achievement of true equality between husband and wife. In fact, the younger Pliny's letter in praise of his much younger wife, Calpurnia, reveals that he evidently regards her much elder aunt as an equal. He even mentions the guidance and encouragement this mature woman, who "respected his mother like a daughter," has given him since his boyhood. But, notwithstanding his reference to the mutual happiness he and Calpurnia share, Pliny defines Calpurnia's "devotion" and "worthiness" as her deferential willingness to admire his writings, law speeches, readings and poetry uncritically. Reporting her miscarriage, Pliny speaks of her to her aunt and grandfather in patronizing tones, claiming that she precipitated this misfortune through foolishness and ignorance.

Testimony to women's submission to their husbands, as both an ideal and a reality, abounds in Roman sources. Tacitus' obituary of Livia singles out her compliant behavior to Augustus. Suetonius even claims that Livia supplied her husband with virgins to deflower. Seneca, who stresses the equal endowment of various virtues in both sexes when consoling Marcia and his mother, Helvia, still admits that actual marital relationships are not conducive to equal partnerships between spouses. In his essay to Helvia, he recalls his father's adherence to traditional ways in limiting his mother's education in philosophy. What is more, he praises his mother's sister for self-effacing and self-sacrificial conduct toward her husband, to the point that she was never seen in public during the sixteen years when he served as governor of Egypt, and that she risked her own life to guarantee him burial.

Evidence on Roman divorces, and why they occurred, also suggests that many Roman husbands would not tolerate self-assertive, noncompliant behavior in their wives, even though wives were expected to show deference and tolerance to their husbands: to put it another way, caring and sharing between partners was not always mutual. Suetonius attributes Augustus' divorce from Scribonia, mother of his daughter Julia, to his intolerance of her merely "annoying ways." Suetonius also claims that this emperor divorced his second wife for offenses "of a trivial sort." Both Plutarch and Suetonius report that Caesar divorced his next-to-last wife, Pompeia, merely because he felt she should be beyond suspicions of adultery, and was not.

Mention of adultery, and of Augustus' wife Livia, remind us of another factor which militated against the realization of an affectively strong and equal marital partnership in classical Rome. Various sources imply that bonds of affection and physical attraction were quite likely to be found in extra-marital relations: the emotional, and physical, investment needed for mutual trust and respect in marriage was not always made by one, or both, partners simply because one of them might have an equally strong or stronger bond with an extra-marital lover. Suetonius' lives of the Caesars attest that virtually all of these leaders had extra-marital relationships; Claudius was even faulted for too

much devotion to his wives. Furthermore, Augustus' love for Livia—as several sources stress—began when she was the wife of another man; indeed, Augustus had this union dissolved, and married her, when she was several months pregnant, presumably by her husband. While it was not as easy for married women to carry on such liaisons as it was for married men, Livia's story alone—and that of Nero's second wife, Poppaea Sabina—make it apparent that politically powerful lovers could, with impunity, have their way with other men's wives. Tacitus' *Annals* indicate that extramarital liaisons were by no means limited to the imperial family, and were both common and tolerated even after Augustus issued legislation forbidding them. For example, Tacitus describes the deportation of the well-born Vistilia, whose husband had refrained from punishing her for the practice of prostitution; he also relates that the adulterous affair between Mutilia Prisca and Julius Postumus allowed the latter to be particularly effective as a slanderer, since his mistress exerted great influence over Livia. Obviously inscriptions about the couplings of more common people, such as the epitaph on Lesbia and her two lovers, document that multiple affectionate and emotionally charged sexual involvements were altogether compatible with the rhetoric of marital ideals; at the same time, they clearly point up the gap between monogamous ideal and physical reality, a gap still to be found in contemporary Western societies.

Evidence from all Roman social classes, moreover, establishes the strong affective ties between parents, particularly mothers, and children of both sexes. These ties, combined with the maternal influence we have previously noted, seem to have furnished Roman women with the potential for wielding authority in a context of mutual affection even if marital relationships did not. Even Augustus' ex-wife Scribonia, whose divorce had legally severed her and Julia from the time of her daughter's babyhood, accompanied the thirty-seven-year-old Julia into exile in 2 B.C. Seneca's consolations to both his mother and Marcia furnish memorable testimony to the powerful emotional bonds between mothers and children, not only those involving the two addressees and their offspring, but also those of numerous women cited by Seneca as examples. While a woman's relationship with her husband might have featured an unequal distribution of authority, respect, and even emotional solicitude, it seems likely that authority over children, and respect and caring from them, could compensate for any feelings of inferiority women derived from subordination to emotionally disengaged spouses.

Women's Important Role in Influencing the Next Generation

Many of the sources which we have examined so far establish that mature Roman women appear to have earned substantial respect from, and wielded influence with, men of a somewhat younger generation, be they men inside or outside of their own blood families. We have seen the younger Pliny recommending Minicius Acilianus as a marital prospect by citing Acilianus' grandmother as a model of propriety, and by implicitly linking her with her grandson's character. So, too, Pliny pays tribute to the guidance and support given him since his boyhood by his wife's aunt. It warrants note that Seneca compliments his mother's sister in his essay consoling his mother for supporting his own political career—and not merely for devoting herself to her husband. Seneca also pays homage to various other older women—Cornelia, mother of the Gracchi; Livia; Rutilia, mother of Aurelius Cotta—by mentioning them in his consolatory essays as examples of admirable behavior in times of sorrow. We have noted Tacitus speaking of the authority possessed by Livia and the younger Agrippina over their emperor sons. Tacitus also testifies to the importance accorded by Nero to his aunt Domitia Lepida, and to the claim—by the father of the future emperor Vitellius—of devoted efforts in behalf of Claudius' mother Antonia. The insistence by Ummidia Quadratilla that her grandson keep at a remove from her frivolous pastimes, reported by the younger Pliny, points to something even further: that the respect

given mature women and the influence they commanded with younger men carried with them responsibilities toward guiding the subsequent generation. Other authors suggest that women were expected to recognize the seriousness of these responsibilities. Certainly Seneca's consoling remarks to both Marcia and Helvia seek to remind these women that they have discharged these obligations well. Seneca stresses to the former that her son "shaped his studies beneath her eyes" and was of an outstanding ability, practically his grandfather's equal. Seneca emphasizes to the latter that she has limited her sons' own spending, although not her generosity to them, and that she did not use her sons' political influence—though she took pleasure and put much money into their careers.

The actual influence enjoyed by Roman women on men younger than themselves cannot, obviously, be measured. Even the fact that male sources ascribe such an impact to various women does not prove that such influence was wielded, merely that it was perceived. But it merits attention that certain sources attribute Roman women with exerting influence over men of a younger generation simply because Roman society valued the wisdom and experience of older males, and attributed just such influence over their juniors to mature males. This perception of women's influence, therefore, was one which assigned them the same positive social value as males.

Such female influence was, of course, expected to be exercised to good end, especially when the younger men in question were the woman's sons. As mothers in Western society today often incur blame for undesirable and disgraceful deeds committed by their offspring, so Roman authors have had harsh words for the mothers of the most disgracefully behaving political leaders. To be sure, Nero's mother, the younger Agrippina, is less favorably portrayed by such Roman sources as Tacitus and Suetonius than is her mother, the elder Agrippina. Yet the despicable conduct of the latter's son, Caligula, caused both women to be similarly categorized by the elder Pliny. For in the passage which describes the younger Agrippina's breach delivery, Pliny first characterizes her maternal grandfather, Agrippa, as also having entered the world feet first, and as having suffered from such a violation of nature in spite of a distinguished career. Agrippa, Pliny says, was not only lame, but also "lived amid arms and death;" in addition, Agrippa is said to have caused "misfortunes to the world through his offspring," especially through the two Agrippinas: after all, they gave birth to "the two firebrands of the human race, the emperor Caligula and Nero."

The repeated insistence, by various Roman sources, on mature women's influence in what might be termed "maternal" roles does not, we should observe, signify that Roman society devalued younger women or the familial roles they occupied. Indeed, it has been argued that Roman culture as a whole placed substantial emphasis on women in their roles as the daughters of their fathers, and that the value assigned women in this role served as a foundation for the respect they commanded as mature, maternal figures. We see this emphasis on the role of daughter in various cultural practices and institutions: the system of identifying women by the feminine form of their fathers' names; the legal stipulation that a married woman either remain under the control of her father and his male kin or in the control of her husband, with the inheritance rights of a daughter to his estate; in the

prominence accorded the Vestal Virgins, who were chosen for their thirty-year posts between the ages of six and ten; in various cherished legends about Rome's founding, which accorded central political importance to females—such as the Sabine women—in their roles as daughters. Obviously, too, Roman women were regarded as important in their capacities as wives, sexual partners, sisters and friends of men, and so regarded by the males who were their contemporaries.

This concept of Roman women as significant figures in many phases of their lives, and in many different familial and social relationships with males, further suggests that they were appreciated as diverse types of individuals. Roman society did not simply categorize women generally, as "the female sex," a monolithic group totally unlike men: in this way, Roman perceptions of women contrast with those of numerous other cultures before and since. Such recognition of these differences meant that Roman women were viewed from a range of different perspectives by men. While it would be far better for Roman women's perspectives on one another to have survived as well, at least these different male viewpoints enable us to recover images of women, and hints about women's reality, that are complex if not comprehensive.

Divorce and Adultery

Beryl Rawson

Dr. Beryl Rawson of the Australian National University is a leading scholar on Roman women and the Roman family. She here treats the public and private aspects of Roman divorce, as well as the laws concerning adultery and their erratic enforcement in the early Roman Empire.

Divorce procedure was probably as informal as that of marriage could be. The decision to separate could be unilateral—either partner or, sometimes, a partner's *paterfamilias*, could bring about the end of a marriage. A simple notification of intent to divorce was sufficient, and no cause need be given: on the whole, the concept of the 'guilty party' was not important. The causes for divorce which we can reconstruct are varied. We have seen that one reason for divorce could be a couple's failure to have children. (It seems to have been assumed that this was the woman's 'fault,' or deficiency, but such divorces seem to have taken place without public recrimination or unpleasantness. The psychological effect on women, however, cannot be assessed. For some it was no doubt a painful and humiliating experience, but others may have welcomed the new freedom it brought, especially as they would have their dowry returned to them and probably gifts from their husband as well.) Political reasons could dictate divorce as they could marriage alliances. In the field of morals, a wife's continuous adulterous behavior seems to have been the reason for some Republican men divorcing their wives (e.g. Lucullus's wife, Claudia, Pompey's wife, Metella). Wives (or their fathers) presumably took the initiative in obtaining a divorce in those cases recorded where the purpose was obviously a new marriage for the woman. The marriage of Sulla's stepdaughter, Aemilia, for instance, was dissolved so that she could marry Pompey and thus give a family basis to the political alliance between these two men. (She was already pregnant by her first husband, and died in childbirth within months of marrying Pompey.) Octavian (the later Augustus) was so anxious to marry Livia that she obtained her divorce while she was still pregnant by her first husband. Although Octavian no doubt put whatever pressure he could on Livia's husband, he had no legal standing in her divorce: she must have taken the initiative, formally or informally.

It is often claimed that there was a double standard for men and women at Rome with respect to adultery and that, because we have few specific references to wives divorcing their husbands on these grounds, wives must have accepted their husbands' adultery as a matter of course. This is possible. But we should remember in the first place that public reasons for divorce were not usually given, and that we do not always know who initiated the divorce. In the second place, it is possible that not many husbands gave their wives cause for complaint on this score—either they were uxorious husbands or discreet ones. It is at least worth noting that, except for Julius Caesar and some of the emperors, adulterous behaviour is not a common accusation hurled at prominent Roman men (even in a period when almost every conceivable kind of abuse was freely used), nor is there evidence of extra-marital affairs being carried on flagrantly in public.

Whatever the causes of divorce, they were normally the private business of the family concerned during the Republican period. Until Augustus, the state normally took no interest in divorce and the relations between married partners, except to recognize a husband's right to kill a wife and her lover if they were caught *in flagrante delicto*. Augustus's moral legislation in 18 B.C. severely restricted this right but made adultery a criminal offence, and a special court was established to hear prosecutions. If a husband had caught a wife in the act of adultery he was required to divorce her and then bring her to trial for adultery. This was his public duty. If he failed to do so, he made himself liable, with the guilty couple, to prosecution by any outsider. In other situations of adultery a husband could, if he chose, merely divorce and leave prosecution to others; or he could take no public action at all and this would protect his wife from outside prosecution. A woman could divorce her husband for extra-marital activities, and could on this count make more rigorous demands for restoration of dowry, but she could not initiate a criminal charge against him. The absolute obligation to divorce a partner caught in the act seems not to have applied to the wife of a guilty husband; but the realities of everyday life probably made such discovery most unlikely. Adultery was more likely to take place at the woman's home than at the man's.

Adultery (*adulterium*) strictly applied only to affairs with married women. There was another crime (for which the more general word came to be reserved) which covered fornication between unmarried 'respectable' women and married or unmarried men. (It also applied to male homosexuality.) The penalty for both crimes was usually exile. There was, then, some discrimination against women in these laws—they could be punished for affairs with slaves and low-class persons while men could not be. But the area of discrimination was much narrower than is sometimes suggested. Augustus's concern was not essentially to ensure the moral purity of marriages. If it had been, he could not have allowed a husband to continue living with a guilty wife. Nor is it clear to me that he particularly wanted to limit divorces (i.e. to strengthen the stability or duration of marriage). In some situations he now made divorce obligatory. His concern seems to have been rather to protect the 'purity,' or official legitimacy, of upper-class family descent. He aimed, first, to guard against married women bearing illegitimate children who would inherit an unsuspecting husband's name and property. (If the husband chose to acknowledge an illegitimate child as his own, that was all right, it kept the situation tidy in the state's eyes.) Second, he aimed to prevent women of good family producing children outside the conjugal family unit—

such children could not inherit a father's name or rank, they were under no paterfamilias, and would not fit naturally into the career structure of equestrian or senatorial families (the ones in whom Augustus surely was interested). In matters of legitimacy, it is the woman's situation that must first be legislated for: but Augustus's laws seldom let the male accomplice go unpunished. Augustus's concern for the orderly workings of public life, which led him to intrude the state into citizens' private lives, opened the way to informers and prosecutors, many of whom probably had political motivation to ruin a rival rather than moral aims of saving society.

Some emperors enforced the adultery law more strictly than others. There seems to have been strong public opinion (at least in the upper classes) against all of Augustus's moral legislation, and a number of women made their own protest in Tiberius's time by registering themselves officially as prostitutes so that the law would not apply to them (the crime of adultery did not apply to slave women or to women of ill repute such as prostitutes and actresses). The motive for this extraordinary action by women (apparently of rank) was surely women's liberation (to free women's private lives from intolerable interference by the state, and perhaps to claim for themselves the freedom granted to men to have 'disrespectable' liaisons without fear of punishment) rather than depraved lust. This seems not to have been an isolated example, because various lawyers recorded action taking account of this situation.

The independence of Roman wives—but also their separateness from their husband's family—is highlighted by the absence of any concept of alimony (beyond restitution of dowry). As we shall see below, the husband almost certainly retained the children of the marriage, so the divorced wife was very much 'on her own.' The effects of this on female attitudes and behaviour should be studied more closely. If a divorced woman found that she was pregnant soon after the divorce, her ex-husband had some rights and obligations towards her; but these were in the direction of his relationship to the child to be born, rather than assisting his former wife financially or otherwise. Certain rules of procedure were laid down, and the father seems to have had the right—and probably the duty—to recognize the newborn child as an heir. As there is no reference to the cause of a divorce in this part of the legal code, and as the idea of 'the guilty party' does not play an important part in Roman divorce, the question of the 'most fit' parent was probably irrelevant to the matter of custody. In fact, a passage in Cicero suggests that a guilty husband would nevertheless keep the children: he would simply have no claims on his wife's dowry for their financial support. Children already born or conceived at the time of divorce belonged to the father in the eyes of the law; they were members of his family rather than of their mother's, they bore his name, and in most circumstances he could retain part of his wife's dowry for the children's maintenance. The father's rights have continued to be strong in western society, until in the twentieth century there developed a belief in the mother's greater fitness to rear a child and in the child's greater need of the female parent. The psychology behind this is changing again, but there was a period when the mother's biological and nurturing functions seemed to give her greater claims to custody. For the Romans, mother and father were equally parents in the natural sense. . . . The Roman family, however, was far more than a biological unit: it was a social and sometimes political unit, and it was important for society (and probably for the individual) to know to whose family the child 'belonged.' The *nomen* (i.e. the inherited family name) determined this. (Illegitimate children belonged to the mother's family on this criterion.)

Perhaps the apparently greater number of references to stepmothers than to stepfathers also reflects the fact that children of a dissolved marriage usually lived with their father (and thus the step-parent, if any, was a stepmother). The stepmother in most periods of history has suffered a bad reputation, and this was true in Rome too, though not uniformly. There were no doubt tensions also between stepfathers and their wives' children. Although widows probably normally raised their own children, they did not inherit the father's role in any legal sense: they had no *potestas* (legal power) over their children. It would be useful to have a thorough examination of all the broken marriages of which we have a record to determine if there is a pattern in the destination of the children of these marriages.

As divorce procedure was so simple in Rome, and did not involve the expensive services of lawyers, the poor might have divorced one another as easily as the rich. In this, Roman society was different from most modern societies, where divorce has been a middle- and upper-class luxury. But even at Rome there may have been financial restrictions on poor couples' freedom to separate. If there were children, it may have required the earnings of both parents living together to support them. On the other hand, many members of the lower-class population who are attested were ex-slaves, and of these many had specialized skills: women of this kind were not dependent on their husbands for financial support and were thus more free to leave them than most wives have been until the twentieth-century phenomenon of the wage-earning wife. But if divorce was frequent in the lower classes we have no record of it. Moreover, as explained above, many of the couples in this sector of the population were probably living in *de facto* rather than legal marriages, because of the slave status of at least one partner at the time the union began. Thus divorce did not technically apply.

The Roman Matron

Sarah Pomeroy

Professor Sarah Pomeroy of Hunter College, the City University of New York, wrote the first survey of women in the Greek and Roman world, Goddesses, Whores, Wives and Slaves: Women in Classical Antiquity *(1975). In an excerpt from this book, Pomeroy discusses the "Facts of Life" known to a Roman matron as well as the possibilities of intellectual achievement open to a small group of the elite.*

Facts of Birth, Life, and Death

Marriage and motherhood were the traditional expectation of well-to-do women in Rome.... The rarity of spinsters indicates that most women married at least once, although afterward a number . . . remain[ed] divorcees or widows.

Augustus established the minimum age for marriage at twelve for girls and fourteen for boys. The first marriage of most girls took place between the ages of twelve and fifteen. Since menarche typically occurred at thirteen or fourteen, prepubescent marriages [were likely to have] taken place.... Marriages of young girls took place because of the desire of the families involved not to delay the profit from a political or financial alliance and, beginning with the reign of Augustus, so that the bride and groom could reap the rewards of the marital legislation, although some of the benefits could be anticipated during the engagement. Sometimes one motive outweighed another. Thus there are cases of dowerless daughters of the upper class who nevertheless found social-climbing men so eager to marry them that the husbands surreptitiously provided the dowry, to save the pride of the girl's family. Another factor . . . [influencing Roman marriage patterns] was the desire to find a bride who was still [a] virgin.

Most upper-class Roman women were able to find husbands, not only for first marriages but for successive remarriages. One reason for this, apparently, was that there were fewer females than males among their social peers.... This disproportion was the result of the shorter lifespan of females, whose numbers fell off sharply once the childbearing years were reached. There were the additional factors of the selective infanticide and exposure of female infants and, probably more important, a subtle but pervasive attitude that gave preferential treatment to boys. This can be surmised from a law attributed to Romulus that required a father to raise all male children but only the first-born female. This so-called law of Romulus—while not to be accepted at face value as evidence that every father regularly raised only one daughter—is nevertheless indicative of official policy and foreshadows later legislation favoring the rearing of boys over girls. The attitude may be criticized as short-sighted in face of the manpower shortage continually threatening Rome....

The law of Romulus incidentally shows that it was not inconvenient for a daughter to be automatically called by the feminine form of her father's name (*nomen*). But it was awkward when the father decided to raise two daughters, who thus had the same name, like Cornelia and her sister Cornelia. The Romans solved the problem with the addition of "the elder" (*maior*) or "the younger" (*minor*). In families where several daughters were raised, numerals, which in earlier times may have been indicative of order of birth, were added (e.g., Claudia *Tertia* and Claudia *Quinta*). A wealthy father might decide to dispose of an infant because of the desire not to divide the family property among too many offspring and thereby reduce the individual wealth of the members of the next generation. Christian authors such as Justin Martyr doubtless exaggerated the extent to which contemporary pagans engaged in infanticide, but, on the other hand, it is clear that this method of family planning was practiced without much fanfare in antiquity. An infant of either sex who appeared weak might be exposed. In *Gynecology* Soranus, a physician of the second century A.D., gives a list of criteria by which midwives were to recognize which newborns should be discarded and which were worth rearing. In deciding to expose a daughter, the provision of a dowry was an additional consideration. However, there was enough of a demand for brides, as we have mentioned, to make even the occasional dowerless bride acceptable.

Additional evidence for a dearth of females in the upper classes is that in the late Republic some men were marrying women of the lower classes. We know of no spinsters, yet upper-class women are not known to have taken husbands from the lower classes. Studies of tombstones generally show far more males than females. This disproportion is usually explained away by the comment that males were deemed more deserving of commemoration. Such a factor might discourage the erection of tombstones for those low on the social scale, but at least among the wealthier classes—the very group where small families were the trend—we could expect that, once having decided to raise a daughter, her parents would commemorate her death. In our present state of knowledge we cannot finally say that women were actually present in Rome in the numbers one expects in an average preindustrial society, and that their lack of adequate representation in the sepulchral inscriptions is totally ascribable to their social invisibility; but it should be noted that the existence of masses of women who are not recorded by the inscriptions is, at most, hypothetical.

The traditional doctrine, enforced by Roman censors, was that men should marry, and that the purpose of marriage was the rearing of children. . . . A decrease in fecundity is discernible as early as the second century B.C., a time when the production of twelve children by Cornelia became a prodigy—probably because her son Gaius harped on it—although only three lived to adulthood. Metellus Macedonicus, censor in 131 B.C., made a speech urging men to marry and procreate, although he recognized that wives were troublesome creatures. The speech was read out to the Senate by Augustus as evidence that he was merely reviving Roman traditions with his legislation.

Augustus' legislation was designed to keep as many women as possible in the married state and bearing children. The penalties for nonmarriage and childlessness began for women at age twenty, for men at twenty-five. Divorce was not explicitly frowned upon, provided that each successive husband was recruited from the approved social class. Failure to remarry was penalized, all with a view to not wasting the childbearing years. Women were not able to escape the penalties of the Augustan legislation as easily as men. A man who was betrothed to a girl of ten could enjoy the political and economic privileges accorded to married men, but a woman was not permitted to betroth herself to a prepubescent male.

But the low birth rate continued, and the Augustan legislation on marriage was reinforced by Domitian and reenacted in the second and third centuries A.D. It appears that women as well as men were rebelling against biologically determined roles. One reason for the low birth rate was the practice of contraception.

Not only infanticide and neglect of infants, but contraception and abortion were used by the married Romans to limit their families, and by unmarried and adulterous women to prevent or terminate illegitimate pregnancies. Among the upper classes, the essential element in contraception—the wish not to have children—was present. Contraception was obviously preferable to abortion and infanticide, since the mother did not endure the burden and dangers of pregnancy and childbirth. There was a long tradition of medical and scientific writing on contraception and abortion, but most of our evidence comes from authors of the early Empire, who collected earlier knowledge and added their own recommendations.

Techniques for contraception were numerous; some were effective, more not. Among the ineffective were potions drunk for temporary or permanent sterility, which could, of course, be administered to unsuspecting parties to render them infertile. Amulets and magic were recommended. Pliny gives a recipe for fabricating an amulet by cutting open the head of a hairy spider, removing the two little worms which were believed to be inside and tying them in deerskin. Aetius recommends wearing the liver of a cat in a tube on the left foot, or part of a lioness' womb in an ivory tube. It was also thought possible to transfer the qualities of the sterile willow or of sterile iron for contraception.

The rhythm method was also practiced, but this was ineffective since the medical writers believed that the most fertile time was just when menstruation was ending, as that is when the appetite was said to be strongest. Conversely, it was thought that conception was not likely to occur when the woman did not have a desire for intercourse. Among other contraceptive techniques mentioned are for the woman to hold her breath at ejaculation, and post-coitally to squat, sneeze, and drink something cold. Lucretius recommends that whores, but not wives, should wriggle their hips and so divert the plow and the seed.

Mixed with ineffective techniques were effective methods, including the use of occlusive agents which blocked the os of the uterus. Oils, ointment, honey, and soft wool were employed.

Contraception was overwhelmingly left to women, but a few male techniques were recommended. Certain ointments smeared on the male genitals were thought to be effective as spermicides or as astringents to close the os of the uterus upon penetration. The bladder of a goat may have been used as an early version of a condom, although this item would have been costly. Whether men practiced coitus interruptus is debatable. The sources do not mention this technique. Two explanations for this omission are equally plausible, but mutually inconsistent: coitus interruptus is not mentioned either because it was not used, or, more likely, because it was so much used and so obvious that it needed no description.

Abortion is closely associated with contraception in the ancient sources, and sometimes confused with it. Keith Hopkins suggests that the reason for the blurring of abortion and contraception was the lack of precise knowledge of the period of gestation. Some Romans believed that children could be born seven to ten months after conception, but that eight-month babies were not possible. A contributing factor in the failure to distinguish between contraception and abortion was that some of the same drugs were recommended for both. Abortion was also accomplished by professional surgical instruments or by amateur methods. Ovid upbraids Corinna: "Why do you dig out your child with sharp instruments, and give harsh poisons to your unborn children."

The musings of philosophers on when the foetus felt life and whether abortion was sanctionable will not be reviewed. In a society where newborns were exposed, the foetus cannot have had much right to life, although it is true that in the early Empire the execution of a pregnant women was delayed until after the birth of her child. Literary testimony, including Seneca, Juvenal, and Ovid, shows both that some men were dismayed about abortions and that some upper-class women and courtesans had them. Not until the reign of Septimius Severus was any legislation enacted curtailing abortion, and this was merely to decree the punishment of exile for a divorced woman who has an abortion without her recent husband's consent, since she has cheated him of his child. In the reign of Caracalla, the penalty of exile (and death if the patient died) was established for administering abortifacients, but this law was directed against those who traded in drugs and magic rather than against abortion itself.

Medical writers were concerned as well with methods of promoting fertility in sterile women and with childbirth. The writings of Soranus, a physician of the second century A.D., cover a sophisticated range of gynecological and obstetrical topics. He did not adhere to the Hippocratic Oath which forbade administering abortifacients, but stated his preference for contraception. At a time when wealthy women usually employed wetnurses, Soranus declared that if the mother was in good health, it was better that she nurse the child, since it would foster the bonds of affection. Of interest are his recommendations for the alleviation of labor pains, his concern for the comfort of the mother, and his unequivocal decision that the welfare of the mother take precedence over that of the infant. In childbirth, most women who could afford professional assistance would summon a midwife, although if the procedure was beyond the midwife's ability, and funds were available, a male physician would be employed. In Rome the skilled midwives, like the physicians, were likely to be Greek. Midwives not only delivered babies, but were involved in abortions and other gynecological procedures, and as we have mentioned, they were supposed to be able to recognize which infants were healthy enough to be worth rearing.

Women—even wealthy women with access to physicians—continued to die in childbirth. Early marriage, and the resultant bearing of children by immature females, was a contributing factor. Tombstones show a marked increase in female mortality in the fifteen-to-twenty-nine-year-old group. In a study of the sepulchral inscriptions, Keith Hopkins claims that death in childbirth is to some extent exaggerated by the reliance upon evidence from tombstones. He suggests that women dying between fifteen and twenty-nine were more likely to be commemorated, because their husbands were still alive to erect tombstones. In his sample he found that the median age for the death of wives was 34; of husbands, 46.5. J. Lawrence Angel's study of skeletal remains in Greece under Roman domination shows an adult longevity of 34.3 years for women and 40.2 for men. Stepmothers are mentioned more than stepfathers, though this may reflect not only early death of mothers but the fact that children stayed with their father after divorce. . . .

Education and Accomplishments

Upper-class women were sufficiently cultivated to be able to participate in the intellectual life of their male associates. A little is known about how girls received their education. The story of Verginia indicates that it was not unusual for the daughter of a lowly plebeian centurion to attend elementary school in the Forum. Both daughters and sons of well-to-do families had private tutors. Pliny the Younger, a senator and author

active in government at the end of the first and the beginning of the second centuries A.D., included in his portrait of a girl who died at thirteen, just before she was to be married:

How she loved her nurses, her preceptors, and her teachers, each for the service given her. She studied her books with diligence and understanding.

Unlike boys, girls did not study with philosophers or rhetoricians outside the home, for they were married at the age when boys were still involved in their pursuit of higher education. Some women were influenced by an intellectual atmosphere at home. Ancient authors give the credit to fathers of girls, as they had to mothers of talented boys. Cornelia, we are told, acquired her taste for literature from her father, Scipio Africanus, noted for his philhellenism. (Cornelia's mother. . . was famous for her displays of wealth.) The eloquence of Laelia and Hortensia was a tribute to their fathers, who were leading orators.

Intellectual and artistic achievements did not endanger a woman's reputation; instead, education and accomplishments were thought to enhance her. Plutarch, in a lost work, discussed the education of women. He wrote in complimentary terms of many women: for example, of Cornelia, the last wife of Pompey, who was particularly charming because she was well read, could play the lyre, and was adept at geometry and philosophy. Pliny the Younger was pleased that his unsophisticated young wife was memorizing his writings, and was setting his verses to music and singing them to the accompaniment of the lyre. Quintilian recommended that for the good of the child both parents be as highly educated as possible. The Stoic Musonius Rufus asserted that women should be given the same education as men, for the attributes of a good wife will appear in one who studies philosophy.

Epictetus, a pupil of Musonius Rufus, reported that at Rome women were carrying around copies of Plato's *Republic* because they supposed he prescribed communities of wives. Women, he noted, were quoting Plato to justify their own licentiousness, but they misinterpreted the philosopher in supposing that he bid people have monogamous marriages first and then practice promiscuous intercourse. Although the Romans saw no essential connection between freedom and education, it was obvious that many cultivated women were also enjoying sexual liberty. Sallust gives a detailed description of the aristocrat Sempronia, who is probably faulted as much for her connection with the conspirator Catiline as for her lack of inhibitions:

Now among these women was Sempronia, who had often committed many crimes of masculine daring. This woman was quite fortunate in her family and looks, and especially in her husband and children; she was well read in Greek and Latin literature, able to play the lyre and dance more adeptly than any respectable woman would have need to, and talented in many other activities which are part and parcel of overindulgent living. But she cherished everything else more than she did propriety and morality; you would have a hard time determining which she squandered more of, her money or her reputation; her sexual desires were so ardent that she took the initiative with men far more frequently than they did with her. Prior to the conspiracy she had often broken her word, disavowed her debts, been involved in murder, and sunk to the depths of depravity as a result of high living and low funds. Yet she possessed intellectual strengths which are by no means laughable: the skill of writing verses, cracking jokes, speaking either modestly or tenderly or saucily—in a word, she had much wit and charm.

The women addressed by the elegiac poets not only possessed the usual attractions of mistresses, but were learned as well. They could be of any class: courtesans or freedwomen or upper-class wives, widows, or divorceés. In any case, they were free to make liaisons with whomever they chose. The poets were drawn to women who would appreciate their work, which was crammed with erudite literary allusions. Catullus called his mistress by the pseudonym Lesbia, while Ovid's poems are addressed to Corinna, both poets alluding to venerated Greek poetesses. Delia and Cynthia, the names given to their mistresses by Tibullus and Propertius, are suggestive of Apollonian inspiration and the Greek poetic tradition.

On the other hand, Juvenal's criticisms make it clear that the bluestocking was not rare:

Still more exasperating is the woman who begs as soon as she sits down to dinner, to discourse on poets and poetry, comparing Virgil with Homer: professors, critics, lawyers, auctioneers—even another woman—can't get a word in. She rattles on at such a rate that you'd think all the pots and pans in the kitchen were crashing to the floor or that every bell in town was clanging. All by herself she makes as much noise as some primitive tribe chasing away an eclipse. She should learn the philosophers' lesson: "moderation is necessary even for intellectuals." And, if she still wants to appear educated and eloquent, let her dress as a man, sacrifice to men's gods, and bathe in the men's baths. Wives shouldn't try to be public speakers; they shouldn't use rhetorical devices; they shouldn't read all the classics—there ought to be some things women don't understand. I myself can't understand a woman who can quote the rules of grammar and never make a mistake and cites obscure, long-forgotten poets—as if men cared about such things. If she has to correct somebody, let her correct her girl friends and leave her husband alone.

Livia

J. P. V. D. Balsdon

The late J. P. V. D. Balsdon of Exeter College, Oxford, provides a portrait of Livia which defends her against the slanders of Tacitus and other ancient writers. Her intelligence and toughness have never been questioned, but Balsdon argues that she also exercised a humanizing influence on her husband Augustus, and that her kindness towards others can be detected even in the prevailing hostility of the misogynist sources.

Few women of real nobility have received such venemous treatment from historians as Livia has received, in particular from Tacitus. Little account was taken of the large contribution which she made to the achievement of Augustus; no account at all was taken of the fact that she was the mother of Drusus, whom posterity idolized, and the grandmother of Germanicus, who was a greater idol still. In the tradition which Tacitus followed and, to which he added his own poisonous distortions, her crime lay in the fact that she was Tiberius' mother. But for his mother, Tiberius might never have been Emperor: that was the fantasy. And, as fantasies take no account of facts, she was described as a Lucrezia Borgia of a woman, who secured the Empire for her son by removing those who stood in his way—Lucius Caesar, Gaius Caesar, Germanicus, and Agrippa Postumus. It was even suggested that she hastened Augustus' end in A.D. 14. All these allegations were as untrue as they were malicious. Gaius and Lucius Caesar and Germanicus certainly died natural deaths; and, if Agrippa Postumus was murdered, Livia had no part in the murder. Tacitus, at his irresponsible worst, reported the slanders, careless whether he described them as rumours or as facts.

If regard is had to the indisputable facts of her life, a very different picture emerges. It is one which Claudius by his acts and the less sensational writers, Valerius Maximus and Velleius Paterculus and Seneca, by their writings, confirm.

Livia's devotion to Augustus, and his devotion to her, were beyond dispute. In their younger years she tolerated, even encouraged, his acts of unfaithfulness, whether it was a stray virgin or Terentia, the wife . . . of his minister Maecenas, who was needed to satisfy his fancy. She nursed him in his numerous and, in his early years, serious illnesses. In a great part of his life he depended on her, and occasions must have been numerous when he sought her advice, even, on serious matters, arriving with written notes of the subjects which he wanted to discuss. This was a subject, naturally, on which Augustus gave no information to the world; and so, in accordance with its own nature, the world made guesses. The sinister critics who, after more than a century, satisfied Tacitus' venomous taste, were prepared to state for fact that Augustus had decided to build up Germanicus and not Tiberius as his successor in A.D. 4, but that Livia persuaded him to change his mind. Wiser people realized that throughout her life her influence on Augustus was likely to have been a humanizing influence; and at some time or other, after they were both dead, this topic was made the subject for free imaginative composition by some educationalist or other. The result was a long discussion, in fact almost a monologue, in which Livia's part was Portia's, her pleading that 'the quality of mercy is not strained.' Forestall a conspirator by winning his respect and affection, not by cutting off his head. This plausible composition was happily preserved and served up for consumption as a piece of true history. It is recorded by Seneca in his *De Clementia* and, at inordinate length, by the loquacious Cassius Dio.

It . . . happened in bed as Augustus tossed sleepless, disturbed by the thought of yet another conspirator to be dispatched. This was Cn. Cornelius Cinna, grandson both of Cinna, the opponent of Sulla, and of Pompey the Great, consul later in A.D. 5. He was detected but, thanks to Livia's intervention, his life was saved. According to Seneca (whose dating is certainly wrong) this happened in Gaul between 16 and 13 B.C.: according to Dio's even more dramatic account, Cinna was arrested in Rome in A.D. 4. Next morning he appeared before the Emperor to receive his sentence. Augustus said, 'I will not only spare you, but will show my confidence in you by making you consul for this very next year.' He should have added, 'You have my wife to thank for this.'

Livia's beauty, which she retained, became with time a somewhat austere beauty; and, though in private she relaxed to a greater degree than convention would once have allowed, she encouraged austerity as well as traditional Roman decorum in the household over which she presided; and she paid high regard to dignity in her public appearances. 'She has the beauty of Venus, the character of Juno'; and for once Ovid's flattery was not altogether inept. Within the family and outside it, she displayed imaginative generosity; for all her brusqueness, she was kind—and even, when she restrained one of his rash literary projects, helpful—to her singularly unprepossessing young grandson Claudius, and she perhaps realized that the boy was not the fool that others thought him. For it is not without significance that, in marrying Plautia Urgulanilla, he married the grand-daughter of one of her most intimate friends. She lived on affectionate terms with her daughter-in-law Antonia, who moved into her house when her husband Drusus died. She even showed pity to her stepdaughter Julia, and did all that she could to alleviate the harsh conditions of her exile: a fact which Tacitus felt bound to record but, naturally, not without a vicious comment. When her son was Emperor, she intervened more than once to save her friends whose husbands were in trouble.

She had, it must be admitted, little interest in culture, and she had no sympathy with emotional weakness. When her son Drusus died, she acknowledged the help which she received from Augustus' philosopher Arcus; but her own native stoicism perhaps counted for as much as his good advice. She had despised Octavia's parade of sorrow when Marcellus died; Livia trampled on her own grief, and showed a smiling face to the world. She was a tough woman, in fact; and so were the women whom she made her friends.

That the public, while finding much in her to respect, never took her to its heart, is understandable. She never sought popularity for herself; she was content to live in the shadow of her husband.

In A.D. 14, when she was seventy years old, he died. Fifteen years of life lay ahead for her, and a new part to play, the part of Dowager-Empress, of Empress-Mother.

She left the palace, naturally; but she had in Rome two houses of her own. One on the Palatine, the so-called 'house of Livia,' is still open to tourists who can even gaze at her pictures on the walls—of Hermes, Argus and Io and of Polyphemus and Galatea. Her name, IVLIAE AVG., is perhaps to be read on one of the drainpipes. It is a modest house, and perhaps it came to her from Augustus. Her other house was a villa at Prima Porta on the way to Veii, nine miles north of Rome on the via Flaminia, known as 'a Gallinas ad primam portam.' This was where the laurel twig held in the beak of a hen (gallina) which an eagle dropped in her lap in 37 B.C. had been planted and had grown into a splendid shrub, from which on triumphal days the laurels were plucked for Augustus'—and indeed for his successors'—wearing.

Thanks to the genius of Italian archaeologists, the wall-paintings of her dining-room have been skimmed off and re-set in the Musco Nazionale in Rome. Here is a woodland glade round four sides of the room, green and bosky, with flowers and with birds galore. But they are small birds, not hens; and the trees are fruit trees, not laurels. There is a lot of fruit on the trees and that—it is made clear—explains the birds. Nowadays the cacciatori would have had them, every one.

She was accustomed to a life of intense business activity, for she was immensely rich, owning property in Asia Minor, Gaul and Palestine as well as in many parts of Italy, and she had complete independence in its administration, for she had been freed from patria potestas in 35 B.C., granted the rights of a mother of three children in 9 B.C. and, on Augustus' death, was exempt from the operation of the law (*lex Voconia*) which restricted the amount which a woman might receive in inheritance. Her personal staff of over a thousand included Burrus, who was later to hold office as Commander of the Praetorian Guard under Claudius and Nero. The extent of her wealth is indicated by the fact that her bequest to Galba (the later Emperor), when she died, was one of fifty million sesterces.

In Roman society she preserved her status as First Lady, for the Emperor Tiberius was a widower.

What of her position in the state?

First of all, she was adopted into the imperial family, and she became not merely Julia but Julia Augusta. The adoption and the title were Augustus' last gifts to her, under his will. And when Augustus was consecrated, she was appointed first Priestess of his cult and given the right, in that capacity, to be accompanied by a public servant (*lictor*) when she appeared in public in Rome.

For the rest, a protocol had to be established; and in the first meeting which the Senate held after Augustus' funeral and consecration, specious flattery and a mischievous desire to embarrass Tiberius combined in a series of awkward proposals: that, as Augustus had been given the title of 'Father of his Country,' his widow should now be called 'Mother of her Country' (*Mater Patriae*); that the Emperor himself, already called 'the son of divine Augustus' should be called, too, 'the son of Julia.' Tiberius acted correctly in refusing to accept these suggestions; he did not want the Julian family at Rome to model itself on the practices of the defunct Hellenistic kingdoms.

Augusta's position, of course, called for recognition. She held levées in her own right, and the names of those who attended them were published. The various priestly colleges celebrated her birthday, and her name was included in the annual vows which were taken for the welfare of the Emperor. Before Augustus had been dead many months, a request came from Gytheion in the Peloponnese for permission to institute an extensive cult to divine Augustus and to living members of the imperial house. Tiberius gave a ruling on the application except in as far as his mother was concerned; in that case he left the decision to her. In A.D. 23 the province of Asia was allowed to erect a temple to a curious and unexampled trinity: Tiberius, his mother and the Senate.

In public the relations of Augusta and the Emperor were studiously correct. Tiberius always spoke of his mother with respect and in public he deferred to her wishes. Nor have we any reason to think that in private she sought to impose her will on him and to determine public policy, or that she even claimed a right to be consulted by him on affairs of state. There is no evidence whatever to support the allegations which Tacitus repeats so smoothly: that she wanted a share in the government, or that she claimed that Tiberius was under an obligation to her, since it was to her that he owed his title of Emperor.

It must not be forgotten that Augusta was becoming a very old lady, and she may never have recovered completely from the serious illness which she suffered in A.D. 22. She was never effusively affectionate and it may well have been the case that even she could not penetrate the hard shell of Tiberius' reserve. Up to the time of her illness in 22, Tacitus himself admits that they got on well together; after this the growth of Tiberius' infatuation for Sejanus—an indication in itself of his personal loneliness—may have injured his close relationship with his mother. We hear nothing of Livia's attitude to Sejanus, or of his attitude to her; and this silence of our sources is interesting, and may well be significant. Certainly Augusta must have been aware that, as the years passed, Tiberius was growing more and more unpopular at Rome, and that she inevitably shared a part of his unpopularity. Whether she tried to warn him, and whether his self-imposed relegation to Capri had, from Sejanus' point of view, the advantage that it broke contact between them, we cannot know and we should be unwise even to guess. Tacitus' suggestion that Tiberius went to Capri with the object of escaping from her dominating influence is both poisonous and silly.

She must have derived great comfort from the affection of her daughter-in-law Antonia, a woman as busy as herself and occupied, like herself, both in the administration of her private property and in attending to the interest of innumerable clients and friends.

Tiberius is portrayed on a large brass coin issued at Rome. The legend (CAESAR DIVI AVG F AVGVST IMP VIII: "Tiberius Caesar Augustus, the son of deified Augustus, proclaimed imperator eight times") provides scholars with a date of A.D. 22–23.

VI

The Reign of Tiberius

INTRODUCTION
Ronald Mellor

Tiberius was born in 42 B.C. and, when his mother married Octavian four years later, he became the stepson of the future emperor Augustus. For decades he served Augustus well on military and diplomatic missions, but he was not seriously considered for the succession. It was only after the deaths of Marcellus and Agrippa that Tiberius was induced to divorce his beloved wife Vipsania and marry Julia to become Augustus' third son-in-law He was to serve as stepfather and guardian for Gaius and Lucius Caesar, whom Augustus intended to be his successors. The marriage was deeply unhappy and the proud, embittered Tiberius withdrew for eight years to the Greek island of Rhodes. In A.D. 2 he returned to Rome where Augustus, after the death of his grandsons, reluctantly invested Tiberius with imperial power and thus designated him for the succession.

The death of Augustus in A.D. 14 brought Tiberius to the throne. He had had an outstanding public career, leading Rome's armies on the northern frontiers, suppressing a military revolt in the Balkans, restoring Roman authority on the Rhine after the annihilation of Varus' three legions in A.D. 9, and negotiating the return of captured Roman standards from the Parthian kings. But despite these public triumphs, Tiberius was a reserved and introspective person. He certainly lacked the personal charm and public charisma of Augustus, as well as the affability of his brother Drusus or Drusus' son Germanicus. His unhappy private life and the public rebuffs to that fierce pride of the Claudians had unquestionably made him dour and melancholic. Such a man, at the age of fifty-five, became master of the Roman world.

Tacitus has provided a description of Tiberius that ranks among the great portraits in historical writing. The hypocritical ruler, exercising power through deception while surrounded by sycophants and a praetorian guard, has been for nineteen centuries the classic picture of tyranny. And yet Tacitus' own account is filled with contradictions, and in recent years scholars have painted a more positive picture of Tiberius and his achievements. In the nine years until the death of his son Drusus in A.D. 23, Tiberius tried to cooperate with the Senate and, even Tacitus admits, governed the Empire well. He resented and despised the growing servility of the senators, and his reluctance to impose his views on every matter under deliberation was interpreted as

---

dissimulation. There was never the wholesale reign of terror later to be seen under Caligula, Nero and Domitian —fewer than two dozen men can be shown to have been executed in Tiberius' reign of twenty-three years. At one point Tacitus uses the phrase "continual slaughter" when there had been two executions (and a number of suicides) in a three-year period. By the standards of bloody despotism—ancient or modern—the reign of Tiberius seems rather mild.

Yet to Tacitus and later Roman writers, Tiberius unmasked the tyranny so carefully disguised by Augustus. And thus later outrages must be laid at his feet. In old age his bitterness and alienation grew. He had withdrawn to Capri and allowed his praetorian prefect Sejanus to rule the city. Tiberius was already in his seventies and the only possible heirs were mere boys, so Sejanus asked to marry Drusus' widow and thus place himself in line for the throne. Tiberius' sister-in-law Antonia, however, was able to slip a letter through to the emperor warning him of Sejanus' imperial ambitions and a possible conspiracy. Slowly and cautiously, Tiberius outmaneuvered his complacent deputy and denounced him to the Senate. After the execution of Sejanus and cruel murder of his children, his widow revealed in a suicide note that Sejanus had murdered the emperor's son Drusus. It was the ultimate betrayal for the bitter Tiberius.

In his bleak, final years the emperor remained at Capri, and his absence (as earlier at Rhodes) gave rise to rumors of perversions (though there is no real evidence). He gloomily wrestled with the problem of succession: his foolish nephew, Claudius; his vicious but talented great-nephew, Caligula; and his still young grandson, Gemellus. Yet through his personal tragedies and his constant bitterness, Tiberius remained an excellent administrator of the Empire. Italy prospered economically under his reign. He defended the frontiers of the Empire, punished his rapacious governors, restrained the growing imperial cult, generously assisted Asia in the wake of a terrible earthquake, and yet left a healthy treasury. Nevertheless, he died hated by the senatorial elite. In exasperation he had once accused the senators of rushing into slavery. And so they were, in their eagerness to please their monarch. But their own shame, as was that of Tacitus who had remained silent during the terrors of Domitian, was transformed into a deep loathing of Tiberius. Tacitus' portrait of Tiberius is an attempt to exorcise his own demons, but we must be more compassionate to that unhappy man. His personal defects and, finally, his moral weakness which placed ambition before love made his own life a tragedy, and yet he labored in public life for half a century to bring security and good government to an Empire of fifty million people. He deserves better from history than to be reviled as a monster.

The Reign of Tiberius

Tacitus *Annals*

Tacitus lived through the terror in the reign of Domitian (A.D. 81–96) and projected that experience and his hatred of informers into his treatment of the reign of Tiberius. In this excerpt, the senatorial historian focuses on the imperial court, in which Tiberius is depicted as the arch-hypocrite surrounded by sycophantic flatterers. It is one of the most powerful portraits of tyranny in all history. Tacitus uses all his dramatic and rhetorical skills to blacken Tiberius' reputation, despite the fact that relatively few executions took place before those last terrible years of the reign. Nor does Tacitus conceal that the senators encouraged Tiberius to take more power upon himself. The political context of factions supporting and opposing Sejanus is clearly delineated, and Tacitus studies the corruption of the courtiers as well as of the emperor himself.

Perhaps the root of Tacitus' hostility lies in his correct perception of the reign of Tiberius as a time of transition between the constitutional principate of Augustus and the ensuing tyranny of Caligula and his successors. Ancient historians attributed political change to the personal virtues or vices of the leading figures, so the growing authoritarianism of the Empire was due to Tiberius' depravity just as the fall of the Republic had been attributed to Julius Caesar's ambition. That Tiberius died a morose and bitter man cannot be doubted; but a modern historian might see that as the result of rejection (by Augustus), disappointment, humiliation (by Julia) and betrayal (by Sejanus) rather than, as Tacitus does, as evidence of innate evil.

Book I

After an appropriate funeral, Augustus was declared a god and decreed a temple. But the target of every prayer was Tiberius. Addressing the senate, he offered a variety of comments on the greatness of the empire and his own unpretentiousness. Only the divine Augustus, he suggested, had possessed a personality equal to such responsibilities—he himself, when invited by Augustus to share his labours, had found by experience what hard hazardous work it was to rule the empire. Besides, he said, a State which could rely on so many distinguished personages ought not to concentrate the supreme power in the hands of one man—the task of government would be more easily carried out by the combined efforts of a greater number.

But grand sentiments of this kind sounded unconvincing. Besides, what Tiberius said, even when he did not aim at concealment, was—by habit or nature—always hesitant, always cryptic. And now that he was determined to show no sign of his real feelings, his words became more and more equivocal and obscure. But the chief fear of the senators was that they should be seen to understand him only too well. So they poured forth a flood of tearful lamentations and prayers, gesticulating to heaven and to the statue of Augustus, and making reverent gestures before Tiberius himself.

At this juncture he gave instructions for a document to be produced and read. It was a list of the national resources. It gave the numbers of regular and auxiliary troops serving in the army; the strength of the navy; statistics concerning the provinces and dependent kingdoms; direct and indirect taxation; recurrent expenditures and gifts. Augustus had written all this out in his own hand. Furthermore, he had added a clause advising that the empire should not be extended beyond its present frontiers. Either he feared dangers ahead, or he was jealous.

The senate now wallowed in the most abject appeals. Tiberius remarked incidentally that, although he did not feel himself capable of the whole burden of government, he was nevertheless prepared to take on any branch of it that might be entrusted to him. 'Then I must ask, Caesar,' called out Gaius Asinius Gallus, 'which branch you desire to have handed over to you.' This unexpected question threw Tiberius off his stride. For some moments he said nothing. Then, recovering his balance, he replied that, since he would prefer to be excused from the responsibility altogether, he felt much too diffident to choose or reject this or that part of it. Gallus, however, who had guessed from Tiberius' looks that he had taken offence, protested that the purpose of his question had not been to parcel out functions which were inseparable; it had been to obtain from the lips of Tiberius himself the admission that the State was a single organic whole needing the control of a single mind. . . .

Livia, too, was flattered a great deal by the senate. It was variously proposed that she should be called 'parent' and 'mother' of her country; and a large body of opinion held that the words 'son of Julia' ought to form part of the emperor's name. He, however, repeatedly asserted that only reasonable honours must be paid to women—and that, in regard to compliments paid to himself, he would observe a comparable moderation. In reality, however, he was jealous and nervous, and regarded this elevation of a woman as derogatory to his own person. . . .

In spite of repeated popular pressure, Tiberius refused the title 'Father of his Country.' He also declined the senate's proposal that obedience should be sworn to his enactments. All human affairs were uncertain, he protested, and the higher his position the more slippery it was.

Nevertheless, he did not convince people of his Republicanism. For he revived the treason law. The ancients had employed the same name, but had applied it to other offences—to official misconduct damaging the Roman State, such as betrayal of an army or incitement to sedition. Action had been taken against deeds, words went unpunished. The first who employed this law to investigate written libel was Augustus, provoked by Cassius Severus, an immoderate slanderer of eminent men and women. Then Tiberius, asked by a praetor . . . whether cases under the treason law were to receive attention, replied: *the laws must take their course* . . . .

Book II

. . . The eastern troubles, [Tiberius] said, could only be put right by the wisdom of Germanicus. For he himself, he said, was of advancing years, whereas Drusus was not yet sufficiently mature. So the senate entrusted the overseas provinces to Germanicus, with powers superior (wherever he might go) to those of all governors of imperial and senatorial provinces alike. But Tiberius had removed Syria's imperial governor . . . replacing him by Cnaeus Calpurnius Piso. This ferocious, insubordinate man inherited his violent character from his father (of the same name), who during the civil war had vigorously helped the revived Republican party in Africa against Julius Caesar, and then supported Brutus and Cassius. . . . In addition to his father's spirit, Piso had his wife Plancina's lineage and wealth to spur him on. He grudgingly allowed Tiberius first place, but looked down on Tiberius' children as far beneath him.

Piso was certain that the purpose of his Syrian appointment was the repression of Germanicus' ambitions. According to one view, he received secret instructions from Tiberius to that effect. Plancina certainly received advice from the Augusta, whose feminine jealousy was set on persecuting Agrippina. For the court was disunited, split by unspoken partisanships for Drusus or Germanicus. Tiberius supported Drusus, as the son of his own blood. But the popularity of Germanicus had increased, partly owing to his uncle's hostility, and partly because his mother's family gave him precedence. He could point to Augustus as great-uncle and Antony as grandfather, whereas Drusus was great-grandson of a knight, Titus Pomponius Atticus, who hardly added lustre to the Claudian genealogy. Besides, Germanicus' wife Agrippina was more distinguished than Drusus' wife Livilla—and had more children. However, the brothers were good friends, unperturbed by the rivalries around them. . . .

On leaving Egypt Germanicus learnt that all his orders to divisional commanders and cities had been cancelled or reversed. Between him and Piso there were violent reciprocal denunciations. Then Piso decided to leave Syria. But Germanicus fell ill, and so Piso stayed on. When news came that the prince was better and vows offered for his recovery were being paid, Piso sent his attendants to disperse the rejoicing crowds of Antioch, with their sacrificial victims and apparatus. Then he left for Seleucia Pieria, to await the outcome of Germanicus' illness. [Germanicus] had a relapse—aggravated by his belief that Piso had poisoned him. Examination of the floor and walls of his bedroom revealed the remains of human bodies, spells, curses, lead tablets inscribed with the patient's name, charred and bloody ashes, and other malignant objects which are supposed to consign souls to the powers of the tomb. At the same time agents of Piso were accused of spying on the sickbed.

Germanicus, alarmed and angry, reflected that if his own house was besieged and his enemies were actually watching as he died, the prospects of his unhappy wife and babies were gloomy. Apparently poisoning was too slow; Piso was evidently impatient to monopolize the province and its garrison. But Germanicus felt he was not so feeble as all that—the murderer should not have his reward. He wrote to Piso renouncing his friendship, and it is usually believed that he ordered him out of the province. Piso now delayed no longer, and sailed. But he went slowly, so as to reduce the return journey in case Germanicus died and Syria became accessible again.

For a time Germanicus' condition was encouraging. But then he lost strength, and death became imminent. As his friends stood round him, he spoke to them. 'Even if I were dying a natural death,' he said, 'I should have a legitimate grudge against the gods for prematurely parting me, at this young age, from my parents, children, and country. But it is the wickedness of Piso and Plancina that have cut me off. I ask you to take my last requests to your heart. Tell my father and brother of the harrowing afflictions and ruinous conspiracies which

have brought my wretched life to this miserable close. My relatives, those who shared my prospects, even those who envied me in my life, will lament that the once flourishing survivor of many campaigns has fallen to a woman's treachery!

'You will have the opportunity to protest to the senate and to invoke the law. The chief duty of a friend is not to walk behind the corpse pointlessly grieving, but to remember his desires and carry out his instructions. Even strangers will mourn Germanicus. But if it was I that you loved, and not my rank, you must avenge me! Show Rome my wife—the divine Augustus' granddaughter. Call the roll of our six children. Sympathy will go to the accusers. Any tale of criminal instructions given to Piso will seem unbelievable or, if believed, unforgivable.' His friends touched the dying man's right hand, and swore to perish rather than leave him unavenged. Turning to his wife, Germanicus begged her—by her memories of himself and by their children—to forget her pride, submit to cruel fortune, and, back in Rome, to avoid provoking those stronger than herself by competing for their power. That was his public utterance. Privately he said more—warning her of danger (so it was said) from Tiberius. Soon afterwards he died.

The province and surrounding peoples grieved greatly. Foreign countries and kings mourned his friendliness to allies and forgiveness to enemies. Both his looks and his words had inspired respect. Yet this dignity and grandeur, befitting his lofty rank, had been unaccompanied by any arrogance or jealousy. At his funeral there was no procession of statues. But there were abundant eulogies and reminiscences of his fine character. Some felt that his appearance, short life, and manner of death (like its locality) recalled Alexander the Great. Both were handsome, both died soon after thirty, both succumbed to the treachery of compatriots in a foreign land. But Germanicus, it was added, was kind to his friends, modest in his pleasures, a man with one wife and legitimate children. Though not so rash as Alexander, he was no less of a warrior. Only, after defeating the Germans many times, he had not been allowed to complete their subjection. If he had been in sole control, with royal power and title, he would have equalled Alexander in military renown as easily as he outdid him in clemency, self-control, and every other good quality.

Before cremation the body of Germanicus was exposed in the main square of Antioch, which was to be its resting-place. It is uncertain if the body showed signs of poisoning. People came to opposite conclusions according to their preconceived suspicions, inspired by sympathy for Germanicus or support for Piso. . . .

Book III

Agrippina pressed on with her journey over the wintry sea. When she reached the island of Corcyra, opposite the Calabrian coast, she paused for a few days to calm herself. Her misery was unendurable. Meanwhile, at the news of her approach, people flocked to Brundusium, the nearest and safest port of disembarkation. Close friends came, and many officers who had served under Germanicus; also many strangers from towns nearby, some to pay duty to the emperor, others (more numerous) imitating them. As soon as her squadron was seen out to sea, huge sorrowing crowds filled the harbours and shallows, walls, house-tops—every vantage point.

They wondered whether they ought to receive her landing in silence or with some utterance. As they still hesitated about the appropriate course, the fleet gradually came nearer. There was none of the usual brisk rowing, but every deliberate sign of grief. Agrippina, with her two children, stepped off the ship, her eyes lowered, the urn of death in her hands. Her companions were worn out by prolonged grieving; so the sorrow of the fresh mourners who now met her was more demonstrative. Otherwise everyone's feelings were indistinguishable; the cries of men and women, relatives and strangers, blended in a single universal groan.

Tiberius had sent two battalions of the Guard, and had ordered the officials of Calabria, Apulia and Campania to pay their last respects to his adoptive son. So, as his ashes were borne on the shoulders of colonels and company-commanders, preceded by unadorned standards and reversed axes, at each successive settlement—in proportion to its wealth—the populace clothed in black and the knights in purple-striped tunics burnt garments, spices, and other funeral offerings. Even people from towns far away came to meet the procession, offering sacrifices and erecting altars to the dead man's soul, and showing their grief by tears and lamentations.

Drusus came out to Tarracina with Germanicus' brother Claudius and those of his children who had been at Rome. The consuls . . . , the senate, and a great part of the population thronged the roadside in scattered groups, weeping as their hearts moved them. There was no flattery of the emperor in this. Indeed everyone knew that Tiberius could scarcely conceal his delight at the death of Germanicus.

He and the Augusta made no public appearance. Either they considered open mourning beneath their dignity, or they feared that the public gaze would detect insincerity on their faces. I cannot discover in histories or official journals that Germanicus' mother Antonia played a prominent part in these happenings, although the names not only of Agrippina, Drusus and Claudius, but of all his other blood-relations as well are recorded. Ill-health may have prevented her. Or perhaps she was too overcome by grief to endure visible evidence of her bereavement. But it seems to me more plausible that Tiberius and the Augusta, who remained at home, kept her there too, so that the dead man's grandmother and uncle might seem, by staying indoors, only to be following the mother's example, and grieving no less than she.

On the day when the remains were conducted to the Mausoleum of Augustus there was a desolate silence—rent only by wailing. The streets were full, the Field of Mars ablaze with torches. Everyone—armed soldiers, officials without their insignia, the people organized in their tribes—reiterated that Rome was done for, all hope gone. In the readiness and openness of their talk, they seemed to forget their rulers. But what upset Tiberius most was the popular enthusiasm for Agrippina. The glory of her country, they called her—the only true descendant of Augustus, the unmatched model of traditional behaviour. Gazing to heaven, they prayed that her children might live to survive their enemies.

Some people missed the pageantry of a state funeral. How different, they said, had been the magnificent rites devoted by Augustus to Germanicus' father, Nero Drusus! . . .

Tiberius heard of all this. Then, to silence the widespread talk, he issued the following statement. 'Many famous Romans have died for their country. But none has ever been so ardently lamented before. That seems admirable to all, myself included—provided that moderation is observed. For the conduct of ordinary households or communities is not appropriate for rulers or an imperial people. Tearful mourning was a proper consolation in the first throes of grief. But now be calm again. Remember how Julius Caesar, when he lost his only daughter, and Augustus, when he lost his grandsons, hid their sorrow—not to mention Rome's courageous endurance (on earlier occasions) of the loss of armies, the deaths of generals, the total destruction of great families. Rulers die; the country lives for ever. . . .'

[Piso was brought to trial in the senate with Tiberius presiding.] Under every head except one the defence faltered. Bribery of the troops, abandonment of the province to every rascal, and insults against the commander, were undeniable. The poisoning charge alone was refuted. No conviction was carried by the story of the accusers that, at a party of Germanicus, Piso, his neighbour at dinner, had himself put poison into his food. It seemed fantastic that he should have attempted this, with many people looking on—including another man's slaves—and under Germanicus' own eyes. Piso offered his own slaves for torture and demanded that the waiters should be tortured too.

But for various reasons the judges were implacable—Tiberius because he had made war on the province, the senate because it

remained unconvinced that Germanicus had died naturally. Both the emperor and Piso refused to produce private correspondence. Outside the senate-house the crowd were shouting that, if the senate spared him, they would lynch him. They dragged statues of him to the Gemonian Steps and began to destroy them; but on the emperor's orders they were saved and put back. Piso was set in a litter and escorted home by a colonel of the Guard, whose role was variously interpreted as protector of his life or supervisor of his execution.

Plancina was equally loathed, but she had more influence. So it was doubted how far Tiberius could act against her. As long as Piso's fate was uncertain, she swore she would share whatever happened to him, and if necessary die with him. But the Augusta's private appeals secured her pardon. Thereafter she gradually dissociated herself from her husband, and treated her defence separately.

Piso saw that this was a fatal sign, and hesitated whether to continue the struggle. Finally, pressed by his sons, he steeled himself to enter the senate again. Renewed charges, hostile cries from senators, relentless enmity everywhere, he endured. But what horrified him most was the sight of Tiberius, pitiless, passionless, adamantly closed to any human feeling. Piso was carried home. He wrote a brief note—ostensibly preparation for the next day's defence—and handed it, sealed, to an ex-slave. Then he performed his usual toilet. Late at night, when his wife had left the bedroom, he ordered the door to be shut. At dawn he was found with his throat cut. A sword lay on the floor.

I remember hearing older men speak of a document often seen in Piso's hands. He never made it known. But his friends insisted that it contained a letter from Tiberius with instructions relating to Germanicus. If, they alleged, Piso had not been deceived by insincere promises from Sejanus, he had intended to disclose this to the senate—thereby convicting the emperor. Moreover, his death, according to this story, was not by his own hand, but by an assassin's. I cannot vouch for either version. But I have felt bound to repeat this account given by people who were still alive when I was young. . . .

Book IV

[In A.D. 23] Tiberius began his ninth year of national stability and domestic prosperity (the latter, he felt, augmented by Germanicus' death). But then suddenly Fortune turned disruptive. The emperor himself became tyrannical—or gave tyrannical men power. The cause and beginning of the change lay with Lucius Aelius Sejanus, commander of the Guard. I have said something of his influence, and will now describe his origins and personality—and his criminal attempt on the throne.

Sejanus was born at Vulsinii. His father, Lucius Scius Strabo, was a Roman knight. After increasing his income—it was alleged—by a liaison with a rich debauchee named Marcus Gavius Apicius, the boy joined, while still young, the suite of Augustus' grandson Gaius Caesar. Next by various devices he obtained a complete ascendancy over Tiberius. To Sejanus alone the otherwise cryptic emperor spoke freely and unguardedly. This was hardly due to Sejanus' cunning; in that he was outclassed by Tiberius. The cause was rather heaven's anger against Rome—to which the triumph of Sejanus, and his downfall too, were catastrophic. Of audacious character and untiring physique, secretive about himself and ever ready to incriminate others, a blend of arrogance and servility, he concealed behind a carefully modest exterior an unbounded lust for power. Sometimes this impelled him to lavish excesses, but more often to incessant work. And that is as damaging as excess when the throne is its aim.

The command of the Guard had hitherto been of slight importance. Sejanus enhanced it by concentrating the Guard battalions, scattered about Rome, in one camp. Orders could reach them simultaneously, and their visible numbers and strength would increase their self-confidence and intimidate the population. His pretexts were that scattered quarters caused unruliness; that united action would be needed in an emergency; and that a camp away from the temptations of the city would improve discipline. When the camp was ready, he gradually insinuated himself into the men's favour. He would talk with them addressing them by name. And he chose their company- and battalion-commanders himself. Senators' ambitions, too, he tempted with offices and governorships for his dependants.

Tiberius was readily amenable, praising him in conversation—and even in the senate and Assembly—as 'the partner of my labours,' and allowing honours to his statues in theatres, public places, and brigade headquarters. Yet Sejanus' ambitions were impeded by the well-stocked imperial house, including a son and heir—in his prime—and grown-up grandchildren. Subtlety required that the crimes should be spaced out: it would be unsafe to strike at all of them simultaneously. So subtle methods prevailed. Sejanus decided to begin with Drusus, against whom he had a recent grudge. For Drusus, violent-tempered and resentful of a rival, had raised his hand against him during a fortuitous quarrel and, when Sejanus resisted, had struck him in the face.

After considering every possibility, Sejanus felt most inclined to rely on Drusus' wife Livilla, the sister of Germanicus. Unattractive in earlier years, she had become a great beauty. Sejanus professed devotion, and seduced her. Then, this first guilty move achieved—since a woman who has parted with her virtue will refuse nothing—he incited her to hope for marriage, partnership in the empire, and the death of her husband. So the grand-niece of Augustus, daughter-in-law of Tiberius, mother of Drusus' children, degraded herself and her ancestors and descendants with a small-town adulterer; she sacrificed her honourable, assured position for infamy and hazard. The plot was communicated to Eudemus, Livilla's friend and doctor, who had professional pretexts for frequent interviews. Sejanus encouraged his mistress by sending away his wife Apicata, the mother of his three children. Nevertheless the magnitude of the projected crime caused misgivings, delays, and (on occasion) conflicting plans. . . .

[Finally] Sejanus decided to act. He chose a poison with gradual effects resembling ordinary ill-health. It was administered to Drusus (as was learnt eight years later) by the eunuch Lygdus. All through his son's illness, Tiberius attended the senate. Either he was unalarmed or he wanted to display his will-power. Even when Drusus had died and his body was awaiting burial, Tiberius continued to attend. The consuls sat on ordinary benches as a sign of mourning. But he reminded them of their dignity and rank. The senators wept. But he silenced them with a consoling oration. 'I know,' he said, 'that I may be criticized for appearing before the senate while my affliction is still fresh. Most mourners can hardly bear even their families' condolences—can hardly look upon the light of day. And that need not be censured as weakness. I, however, have sought sterner solace. The arms in which I have taken refuge are those of the State.'

After referring sorrowfully to the Augusta's great age, his grandson's immaturity, and his own declining years, he said that the sons of Germanicus were his only consolation in his grief; and he requested that they should be brought in. The consuls went out, reassured the boys, and conducted them before Tiberius. He took them by the hand, and addressed the senate. 'When these boys lost their father,' he said, 'I entrusted them to their uncle Drusus, begging him—though he had children of his own—to treat them as though they were his blood, and, for posterity's sake, to fashion them after himself. Now Drusus has gone. So my plea is addressed to you. The gods and our country are its witnesses.

'Senators: on my behalf as well as your own, adopt and guide these youths, whose birth is so glorious—these great-grandchildren of Augustus. Nero and Drusus Caesars: these senators will take the place of your parents. For, in the station to which you are born, the good and bad in you is of national concern.' This speech was greeted by loud weeping among the senators, followed by heartfelt prayers for the future. Indeed, if Tiberius had stopped there, he would have left his audience sorry for him and proud of their responsibility. But by reverting to empty discredited talk about restoring the Republic and handing the government to the

consuls or others, he undermined belief even in what he had said sincerely and truthfully. . . .

When Tiberius pronounced his son's funeral eulogy from the platform, the attitudes and tones of mourning exhibited by the senate and public were insincere and unconvincing. Secretly they were glad that the house of Germanicus was reviving. However, this awakening popularity, and Agrippina's ill-concealed maternal ambitions, only hastened the family's ruin. For when Sejanus saw that Drusus' death brought no retribution upon the murderers and no national grief, his criminal audacity grew. The succession of the children of Germanicus was now certain. So he considered how they could be removed. . . .

[Sejanus requests marriage to the emperor's daughter-in-law Livilla, but Tiberius discourages the match and suggests it would arouse envy and resentment against Sejanus.] Sejanus was alarmed, not just for his marriage but on graver grounds. He replied urging Tiberius to eschew suspicion and ignore rumour and malignant envy. Then, unwilling either to shut out his stream of visitors—which would mean loss of influence—or by receiving them to give his critics a handle, he turned his attention to persuading Tiberius to settle in some attractive place far from Rome. He foresaw many advantages in this. He himself would control access to the emperor—as well as most of his correspondence, since it would be transmitted by Guardsmen. Besides, the aging monarch, slackening in retirement, would soon be readier to delegate governmental functions. Meanwhile Sejanus himself would become less unpopular when his large receptions ceased—by eliminating inessentials, he would strengthen his real power. So he increasingly denounced to Tiberius the drudgeries of Rome, its crowds and innumerable visitors, and spoke warmly of peace and solitude, far from vexation and friction: where first things could come first. . . .

Now, after long consideration and frequent postponements, Tiberius at last left for Campania. His ostensible purpose was the dedication of temples to Jupiter and Augustus at Capua and Nola respectively. But he had decided to live away from Rome. Like most historians, I attribute his withdrawal to Sejanus' intrigues. Yet, since he maintained this seclusion for six years after Sejanus' execution, I often wonder whether it was not really caused by a desire to hide the cruelty and immorality which his actions made all too conspicuous. It was also said that in old age he became sensitive about his appearance. Tall and abnormally thin, bent and bald, he had a face covered with sores and often plaster. His retirement at Rhodes had accustomed him to unsociability and secretive pleasures.

According to another theory he was driven away by his mother's bullying: to share control with her seemed intolerable, to dislodge her impracticable—since that control had been given him by her. For Augustus had considered awarding the empire to his universally loved grand-nephew Germanicus. But his wife had induced him to adopt Tiberius instead (though Tiberius was made to adopt Germanicus). The Augusta harped accusingly on this obligation—and exacted repayment. . . .

A dangerous accident to Tiberius at this time stimulated idle gossip, and gave him reason for increased confidence in Sejanus' friendship and loyalty. While they were dining at a villa called The Cave, in a natural cavern between the sea at Amyclae and the hills of Fundi, there was a fall of rock at the cave-mouth. Several servants were crushed, and amid the general panic the diners fled. But Sejanus, braced on hands and knees, face to face, warded the falling boulders off Tiberius. That is how the soldiers who rescued them found him. The incident increased Sejanus' power. Tiberius believed him disinterested and listened trustingly to his advice, however disastrous. . . .

. . . So he took refuge on the island of Capri, separated from the tip of the Surrentum promontory by three miles of sea. Presumably what attracted him was the isolation of Capri. . . . In winter the climate is mild, since hills on the mainland keep off gales. In summer the island is delightful, since it faces west and has open sea all round. The bay it overlooks was exceptionally lovely, until Vesuvius' eruption transformed the landscape. . . .

On this island then, in twelve spacious, separately named villas, Tiberius took up residence. His former absorption in State affairs ended. Instead he spent the time in secret orgies, or idle malevolent thoughts. But his abnormally credulous suspicions were unabated. Sejanus, who had encouraged them even at Rome, whipped them up, and now openly disclosed his designs against Agrippina and Nero Caesar. Soldiers attached to them reported with a historian's precision their correspondence, visitors, and doings private and public. Agents incited them to flee to the German armies, or—in the Forum at its peak hour—to grasp the divine Augustus' statue, and appeal to senate and public. They dismissed such projects: but were accused of them. . . .

. . . [In A.D. 29] the aged Augusta died. . . . Her private life was of traditional strictness. But her graciousness exceeded old-fashioned standards. She was a compliant wife, but an overbearing mother. Neither her husband's diplomacy nor her son's insincerity could out-manoeuvre her.

The implementation of her will was long delayed. At her modest funeral, the obituary speech was pronounced by her great-grandson Gaius, soon to be emperor. Tiberius did not interrupt his own self-indulgences for his mother's last rites, but wrote excusing himself and pleading important business. Moreover, when the senate decreed extensive honours to her memory, he curtailed them in the name of moderation, conceding only a few. Tiberius added that she was not to be deified—she herself had not wished it. . . .

. . . Now began a time of sheer crushing tyranny. While the Augusta lived there was still a moderating influence, for Tiberius had retained a deep-rooted deference for his mother. Sejanus, too, had not ventured to outbid her parental authority. Now, however, the reins were thrown off, and they pressed ahead. A letter was sent to Rome denouncing Agrippina and Nero Caesar. It was read so soon after the Augusta's death that people believed it had arrived earlier and been suppressed by her. . . .

[There is now a gap of two years in our manuscript of Tacitus. First Agrippina, Nero

Caesar, and Drusus Caesar are exiled; and Nero Caesar dies. Then Tiberius, believing Sejanus himself (now consul) guilty of conspiracy, has him arrested in the senate and executed. Sejanus' divorced wife Apicata now reveals to Tiberius that his own son Drusus had been poisoned by Sejanus and Livilla; and Livilla too is killed or kills herself.]

Book VI

The general rage against Sejanus was now subsiding, appeased by the executions already carried out. Yet retribution was now decreed against his remaining children. They were taken to prison. The boy understood what lay ahead of him. But the girl uncomprehendingly repeated: 'What have I done? Where are you taking me? I will not do it again!' She could be punished with a beating, she said, like other children. Contemporary writers report that, because capital punishment of a virgin was unprecedented, she was violated by the executioner, with the noose beside her. Then both were strangled, and their young bodies thrown on to the Gemonian Steps. . . .

Tiberius' health and strength were now failing. But his stern will and vigorous speech and expression remained. So did his powers of dissimulation. To conceal his obvious decline, he assumed an affable manner. After numerous moves he settled in a villa on Cape Misenum which had belonged to Lucius Licinius Lucullus. There his end was discovered to be approaching. For an eminent doctor called Charicles, though not employed to treat the emperor's illnesses, had made himself available for consultation. Ostensibly taking his leave to attend to private affairs, he grasped the emperor's hand—and under cover of this respectful gesture felt his pulse. Tiberius noticed, ordered the dinner to be prolonged, and stayed up later than usual. This was allegedly in honour of his departing friend. But he may well have been annoyed, and so taken special pains to conceal his annoyance.

However, Charicles assured Macro that Tiberius was sinking and would not last more than two days. There were conferences, and dispatches to imperial governors and generals, hurriedly making all arrangements. On March 16th the emperor ceased to breathe, and was believed to be dead. Gaius, surrounded by a congratulatory crowd, issued forth to begin his reign. But then it was suddenly reported that Tiberius had recovered his speech and sight, and was asking for food to strengthen him after his fainting-fit. There was a general panic-stricken dispersal. Every face was composed to show grief—or unawareness. Only Gaius stood in stupefied silence, his soaring hopes dashed, expecting the worse. Macro, unperturbed, ordered the old man to be smothered with a heap of bed-clothes and left alone.

So Tiberius died, in his seventy-eighth year. The son of Tiberius Claudius Nero, he was a Claudian on both sides (his mother was successively adopted into the Livian and the Julian families). From birth he experienced contrasts of fortune. After following his proscribed father into exile, he entered Augustus' family as his stepson—only to suffer from many competitors, while they lived: first Marcellus and Agrippa, then Gaius Caesar and Lucius Caesar. His own brother Nero Drusus was more of a popular favourite. But Tiberius' position became most delicate of all after his marriage to Augustus' daughter Julia. For he had to choose between enduring her unfaithfulness or escaping it. He went to Rhodes. When he returned, he was undisputed heir in the emperor's home for twelve years. Then he ruled the Roman world for nearly twenty-three.

His character, too, had its different stages. While he was a private citizen or holding commands under Augustus, his life was blameless; and so was his reputation. While Germanicus and Drusus still lived, he concealed his real self, cunningly affecting virtuous qualities. However, until his mother died there was good in Tiberius as well as evil. Again, as long as he favoured (or feared) Sejanus, the cruelty of Tiberius was detested, but his perversions unrevealed. Then fear vanished, and with it shame. Thereafter he expressed only his own personality—by unrestrained crime and infamy.

Life of Tiberius

Suetonius

Suetonius collected a great deal of material from a variety of sources ranging from slanderous gossip to reliable documents. But Suetonius is not inclined to be critical of these sources; he simply arranges the stories under different headings and thus constructs a biography. In his attempt to provide a catalogue of Tiberius' cruelties, the political context that Tacitus provides is entirely absent, and the savagery therefore seems unmotivated. Suetonius recounts events of the bloody aftermath of Sejanus' fall as though they were typical of Tiberius' entire reign. Tacitus also sees Tiberius as a monster; his own account, however, also provides the evidence that there were few executions before the rise of Sejanus. But if Suetonius fails to provide a balanced picture of the reign, he does provide useful specific information in a number of areas (e.g., Tiberius' cultural tastes, which demonstrate his interest in Greek civilization).

4.   [The father of the emperor Tiberius was Tiberius Claudius Nero who had supported Marc Antony.] He returned to Rome in 39 B.C. at the conclusion of the general truce, and he relinquished to Augustus his wife Livia Drusilla, who was pregnant at the time and had already borne him a son. He died soon afterwards leaving two sons, Tiberius Nero and Drusus Nero.

6.   Tiberius passed his infancy and youth amid hardship and tribulation, since he accompanied his parents in flight. . . . At the age of nine he delivered his father's eulogy on the rostra. Then, just as he was arriving at puberty, he accompanied the chariot of Augustus in the triumph after Actium, mounted on the left trace-horse, while Octavia's son Marcellus rode the right one. . . .

7.   . . . He married Vipsania, daughter of Marcus Agrippa. Though that happy marriage had produced a son, Drusus, and Vipsania was again pregnant, Tiberius was forced to divorce her and contract a hurried marriage with Julia, daughter of Augustus. He took this badly, for he was living happily with Vipsania and disapproved of Julia's character, since he knew that she had an obvious passion for him while her former husband Agrippa was still alive. After the divorce he regretted his separation from Vipsania, so that the only time that he chanced to see her, he pursued her with such tearful look that he was never allowed to see her. At first he lived harmoniously with Julia and returned her love. But

he soon grew cold, and ceased to live with her at all, after their child died in infancy.

9.   He first served as military tribune in the Spanish war, and then he led an army to the East and crowned Tigranes as king of Armenia. He also recovered the standards which the Parthians had taken from Marcus Crassus. Then for a year he was governor of Gaul, where barbarian raids and the bickering of the chiefs had caused unrest. He fought in the Alps, Pannonia, and finally in Germany, whence he brought forty thousand prisoners over into Gaul and settled them near the bank of the Rhine. For these exploits he received an ovation and a triumph. . . . He became in turn quaestor, praetor, and consul before the usual age, and he soon became consul again, at the same time receiving the tribunician power for five years.

10.   At the peak of success and in the prime of life, he suddenly decided to withdraw as far as possible from public business. He was perhaps disgusted with his wife whom he could no longer endure, but he dared neither to accuse her nor to divorce her. Or perhaps he wished to bolster his prestige by a prolonged absence from Rome, in case his country should ever need him. Some think that, since the grandsons of Augustus were now of age, he voluntarily gave up the second position in the state which he had long held, thus following the example of Marcus Agrippa, who withdrew to Mytilene when Marcellus

began his public career, so that he might not seem either to oppose or diminish him by his presence. This was actually the reason which Tiberius himself gave afterwards, but at the time he asked for leave of absence on the ground of the strain of public office and a desire to rest. Neither his mother's entreaties nor his step-father's complaint of desertion caused him to relent. . . . He left his wife and son in Rome and hastened to Ostia without saying a single word to any of those who saw him off, and kissing only a very few when he left.

11. . . . On Rhodes he only once exercised his tribunician authority. He constantly attended the lecture-halls of the professors of philosophy, where a fellow had the audacity to abuse him when he appeared to favor one side in a heated debate. Thereupon Tiberius returned to his house, and brought back his lictors and attendants, and ordering his herald to summon the foul-mouthed fellow before his tribunal, he had him taken off to prison.

Shortly afterwards Tiberius learned that Augustus had banished Julia for adultery, and had sent her a bill of divorce in his name. Though this was welcome news, he thought he should try by letters to reconcile father and daughter, and he allowed her to keep any gifts he had given to her whether she deserved them or not. Moreover, at the end of his term of tribunician power, he finally admitted that he had left Rome to avoid the suspicion of rivalry with Gaius and Lucius. Now that they were grown and the succession was secure, he asked that he be allowed to visit his relatives, whom he missed. But Augustus refused, and said that since he had so eagerly abandoned his family, he should forget about them.

12. So Tiberius remained in Rhodes unwillingly, and Livia barely secured the title of ambassador to conceal his disgrace. He then lived in privacy and anxiety. . . .

13. When his name was mentioned at a private dinner party, a man assured Gaius that if he would say the word, he would at once sail to Rhodes and bring back the head of the exile, as Tiberius was commonly called. It was this act especially—which made his position no longer one of mere fear but of actual peril—that drove Tiberius and his mother to plead urgently for his recall. He obtained it . . . although on the understanding that he should not take part in public affairs.

14. A few days before his recall an eagle, never before seen in Rhodes, perched upon the roof of his house; and the day before the news arrived his tunic seemed to blaze as he was changing his clothes. It was then that he became convinced of the powers of the astrologer Thrasyllus, who had declared that the eagle brought good news—this too at the very moment when Tiberius had made up his mind to push the man off the cliff into the sea as they were strolling together, believing him a false prophet and too hastily made the confidant of his secrets, because things were turning out adversely and contrary to his predictions.

15. After Tiberius returned to Rome and introduced his son Drusus to public life, he led a quiet life attending to his personal affairs and exercising no public functions. But when Gaius and Lucius died within three years, he was adopted by Augustus along with their brother Agrippa Postumus, though he first had to adopt his nephew Germanicus. . . . From then on Augustus tried to promote his prestige, especially after the banishment of Postumus made it clear that he would be the successor.

16. He was given the tribunician power for another three years, with the task of subjugating Germany. . . . But when the Illyrian revolt broke out, Tiberius was sent to suppress what developed into the most serious of all foreign wars since those with Carthage. He fought it amid difficult conditions with scarce supplies for three years with fifteen legions and a corresponding force of auxiliaries. . . . He reaped an ample reward for his perseverance, for he completely subdued the whole of Illyricum.

17. This exploit seemed more glorious when Varus perished with three legions in Germany, since everyone knew that the victorious Germans would have united with the Pannonians, had not Illyricum been subdued first. Consequently Tiberius was voted a triumph and other high honors. . . .

18. The next year he returned to Germany. Although he had always been independent in

judgment, he realized that the disaster to Varus was due to that general's rashness and lack of care and so he took no step without the approval of his military council. He also became more careful about matters of detail. . . . He gave his standing and emergency orders in writing with the injunction that if any officer had any question about them, he was to consult him personally at any hour of the day or night.

20. After two years in Germany Tiberius returned to Rome and celebrated the postponed Illyrian triumph. . . .

21. Since the consuls introduced a law that he should govern the provinces jointly with Augustus and hold the census with him, he set out for Illyricum on the conclusion of the lustral ceremonies; but he was at once recalled, and finding Augustus in his last illness but still alive, he spent an entire day with him in private.

The story goes that when Tiberius left the room after this confidential talk, Augustus was overheard by his attendants to say: Alas for the Roman people, to be ground by jaws that chew so slowly! I also am aware that some have said that Augustus so openly disapproved of his dour manner that he sometimes broke off his own light conversation when Tiberius appeared, and also that he only adopted him at Livia's request, with perhaps the notion that with such a successor he would himself be more sorely missed. But I cannot believe that such a prudent emperor acted so rashly on this important issue. I think that he weighed the pros and cons and decided that Tiberius' virtues tipped the balance. After all, he swore publicly that he adopted Tiberius in the national interest, and often called him in letters a capable general and the sole defense of the Roman people. Here are some selections:

Farewell, my dear Tiberius, and good luck in your battles on my behalf and for the Muses. Farewell, dearest of men and bravest of generals. My happiness rides on you!

When I hear and read that you are worn out by constant campaigning, I swear that my own body aches in sympathy. I beg you to spare yourself, so that a report of your illness does not kill your mother and me, and endanger the Roman people in the person of their future ruler.

It doesn't matter whether I am well or not, if you are not well. May the gods protect you and grant you good health now and forever, if they do not utterly hate the people of Rome.

22. Tiberius only announced the death of Augustus after he had got rid of Agrippa Postumus. He was killed by a military tribune appointed to guard him, who received written orders. It is not known if Augustus left the orders to remove a future source of discord, or whether Livia wrote it in Augustus' name (with or without the knowledge of Tiberius). When the tribune reported what he had done, Tiberius replied that he had given no such order, and that the man must render an account to the Senate. He was trying to avoid suspicion; later he allowed it to be forgotten.

23. When Tiberius used his tribunician power to convene the Senate and began to speak, he suddenly groaned aloud, as if overcome by grief, and wishing that not only his voice, but also his life might leave him, handed the written speech to his son Drusus to finish. Then a freedman read aloud the will of Augustus, . . . which began thus: "Since a cruel fate has bereft me of my sons Gaius and Lucius, let Tiberius Caesar be heir to two-thirds of my estate." This preamble strengthened the suspicion that Augustus had named Tiberius his successor from necessity rather than from choice.

24. Tiberius did not hesitate to exercise the imperial authority by surrounding himself with a guard of soldiers, the actual indication of imperial power. But he refused the title of "Emperor" for a long time, with barefaced hypocrisy now upbraiding his friends who urged him to accept it, saying that they did not realize what a monster the empire was, and now by evasive answers and calculating hesitancy keeping the senators in suspense when they begged him to yield and threw themselves at his feet. Some finally lost patience, and one man cried out in the confusion: "Let him take it or leave it." Another openly voiced the taunt that others were slow in doing what they promised, but that he was slow to promise what he was already doing. At last, as though on compulsion and complaining that he was being forced to be an overworked slave, he accepted the empire while

suggesting that he would one day lay it down. His own words are: "Until I come to the time when you might wish to grant an old man some rest."

26. Once relieved of fear, Tiberius at first behaved with such restraint as though he were a private citizen. He only accepted a few modest honors of the many that were proposed. He forbade the voting of temples and priests in his honor, and he would only allow his statues and busts to be set up as decorations but not among the images of the gods. He would not allow an oath to be taken ratifying his acts, nor the name Tiberius to be given to the month of September, or that of Livia to October. He also declined the name Imperator, and the title "Father of his Country."

30. He even pretended to introduce free government by keeping the old dignity and powers of the Senate and the magistrates. He referred all public business, whether important or trivial, to the senators, and consulted them about revenues and monopolies, the construction and upkeep of public buildings, and even about the draft, discharge and assignment of soldiers. He also asked them about appointing generals and his correspondence with foreign kings. When a cavalry commander was charged with armed robbery, he made him plead his case before the Senate. He always entered the Senate alone; and once when he was sick and was carried there in a litter, he dismissed his attendants.

31. Much public business was left to the magistrates and the ordinary process of law, while the consuls grew so important that some envoys from Africa came to them complaining that they were wasting time with Caesar, to whom they had been sent. And this was not surprising, for everyone knew that he himself actually rose in the presence of the consuls, and made way for them on the street.

33. Tiberius gradually revealed his control, and yet, though he was inconsistent, he often was kind and devoted to the public good. At first he intervened only to prevent abuses. Thus he revoked some regulations of the Senate and sometimes offered the magistrates his services as adviser, when taking a place with them on the tribunal. If it was rumored that any defendants were being acquitted through influence, he would suddenly appear, and either from the floor or from the judge's tribunal remind the jurors of the laws and of their oath, as well as of the nature of the crime on which they were sitting in judgment. Moreover, he tried to correct any decline in public morals due to laziness or bad habits.

36. Tiberius abolished foreign cults, especially the Egyptian and the Jewish rites, compelling all who were addicted to such superstitions to burn their religious vestments and all their paraphernalia. Jews of military age he sent to less healthy provinces, ostensibly to serve in the army, and he banished other Jews from Rome on pain of slavery for life if they did not obey. He banished the astrologers as well, but pardoned such as begged his forgiveness and promised to give up their art.

43. When Tiberius withdrew to Capri in A.D. 26, he devised an orgy-room where flocks of girls and male prostitutes, specialists in unnatural sex, were brought from all over the Empire. They performed before him in groups of three to excite his now flagging lust through voyeurism. Small bedrooms were decorated with the most indecent pictures and sculpture, and there were Egyptian pornographic manuscripts so that they could see what they should do. Tiberius also created sexual hideaways in the woods where boys and girls dressed as Pan and the nymphs stood guard in front of the grottos. Now the island is openly called not Capri but "Caprineum"—because of his goat-like (caprinus) behavior.

50. He first showed his hatred toward his relatives when he produced a private letter in which his brother Drusus suggested that they compel Augustus to restore the Republic; later he showed his hostility towards the rest of his family. So far from showing any courtesy or kindness to his wife Julia after her banishment (which is the least one might expect), Tiberius kept her in the seclusion of her house though Augustus had merely confined her to one city. In fact he even deprived her of the annual income allowed by Augustus, on the pretext that Augustus had made no provision for it in his will. Tiberius complained that his mother Livia

annoyed him by wanting to share power, and though he sometimes needed her advice, he avoided long conversations with her lest he seem to follow it. The senatorial decree providing that "son of Livia," as well as "son of Augustus," should be inscribed among his titles so upset him that he did not allow her to be called "Mother of her Country," nor other inflated title. And he also warned her not to meddle in public matters inappropriate for women, especially after he learned that she urged on the people and soldiers of the fire-brigade to extinguish a fire at the temple of Vesta, as she had when Augustus was still alive.

51. Later there was open enmity between Tiberius and Livia.... Livia produced and read some old letters written to her by Augustus with regard to Tiberius' dour and stubborn disposition. And he was angry that she had kept them for so long and used them in such a spiteful spirit, that some think that this was the chief reason for his withdrawal to Capri. He saw her only once in her last three years, and then only for a few hours.... When she died, ... he forbade her deification, alleging that he was acting according to her own instructions. He further disregarded the provisions of her will, and within a short time caused the downfall of all her friends and intimates....

52. He had a father's affection neither for his own son Drusus, whose dissolute life offended him, nor his adopted son Germanicus.... He did not like Germanicus, so he made light of his illustrious deeds and even complained in the Senate when Germanicus, on the occasion of a sudden and terrible famine, went to Alexandria without consulting him. Some even think he encouraged Gnaeus Piso, governor of Syria, to poison him and, when Piso was tried on that charge, he would have produced his instructions had not Tiberius caused them to be taken from him when Piso privately showed them, and the man himself to be put to death....

54. By Germanicus he had three adoptive grandsons, Nero, Drusus, and Caligula, and by Drusus one, called Tiberius Gemellus. [Though he recommended Nero and Drusus to the Senate when they came of age, they were eventually declared public enemies and killed.]

55. In addition to his old friends and intimates, he asked for twenty leading men to be his advisers. Only two or three died naturally; the others he destroyed one way or another, including Aelius Sejanus, whose downfall involved the death of many others. The emperor had advanced that creature to destroy the children of Germanicus and secure the succession for his own grandson, the child of his son Drusus.

61. Tiberius soon vented his cruelty on the friends and even the acquaintances, first of his mother, then of his grandsons and daughter-in-law, and finally of Sejanus. After the death of Sejanus he was more cruel than ever, which showed that the prefect did not incite him but merely provided welcome opportunities. Yet in his brief autobiography he asserted that he had punished Sejanus because he vented his hatred on the children of his son Germanicus. Whereas in fact Tiberius had himself put one of them to death after he had begun to suspect Sejanus and the other after the latter's downfall....

62. He became more savage when he learned that his son Drusus had not died from dissipation, but was poisoned by the treachery of his wife Livilla and Sejanus.... On Capri they still point out the place where Tiberius had his victims cast into the sea after long tortures.... Even more would have died but he delayed some executions, when the astrologer Thrasyllus convinced him that he still had long to live. And it is thought that he would not even have spared his grandsons Caligula and Tiberius Gemellus....

65. Though Tiberius was aware that Sejanus' birthday was publicly celebrated and gold statues were erected in his honor as he prepared to seize the throne, the emperor removed him by guile rather than by his imperial authority. He first removed Sejanus from his immediate entourage by making him his colleague in the consulship, which Tiberius entered in absentia. When Sejanus went to Rome beguiled with hope of a royal marriage to Livilla and of imperial power, he was accused in Tiberius' shameful message to the Senate begging them

among other things to send one of the consuls to bring him, a lonely old man, into their presence under military protection. . . . The emperor even prepared ships and considered fleeing to the legions, constantly watching from a high cliff for the fire signals which he had ordered in case the messengers were delayed. But even when the conspiracy of Sejanus was crushed, he was no more confident, and for the next nine months he did not leave his villa on Capri.

68. Taller than average, Tiberius had a strong and heavily-built, though well-proportioned, body with a broad chest and shoulders. His left hand was the more nimble and stronger, so powerful that he could bore through a fresh apple with his finger, and break the head of a boy or a young man with a fillip. He was of fair complexion and wore his hair rather long at the back, so much so as even to cover the nape of his neck as was the Claudian custom. His face was handsome, but would suddenly break out in pimples. . . . He walked stiff-necked leaning forward, usually with a stern countenance and for the most part in silence, very rarely talking with his companions, and then speaking with great deliberation and with prissy gesturing of his fingers. Augustus put these mannerisms

down to arrogance, but he often tried to excuse them to the Senate and people by declaring that they were natural failings, and not intentional. Tiberius enjoyed excellent health, which was all but perfect during nearly the whole of his reign, although from the thirtieth year of his age he took care of it himself, without the aid or advice of physicians.

69. Although neglectful of the gods and religion, his belief in astrology convinced him that everything was ruled by fate. But he was absurdly frightened of thunder so that in threatening weather he always wore a laurel wreath, because it is said that kind of leaf is not struck by lightning.

75. The people were so happy to hear of his death, that at the news some ran about shouting, Tiberius to the Tiber, while others prayed to Mother Earth and the Spirits of the Dead to allow the dead man no abode except among the damned. . . .

76. Two years before his death he had made a will . . . in which he named his grandsons, Caligula, son of Germanicus, and Tiberius Gemellus, son of Drusus, heirs to equal shares of his estate, each to be sole heir in case of the other's death. . . .

In Praise of Tiberius and Sejanus

Velleius Paterculus

Velleius here provides a panegyric to his hero and old commander Tiberius and his right-hand man Sejanus. The historian published the book in A.D. 30—the year before the fall of Sejanus and the terrible last years of Tiberius on Capri. But it provides an extraordinary contrast to the accounts of the resentful senatorial historians.

CXXI.   Tiberius showed the same valour, and was attended by the same fortune, when he entered Germany on his later campaigns as in his first. After he had broken the force of the enemy by his expeditions on sea and land, had completed his difficult task in Gaul, and had settled by restraint rather than by punishment the dissensions that had broken out among the Viennenses, at the request of his father that he should have in all the provinces and armies a power equal to his own, the senate and Roman people so decreed. For indeed it was incongruous that the provinces which were being defended by him should not be under his jurisdiction, and that he who was foremost in bearing aid should not be considered an equal in the honor to be won. On his return to the city he celebrated the triumph over the Pannonians and Dalmatians, long since due him, but postponed by reason of a succession of wars. Who can be surprised at its magnificence, since it was the triumph of Caesar? Yet who can fail to wonder at the kindness of fortune to him? For the most eminent leaders of the enemy were not slain in battle, that report should tell thereof, but were taken captive, so that in his triumph he exhibited them in chains. It was my lot and that of my brother to participate in this triumph among the men of distinguished rank and those who were decorated with distinguished honours.

CXXII.   Among the other acts of Tiberius Caesar, wherein his remarkable moderation shines forth conspicuously, who does not wonder at this also, that, although he unquestionably earned seven triumphs, he was satisfied with three? For who can doubt that, when he had recovered Armenia, had placed over it a king upon whose head he had with his own hand set the mark of royalty, and had put in order the affairs of the east, he ought to have received an ovation; and that after his conquest of the Vindelici and the Raeti he should have entered the city as victor in a triumphal chariot? Or that, after his adoption, when he had broken the power of the Germans in three consecutive campaigns, the same honour should have been bestowed upon him and should have been accepted by him? And that, after the disaster received under Varus, when this same Germany was crushed by a course of events which, sooner than was expected, came to a happy issue, the honour of a triumph should have been awarded to this consummate general? But, in the case of this man, one does not know which to admire the more, that in courting toils and danger he went beyond all bounds or that in accepting honours he kept within them. . . .

CXXVI.   Who would undertake to tell in detail the accomplishments of the past sixteen years, since they are borne in upon the eyes and hearts of all? Caesar deified his father, not by exercise of his imperial authority, but by his attitude of reverence; he did not call him a god, but made him one. Credit has been restored in the forum, strife has been banished from the forum, canvassing for office from the Campus Martius, discord from the senate-house; justice, equity, and industry, long buried in oblivion, have been restored to the state; the magistrates have regained their authority, the senate its majesty, the courts their dignity; rioting in the theatre has been suppressed; all citizens have either been impressed with the wish to do right, or have been forced to do so by necessity. Right is now honoured, evil is punished; the humble man respects the great but does not fear him, the great has precedence over the lowly but does not despise him. When was the price of grain more reasonable, or when were the blessings of peace greater? The *pax augusta* (Augustan peace) which has spread to the regions of the east and of the west and to the bounds of the north and of the south, preserves every corner of the world safe from the fear of brigandage. The munificence of the emperor claims for its province the losses inflicted by fortune not merely on private citizens, but on whole cities. The cities of Asia have been restored, the provinces have been freed from the oppression of their magistrates. Honour ever awaits the worthy; for the wicked punishment is slow but sure; fair play has now precedence over influence, and merit over ambition, for the best of emperors teaches his citizens to do right by doing it, and though he is greatest among us in authority, he is still greater in the example which he sets.

CXXVII.   It is but rarely that men of eminence have failed to employ great men to aid them in directing their fortune, as the two Scipios employed the two Laelii, whom in all things they treated as equal to themselves, or as the deified Augustus employed Marcus Agrippa, and after him Statilius Taurus. In the case of these men their lack of lineage was no obstacle to their elevation to successive consulships, triumphs, and numerous priesthoods. For great tasks require great helpers, and it is important to the state that those who are necessary to her service should be given prominence in rank, and that their usefulness should be fortified by official authority. With these examples before him, Tiberius Caesar has had and still has as his incomparable associate in all the burdens of the principate Sejanus Aelius, son of a father who was among the foremost in the equestrian order, but connected, on his mother's side, with old and illustrious families and families distinguished by public honours, while he had brothers, cousins, and an uncle who had reached the consulship. He himself combined with loyalty to his master great capacity for labour, and possessed a well-knit body to match the energy of his mind; stern but yet gay, cheerful but yet strict; busy, yet always seeming to be at leisure. He is one who claims no honours for himself and so acquires all honours, whose estimate of himself is always below the estimate of others, calm in expression and in his life, though his mind is sleeplessly alert.

CXXVIII.   In the value set upon the character of this man, the judgement of the whole state has long vied with that of the emperor. Nor is it a new fashion on the part of the senate and the Roman people to regard as most noble that which is best. For the Romans who, three centuries ago, in the days before the Punic war, raised Tiberius Coruncanius, a new man, to the first position in the state, not only bestowing on him all the other honours but the office of pontifex maximus as well; and those who elevated to consulships, censorships, and triumphs Spurius Carvilius, though born of equestrian rank, and soon afterwards Marcus Cato, though a new man and not a native of the city but from Tusculum, and Mummius, who triumphed over Achaia; and those who regarded Gaius Marius, though of obscure origin, as unquestionably the first man of the Roman name until his sixth consulship; and those who yielded such honours to Marcus Tullius that on his recommendation he could secure positions of importance almost for anyone he chose; and those who refused no honour to Asinius Pollio, honours which could only be earned, even by the noblest, by sweat and toil—all those assuredly felt that the highest honours should be paid to the man of merit. It was but the natural following of precedent that impelled Caesar to put Sejanus to the test, and that Sejanus was induced to assist the emperor with his burdens, and that brought the senate and the Roman people to the point where they were ready to summon for the preservation of its security the man whom they regarded as the most useful instrument.

The Psychology of Tiberius

Gregorio Maranon

The psychoanalyst Gregorio Maranon has provided a controversial psychological portrait of the emperor Tiberius. His book, published in 1956, has been criticized for its uncritical acceptance of nearly every personal quirk reported in the ancient sources, and for its reductive use of this material in a rigid psychological system. Yet Maranon is constantly stimulating as he discusses Tiberius' timidity and his need to depend on other strong personalities such as Livia and Sejanus, as well as the emperor's own personal anguish. The ancient sources show clearly enough that Tiberius was an inadequate and troubled man; Maranon attempts to describe the pathology of the tyrant as described by Tacitus and Suetonius.

Tiberius's Timidity

The classical historians themselves refer to Tiberius's timidity, which, mingled with his more elemental emotions, makes its appearance at every turn of his life. Tacitus tells us, for example, that the emperor 'at one and the same time loved and feared Sejanus': a typical expression of Tiberius's ambivalence. . . .Tiberius's timidity and its importance in his public and private life are not to be denied.

Men of tall stature, including giants, are especially predisposed to suffer from the defect of timidity, sexual and social, both closely linked. Such was the case with Tiberius, who was a tall man. Even in his military life, his well-known desire to spare the lives of his men was often interpreted as lack of decision. The failure of the Roman legions against the insurrection of the Dalmatians during Augustus's lifetime was attributed to his irresolution, and so was the unsuccessful campaign in Gaul in A.D. 21. I have already said that these criticisms must have wounded him. His forte was diplomacy rather than military assault; perhaps because he did not feel himself to be sufficiently strong for it. Cleverness is the resource of the weak; and some men have been great diplomats simply because they were fundamentally weak.

But it was above all in Tiberius's civilian life that evidence abounds about the timidity which he hid behind his severe cast of countenance. I have already mentioned several instances of it, some apparently trivial, but all of great significance in the march of events. I may recall the absence of the emperor and his family from the funeral of Germanicus, which was undoubtedly due to fear, and the notoriously unjust condemnation of Piso, which was dictated by the emperor's timorous yielding to public clamour. . . .

His Mother and His Favorites

But what most clearly conveys his weakness of will was his constant need to lean on someone else's will. Tiberius lived always in the shadow of other people's imperious strength. In the first place, there was that of his mother and also that of Augustus, semi-divine. We have seen how he was dragged along by Livia's manoeuvres and protection in the long struggle between the two imperial families. His present and his future swung backwards and forwards, like an inert object, at the mercy of two contrary forces, that of Livia, who pushed him forward, and that of Augustus, who pushed him back.

When he became master of the empire he was past fifty: an age at which the mind, at its maturity, may still yield its best fruits, but at which it is hard for it to be cast in a new mould; and this was what was needed in Tiberius's case. The long apprenticeship of his youth and middle age had been excellent for his training as an administrator, but fatal for the strengthening of his will.

He could give orders to the whole Roman empire, but he could not make himself independent of his mother. Ambitious Livia, toughened by her years, was ever his empress. We have already seen how he tried to react against her tutelage, but beneath his superficial rebellion we can sense that her yoke, forged and tightened over so many years, was stronger than he thought. To gain his independence he had to break openly with his mother. He had first to absent himself from Rome, and then to sever all relations with her. In short, like all timid men, he sought refuge in flight.

But, fleeing from one slavery, he fell into a worse one. Like all weak tyrants, he had a constant need for an omnipotent minister, a favorite. Sejanus became his favorite. Dio tells us that during the latter years of his reign it was said that 'Sejanus was the emperor of Rome, and Tiberius was merely the governor of Capri.' Like all favorites, Sejanus sought to devour his master—this is a just biological law—but, as happens to many a man, he died the victim of one of those sudden violent reactions of a weak man. When his minister carried his tyranny too far, and thereby attracted the lightning-stroke of public wrath, the submissive emperor turned on him with the support of popular opinion.

To rid himself of Sejanus, Tiberius found another support also, that of Macro, a useful man though a bad one, who took the place of the fallen favorite in the command of the praetorian cohorts, and in the ruling of the empire by his influence over the emperor's will. To obtain some idea of the laxity of Tiberius's will, we need only consider this absolute submission of his to second-rate minds, vacuous and intriguing, like those of Sejanus and Macro, whereas he put to death men of political talent like Nerva. We may also compare this excessive influence of his favorites over Tiberius with the strictly defined and never excessive rank allotted to ministers of the stature of Maecenas and Agrippa by an emperor of strong will and real political talent like Augustus. Augustus, let us not forget, also had Livia at his side for the greater part of his life, and, what was worse, during the nights of many a long year. Nevertheless, he managed to evade the same danger from this imperious woman who made a prisoner of Tiberius.

Crises of Will-Power

The most characteristic crises of Tiberius's wavering will were his doubts about accepting the emperorship, and, above all, his flights, to Rhodes in his youth and to Capri in his old age. These two latter episodes belong to the nebulous region of his abnormalities and I shall deal with them later. As to his dallying about accepting power, the references of the classic authors present it as one of the typical manifestations of his hypocrisy, since while he was resisting in the Senate he was handling the troops as though he were already emperor. But close reading of these references conveys the impression that his doubts were sincere, being the offspring of his indecision, and that what he was trying to conceal with his confused language and his mysterious attitude was his own weakness. . . .

Tiberius's Ambivalence

. . . I have stressed Tiberius's dual personality: on the obverse, his strictness as an administrator, his zeal for order, his qualities as a general; on the reverse, the dark passions of his soul. If we try to judge him in modern terms we might say that he was an excellent technical expert with a depraved soul: a combination, to be sure, in no way exceptional. His glorification by recent authors is a typical expression of modern ethics, which, so long as a man is efficient, will forgive him all else.

This dual personality of Tiberius is interesting because it very well explains the ambivalence of his soul: his respect, as a subject and a son, for Augustus and Livia, and his hatred of them, because they had built the virtue and the glory of the imperial home on the foundation of his father's sorrow; his compassion for Julia, his lawful wife, when she was exiled, and his implacable rancour against her for the ridicule with which she had covered him; his alternations of protection and persecution towards Germanicus and Agrippina and her children; his attitudes of friendship and mortal enmity towards Sejanus, his friend and his enemy at one and the same time; and so on, always the same.

All the time, through the chinks of his excellent administrative armour, we can see the fumes of his resentment escaping, and so giving his life that ambiguous aspect which his contemporaries interpreted as hypocrisy and later historians have been unable to confine within the definition of a personality all of a piece.

The Cycle of Resentment

As we survey Tiberius's life, we can see clearly how, in proportion as his resentment fermented, the troubled, passionate reverse of his personality gradually overcame the clear obverse of his political life. For this reason the ancients regarded him as a disconcerting man who kept on changing all the time. Let me again recall the words of Pliny, who described him as an austere, but sociable prince, who as the years went by turned severe and cruel. Some of the classical historians assign a fixed date for his change from good to evil, associating it with the death of his son Drusus, or that of Germanicus, or that of Livia. These misfortunes, indeed, gave sudden spurts to the cycle of his passion of resentment. But, still more than any of them, what brought about its final paroxysm was Sejanus's treachery and the alleged assassination of his son.

This outburst of his later years was also influenced by the intoxication of power. It is typical of the resentful man, and especially of the man both timid and resentful, as I have already remarked, that, when he acquires a power dependent alike on force and cunning, he makes a barbarously vindictive use of it. The test of power divides men who achieve it into two great groups: those who are sublimated by the responsibility of ruling, and those who are perverted. The reason for this difference resides solely in the capacity for magnanimity of the first, and in the resentment of the second.

To quote only examples historically close to Tiberius, among the great leaders who were ennobled by the exercise of power I may recall Julius Caesar, an immoral demagogue at the beginning of his career, and a fine ruler in the second part of his short official life. Then there was Augustus himself, whose youth, full of profound and shameful moral failings, was transformed by the imperial responsibility into a balanced, patriarchal middle age, with unquestionable gleams of greatness. Examples of the degenerating influence of power, on the other hand, are to be found in Tiberius, Caligula, Claudius, Nero and Domitian.

It is no fancy of the ancient historian . . . but a positive fact, this change which, in all cases of weak-willed and especially resentful men, is brought about by the intoxication of power, and indeed gives their reigns a clear appearance of two phases: a first, which is good, and a second, which is bad.

We must bear in mind what the supreme power meant at the time of the Roman emperors. Nothing can give us a better idea of it than the words which Seneca puts into Nero's mouth at the beginning of his emperorship: 'I am the arbiter of the life and death of peoples. The destiny of everyone is in my hands. What fate is to befall everyone, it rests with me to say. On one reply of mine depends the happiness of cities. Without my consent, none of them can prosper.' It would be understandable that demigods should stand this almost supernatural power without its going to their heads; but not men of flesh and blood.

Finally, it is not certain that in his later years, when he was an old man, hurt by so much misfortune, and perhaps syphilitic, Tiberius's mind remained normal. I shall deal a little later with his flights, his incessant comings and goings between his retreat in Capri and Rome, which have a suspicious appearance of madness. Only Antonia's sound sense linked him with normality. But it was a link too weak by contrast with the forces that impelled him, without reason or justice, into his reign of terror: a reign of terror which sent a shudder through history and possessed all the characteristics of the spite of a resentful man, because it was not directed—like the spite of hatred or envy—against those who had offended him, but against everyone; for everyone, human and divine, was his enemy. . . .

'Island' Psychology

So it was that Tiberius was alone in the great, bustling swarm of Rome; and in his loneliness he instinctively sought solitude, where he might encounter his own company, hard to find amid the multitude. This is the main explanation of his retirement, while still a young man, to the island of Rhodes, and now, as an old man, to the island of Capri.

Every misanthropic man has this same tendency towards 'the island,' which separates him from the outside world, yet at the same time gives him a limited world in which his sense of inferiority may breathe with less distress. If the misanthropic man is also a resentful man, this attraction becomes all the stronger. Indeed, a man born in an island, even if he be a normal man, suffers from the influence of an island environment, which is full of a dangerous ambivalence. In the island he may be self-sufficient—like Robinson Crusoe—better and more easily than on the immense mainland; but this self-sufficiency is irremediably limited. The stress of this twofold influence weighs upon the minds of almost all islanders. By way of relieving it they are very often alcoholics.

But the problem is clearer in the case of the man who deliberately seeks the island. I doubt whether this question has been studied with the attention which it deserves. The man from the mainland who shuts himself up in an island does so precisely because his soul needs a little, limited cosmos, just as certain birds prefer the gilded world of their cages to the outside world, full of effort and danger. Any observer may catch that unmistakable glance, expressive of repression and resentment, in the eyes of a settler in one of those islands that are ports of call for light-hearted tourists but refuges for those whose lives have been shipwrecked on the mainland. . . .

Abnormality and Madness

What did Tiberius do in Capri during those last eleven years of his life? Let me repeat here my agreement with those who believe the story of his repulsive vices, which Suetonius describes in such detail and with almost ingenuous shamelessness, together with the story of his refined cruelties, to be a mere legend. Tiberius retired to the island sick of the whole of humanity, concentrated upon himself, fleeing into himself, to the point of anguish; irremediably isolated, not only from his living environment, but also from his memories and his hopes; by now without a past and without a future. With a mind in such a state, a body is in no mood for orgies.

It was said, even at that time, that Tiberius had lost his reason, and some modern commentators repeat this. But, in the data which his contemporaries have handed down to us, there are no grounds for making an exact psychiatric diagnosis of the emperor, even taking into account the suspicion that he may have been syphilitic. Tiberius was—so much is certain—a schizoid; but he was not mad. The terrible anguish of his resentment gave the last years of his life the accent of abnormality, which is not madness, though it may be confused with it. His flight from Rome was not the act of a madman, but it was the act of an abnormal man. So was his refusal to return for eleven years, despite all the advantages of doing so. Abnormal, above all, were his tragic attempts to approach the city, with which I shall deal in a moment. He was not, in short, a sadistic madman.

Equally inadmissible, however, is the picture which some simplifying historians paint for us of an almost patriarchal old man, seeking rest after a long, sad life, and relief for his senses and his soul by plunging them in the incomparable sunsets of the Bay of Naples. Tiberius was simply a man whom the passion of resentment had made abnormal.

The most conclusive proof that he was merely abnormal is provided by the legend about him. Abnormality is not madness; but, precisely because of its element of ambiguity, and because it does not produce the definite attitudes of vigilance or pity which madness brings into play, those who are simply abnormal in mind often perturb homes or nations much more frequently and much more gravely than downright madmen. Legends do not grow around a madman. Madness is, in itself, a legend for the multitude; but the great legends grow around the abnormal man whose conduct, with its chiaroscuro, we cannot understand.

Around this man, who was not mad and yet was not entirely in his right mind; who kept on leaving Capri and coming back without apparent reason, always shutting himself up again in his inaccessible island mansions; who passed along the paths surrounded by soldiers who drove the curious away with blows; who was a rational and at the same time an incomprehensible ruler; who implacably carried on his life despite the death of his nearest relatives; who cast his favourite, within a few hours, from absolute power to destruction; who persecuted Agrippina's and Sejanus's friends with a cruelty disguised as strict legality; who saw his best friend deliberately commit suicide beside him; who was the prudent governor of a people ruled with shrewdness and at the same time terrorized by informing—around such an indecisive personality, complex and mysterious, legends were bound to grow.

So grew the legend of his cruelty in Capri, full of nice refinements, obviously invented by the populace. There was, for example, the story of the fisherman who startled the emperor by suddenly approaching him and offering him a fish. Tiberius had his face fiercely rubbed with it. When the poor fellow, who, like his emperor, was a humorist, congratulated himself, amid groans of pain, that he had not offered him a lobster, Tiberius, by way of capping the joke, sent for a lobster, and continued the cruel rubbing with its scaly shell.

The legend of such subtle cruelty created in turn the legend of his sexual vices and aberrations. The public's sense of sadism is always on the watch. To associate sexual pleasure with pain is instinctive in people in times of collective depravity or political terrorism. During the recent Spanish revolution, the legend that grew up around the unquestionable fact of cruelty became immediately associated with a complicated series of sexual aberrations, which people hitherto truthful declared they had witnessed and doubtless believed that they had. It was

with the same dubious brand of truth that gossipers in Rome related stories about erotic mysteries in the grottoes of Capri. In all periods of social disturbance there are similar stories; and I am convinced that in every case they should be accepted with the same reserve.

Similarly legend must have exaggerated the fear which Tiberius undoubtedly displayed during his latter years; for the fact that he displayed it is unquestionable. Some authors . . . suggest that it reached the point of regular persecution mania; and doubtless it sometimes looked like it. An imperial edict forbade anyone to approach the emperor along the paths, even at a distance; soldiers in his confidence escorted him everywhere; and even his letters to the Senate betray the fear in which he continually lived, suspecting ambushes and conspiracies all round him. But this was worry rather than real fear; the worry of old age, which increased his inborn timidity.

An infinite anguish marked the last phase of his life and his reign. It was the anguish of a resentful man who could find no relief either in revenge or in pardon, because the thorn of his anguish was in the essence of his own soul, incapable of generosity. He fled the world only to find himself in solitude; and solitude terrified him, because it was too close to his despair. It was an ambivalence of wanting and not wanting, of being able and being unable, which lived in his soul like two brothers, at one and the same time twins and deadly enemies.

The Tragic Round

We have often witnessed this same spectacle in outlaws or in historical personages. But in the case of Tiberius his anguish attained the dimensions of tragedy: a dreadful tragedy of sheer horror, such as has never yet been adequately described. He was the emperor of the world; and the whole world meant, to his uneasy spirit, what the cramped space of his cell means to an unhappy prisoner. He went from Capri to Rome and returned to Capri without entering the city, which attracted him and repelled him with one and the same force. 'He circled around Rome,'

Tacitus tells us, 'almost always by lonely roads, seeming at once to seek it and to flee from it.'

Twice he all but managed to touch its immemorial walls with his hands tremulous with terror and old age. On one occasion, onboard a trireme, he ascended the Tiber to the naumachy which lay off his gardens; and then, for no known reason, he suddenly turned his back on that city peopled with ghosts and returned to Capri. On the other occasion, travelling by land, he got as far as the Appian Way. There he encamped, replied to letters from the consuls, and surveyed the trembling city, crushed by informing and executions. He sought to overcome his fear and approach it more closely. But one morning he found in his own hand the corpse of a snake, a festering feast for ants: a bad omen which meant the hatred of the people towards him; and he returned trembling to his exile. On both occasions, as usual, soldiers drove away the crowds from the banks of the river and the sides of the road. Only from a distance could his silent people catch a glimpse of him and furtively point out to their children the tall, bent figure of the sinister Caesar.

Rarely has history given us a picture of superhuman anguish such as that of this emperor, prowling like a criminal around the scene of his crimes, without realizing that it was to be found, not in Rome, but in his own lost soul.

There are two sayings of his which depict his infinite spiritual solitude, without anchorage in the past or in the future. Seneca tells us about both of them. On one occasion, someone approached Tiberius and started speaking to him, asking: 'Do you remember, Caesar? . . . ' Tiberius cut him short. 'No,' he replied, sombrely, 'I remember nothing about what I have been.' The other saying was a Greek verse. Tiberius repeated it often. It meant his renunciation of all hope. 'After me, let fire destroy the earth!'

Such was Tiberius.

The Politician Sejanus

Thomas Africa

Thomas Africa of the State University of New York at Binghamton provides a fascinating picture of the rise and fall of an ambitious politician. He quotes Velleius' panegyric of Sejanus, the attempts by former friends to distance themselves from him after his fall, and the satirist Juvenal's mockery as the statues of Sejanus are consigned to the flames. It is a salutary morality tale. Tacitus might lead us to believe that Sejanus was obviously a monster for all to see, and so it might seem in retrospect. But his contemporaries at first saw him as little more than another ruthless politician eager to curry favor and power with the monarch. His most heinous crimes were revealed only after his death. Those who grasp for power and fail are doomed, like Antony and Sejanus, to vilification by their victors. The question remains whether the victorious were any more virtuous. Sejanus did not fall because he was bad, but because he was outsmarted in the dangerous and deadly game of imperial politics.

The career of Sejanus, right-hand man of the emperor Tiberius, was a model for aspiring politicians in any era. With ability, agility, and cunning, he pushed his way through the power structure to a position second only to the emperor himself. Sejanus would have been equally successful under the cold and suspicious Stalin. However, the wily Sejanus succumbed to ambition and was crushed by the master whom he threatened. The ultimate fate of Sejanus had elements of tragedy, and his meteoric fall from power excited Roman moralists of later generations. While the rise and fall of agile schemers is a common theme in world history, the career of Sejanus was conditioned by factors which Augustus had set in motion. . . .

. . . Despite his achievements as a ruler, Tiberius was an unhappy and lonely man. For decades, resentment had eroded his personality until the emperor was close to misanthropy. The few people whom Tiberius trusted sooner or later disappointed or betrayed him. His mother, the dowager empress Livia, was a domineering old woman who had hoped to control the state through him. However, Tiberius sent Livia into retirement and would not attend her funeral when she died. The emperor's son Drusus was a mediocrity, and his official heir Germanicus was a vain prince with an ambitious wife, Agrippina. The court seethed with intrigue and a dangerous faction formed around Agrippina, who was impatient for Germanicus to reach the throne. The emperor respected his astrologer Thrasyllus but loathed the other courtiers, whose smiles masked envy and hatred. Bored with social affairs, Tiberius preferred pedantic discussions with Thrasyllus but turned to the bottle whenever the conversation palled. As age and disappointment overtook him, the emperor became increasingly dependent on wine, but the administration of the empire never suffered from his indulgence in alcohol. Weary with power and isolated by suspicion, Tiberius had only one friend on whom he relied to share the burdens of state—the prefect Sejanus, who commanded the Praetorian guards.[1]

The Augustan era was an age of social mobility and many men had risen in status through faithful service to the Princeps. The old nobility was debilitated and many famous families had perished in the civil wars. The

---

1 Two Equites with the rank of prefect commanded the 9,000 Praetorian guards who protected the palace and the emperor. The senior Praetorian prefect held a position of great potential power, and occasionally there was only one prefect in charge of the guards.

future lay with the minor gentry, or Equites, who had controlled the financial life of Rome during the Republic. Under the emperors, Equites increasingly dominated the civil service and earned noble status through promotion to consular rank. Most Equites were loyal public servants, but a few were ambitious schemers, like Lucius Aelius Sejanus. His father, Seius Strabo, was from Tuscany and served as Praetorian prefect in the last years of Augustus. To improve his social status, Strabo had married a lady from a powerful noble family, and their son Sejanus was later adopted into another noble clan, the Aelian family. Such adoptions were common practice among social climbers at Rome. While Strabo typified the revolutionary elite who rose with Augustus, Sejanus represented the second generation of Equites, who built on the achievements of their fathers. In his first official position, Sejanus served as an aide to a grandson of Augustus and may have met Tiberius while the future emperor was in self-imposed exile on Rhodes. Soon the able Sejanus became his father's colleague in the Praetorian guards. In A.D. 14, Tiberius appointed Strabo to a lucrative governorship in Egypt and promoted Sejanus to be the sole prefect of the Praetorians. Having won the confidence of Tiberius, Sejanus persuaded the emperor to move the guards to a permanent barracks on the outskirts of Rome. Since he held the life of the emperor in his hands, Sejanus was well aware of the political implications of his position as Praetorian prefect.

Like most successful politicians, the prefect gave an impression of great sincerity. Impressed by his ability and apparent loyalty, the lonely Tiberius trusted Sejanus implicitly and called him "companion of my labors." A contemporary view of the Praetorian prefect was expressed by a retired colonel, Velleius Paterculus, who admired Tiberius and praised Sejanus without reservations. [Cf. pp 175-6 above for the text of Velleius.]. . . While typical of the new men who served the Principate, Sejanus unfortunately was not the paragon of virtue which he seemed to be in the uncritical judgment of Paterculus.

In reality, Sejanus had most of the unpleasant characteristics of Faulkner's scheming Flem Snopes. The historian Tacitus sneered that Sejanus was a "small town adulterer" as well as a prototype of the Praetorian kingmakers who often disrupted Roman politics. Though a few contemporaries were aware of his duplicity, the Praetorian prefect planned his political moves with consummate skill and carefully hid his ambitions from the aged and trusting Tiberius. As commander of the palace guards, Sejanus made every effort to win the personal loyalties of the Praetorians. He screened the selection of all officers and took care to address enlisted men by name. In the days of the Republic, Cicero had used similar tactics to win the loyalty of voters.

Not content with Tiberius' trust, Sejanus wanted absolute control over the emperor. The first obstacle was Germanicus, the nephew and adopted heir of Tiberius. On the German frontier, Germanicus had won fame in battles and his wife Agrippina impressed Roman troops with her courage during a mutiny. Sejanus persuaded the emperor that the growing popularity of Germanicus and Agrippina might prove a threat to Tiberius. When Germanicus died of fever in 19, rumor implicated Tiberius and Sejanus in his death, and Agrippina was convinced that her husband had been poisoned. With the death of Germanicus, Tiberius was free to show favor to his own son and began to groom Drusus for the succession. However, Sejanus resented Drusus' influence with Tiberius and often quarreled with the prince, who finally struck the prefect in anger. Intent on revenge, Sejanus seduced Drusus' wife Livilla, who had developed into a great beauty. Whatever reason drove her into Sejanus' arms, Livilla was only a tool for the prefect's far-reaching schemes. In 23 Tiberius suffered a great personal loss, the sudden death of his son Drusus, and turned again to Sejanus for comfort and support. . . .

Confident of his privileged position, Sejanus hoped to marry Livilla, whose son Gemellus was Tiberius' only grandson and would likely be his heir. When the prefect asked Tiberius for approval, the emperor dryly replied that public opinion was not yet ready for such an alliance. In 26 Tiberius also rejected Agrippina's request to remarry, for he feared the marriage would add strength to her faction. The aged Livia constantly criticized the haughtiness and sharp tongue of Agrippina, and Sejanus' agents trapped the princess into offending the emperor. Posing as friends, they warned Agrippina that Tiberius planned to poison her; accordingly, she refused to eat the food which he handed to her at a banquet. The old despot interpreted her behavior as proof that she was planning to poison him. Since the city of Rome had always depressed him and court intrigues had become unbearable, the emperor withdrew from the noisy capital, never to return. While traveling in southern Italy, Tiberius was again impressed by the loyalty of Sejanus. When the emperor's entourage was dining in a scenic grotto, part of the roof collapsed and the prefect shielded Tiberius from falling rocks by throwing himself over the ruler. Confident that Sejanus would guard his interests at Rome, Tiberius retired to the Isle of Capri with a small clique of intellectuals and astrologers. After 27, Sejanus was the principal link between the emperor on Capri and the Senate and court at Rome. Nevertheless, the wary Tiberius kept a careful watch on events in the capital and received reports from sources other than Sejanus.

At Rome, Sejanus devoted himself to the destruction of the family of Germanicus. With his usual skill, the prefect played Agrippina's two older sons against each other, and he seduced their wives in order to learn the secrets of Agrippina's faction. Since the armies were loyal to Tiberius, Agrippina did not dare to appeal to the legions for support, for she was not inclined to the desperate gambles of civil war. In 29 Livia died at the age of eighty-six, but Tiberius did not attend her funeral, where the principal oration was delivered by the eloquent Gaius "Caligula," the youngest son of Germanicus. Though she had never liked Agrippina, the old dowager empress would not have tolerated harsh treatment of her granddaughter. With the death of Livia, Sejanus was free to attack Agrippina openly, and Tiberius was easily persuaded that she was guilty of treason. On the orders of the emperor,

Sejanus imprisoned Agrippina and her two older sons as traitors. Only Gaius was left undisturbed until Sejanus could devise a trap for him. The prefect had every reason to be satisfied, for his statues were now placed in the legionary camps, and public prayers were offered for the continued good fortune of the emperor's indispensable aide. Covered with honors at Rome, Sejanus was surrounded by senators whose flattery hid subtle malice. Later, Gaius would remark that "the Senate had corrupted Sejanus," and many anecdotes suggest that his secret enemies deliberately praised the prefect and hoped that he would overplay his hand.

In 31 Sejanus was at the height of his career and shared the consulship with the absent Tiberius. Intoxicated with power, the prefect formed an elaborate plan to win the throne. Discarding his mistress Livilla, he extracted a promise from the emperor that he could marry her daughter Julia, who was Tiberius' granddaughter. As the husband of an imperial princess, Sejanus could then force the elderly Tiberius to adopt him as the official heir. However, the prefect's threats against Gaius brought about his downfall before the marriage or the coup could take place. Sejanus had reckoned without Tiberius' sister-in-law, the wily old Antonia, who feared for the safety of her grandson Gaius. Unknown to Sejanus, Antonia sent her freedman Pallas to Capri with a report that the prefect planned to kill Gaius and wrest the succession from Gemellus. Convinced by Antonia's charges, the emperor removed Gaius to the safety of Capri and arranged a counterplot to outwit Sejanus. To gain time and throw the prefect off guard, Tiberius beguiled Sejanus with hints of another promotion. Though he suspected that something was afoot, Sejanus tried to hide his anxiety from the Senate and the court. Finally, Tiberius' agent Sertorius Macro arrived from Capri with a letter for the Senate. He reassured the prefect that the letter contained an order to endow Sejanus with tribunician powers, but actually Macro bore a commission from Tiberius and secretly won over the Praetorian guards. On October 18, 31, the unsuspecting Sejanus presided over the Senate to hear a reading of the document which he expected would give him even greater authority. Slowly, Macro read the long letter which began with an appreciation of Sejanus' many services to the state, then gradually cooled in tone, and culminated in a flat accusation of treason against Sejanus and a plea that the Senate would take immediate action. His world collapsing about him, the former favorite sat dumbfounded, but the senators erupted with long-repressed hatred. Immediately, Sejanus was reviled, condemned as a traitor, and dragged to execution. Later, the city mob was given his corpse which they abused and threw into the Tiber. However, though the emperor had outwitted his crafty prefect, Sejanus dealt him a final blow. When the vindictive Senate ordered the execution of Sejanus' children, their mother[2] sent a bitter letter to Capri and committed suicide. Her letter informed Tiberius of the affair between the prefect and Livilla and their complicity in the death of Drusus who had died by poison at the hands of his unfaithful wife. Contrary to Acton's dictum, power had not corrupted Sejanus but power had made him careless. The wily prefect had never been Tiberius' friend and had always played the old emperor for a fool.

In his memoirs, Tiberius offered the lame explanation that Sejanus had been destroyed because he had attacked the family of Germanicus. In reality, the emperor had little love for Agrippina or her family. Though he had rescued Gaius, Tiberius left Agrippina and her other sons to die in prison. His faithless daughter-in-law Livilla was placed under house arrest and soon starved herself to death. The morose emperor painfully resumed the burdens of government which once had been shared by the "companion of my labors." Formerly, the enemies of Sejanus had lived in fear but now the bitter Tiberius allowed the Senate to hound and punish the friends of Sejanus. However, the emperor often intervened to prevent the purge from turning into an unrestrained witch hunt. Tacitus reports the successful defense of a former supporter of Sejanus.

When everyone else was untruthfully disclaiming friendship with Sejanus. . . . Marcus Terentius bravely accepted the imputation. "In my position," he observed to the Senate, "it might do me more good to deny the accusation than to admit it. And yet, whatever the results, I will confess that I was Sejanus' friend. I sought his friendship and was glad to secure it. I had seen him as joint-commander of the Guard with his father. Then I saw him conducting the civil as well as the military administration. His kinsmen, his relations by marriage, gained office. Sejanus' ill will meant danger and pleas for mercy. I give no examples. At my own peril only, I speak for all who took no part in his final plans. For we honored, not Sejanus of Vulsinii, but the member of the Claudian and Julian houses into which his marriage alliances had admitted him—your 'son-in-law,' Tiberius, your partner in the consulship, your representative in state affairs. It is not for us to comment on the man whom you elevate above others, or on your reasons. The gods have given you supreme control—to us is left the glory of obeying! Besides, we only see what is before our eyes: the man to whom you have given wealth, power, the greatest potentialities for good and evil—and nobody will deny that Sejanus had these. Research into the emperor's hidden thoughts and secret designs is forbidden, hazardous, and not necessarily informative. Think, senators, not of Sejanus' last day, but of the previous sixteen years. . . . We thought it grand even if Sejanus' ex-slaves and door-keepers knew us. You will ask if this defense is to be valid for all without discrimination. Certainly not. But draw a fair dividing line! Punish plots against the state and the emperor's life. But, as regards friendship and its obligations, if we sever them at the same time as you do, Tiberius, that should excuse us as it excuses you." This courageous utterance, publicly reflecting everyone's private thoughts, proved so effective that it earned Terentius' accusers, with their criminal records, banishment and execution.

---

2 Earlier, Sejanus had divorced his wife Apicata when he had hoped to mary Livilla.

Because of his candor, Terentius was exonerated by Tiberius. His frank confession of careerism expressed the means whereby most men succeeded in politics at Rome or anywhere else.

To Roman moralists, the spectacular fall of Sejanus provided many sermons on the themes that Fortune is fickle and ambition digs its own grave. The poet Juvenal mocked the destruction of Sejanus' bronze statues:

Now the fires hiss hot—in the roar of bellows and furnace
Burns the head adored by the people. The mighty Sejanus
Makes a crackling sound, and out of that countenance, second,
Not so long ago, in the whole wide world, there are fashioned
Wine jars, frying pans, basins, and platters, and . . . pots.
Laurel your doors and lead the great chalked bull to Jove's altar!
Sejanus gets the hook, he is dragged along. What a picture!
Everybody is glad. "Believe me, I never could stand him.
What a puss he had! But what were the charges against him?
Who were the witnesses, the informant? How did they prove it?"
"Nothing like that at all: the only thing was a letter,
Rather wordy and long; it came from Capri." "That's allright, then.
That's all I wanted to know."

And what are the people of [Rome]
Doing now? What they always do; they are following fortune,
Hating her victims, as always. Had [Fate] favored Sejanus,
Had the leader's old age been unexpectedly stricken,
This same mob would have hailed as Augustus the man now doomed.

. . ."Allright, let's go, in a hurry—
While he lies on the bank, let's give Caesar's foeman a few kicks.
Yes, and be sure the slaves can see, so that all must admit it.
We don't want to be dragged to court at the end of a halter."
That was how they talked, at the time, about their Sejanus.
That was the way the crowd muttered and grumbled about him.

In the fall of Sejanus, the satirist found a more useful moral than the mere fickleness of the crowd:

So—would you like to have been Sejanus, popular, courted,
Having as much as he had, appointing men to high office,
Giving others command of the legions, renowned as protector
Of that Prince who's perched on the narrow ledges of Capri
With his Eastern seers and fortune tellers around him?
You would certainly like the spears, the horsemen, the cohorts,
The camp all your own. Why not? Even those with no craving for murder
Wish that they had the power. But what good would it be if it brought you
Risk in equal amount? Would you rather be robed like Sejanus,
Dragged along the streets like him, or would it be better

Taking charge of affairs in some little town like Fidenae,
Mayor of Gabii, or Inspector of Weights at Ulubrae?
So you acknowledge Sejanus did not know what to pray for,
Seeking excessive renown, excessive wealth, and preparing,
All the time, a tower whose stories soared to the heaven,
Whence he had farther to fall, a longer plunge to his ruin.

Juvenal's cautionary verses echoed the sentiments of most Roman politicians.

In imperial Rome competitive politics was dangerous and the risks outweighed the profits. Civil service was far safer and ultimately more rewarding. Many Equites served the state with distinction and later entered the Senate and earned nobility by elevation to the consulship. Under the emperors, organization men prospered and mavericks perished. In the provinces and at Rome practical men avoided political intrigue and left the dangerous game to members of the imperial family. Though savage power struggles took place in the palace, the armies held aloof and civil servants were indifferent to the outcome. Unless the ruler became psychopathic or was an extravagant spender, the personality of the emperor was not as important as the imperial system itself. The apparatus of Roman government was a highly efficient machine even under Caligula or Nero. The loyalty of the able men who performed the many tasks of government was reinforced by a common distaste for civil war and a healthy awareness of the perils of ambition. The memory of Sejanus was a constant reminder that the will to power can be fatal to even the most cunning of men.

Judgment on Tiberius

Robin Seager

Robin Seager of Liverpool concludes that certain character traits of Tiberius served to weaken the senatorial class and to pave the way for the despotism of Caligula. He believes that the personality of Tiberius—his personal fear and his reluctance to make decisions—provided the key to his principate. Those weaknesses allowed Sejanus and others to play upon him and make of a lonely and suspicious old man a cruel despot.

The twenty-two years of Tiberius' principate are a period of transition as well as of consolidation. The fortunes of the governing class were mixed. Tiberius always showed himself ready to advance men who like himself belonged to the nobility of the old republic, as he did the sons of newer consular families whose rise had been contemporaneous with that of Augustus. Yet his fears for his own security and the readiness of unscrupulous opportunists to exploit his suspicions made high birth a perilous distinction, as Tacitus delights in pointing out. However exaggerated the historian's claims may be, consulships and governorships must have seemed small compensation to those of the nobility whose talents and temper matched their birth. Only by accepting the major restraints that the principate imposed on independent action could they preserve some semblance of dignity. Greater freedom Tiberius the republican was powerless to grant. Those who understood, like M. Lepidus, might flourish within limits—others, like Cn. Piso, learned the hard way. But worse than the curbs on individual achievement and glory was the insecurity. . . . Thus, despite Tiberius' ingrained respect for birth and ability and his overall traditionalism, the effects of certain traits in his character combined with the very nature of the principate to weaken and demoralize the governing class and so to prepare the way not only for the undisguised despotism of Gaius but also for the bureaucracy of Claudius.

The same paradox marks the position of the magistrates and the senate. Tiberius made repeated efforts in the early years of his reign to force the senate to assume its responsibilities, and his sincerity cannot be doubted. The principal reason for his failure was that he was too late. Augustus had already irrevocably undermined the senate's capacity for independent action. Unlike Tiberius, he had had no respect for the traditions of senatorial government. But open contempt for the authority of the senate had caused the downfall of Julius Caesar, and so he had thought it prudent to shelter behind an elaborate pretence of republicanism. During the long years of his reign the senate and magistrates had learned to be content with this outward show, to be satisfied with the trappings of importance without the realities of power. By the time that Tiberius offered them power once again, they had grown so used to dignified impotence that the chance to govern reduced them to quaking confusion. Yet Tiberius must bear some of the blame, even during the 'good years'. . . . Whenever Tiberius intervened to force his wishes on the senate, even if his object was to check adulation or to prevent the condemnation of an innocent man, he was depriving the senate of that power of decision it was already only too reluctant to use and encouraging it in its lamentable habit of decreeing only what it thought would be pleasing to the princeps. Any such exertions of his authority, even in a good cause, were inevitably detrimental to the republican freedom that Tiberius professed and honestly desired to encourage. The final blow to senatorial government was delivered by his withdrawal to Capreae. Had the senate not been so cowed already, it might have seized this chance to recover its independence, but instead its initiative became totally extinct, as it found itself reduced to ratifying decisions taken miles away by the princeps and a handful of advisers. Again the ultimate result was ironically to leave the way clear for open autocracy.

There is little sign that Tiberius' principate had profound effects on other strata of society. It may be presumed that the power of the equestrian order in the army and the imperial civil service continued to grow in preparation for its flowering under Claudius, but apart from outstanding individuals in the highest posts— Sejanus and Macro of course above all—there are few indications of equestrian influence. The imperial freedmen, who similarly come to open prominence in the time of Claudius, are even less in evidence: only a hint in Fulcinius Trio's will. But again the increasing demoralization of the upper ranks of the senatorial order and the development in the last years of government by cabal will have produced a climate that fostered the changes to come. Of the masses there is almost nothing to say. They disliked Tiberius because he made no secret of the fact that he did not value their circuses. But their absence of interest in political developments is shown by their ready acceptance of the transference of elections to the senate. They sometimes manifest certain basic tendencies—love of lords, hatred of upstarts and loyalty to the Caesars— but they may fairly be said to have influenced nothing except on occasion Tiberius' suspicions.

It is Tiberius' character that provides the key to the paradoxical appearance of his reign. Ancient theories of a stage-by-stage decline are nonsense, and his notorious dissimulation is largely a red herring. But his fear for his own security and his reluctance to make decisions are at the root of the outstanding evils of the reign

and the failure of his republican good intentions. For years he had been the instrument of another man's will, and his career and even his life had been in danger. His submission to Augustus in accepting the principate at all brought a first measure of unreality to his efforts to put republican principles into practice, for his love of freedom was in constant friction with the awkward awareness that his safety depended on his status as princeps, as Augustus' chosen successor—yet if anyone was in a position to know that the republican exterior of the Augustan principate was a sham, it was Tiberius. But it was fear that ultimately made his republicanism too completely hollow: the gnawing fear of conspiracy and assassination that rendered possible the abuse of the law of maiestas, despite the efforts of his reason to hold it in check, and, combined with his eagerness to shed responsibility, gave Sejanus his chance. As a private citizen he would merely have been a lonely, suspicious, frightened old man. But because of the power that circumstances had forced on him, his suspicions and fears were transformed into lethal weapons, at first forged and skillfully directed by Sejanus, then in the last years scattered at random by a warped and haunted mind. There is a kernel of truth in Arruntius' claim that Tiberius was changed and twisted by imperial power, for empire deprived his virtues of the only climate in which they could flourish freely and condemned them to a barren and stunted growth, while it nurtured his faults to an unnatural increase that yielded a grim harvest. Such suffering as Tiberius' principate brought upon Rome was but a sombre echo of the desolation that it wrought in Tiberius' own mind.

*The goddess Roma is depicted in armor
seated on a breastplate and holding a
small figure of Victory in her hand.*

VII

Emperors As Gods: The Transformation of Roman Religion

INTRODUCTION
Ronald Mellor

The focal point of Roman religion was the relationship between the Romans and their gods. Though there were family shrines in houses and humble sanctuaries in the countryside, the most important religious manifestation was the official cult in which state officials approached the gods on behalf of the entire Roman people. The modern assumption that religion satisfies emotional needs or provides a guide to private morality would have puzzled the ancient Romans. For them the formal acts of ritual—prayers, festivals, sacrifices, auguries—ensured the pax deorum *("peace of the gods") through which the gods rewarded and protected the Roman people and supported the enterprises of the Roman state. The traditional state cult of the Republic may appear to modern eyes to be an arid, legalistic religion which offered little in the way of spiritual comfort, but Roman religion was a reflection of Roman society and its reliance on formalism mirrored the legal system as well as aspects of political and social life. We have been conditioned to see religion as a matter of individual commitment, and the solace we seek from religion is of a personal, emotional nature. But that was not the Roman way, and it was only when the social or political circumstances changed that the Romans adapted their beliefs to other forms of religious practice.*

The religion of the Roman Republic was a part of public business and, as such, it was inevitably political. While highly politicized religion seems distasteful to our modern idealization of religion as an exclusively spiritual phenomenon, many other religions (phases of Judaism, Islam, certain Christian denominations) have been highly political while being no less sincere. The Senate served as the mediator between men and gods, and the Romans perceived politicians as favored by, or opposed by, the gods. Roman religion was highly political long before the deification of the dead Julius Caesar.

Just as Augustus represented himself as a restorer of the social mores and political institutions of the Roman Republic, he also boasted of his support for traditional religion. The Res Gestae says that he repaired eighty-two temples, and he also revived ancient rituals and priestly offices which had long been ignored. He closed the doors of the temple of Janus (to signify peace) for the first time in centuries. He re-established the ancient priesthood called the Arval Brethren, and in 17 B. C. he lavishly celebrated the Secular Games to commemorate the 700th anniversary (by the emperor's calculations) of the founding of Rome.

Despite Augustus' emphasis on traditional religious practice there were, of course, many religious innovations in his reign. The temple of Mars Ultor celebrated Augustus' defeat of Brutus and Cassius, and that of Apollo on the Palatine recalled his defeat of Antony beneath the temple of Apollo at Actium. But the most startling novelty was surely the temple of the Deified Julius in the Forum itself and Augustus' own adoption of the title Divi filius ("son of the deified"). The popular enthusiasm for Julius Caesar allowed Augustus to establish the new cult and to link himself and his family closely to this new Roman divinity.

Although ruler-worship had just reached Rome, it had long been known in the Greek world. With Alexander's conquest of the East, Persian and Egyptian worship of god-kings were offered to Alexander and his successors. The bestowal of divine honors became a political and diplomatic act in the Greek world, and even Roman magistrates were voted temples, priesthoods and cults. The Greek city of Chalcis established a cult in honor of the goddess Roma and Titus Quinctius Flamininus, the "liberator" of Greece from Macedonian domination, in 197 B.C., and the cult with its annual festival survived more than three centuries. Other republican magistrates were so honored, sometimes in conjunction with the goddess Roma, whom the Greeks created as a divine personification of the Roman people who had become their political masters. With Augustus' defeat of Antony and Cleopatra, and his incorporation of Egypt into the Empire, the emperor allowed himself to be worshipped there as a god like the Pharaohs and Ptolemies before him.

Augustus permitted himself to be worshipped in the provinces in association with Roma. The League of 64 Gallic cities established an altar of Roma and Augustus at the Gallic capital of Lyon, and the Greek cities of Asia founded similar cults. The annual festivals became a demonstration of political loyalty to Rome. Such cults spread throughout the empire and eventually included other members of the imperial family. But Augustus and the more responsible of his successors did not allow divine worship of the living emperor in Rome itself. It was only after death that an emperor underwent apotheosis—transformation into a god—and could be incorporated into the Roman pantheon and receive a temple within the capital. Thus the behavior of Caligula in displaying himself as a god was shocking because it violated the Augustan precedent: only provincials were allowed to worship the living emperor.

Eastern religions had for long made their way to Rome. The cult of Cybele came from Asia in the third century B.C., the worship of Dionysus (Bacchanalia) had to be suppressed in the second century because its orgiastic rituals were thought to threaten public order, and the devotees of the Egyptian goddess Isis were persecuted several times in the closing decades of the Republic. But the Julio-Claudians were more tolerant; Caligula built a temple to Isis and Claudius one to Cybele. The Jews were protected by Julius Caesar, Augustus and Claudius though Tiberius exiled some from Rome and Caligula demanded divine worship in the Temple at Jerusalem. The Christians, however, remained a minor sect, one hardly noticed at Rome until Nero blamed them for the great fire of A.D. 64 and launched the first persecution in which Peter and Paul were said to have been martyred.

The Julio-Claudian emperors were more concerned with the political dangers posed by astrology and magic than with religion. Astrology had become fashionable with the aristocratic elite and, while the emperors sought assistance from personal astrologers, they saw horoscopes of the imperial family as an obvious threat. Astrologers were occasionally exiled and even executed.

Magic likewise appears with some regularity in the histories of Tacitus and Suetonius, most notably in the strange events surrounding the death of Germanicus. It is clear that magic and astrology had a wide following in Rome and the emperors sometimes found it necessary to place restrictions upon them.

The traditional republican state religion did not disappear, but as Roman political and social life was transformed by the Empire, religion changed as well. The state religion increasingly focused on the emperor and the imperial family—both as representatives of the Roman people before the gods and, after their deaths, as gods themselves. But as the emperors came to be regarded as divinities, they themselves perceived other gods—Jupiter, Isis, Jehovah, or Jesus—as allies or rivals.

The Deification of Augustus

Dio Cassius

The third century historian Dio Cassius here describes the establishment of the cult to the deified Augustus with priests, rituals and a shrine. Dio makes it quite clear that it was Livia who was the guiding force behind these actions: she built the shrine, she held the festival, and she and Tiberius formulated the decrees that were nominally passed by the Senate.

At the time they declared Augustus immortal, assigned to him priests and sacred rites, and made Livia, who was already called Julia and Augusta, his priestess; they also permitted her to employ a lictor when she exercised her sacred office. On her part, she bestowed a million sesterces upon a certain Numerius Atticus, a senator and ex-praetor, because he swore that he had seen Augustus ascending to heaven after the manner of which tradition tells concerning Proculus and Romulus. A shrine voted by the senate and built by Livia and Tiberius was erected to the dead emperor in Rome and others in many different places, some of the communities voluntarily building them and others unwillingly. Also the house at Nola where he passed away was dedicated to him as a precinct. While his shrine was being erected in Rome, they placed a golden image of him on a couch in the temple of Mars, and to this they paid all the honors that they were afterwards to give to his statue. Other votes in regard to him were that his image should not be borne in procession at anybody's funeral, that the consuls should celebrate his birthday with games like the Ludi Martiales, and that the tribunes, as being sacrosanct, were to have charge of the Augustalia. These officials conducted everything in the customary manner—even wearing the triumphal garb at the horse-races—except that they did not ride in the chariot. Besides this, Livia held a private festival in his honor for three days in the palace, and this ceremony is still continued down to the present day by whoever is emperor.

Such were the decrees passed in memory of Augustus, nominally by the senate, but actually by Tiberius and Livia. For when some men proposed one thing and some another, the senate decreed that Tiberius should receive suggestions in writing from its members and then select whichever he chose. I have added the name of Livia because she, too, took a share in the proceedings, as if she possessed full powers.

Emperor Worship at Rome

Keith Hopkins

Professor Keith Hopkins of Cambridge University provides a sociological analysis of emperor worship in imperial Rome. He shows that individual Romans had been honored "like the immortal gods" but never as part of the public state cult until Julius Caesar. The early emperors were far more willing to be worshipped in the provinces than they were to allow cults to be introduced into Rome, where they would inflame the senatorial opposition. Those who did permit emperor worship in Rome—Gaius, Nero and later Domitian—were all also murdered. But Augustus, Tiberius and Claudius are all on record as discouraging excessive adulation and religious worship. Many cults were founded on local initiative and do not fit into any easy generalization about the ruler cult. Where the cults did exist, however, Hopkins shows that their rituals could help to honor the local elite as well as the emperor himself.

Absolutist kings of large pre-industrial states have almost always ruled with divine aid. The nature and degree of their divinity have varied: for example, the Pharaohs of Egypt were god-kings, Chinese emperors ruled by the mandate of heaven, Abbasid Caliphs called themselves Shadows of God on Earth, Byzantine emperors ruled as the vicegerents of god on earth, English and French kings claimed divine right. The list could be extended, but the basic point is clear. The king of a large empire, never seen by most of his subjects, legitimates his power by associating himself and his regime with the mystic powers of the universe. Reciprocally, subjects who rarely see an emperor come to terms with his grandeur and power by associating him with the divine. . . .

The Beginnings of Emperor Worship in Rome, Its Establishment and Diffusion

Originally, the divinity of the living emperor was alien both to traditional Roman religion and to Roman oligarchic politics. Its eventual acceptance even by the elite in the city of Rome was a symptom of the growth of emperors' power and of the changes which took place in Roman political culture; these changes made it possible to express individual emperors' political power

in religious terms. But the emperor's divinity was only one aspect, albeit the most impressive aspect, of the emperors' association with the gods. The intricate relationship of emperors and gods and its political significance can be understood only against the backcloth of Roman religious beliefs and rituals. Religion and politics were intertwined.

In metaphors, myths and sacred rites, Romans frequently bridged the great divide which in puritan Christianity separates man from God. The every-day world of the Romans (not simply their mystic world) was populated by a host of divine intermediaries who stood between men and the great gods of Heaven and Hades. They ranged from demi-gods and divine heroes such as Castor and Hercules to divine forces such as Victory, Fortune and Hope and even to portents and omens of good and evil. Each household had its private cults in which men placated the spirits of the living (*Genius*) and the dead (*Lares*) with sacrifice and ritual, and invested them with such divinity as they chose. Cicero, for example, wanted to build a shrine, not a tomb, to his dead daughter in order "to achieve deification as far as possible." This was a private act, and therefore consistent with his violent public objection to the official deification of Julius Caesar.

Earlier in the Republic, Romans had associated several of their leaders with gods, but not in the state cult. For example, after the political murder of the Gracchi brothers, statues of them were set up in a prominent place in the city of Rome; 'many people sacrificed at and worshipped their statues every day, as though they were visiting the shrines of the gods' (Plutarch). Other leaders were similarly honored, while they were still alive. For example in 102-10 B.C., the general Marius achieved a crushing victory over the Celtic tribes which had for several years defeated Roman armies in northern Italy. He was honored in the city of Rome with libations 'just like the immortal gods' (Valerius Maximus). Exceptional ability or success or the spark of genius was commonly recognized as having something divine about it. The dictator Sulla took the sobriquet *Felix*, Fortunate, to reflect his protection by divine forces. Republican poets such as Ennius, Lucretius and the early Virgil each referred to great men (Scipio, Epicurus and Octavian) as though they were gods or god-like.

Emperor worship involved the transfer of what had previously been private and unofficial rites to the public domain; it involved the inclusion of the emperor in private household rites; and it involved paying honors to the living which had customarily, though not exclusively, been given to the dead. For example, a wall painting has been discovered in a private house in Pompeii, which shows the spirit (*Genius*) of the head of the household, surrounded by his family, pouring a libation; a second figure was added to this picture, and was carefully preserved in ancient times. Mau [the great scholar of Pompeii] interpreted this figure as the Genius of the emperor Augustus, since beneath the picture were the letters EX SC 'by decree of the senate,' which Mau took to be the decree of the senate which ordained that a libation should be poured to the emperor at all public and private meals—like a Christian grace or an English royal toast. And we know from literary sources that this toast, 'To Augustus, Father of the Fatherland, hail,' became common practice.

Julius Caesar was the first Roman to be recognized as a god in a public state cult. He had also been more powerful than any Roman before him. His divinity followed from his political power. Julius Caesar had also been the first living Roman noble to claim descent from a god, through Aeneas from Venus. Even during his life-time, when he was a dictator, he was given honors similar to those given to a god. For example, a statue of Caesar was set up in the temple of Quirinus with the inscription 'To the Unconquered God.' At the circus games, an ivory statue of Caesar was carried in solemn procession along with those of the gods. The senate ordered that a temple be built 'To Julius Caesar and his Clemency,' and that a special priesthood be instituted in his honor similar to Jupiter's. But his elevation provoked opposition. He was assassinated by a band of nobles who could not endure his supreme power and quasi-divinity.

Julius Caesar's deification after his death was partly a legitimating maneuver by his political successors, particularly by his adopted son and heir Octavian, who thus became 'Son of God.' Deification after death was also a continuation of Caesar's life-time ambitions and of popular belief. An angry crowd reacted to his assassination by burning down the senate-house in which he had been murdered and then attempted 'to bury his body in the temple of Jupiter on the Capitol along with the gods.' The priests turned the crowd back and so they burnt the body on a hastily built pyre in the Forum. Caesar's power, his popularity, the manner of his death and the political sagacity of his heir, all combined to make his funeral and his memory more a public than a private family matter. Julius Caesar was numbered among the state gods, wrote Suetonius,

not only by public decree but also by popular belief. At the first games, which his heir Augustus gave in honor of his consecration, a comet shone for seven successive days. It was believed to be the soul of Julius Caesar which had been taken to heaven. And this is why a star is set at the top of his statue. (Julius Caesar)

Augustus and the emperors who succeeded him were the first Romans to be widely acknowledged as gods during their life-time. Several emperors found this personally embarrassing, and in the city of Rome it was politically awkward; it cut across the constitutional mask which disguised the emperors' supremacy. They did not want to be assassinated. Members of the elite, who suffered most from the emperor's human weaknesses, were most skeptical of his divinity. Hence, for example, Seneca's savage skit on dead Claudius' arrival in heaven and his open scorn for the senators who had seen the soul of the imperial dead rising in the sky and had been richly rewarded for the speed of their vision.

Emperors were caught in a cleft stick. In the eastern provinces rulers were traditionally honored as gods. Emperors could not refuse the honors and prayers of the eastern provincials without giving gratuitous offense which might undermine the provincials' loyalty. Equally, they could not afford to be seen, especially by the Roman elite, to welcome divinity. Augustus and his immediate successors tried to cope with this clash of cultures by a compromise which they enforced in the provincial state cults; in these, they allowed temples and priests to be established in their honor, but only in association with an established deity, usually *Roma*. Or they diverted the direct imputation of personal divinity by allowing sacrifices only to the living or divine spirit of the emperor (*Genius, Numen Augusti*). In this way, religious rites and feelings were harnessed to the political order as well as to the individual emperor.

Several sources reveal the awkwardness of this solution, as emperors rejected unwanted honors proffered by deferential provincials or defended themselves to Romans for the honours which they had accepted. The extract which follows is from a papyrus, first published in 1924, which contained a letter from the emperor Claudius to the Alexandrians sent in A.D. 41:

. . . First, I allow you to keep my birthday as a sacred day as you have requested, and I permit you to erect. . . a statue of me and my family. . . . But I decline the establishment of a high-priest and temples to myself, not wishing to be offensive to my contemporaries and in the belief that temples and the like have been set apart in all ages for the gods alone.

But in the proclamation publicizing this very letter, the Roman prefect of Egypt referred to 'the greatness of our God Caesar,' apparently in direct defiance of the emperor's explicit wishes. The conventional explanation of this inconsistency is persuasively simple; it was considered all right publicly to entitle Caesar 'God,' provided it happened in the provinces. But decisions about emperor worship in the provincial state cults were often made in the city of Rome. The contradictory expectations of Roman aristocrats and of provincials therefore could not be segregated. And when a decision was made in public in the city of Rome, the emperor often took the Roman elite's view into account. Besides, the emperor was a member of that elite. Tacitus records the following debate which took place in the senate in A.D. 25:

Farther Spain sent a delegation . . . (which applied) to follow Asia's example and built a shrine to Tiberius and his mother. Disdainful of compliment, Tiberius saw an opportunity to refute rumors of his increasing self-importance.

I am aware, senators, he said, that my present opposition has been widely regarded as inconsistent with my agreement to a similar proposal by the cities of Asia. So I will justify my silence then and my intentions from now on.

The divine Augustus did not refuse a temple at Pergamum to himself and the city of Rome. So I, who regard his every action and word as law, followed the precedent thus established, the more since the senate was to be worshipped together with myself. One such acceptance may be pardoned. But to have my statue worshipped among the gods in every province would be presumptuous and arrogant . . . senators, I emphasize to you that I am human, performing human tasks. I am content to occupy the first place among men.

Later too, even in private conversation, (Tiberius) persisted in rejecting such veneration. Some attributed this to modesty, but most people thought it was uneasiness.

Such public protestations had little effect, in Italy or the provinces. We can see this, for example, in the public proclamation made by Germanicus Caesar, the nephew and adopted son of Tiberius, in Alexandria in A.D. 19. He refused divine honors for himself, although the offer was very restrained by Egyptian standards.

I welcome the good-will which you always display when you see me, but I totally reject your acclamations which are invidious and appropriate to the gods. They belong exclusively to the real Saviour and Benefactor of the Human Race, my father [the emperor Tiberius], and to his mother, my grandmother [Livia]. . . .

He was perhaps afraid that exaggerated reports of the honors accepted by him would reach the jealous emperor's ears.

Emperor worship in a broad sense, that is the public association of emperors with gods, divine forces, sacred rites, altars and temples, flourished almost everywhere. Even the elite in the city of Rome repeatedly elevated living emperors to the level of a god. The list of honors voted to Octavian is extraordinary: in 29 B.C., the senate decreed that his name be included in its hymns equally with the gods. They decreed 'that a tribe should be called the Julian tribe after him, that he should wear the triumphal crown at all festivals . . . that the day on which he entered the city of Rome should be honored with sacrifices by the whole population and be held sacred for evermore.' In 27 B.C. he took the name Augustus, which like 'Son of God,' symbolized his superiority over the mass of humanity. An altar was set up in Rome to his Victory, temples were built to Fortune which vouchsafed his Safe Return (*Fortuna Redux*), and to the Augustan Peace. His statue was placed in the entrance to the Pantheon while another statue of him, dressed in all the insignia of Apollo, was set up in the library attached to the new temple of Apollo.

Stories about the connections between Augustus and Apollo circulated even in sophisticated circles and have survived in the histories of Suetonius and Dio. In the book *About the Gods* by Asklepias of Mendes, the story was told that Augustus' mother once spent the night in the temple of Apollo with other matrons. While she slept, a snake came to her (by Roman convention, a snake was apparently used on household altars to represent the Genius—but Freudians will also make speculations about the imagery in the story); when she awoke, she washed herself as though after intercourse with her husband, but she could not wash away the mark of the snake which she found on her body. In the tenth month afterwards, Augustus was born and was

therefore considered to be the son of Apollo. (Suetonius, *Augustus*)

To continue the saga, Augustus eventually in 12 B.C. became High Priest. He did not move into the traditional High Priest's house, but gave it to the Vestal Virgins. In compensation he made part of his own house into a public shrine with an ever burning fire. In this way the household gods of the state and Augustus' own household gods were under the same roof. Augustus was Father of the Fatherland (*pater patriae*) as well as head of his own family (*paterfamilias*). The headship of state was fused with the office of High Priest; the regime had the ostensible support of the gods.

Outside Rome, in Italy and in the provinces, eastern and western towns and town-councilors competed in their search for the appropriate honors to pay their monarch. They looked for honors which would cast most glory upon themselves, in their own eyes, in the eyes of the distant monarch, and in the eyes of the commonfolk who watched the sacrifices and participated in the festivals held in the emperor's honor. The emperor's birthday and other anniversaries were celebrated by public games and in other ways. In 9 B.C., for example, 'the cities of Asia [Minor] decreed . . . that a crown be awarded to the person suggesting the highest honors for the god [Augustus]. . . .' Discreetly enough, they then awarded the prize to the Roman governor of the province for suggesting 'an honor for Augustus hitherto unknown among the Greeks, namely to start the year on his birthday.' The idea was taken up with public enthusiasm. 'The birthday of the most divine emperor is the fount of every public and private good. Justly would one take this day to be the beginning of the Whole Universe. . . . Justly would one take this day to be the beginning of Life and Living for everyone. . . .'

In other cities also, the emperor's birthday and other anniversaries were publicly celebrated by sacrifice, rituals, ceremonies and games. . . .

These examples illustrate three general points. First, the style of public celebrations held in honor of the emperor varied considerably from town to town, as it did between provinces. This variety demonstrates that the festivals were not instituted by Augustus himself or by the dictate of the central government. The varied arrangements reflected local initiatives or competitive innovations rather than imperial decree. The strength of local feelings and beliefs, the sense of obligation to the emperor, the belief in the benefits to be derived from his propitiation far outweighed the effect of any imperial regulation. The evidence simply does not match the model which consciously or unconsciously still seems to underlie some modern discussions of the imperial cult, especially in the western provinces: namely that it was initiated, licensed, controlled and maintained primarily by the emperors themselves in the interest of some overall policy of political control, and that western provincials were far too sensible to believe in such eastern superstitions.

Caligula's Conflict with the Jews

Josephus

The aristocrat Josephus was the Jewish commander in Galilee during the great revolt, but he was captured early and became part of the entourage of the Roman general Vespasian. After Vespasian became emperor in A.D. 69, Josephus was generously supported as he wrote his Jewish Antiquities, a history of the Jews from the Creation to the outbreak of the war in A.D. 66 and his Jewish War about the revolt itself. Though pro-Roman, Josephus remained a defender of Jewish culture and traditions. This passage examines Caligula's famous attempt to have his own images set up in the Temple at Jerusalem. He was incited by the Jew-hating Alexandrian Apion, while his governor of Syria, Petronius, and his friend King Agrippa counseled restraint, since such an action would surely provoke a rebellion. The emperor's fortuitous death avoided a major conflict and Josephus credits Petronius with courage and principles in his attempt to respect Jewish religious scruples.

1. Meanwhile, there was civil strife in Alexandria between the Jewish inhabitants and the Greeks. Three delegates were chosen by each of the factions and appeared before Gaius. One of the Alexandrian delegates was Apion, who scurrilously reviled the Jews, asserting, among other things, that they neglected to pay the honors due to the emperor. For while all the subject peoples in the Roman empire had dedicated altars and temples to Gaius and had given him the same attentions in all other respects as they did the gods, these people alone scorned to honor him with statues and to swear by his name. And so Apion spoke many angry words by which he hoped that Gaius would be moved, as might be expected. Philo, who stood at the head of the delegation of the Jews, a man held in the highest honor, brother of Alexander the alabarch and no novice in philosophy, was prepared to proceed with the defense against these accusations. But Gaius cut him short, told him to get out of his way, and, being exceedingly angry, made it clear that he would visit some outrage upon them. Philo, having thus been treated with contumely, left the room, saying to the Jews who accompanied him that they should be of good courage, for Gaius' wrath was a matter of words, but in fact he was now enlisting God against himself.

2. Indignant at being so slighted by the Jews alone, Gaius dispatched Petronius as his legate to Syria to succeed Vitellius in this office. His orders were to lead a large force into Judaea and, if the Jews consented to receive him, to set up an image of Gaius in the temple of God. If, however, they were obstinate, he was to subdue them by force of arms and so set it up. Petronius took over Syria and hastened to carry out the commands of the emperor. Gathering together as many auxiliaries as possible, he marched at the head of two legions of the Roman army to Ptolemais, intending to spend the winter there and towards spring to engage in war without fail. He wrote Gaius what he had in mind to do. The

latter commended him for his zeal and bade him abate nothing but wage war vigorously against them if they persisted in disobedience. Meanwhile, many tens of thousands of Jews came to Petronius at Ptolemais with petitions not to use force to make them transgress and violate their ancestral code. "If," they said, "you propose at all costs to bring in and set up the image, slay us first before you carry out these resolutions. For it is not possible for us to survive and to behold actions that are forbidden us by the decision both of our lawgiver and of our forefathers who cast their votes enacting these measures as moral laws." To this Petronius indignantly replied: "If I were the emperor and intended to take this action of my own choice, you would have a right to speak as you do. As it is, I am Caesar's emissary and bound to carry out the decision he has already made, since to disregard it would bring on me irretrievable punishment." "Equal to this determination of yours, O Petronius," replied the Jews, "not to transgress the orders of Gaius, is our determination not to transgress the declaration of the law. We have put our trust in the goodness of God and in the labors of our forefathers and have thus hitherto remained innocent of transgression. Nor could we ever bring ourselves to go so far in wickedness as by our own act to transgress, for any fear of death, the law bidding us abstain, where He thought it conducive to our good to do so. In order to preserve our ancestral code, we shall patiently endure what may be in store for us, with the assurance that for those who are determined to take the risk there is hope even of prevailing; for God will stand by us if we welcome danger for His glory. Fortune, moreover, is wont to veer now toward one side, now toward the other in human affairs. To obey you, on the other hand, would bring on us the grave reproach of cowardice, because that would be the explanation of our transgressing the law, and at the same time we should incur God's severe wrath—and He even in your eyes must be accounted a higher power than Gaius."

3. Now Petronius saw from their words that their spirit was not easily to be put down and that it would be impossible for him without a battle to carry out Gaius' behest and set up his image. Indeed there would be great slaughter. Hence he gathered up his friends and attendants and hastened to Tiberius, for he wished to take note of the situation of the Jews there. The Jews, though they regarded the risk involved in war with the Romans as great, yet adjudged the risk of transgressing the Law to be far greater. As before, many tens of thousands faced Petronius on his arrival at Tiberius. They besought him by no means to put them under such constraint nor to pollute the city by setting up a statue. "Will you then go to war with Caesar," said Petronius, "regardless of his resources and of your own weakness?" "On no account would we fight," they said, "but we will die sooner than violate our laws." And falling on their faces and baring their throats, they declared that they were ready to be slain. They continued to make these supplications for forty days. Furthermore, they neglected their fields, and that, too, though it was time to sow the seed. For they showed a stubborn determination and readiness to die rather than to see the image erected.

4. At this juncture Aristobulus, the brother of King Agrippa together with Helcias the Elder and other most powerful members of this house, the civic leaders, appeared before Petronius and appealed to him, since he saw the deep feeling of the people, not to incite them to desperation but to write to Gaius telling how incurable was their opposition to receiving the statue and how they had left their fields to sit protesting, and that they did not choose war, since they could not fight a war, but would be glad to die sooner than transgress their customs. Let him point out that, since the land was unsown, there would be a harvest of banditry, because the requirement of tribute could not be met. For perhaps Gaius would relent and not adopt a cruel plan or have the heart to exterminate the nation. But if he remained firm in his present policy of war, let Petronius then proceed with operations. When Aristobulus and the rest appealed to Petronius along such lines, he was influenced by them, for they brought pressure to bear upon him in every way, since the question at issue was of such importance, and employed every device to make their plea effective. Furthermore, he beheld the stubborn determination of the Jews to resist and

thought it a terrible thing to bring death upon so many tens of thousands of men in carrying out the mad orders of Gaius, and to hold them guilty for their reverence to God, and thus to spend the rest of his life in foreboding. He considered it far better to send a letter to Gaius and to endure the latter's inexorable wrath aroused by his not carrying out the orders at once. Perhaps, moreover, he might even convince him. Nevertheless, if Gaius persisted in his original lunacy, he would undertake war against them. But if, after all, Gaius should turn some of his wrath against him, a man who made virtue his goal might well die on behalf of such a multitude of men. And so he decided to recognize the cogency of the plea of the petitioners.

5. He now convened the Jews, who arrived in many tens of thousands at Tiberias, stood up before them and explained that the present expedition was not of his own choosing but by command of the emperor, whose wrath would descend instantly and without any delay upon those who assumed the audacity to disobey his commands. "It is only right that one upon whom such high position had been conferred by grant of the emperor should thwart him in nothing. I do not, however," he said, "deem it right not to hazard my own safety and position in order to save you, who are so numerous, from perishing. You are carrying out the precepts of your law, which as your heritage you see fit to defend, and serving the sovereign of all, almighty God, whose temple I should not have had the heart to see fall a prey to the insolence of imperial authority. Rather I am sending a dispatch to Gaius fully explaining your determination and also in some way advocating my own case for compliance, contrary to his decree, with the good object which you have proposed. May God assist you, since His might is above any human ingenuity or strength; may He enable you to maintain and to preserve your ancestral laws without His being deprived of His customary honors by capricious human plots. If, however, Gaius is embittered and makes me the object of his inexorable wrath, I will endure every form of danger and every form of suffering that may be inflicted upon my body and my fortune rather than behold you who are so numerous destroyed

for deeds so virtuous. Go, therefore, each to your own occupation, and labor on the land. I myself will send a message to Rome and will not turn aside from doing every service in your behalf both by myself and through my friends."

6. With these words he dismissed the assembly of the Jews and requested those in authority to attend to agricultural matters and to conciliate the people with optimistic propaganda. He thus did his best to encourage the masses. God, on His part, showed Petronius that He was with him and would lend His aid in all matters. For as soon as Petronius had finished delivering this speech before the Jews, God straightway sent a heavy shower that was contrary to general anticipation, for that day, from morning on, had been clear and the sky had given no indication of rain. Indeed, that entire year had been beset by so great a drought that it caused the people to despair of rainfall even if at any time they saw the sky overcast. The result was that, when much rain fell at that moment exceptionally and unexpectedly, the Jews were hopeful that Petronius would by no means fail in his petition on their behalf. Petronius, on his part, was struck with great amazement when he saw unmistakable evidence that God's providence was over the Jews and that He had shown His presence so abundantly that not even those who actually proposed to take the opposite view had any heart left to dispute the fact. He included this occurrence along with the other things of which he wrote to Gaius. It was all designed to induce him and entreat him in every way not to drive so many tens of thousands of men to desperation. For if he should slay them—and they would certainly not give up their accustomed manner of worship without war—he would be deprived of their revenue and would be put under the ban of a curse for all time to come. He said, moreover, that the Divinity who was in charge of them had shown His power to be unimpaired and was quite unambiguous in displaying this power. So much for Petronius.

7. Meanwhile King Agrippa, who, as it happened, was living in Rome, advanced greatly in friendship with Gaius. Once he made a banquet for him with the intention of surpassing everyone both in the expenditure on the

banquet and in provision for the pleasure of the guests. He was so successful that, to say nothing of the others, even Gaius himself despaired of equalling, much less surpassing it, if he should desire to do so. So far did this man surpass everyone in his preparations and in devising and providing everything for the emperor. Gaius thoroughly admired his ingenuity and magnificence and his forcible way of employing, in order to give him pleasure, an abundance of money even beyond his means. Gaius therefore wished to imitate the ambitious display that Agrippa had made to please him. Hence while he was relaxed with wine and while his mood was unusually genial, he said during the banquet when Agrippa invited him to drink: "Agrippa, I have known in my heart before how highly you regarded me and how you have proved your great loyalty even amidst the dangers with which, because of it, you were encircled by Tiberius. And now you never fail to show kindness to us, going even beyond your means. Consequently, inasmuch as it would be a stain on my honor to let you outdo me in zeal, I wish to make amends for past deficiencies. Indeed, all the gifts that I have allotted to you are but slight in amount; any service that can add its weight in the scale of prosperity shall be performed for you with all my heart and power." He spoke these words thinking that Agrippa would ask for a large accession of territory adjoining his own or for the revenues of certain cities. As for Agrippa, although he was quite ready to make his request, he did not reveal his intention. On the contrary, he at once replied to Gaius that it was not in expectation of any benefit from him that he had in the past paid court to him in spite of Tiberius' orders; nor were any of his present activities in giving him pleasure designed as a road to personal gain. He said that the gifts that Gaius had already presented to him were great and went beyond any expectations that he would dare to cherish. "For even if they have been inferior to your capacity, they exceeded my thoughts and my claims as a recipient." Gaius, amazed at his character, insisted all the more on his telling what he might grant to please him. Agrippa

replied: "Since, my lord, in your kindness you declare me worthy of gifts, I shall ask for nothing that would make me richer inasmuch as I am already extremely conspicuous because of the gifts that you have hitherto bestowed upon me. But I shall ask for something that will bring you a reputation for piety and will induce the Deity to help you in everything that you wish; and it will bring me the renown, among those who hear of it, of never having known failure in anything that I desired your authority to obtain for me. Well, I ask you to abandon all further thoughts of erecting the statue which Petronius has your orders to set up in the temple of the Jews."

8. Hazardous as he considered this petition—for if Gaius did not regard it with favor, it would bring him certain death—yet, because he thought the issue important, as it truly was, he chose to make the gamble on this occasion. Gaius was bound by Agrippa's attentions to him. Furthermore, if he repented quickly of his offer, he regarded it as unseemly to break his word before so many witnesses, when he had by his zealous constraint compelled Agrippa to make his request. At the same time he admired the character of Agrippa in that he set little store on adding to his personal authority either by increasing his revenue or by other privileges, but had regard to the happiness of the commonwealth, by giving precedence to religion and the law. So he yielded and wrote to Petronius commending him for having assembled his army and for having sent him his dispatch on the subject. "Now, therefore," he said, "if you have already set up my statue, let it stand. If, however, you have not yet dedicated it, do not trouble yourself further but dismiss the army and betake yourself to those matters for which I originally dispatched you. For I no longer require the erection of the statue, showing favor to Agrippa in this, a man whom I hold in too high esteem to gainsay his request and his bidding." Gaius had written this to Petronius before reading the latter's message from which he wrongly concluded that the Jews were bent on revolt and that their attitude indicated no other intent than a threat of downright war against the Romans. Upon receiving this letter, he was in agony at the

thought that they had dared to put his authority to the test. Since he was a man who always yielded to baseness but was strong in resisting the claim of an ideal, one who beyond all others rushed into a rage against anyone who came under his censure, exercising no control over it whatsoever but considering the pleasure derived from indulging it his criterion of happiness, he wrote to Petronius as follows: "Since you have held the gifts that the Jews have bestowed upon you in higher regard than my orders and have presumed to minister in everything to their pleasure in violation of my orders, I bid you act as your own judge and consider what course it is your duty to take, since you have brought my displeasure upon yourself. For I assure you that you shall be cited as an example by all men now and all that will come hereafter to point the moral that an emperor's commands are never to be flouted."

9. Such was the letter that he wrote to Petronius. But Petronius did not receive it while Gaius was alive since the voyage of those who brought the message was so delayed that before it arrived Petronius had received a letter with news of the death of Gaius. Indeed, God could never have been unmindful of the risks that Petronius had taken in showing favor to the Jews and honoring God. No, the removal of Gaius in displeasure at his rashness in promoting his own claim to worship was God's payment of the debt to Petronius. In fact, Rome and all the empire, and especially those of the senators who were outstanding in merit, favored Petronius, since Gaius had vented his wrath against them without mercy.

Anti-Semitism in the Ancient World

Louis Feldman

Louis Feldman, Professor of Classics at Yeshiva University, surveys the differing attitudes about the Jews among the Greeks and Romans in the ancient world. He differentiates among the attitudes of the government, the masses, and the intellectual elite to paint a more complex picture of ancient anti-Semitism. In the section of his article concerning the Roman period, Feldman shows that governmental anti-Semitism was not a significant problem and the Jews were often allied with Roman officials. However the masses in the Greek-speaking cities of the Roman Empire (Alexandria, Antioch) launched provocations and pograms against the local Jewish communities, though interestingly this does not seem to have happened in Rome, where the emperor was often viewed as a protector of the Jews. But if officials seem positive and the masses negative the writings of intellectuals show both disparaging remarks (which Greeks and Romans made of nearly all peoples including each other) about the Jews, as well as much that is favorable. It is striking that many pagans embraced Judaism during this period—evidence of considerable admiration of the people and their religion.

"Almost every note in the cacophony of medieval and modern anti-Semitism was sounded by the chorus of ancient writers"[1] This observation is perfectly valid, but the phenomena that underlie it must be examined with meticulous care if we are to avoid hasty and exaggerated conclusions about the scope and intensity of classical anti-Semitism. First, the literary material itself is not unrelievedly hostile, and positive statements about Jews and Judaism must not be ignored. In addition, discussions of this subject often rest upon the assumption that the remarks of ancient intellectuals faithfully reflect societal attitudes in

1 Salo W. Baron, A *Social and Religious History of the Jews*, vol. 1 (New York, 1952), p. 194.

general. Thus a recent analyst declares that, "a survey of the comments about Jews in the Hellenistic-Roman literature shows that they were almost universally disliked, or at least viewed with an amused contempt."[1] In fact, a separate analysis of the positions of government, the masses, and the intellectual elite will reveal a far more nuanced picture ranging from admiration to hostility to a toleration born of Realpolitik. Ancient anti-Semitism was significant and widespread, but it was part of a varied and complex reality. . . .

Governmental Anti-Semitism

. . . Under the Romans, the Jews maintained and even strengthened their vertical alliance with the ruling power. At the outset it was in the Roman interest to support the Maccabean rebellion against the rule of the Syrian Greeks, Rome's chief rival in the eastern Mediterranean, and, in fact, Judah Maccabee contracted an alliance with the Romans. Moreover, as Judaism spread through the next two centuries, the realistic Romans no doubt perceived that the Jews were too numerous (perhaps 10 per cent of the population of the Roman Empire as a whole during the reign of Augustus and 20 per cent of the eastern half of the Empire) to risk antagonizing.

There is one significant report of an expulsion of Jews from the city of Rome itself in 139 B.C.E. as a reaction against Jewish efforts to attract pagans to Judaism or Jewish rites. Such an expulsion, however, must have been short-lived, since by the following century the Jewish presence in Rome was noted bitterly by such writers as Cicero and Horace. Indeed, it is of special interest that the law of B.C.E. 65 that demanded the general expulsion of all non-citizens from Rome does not seem to have affected the Jews, since a few years later, in B.C.E. 59, Cicero noted, "how numerous they are, their clannishness, and their influence in the assemblies." Cicero was defending a client, and

lawyers have been known to exaggerate, but it is self-evident that this courtroom tactic was possible only in a city with a Jewish community of some visibility and at least a modicum of influence.

Shortly after Cicero's remarks, the standing of the Jews in the Empire was enhanced significantly by no less a figure than Julius Caesar himself. Caesar, whose actions served as weighty precedents in the eyes of his successors, was grateful for Jewish assistance rendered during his civil war with Pompey, and he consequently granted the Jews numerous privileges. In city after city in Asia Minor, decrees were issued exempting the Jews from military service, permitting them to send money to the Temple in Jerusalem, and allowing them to form corporate groups, a concession granted uniquely to the Jews that must have seemed remarkable to the non-Jewish inhabitants. Not surprisingly, such preferential treatment did not leave inter-communal relations unscathed. The fact that no fewer than eight cities in Asia Minor were pressured by the Romans to stop their harassment of the Jews (if we assume, as most scholars do, that the Roman documents are authentic) indicates that such privileges were deeply resented.

Relations between Jews and the Roman authorities were not, of course, without grave and ultimately explosive tensions, but before the great revolt of C.E. 66-74 even the most serious incidents were relatively short-lived. In C.E. 19, 4,000 Jews were reportedly expelled from Rome after Jewish embezzlers defrauded a noble proselyte. As in the earlier expulsion, there is reason to believe that Jewish conversionary activity played a role in this decision; in any event, the banishment was brief, it was connected with the activities of a particularly notorious anti-Semite, and it is even possible that it affected only proselytes. The later attempt by Caligula to force the Jews to worship him was regarded as the act of a madman, and despite an enigmatic remark by Suetonius, it appears highly unlikely that Claudius ever expelled them from Rome.

---

1 Jerry L Daniel, "Anti-Semitism in the Hellenistic-Roman Period," *Journal of Biblical Literature* 98 (1979): 45-65.

In the land of Israel, the pressures that led to revolution cannot be perceived in the main as a result of anti-Semitism, although some of the special characteristics of Judaism certainly contributed both to Jewish resistance and to Roman irritation and repression. In the crucial decades before the revolt Jews were often successful in pressing appeals to the governor of Syria and even the emperor himself, and there are various indications that Jewish influence in the royal court was not negligible. Still more striking is the Roman failure to reverse the policy of toleration even after the conclusion of the bloody and unsuccessful revolt. It is true that the Temple tax was converted into the humiliating *fiscus Ludaicus* for the upkeep of the temple of Jupiter and that this tax was collected very strictly, especially during the reign of Domitian (81-96 C.E.). Nevertheless, immediately after the revolt, a number of indications point to the fact that Jewish influence remained in high places: The Jewish king Agrippa II was given the rank of praetor, his sister Berenice became the mistress of the Emperor Titus himself, and the historian Josephus was given a pension and a residence in the former mansion of the emperor.

After the death of Domitian, there was again a relaxation of anti-Jewish pressure, and even the great Diaspora revolt of 115-117 C.E. does not appear to have caused fundamental changes in Roman policy. Finally, the Hadrianic prohibition of circumcision, which probably precipitated the Bar-Kokhba revolt of 132-135 C.E., was not directed only against Jews; the revolt itself was, of course, followed by a series of draconian decrees against many Jewish observances, but these too were alleviated by Hadrian's immediate successor.

The essential toleration extended to the Jews does not go unappreciated in rabbinic literature. It is hardly necessary to point out that various rabbinic comments denounced Rome as a wicked kingdom, but these were balanced in part by a significant number of favorable remarks. Esau's descendants were rewarded for his filial piety, the founding of Rome was placed even earlier than it is by Roman tradition itself, and Roman justice was cited with admiration as

a central reason for God's positive evaluation of His own act of creation.

None of this should obscure the fact that the Jews, alone among all the subjects of the Empire, erupted into revolt three times between the middle of the first and the middle of the second centuries. This is hardly the symptom of an idyllic relationship. Nevertheless, the revolts were not the norm. They took place against the backdrop of an essentially tolerant policy that was a manifestation, at least in the Diaspora, of a vertical alliance between Jews and the government. It is especially striking that even in revolt Jews did not appear to have sought horizontal alliances with other oppressed people. Relations between Jews and the Roman government were marked by alliance, persecution, and revolt, but it is the alliance that was dominant. Government anti-Semitism was not a significant phenomenon in the ancient world.

Popular Anti-Semitism

When we turn to the attitudes of the masses, the picture changes radically. We do not, of course, possess any writings by ordinary people except for a few fragments of papyri, and the intellectuals who produced our literary sources generally express the utmost contempt for the mob. Nevertheless, the sources leave no room for doubt about the widespread hatred and fear of Jews among the masses in the Roman Empire.

We have already noted that the Roman government had to prevent various cities in Asia Minor from interfering with Jewish observance, but such local persecution was but a mild expression of popular anti-Semitism. The hatred of the mob came into boldest relief during a series of riots that can legitimately be described as anti-Semitic pogroms.

The first of these took place in Alexandria in the year 38 C.E. Philo reported that when the Jews refused to obey Caligula's decree that he be worshiped as a god, the promiscuous mob gave full expression to its long-smoldering hatred of the Jews. Ralph Marcus has already noted that this riot illustrates a typical pattern of ancient pogroms: first, long-standing resentment at the privileged position and influence of the Jews, whether political or economic; second and more immediate, the accusation that the Jews were unpatriotic, inasmuch as they refused to participate in the state cults, which, like a flag, united all the diverse peoples of the Empire; third, the rousing of the passions of the mob by professional agitators (though this is perhaps exceptional); fourth, the intervention of the government to preserve order while blaming the Jews for causing the riot. In the case of the riot of 38 C.E., there were additional, special circumstances. Even with the mad Caligula as emperor, the pogrom was hardly inevitable, since the Jewish king Agrippa I had so much influence with the emperor and since Caligula himself had attributed Jewish recalcitrance to stupidity rather than evil. What determined the course of events in this instance was the behavior of Flaccus, the Roman governor of Egypt.

In the first five of the six years of his administration, Flaccus was a model administrator who showed no sign of anti-Jewish animus. Philo conjectured that the change in attitude reflected during the pogrom of 38 C.E. resulted from transformations in the Roman administration that made Flaccus insecure about his standing with the emperor.

The immediate pretext for the riot was the visit of Agrippa I to Alexandria and his ostentatious display of his bodyguard of spearmen, decked in armor overlaid with gold and silver. To the envious anti-Semites this highlighted Jewish wealth and power. The mob responded by dressing up a lunatic named Carabas in mock-royal apparel with a crown and bodyguards and saluting him as "Marin," the Aramaic for "lord." The implied charge was that the Alexandrian Jews, in giving homage to Agrippa as a king, were actually guilty of dual loyalty and of constituting themselves, in effect, as a state within a state. It may even be that the use of the Aramaic word was intended to emphasize the allegation that the Jews' first loyalty was to the Aramaic-speaking ruler of Palestine. Flaccus's response was not merely to seize the meeting house of the Jews but also to deprive them of civic rights, to denounce them as foreigners and as aliens, and to herd them into a

very small part of one of the quarters of the city, the first ghetto in history. Ancient writers rarely stressed or even indicated economic causes of events, and this riot was no exception; nevertheless, the fact that the anti-Semites then pillaged Jewish homes and shops with abandon may indicate that economic considerations were far from insignificant. Indeed, one immediate result of the pogrom was the mass unemployment that occurred because Jewish merchants, artisans, and shipmen lost their stocks and were not allowed to practice their usual business. The sheer savagery of the anti-Semitic mob in binding Jews alive, burning them slowly with brushwood, dragging them through the middle of the marketplace, jumping on them, and not sparing even their dead bodies further indicates the release of pent-up fury reminiscent of the massacres of Polish Jews in the seventeenth century.

Flaccus, according to Philo, could have halted the pogrom in an hour if he had desired, but did nothing. Once they knew that the governmental authority would take no action, the mob attacked the synagogues and placed portraits of Caligula in all of them, while Flaccus himself made a special point of arresting the members of the Gerousia, the body of Jews responsible for their self-government, and stripped and scourged them. Both of these acts were intended to underscore Jewish separatism and lack of patriotism, and the fact that the Jews were accused of storing arms—an accusation that was disproved when absolutely nothing was found—may be an indication that the Jews were perceived as plotting a revolution, perhaps in conjunction with Palestinian revolutionaries. In the end, what must have seemed to the anti-Semites like an instance of "international Jewish power" was recalled in disgrace, banished, and eventually executed. . . .

Josephus noted that the non-Jewish inhabitants of Caesarea slaughtered the Jews of that city at the very same hour that the Roman garrison in Herod's palace in Jerusalem was massacred. The break in the tie between the Jews and their rulers meant that the anti-Semitic mobs were, in effect, given *carte blanche* throughout the Empire for their murderous assaults. Indeed, it was presumably the fact that the Romans ceased to act as "honest brokers" between the two groups and instead favored the non-Jews that led the Jews to the painful conclusion that they could no longer count on the vertical alliance with their rulers to protect them. In any event, the fact that 20,000 Jews were slaughtered in Caesarea within one hour (a kind of Jewish St. Bartholemew's Day in more concentrated form, even if the figure is an exaggeration) indicates the premeditated nature and ferocity of the assault. This, in turn, set in motion a series of reprisals by Jews against non-Jews in a number of Palestinian and Syrian villages and cities, after which the Syrians retaliated with a massacre of Jews.

Significantly, Josephus cited the presence of "Judaizers" in each Syrian city; and one may guess that one of the causes of the Jew-hatred was precisely the Jewish success in winning converts and gaining "sympathizers," as well as the eagerness of the Jews to expand their civic rights. Josephus himself ascribed three motives to the anti-Semites: hatred, fear, and greed for plunder. Josephus's declaration that the Jews of Caesarea were superior in wealth and physical strength is especially revealing. One may reasonably infer that Jewish wealth created jealousy; and, indeed, we find that when the procurator Felix let loose his soldiers against the Caesarean Jews, he permitted his troops to plunder certain houses of the Jewish inhabitants that were laden with very large sums of money. Finally, by pointing to the Jews' physical strength, Josephus was doubtless including their sheer number; and we may surmise that the non-Jews were frightened by the increase in the Jewish population that resulted at least in part from success in proselytism.

Despite this series of disasters, it is striking that the Jews could ultimately count on the support of the rulers against the mob. Antioch was one of only three Syrian cities that, according to Josephus, had not indulged in popular anti-Semitic massacres of the Jews on the eve of the war. After the outbreak of the fighting, however, the security of the Jews was ended, and a renegade Jew named Antiochus incited a riot when he accused the Jews of planning to burn the city. Now that the revolution had broken out in Judaea, the Roman general no longer protected the Jews and instead sent troops to aid Antiochus in forcing the Jews to violate the Sabbath. Nevertheless, when Antiochus incited a second attack after the capture of Jerusalem, the results were quite different. Once the revolt of the Jews in Jerusalem was over, the Roman administrator restrained the fury of the mob. Shortly thereafter, when the victorious Roman general Titus passed through Antioch, the non-Jewish population greeted him enthusiastically and petitioned him to expel the Jews from the city. Titus, however, was unmoved by this request and listened in silence. When the people of the city persisted, Titus declined, stating that since the country of the Jews had been destroyed, they had nowhere to go. When the people asked that at least the privileges of the Jews should be removed, Titus again refused, leaving the status of the Jews as it formerly was. . . .

In Rome itself, despite the insinuations about Jewish clannishness and influence in Cicero's defense of Flaccus, there was apparently no history of virulent anti-Semitism on the part of the mob, noted though it was for its size and unruly nature. We may conjecture that this may have been because the Jews in the city, unlike those in Alexandria or Antioch or Caesarea, did not have or seek special political privileges, so far as we know. Moreover, the fact that Rome was the seat of the emperor, who had regarded himself since the days of Julius Caesar as the protector of the Jews, may have served as a deterrent. Finally, because the emperor constantly had his own bodyguard and a sizable number of troops in readiness to protect him from assassination or violent outbreaks, such popular uprisings would have been difficult to carry out.

Intellectual Anti-Semitism

Though it is perhaps hard for us to imagine a time when the world was not preoccupied with the "Jewish question," for many centuries in antiquity this was the case. Thus it is not until Herodotus in the fifth century B.C.E.. that any extant Greek writer mentioned the Jews at all, and the first mention of them was oblique, in a discussion of circumcision. Stern's monumental three-volume collection of testimonia to the Jews in pagan writers seems large, but the truth is that many of the quotations deal only peripherally with the Jews as such. Indeed, if Josephus's reply *Against Apion* had been lost, we would be lacking a large proportion of the most virulent anti-Semitic texts.

Scholars who have examined this corpus have emphasized the almost universal prevalence of virulent anti-Semitism in the remarks of these writers. In Germany it became fashionable to cite these passages in promoting the thesis that the Jew's inherent characteristics produced anti-Semitism wherever he went, especially among men of intellectual attainments. And yet, as I have tried to indicate elsewhere, Jews were admired as possessing the four cardinal virtues of wisdom, courage, temperance, and justice; and the list of their admirers included figures of the stature of Aristotle, his successor Theophrastus, and Varro, who was to be termed by the great literary critic Quintillion "the most learned of the Romans." Indeed, one of antiquity's most distinguished literary critics, the first-century pseudo-Longinus, praises the opening of Genesis as an example of the most lofty style. Moreover, many of the hostile passages come from rhetorical historians or satirists, where the references are clearly colored and exaggerated. In addition, other peoples of antiquity, such as the Egyptians, Syrians, Thracians, Spaniards, Gauls, Germans, Phrygians, and Carthaginians, as well as the Greeks and Romans themselves, are also objects of detestation and derision. Thus, for example, two of the charges made against Jews, that they are lazy and superstitious, were also made by Tacitus against the Germans. The fact that so many pagans embraced Judaism during this period shows that Jews were by no means universally unpopular and that they had more contacts with non-Jews than is generally recognized. Finally, according to my own count, 101 (18 per cent) of the comments by pagans in Stern's collection are substantially favorable, 339 (59 per cent) are more or less neutral, and only 130 (23 per cent) are substantially unfavorable. Nonetheless, it must be granted that a number of serious charges are made by the intellectual Anti-Semites.

Conclusion

During the Hellenistic and Roman periods, the Jews encountered hostility from governments, mobs, and intellectuals. The anti-Semitism of the last group was by no means universal; and in no case, with the exception of one or possibly two incidents at Alexandria, do we find that intellectuals had any influence in arousing the masses against the Jews, so great, apparently, was the gulf between these teachers and the masses. Indeed, this lack of communication between the intellectuals and the mob may explain why the blood libel, which is found in ancient writings as early as the beginning of the first century, was apparently never an occasion for a pogrom. Nevertheless, there is a good deal of evidence that the anti-Semitism of the masses was deep-seated and that little was needed to trigger it into violence. It was basically the vertical alliance of the Jews with governments, starting with the Persians, continuing through Alexander and his successors the Ptolemies and the Seleucids, and further continuing with the Romans that, on the whole, restrained the masses from violent outbreaks. The position of the Jews was certainly strengthened by their sheer numbers, constantly increasing through highly successful proselytism, so that we may even conjecture that if the three great revolts against the Romans had not occurred and if Christianity had not lowered the price of admission, so to speak, Judaism might have become the major religion of the Roman Empire. The masses, however, established a love-hate relationship with the Jews; and many of these who remained unconverted were fearful of the prospect that Judaism would bring about the end of their pagan religions. The governments, with few exceptions, did not wish to antagonize so large and important a group and maintained the privileged position of the Jews.

The Church and the Early Empire

Harold Mattingly

The late Harold Mattingly here provides a survey of Roman relations with the Christians through the first century A.D. He points out that the Christians initially saw the Jews as the persecutors while St. Paul often was protected by local Roman officials. Nero's use of the Christians as scapegoats for the disastrous fire at Rome in A.D. 64 must have come as a terrible shock to that young religion. Even now it is not certain on what grounds the Christians were initially persecuted or when the Romans actually began to see them as distinct from the Jews. Though the better emperors did not encourage active persecution of the Christians, Christians were considered to be traitrs because they refused to pray to Roman gods.

Jesus Christ 'suffered under Pontius Pilate,' as one among many suspected of leading national risings against Rome (A.D. 29?). The story in Eusebius, which he quotes from Tertullian, tells of how Tiberius received a report from Palestine about the death and resurrection of Jesus and sent it on to the senate, with indications of his approval of the new doctrine; but the senate, not having tested the matter itself, rejected the report. However, Tiberius threatened death to the accusers of the Christians. This story is generally rejected today as not being consistent with what we know in general of the early days of the Church. Tacitus, in his *Annals*, may have referred to the Crucifixion—he does occasionally refer to events of not dissimilar character in the provinces—but the passage would have stood, if at all, in the gap between Books V and VI. If Pilate reported to Tiberius, one might suppose that it would be through his superior on the spot, the governor of Syria.

We are familiar with the Christian witness about the empty tomb—also with the Jewish account, that the disciples came by night and took the body away. The ordinary Roman would shrug his shoulders; men once crucified do not rise again. . . . We know how the Athenians, when St. Paul spoke to them on Mars' Hill of the resurrection, at once said 'that they would hear him another day.' There is one curious piece of evidence which might have some reference, if only indirectly, to the case. It is an imperial edict from Nazareth, decreeing the death penalty for tomb robbery for anyone who destroys a tomb or casts out the buried or 'with evil intent, removes them to some other spot.' Momigliano relates the edict to the quarrels between Jews and Christians under Claudius in Rome. The edict certainly seems to fit that date: before Claudius, one could not expect an imperial edict in Galilee.

The picture . . . of Christianity already attracting serious attention in the reigns of Tiberius and Caligula is probably false. Tacitus tells us how the 'awful superstition,' repressed for a time, revived and spread. Suetonius reports that Claudius expelled from Rome the Jews who were rioting at the instigation of Chrestus. The 'e' for 'i' in the names Christ, Christians, occurs not uncommonly; so there is hardly room to doubt that Suetonius had a confused reference to riots between Jews and Christians in Rome. Christianity, then, early reached Rome. It took root in the Emperor's own guard. The noble lady, Pomponia Graecina, wife of Plautius, the conqueror of Britain, was probably a Christian. She was accused of a foreign superstition, tried by her husband before a domestic court and acquitted.

Our knowledge of the Apostolic Age comes to us mostly from the Christian side, from the Acts of the Apostles, from the Epistles of St. Paul and other New Testament writings and, with much less certainty, from sundry Apocryphal Gospels and Epistles. The faith of the disciples revives with the conviction that Christ is risen. Bitter persecution by the Jews fails to crush the growth of the Church. St. Paul is converted and learns of his life mission—to carry the Gospel to the Gentiles. And so the Christian Churches are one by one planted, sometimes very humble meetings in private houses. They arise in many of the cities of the East—in Jerusalem, Antioch, Ephesus, Philippi, Corinth and the rest; there are some notable exceptions, Alexandria for example. The call is to the poor and oppressed; not many wise, not many noble, not many rich are called.

It is the Jews that are the enemy. The Roman government is seen as protector, rather than persecutor. St. Paul is a friend of Sergius Paulus, governor of Cyprus. At Philippi he is scourged and imprisoned by the magistrates; but they discover their grave error—he is a Roman citizen and they had not realized it—and have to appeal to his generosity to pass it by. At Ephesus, when Demetrius the silver-smith rouses the mob against St. Paul, the town clerk tries to still the tumult with appeals to the Roman authority. In Achaea Gallio, the Roman governor, 'cares for none of these things,' when the Jews try to interest him in their quarrel with Paul. Rome is concerned with the public order, not with petty disputes on religion which no one not closely concerned in them can understand. Christians are often reminded of their duty to honor lawful authority.

The persecution of Nero fell like a thunderbolt on the Church. It seems to have lasted several years and not to have been confined to Rome. A confident tradition assigns to it the martyrdoms both of St. Peter and St. Paul. Tacitus alone in his very particular account gives the initial year, A.D. 64, and connects the persecution with the Great Fire of Rome. Suetonius (Nero) only knows of the torments inflicted on the Christians, a new, vile and pernicious superstition. We turn to the evidence of Tacitus. In A.D. 64 a large part of Rome was destroyed by a terrible fire; the Emperor, Nero, already horribly notorious as murderer of half-brother, mother and wife, was suspected of having fired his city; he had, they said, dressed up as a lyrist and sung a 'Sack of Troy' over burning Rome. Tacitus then reports the sequel—it may be said, by the way, that the passage is unquestionably by Tacitus if any part of the Annals is; the attempts of the old 'Higher Criticism' to discredit the passage have failed completely:

Annals. XV. 44. . . . 'But no human effort, no generosity on the part of the Emperor, no atonement of the gods could rid Nero of the disgraceful imputation of having ordered the fire. To silence these rumors Nero found scapegoats on whom to fix the guilt and punished them with the most exquisite torments. These were the people called Christians by the mob and hated for their abominations. The originator of the name, Christus, was put to death by the procurator, Pontius Pilate, in the reign of Tiberus. For the time the horrible superstition was suppressed, but it tended to break out again not only in Judaea, the source of the mischief, but in Rome, whither all that is monstrous flows and finds a ready welcome. First to be arrested were the men who admitted the charge; then, on their information a vast multitude were seized—not exactly on the charge of incendarism, but of hatred of the human race. The deaths they died were aggravated by cruel mockeries. They were wrapped in the skins of wild beasts to die under the mangling of hounds, or nailed to crosses or set to burn like torches so that when day-light failed, they might illuminate the night. Nero had ordered his gardens for this spectacle and also gave a circus show, mingling with the crowds in the dress of a charioteer or riding in his car. All this gave birth to pity for his victims guilty though they were and deserving of the worse possible punishments; men felt that they were being spent, not in the public interest, but to glut the cruelty of an individual.'

Tacitus, when we can check his accounts against other sources, is always—nearly always—reliable. When he connects the persecution with the Great Fire, he can hardly be mistaken. But the rest of our tradition, which extends the persecution to a wider range and knows of no special connection with the Fire, cannot be ignored. Suetonius reports the persecution not as an atrocity, but as one of a series of salutary reforms. We shall also see, very soon, that the action of Nero as persecutor seems to have become a model for later Emperors. Tacitus, I believe, has misled us, as he often misleads, not on point of fact, but on its interpretation. The Great Fire had occurred, Nero was suspected of guilt, the Christians, with their talk of an approaching end of the age in fire, might seem very suitable scapegoats. But the examinations of the persons arrested soon took the question right away from the original occasion. The government claimed to have unearthed a sort of minor conspiracy against the human race; as we shall see, it seems to have won general approval for its action. Tacitus wants to throw mud at Nero and finds a most unfriendly interpretation of his persecution. He used the Christians as sticks to beat Nero with. For the Christians themselves he has no real sympathy or understanding. Yet he was governor in Asia the year after Pliny in Bithynia had raised the question of the Christians with the Emperor Trajan; he knew, then, that Pliny had discovered that the horrible charges of crime brought against the Christians were, normally, false. No hint of this is allowed to color his narrative here. He is guilty of telling something less than the truth. The Christians lay outside the possible range of his approval—low, unusual, no class people—it never even occurs to him that they may be right.

On what grounds were the Christians persecuted? A much disputed question—not yet certainly answered. Paganism was usually carelessly tolerant. Rome herself interfered now and then against foreign cults, but normally in the name of threatened morality. What was there in Christianity to make Rome break her general rule? [The historian] Mommsen in a famous paper urged that persecution was commonly a part of police control, *coercitio*, determined not by law, but by the decision of authority from time to time that intervention was necessary to ensure public order. Another view is that the Church was persecuted as an unlicensed society.

The Empire was very jealous of private societies, seeing in them sources of trouble, and therefore insisted that they should be licensed. An unlicensed club, continuing to meet after warning, would certainly expose itself to extreme penalties. Others think that the charge was High Treason, *maiestas*. It was a charge very commonly tacked on to others in the Early Empire. Or the supposed crimes of the Christians might have furnished the grounds for prosecution. Cannibalism and incest were supposed to be regular features of Church life.

None of these explanations is quite satisfactory. All may contain some element of truth. Very early, persecution 'for the name,' is certain. That is to say, to confess yourself a Christian is enough to condemn you. The principle is recognized when Pliny consults Trajan from Bithynia. It must, then, have been established by test cases, who the Christians were and how they were to be dealt with. Our evidence for events between the years A.D. 64 and A.D. 111 is so slight that we must admit that the decision against the Christians *may* have fallen within them. It seems more probable that the action of Nero against the Christians was not, in the imperial records, associated specifically with the Great Fire, or regarded as one of his more irresponsible freaks, but that it furnished a precedent for further trials and at once made persecution 'for the name' an immediate possibility for every loyal Christian. Even if the Christians were not guilty of cannibalism and incest, even if they had not fired Rome, they were, by common consent, an uncouth, uncomfortable set of killjoys, hating the normal pleasures of life and denying the people's gods. They seemed to be Jews of a kind—and yet the Jews would have none of them. The Empress Poppaea was addicted to Jewish practices; and it has been most plausibly suggested that she, to divert hatred from the Jews, used her influence with Nero to turn him against the Christians. This is only a guess—but it seems to be a reasonable one.

Close on the persecution of Nero followed the first revolt of the Jews, ending in the destruction of Jerusalem. The Church had to adapt itself to new conditions. The Empire, long seen as a friend, might at any moment turn persecutor. The disastrous end of the Jewish fight with Rome might seem to mean the catastrophic end of the age of which Jesus had spoken. Perhaps the thought that the end of the world itself was now imminent may now have begun to arise. It was in this new era that our Gospels were written. The three Synoptic Gospels set out in due order for the faithful what was known and accepted of our Lord's life and ministry. They all—including St. Mark—are written under the impression of the Fall of Jerusalem, accomplished or imminent. That Jesus spoke His warnings of the coming judgment is not to be questioned; but the fresh interest in these sayings, nowhere apparent in the Acts or the Epistles of St. Paul, tells its tale. St. Luke was perhaps presenting the Christian case to sympathizers in the Greek world. St. John, of course, is years later than the Synoptics; he tells the Gospel story again with new emphasis for a new age.

The position of the Jews in the Empire was seriously changed for the worse. The didrachm, due to the Temple, had now to be paid to Jupiter of the Capitol; a special chest, the *fiscus Iudaicus*, dealt with this revenue, and became notorious for brutality and chicanery over the collection of the tax. It is most probable that, during the course of examinations to decide whether a man was a Jew and so liable to the tax, the difference between Jew and Christian became generally known as never before. Suppose a man is found to be circumcised and yet denies that he is a Jew. Who is he then? A Christian. Has he a special charter as the Jew has? No. Has he the right, then, to exist as a Christian? No. In this way, the original judgment of Nero against Christians may have been repeated and confirmed. There is a passage in Sulpicius Severus, a later writer thought to be copying Tacitus, about Titus holding a Council of War to decide whether or not to destroy the Temple. He himself is for destruction; the religions of the Jews and Christians will be the easier undermined. This suggests that the Jews and Christians were indeed known to be distinct, but still not clearly distinguished.

Of the second persecution, that of Domitian, late in his reign, c. A.D. 95, not much is known. Among the victims were Flavia Domitilla, cousin of the Emperor, banished to an island; she was certainly a Christian. Probably her husband, Flavius Clemens, put to death on this occasion, was one also; he was executed for 'atheism'. . . . The persecution extended to Asia. The Apocalypse is full of the sufferings of those who would not bear the mark of the Beast on their foreheads; it speaks of Pergamum 'where the seat of Satan is.' There is a clear reference to the Pergamene temple of Rome and Augustus. Persecution is clearly for refusal to worship the Emperor—the Beast. There is a curious story that Domitian, anxious to learn more of the truth, sent for the descendants of the family of the Lord from Palestine and interrogated them. When he found them to be poor, unambitious and humble people, he sent them home unharmed. Our record of this persecution is very imperfect. The Apocalypse, it seems, preserves the impression that it made—mixed, no doubt, with memories of the persecution of Nero; but we cannot read certainties out of deliberately riddling prophesies. . . .

We come now to the most interesting of all pagan *testimonia* to the early history of the Church. In A.D. 110 Trajan . . . sent out as governor on a special mission his friend, the Younger Pliny. We know of Pliny as a barrister and man of letters, a great friend of Tacitus and a man of liberal and kindly character. Pliny found serious difficulties awaiting him, about many of which he consulted Trajan. Among them was the question of the Christians. Let us give Pliny himself the word:

Epistle of Pliny to the Emperor Trajan

. . . *Pending your advice, the method I have followed with those who were brought before me as Christians is this. I have asked them in person whether they were Christians. If they have confessed I have repeated my inquiry a second and third time; when they persisted, I have ordered them to execution. I had no uncertainty in my mind, that whatever the character of their confession was, their persistence, their unbending obstinacy, deserved extreme punishment. There were others, similarly afflicted, to whose cases, as they were Roman citizens,*

I added the note that they should be sent to Rome. Then as the cases were being tried and the charges spread as they will, more types of conduct met me. An anonymous document was produced in public, containing many names. Such of these as declared that they were not and never had been Christians, I thought fit to discharge, after they, following my recital, had invoked the gods and had prayed with wine and incense before your statue. . . .

Epistle of Trajan, to his friend Pliny

"My dear Secundus, you have pursued the correct course of conduct in investigating the cases of those who were brought before you as Christians. Indeed, no general regulation can be given that would have anything like a clear-cut form. They are not to be sought out; if they are denounced and proved guilty, they must be punished—providing only this, that a man who denies that he is a Christian and proves it by his act, that is to say, by praying to our gods, however suspect he may have been in the past, may obtain forgiveness through repentance. Anonymous documents must not figure in any charge. That would be a vile precedent, not permissible in our age."

. . . Trajan could be represented either as a persecutor or as a friend. As a matter of fact the knowledge that the Emperor was personally unwilling to hunt down Christians certainly acted as a deterrent on accusers, but we have only to look back to the experiences of St. Paul to see how far things have moved since his day. Then the Christian might expect protection, if not positive favor, from the Roman government. Now he must be thankful if he is permitted to escape notice. Let us sum up the development that we have been considering. The early Christians attracted little attention from the Roman government, were not persecuted, might even be protected against their enemies, the Jews. This happy state of things came to a sudden close under Nero. Tacitus has probably confused the picture by connecting the persecution too closely with the Great Fire of Rome. If the persecution had been merely one of Nero's brutal vagaries, it would not have continued to supply a precedent for Emperors after him. It is strange but true that Romans of character and position continue to speak of Christianity as a horrible superstition and have no doubt that mere persistence in it merits death. It may be as early as Nero that persecution 'for the name' began. . . .

It may be noted that Christian apologists made much of the fact that only bad Emperors persecuted. This was an exaggeration of the truth. Trajan continued the practice of Nero. There was something of a moral reform at Rome, beginning with the sound old Sabine countryman, Vespasian. But the better men who now tended to rise to high positions in the State still maintained the harsh verdict on the Church.

Astrology and Magic in Public Life

J. H. W. G. Liebeschuetz

Professor Wolf Liebeschuetz of Nottingham surveys the use of astrology in Roman political life. Though the Romans had long used astrology, it was only under the Julio-Claudians that belief in its efficacy became widespread. Augustus and his successors consulted astrologers regularly, and Thrasyllus even became a close friend of Tiberius. But the astrologers' predictions obviously had political importance, and they understandably unsettled the emperors, who feared the implications of an unfavorable horoscope.

Magic also appeared in public life in the early Empire. Scribonius Libo was forced to commit suicide after he was suspected of using magic against Tiberius, while Piso was accused of magic in the death of Germanicus. Tacitus recounts a number of cases of magic and there was increasing legislation against magic as the Julio-Claudian emperors tried to protect themselves.

Astrology in Public Life

A feature of life in senatorial and court circles in the early empire was the influence of astrology. Astrology was not new. It had been used by many Romans for a long time to help them in private concerns. But the end of the republic and the establishment of the principate gave it a place in public life which it had not had before.

The belief that human destinies can be predicted by observation of the stars originated in Mesopotamia and was known in Greece before the time of Plato. It made great progress in the Hellenistic world. It was in Hellenistic Egypt that a sophisticated science was evolved from Mesopotamian astrology and Greek astronomy and mathematics. The claims of astrology were given plausibility by the fact that the annual rising and setting of constellations had long been associated with the seasonal changes of the weather, and had indeed been held to be the cause of the changes.

Practical exploitation of the theory that the stars which dominated at the time of a man's birth would influence the whole of his life was encouraged by advances in astronomy and mathematics, which made possible accurate observation of the positions of stars and calculation of their positions in the past. Astrology was of course a pseudo-science. The true nature of the forces that operate between different parts of the universe (gravitation, radiation, etc.) remained unknown, and the astrologers' arbitrary procedure of endowing stars with personalities, and postulating the existence of mysterious emanations through which these stellar personalities could exert their influence over huge distances, could in no way fill the gap in knowledge. Nevertheless the prestige of philosophy and mathematics led men to indulge in wishful thinking and believe what they wanted to believe. . . .

. . . One feels that astrology was still of very little public importance at Rome. The situation was to be quite different under the empire. In the reign of Augustus, belief in astrology was widespread. Maecenas, the emperor's friend, and patron of the Augustan poets, believed that his fate was determined by the stars that had dominated the hour of his birth. The architect Vitruvius accepted the truth of astrology in a matter-of-fact way. It was just one of a long series of scientific discoveries. The age saw the writing of an astrological epic by Manilius, and the poets occasionally assume knowledge of astrological terms on the part of their readers. All through the first and second centuries there was a vast amount of consultation concerning everyday matters of private life or business. But a new and influential development, now that government of Rome revolved round one man, was that the emperor almost invariably used the services of astrologers. Augustus was converted by an astrological forecast of greatness made at the very start of his career. Sometime later he publicized the astral circumstances of his birth, obviously hoping that this would win him supporters. In A.D. 11 when many thought that Augustus' death was imminent, he published a horoscope which suggested that he would live longer. Astrology retained the esteem which it had won under Augustus. Most of his successors consulted one or more astrologers regularly. Thrasyllus, a man of learning in many fields, was a friend as well as the astrologer of the emperor Tiberius. His descendants rose into the senatorial order. . . .

A second development of the principate was that astrology came to be linked with conspiracy. The authorities could assume that an attempt at political innovation would generally be preceded by some inquiry as to whether fate favored the revolutionaries, and that this would normally involve consultation of an astrologer. Hence astrology was repressed repeatedly by the government. Astrologers were expelled from Rome in 33 B.C. In A.D. 11 Augustus made it illegal to consult a diviner about the date of the death of any person, a topic on which Balbillus was to write a book. It was also forbidden for a diviner and his client to meet without witnesses. In A.D. 15, following the suppression of the plot of Scribonius Libo, astrologers were expelled from Italy. After this we hear fairly regularly of the prosecution of men who were accused of having consulted an astrologer about the future of the emperor. Ulpian explained the principle: 'those who consult about the health of the emperor are punishable by death or some still heavier sentence; and about their own or relatives' 'affairs by a lighter sentence.' That such consultation might in fact encourage a man who was in any case eager to attempt a coup détat is shown in Tacitus' account of how Otho overthrew the emperor Galba.

The political importance of astrology was something new. Republican politicians might employ astrologers, but there is no evidence that astrological advice influenced political behavior. . . . It was certainly no coincidence that the early empire should witness an increase in the public importance of astrology. One factor was the transformation of political action. As long as the republic lasted, political change could be brought about by more or less political means, and judgments about the future could be formed on the basis of the facts and rumors of (again more or less) open politics. After Augustus, things were different. Political change required revolution, a daunting task for which the would-be rebel required all possible human and superhuman encouragement. In addition, information about the political situation was much more difficult to obtain, since important decisions were made by the emperor and his advisers in private. No wonder public figures snatched at the information which astrologers offered. The emperor himself had to bear a heavy weight of decision-making, since no matter how many advisers he consulted, he could not avoid the full responsibility. He needed reassurance, and perhaps sometimes obstruction, that was both confidential and independent. Hence the employment of a court astrologer. There was the additional consideration that astrology was thought to be scientific, for it benefited from the prestige of the great names in Greek mathematics and philosophy.

The other factor favoring the progress of astrology under the empire was philosophic. Astrology, whatever its claims, would not have been widely adopted unless people had thought the claims valid. But men in the political classes were predisposed to find astrology true because, as we have seen, Stoic philosophy had in a sense become their religion. In fact astrology, quite apart from its supposed usefulness, reinforced the appeal of Stoic philosophy as a doctrine which asserted the dignified place of rational man in a rational universe. For the Stoic believer in astrology each individual man is a small-scale model of the universe, and the heavens revolve around man in order that he may read his future. This picture of himself gave back to a Roman noble the dignity lost through humiliating submission to an emperor.

The widespread use of astrology had consequences both in politics and in thought. In the first place, astrology could not be controlled as the traditional Roman divination had been. Dangerous knowledge about the future was available for whoever could pay a prestigious astrologer. Hence, astrology made for political restlessness, encouraging would-be rebels and feeding a sense of insecurity in emperors. Claudius' death was frequently predicted; so was Nero's. Both emperors executed numerous senators. Nero was certainly terrified by the mass of predictions. So was Domitian.

Astrology affected the way men looked at the world because its validity required the existence of unseen connections to transmit the influence of the stars to earth. Once the existence of invincible but powerful forces running through the world was admitted, plausibility was given to techniques that might manipulate such forces: in other words, magic and magicians.

Astrology and magic were not absolutely distinct. The same man might practice both. Thrasyllus, the court astrologer of Tiberius, wrote a lapidary, a text-book on the arcane properties of stones. Divination was a principal object of magic no less than of astrology. The sun, as 'ruler of the universe', played an important role in the theory of both astrology and learned magic.

Astrology could be presented as an empirical science but also as an arcane doctrine ultimately resting on revelation. It is not therefore surprising that magic appears in public life at Rome not much later than astrology.

Magic in Public Life

The use of a combination of words and ritual to achieve a result which would otherwise be beyond a person's power to bring about by physical action is as old as Graeco-Roman civilization—perhaps as old as mankind. But the concept of magic was a much less sharply defined one for the ancients than it is for us.

The behavior of matter was poorly understood, and in many cases, particularly in the field of healing, men would have been hard put to distinguish between a natural and a magical

cause. Moreover, since a very large part of everyday life was accompanied by ritual words and actions and the rites were thought essential for the successful accomplishment of one's purpose, it was difficult to maintain on principle that ritual could not achieve physical effect. Nevertheless distinctions were made: some rites were acceptable, others were not. One criterion was provided by the objective. Ritual intended to benefit crops or heal disease was good, but directed to harm individuals or crops it was bad, and from an early time punishable. . . .

Magic found its way into literature and produced commonplaces for the description of magical rites which recur in the writings of generation after generation of poets, but nevertheless retain a relationship to practices that were actually carried out. . . .

The poets leave no doubt of the prevalence of witchcraft. At the same time they exploit the black science to make their reader's flesh creep agreeably. The poets make it quite clear that they do not take magic very seriously. The topic lends itself to the production of literary horror, or black humor, but it is not important. It is not linked with any of the activities that really mattered, or were practiced by people that mattered.

This was changing. One can see the first traces of the change in the late republic but its effects only become visible in political life under the emperors. One can isolate a number of factors which favored this development. These include, not necessarily in this order of importance, the emotional needs which induced leading men of Rome to favor Pythagoreanism, the appearance of a magical literature which could benefit from the prestige of learning, the intellectual respectability of astrology, and the political change from republic to monarchy. . . .

We see that learned magic was one of a succession of ideological imports from the Hellenistic world that gradually revolutionized the outlook of the Romans. It belongs together with the rationalist Stoic philosophy and astrology on the one hand, and with mystery religions and, eventually, Christianity on the other and like astrology and the mystery religions it only began to play a significant part in public life under the empire. . . . Early in the reign of

Augustus, Anaxilaus of Larissa, a Pythagorean, a natural philosopher and a *magus*, was expelled from Rome. Under Tiberius consultation of *magi*, like the consultation of astrologers, is found among charges against men on trial for conspiring against the emperor. The earliest case was that of M. Scribonius Libo, a rich young man who was directly descended from Pompey and had family links with the imperial house. Libo had had dealings with astrologers, *magi*, and interpreters of dreams. A personal friend, a senator, informed the emperor. Later, accusers of lower rank appeared. It was claimed that he had consulted a diviner whether he would ever be rich enough to cover the Appian way with money. But among his papers there was also found a list of names, including the emperor's, with mysterious signs attached to them. Immediately, Tiberius took the affair very seriously. Slaves were tortured and Libo was compelled to commit suicide. A public supplication of thanksgiving was decreed by the senate. Astrologers and magicians were expelled from Italy.

In A.D. 20 the death of the emperor's nephew Germanicus followed soon after a quarrel with the highly aristocratic governor of Syria. Piso was accused of murder and treason. The murder was alleged to have been attempted through magic as well as straight-forward poisoning. At any rate the charge of poisoning was refuted. . . .

In 53 Statilius Taurus was accused of extortion but there was the additional charge—probably the real charge—of magic rites. The motive behind the charge was said to have been that the Empress Agrippina desired the accused's gardens. The informer was expelled from the senate after Taurus had anticipated the verdict with suicide.

The number of magic trials is not great. But there would not have been any at all if the employment of magic had not been a feature of life in the highest class, and one which was considered a public danger. But what precisely was the danger. Magic could be used to harm people. This was a charge against Piso. But the reader of Tacitus does not feel that Roman emperors or Roman nobles of the Julio-Claudian period were afraid of the harm that they might suffer from sympathetic magic. One suspects that the ultimate threat of magic was the same as that of astrology; namely, that it was thought to provide reliable information about the future. It would enable a would-be conspirator to estimate whether his scheme had a chance of success. In the case of a discontented noble—and there always were such—the encouragement of the astrologer or magus might just be the incentive to remove the last inhibition. . . .

The accusation of magic must not be considered in isolation. Together with the *maiestas* charge itself, it was part of the armory of the prosecution in the treason trials that were so prominent and disagreeable a feature of the early principate. We have seen that magic was often linked with astrology and with the, to modern minds, much more commonplace adultery. The charges could be made on their own or in various combinations. Magic, and to a lesser degree adultery, had the advantage that they could be used for character assassinations as well as to achieve conviction.

One suspects that many of the charges were preferred because ambitious men exploited tensions in the political system, between the emperor and the old noble families, between Tiberius and the house of Germanicus, between Nero and the 'philosophical' opposition, or the tension resulting from public indignation, as after the suspicious death of the popular prince Germanicus, to further their own rise to power and wealth. Moreover, if recourse to the expertise of magicians was anything like as common as recourse to astrologers, or adultery, are known to have been it will have been fairly easy to get evidence on which to base the charge. Thus accusations of this kind provided an ideal means for bringing down men who were unlikely to risk genuinely treacherous activity. Nero's mother, the empress Agrippina, made free use of such prosecutions to clear the way to power for herself and her son.

This medal depicts four chariots racing around the central spina (with statues and the central obelisk) in the Circus Maximus. This late fourth-century brass "contorniate" is not a coin, but a special issue perhaps used for circus prizes or memorials of the games.

VIII

Bread And Circuses:
The Politics Of Entertainment

INTRODUCTION
Ronald Mellor

The tutor of the emperor Marcus Aurelius once wrote: "The Roman people is held together by two things: wheat doles and public shows. Control is secured as much by amusements as by serious things." This had long been known, and many prudent rulers had pursued the same strategy in the 1,800 years since Fronto wrote these lines, but never has that philosophy been so relied upon as in the Roman Empire. Horse races, theatrical events, wild beast hunts, mock sea battles, public executions and gladiatorial combat—all were sponsored by the emperors to entertain and pacify the dangerous urban mob.

Jo-Ann Shelton describes the most important of the Roman games at which, unlike the Greeks, the Romans were normally spectators rather than participants. Her essay provides the historical and political context of the Roman spectacles and prepares for Suetonius' description of specific games sponsored by the Julio-Claudian emperors. Other essays in this chapter examine the psychological, sociological and political basis for this entertainment, which played such a central role in Roman imperial civilization.

But Fronto, and the satirist Juvenal in his famous phrase "bread and circuses," place the paramount human need for food before entertainment. All ancient cities were parasites which were supported by the masses who toiled in the countryside. More than 90 percent of the population of the Empire was engaged in agriculture and we should not allow the urban setting and orientation of most ancient literary texts to conceal that central economic fact. Rome was the parasite par excellence supported by the taxes and trade of the entire Empire. To provision a city of a million mouths and bellies was a formidable logistical task in a technologically underdeveloped society, but Augustus and his successors went further: the emperors provided a free grain dole for the several hundred thousand free men and their families who constituted the Roman plebs. The demands of the capital (both the grain dole as well as the sustenance of hundreds of thousands of soldiers) were greater than those of any previous empire in the Mediterranean world, yet these needs could be met by the resources of an Empire of over fifty million souls as long as the central government remained firmly in control and the grain supply was kept under close imperial scrutiny.

Roman Spectacles

Jo-Ann R. Shelton

Jo-Ann Shelton, who is Professor of Classics at the University of California Santa Barbara, has published and lectured on Roman spectacles, particularly on Roman horsemanship and the circuses. She here presents a detailed introduction to Roman popular entertainment in the early Empire. Her discussion traces the history of theatrical performances, gladiatorial shows and circuses, and it is richly supplemented with quotations from contemporary sources, so that we are not only given a detailed description of the spectacles but we can also glimpse the Roman attitudes to them. The quotations from Professor Shelton's own translations from her sourcebook, As The Romans Did (Oxford, 1988), are her own translations.

"The particular and peculiar vices of the Romans—a partiality toward actors and a passion for gladiators and horses—seem almost to be conceived in the mother's womb." So lamented one of the speakers in Tacitus' *Dialogues*. The satirist Juvenal grumbled that the populace of Rome was interested only in bread and circuses, that is, in the distribution of free grain and the display of chariot races, both provided by the government with state funds. The ancient Romans were indeed avid spectators, and their favorite spectacles (Latin *spectare*, "to look at") were chariot races, dramas, musical and dance performances, gladiatorial combats, and the slaughter of men and animals. These spectacles were "popular" in a number of senses: they were enjoyed by the common people, and they were organized for the enjoyment of these people by public officials. ("Popular" and "public" are both cognate with the Latin *poplicus*, "of the people.") Today we think of entertainment as a private concern; we pay for the entertainment we choose to watch. In the Roman world, there were no admission fees to popular entertainments. Funding was provided from the public treasury, and the producer was a public official, although at times a wealthy individual might finance spectacles.

The state was involved in the production of spectacles because they were presented in honor of the gods, and the propitiation of the gods—religion—was a function of the state. The gods whom the Romans worshipped had made, and could continue to make, their state prosperous. The continuous military successes and territorial expansions of the republican period had proved to the Romans the efficacy of their religion. Religion protected the state, and the state protected religion.

Early in Roman history, perhaps as early as the monarchy, military commanders embarking on a campaign would vow to Jupiter, chief of the gods, that if they were successful in battle they would celebrate their triumph by honoring him with a display of games (*ludi*). Financing would be provided from the war booty. Since the campaign season usually ran from March to September, September was a common month for the *ludi*. Eventually these occasional triumphal games became a regular annual event, the *Ludi Romani* ("Roman Games"), held from September 5 to 19. By the beginning of the second century B.C., five more sets of games had been added to the Roman calendar, honoring the Great Mother; Ceres, the goddess of cereal grains; Flora, goddess of flowers; and Apollo. The fifth set were the "Plebeian Games," held in November. In the first century B.C., public games celebrating military victories were added to the calendar by Sulla and by Julius Caesar. In 11 B.C., at the beginning of the imperial period, Augustus instituted the *Ludi Augustales*. The number of days during the year on which regular public games were celebrated continued to increase. At the time of Augustus, there were 77 days of public games on the calendar; by the mid-third century A.D. there were 177.

In the republican period, the entertainments presented at the games were chariot races and theatrical performances. There were more days of theater events than of races, but the latter attracted larger crowds. (Gladiatorial contests, which had an origin and development quite distinct from that of *ludi*, will be discussed below.) Wild animal "hunts" (*venationes*) were also presented occasionally. Athletic competitions for citizens, which had a long tradition in the Greek world, received little support in the Roman world, where the law courts, the senate house and the battlefield were considered the proper arenas for competition and displays of talent by citizens. The Romans enjoyed theatrical performances and chariot races as spectators, not participants.

Chariot Racing

Chariot racing was the oldest of the spectator events, as old as the city of Rome itself, according to the legend which associates it with Romulus. After founding Rome in 753 B.C., he sought wives for his men. He invited his neighbors, the Sabines, to come to a day of chariot racing in the valley between the Palatine and Aventine Hills, which later became the site of the Circus Maximus. While the Sabine men were intently watching these races, Romulus' men carried off the Sabine women ("the rape of the Sabine women"). Whatever the origin of horse races at Rome, they became a regular feature at the annual games. The earliest drivers may have been the wealthy horse owners themselves, but, by the first century B.C., driving chariots at the *ludi* was an occupation for the lowest classes. The horses were still owned by the wealthy, but supplying teams for the races had evolved from a sporting venture to a business enterprise.

All horses entered in the races were owned by four professional organizations, called "factions," which were distinguished by colors: Red, White, Blue and Green. A faction might be owned by an individual businessman or, more likely, a group of businessmen, who would profit financially from the success of their horses. The factions owned not just the horses, chariots, stables and other equipment, but often even the drivers and grooms, most of

whom were slaves. The public officials responsible for producing the entertainment at the *ludi* would negotiate with the faction owners a contract to supply chariots, teams and drivers for the days of racing.

Although only four factions competed at each meet, there were usually more than four teams in each race. For a twelve-team race, for example, each faction supplied three starters. Often the drivers from the same faction worked together to ensure their faction's victory. A Blue driver, for example, might set a fast pace for the early laps in order to tire the competitors' horses. He would then drop back and allow another Blue driver, who had reserved the strength of his horses, to pull ahead in the final laps. Or a Green driver might deliberately veer towards an opponent, forcing him to make too sharp a turn and thus to crash, so that his fellow Green driver would have an unhindered run to the finish line. Some of the races were for two-horse or three-horse chariots. Most were for four-horse chariots, but teams of six or even eight or ten horses occasionally appeared. Sidonius Apollinaris, a writer of the fifth century A.D., produced a vivid account of a chariot race in the Circus Maximus. There were four chariots in this race, but they represented only two factions. Sidonius' account provides valuable information about driving techniques, and, in particular, about the ways in which drivers from one faction worked together to defeat the opposing faction.

Grooms are holding the heads and the bridles of the horses . . . calming them with soothing pats and reassuring them with words of encouragement. Still the horses fret in the gates, lean against the starting barrier, and snort loudly . . . They rear up, prance, and kick impatiently against the wood of the gates. A shrill blast of the trumpet and the chariots leap out of the gates, onto the track. . . . The wheels fly over the ground, and the air is choked with the dust stirred up on the track. The drivers urge their horses with whips. Standing in the chariots they lean far forward so that they can whip even the shoulders of the horses. . . . The chariots fly out of sight, quickly covering the long open stretch. . . . When they have come around the far turn, both the rival teams have passed Consentius, but his partner is in the lead. The middle teams concentrate now on taking the lead in the inside lane. If the driver in front pulls his horses too far right toward the spectator stands, he leaves an opening on his left in the inside lane. Consentius, however, redoubles his efforts to hold back his horses and skillfully reserves their energy for the seventh and last lap. The others race full out, urging their horses with whip and voice. The track is moist with the sweat of both horses and drivers. . . . And thus they race, the first lap, the second, the third, the fourth. In the fifth lap, the leader is no longer able to withstand the pressure of his pursuers. He knows his horses are exhausted, that they can no longer respond to his demand for speed, and he pulls them aside. When the sixth lap had been completed and the crowd was already demanding that the prize be awarded, Consentius's opponents thought they had a very safe lead for the seventh and last lap and they drove with self-confidence, not a bit worried about a move by Consentius. But suddenly he loosens the reins, plants his feet firmly on the floorboard, leans far over the chariot, . . . and makes his fast horses gallop full out. One of the other drivers tries to make a very sharp turn at the far post, feeling Consentius close on his heels, but he is unable to turn his four wildly excited horses, and they plunge out of control. Consentius passes him carefully. The fourth driver is enthralled by the cheers of the spectators and turns his galloping horses too far right toward the stands. Consentius drives straight and fast, and passes the driver who has angled out and only now, too late, begun to urge his horses with the whip. The latter pursues Consentius recklessly, hoping to overtake him. He cuts in sharply across the track. His horses lose their balance and fall. Their legs become tangled in the spinning chariot wheels and are snapped and broken. The driver is hurled headlong out of the shattered chariot which then falls on top of him in a heap of twisted wreckage. His broken and bloody body is still. . . . And now the emperor presents the palm branch of victory to Consentius. (Sidonius Apollinaris, *Poems* 23.323-424)

Racing was a team sport, and each team, or faction, had devoted fans, as do football or hockey teams today. Drivers wore tunics dyed the color of their factions, and spectators cheered for the success of the faction rather than for an individual driver or horse. Faction members often sat together. Fights between members of rival factions were not uncommon, and soldiers were stationed in the Circus Maximus to control unruly crowds and prevent riots. Even the most devoted fan, however, had only a limited number of occasions to cheer his beloved Greens or his cherished Blues. At the time of Augustus, chariot races were presented on only seventeen days during the year, though by the fourth century A.D., the number of days had increased to sixty-six.

The majority of Romans were devoted to chariot races; but not quite everyone shared this enthusiasm. Pliny, a statesman and writer of the late first century A.D., scoffed at factional loyalties and the public passion for horse racing.

I have spent the past few days quietly, but very pleasantly, involved with my notes and books. "In Rome?" you say "How could you?" There were of course, chariot races, but I am not the least bit interested in that kind of entertainment. There's never anything new or different about them, nothing which you need to see more than once. And so I am amazed that so many thousands of men time after time have such a childish desire to see horses racing and men driving chariots. Now, if they were attracted by the speed of the horses or the skill of the drivers, this would not be unreasonable. But as it is, they are interested only in the team uniforms. It's the team colors they love. In fact if, during the race itself right in the middle of the race, the team colors were suddenly switched, the spectators would immediately transfer their interest and support and abandon those drivers and those horses which they recognized from afar and whose names they had been shouting just a moment before. One cheap little tunic has so much power, so much influence, and not just with the rabble, which is cheaper even than the tunic but with certain men of weight and dignity. When I consider these men, and their insatiable interest in something so silly, so dull, and so common, I take some pleasure in the fact that I am not taken in by a pleasure such as that. And so, during the past few days, which other men have wasted on the most vacant pursuits, I have used my vacant time very cheerfully for literary work. (Pliny the Younger, *Letters* 9.6)

The Latin word for race track is circus, and the largest, and oldest, track in Rome was the Circus Maximus. By the early imperial period, it seated 250,000 people, one-quarter of Rome's one million population. The track was about 600 yards long and 100 yards wide. A low wall (spina) running lengthwise separated the "up" stretch and "down" stretch, preventing head-on collisions. At each end of the spina was a turning post. Teams leaving from the twelve starting boxes at the north end of the track made seven laps and thirteen very tight turns around the posts. By the time of Caligula, there were sometimes twenty-four races in a day, although twelve races was the usual number. In addition to the Circus Maximus, there were three other tracks in or near Rome: The Circus Flaminius in the Campus Martius, the Circus Vaticanus, where the basilica of St. Peter now stands, and the Circus of Maxentius, just south of Rome, near the Appian Way.

The poet Ovid, writing during Augustus' reign, was interested in the circus as a place to meet women. At the circus, men and women could sit together, whereas at the theater and the amphitheater the seating was segregated. Ovid's account includes a description of the procession with which each day of racing began. It reminded spectators of the religious origin of the event. The races had, after all, originated as a display in honor of the gods, and the gods were therefore invited to attend the day's events. Carriages holding statues of the gods were driven into the circus and around the track, and spectators would applaud enthusiastically as their favorite god passed by.

I'm not sitting here because of my enthusiasm for race horses; but I will pray that the chariot driver you favor may win. I am here, in fact, so that I might sit beside you and talk to you. I didn't want the love which you stir in me to be concealed from you. So, you watch the races, and I'll watch you. Let's each watch the things we love most, and let's feast our eyes on them.

Oh, how lucky is the chariot driver you favor! Does he have the good fortune to attract your attention? Let me, please, have that good fortune. Carried out of the starting gate by galloping horses, I will drive aggressively, sometimes giving the horses their heads, sometimes whipping their backs. Then I will graze the turning post with my inside wheel. But if I catch sight of you as I race along, I will stop and let the reins slacken and fall from my hands. . . .

Why are you edging away from me? It's no use. The seat marker forces us to touch. Yes, the Circus does offer some advantages in its seating rules.

Hey, you, on the right, whoever you are, be more considerate of the lady! You're hurting her by pressing up against her. And you, too, behind us. Draw in your legs, if you have any sense of decency, and don't stick your bony knees in her back.

Oh dear, your skirt is trailing a bit on the ground. Lift it up, or here, I will do it . . . (But what will happen when I see her ankles? Even when they were hidden I burned with passion. Now I am adding flames to a fire, water to a flood. From the sight of her ankles I can well imagine the other delights which lie carefully hidden under her clothing.) Would you like me to stir a light breeze by using my program as a fan? . . .

But look, the procession has arrived. Quiet, everyone! Pay attention! It's time for applause. The golden procession has arrived. Victory is riding in front, her wings outstretched. Be with me, Victory, and make me victorious in love. You who trust yourselves to the sea can clap for Neptune. I have no interest in seafaring; I'm a landlubber. And you, there, soldier, clap for Mars, your patron god. I hate warfare. It's peace I like, and it's in peace that you find love. Let Phoebus help the augurs, and Phoebe the hunters. Minerva, seek applause from the craftsmen. Farmers stand up! Here comes Ceres and delicate Bacchus. Boxers should show reverence to Pollux and horsemen to Castor. Now it's my own turn to applaud, sweet Venus, for you and your archer cupids. Nod in support of my plans, oh goddess. Make my new girlfriend receptive to my advances and willing to be loved. Look, she nodded and gave me a favorable reply. Well, then, I'm only asking you to agree to what the goddess has already promised . . . . I swear, in front of all these witnesses and by this procession of the gods, that I will cherish you as my girlfriend forever.

Oh, but your legs are dangling. You can, if you wish, rest your toes on the railing.

Good, the track is clear and ready for the first big race. The praetor gives the signal and the four-horse chariots break from the starting gates. I can see the driver you're cheering for. I'm sure he'll win. Even his horses seem to know what you want.

Oh no, he's swinging wide around the turning post. What are you doing? The driver in second position is coming up from behind. Pull on the left rein with your strong hand! Oh, we're cheering for an idiot and a coward.

Come on, call them back, citizens. Wave your togas and give them the message. Good, they're calling them back. Oh dear, don't let the waving togas mess your hair. Here, you may hide under the folds of my toga.

The starting gates are opening again, the horses break and the different-colored teams fly onto the track. Now, gallop ahead and take a clear lead! Fulfill my girlfriend's hopes, and my own. (Good! Her wishes have been granted, mine remain to be granted. He has won the palm, I am still reaching for mine. Ah, she smiled, and promised me something with her sly eyes.) Enough for this place. Satisfy the rest of my desires elsewhere. (Ovid, *Amores* 3.2.1-14, 19-26, 33-38, 43-59, 61-84)

Many chariot drivers were slaves purchased by one of the four factions, and they were purchased when quite young, often only twelve or thirteen years old. Faction owners undoubtedly preferred lightweight drivers for the same reasons that horse-owners today choose lightweight jockeys. And many drivers died young. On one tombstone, a relief of a small boy falling from a fast-moving chariot is accompanied by this inscription: "Here I lie, Florus, a child driver. While I was trying to race quickly, I quickly fell into the shadow of death. Januarius erected this to his beloved pupil." Another epitaph honors Crescens, a North African youth, who started driving at the age of twelve, and died when only twenty-two years old.

Chariot racing was an extremely dangerous occupation. The chariots were small and flimsy, made primarily of lightweight wood and wicker in order to minimize the burden on the horses. As a consequence, however, they were easily shattered. The drivers, who stood, or rather balanced, on narrow floorboards close to the hindquarters of the horses, and tried to control their wildly excited horses around the very sharp turns, were lucky to finish a race without an accident. Since these same drivers did not hesitate to force one another into crashes, it is amazing that anyone survived even one race. Adding to the danger was the fact that drivers wrapped the ends of the reins around their waists, which freed their whip hands but also made it likely that they would be dragged to death if they fell from the chariot.

Many drivers did not wait until the actual race to begin endangering the lives of their opponents. In addition to sabotaging the equipment and poisoning the horses of their opponents, they invoked evil spirits and put curses on the drivers of the other factions. The following inscription was discovered in North Africa, an area renowned for the quality of its horses,

I call upon you, O demon, whoever you are and ask that from this hour, from this day, from this moment, you torture and kill the horses of the Green and the White factions and that you kill and crush completely the drivers Clarus, Felix, Primulus, and Romanus, and that you leave not a breath in their bodies. (*Inscriptiones Latinae Selectae* 8753)

For the spectators, the attraction of a chariot race was not unlike that of a gladiatorial combat. At both events the spectators appreciated the skills of the competitors and enjoyed the tension of the competition, but their enjoyment was enhanced by the deadly nature of the event. They loved to know that the competitors faced death at every moment, and they expected to see bloodshed, gore and mangled bodies. For only a fortunate few drivers was racing a rewarding occupation. The prize money for the races went, of course, to the faction owners. However, a happy owner might reward the slave who drove the winning chariot with a gift of money. Successful drivers sometimes managed to save enough money to purchase their freedom from their owners. Once freed, or manumitted, they might choose to continue driving, and they would then be paid for their skills. A very talented—and lucky—driver could earn a comfortable living. In addition, successful drivers won the affection of the crowds, as do successful athletes today. They were admired by the men and adored by the women. They were invited to the homes of the wealthy and befriended even by emperors such as Caligula. They could not, however, gain any real social acceptance in a society which considered entertaining a degrading occupation, for they were, after all, considered entertainers—slaves or freedmen provided by the state for the amusement of the masses. And yet for a young slave, the possibility of public adulation and patronage by the wealthy must have inspired courage. Many drivers displayed reckless bravado on the track, hoping to win glory and to become the current pet of the circus crowd. One of the best-loved drivers of the early imperial period was a man named Scorpus. He won 2,048 races and a large following of devoted fans, but he died in a crash on the track when he was only twenty-five years old. His death was recorded by the poet Martial.

Here I lie, Scorpus, the pride of the noisy Circus, the darling of Rome, wildly cheered, but short-lived. Spiteful Lachesis snatched me away in my twenty-sixth year. She counted my victories, not my years, and decided that I was an old man.

Alas, what a crime! You were cheated of your youth, Scorpus. You have fallen and died. Too soon have you harnessed the dark horses of death. Why did the finish line of the race, which you time and again hastened to cross, quickly covering the distance in your chariot, now become the finish of your life? [Martial *Epigrams* 10.53, 50(5-8)]

Chariot racing was not only the oldest but also the most enduring of Rome's spectacles. It was popular not only in Rome, but throughout the Roman Empire, in the more civilized areas such as Greece, Egypt and Asia Minor, and in the less urbanized areas such as Africa, Spain and Gaul. And apparently the same four colors—Red, White, Blue and Green—appeared on tracks throughout the Empire. Even after the fall of the Roman Empire in the west, chariot-racing remained popular in the eastern empire and was an important element in Byzantine society.

Theatrical Entertainments

Most days of the *ludi* were occupied not by chariot races but by theatrical entertainments. At the time of Augustus, these entertainments were presented on fifty-six of the seventy-seven regular days of *ludi*. The types of entertainment on these days were varied. There was a native Italian form of comic drama called Atellan farce in which broadly drawn stock characters ("the glutton," "the buffoon," "the hunchback") performed in conventional plots with an emphasis on visual humor. Atellan farces were popular in Rome from a very early period until at least the second century A.D.

After the First Punic War (264 to 241 B.C.), playwrights in Rome began to compose dramas whose plots and characters were borrowed from the work of earlier Greek playwrights. Unfortunately, very few of the plays have survived. No tragedies from this period are extant, and we have only twenty comedies by the playwright Plautus and six comedies by Terence. The characters in these plays invariably included cruel pimps, good-hearted prostitutes, irresponsible young men, stern, doddering or miserly fathers, and clever slaves. Typically the shrewd slave helps the foolish young man to deceive his difficult father and to win the heart of a beautiful prostitute, who turns out to be not a prostitute after all but a citizen's daughter whom the young man can then marry. Most of the comedies end with at least one marriage and everyone lives happily ever after. Much of the humor in the play depends on the presentation of a topsy-turvy household, where slaves and sons plotted successfully against fathers. Music was a prominent element in these comedies and many of the parts were sung rather than recited; these plays may have been similar to Gilbert and Sullivan operettas. The popularity of these plays gradually waned during the first century B.C.

Our only extant Roman tragedies were composed by Nero's tutor and advisor, Seneca the Younger, and were probably not intended for the audience which the games attracted. In the imperial period, revivals of comedies were sometimes presented at the *ludi*, or individual scenes or speeches from a tragedy might be performed.

The emperor Nero, who considered himself a fine actor and welcomed opportunities to perform in public, appeared on stage performing scenes from tragedies about Orestes, Oedipus and Hercules. However the Roman audiences now preferred a different type of theatrical entertainment.

By the time of Augustus, balletic performances known as pantomime (*pantomimus*), derived perhaps from the Etruscans, had become extremely popular. The themes of these ballets were usually drawn from Greek mythology or epic. Most of the dancers were men, but women dancers did sometimes appear on stage. The dancers wore masks, and each took several roles in the performance. Flute and pipe music accompanied their movements. Pantomime had many enthusiastic supporters among all classes of imperial Roman society, but also a few critics, including Pliny the Younger (the same writer who scoffed at chariot races), who considered pantomime morally degenerate. We have a description of a pantomime in the writing of the second century A.D. writer, Apuleius. In it Paris, prince of Troy, was asked to decide which goddess was most beautiful: Juno, Minerva, or Venus.

There appeared on stage a young man representing the Trojan prince, Paris, gorgeously costumed in a cloak of foreign design which flowed down from his shoulders. On his head was a gold tiara. He pretended to be a shepherd tending his flock. Next there appeared a radiantly fair young boy, naked except for a small cloak which covered his left shoulder. His long golden hair attracted everyone's eyes. It flowed down his back but did not conceal his beautiful little golden wings. These wings and the herald's staff he held in his hand indicated that he represented Mercury, the messenger god. He danced toward the actor representing Paris and offered him the golden apple which he was holding in his right hand. By his gestures, he informed him of Jupiter's command and then immediately danced gracefully away, out of our sight.

[Actresses representing Juno and Minerva appear on stage.]

Then Venus appeared, displaying to all her perfect beauty, naked, unclothed except for a sheer silk scarf which covered, or rather shaded, her quite remarkable hips and which an inquisitive wind mischievously either blew aside or sometimes pressed clingingly against her. . . . .Then two groups of attractive young maidens danced onto the stage. On the one side was the very graceful Graces, on the other the very beautiful Seasons, who honored the goddess by scattering flowers and bouquets around her. They danced with great skill an intricate ballet movement, paying tribute to the goddess of pleasure with the blossoms of spring. The flutes played sweet Lydian melodies which soothed and delighted the minds of the spectators. But far more delightful was Venus, who began to move forward gracefully, rhythmically, slowly, swaying softly from side to side, gently circling her head, answering the tender sound of the flutes with her delicate movements . . . . As soon as she came face to face with the judge, she appeared by her gestures to promise him that if he would choose her above all the other goddesses she would give to him, Paris, a bride who was the most beautiful of all mortals and similar in appearance to Venus herself. And then the young Trojan prince gladly handed to Venus the golden apple, thus pronouncing her victor in the beauty contest. (Apuleius, *The Golden Ass* 10.30-32)

Another type of theatrical entertainment was the mime. The word "mime" means "imitation," and mimes were intended to be imitations of everyday life. Quite unlike modern mime, which is a silent performance, Roman mime was a combination of spoken words, song, dance, and even acrobatics. Women performers were as common in mimes as men; in contrast to the actors in comedy and tragedy, none of the performers wore masks. There were written plots, but also a great deal of improvisation. The mimes were often melodramatic, although they were meant to represent events which might befall the average man. Sex and violence were staple elements in the mimes, and the coarser and more indecent the performance was, the louder the crowd cheered its approval. The spectators also demanded realism. During the time of Nero, the stage was set on fire during a mime whose theme was the burning of a house. At a performance in the Coliseum of a mime whose theme was crucifixion, a condemned criminal was nailed to a cross and torn apart by a bear. It is little wonder that mimes were condemned by more sensitive souls, but they remained a favorite spectacle for many people.

The Romans had enjoyed theatrical performances from an early period in their history, yet there was no permanent theater in Rome until 55 B.C., when the triumvir Pompey had a permanent theater which could seat 10,000 spectators built in the Campus Martius with funds secured from the spoils of the Mithridatic War. Earlier proposals for a permanent theater in Rome had met with resistance from the powerful senatorial class, which claimed that such a theater would lead to the moral decay of the Roman people. In reality, the politically powerful upper-class opposed permanent theaters because they feared that theaters, which brought together a large mass of people in a small area, would allow political discontent to fester and would become settings for civil disturbances. But the lower classes, which had few other forms of entertainment besides the public spectacles, were delighted by the construction of a permanent theater and did not apparently worry about the moral decline that the upper-class predicted. Indeed the fact that politicians could curry favor with the voters by sponsoring lavish spectacles indicates the true feelings of the Roman masses.

Prior to the construction of the theater of Pompey (at which Julius Caesar was assassinated in 44 B.C.), theatrical entertainments were usually presented in front of the temple of the deity being honored by the ludi. If seating was provided (it sometimes was not), it was on temporary wooden bleachers. A carnival atmosphere prevailed at the ludi, and the crowds were happy, restless and eager to be amused. If the theater performances did not hold their interest, people would wander off to see jugglers, conjurers, dancing bears, boxers or acrobats. Once permanent theaters separated the audience and performance from the outside world, spectators demanded, according to Horace, that bears and boxers be brought to the theater. There was considerable banter between the audience and the actors. For example, a character in a play by Plautus interrupted his monologue to address a spectator in the rear.

"Did you get that? Good. The fellow at the back says he didn't. Come up front, then. There's no place for you to sit down? There's room for you to walk around. Don't think I'm going to rupture myself for your sake!" (Plautus, *Captivi* 10-14)

Like chariot drivers, most actors and actresses were slaves or freedmen and freedwomen. They were rented out by their owners to the public official responsible for producing the *ludi*. Since it was much less expensive to own a troupe of actors than a circus faction, acting companies might be owned by an individual rather than a corporation, and even by a woman as well as a man. Pliny the Younger tells of a lively and wealthy old woman named Ummidia Quadratilla who owned a troupe of pantomimists and enjoyed watching their performances, but forbade her grandson to watch because his morals might be corrupted. An individual who owned actors could bequeath them in his will to his heir, just as he bequeathed his household slaves.

The amusing ambivalence towards pantomimists which Pliny revealed in Ummidia—she enjoyed the performances, but believed they were corrupting—was common among the Romans. They loved watching theatrical shows, and they appreciated the skill of the actors, but nonetheless considered acting a shameless and sordid profession, perhaps even more so as mime and pantomime increased in popularity. A Roman citizen who appeared on stage would be criticized for making a public spectacle of himself. The Julian Laws forbade senators and the sons and daughters of senators to marry prostitutes or members of the acting profession, obviously considering both occupations to be similarly disreputable, although a few actors won the affections of both the lower and upper classes and were invited into the homes of the wealthy.

Actors and actresses no doubt received gifts from their fans, and, if they were slaves, may have been able to purchase their freedom (and continue acting as freedmen). Sometimes the fans in the theater would demand with persistent shouts that the emperor manumit (free) a popular actor. If the emperor acceded to his request, he then compensated the owner of the actor for the purchase price. A freedman, who would be paid for his performance, might earn a comfortable living if he were very talented and charming. Cicero's friend Roscius earned one-half of a million sesterces one year, at a time when rank and file soldiers earned 900 sesterces. Yet most theater performers lived in poverty and were considered at the bottom of the social ladder by the public which flocked to their performances.

Gladiatorial Combats

The type of entertainment for which Rome has been most widely remembered is the gladiatorial combat. Gladiatorial combats (*munera*) originated as services performed to honor the dead. Among the Etruscans, who had dominated much of Italy, including Rome, in the seventh and sixth centuries B.C., these combats were produced as funeral rites. Armed men fought at the tomb of a dead leader, perhaps to provide his spirit with a sacrifice of blood. Aristocratic Roman families preserved Etruscan custom by occasionally presenting exhibitions of fighting at funerals, or at events honoring the memory of a dead family member. The number and size of such exhibitions continued to grow. In 65 B.C., Julius Caesar presented 320 pairs of gladiators to honor the memory of his father. By this time, *munera*, which may originally have been witnessed only by the aristocratic families which produced them, had become popular entertainment, enjoyed by as many of the common people as could gain entrance to them. They retained their private character, however, and were not financed by state funds until 42 B.C., when the magistrates substituted gladiatorial combats for chariot races.

In the imperial period, although they received state funding, gladiatorial shows usually were presented only on special occasions, at spectacles sponsored by the emperor, not at the regular *ludi*. For example, Augustus sponsored eight gladiatorial shows (involving a total of 10,000 fighters) during his reign, and all

eight shows marked a particular event, such as the death of Agrippa or the death of Augustus' stepson Drusus. Similarly, when the emperor Titus celebrated the opening of the Coliseum in A.D. 80 with one hundred days of slaughter of men and animals, he probably dedicated these spectacles to the memory of his father Vespasian, who had initiated construction of the arena.

The first gladiators may have been enemy soldiers captured in war, or Roman soldiers convicted of cowardice or desertion. Spartacus, who led a revolt of gladiators in 73 B.C., was a Thracian who had been conscripted into the Roman army, deserted the army, and been captured and sold to a gladiatorial troupe in Italy. Most gladiators were slaves purchased by the owner of a gladiatorial troupe. Some had been enslaved in war; others were domestic slaves who had displeased their owners and been sold to a gladiatorial troupe as punishment (female slaves were sold to brothels). There were also free men in the troupe. Some were criminals who were sentenced to the troupe as punishment, others were men who joined voluntarily, probably because of economic constraints. The criminals and volunteers were signed for a term of service, usually five years, but they swore an oath to submit to being burned, shackled, whipped and killed by the sword.

The novice was sent to "school" for training, and was evaluated for particular skills, for there were different types of gladiators. Men of speed and agility were marked out to be net-fighters, gladiators who wore no defensive coverings and who were armed with only a trident, a dagger and a net in which to entangle their opponents. Strong but slower-moving men were destined to be gladiators (Latin *gladius*, "sword") equipped with swords, shields, helmets and greaves. The most heavily armed gladiators wore vizored helmets and body armor. Differences in equipment may reflect the fact that gladiators originated as prisoners of war fighting with their native equipment. For example, in the imperial period, gladiators with one type of weapon were called "Thracians," with another type, "Samnites," although few now were actually Thracian or Samnite by birth.

There were special trainers for each type of fighter. The gladiatorial schools, like the circus factions, employed large staffs. In addition to the performers and the trainers, there were doctors, equipment makers, cooks, cleaners and accountants, all under the supervision of the *lanista*. Living conditions at the school were austere. A gladiatorial barrack which has been excavated at Pompeii reveals that the men were confined in tiny cells surrounding a courtyard training arena. There are almost one hundred cells in the two-story structure; each cell is only twelve feet wide and has no windows. Yet there has also been discovered at Pompeii a building which appears to have been the home of gladiators. Perhaps the slaves were confined to barracks, but freedmen and free men were allowed to live elsewhere. We know that some gladiators married and had children.

In the republican period, a troupe was owned by an individual or a group of investors. Julius Caesar, for example, owned gladiators, as did Cicero's friend Atticus. Privately-owned troupes of gladiators were still allowed in the Julio-Claudian period, but such ownership provoked the suspicion of the emperors who feared, not unreasonably, that privately-owned gladiators might form a private army and be used in a coup détat. Soon the presentation of gladiatorial shows, in Rome at least, became a prerogative of the emperor and the imperial family. Elsewhere in Italy, an individual wishing to present combats as a public spectacle needed the emperor's permission. Outside of Italy—for gladiatorial combats became a very popular entertainment everywhere in the Roman Empire, not only in the west, but also in Greece and Asia Minor—there were fewer restrictions, but a private citizen with the money to purchase gladiators had to be careful not to arouse the suspicions of the Roman governor. The revolt of the gladiators led by Spartacus in 73 B.C.—a revolt that lasted two years, occupied the best Roman legions and took the lives of thousands of Roman citizens—had made Roman officials painfully aware of the potential threat of gladiatorial schools, even under the most brutally stringent restrictions.

Gladiatorial combats took place on sand (Latin *arena*, "sand") which soaked up the blood of the fighters. In the republican period, combats were presented in the Circus Maximus or in a temporary arena with temporary bleachers in the Forum. Although the town of Pompeii had a permanent amphitheater by about 80 B.C., the first permanent amphitheater in Rome was not dedicated until 29 B.C. In A.D. 80, Titus opened the amphitheater that the Romans called the Amphitheatrum Flavium, but is best known to us as the Colosseum. The arena was surrounded by seating for 50,000 spectators. Like the theater (but unlike the circus), the amphitheater provided segregated seating, in the imperial period at least, and women sat in the top rows, although women of the imperial family and Vestal Virgins were given good seats in the front rows. Underneath the arena was a honeycomb of tunnels and cells for men and animals awaiting their fates. After its opening in A.D. 80, the Colosseum became the site for all public gladiatorial spectacles in Rome. Perhaps the most extravagant of contests were the mock sea battles, in which gladiators fought on ships. In a testament to the skills of Roman engineers, the design of the Colosseum allowed it to be flooded and drained so that spectators might enjoy sea battles in the heart of Rome. These events resembled historical pageants, with gladiators dressed in costume, but with a very real flow of blood and loss of life.

In Pompeii, and undoubtedly in Rome as well, forthcoming spectacles were advertised by signs painted on walls.

Twenty pairs of gladiators sponsored by Decimus Lucretius Satrius Valens, lifetime priest of Nero Caesar, and ten pairs of gladiators sponsored by Decimus Lucretius Valens, his son, will fight in Pompeii on April 8, 9, 10, 11, and 12. There will also be a suitable wild animal hunt. The awnings will be used. Aemilius Celer wrote this, all alone, in the moonlight. (Corpus Inscriptionum Latinarum 4.3884)

On the night before the event, the patron who was paying for the spectacle provided a banquet for the gladiators. We have no idea whether men who were preparing to face death enjoyed such a feast. The next day, they paraded into the arena for the official procession, dressed in gorgeous outfits of purple cloth with gold embroidery, and they saluted the patron with the words *morituri te salutant,* "those who are about to die salute you." They withdrew to change into their fighting outfits, and then the combats began. Sometimes two fighters with similar equipment were matched, sometimes a slow, heavily-armed fighter was sent against an agile but vulnerable net-man. The combats were accompanied by the music of trumpets, horns, pipes and flutes. Fight officials "encouraged" reluctant fighters by whipping them or burning them. A fighter who had received a serious wound might wait for the death blow or appeal to the spectators for mercy. Spectators shouted out their decisions, and also pointed their thumbs up if they wanted the fighter spared, thumbs down if they wanted him finished off. The final decision rested with the patron, for whom the death of the gladiator represented a loss of money. If the injured fighter's appeal failed, his opponent delivered the fatal blow. A fight official then applied a hot iron to his body to make sure that he was really dead, and his body was dragged out of the arena. Arena workers raked over the blood-stained sand while the victorious gladiator paraded through the arena with his palm branch of victory.

Although many gladiators were killed in the arena or died later from wounds, not every loser of a match met death. A patron who had invested considerable amounts of money for the purchase, training, boarding and equipping of gladiators would probably not want to see half his men killed at the spectacle. A graffito from Pompeii indicates that in an exhibition of eighteen gladiators (nine matches), nine were victorious, six were spared and three were killed. Each gladiator was put in the arena only once or twice a year, and some gladiators had long careers. Inscriptional evidence informs us that some gladiators fought in more than thirty matches. Condemned criminals who were sentenced to serve in a gladiatorial school were generally given five year terms, and expected to spend three years of the term as fighters and two years as workers in the school. Those who did not die in the arena would be freed at the end of five years, but might choose to re-enlist. Successful fighters could demand high prices for their performances.

The Romans showed the same ambivalence toward gladiators that they did toward chariot drivers and actors. Gladiators were considered the vilest element of society, but successful fighters were adored by the crowds. Pompeian inscriptions attest to the adulation of the masses.

Celadus, the Thracian, makes all the girls sigh.
Crescens the net fighter holds the hearts of all the girls. (CIL 4.4397 and 4356)

Respectable Roman matrons were sometimes infatuated by gladiators. Juvenal tells a tale of a woman who abandoned her husband and children for a gladiator, and an ugly one at that:

What was the youthful charm that Eppia found so
enchanting? What did she see worthwhile being labelled 'The Gladiatress'?
This dear boy had begun to shave a long while ago and one arm,
Wounded, gave hope of retirement; besides, he was frightfully ugly,
Scarred by his helmet, a wart on his nose, and his eyes always running.
Gladiators, though, look better than any Adonis:
This is what she preferred to children, country, and sister,
This to her husband. The sword is what they dote on, these women.
(Juvenal, *Satires* 6.104-110; tr. by Rolfe Humpheries)

Yet most spectators did not long mourn the death of a favorite gladiator. It is difficult for us today to understand how a man who had won the admiration and affection of the crowd could nonetheless be considered by this crowd as a dispensable commodity. But Roman spectators came to the arena to be entertained, and they expected a good show. They showed no compassion for fighters who were sick, wounded, exhausted or frightened, as this passage from Petronius reveals.

What good has Norbanus ever done us? He arranged a show with gladiators, sure! They were worth about two cents, the whole lot. So old and decrepit they would have fallen over if you blew on them. I've seen better wild animal fighters. . . . There was one with a bit of spirit in him. He was a Thracian. But even he fought in a very perfunctory way. Finally, at the end of the show they were all soundly flogged. They had heard the whole audience shouting, "Hit him! Hit him!" They were clearly cowards, pure and simple. (Petronius, *Satyricon* 45.11 and 12)

Gladiators were men. There are a few accounts of female gladiators, but their performances were novelties and probably part of the warm-up events that preceded the real combats. Many involved bloodless contests; some had an amusing, some a sadistic, intent. For example, Domitian put on a display of combats between women and dwarfs, and Caligula forced crippled and deformed men from respectable families to fight in the arena.

Executions and Slaughters

The most sadistic of events, however, were not the gladiatorial combats. Gladiatorial combats, although frequently fatal, could at least be described as contests of skill. Other events, however, offered only the unremitting spectacle of agonizing death. While some criminals were sentenced to a term in a gladiatorial school, others were sent to the arena for a cruel execution. These condemned men might be matched against one another, with no training and no defensive armor. If a man killed one opponent, he immediately faced another, and then another, until he became exhausted and was himself slain. Seneca provides a vivid account of such executions.

Recently I happened to stop at a noon-hour entertainment, expecting humor, wit, and some relaxing intermission when men's eyes could rest from watching men's blood. But it was quite the opposite. The morning matches had been merciful in comparison. Now all niceties were put aside and it was pure and simple murder. The combatants have absolutely no protection. Their whole bodies are exposed to one another's blows, and thus each never fails to injure his opponent. Most people in the audience prefer this type of match to the regular gladiators or the request bouts. And why not! There are no helmets or shields to deflect the swords. Who needs armor anyway? Who needs skill? These are all just ways to delay death. In the morning, men are thrown to the lions and the bears; at noon they are thrown to the spectators. The spectators demand that combatants who have killed their opponents be thrown to combatants who will in turn kill them and they make a victor stay for another slaughter. For every combatant, therefore, the outcome is certain death. They fight with swords and with fire. And this goes on while the arena is supposedly empty. "But one of these men is a robber." And so? "But he killed a man." Well, since he killed a man, he deserves capital punishment. But what did you do, you wretch, to deserve the punishment of watching?— "Kill him, whip him, burn him! Why does he approach combat so timidly? Why does he kill so reluctantly? Why does he die so unwillingly? Why must he be driven with whiplashes to face sword wounds? Let them expose their naked chests to one another's weapons. This is the intermission for the gladiators. So let's have some men murdered. Don't just stop the entertainment!"—Don't you understand that bad examples recoil upon those who set them? (Seneca the Younger, *Letters* 7.2-5)

The Romans loved displays of animals, the more exotic the better. And they enjoyed watching these animals either slaughtering or being slaughtered. One popular spectacle was the "hunt." Animals were herded into the arena and killed by trained hunters armed with javelins, hunting spears or bows and arrows. The task was extremely dangerous and required great skill, but the hunter, like the gladiator, had a chance of survival. The earliest hunts involved local animals, such as deer and rabbits, but, as the Empire expanded, producers began to import animals such as elephants, large cats (lions, panthers and leopards), and ostriches. Sometimes animals were let loose to attack other animals; large cats or dogs were turned out among deer, for example. As the decades passed, Roman audiences became bored with simple acts of slaughter and familiar animals. Producers began to chain together bears and bulls, or lions and bulls so that the audience might enjoy new forms of mutilation and death. And enterprising producers brought to Rome rhinoceroses, hippopotamuses and even crocodiles to stimulate the interest of jaded spectators. Cicero commented on the slaughter of elephants at a spectacle sponsored by Pompey in 55 B.C.

There were wild animal hunts, two a day for five days, very expensive ones—no one can deny that. But what pleasure can a civilized man find when either a helpless human being is mangled by a very strong animal, or a magnificent animal is stabbed again and again with a hunting spear? Even if this was something to look at, you have seen it often enough before, and I, who was a spectator there, saw nothing new. The last day was the day for elephants. The mob of spectators was greatly impressed, but showed no real enjoyment. In fact a certain sympathy arose for the elephants, and a feeling that there was a kind of affinity between that large animal and the human race. (Cicero, Ad Familiares 7.1.3)

Despite Cicero's criticism, the slaughter of animals continued, and even increased. When Titus opened the Colosseum in A.D. 80 with 100 days of spectacles, 9,000 animals died.

The spectacles whose appeal is perhaps the most difficult for us to understand are the executions. Frequently the condemned person was tied to a stake, wheeled into the arena and left exposed to a starved animal such as a lion or bear which would mangle and eat him. The arena audiences were without pity, without compassion. In the imperial period, producers seeking novel forms of execution began to integrate the slaughter into mythological dramas. In one such drama, an elaborate setting of trees was moved into the Colosseum to create forest scenery. A condemned criminal forced to play the role of Orpheus moved through the forest trying to soothe the wild animals with his music. In the end, he was mangled and killed by a bear. So agonizing were these deaths that some men who were condemned to such executions tried to kill themselves rather than enter the arena. They were kept under close guard until the time of the spectacle so that they could not, by their suicides, deprive the spectators of the gruesome sight they craved. Seneca reports, however, that a few of these desperate men managed to take their own lives and thus escape the torture that awaited them in the arena.

The Politics of Entertainment

From a very early period in their history, the people of Rome knew that shows would be presented by wealthy politicians and provided to them free of charge. It is therefore not unfair to say that the common people expected to be entertained. Although these spectacles had a religious origin, most people came to consider them primarily as entertainments. It is incorrect, however, to assume that in the early imperial period mobs of lazy or underemployed people roamed the streets of Rome demanding food and entertainment. The comments of Tacitus, that a passion for actors, gladiators and horses was almost innate to the Romans, and of Juvenal, that the people of Rome were interested only in bread and circuses, must be read as the moralizing comments of upperclass conservative writers. Even if shows were given concurrently in Rome's three theaters (and we have no evidence to suggest that they were), since each theater did not hold more than 10,000 spectators, only 3 percent of Rome's one million population could attend a show on one of the fifty-six regular days of the ludi that were devoted to theatrical events. And even after the opening of the Colosseum in A.D. 80, only 5 percent of the population could watch a show there. Only the Circus Maximus offered seating for a substantial number of people. Nor were people given a choice of entertainments on a single day; on theater days, for example, there were no races. Obviously only a small proportion of the population could attend theater and amphitheater events on the days they were produced.

We do not know, moreover, how many people were free to attend the shows. We should

---

233

not assume that most people were "off work" even during the regular festivals. And surely during special events, such as Titus's one hundred days of spectacles at the opening of the Colosseum, most people continued their regular day's activities and expected to attend the spectacles only once or twice. Today most people are free of work on 104 weekend days, as well as vacation days and holidays. And in any city of a million people, there occur at one time a multitude of sports events, for both participants and spectators, at various levels of competition, in addition to presentations of movies, concerts and stage shows. Those who do not wish to leave home can be entertained by television and movie rentals. To future historians, our own generation may appear far more idle and underemployed than the ancient Romans.

And yet the people of Rome were indeed dependent on their government for entertainment and races; theatrical performances and gladiatorial combats provided politicians with an opportunity to advance their careers. In the republican period, these shows became an expensive way to curry public favor and win votes. By the late republican period, competition was fierce among Roman politicians to produce the most lavish and most crowd-pleasing spectacles. As a result, the upper-class, to which all politicians belonged, found itself in a peculiar situation. Politicians had encouraged the development of a system in which the presentation of spectacles became a major device for winning popular support and thus votes. Yet, as members of the upper-class, they also feared gatherings of lower-class people as threats to their own security, particularly in an emotionally stimulating environment such as a spectacle. A restless crowd in a confined area was always a volatile combination. Even as the upper-class had learned how to manipulate the affections of the lower-class by the production of games, so the lower-class crowds had in turn learned how to manipulate the situation at the games to provide themselves with an opportunity to express their opinions—and not just their views about the entertainment. Cicero wrote that the Roman people made their wishes known at three places: public meetings, popular assemblies and spectacles. He added that the most honest and spontaneous expression of their wishes was given at the spectacles, rather than at the meetings and assemblies, which were controlled by politicians. Cicero was not the only politician to understand the importance of the games. Any politician who wished to gain and retain public support needed not only to sponsor entertainments, but also to attend the entertainments and to listen to the opinions expressed there by the crowds.

Once Augustus had assumed supreme control of the Roman state, he could not allow the senatorial class, from which his main opposition arose, to continue to curry favor with the lower-class by the lavish production of spectacles. He worried that a popular individual might persuade the city mob to join him in an uprising against the new regime. Most games during the Principate were sponsored by the imperial family, and, by the end of the first century A.D., private ownership of gladiators was forbidden in Rome. The emperors curtailed the opportunities for political popularity which the presentation of games might offer an ambitious man, but they certainly did not curtail the games; indeed the number of games, both regular and special, increased as the imperial period proceeded. The emperors, like the republican senators, perceived that the political advantages of sponsoring games outweighed the threat of unruliness in the crowds. And the crowds, for their part, continued to use the theater, circus and amphitheater as the sites for public expression of opinion. Indeed, with the abolition of popular assemblies, the entertainment sites became the only places where the common people could confront their ruler and make their views known. And they expressed their opinions strongly. On some occasions, a group representative might present the emperor with a written petition, and the crowd would wait for a response. Frequently the crowd shouted its demand loudly and in unison. Sometimes an actor would make a remark which the crowd interpreted as a critical comment about a contemporary event and it would roar its approval. At times a performer might caricature the emperor's physical appearance. A surprising degree of license was permitted to the audience. Of course, the emperor always had the upper hand. He was protected by armed guards, he could attend the spectacles when and for as long as he wished, and he could threaten disruptive individuals with execution. Yet the common people expected the emperor to appear, to listen to criticism and to accede to at least some of their demands. And most emperors did. However, each of the Julio-Claudian emperors treated the crowds at the public spectacles differently.

Augustus took very seriously his responsibilities as a provider of many and lavish shows. Moreover he regularly attended these shows and appeared greatly interested in them. He watched the events intently, and was careful to avoid the criticism which had been directed at Julius Caesar who attended the games but read letters instead of watching the events. On one occasion when he was ill, Augustus nonetheless insisted on attending some circus events and was carried in the procession on a litter. He also encouraged members of his family to fill the imperial box. If he was unable to be present, he was careful to appoint an official to preside in his place.

The notoriously thrifty Tiberius was remembered as the emperor who reduced the financial allotments for public spectacles. Early in his reign, he attended the spectacles frequently and listened to the protests of the crowd. On one occasion, when the theater audience complained about the high price of grain, Tiberius took the complaints seriously and tried to rectify the situation. Later, however, he refused to attend spectacles, particularly after he was pressured by shouting spectators to manumit a favorite actor and compensate his owner for the purchase price. It is possible, of course, that Tiberius avoided these spectacles simply because they did not amuse him. But his own and later generations could not forgive his disinterest in the events and his reluctance to grant audience requests. Tacitus, for example, attributed Tiberius's absence from public spectacles to serious character flaws: an innate sullenness and a dislike of crowds.

Caligula was very popular at the beginning of his reign, in part because he sponsored many shows, at which he distributed gifts and food among the crowd. Nor was he merely an interested spectator of events. He trained as a Thracian gladiator, sang, danced and drove racing chariots. He dined with the professional chariot drivers in their faction dining room, and housed his favorite horse, Incitatus, in an ivory stall in a marble stable. (So fond was he of the horse that he wished to make it consul of Rome.) At first, Caligula appeared to the common people as an emperor who shared their amusements and interests. They were soon disenchanted, however, when Caligula's contempt for the Roman populace and his sadistic nature became manifest. He enjoyed watching people suffering, and did not restrict the torture to slaves and criminals. For example, he found it amusing to remove the awnings, which provided shade for spectators at gladiatorial matches, at the hottest period of the day, and then forbid anyone to leave the arena. On some occasions he forced crippled or deformed citizens to fight in the arena. Nor did he conceal his hatred for the crowd at the spectacles. Once he threatened the audience at the circus with the comment: "I wish all you Romans had only one neck." Less than four years after he assumed power Caligula was assassinated, perhaps suitably at the theater. Just a few weeks before his assassination he had not only refused to grant a request by the audience to reduce taxes, but had even executed the people involved in the protest. Caligula's assassins were military men, not leaders of a popular uprising, but the common people did not mourn his death. They hated the emperor who refused to abide by the tradition of popular petitions at the public spectacles.

Claudius exhibited his interest in the public amusements not only by sponsoring games, but also by rebuilding and improving the sites. His favorite spectacles were the wild animal hunts, and he would stay at the arena during the lunch break so as not to miss any of the slaughter. The spectators, in turn, were well-disposed toward an emperor who shared their amusements and seemed so accessible. Apparently Claudius was never more relaxed and friendly than at spectacles, where he liked to exchange banter with the crowd.

Nero had a passion for performances—but mainly his own. He appeared in public as an actor, singer, poet and lyre-player. He entered competitions in Italy and even in Greece, with predictable success. What municipality would dare to refuse the emperor the prize for first place? Sometimes he was awarded the prize before he had even performed. He drove chariots in the Circus Maximus and even entered a race for ten-horse teams at Olympia. Although he fell out of his chariot, was helped back in, and still failed to finish the race, he was awarded the prize. The upper-class was not amused by Nero's antics, but he remained popular among the common people because his generous sponsorship of games and his personal interest in performing indicated that he understood their interests. Moreover he allowed a relatively free expression of criticism at the spectacles. When an actor at the theater accompanied the words in the script, "Good-bye, Mother," with swimming gestures, a blatant allusion to the rumor that Nero had tried to drown his mother, Nero was angered and sent the actor into exile, but did not execute him.

It is surely more than coincidence that the Julio-Claudian emperors most reviled after their deaths—Tiberius and Caligula—were those who showed disdain for the spectacles or the audience, and who did not tolerate the appeals and the criticisms of the common people at the spectacles. Yet even these emperors did not abolish the spectacles.

And why did any emperor feel compelled to attend spectacles and expose himself to the shouts of the crowd? The emperors were not elected officials and did not therefore need to win votes. There are a number of reasons for the emperors' support of public spectacles. These spectacles helped to divert the attention of the masses from serious problems, such as poverty and hunger. People who were amused were less likely to complain. And quarrels in the circus between supporters of rival factions would channel frustrations and aggressions into factional disputes rather than riots in the streets of Rome. But more important, public spectacles gave the emperors the opportunity to manipulate the affections of the common people by their responses to petitions and criticisms. If the emperor allowed people to protest real issues, such as grain shortages, in a restricted and heavily guarded area such as the theater, he could actually prevent a widespread violent demonstration. If he listened politely to their demands and promised to take action, the people were often satisfied that they had been heard and would cease their protest. The people made many demands on the emperors, from manumitting a favorite actor to distributing more grain. If the emperor granted some of these requests—and paying the manumission price for an actor was an easy request to grant, despite Tiberius's reluctance to do so—the crowd perceived the emperor as a generous and gracious man. And if the emperor listened without angry response to veiled criticism from performers, he was considered tolerant and kind. Although the emperor did not need to worry about being voted out of office, he knew that it was best to keep the people pacified. Moreover an emperor who seemed accessible, generous, and eager to share the interests of his people was accepted by them as a benevolent ruler, a first among equals, a princeps rather than a hated despot. When he entered the theater, circus or amphitheater, he was greeted with loud shouts of approval and affection, which reinforced the stability of his regime.

The interaction between the emperor and the audience at public spectacles provides a fascinating example of political accommodation. Each side played a role in a drama more interesting to us than any of the events they watched. The common people, who had lost their right to political assemblies in Tiberius's reign, retained the privilege of expressing their opinions at spectacles. Yet they knew that there were limits to this privilege, and they seldom went beyond these limits, and were therefore seldom punished. Their protests were expressed loudly and emotionally, but usually in an orderly fashion. The wise emperor, for his part, encouraged controlled dissent so that he did not face the threat of violent popular uprisings.

The Emperors and Their Games

Suetonius

Suetonius had a fondness for catalogues and lists, and he provides comments on the games sponsored by each emperor together with any exceptional happening. The anecdotes show Augustus' affability in public, which is but one aspect of his political shrewdness while Tiberius and Caligula reacted badly to the pressures involved in public appearances at the games. Suetonius is contemptuous of Claudius' terrible jokes and his ludicrous hobble, but the jokes (considered as spontaneous political humor) are not at all bad and we can detect through the biographer's hostility Claudius' genuine ease with the crowds. Any discussion of Nero's games must recount his grand, triumphant tour as he sang and acted at festivals across the Greek world. It delighted the provincials to see an emperor so enamored of their culture, but the Romans saw it as disgraceful for an emperor to stoop to public performances.

From Life of Augustus

43. Augustus surpassed all his predecessors in the frequency, variety, and magnificence of his public shows. He says that he gave games four times in his own name and twenty-three times for other magistrates, who were absent from Rome or short of money. He gave them on stages all over the city with actors speaking several languages, and he presented gladiatorial combats in the Forum, the amphitheater, and in the Circus as well. Sometimes, however, there was only a wild beast fight. He also gave athletic contests in the Campus Martius, erecting bleachers, and a sea-fight, constructing an artificial lake near the Tiber. . . . On such occasions he placed guards around the city to deter burglars since few people remained at home. In the Circus he exhibited charioteers, runners and wild-animal hunters, who were sometimes aristocratic young men. . . .

Before the Senate forbade it, Augustus sometimes used even Roman knights in plays and gladiatorial contests. After that he exhibited no one of respectable parentage, with the exception of a young man named Lycius, who was a dwarf with an enormous voice. He did however on the day of one of the shows make a display of the first Parthian hostages that had ever been sent to Rome, by leading them through the middle of the arena and placing them in the second row above his own seat.

Furthermore, if anything rare was ever brought to the city, it was his habit to make a special exhibit of it in any convenient place on days when no shows were appointed: for example, a rhinoceros, a tiger, and an eighty-foot long snake which was shown where assemblies were held. . . .

44. He promulgated new rules to control admission to games, annoyed at the insult to a senator, to whom no one gave a seat at a crowded festival in Puteoli. The Senate consequently decreed that, whenever any public show was given anywhere, the first row of seats should be reserved for senators. At Rome the emperor would not allow the envoys of allied nations to sit in the orchestra when he learned that some were freedmen. . . . He would not allow women to view even the gladiators except from the upper seats, though it had been the custom for men and women to sit together at such shows. Only the Vestal Virgins were assigned a place to themselves, opposite the praetor's tribunal. Women were excluded from the athletic contests [where the men competed in the nude], so that when the people called for a boxing match at the games in honor of his appointment as pontifex maximus, he postponed it until early the following day and proclaimed that women should not come to the theatre before ten o'clock.

45. He himself usually watched the games in the Circus from the upper rooms of his friends'

houses, but sometimes from the imperial box, and even in company with his wife and children. He was sometimes absent for several hours, and now and then for whole days, making his excuses and appointing presiding officers to take his place. But whenever he was present, he gave his entire attention to the contest, either to avoid the criticism levelled at Julius Caesar who spent his time reading or answering his letters and petitions, or because he honestly enjoyed the spectacle, which he never denied but often frankly confessed. For this reason he offered special prizes and many valuable gifts from his own purse at games given by others, and he appeared at no Greek dramas without making an appropriate present to each of the participants. He especially liked to watch boxers, particularly those of Latin birth, not merely such as were recognized and classed as professionals, whom he matched even with Greeks, but the common untrained townspeople that fought rough and tumble and without skill in the narrow streets. In conclusion, he showed his interest in all classes who performed in the public shows, maintaining the privileges of athletes; and even increasing them. He forbade the gladiator matches without the right of appeal for mercy, and he deprived magistrates of their ancient power of punishing actors anywhere, restricting it to the time of games and the theatre. Nevertheless he exacted the severest discipline in the contests in the wrestling halls and the combats of the gladiators. In particular he was so strict in curbing the lawlessness of the actors, that when he learned that Stephanio, an actor of Roman plays, was waited on by a matron with hair cut short to look like a boy, he had him whipped with rods through the three theatres and then banished him.

From Life of Tiberius

34. Tiberius reduced the cost of the games and shows by cutting down on the pay of the actors and limiting the pairs of gladiators to a fixed number. . . .

47. While emperor he built no magnificent public works. . . . He gave no public shows at all, and he very seldom attended those given by others, for fear that some request would be made of him, especially after he was forced by the crowd to buy the freedom of a comic actor named Actius.

From Life of Caligula

18. Caligula gave several gladiatorial shows, and he also introduced pairs of African and Campanian boxers, the best of both regions. He did not always preside at the games in person, but sometimes assigned the honor to the magistrates or to friends. He exhibited plays continually, of various kinds and in many different places, sometimes even by night, lighting up the whole city. . . . He also gave many games in the Circus, lasting from early morning until evening, introducing between the races now a baiting of panthers and now the manoeuvres of the Troy game; some games were of special splendor, in which the Circus was decorated with red and green, while the charioteers were all men of senatorial rank. He also organized some games on the spur of the moment, when a few people called for them from the neighboring balconies, as he was inspecting the equipment of the Circus.

19. He once devised an extraordinary pageant: he bridged the Bay of Naples between Baiae and the breakwater at Puteoli, a distance of about three Roman miles, by bringing together merchant ships from all sides and anchoring them in a double line, after which dirt was heaped upon them as though it was the Appian Way. Over this bridge he rode back and forth for two days, the first day on a caparisoned horse, himself resplendent in a crown of oak leaves, a shield, a sword, and a cloak of cloth of gold; on the second, in the dress of a charioteer in a car drawn by a pair of famous horses, carrying before him a boy named Dareus, one of the hostages from Parthia, and attended by the entire praetorian guard and a company of his friends in Gallic chariots. I know that many have supposed that Gaius devised this kind of bridge in rivalry of Xerxes, [the king of Persia who in his great

expedition against Athens in 480 B.C. excited no little admiration by bridging the much narrower Hellespont between Europe and Asia]; others, that such a stupendous work would inspire fear in Germany and Britain whom he wished to invade. But when I was a boy, my grandfather used to say that the reason for the work, as revealed by the emperor's own courtiers, was that Thrasyllus the astrologer had declared, when Tiberius was worried about his successor and inclined towards his natural grandson, that Gaius had no more chance of becoming emperor than of riding about over the gulf of Baiae with horses.

26. . . . Caligula treated all with insolence and cruelty. Being disturbed by the noise made by those who came in the middle of the night to secure the free seats in the Circus, he drove them all out with cudgels; in the confusion more than twenty Roman knights were crushed to death, with as many matrons and a countless number of others. At the plays in the theatre, sowing discord between the commons and the knights, he scattered free tickets early to induce the rabble to take the seats reserved for the equestrian order. At a gladiatorial show he would sometimes draw back the awnings when the sun was hottest and give orders that no one be allowed to leave; then he would match worthless and decrepit gladiators against mangy wild beasts, and have sham fights between respectable, but physically disabled, citizens. . . .

55. He was so passionately devoted to the Green faction of charioteers that he constantly dined and spent the night in their stable, and in one of his revels with them he gave the driver Eutychus two million sesterces in gifts. He used to send his soldiers on the day before the games and order silence in the neighborhood, to prevent his favorite horse Incitatus from being disturbed. Besides a stall of marble, a manger of ivory, purple blankets and a collar of precious stones, he even gave this horse a house, a troop of slaves and furniture, for the more elegant entertainment of the guests invited in his name; and it is also said that he planned to make him consul.

From Life of Claudius

21. He often gave games in the Vatican Circus, at times with a beast-baiting between every five races. But at the Great Circus he decorated the starting gate with marble and gilded the turning posts, whereas before they had been of limestone and wood, and he assigned special seats to the senators, who had been in the habit of viewing the games with the rest of the people. In addition to the chariot races he exhibited the Troy game and also panthers, which were hunted down by a squadron of the praetorian cavalry under the lead of the tribunes and the prefect himself; likewise Thessalian horsemen, who drove wild bulls all over the arena, leaping upon them when they were tired out and throwing them to the ground by the horns.

He gave many gladiatorial shows in many locations: an annual one in celebration of his accession was held in the Praetorian Camp without wild beasts and fine equipment. . . . On occasion the emperor would address the audience, and urge them to be merry, calling them "masters" from time to time, and interspersing feeble and far-fetched jokes. For example, when they called for a gladiator nicknamed "Dove," he promised that they should have him, "if he could be caught." But the following joke was both exceedingly timely and salutary: when he had granted the wooden sword to a chariot racer, for whose discharge four sons begged, and the act was received with loud and general applause, he at once circulated a note, pointing out to the people how greatly they ought to desire children, since they saw that they could protect even a gladiator.

From

Life of Nero

12. The emperor compelled four hundred senators and six hundred Roman knights, some of whom were rich and distinguished, to fight in the arena. . . . He also exhibited a naval battle in salt water with sea monsters swimming about in

it. After some Greek youths performed a ballet, the emperor presented each of them with certificates of Roman citizenship. In one scene of their ballet . . . Icarus at his very first attempt at flight with artificial wings fell close by the imperial couch and spattered the emperor with his blood, for Nero very seldom presided at the games, but used to view them while reclining on a couch in the imperial box. . . . He established at Rome a Greek-style festival every four years called the Neronia which had competitions in music, gymnastics, and horseracing; at the same time he dedicated his baths and gymnasium, supplying every member of the senatorial and equestrian orders with oil. He appointed ex-consuls, chosen by lot, to preside over the whole contest. Then Nero went down into the orchestra among the senators and accepted the prize for Latin oratory and verse, for which all the experts had competed but which they all agreed he deserved. But when the judges also gave him the prize for lyre playing, he knelt and laid it at the feet of Augustus' statue. . . .

20. Nero had learned some music as part of his early education, and when he became emperor he sent for Terpnus, the leading lyre player of the time, and listened to him sing after dinner night after night. He then little by little began to practice himself, neglecting none of the exercises which singers use to preserve or strengthen their voices. For he used to lie upon his back and hold a leaden plate on his chest, purge himself by enemas and vomiting, and avoid fruit and all food harmful to the voice. Finally encouraged by his progress (although his voice was weak and husky), he wished to appear on the stage, and occasionally among friends he quoted the Greek proverb: "Hidden music counts for nothing." He made his debut at Naples, where he sang the number through to the end even though the theatre was being shaken by an earthquake. He often sang there, and even when he gave his voice a brief rest, he could not stay away from the theater but went there after bathing and dined in the orchestra with the people all about him, promising them in Greek, that when he had had a drink, he would sing something good and loud. He was captivated by the rhythmic

applause of some Alexandrians, . . so he selected some young knights and more than five thousand sturdy young commoners, to be divided into groups to learn the Alexandrian styles of applause and to do it loudly whenever he sang. . . . Their leaders were paid handsomely.

21. He wished to appear in Rome so badly that he held the Neronia festival years early, and when there was a general call for his "divine voice," he replied that if any wished to hear him, he would favor them in the gardens; but when the guard on duty joined the entreaties of the people, he gladly agreed to appear at once. So without delay he had his name added to the list of the lyre players who entered the contest, and casting his own lot into the urn with the rest, he came forward in his turn, attended by the prefects of the Guard carrying his lyre, and followed by the tribunes of the soldiers and his intimate friends. Having taken his place and finished his preliminary speech, he announced through the ex-consul Cluvius Rufus that "he would sing Niobe;" and he kept at it until late in the afternoon. . . . He also wore masks and sang tragedies representing gods and heroes and even heroines and goddesses, having the masks made in the likeness of his own features or those of women with whom he was in love. . . . There is a story that a young recruit seeing Nero dressed in rags and bound in chains as the mad Hercules, rushed forward to rescue him.

22. Horses had been Nero's special passion from childhood, and he was always talking about the circus games. Once when he was lamenting with his fellow pupils the fate of a charioteer who was dragged by his horses, and his tutor scolded him, he told a lie and pretended that he was talking of Hector in Homer's *Iliad*. At the beginning of his reign he used to play every day with model ivory chariots on a board, and he came from the country to all the races. . . . He soon longed to drive a chariot himself in a public race and, after a trial run in his palace gardens before his slaves and the rabble, he presented himself before all in the Circus Maximus where one of his freedmen gave the

starting signal from the place usually occupied
by the magistrates. . . .

Gladiators and Their Public

Michael Grant

Michael Grant, formerly Professor of Humanities at Edinburgh and President of the Queen's University, Belfast, is perhaps the most prolific living writer on the history and civilization of Greece and Rome. His essay analyzes the attitudes of rulers and spectators from a psychological perspective and he comments on the obvious sadism in gladiatorial contests. The essay closes with a brief treatment of Roman writers who were critical of this barbaric practice.

The Attitudes of Rulers and Spectators

Gladiatorial duels had originated from funeral games given in order to satisfy the dead man's need for blood; and for centuries their principal occasions were funerals. Accordingly a religious aura continued to hang about such contests—if only in the eyes of educated traditionalist.

There were other motives, too, which inspired the Roman ruling classes to view these contests with a favourable eye. The ancient excuse of encouragement to warlike toughness continued to be put forward until the eve of the Middle Ages, although it came to sound increasingly lame and inhumane. Another purpose present in the minds of Rome's rulers was the desire that the potentially unruly and dangerous city population should be amused and kept quiet, by being given the entertainment that they wanted, however repulsive it might be.

Indeed, the principal attraction of such combats was this very nastiness. The Romans' enjoyment of the sport was horrifyingly brutal and perverted. If this needs documenting, we can direct a glance or two at the imperial platform, since its occupants' reactions were seen and have consequently come down to us. There we can note the embarrassingly keen interest in bloodshed displayed by Tiberius' son Drusus; or the macabre unpleasantnesses of Caligula. . . .

If rulers of the empire committed such detestable extravagances, the reactions of other spectators were unlikely to be any more high-minded. Many of them, it is true, must also have been capable of appreciating the finer technical points of combat. But nearly all of them also wallowed unrestrainedly in bloodlust. Petronius'

Echion entertains high hopes of a forthcoming display, because its patron 'will give us cold steel, no quarter and the slaughterhouse right in the middle where all the stands can see it.' And nothing can be more frank than the Minturnae inscription on which Publius Baebius Justus—in connection, as it happens, with a slaughter not of gladiators but of ten bears—is explicitly credited with having these animals killed CRVDLiter—cruelly. The word is apparently inserted as an expression of praise! More cruelty was openly equated with more fun.

The constant recurrence of this unrestrained blood-thirstiness throughout long centuries is one of the most appalling manifestations of evil that the world has ever known. The reactions of spectators unmistakably assumed that form of perverted sexuality known as sadism—which is likewise a major feature of our own modern community. Occasional sadistic murders shock and alarm the public, and bloodsports are accused of ill-effects on some of their participants, but the principal manifestation of the tendency is cheap literature incorporating sadistic phantasies and their masochistic counterparts. Other societies have operated different safety-valves. The Spanish taste for excitement and blood finds its outlet in bullfighting; the Nazis slaughtered human beings on a scale exceeding even the Romans.

Our knowledge of the correlation between literary or visual sadistic entertainments, crimes of violence, and social conditions, is still rudimentary. Schopenhauer believed that man outdoes the tiger and hyena in pitiless cruelty, and Sigmund Freud, seeing sadism and masochism as innate, evolved several different theories regarding the impulses which make men 'savage beasts to whom the thought of sparing their kind is alien.' Against this, Karen Horney cited the Arapesh tribe of New Guinea and the Zuni of New Mexico, in whom the nastier tendencies seem to be lacking. But now Konrad Lorenz has argued that, although by nature man was not very aggressive, his discovery of weapons long since provided a terrible substitute for his natural lack of animal rage.

Freud's associate and rival Wilhelm Stekel maintained, like him, that 'in the human soul cruelty lies, like a beast, chained, but eager to spring.' In studying the subject, he turned his attention to the gladiators of ancient Rome, seeing the institution as an expression of hatred and the will to power—a part of those qualities in the Romans which also led to their conquests (and the *pax Romana*). And it is true that conquering powers exhibit crude or aggressive sporting tastes. But this hardly accounts, in itself, for the intense, continuous carnage and blood-lust of the arena. Moreover, as Otto Kiefer points out in his study of Roman sexuality, it is not accurate to look only at the proliferation of *later* imperial bestialities, and then to claim that they were the sign of a degenerate society. On the contrary, they had been present from very early times, for example in an abundance of tortures and floggings, and in execution customs so repellent that they have had to be ascribed to the victim's ritual representation of a sacrificial animal. These were not late degenerate horrors but early, endemic, and never far from the surface. . . .

As Freud's successors shifted the emphasis from biological to sociological and cultural factors, universal aggression and brutality were attributed to frustration, disastrous social conditions, and the 'failure to obtain love.'

Erich Fromm's view of sadism as one of the things that arise from unconscious attempts to escape from intolerable helpless isolation has a bearing on the Roman predicament. Already earlier, when the parochial Greek city-states had been absorbed or eclipsed by huge Hellenistic kingdoms, the resultant lonely defenselessness of the individual had created a widespread 'collapse of nerve.' In the vast Roman world these symptoms became accentuated, permanent and ubiquitous. Millions of people felt shiftless, unsupported, un-looked after, lost—and above all bored.

The plunge into religion was one compensatory reaction. But another was immersion in sanguinary sadism. Religion had its share of this, notably in the ghastly drenchings in bull's blood which comprised the very popular pagan baptism rite known as the *taurobolium*. But nothing could touch the gladiatorial combats for excitement. And into these plunged the millions of Rome's citizens and subjects all the more keenly because they were encouraged to adopt this outlet by their rulers, as an apparently inconsiderable evil, or no evil at all, in comparison with the political insecurity and sedition which might result from the absence of such distractions.

The Attitudes of Writers

The attitude of many Romans, even men of the highest culture, towards the arena was flawed and inhumane—or, if disapproving, not disapproving enough. Cicero says people are bored by excess of gladiatorial shows. 'This type of display,' he remarks 'is apt to seem cruel and brutal to some eyes, and I incline to think that it is so, as now conducted. But in the days when it was criminals who crossed swords in the death struggle, there could be no better schooling against pain and death—at any rate for the eye, though for the ear perhaps there might be many.' The suggestion, then, is that the combats have deteriorated and become unproductive of pleasure but that they were originally a noble and educational art—good virile training, as the rulers of the Republic had thought. This is typical of a certain equivocation in Cicero who, although steeped in Greek culture, often criticized its anti-Roman softness, partly for appearance's sake but partly because of a genuine ambivalence.

A century and a half later, Pliny the younger is equally disappointing. He praises a friend who gave a gladiatorial display and approves of the disdain of death and love of honourable wounds which such combats encouraged, inspiring, he said, ambition in the hearts even of criminals and slaves. Nowhere do we see more clearly than in the inadequate comments of this usually kind-hearted man what it was to live in a society where some people had no rights at all; and where policy and tradition had institutionalized the brutalities inherent in this situation.

Equally unattractive, at the very end of antiquity and in a time of growing Christian humanitarianism, is the attitude of the highly educated pagan Symmachus. Reference has been made of the heart-rending incident when twenty-nine Saxon prisoners of war succeeded in strangling one another rather than fight duels in Symmachus' games. But his comment is merely this: 'evidently no guard, however efficient, can restrain that desperate race.' The climate of opinion still encouraged Constantine the Great, the first Christian emperor, to throw masses of German prisoners (Bructeri) into the arena and have them torn to pieces by wild animals—the fate that Christians had suffered for centuries. The comment of his cultured panegyrists is that he 'delighted the people with the wholesale annihilation of their enemies—and what triumph could have been finer?'

On the other hand, from the time of the early principate onwards, the rhetorical schools which comprised Rome's higher educational system had been building up a series of stock themes criticizing the barbarians of gladiatorial combats. The practical effect of these objections was slight or non-existent. Yet it is important that they were voiced; and they were translated into significant literary denunciations. The earliest and most notable protest comes from the Romano-Spanish philosopher, essayist and dramatist, Seneca the younger. Whatever his equivocations as Nero's minister, he must be credited with the first known unambiguous attack upon the whole institution of gladiators, and the popular enjoyment of its human bloodshed. Seneca invokes the Stoic Universal Brotherhood. 'Man,' he asserts, 'is a thing which is sacred to mankind. But nowadays he is killed in play, for fun. It was once a sin to teach him how to inflict wounds or receive them. But now

he is led out naked and defenceless—and provides a sufficient show by his death. . . .'

Such an appeal against this degradation of the human spirit was a mere drop in the ocean of universal savagery fomented by official support. Yet there were other philosophers and thinkers of the imperial epoch, Greeks and Orientals rather than Romans, who spoke out as uncompromisingly as Seneca. Artemidorus of Daldis . . . described the gladiators' profession as a dishonourable, cruel and impious career founded on human blood. He was probably a Stoic like Seneca; and the far greater Stoic Epictetus, a crippled Phrygian slave, was like-wise nauseated by the whole business—writing with bitter irony of the elegant high-priest who takes meticulous care of his fine gladiatorial troop in which he has invested. . . .

But the most explicit condemnation of all comes from an unidentifiable follower of the ancient school of Pythagoras, whose work, *On the Eating of Flesh*, written in imperial times, contains a warning even more specific than Seneca's about the moral corruption with which a taste for gladiator shows infects the spectators. For these results are correctly defined by the anonymous Neo-Pythagorean as 'insensibility to human beings, and cruelty.'

Such were the few and scattered voices that protested against the destructive effects of this never-ending flow of gladiatorial slaughter upon the watching crowds. But the objectors could not fail to receive adherents from among the rapidly increasing Christians, whose doctrines both respected human life and paid attention to the lost and oppressed. In about A.D. 200 the fiery anti-pagan eloquence of the African Tertullian is devoted to this theme, with particular reference to the infamous custom or pretence that death in the arena was regarded as a justifiable punishment for crime.

'*He who shudders at the body of a man who died by nature's law the common death of all will in the amphitheatre, gaze down with most tolerant eyes on the bodies of men mangled, torn in pieces, defiled with their own blood; yes, and he who comes to the spectacle to signify his approval of murder being punished, will have a reluctant gladiator hounded on with lash and rod to do murder. . . .*

'If we can plead that cruelty is allowed us if impiety, if brute savagery, by all means let us go to the amphitheatre. If we are what people say we are, let us take our delight in the blood of men. 'It is a good thing, when the guilty are punished.' Who will deny that, unless he is one of the guilty? And yet the innocent cannot take pleasure in the punishment of another, when it better befits the innocent to lament that a man like himself has become so guilty that a punishment so cruel must be awarded him.'

But it remained for Augustine, writing in his *Confessions* nearly two hundred years later, to depict in final and unforgettable terms . . . the dreadful fascination which gladiatorial bestialities had exerted upon a previously innocent spectator, his young friend Alypius.

'He had gone to Rome before me in order to study law, and in Rome he had been quite swept away, incredibly and with a most incredible passion, by the gladiatorial shows. He was opposed to such things and detested them; but he happened to meet some of his friends and fellow pupils on their way back from dinner, and they, in spite of his protests and his vigorous resistance, used a friendly kind of violence and forced him to go along with them to the amphitheatre on a day when one of these cruel and bloody shows was being presented. As he went, he said to them: 'You can drag my body there, but don't imagine that you can make me turn my eyes or give my mind to the show. Though there, I shall not be there, and so I shall have the better both of you and of the show.'

'After hearing this his friends were all the keener to bring him along with them. No doubt they wanted to see whether he could actually do this or not. So they came to the arena and took the seats which they could find. The whole place was seething with savage enthusiasm, but he shut the doors of his eyes and forbade his soul to go out into a scene of such evil. If only he could have blocked up his ears too! For in the course of the fight some man fell; there was a great roar from the whole mass of spectators which fell upon his ears; he was overcome by curiosity and opened his eyes, feeling perfectly prepared to treat whatever he might see with scorn and to rise above it.

'But he then received in his soul a worse wound than that man, whom he had wanted to see, had received in his body. His own fall was more wretched than that of the gladiator which had caused all that shouting which had entered his ears and unlocked his eyes and made an opening for the thrust which was to overthrow his soul—a soul that had been reckless rather than strong and was all the weaker because it had trusted in itself when it ought to have trusted in You. He saw the blood and he gulped down savagery. Far from turning away, he fixed his eyes on it. Without knowing what was happening, he drank in madness, he was delighted with the guilty contest, drunk with the lust of blood. He was no longer the man who had come there but was one of the crowd to which he had come, a true companion of those who had brought him.

'There is no more to be said. He looked, he shouted, he raved with excitement. He took away with him a madness which would goad him to come back again, and he would not only come with those who first got him there; he would go ahead of them and he would drag others with him. . . .'

Murderous Games

Keith Hopkins

Keith Hopkins, Professor of Ancient History at Cambridge University and formerly Professor of Sociology at Brunel University, combines his specialties to analyze Roman gladiatorial shows from a sociological perspective. He traces their origins to the public executions of prisoners of war and comments on the importance to the Romans of maintaining an atmosphere of violence, even during peacetime. He argues that, though infrequent, gladiatorial shows had a great impact on Roman society. His essay examines the social role of the gladiator as object of admiration and even of love.

Rome was a warrior state. During two centuries of imperial expansion following the second war against Carthage, that is in the last two centuries B.C., Rome conquered the whole of the Mediterranean basin, and incorporated the conquered territory and its inhabitants, perhaps one fifth or one sixth of the world's then population, within the Roman state. These victories were bought at a price, paid by hundreds of thousands of men killed in war, and by captive slaves, and by soldiers who owed their victory to training and discipline. Decimation illustrates the point well. If an army unit was judged disobedient or cowardly in battle, one soldier in ten was selected by lot and cudgelled to death by his former comrades. Decimation was not merely a terrifying myth, told to enforce compliance among fresh recruits. Decimation actually occured, and often enough not to be particularly remarked on. Roman soldiers killed each other for their common good. Small wonder then that they executed military deserters without mercy; or that prisoners of war were sometimes forced to fight in gladiatorial contests, or were thrown to wild beasts for popular entertainment.

Public executions of prisoners helped inculcate valour and fear in the men, women and children left at home. Children learned the lesson about what happened to soldiers who were defeated. These were the rituals which helped maintain an atmosphere of violence, even in peace. Bloodshed and slaughter joined military glory and conquest as central elements in Roman culture. They persisted as central elements, even when the Roman peace (*pax Romana*) was established under the emperors in the first two centuries A.D. It was a period when the mass of Roman citizens living in the capital were divorced from the direct experience of war. Real-life battles occurred much less frequently. And those which did occur were fought on distant frontiers.

Then, in memory of their warrior traditions, the Romans set up artificial battlefields in their cities and towns. They re-created battlefield conditions for public amusement. The custom spread from Italy to the provinces. Nowadays, we admire the Colosseum in Rome and other great Roman amphitheatres, such as those at Verona, Arles, Nimes and El Djem (Tunisia), as architectural monuments, while choosing to forget, I suspect, that this was where Romans regularly organized fights to the death between hundreds of gladiators, the mass execution of unarmed criminals and the indiscriminate slaughter of domestic and wild animals. The enormous size of the amphitheatres indicates how popular these exhibitions were. The Colosseum which seated about 50,000 people is still one of the most impressive buildings in Rome. It is also a magnificent feat of engineering and design. In ancient times, amphitheatres must have towered over cities, much as cathedrals towered over medieval towns. Public killings were a Roman rite, legitimated by the myth that gladiatorial shows 'inspired a glory in wounds and a contempt of death, since the love of praise and desire for victory could be seen, even in the bodies of slaves and criminals' (Pliny, *Panegyric* 33). . . .

Gladiatorial Shows: Origins and Developments

Gladiatorial fights originated apparently as an element in funeral games. 'Once upon a time,' wrote the Christian critic Tertullian at the end of the second century, 'men believed that the souls of the dead were propitiated by human blood, and so at funerals they sacrificed prisoners of war or slaves of poor quality bought for the purpose.' It was also thought that gladiators were originally imported from Etruria or from Campania. Stories about origins are notoriously unreliable. Yet repeated evidence confirms the close association of gladiatorial contests with funerals. The first recorded gladiatorial show in the city of Rome is attributed to . . . D. Iunius Brutus Pera and his brother in 264 B.C.; it was held in the ox-market in honour of their dead father. Only three pairs of gladiators took part. Over the next two centuries, the scale and frequency of gladiatorial shows steadily increased. In 65 B.C., Julius Caesar gave elaborate funeral games for his long dead father, involving 320 pairs of gladiators, and condemned criminals equipped with silver weapons who were forced to fight with wild beasts. At his next games in 46 B.C., in honour of his dead daughter and of his recent triumphs in Gaul and Egypt, Caesar presented not only the customary fights between individual gladiators, but also fights between detachments of infantry and between squadrons of cavalry, some mounted on horses and others on elephants; the contestants were gladiators, prisoners of war and criminals condemned to death.

Up to this time, gladiatorial shows had always been put on by individual aristocrats at their own initiative and expense, in honour of dead relatives. The religious component in gladiatorial ceremonies continued to be important. For example, attendants in the arena were sometimes dressed as gods; slaves who tested whether executed criminals or dead gladiators were really dead or just pretending, by applying a red-hot cauterising iron, were dressed as the god Mercury, while those who dragged the dead bodies away were dressed as the god of the underworld, Pluto, or as Charon. During the persecutions of Christians, from the second century A.D., the victims were sometimes led in a procession around the arena dressed up as priests and priestesses of pagan cults, before being stripped naked and thrown to wild beasts. The welter of blood in gladiatorial and wild beast shows, the squeals of the victims and of slaughtered animals, are completely alien to us and almost unimaginable. For some Romans, there must have been associations with battlefields, and more immediately for everyone, associations with religious sacrifice—except that after gladiatorial shows the victims were not eaten. In gladiatorial contests and in wild beast shows, the Romans came very close, even at the height of their civilization, to performing human sacrifice. Purportedly it was done in commemoration of their dead.

In the city of Rome, in the late Republic and early Principate, the religious and commemorative elements of gladiatorial shows were increasingly fused with, even eclipsed by, the political and the spectacular. Gladiatorial shows at Rome were public performances, held mostly, before the amphitheatre was built, in the ritual and social centre of the city, in the Forum. Public participation, attracted by the splendour of the show and by the distributions of meat, magnified the respect paid to the dead and the honour of the whole family. Aristocratic funerals were political acts. And funeral games had political overtones, particularly during the Republic, because of their popularity with citizen electors. Indeed, the growth in the splendour of gladiatorial shows was largely fueled by political competition between ambitious aristocrats. It spilled over from their traditional competition in the provision of regular games, which included theatrical shows and chariot races. . . .

In 42 B.C. for the first time, gladiatorial fights were substituted for chariot races in official games. In the city of Rome, thereafter, regular gladiatorial shows, like theatrical shows and chariot races, were given by officers of state as part of their political careers. . . . Extra gladiatorial shows and wild-beast hunts were given by the emperors themselves. The first emperor, Augustus, as part of his general policy of limiting aristocrats' opportunities to court favour with the Roman populace, severely restricted the number and size of the regular gladiatorial shows. So after 22 B.C., in his reign there were perhaps only two regular gladiatorial shows per year. In the fourth century A.D., we know from an official calendar that there were ten per year. . . . Gladiatorial shows were always something special, and happened regularly only a few times each year.

The actual events were magnified beforehand by expectations and afterwards by memory. Street advertisements painted on plastered walls stimulated excitement and anticipation. In surviving literature, art and artifacts (frescoes, mosaics, sculptures, graffiti, bronze figurines, glazed vases, terra cotta lamps and engraved glasses), there are frequent references to and depictions of gladiatorial fights and of wild beast shows. In Latin proverbs and sayings, and even in our own language, gladiatorial contests have left their mark: thumbs down—*verso police*. In conversation, in daily life, chariot-races and gladiatorial fights were all the rage; the historian Tacitus commented, presumably with some rhetorical exaggeration: 'How often will you find anyone who talks of anything else at home? And when you enter the lecture-halls, what else do you hear the young men talking about?' A baby's nursing bottle, made of clay, and found at Pompeii was stamped with the figure of a gladiator. It presumably symbolized that the baby should imbibe a gladiator's strength and courage. Gladiatorial shows suffused Roman life. . . .

Gladiatorial Shows as Political Theatre

. . . Under the emperors, as citizens' rights to engage in politics diminished, gladiatorial shows, games and theatre together provided repeated opportunities for the dramatic confrontation of rulers and ruled. Rome was unique among large historical empires in allowing these regular meetings between emperors and the massed populace of the capital, collected together in a single crowd, not just strung along the public streets. To be sure emperors could mostly stage-manage their own appearance and their reception; they gave extravagant shows, threw gifts to the crowd, occasionally had their own claques, and were attended by armed guards. Mostly they received standing ovations and ritual acclamations. . . .

Gladiatorial shows were political theatre. The dramatic performance took place not only in the arena, but also between different sections of the audience. Their interaction was part of Roman politics, and should be included in any thorough account of the Roman constitution. They are usually omitted, simply because in our own society, mass spectator sports count as leisure. The politics of metropolitan control included 'bread and circuses' (Juvenal). ' The Roman people,' wrote Fronto, 'is held together by two things: wheat doles and public shows. Control is secured as much by amusements as by serious things.'

Consider how the audience in the amphitheatre sat: the emperor in his gilded box, surrounded by his family; senators and knights had special seats, and came properly dressed in purple-bordered togas. Soldiers were separated from civilians. Even ordinary citizens had to wear the heavy white woollen toga, the formal dress of a citizen, and sandals if they wanted to sit in the bottom two tiers of seats; married men sat separately from bachelors, boys sat in a separate block with their tutors in the next block. Women, and the very poorest men, dressed in the drab grey cloth associated with mourning, could sit or stand only in the top tier. Priests, such as the Arval Brethren and the Companions of Augustus and the Vestal Virgins (honorary men), had reserved seats at the front. The formal dress and the segregation of ranks underlined the formal, ritual elements in the occasion, just as the steeply banked seats reflected the steep stratification of society. It mattered where you sat and where you were seen to be sitting.

The emperor was the centre of everyone's attention, usually welcomed, cheered with ritual chants of praise. In return, the crowd was showered with gifts and often provided with food and drink. Ideally, gladiatorial shows put the whole metropolitan population in a good humour. When a gladiator fell, the crowd would shout for mercy or dispatch. The emperor might be swayed by their shouts or gestures, but he alone, the final arbiter, decided when the fighting was to stop and who was to live or die. This dramatic enactment of imperial power, repeated several times a day on several occasions a year, before a mass audience of citizens, conquerors of the world, helped legitimate the emperor's position. And yet, the crowd's potential for legitimation and support contained an inherent risk of subversion and resistance. To be sure, the crowd could be placated, bought off with tokens, commanded or bullied into silence. But it could also resist, or slip out of control. Yet the dangers of political confrontation were lessened by the crowd's lack of coherence, by its own volatility, and by the absence of an ideology which could bind it together in a sustained programme of action. If the crowd became too vociferous, emperors could just stay away or leave the city; for example, Nero, immediately after he had killed his mother in A.D. 59, delayed returning to Rome, reportedly because he was anxious about popular reaction. Tiberius, who had little interest in public shows, withdrew for several years to the island of Capri, and by his absence disfranchised the crowd.

Even so, given the decline under the emperors of all the other Republican traditions of popular participation in politics, it is surprising that the tradition of the emperor's attendance at the Games persisted. . . . Augustus set the style of overt respect by emperors to the only surviving assembly of citizens. Tiberius attended public shows assiduously in the early years of his reign, in spite of not being interested in them, 'both in order to honour those who put them on and to keep the populace in order, by seeming to share their festivities with them. . . .' Claudius called the people 'My masters' and joked with them, sometimes explaining his decision to them on placards. He gave frequent gladiatorial shows, during which 'he acted as one of the people and was quite relaxed; he even counted out loud in time with the crowd, and on the fingers of his outstretched left hand, marked off the number of gold coins paid to the victors.' By

his enthusiastic involvement, he outperformed expectations and so earned censure from some aristocrats and historians who thought that emperors should be more discreet and discriminating in their pleasures.

Gladiators as Heroes

Enthusiastic interest in the games and in gladiatorial shows occasionally spilled over into a desire to perform on the stage or in the arena. Two emperors were not content to be spectators-in-chief; they wanted to be prize performers as well. Nero's histrionic ambitions and success as musician, singer, actor and dancer were notorious; he also prided himself on his abilities as a charioteer, and after a private exhibition in front of 'his slaves and the dregs of the plebs' he gave a public performance in the Circus Maximus. Commodus also fancied himself as a charioteer, but as such performed only in private. He practiced as a gladiator at home, killing or maiming several opponents; in the amphitheatre itself, he took part as a gladiator in preliminary bouts with blunted weapons and won all of his fights; he charged the treasury a million HS for each appearance. Eventually, he was assassinated, when he was planning to be inaugurated as consul (for A.D. 193) dressed up as a gladiator. Such behaviour was even then regarded as a reflection of 'madness and paranoia.'

Commodus' gladiatorial exploits were an idiosyncratic fall-out from a cultural obsession with fighting, bloodshed, ostentation and competition. After all, Commodus was not alone. At least seven other emperors (Caligula, Titus, Hadrian, Lucius Venis, Didius Julianus, Caracalla, Geta) practiced as gladiators or fought in gladiatorial contests. And so did senators and knights, occasionally but repeatedly. Attempts were made to prohibit senators and knights from appearing in the arena by law, but the laws were evaded. Our sources are uniform in their moral condemnation, and try to explain away their behavior by calling them desperadoes, forced into the arena by degenerate emperors, or by the dissipation of their patrimony. In such a steeply stratified society, it seemed outrageous for men of high status to throw away privilege, to declass themselves, even if 'in this way they achieved death instead of dishonour.'

It is difficult to know why senators and knights performed as gladiators. I suspect what attracted them was the opportunity to display their military prowess, their courage and their skill, plus the desire for victory, and the shouts of the crowd. At the risk of death, it was their last chance to play soldiers in front of a large audience. In spite of the opprobrium and perhaps because of the risk, a minority tried. The emperor Septimius Severus openly rebuked the senate for its hypocrisy in criticising Commodus so severely for his activities as a gladiator: 'And do none of you fight as gladiators? Why then have some of you bought his shields and those golden helmets of his?' Gladiatorial fighting was more popular among the Roman upper classes than modern scholars readily admit.

Gladiators were glamour figures, cultural heroes. The probable life-span of each gladiator was short. Each successive victory brought further risk of defeat and death. But for the moment I am concerned more with image than with reality. Modern pop-stars and athletes (tennis-players, gymnasts and football players) have only a short exposure to full-glare publicity. Most then fade rapidly from being household names into obscurity, fossilised in the memory of each generation of adolescent enthusiasts. The transience of the fame of each does not diminish their collective importance. So too with Roman gladiators. Their portraits were often painted; and occasionally even walls in public porticoes were covered with 'life-like portraits of all the gladiators' in a particular show. Names of individual gladiators survive in dozens, scratched or painted on the plastered walls of Pompeii. The ephemera of A.D. 79 have been preserved by volcanic ash. For example:

Celadus the Thracian, thrice victor and thrice crowned, the young girls' heart-throb Crescens the Netter of young girls by night. (CIL 4.4342 and 4353)

The victorious gladiator, or at least his image, was sexually attractive. The word *gladius*—sword—was vulgarly used to mean penis. Even the defeated and dead gladiator had something sexually portentous about him. It was customary for a new bride to have her hair parted with a spear, at best one which had been dipped 'in the body of a defeated and killed gladiator.' A stone relief from southern Italy (Beneventum) shows a heavily armed gladiator fighting a huge penis; beside him are written the words of the crowd: 'Free him. Kill him.' I am not at all sure how to interpret the significance of all this; such customs and artifacts can mean so many different things to different people, and even to the same person. But this evidence suggests that there was a close link, in some Roman minds, between gladiatorial fighting and sexuality.

Other evidence corroborates this association: for example, a terra cotta gladiatorial helmet shaped suggestively like a penis, and a small bronze figurine, from Pompeii, of a cruel looking gladiator, fighting off with his sword a dog-like wild-beast which grows out of his erect and elongated penis; five bells hang down from various parts of his body and a hook is attached to the gladiator's head, so that the whole ensemble could hang as a bell and perhaps as a talisman in a door-way or from a ceiling. Once again, interpretation is speculative. It seems as though gladiatorial bravery for some Roman men represented an attractive yet dangerous, almost threatening, macho masculinity.

Gladiators' strength and bravery, their risk of death, attracted some Roman women. Yet to pursue and love slave gladiators was socially dangerous, even disastrous. Even if they were free men by birth or socially distinguished by origin, as gladiators they were déclassé, outcasts. Indeed, because they were in such close contact with death, they were polluted and sometimes therefore, like suicides, excluded from normal burial. They were, according to Tertullian, both loved and despised; 'men give them their souls, women their bodies too. . . they are both glorified and degraded. . . .'

Behind the brave facade and the hope of glory at the best shows, there still lurked the fear of death. 'Those about to die salute you, Emperor.' Only one account survives of what it was like, from the gladiator's point of view. It is from a rhetorical exercise; the raconteur, typically enough, is a rich young man who had been captured by pirates and then sold on as a slave to a gladiatorial trainer:

'And so the day arrived. Already the populace had gathered for the spectacle of our punishment, and the bodies of those about to die had their own death-parade across the arena. The presenter of the show who hoped to gain favour with our blood, took his seat. . . . Although no one knew my birth, my fortune, my family, one fact made people pity me; I seemed unfairly matched. I was destined to be a certain victim in the sand. . . . All around I could hear the instruments of death: a sword being sharpened, iron-plates being heated in a fire [to stop fighters' retreating and to prove that they were not faking death], birch-rods and whips were prepared. One would have imagined that these were the pirates. The trumpets sounded their foreboding notes; stretchers for the dead were brought on, a funeral parade before death. Everywhere I could see wounds, groans, blood, danger. . . .' (Quintillian, *Rhetorical Exercises* 9.6)

Conclusions

Why did Romans popularize fights to the death between armed gladiators? Why did they encourage the public slaughter of unarmed criminals? What was it, asked Tertullian, which transformed men who were timid and peaceable enough in private and made them shout gleefully for the merciless destruction of their fellow men? Part of the answer may lie in the social psychology of the crowd, which helps relieve the individual of responsibility, and in the psychological mechanisms by which some spectators identify more readily with the victory of the aggressor than with the sufferings of the vanquished. Slavery and the steep stratification of society must have helped. Slaves were at the mercy of their owners. Those who were destroyed for public edification and entertainment were considered worthless, as non-persons; or like the Christian martyrs, they were considered social outcasts and were tortured as if 'we no longer existed.' The brutalization of the audience fed on the dehumanization of the victims.

Rome was a cruel society. Brutality was built into its culture, in private life as well as in public shows. The tone was set by military discipline and by slavery, to say nothing of wide-ranging paternal powers. Perhaps because of this paternal independence and slave-owner's rights over their slaves, the state did not establish an early monopoly of legitimate violence, and only in the second century A.D. did it acquire a legal monopoly of capital punishment. So, for example, rich Romans could give and regularly gave private gladiatorial shows of two or three pairs at dinner-parties: 'when they have finished dining and are filled with drink, they call in the gladiators; as soon as one has his throat cut, the diners 'applaud with delight.' At their master's whim, as we have seen, slaves could be sold to gladiatorial schools or sentenced without trial and thrown to wild beasts. Owners could, if they wanted, on their own initiative, crucify their slaves publicly. Seneca recorded from his own observations the various ways in which crucifixions were carried out, in order to increase pain.

But there were limits, even though the limits were not where we would set them. For example, the story is told that a Roman knight, Vedius Pollio, had a fish-pond stocked with huge lampreys which he fattened on the flesh of slaves who offended him in any way. Once when Augustus was dining with him, a young slave dropped a precious crystal bowl. His master ordered him to be seized and thrown alive to the lampreys. The boy slipped from his captors' grasp and threw himself at the emperor's feet to ask only that he be allowed to die some other way, not as human bait.' Augustus was so shocked at Vedius' cruelty that he pardoned the boy, and ordered that all Vedius' crystal bowls be smashed there and then, and that the fish-pond be filled in. The truth or falsity of the story does not matter much. There are numerous other examples of cruelty, most of them reported casually, without critical comment. What matters here is that these stories circulated. They were instruments of social control. Feeble enough in all conscience, but they helped set the boundaries to the open cruelty which could be socially condoned in the private domain. It is worth stressing that we are dealing here, not with individual sadistic psychopathology, but with a deep cultural difference. Roman commitment to cruelty fueled popular interest in gladiatorial shows. The cultural divide makes the modern historian's normal tactic of empathetic imagination particularly difficult.

The popularity of gladiatorial shows was a by-product of war, discipline and death. Rome was a militaristic society. For centuries, it had been devoted to war and to the mass participation of citizens in battle. They won their huge empire by discipline and control. Public executions were a gruesome reminder to noncombatants, fellow-citizens or subjects, that vengeance would be exacted if they betrayed their country, rebelled or were convicted of serious crimes. For example, in 70 B.C., after the slave rebellion led by Spartacus, himself an escaped gladiator, had finally been crushed, 6,000 slaves captured alive were crucified all the way along the road from Capua to Rome, a distance of about 200 km. The objective was deterrence. Public punishment ritually re-established the moral and political order. The power of the state was dramatically reconfirmed.

When long-term peace came to the heartlands of the empire, particularly after 31 B.C., these militaristic traditions were preserved at Rome in the domesticated battlefield of the ampitheatre. War had been converted into a game, a drama repeatedly replayed, of cruelty, violence, blood and death. But order still needed to be preserved, and the fear of death still had to be controlled or assuaged by ritual. In a city as large as Rome, without an adequate police force, disorder always threatened. And without effective medicine, death rates must have been very high; no one was safe. Sickness spread occasionally like wildfire through crowded apartment blocks. Gladiatorial shows and their accompanying executions provided opportunities for the reaffirmation of the moral order through the sacrifice of criminal victims, of slave gladiators, of Christian outcasts and wild animals. The enthusiastic participation by spectators, rich and poor, raised and then released collective tensions, in a society which traditionally idealized impassivity. The gladiatorial shows provided a psychic and political safety valve for the population of the capital. The risk for the emperors, as we have seen, was an occasional policital conflict, but the populace could usually be diverted or fobbed off. At the psychological level, the gladiatorial shows provided a state (as television news does for modern viewers) for shared violence and tragedy. They also gave spectators the reassurance that they themselves had yet again survived disaster. Whatever happened in the arena, the spectators were always on the winning side. They found comfort for death, wrote Tertullian, in murder.

The Emperor and his People at the Games

Alan Cameron

Alan Cameron, Professor of Greek and Latin at Columbia University, has published widely on the literature, history and culture of the Roman Empire. In this chapter from his book on circus factions, he examines the political importance of games in the relations between the emperor and the Roman populace. Public appearances by the emperor both served his vanity and also provided for the only direct interchanges between the ruler and the ruled, and on many occasions the emperor wisely responded to popular concerns. It was also a pressure valve and the more prudent emperors realized that popular protest was preferable to assassination.

It has long been customary to draw a sharp contrast between the feckless, degenerate, work-shy plebs of early imperial Rome concerned only with its bread and circuses, and the alert, fearless, freedom-loving people of Constantinople, represented by the circus factions. It would be hard to say which side of the contrast is more false.

Naturally enough this one chapter cannot hope (and does not attempt) to treat the relationship between plebs and princeps in all its manifestations throughout the Principate. In keeping with the purpose of this book it will concentrate on their common meeting place in the theatres and circuses of Rome. Not the only approach to the question, of course, but a more direct route to the wider issues than might at first sight appear.

'The hundreds of thousands of Roman citizens who lived in Rome,' wrote Rostovtzeff, '... readily acquiesced in the gradual reduction of the popular assembly under Augustus to a mere formality; they offered no protest when Tiberius suppressed even this formality, but they insisted on their right, acquired under the civil war, to be fed and amused by the government.' This is not untrue, but it is a rather misleading formulation. It is of course true enough that in A.D. 15 the people lost the right to elect praetors and consuls. But what were praetors and consuls to the people of A.D. 15? It was to the princeps that the people now turned in their hour of need. The vote which they lost had long since ceased to be a valid or significant means either of expressing their will or attaining their ends.

Nothing illustrates this more clearly than Gaius' unsuccessful attempt to reintroduce popular elections in 38; the people were not interested, nor were there even enough candidates forthcoming. On matters which really concerned them (the price of corn, high taxes, unjust decisions) they could—and did—address specific complaints directly to the one person who could—and often did—offer some redress: the emperor.

Let us begin with what Cicero had to say a century before Gaius discovered the same truth. 'There are three places above all,' he wrote in 56 B.C., 'where the will of the people makes itself known: public assemblies, elections, and the games.' The first two had degenerated so far, Cicero roundly declared, that it was only at the games that the true feelings of the people could be discerned: 'the expression of popular opinion which we see at elections and public meetings is sometimes spurious and rehearsed; and while it may be possible to raise a thin smattering of cheers at the theatres or gladiatorial shows with a rented crowd, nonetheless it is easy enough to see how it is done and who is behind it—and how the majority of honest citizens react.'

The validity of Cicero's instinct is confirmed by the fact that, long after *contiones* and *comitia* had disappeared, the people continued to express their hopes, fears, and resentments freely and often forcibly at the public shows. No emperor was able to curb this 'theatri licentia' and many had to bow before it, in matters large and small. To take the sort of phenomenon that Cicero had always felt to be particularly representative of public opinion, nothing, it seems, could dampen the enthusiasm of mime-writers and actors for contemporary allusions—or the readiness with which Roman audiences picked them up. . . .

It is a sure index of the quasi-official licence allowed in the theatres that it is only the traditional 'bad' emperors who reacted violently to such ribaldries. For example, Gaius and Domitian are the only emperors recorded to have actually executed actors for double entendres. The most outrageous example is the occasion, soon after Agrippina had joined Claudius in untimely death, when a certain Datus sang the popular song 'Goodbye father, goodbye mother' before Nero, miming first drinking and then swimming gestures. All Nero did was exile the man from Italy, 'either because he did not care about such insults,' remarks Suetonius, 'or so as not to encourage others by showing himself offended.' Nero understood better than any emperor since Augustus (and most of his successors too) how to win the people's favour, or (in crises where favour was beyond reach) how least to incur their hostility. The good Marcus stolidly sat through the most excruciating puns on the name of his wife's supposed lover, and even his even less tolerant son Commodus merely exiled actors who poked fun at his debauchery. It was probably in part at least this sort of thing that Tacitus had in mind when he wrote of the 'seditious' behaviour of actors that led Tiberius to suppress the 'Oscan farce' in 23. . . .

From Augustus on it became normal and common for the people to make requests of the emperor at the circus and theatre—requests to which he was morally obliged to at least reply. This was not (of course) the only place where such petitions might be presented, but whereas it was easy enough to deal with petitions presented by individuals or small groups strictly in accordance with the merits of the case, any request made publicly in front of up to 250,000 fellow citizens was potentially political—and not easy to resist. And there can be no doubt that it was at the circus and theatre above all that the Roman emperor was answerable to the voice of his people, on matters great and small alike.

No text better illustrates both the thing itself and the consequences of its injudicious handling than Josephus' account of a circus meeting held a few weeks before the murder of Gaius in January 41:

At this time occurred chariot races. This is a kind of sport to which the Romans are fanatically devoted. They gather enthusiastically in the circus and there the assembled throngs make requests of the emperors according to their own pleasure. Emperors who rule that such petitions are to be granted automatically are highly popular. So in this case they desperately entreated Gaius to cut down imposts and grant some relief from the burden of taxes. But he had no patience with them, and when they shouted louder and louder, he also dispatched agents among them in all directions with orders to arrest any who shouted, to bring them forward at once and put them to death. The order was given and those whose duty it was carried it out. The number of those executed in such summary fashion was very large. The people, when they saw what happened, stopped their shouting and controlled themselves, for they could see with their own eyes that the request for fiscal concessions resulted quickly in their own death. This strengthened still further Chaerea's determination to embark on the plot and to put an end to Gaius and his brutal fury against mankind. . . .

Yet there was no mistaking the significance of such manifestations as a guide to the waning popularity of Gaius, and there can be little doubt that Josephus was right about the effect of the demonstration of 41 on the resolve of his future assassin. Nor will the praetorians who dragged Claudius out from behind his curtain after the deed was done have forgotten that when he had presided at the games in Gaius' place, the people greeted him with the cry 'Hail, brother of Germanicus.' However unsuitable Claudius might have seemed to those who knew him, his reception in the circus plainly marked him out as a candidate acceptable to the masses. . . .

Indeed, Josephus' remark that the emperors normally granted petitions made at the games is amply borne out by the examples that have come down to us. The complaisant Titus made a promise (which he kept) before a gladiatonal show that he would grant *anything* he was asked. The stern Tiberius once made the mistake of moving a statue he happened to like from the baths of Agrippa to his own palace. At his next visit to the theatre the people insisted that he put it back.... He simply gave up attending the games 'so that he should not be faced with petitions'—an omission for which he was never forgiven by the people....

No less illuminating, when refusing petitions emperors were evidently expected to offer an explanation or justification of their refusal, even in the most (apparently) trifling cases. For example, when asked to manumit a charioteer, Hadrian replied that it was not proper for him to free another man's slave. Marcus refused repeated requests to free the trainer of a man-eating lion because (he said) he did not approve of what the man had taught his pet. When the people clamoured incessantly, in all the theatres and circuses for the head of Tigellinus, Galba justified his refusal to comply by issuing a statement weakly (and falsely) alleging that Tigellinus would soon be dead of consumption anyway. A long exchange is reported between Claudius and a theatre audience concerning the whereabouts of the pantomime Mnester (popularly believed to have been closeted at the time with the Empress Messalina). In order to convince the crowd that he really did not know where Mnester was, Claudius was reduced to swearing a public oath. When Augustus was faced with a demonstration from the equites against his law encouraging marriage, he replied by 'sending for the children whom his granddaughter Agrippina had borne to Germanicus, and publicly displayed them, some sitting on his own knee, the rest on their father's—and made it quite clear by his affectionate looks and gestures that it would not be at all a bad thing if the knights imitated that young man's example, ...

... Before proceeding to the more violent popular disturbances of the early imperial circuses and theatres, demonstrations which go way beyond the limits of such permitted licenses as formal petitions from the people and double entendres from the stage, let us consider why it is that the emperors not only tolerated but in effect positively encouraged such manifestations.

It was not inevitable that they should have behaved thus. To say that it was a long-established tradition may be true; but that is hardly an explanation.

The emperors could, for example, simply have stopped attending the games. Or they could have removed themselves more decisively from such popular pressures by retiring to a Versailles (something of the sort did happen eventually, when court was moved to Ravenna early in the fifth century). But by the mere act of regularly and frequently attending the games, they automatically put themselves in a vulnerable position: either they granted the petitions they had encouraged by their very presence, or they solicited unpopularity by refusing. Why then did they attend? Three basic reasons may be suggested:

1. It is in the nature of things that our sources tend to record cases where an emperor was booed in the circus or theatre. That was news. In reality it was here more than anywhere that he normally expected to be *cheered*. ...

Acts likely to be popular or designed to win favour or support could be given the maximum publicity if performed in the theatre or circus. Titus, for example, had informers arrested and paraded in the Colosseum, as later did Trajan. It was of course an old established Roman practice to throw criminals and prisoners to the beasts. ...

Titus had planted stooges in theatre audiences to clamour for the arrest of men he wanted out of the way. And at a much more mundane level, we may without undue cynicism guess that when announcements were made there about the price and availability of corn and wine, the government would often have foreseen the request and carefully calculated how far they could go, so that the emperor could present what concessions were possible in the most favourable light.

It is of course a time-honoured device of the dictator to exploit his subjects' loyalty at mass celebrations—but normally on occasions of his own choosing. The difference—and danger—at Rome was that from time to time circumstances might evoke a less favourable reaction from the people. But this was no doubt sufficiently uncommon to make the price well worthwhile.

2.   Provided that it did not get out of hand (and in the early empire there were normally police provisions adequate to ensure that it did not), even a hostile demonstration could ease a difficult situation. A grievance aired, even if fruitlessly, is a grievance halved. Imagine the tension the first time Nero entered the theatre after the murder of Agrippina. A joke against him (like the one quoted above), if tolerated, could help to defuse indignation that, if suppressed, might have smouldered and grown to explode in a much more dangerous way. The emperor who allowed the people to get away with murder in the theatre was seldom troubled by real plots. It is at any rate suggestive that those who suppressed such verbal treason most harshly—Gaius and Domitian—eventually succumbed to the real thing. It was scarcely freedom of speech in the true sense, since it did not extend to the upper classes (who had to be much more careful what they said). But the people were not likely to mind if the heads of their betters rolled so long as they felt that they could say what they liked. An emperor's less popular ministers might have had more cause for anxiety; emperors were not above diverting the people's indignation with a scapegoat. At a more modest level, circus and theatre complaints could provide an emperor with useful information, even if he was unable (or unwilling) to act upon it at the time. If he could show himself thick-skinned enough, a prudent emperor could derive the same sort of lessons from the theatre or circus as a modern politician does from the popular press or public opinion polls—favourable or unfavourable. This was exactly how Cicero had treated them. . . .

3.   The ideology of the early Empire has attracted much attention of late. Yet of all the virtues (real and imaginary) credited at different times to different emperors, perhaps the most important yet the least discussed is his *civilitas*. It is a commonplace of imperial panegyric to contrast Rome, where a *princeps* governed free men, with Parthia, where a despot ruled over slaves. And nowhere did the emperor take more pains to appear first citizen among his fellows than at

the games. If he could but master the popular touch, there he could be his own propaganda incarnate.

This great truth was early seen and exploited by Augustus, profiting from an error of Caesar. For Caesar, as Augustus himself (significantly enough) used to relate, was criticized for dealing with his correspondence while watching the games. Augustus was careful to do nothing but watch.

It is interesting to see that exactly the same reproach was levelled at another conscientious ruler, Marcus Aurelius. Both Marcus and Caesar recognized their duty to attend the games, but could not bring themselves to abandon all their other duties for days on end. For we must remember that festivals sometimes lasted for a week or more, and as early as Augustus, 77 days a year were wholly given over to public games—a total that by the fourth century had risen to 177. No responsible ruler could afford (whatever his inclination) to give up this much time to public relations. Even Augustus would 'absent himself from a show for several hours, sometimes for several days' (whence it would appear that several days' attendance would have been considered desirable), but to avoid offense he always sent his apologies (*petita venia*)—and a substitute too. Gaius also sent a deputy when unable to be present, often his uncle Claudius. Thus the principle was established that a representative of the imperial family should normally attend at any rate the major festivals. . . .

We come now to violent protests and riots. Our purpose is to compare the violence of the early Empire with that of the late Empire. But first a general point. This combination of frequent riots and a close relationship between ruler and ruled is by no means unique to ancient Rome.

The pattern has been brilliantly sketched by Eric Hobsbawm on evidence from eighteenth- and nineteenth-century Southern European cities like Naples, Palermo, Vienna, and (even then) Rome and Constantinople, capital cities with a long tradition of direct rule by a resident prince or duke.

'In such cities,' writes Hobsbawm, 'the [people] lived in an odd relationship with its rulers, equally compounded of parasitism and riot.' It was the ruler's business to provide food and employment for his people. So long as he did this, he would receive their active and enthusiastic support. If he failed to provide, the people would simply riot until he did. Both sides knew exactly how far they could go, and provided the ruler did not default too long or too seriously, the people would always return to their allegiance. It was in their interest to do so, since normally they took a positive pride in identifying with the greatness and splendour of their prince. And the prince could afford to tolerate what by modern standards might seem an alarming number of riots because they never threatened the system; at bottom the people were a thoroughly conservative force. So satisfactory a means of negotiation did this prove at Parma down into this century that the people found it very difficult to adjust to trade unions.

It will, I think, be obvious that early imperial Rome is a classic illustration of this pattern. Except that this curious 'symbiosis' between ruler and ruled was even more highly developed at Rome, thanks to their regular personal confrontations at the games. . . .

It was normally in the theatre or circus that such protests took place; partly because of the license traditionally allowed at the games, partly because of the 'feeling of power' and 'absence of a sense of individual responsibility' encouraged at a mass gathering. Add to these three categories the sheer excitement generated by the games themselves—something the football fan can perhaps appreciate more readily than the sober historian and it is not difficult to see why.

It would be far beyond the scope of this chapter to assess either the significance or the success of such varied popular manifestations over so long a period. For one thing, we have almost no evidence as to how representative they were even of the population of Rome; our sources tend to use loaded terms (*plebs sordida, imperita multitudo, vulgus credulum*) which tell us more about their own outlook than the composition of the body in question, and it would be naive to imagine that bodies of people however constituted are never manipulated. Nor is it easy to judge what counts as success in such cases; a protest suppressed with blood may nevertheless make its point. Governments cannot always afford to lose face by admitting mistakes too promptly and openly. But even by the strictest criteria, many of the protests were surely successful.

The Roman Economy and the Grain Supply

Peter Garnsey and Richard Saller

Peter Garnsey of Jesus College, Cambridge, and Richard Saller of the University of Chicago, are among the leading scholars of the social and economic history of the early Roman Empire. These excerpts from their recent book, The Roman Empire: Economy, Society and Culture *(1987), examine the agricultural basis of the Roman economy, which manifests the lack of development characteristic of pre-industrial societies. This ecomomy had to provide food for the capital city, and the authors here examine the expansion of provincial agriculture during the early empire. They also demonstrate that, despite the well-known reluctance of the Roman state to direct the economy, the emperors' personal security demanded that they ensure the reliability of the grain supply.*

An Underdeveloped Economy

We know little in detail about the economy of the Roman world. There are no government accounts, no official records of production, trade, occupational distribution, taxation. A systematic account of the Roman economy is therefore beyond our reach. Economic historians, more even than those historians with traditional interests, must set themselves limited objectives and be imaginative and discriminating in their pursuit of them.

We begin with a simple model of the Roman economy, arrived at by setting that economy against the background of other, better known, pre-industrial economies. . . .

The Roman economy was underdeveloped. This means essentially that the mass of the population lived at or near subsistence level. In a typical underdeveloped, pre-industrial economy, a large proportion of the labour force is employed in agriculture, which is the main avenue for investment and source of wealth. The level of investment in manufacturing industries is low. Resources that might in theory be devoted to growth-inducing investment are diverted into consumption or into unproductive speculation and usury. Demand for manufactured goods is relatively low, and most needs are met locally with goods made by small craftsmen or at home. Backward technology is a further barrier to increased productivity. Finally, there is no class of entrepreneurs who are both capable of perceiving opportunities for profit in large-scale organization of manufacture and prepared to undergo the risks entailed in making the necessary investment. In ancient Rome, small-scale handicraft industry was pre-dominant. Some goods were made in quantity, notably pottery and textiles. But little technical expertise or accumulation of capital was required for their production. They were in constant demand as basic and inexpensive consumer goods. However, no one producer or group of producers could be sure of a steady or expanding non-local market.

In Rome as in other pre-industrial economies, commerce received some of the capital that could not find an outlet in industrial enterprise. But the riskiness of trade acted as a disincentive to potential investors. In addition, transport facilities were backward. Land transport was slow and costly, even as it was after Roman times, when the collar harness and nailed shoes were invented. Water transport was altogether cheaper and faster, although goods could not be moved with speed and efficiency in

all seasons until the invention of the steamship in the nineteenth century. Most agricultural areas inevitably aimed at subsistence rather than the production of an exportable surplus. In the case of manufactures, too, proximity or ease of access to markets was essential. The emergence of Pisa and then Lyon as centres for the production of fine tableware illustrates the problems faced by the potters of Arezzo in the early decades of the first century A.D. in selling their product on the northern frontiers where the Roman army offered a ready market. In general, the backwardness and expense of transport and the relatively low level of demand limited opportunities for profitable investment in commerce.

Trading profits were attracted into land and money-lending. Money-lending brought the better return. Interest rates were especially high where the risks were great, as was the case with nautical loans and loans abroad (an empire afforded opportunities for exploitation). Money-lending was also unproductive: loans to aristocrats, for example, were used for purposes of consumption rather than land improvement and increased productivity.

Land investment offered security and a steady income. In modern developing countries, the scale of speculation in land suggests that many of those who have wealth find alternative opportunities for investment limited, or consider anything but a marginal investment in trade (or industry) unsafe or undesirable. In such societies, as was the case in pre-industrial Europe, land is valued also as a source of prestige and political power. The conversion of profits won in commerce into landed wealth often heralds the arrival of a new family in the ranks of the aristocracy. In such cases, the acquisition of property may be followed by the purchase of office and the forging of marriage connections with the upper class. The process of assimilation into the aristocracy might take one generation or more. As regards Rome, the best-known example of the merchant turned landowner is fictional, the freedman Trimalchio in Petronius' mid-first-century A.D. novel; and he, notoriously, failed to found a family that might have secured the status that was denied to Trimalchio himself. Freedmen were barred from political office. However, as many insciptions from Italy and elsewhere demonstrate, sons of freedmen could enter a city council and hold magistracies and priesthoods on the basis of their father's wealth and generosity. The source of their wealth is not generally specified on these inscriptions, which are intended to be honorific, nor is the form in which it was invested.

Finally, in pre-industrial societies the prevailing value system is that of a landed aristocracy. A prosperous merchant class, the source of whose wealth was not land, and whose success rested on enterprise and skill rather than traditional precepts and modes of behaviour, provides a potential threat to aristocratic values. But successful merchants fall easy prey to the dominant ideology: they buy or marry their way into the aristocracy and seek political office. Only the rise of a class of industrial owners, who possess social prestige and economic power independently as profit-makers and employers of labour, endangers the traditional social order.

In ancient Rome there was no prospect of the emergence of such a class. Moreover, economic realities, in particular the limitations of the market, virtually ruled out the possibility of the formation of a competing social hierarchy based on commercial wealth. Nevertheless, the landed aristocracy perceived a threat to their supremacy in the growth of commerce that followed Republican Rome's expansion beyond Italy. It is this which explains the reactionary and defensive tone colouring Roman social attitudes from the early second century B.C., when Latin literature begins. Treatises on agriculture and morality defend landowning as the safest occupation (the least likely therefore to impoverish the aristocracy and weaken its position) and as the most honourable (the most conducive to the lifestyle appropriate for the senator), and manifest hostility in differing degrees to trade as a source of income. . . . It is not a purely Republican phenomenon; Columella in the mid-first century A.D. affirms in stronger terms than any preceding writer the superiority of agriculture over trade.

The limitations of an analysis of the kind we have just attempted are obvious. The search for points of similarity between societies, when coupled with the tendency to pass over differences both between and within societies, produces a picture of any particular society that is grossly oversimplified. The arguments are set at a high level of generality. Thus, for example, the supremacy of agriculture over other forms of investment and income has been established, but only at a very general level. A sceptic might question whether it is in fact possible to offer a more penetrating analysis for the role of agriculture, and of its importance in relation to other sections of the economy, on the basis of the existing, non-quantitative, evidence. . . .

It remains to consider the effect of the city of Rome itself on agricultural production. A city of one million people could only have grown so big, and remained so big, by drawing on the resources of the whole empire. It is customary, and accurate, to view the western provinces as the main suppliers of Rome (leaving aside grain-rich Egypt): African and Sicilian grain, Gallic wine, African oil, Spanish wine and, more particularly, oil were consumed in quantity in Rome. Spanish oil alone came in at the rate of about four million kg per annum in around 55,000 amphorae, as Monte Testaccio, a hill of broken pottery, bears witness. The western provinces were closer to Rome and had made greater advances in agricultural production than the eastern provinces, which were already more or less completely developed, were only lightly garrisoned and experienced no significant spread of cities; Italy's contribution is usually overlooked, or played down. Worse still, Italy is commonly held to have fallen into gradual and inexorable decline, a victim of provincial competition. Yet one might have expected Italy to have prospered in the early empire, or at least those areas of Italy well placed to supply the capital city, once civil war and associated dislocations (notably the settling of large numbers of veterans) had ended, and the countryside could enjoy the benefits of freedom from the land tax, absence of an army to supply or man, and a reduced rural population. These expectations are to some extent realized, if one studies the performance of Italy, not so much in cereals—though as much as 10 per cent of

Rome's grain may have come from Tuscany, Umbria, Campania and Apulia under the Principate—as in the products that Rome's inhabitants were able to buy with the money they did not have to spend on grain, because of the stability and generous dimensions of the grain distribution system.

Foremost among these products was wine. Rome under Augustus needed more wine than ever. Italian wine producers responded in two ways, by the development of popular wines, particularly in Campania and the north Adriatic region from Veneto to Piceno, and by the diversification of *grands crus*. The early empire was a period of modest innovations in agricultural technology, to judge from the rather patchy accounts of Columella and the elder Pliny, more particularly the latter. Thus Pliny refers to Greek-invented devices for raising water, such as the water wheel and pump, in his discussion of the irrigation of a market-garden; and he presents stages in the development of the lever press in some detail and with attention to chronology. Columella's forte was arbonculture, especially viticulture. He himself introduced refinements of technique (for example, an improved auger for boregrafting) and as one of a new breed of provincial farmers 'who bought up farms in Italy. . . was well informed about and perhaps personally involved in the importation and acclimatization of more productive foreign vines and other fruit-bearing trees' . . . .

Rome, as far as we know, remained a city of around one million people at least until the second half of the second century. Provincial products poured in. Agricultural writers led the chorus of ritual complaint, but it must have been obvious to all that Italy with Rome in its midst could not be self-sufficient in the main products, let alone the luxury items required by the elite. On the other hand, it is difficult to believe that Italian farmers, those with easy access to Rome by river, sea or land, ever lost their share of the huge market provided by the capital city, whatever the quality of their products. Rome must always have absorbed most of whatever surplus remained, whether of wine or of some other product, after local and regional needs had been satisfied.

The period of the Principate, then, saw in the first place the expansion of provincial agriculture, especially in the West. To be sure, this was partly a consequence of public policies, and the fruits were tapped by successive Roman governments in the form of taxes and rents, and more directly through the extension of imperial landholdings outside Italy. Secondly, it saw a period of recovery followed by moderate prosperity in Italy, for example in the northern provinces from Lombardy to Histria, in the central areas of Umbria and inland Tuscany and in Campania and parts of Latium. Our sources for provincial agriculture are of course very limited, and archaeology does not and cannot fill the gaps in our knowledge left by literature. The treatise on agriculture that survives from the period, that of Columella, is Italy-centred, but by no means presents a full and accurate picture of the state of agriculture in Italy in the middle of the first century. The evidence that we have, however, is compatible with the hypothesis that in at least some areas of the agricultural economy of Italy and the provinces, step-by-step advances in techniques and knowledge were made, better crop-combinations and seed selections were practised, more efficient units of exploitation were arrived at and labour was more effectively utilized. Such changes represented progress, but within limits: they are consistent with a rise in productivity, but one of only modest dimensions. From a comparative perspective, that is to say, set against historical periods that saw major technological breakthroughs, the period of the Principate deserves to be categorized as one of relative stagnation.

Supplying the Roman Empire

Under the Principate, the Roman government was in a position to exploit the whole of the Mediterranean basin, north-western and central Europe and the Balkans. The existence of this massive empire had implications for distribution and consumption in Rome, Italy and the empire at large. Under the heading of distribution, one might ask: How did the city of Rome, the central government and the Roman army secure the consumption items they needed? How far was the government involved in the supply of essential foodstuffs? . . .

Augustan Rome was a city of around one million residents, and there may have been more. Recipients of Augustus' handouts of cash or grain numbered at various times 320,000, 250,000 and 200,000, by his own reckoning (*Res Gestae* 15). These were exclusively male citizens. The middle figure of 250,000 recipients, if eligibility began at the age of ten, implies a population affected by the grain dole of around 670,000. A slave population of 30 per cent, a reasonable estimate, brings us not far short of one million inhabitants, without counting in, on the one hand, resident free foreigners, and, on the other hand, citizens of both high and low status not involved in the grain dole.

One million people is a large number of consumers. No city in the western world grew so big again until London topped the one million mark in the eighteenth century. Rome could only grow so big, and remain so big, by drawing heavily on the resources of the whole empire.

. . .The interest of the government and the initiative of private traders combined to ensure that much more grain would come into Rome than that which was earmarked for the distributions, which fell far short of the requirements of the population at large. The government appreciated that there was a short-fall, even if it was not equipped to calculate its size, and was interested in making it up. The consumption needs of the court, administration and resident soldiers (around 21,000 men) had to be catered for. Then, families of three or more on the list of grain receivers, unless represented by more than one person, had to supplement from other sources a dole sufficient only for two people. Augustus showed an awareness of this when he issued double rations during the shortage that began in A.D. 6. The lowering of the age of eligibility was a more permanent strategy, followed by Trajan and possibly one or more of his predecessors. Finally, no emperor could disregard the rest of the population altogether. The political risks were too great. The whole Roman plebs was a privileged category.

Roman governments did not operate with the figures cited above, with the exception of the grain for the dole. They might, however, have had rough import targets. Perhaps not Augustus. His record suggests a lack of system and a dangerous degree of improvisation. Crises were resolved, not always very fast, rather than averted. It looks as if he did not always have adequate reserve stocks available, but was able to produce grain in emergencies by putting pressure on private grain holders and distributors. He did, however, bequeath to his successors a permanent office headed by a prefect of the grain supply. There are signs that the more responsible post-Augustan emperors were interested in introducing more order and regularity into the supply system than Augustus was able to achieve. Tiberius on one occasion dismissed contemptuously talk of crisis, pronouncing himself satisfied that he had succeeded in increasing the flow of grain from the provinces. In Tacitus' report of the incident Tiberius does not say how this was achieved, but it is likely that in his measures he was anticipating Claudius' panicky drive to add to the number of regular, bulk suppliers. This policy, extended no doubt by later emperors, and combined with an increase in the amount of tax- and rent-grain, brought stability to the system of supply, and ensured that Rome would avoid dangerous shortages except in conditions of civil war. It is in this context that we can begin to talk of government import targets.

At what levels would such targets have been set? Emperors and prefects of the grain supply appreciated that the amount of grain flowing into Rome varied from year to year in accordance with fluctuations in harvest levels in surplus-producing areas and the vagaries of the weather at sea. To be sure of building up adequate reserve stocks in all years, and to allow for damage to grain in transit or storage, the government had to set high targets, higher than estimates of real consumption, whatever rough-and-ready estimates existed.

Import targets or no, the consequence is the same. Rome imported much more grain than it needed. . . .

The government did not exercise direct control over the grain supply system at all stages.

The production, storage and processing of the grain can be dealt with briefly; collection and transport are more problematic. The bulk of the grain that reached Rome was grown on private property. It was exacted (as tax or requisition) or bought by the government or sold, in the market. The contribution of rent-grain from public and imperial estates (unattested but probable) is likely to have been much less significant. On the other hand, it is also likely to have increased, as confiscations and legacies brought more good quality arable land into imperial possession. In the matter of storage, too, one can envisage a steady extension of state ownership and control at the expense of private, so that whereas state grain overflowed into private granaries in the age of Augustus, state granaries were holding stocks of private suppliers in the age of Septimius Severus. Finally, once the grain earmarked for distribution was taken out of storage and handed out by officials of the government, the profitable business of converting the distributed grain and other unmilled grain into flour and then bread was in the hands of independent millers and bakers. Some of these were very prosperous, as the impressive private tomb of the baker Eurysaces at the Porta Maggiore in Rome bears witness. . . .

Conclusion

The cities of the Roman world were apparently able to cope with the periodic food shortages that they suffered, although there was a tendency, perhaps a growing tendency, to lean on the authority and charity of the imperial power. This was an ominous development.

This general conclusion must be qualified. The evidence is thin. Few cities are visible, and when they come into focus, we are given only a partial glimpse of their condition. The inscriptions that inform us about individual food shortages are honorific. Their function was to advertise the generosity of men who by their benefactions had averted crisis. They issued from communities that were not in serious disaray or slow decline. The latter did not expose their weaknesses through the medium of epigraphy.

The problem recedes once it is recognized that the central government had a firm stake in the survival and welfare of cities in general, less so in those of individual cities, with some exceptions. Cities were needed to perform a narrow range of essential administrative duties, and for this their economic viability and demographic base had to be preserved. But this general commitment to cities did not extend to the preservation of any individual community at a given level of prosperity. So the territories of cities and their revenues were increased or diminished; some were demoted and became subservient to others, some were promoted or created out of nothing, for a variety of reasons, often trivial. The continually changing pattern of urbanization in the empire is not to be mistaken for an endemic weakness in the administrative infrastructure of the empire.

A conclusion relating to the peasantry follows similar lines. The ebb and flow in the countryside, as peasant households collapsed, survived, migrated and prospered, should not be confused with the issue of the survival of the peasantry as a class. If there was no group survival of the farming population, then the cities, dependent upon the agricultural resources of the countryside, would certainly have been in a state of collapse. As a fourth-century prefect of the city of Rome put it to the Roman senate in time of famine in Italy: 'If so many cultivators are starved, and so many farmers die, our corn supply will be ruined for good. We are excluding those who normally supply our daily bread.'

It remains to bring these conclusions to bear on the issues raised earlier, the demands of the government and the way they were distibuted.

Taxation, tribute, impositions under some other name, were not a new phenomenon in the regions that made up the Roman empire. What occured as a result of imperial conquest and the imposition of empire-wide censuses was that tax was raised somewhat more efficiently and from a wider area than ever before. Tax rates remained relatively low, at least outside Egypt, and Vespasian is the only emperor known to have raised them. A high level of taxation was unnecessary. The requirements of the government were very limited, because its concerns were few.

Thus, the demands of the central government were not such as to threaten the future of Rome's subjects. Moreover, although those demands were greater in aggregate than those made by any previous imperial state in the Mediterranean region, they were also distributed throughout the empire, and the empire was big enough to absorb them.

The emperor Gaius (Caligula) is portrayed on a brass sestertius issued at Rome in A.D. 39 The legend C(aius) CAESAR identifies the emperor and the letters TR (ibunicia) P (otestate) III dates the coin to the third year of his reign.

IX

Caligula and the Politics of Madness

INTRODUCTION
Ronald Mellor

Gaius Caesar had the most distinguished genealogy of the Julio-Claudian emperors. Born in A.D. 12 to Agrippina and Germanicus, he was the great-grandson of Livia, Augustus and Marc Antony. The boy grew up with his parents in the military camps along the Rhine, where the soldiers called him "Caligula" after his tiny military boots. After the death of his father in 19 and the persecution of his mother and older brothers by Tiberius and Sejanus, the adolescent Caligula was brought to live on Capri with the reclusive emperor Tiberius, who named Caligula and his weak grandson Gemellus as his heirs.

At the death of Tiberius in 37, the will was set aside and Caligula alone was acclaimed emperor. There was genuine popular enthusiasm: a misanthropic hermit had been replaced by the son of the much-beloved Germanicus. The sources depict Caligula's beneficence during the first months of his reign: the sales tax was abolished; treason trials were controlled and political exiles were recalled to Rome; and the emperor was generous in sponsoring games. Though there is certainly evidence of cruel and erratic behavior in his boyhood, the ancient sources attribute his transformation to a severe illness he suffered in the autumn of 37 from which he emerged the monster and madman that the name "Caligula" has evoked for the last nineteen centuries.

His cousin Gemellus and the praetorian prefect Macro (who had helped him to the throne) were soon killed, and his uncle Claudius may only have survived as a butt for the emperor's vicious sense of humor. Treason trials were resumed, but with a new twist: senators were persecuted and executed so that their property could enrich the depleted imperial coffers. The emperor's prodigality entertained the Roman mob and enriched the praetorians, yet it emptied the treasury of Tiberius' hard-won surplus.

Although Marc Antony had died more than four decades before Caligula's birth, his influence on his great-grandson was remarkable. Caligula had been raised in his grandmother Antonia's house surrounded by Egyptian slaves, and his court assumed the trappings of Hellenistic monarchy. Incest with his sister Drusilla, performances as a singer and a charioteer, and his pretensions to divinity all outraged the Senate. He disposed of provinces and kingdoms as his personal possessions, as when he gave remote kingdoms to each of the three sons of King Cotys of Thrace,

---

the emperor's boyhood playmates in the imperial palace. His erratic behavior provoked confusion in Germany, rebellion in Mauretania (where he removed a popular king), and constant strife between Greeks and Jews in Alexandria.

The only solution was assassination, and we see here for the first time the surprising alliance between senators and praetorians which also paved the way for the murders of Nero and Domitian. In A.D.41 Caligula was struck down by the praetorian tribune Cassius Chaerea. Yet the dead emperor retained enough popularity that mobs demanded revenge, and his successor Claudius executed the assassins. Some scholars have been skeptical of the ancient version of Caligula's transformation; his early years displayed cruelty and there may have been more method in his later madness than Suetonius would accept. But these interpretations cannot now change the imprint that Caligula has left on the Western tradition: a lunatic with absolute power in which the state, the court and even the army must engage in the politics of madness to survive.

Life of Caligula

Suetonius

Suetonius' Life of Gaius Caligula is a particularly important source, since Tacitus' account of this reign was contained in the missing books 7–10 of his Annals. The biographer recounts the widespread delight that greeted the accession of this son of the popular Germanicus. But the reign soon took a turn for the worse; as Suetonius says, "So much for Caligula the Emperor; the rest of the history must deal with Caligula the Monster."

Suetonius' life of Caligula is a catalogue of repulsive depravity: incest with each of his three sisters, murders, a brothel of aristocratic women and boys in the imperial palace, and numerous instances of horrible cruelty. But we cannot resist smiling at the emperor's flamboyant gestures: an obscene password for his prim commander of the palace guard; a prohibition (under penalty of death) of the mention of "goat" in the emperor's presence—so sensitive was he of his balding head and hairy body; the emperor forcing Gauls to dye their hair red and learn a few words of German so he could parade them as German captives; and his desire to make his favorite racehorse consul. Suetonius is in his element as a chronicler of the bizarre.

The Youth of Caligula

1.   Caligula's father Germanicus, son of Drusus and the younger Antonia, was adopted by his paternal uncle Tiberius. . . .   •

4.   He was so respected and loved by his family that Augustus (to say nothing of the rest of his relatives) wondered for a long time whether to appoint him his successor, but finally had him adopted by Tiberius. He was so popular with the masses, that many writers report that he was in danger of being mobbed by crowds when he went anywhere; in fact, when he returned from putting down the rebellion in Germany, the entire praetorian guard went to meet him, despite orders that only two cohorts should go, and the whole populace, regardless of age, sex, or rank, poured out of Rome as far as the twentieth milestone.

7.   He married Agrippina, daughter of Marcus Agrippa and Julia, who bore him nine children. Two died in infancy, and one charming boy in childhood. . . . The other children survived their father: three girls, Agrippina, Drusilla, and Livilla, born in successive years, and three boys, Nero, Drusus, and Gaius Caesar. Much later, at Tiberius' instigation, the Senate proclaimed Nero and Drusus public enemies.

8. Gaius Caesar was born August 31, A.D. 12 while his father was consul. . . .

9. The troops called him "Caligula" ("Bootkins"), because he was brought up in their midst and wore little military boots. Their affection for him was evident for when they were running wild after the death of Augustus; the mere sight of Gaius calmed them down. They only became quiet when they saw him being taken to a nearby town for protection from their violence. Then they became contrite, grabbing the carriage to stop it and begging to be spared this disgrace.

10. Caligula accompanied Germanicus to Syria. On his return from there he first lived with his mother and, after her exile, with his great-grandmother Livia, whose eulogy he spoke from the Rostra, though he was not yet of age. Then he lived with his grandmother Antonia until, at nineteen, he was called to Capri by Tiberius where he assumed the gown of manhood and first shaved his beard. . . . At Capri many intrigued to get him to criticize Tiberius, but the young man treated the destruction of his family and his own ill-treatment with an incredible pretence of indifference, and he remained so obsequious towards the emperor and the court, that it was well said of him: "No one had ever been a better slave or a worse master."

11. Yet even then Caligula could not control his natural cruelty; he enjoyed watching the tortures and executions, and liked to revel at night in gluttony and adultery, disguised in a wig and a long robe. Tiberius indulged his passion for theatrical dancing and singing, hoping that these might soften his savage nature. The shrewd old man perceived his viciousness and used to say that to allow Gaius to live would prove the ruin of himself and of all men, and that he was rearing a viper for the Roman people.

12. Gaius soon married Junia Claudilla, daughter of Marcus Silanus, a man of noble rank. He was appointed augur in place of his brother Drusus, and immediately advanced to the office of pontiff with strong commendation of his dutiful conduct and general character. Since the court was depleted after the fall of Sejanus, Caligula was encouraged to hope for the succession. To improve his chances, after Junia died in childbirth, he seduced Ennia, wife of Macro, the praetorian prefect, even promising to marry her if he became emperor, and guaranteeing this promise by an oath and a written contract. Having through her wormed himself into Macro's favor, some think he poisoned Tiberius and ordered that the imperial ring be taken from him while he was still alive, but when the old man held it tight, that a pillow be put over his face. Another story reported that he strangled him with his own hands, immediately ordering the crucifixion of a freedman who protested the awful deed. And this may be true; for some writers say that Caligula himself later admitted that he had at least thought about parricide. They say that he often boasted, in speaking of his filial piety, that he had entered the bedroom of the sleeping Tiberius dagger in hand, to avenge the deaths of his mother and brothers; then, seized with pity, he dropped the dagger and left.

The Accession of Caligula

13. By thus gaining the throne Caligula fulfilled the highest hopes of the Roman people, or I may say, of all mankind. The memory of his father Germanicus and pity for his decimated family made him popular with the provincials and soldiers, many of whom had known him in his infancy, as well as with the entire population of Rome. Accordingly, when he set out from Misenum, though in funeral dress and escorting the body of Tiberius, yet his progress was celebrated by altars, sacrifices, and blazing torches, and the large, happy crowd called him such endearments as "star," " chick," "baby," and "nursling."

14. When he entered the city, the Senate and a mob which had forced its way into the senate-house unanimously gave him full and absolute power, and no attention was paid to the wish of Tiberius, who in his will had named his young grandson, Tiberius Gemellus, joint heir with Caligula. So great was the public rejoicing, that within the next three months, more than a

hundred and sixty thousand victims are said to have been sacrificed. A few days after this, when Caligula crossed to the islands near Campania, vows were put up for his safe return, while no one passed up the slightest opportunity of professing concern about his safety. When he fell ill, the crowd swarmed around the Palace; some vowed to fight as gladiators, and others posted placards offering their lives, if the ailing emperor were spared. . . .

15.   Gaius himself courted popularity in every way. After eulogizing Tiberius with many tears before the assembled people and giving him a magnificent funeral, he immediately sailed to the prison-islands to bring the ashes of his mother and brother back to Rome; and in stormy weather, too, to publicize his family loyalty even more. . . .He established annual Circus games in honor of his mother Agrippina where her statue would be carried in a carriage. In memory of his father he called September "Germanicus." Then by single decree of the senate, he heaped upon his grandmother Antonia all the honors Livia Augusta had enjoyed; he took his uncle Claudius, who until then had only been a Roman knight, as his colleague in the consulship; and he adopted his "brother" Tiberius Gemellus on the day that he assumed the gown of manhood, and gave him the title of Chief of the Youth. He included the names of his sisters in all oaths: "I will not hold myself and my children dearer than I do Gaius and his sisters;" as well as in the consular motions: "Good fortune attend Gaius Caesar and his sisters." To equal acclaim he recalled those who had been banished, and dismissed criminal charges still pending from Tiberius' reign.

16.   He banished certain sexual perverts from Rome, barely persuaded not to drown them. He allowed the works of Titus Labienus, Cremutius Cordus, and Cassius Severus, all suppressed by decrees of the senate, to be hunted up and published, saying that he wished that posterity know everything that had happened. He published the imperial budget, which had regularly been made public by Augustus, a practice discontinued by Tiberius. He allowed the magistrates unrestricted jurisdiction, without appeal to himself. He carefully revised the roll of the Roman knights, publicly ejecting those guilty of any scandalous act, but merely omitting to read the names of men convicted of lesser offenses.

Caligula the Monster

22.   So much for Caligula as emperor; we must now tell of his career as a monster. He assumed such titles as "Pious," "Child of the Camp," "Father of the Armies," and "Caesar, Greatest and Best." When he heard some kings disputing at dinner whose family was most noble, Caligula quoted Homer's line: "Let there be one Lord, one King." And he nearly took a crown at once and changed the semblance of a principate into the form of a monarchy. But on being reminded that he had risen above princes and kings, he then began to claim to divine majesty, and ordered that the most revered and beautiful statues of the gods (including that of Jupiter of Olympia) should be brought from Greece, in order to remove their heads and put his own in their place. He next extended his Palace to the Forum, and made the temple of Castor and Pollux its vestibule where he often stood between the divine twins to be worshipped by all visitors, some of whom hailed him as Latian Jupiter. He also set up a temple to himself as god, with priests and choice sacrifices. There was a life-sized statue of the emperor in gold, which was dressed each day in clothing such as he wore himself. The richest citizens used their influence and bribery to become priests of his cult. . . . At night he used to invite the full and radiant moon-goddess to his bed, while in the daytime he would talk confidentially with Jupiter Capitolinus, now whispering and then putting his ear to the mouth of the god, now in louder and even angry language; for he was heard to threaten in Homer's words: "Take me to heaven, or I'll get you!" He finally announced that Jupiter had persuaded him to share his home, so he joined his Palace to the Capitol with a bridge. . . .

23.   Due to Agrippa's humble origin, Caligula did not wish to be thought to be his grandson, and he grew very angry if anyone in a

speech or a song called Agrippa an ancestor of the Caesars. He even boasted that his own mother was born of an incestuous union between Augustus and his daughter Julia. . . . He often called his great grandmother Livia "a wily female Ulysses," and he dared to accuse her of low birth in a letter to the senate. . . . When his grandmother Antonia asked for a private interview, he refused it except in the presence of the praetorian prefect Macro, and by such insults he hastened her death, though some think that he also gave her poison. After she was dead, he paid her no honor, but watched her funeral pyre burn from his dining-room. He suddenly sent a tribune to kill his adoptive brother Tiberius Gemellus, on the pretext that he had insulted the emperor by drinking an antidote against poison while it was in fact medicine for a chronic cough. He also forced his father-in-law Silanus to cut his throat with a razor. He charged that Silanus had not followed Caligula when he sailed in a storm, but had remained hoping to seize Rome if the imperial ship sank, while he was in reality merely subject to seasickness and wished to avoid the discomforts of the voyage. As for his uncle Claudius, he spared him merely as a laughing-stock.

24.   He lived in habitual incest with all his sisters, and at large banquets he placed each of them in turn in the place of honor. They say he violated Drusilla when he was still a minor, and even that his grandmother Antonia, who brought them up together, caught them in bed. He later took her from her husband Cassius Longinus and openly treated her as his lawful wife, and when he was ill he made her heir to his property and the throne. When she died, he made it a capital offence to laugh, bathe, or dine in company with one's parents, wife, or children during the mourning period. He was so beside himself with grief that he suddenly fled Rome by night, crossed southern Italy and went to Syracuse; and returned as hurriedly without cutting his hair or shaving his beard. And later he always swore in important matters by the divinity of Drusilla, even before the assembly of the people or in the presence of the soldiers. He did not so love or so honor his other sisters, but he often prostituted them to his favorites. At

the trial of Aemilius Lepidus, he condemned them as adulteresses who conspired against him; and he not only made public letters in the handwriting of all of them, procured by fraud and seduction, but also dedicated to Mars the Avenger, with an explanatory inscription, three swords with which they planned to take his life.

25.   . . . Though Caesonia was neither beautiful nor young, and was already mother of three daughters by another, besides being a woman of reckless extravagance and wantonness, he loved her not only more passionately but more faithfully, often exhibiting her to the soldiers riding by his side, decked with cloak, helmet and shield, and to his friends even in a state of nudity. He did not honor her with the title of wife until she had borne him a child, announcing on the same day that he had married her and that he was the father of her baby. He took this baby Julia Drusilla to the temples of all the goddesses, finally placing her in the lap of Minerva and commending to her the child's education and training. And he was only convinced that he was her father when he saw her savage temper, which was even then so violent that she would try to scratch the faces and eyes of her little playmates.

26.   . . . He was disrespectful toward senators, making distinguished men run in their togas for miles beside his chariot and wait on him at table. Others he secretly put to death, yet continued to send for them as if they were alive, after a few days falsely asserting that they had committed suicide. . . .

27.   . . . He forced parents to attend the executions of their sons, sending a litter for one man who pleaded ill health, and inviting another to dinner immediately after witnessing the death, and trying to rouse him to gaiety by a great show of affability. . . .

30.   . . . When a different man than he had intended had been killed, through a mistake in the names, he said that the victim had also deserved the same fate. He often uttered the familiar line of the tragic poet: "Let them hate me, as long as they fear me."

31.   He even openly used to deplore the state of his times, because there were no public disasters, saying that the rule of Augustus had been

made famous by the Varus massacre, and that of Tiberius by the collapse of the amphitheater at Fidenae, while his own reign was threatened with oblivion because of its prosperity; and every now and then he wished for the destruction of his armies, for famine, pestilence, fires, or a great earthquake.

33.   As a sample of his humor, he stood beside a statue of Jupiter, and asked the tragic actor Apelles which of the two seemed the greater, and when he hesitated, Caligula had him flayed with whips, extolling his voice from time to time, when the wretch begged for mercy, as being sweet even in his groans. Whenever he kissed the neck of his wife or sweetheart, he would say: "Off comes this beautiful head whenever I give the word." He even used to threaten now and then that he would resort to torture to find out from his dear Caesonia why he loved her so passionately.

34.   In envy and cruelty he attacked men of almost every age. He demolished statues of famous men which Augustus had moved to the Campus Martius, so that they could not be set up again with their inscriptions intact; and afterwards he forbade the erection of the statue of any living man anywhere, without his knowledge and consent. He even thought of destroying the poems of Homer, asking why he should not have the same privilege as Plato, who excluded Homer from his ideal commonwealth. More than that, he all but removed the writings and the busts of Virgil and of Livy from all the libraries, railing at the former as a man of no talent and very little learning, and the latter as a verbose and careless historian. He also seemed intent on abolishing the legal profession, but at least he often threatened that lawyers would give no advice contrary to his wishes.

36.   He respected neither his own chastity nor that of anyone else. He is said to have had unnatural relations with Marcus Lepidus, the pantomimic actor Mnester, and certain hostages. . . . In addition to incest with his sisters and his notorious passion for the concubine Pyrallis, there was scarcely any woman of rank whom he did not approach. These as a rule he invited to dinner with their husbands, and as they passed by the foot of his couch, he would inspect them critically and deliberately, as if buying slaves, even putting out his hand and lifting up the face of anyone who looked down in modesty. Then when he felt like it he would leave the room, sending for the one who pleased him best, and returning soon afterward with evident signs of what had occurred, he would openly commend or criticize his partner, recounting her charms or defects and commenting on her conduct. To some he personally sent a bill of divorce in the name of their absent husbands, and had it entered in the public records.

37.   He exceeded all in reckless extravagance, inventing a new sort of bath and unnatural varieties of food and feasts; for he would bathe in hot or cold perfumed oils, drink pearls of great price dissolved in vinegar, and set before his guests loaves and meats of gold, declaring that a man ought either to be frugal or Caesar. He even scattered large sums of money among the commons from the roof of the basilica Julia for several days in succession. . . . He built villas and country houses with utter disregard of expense, caring for nothing so much as to do what men said was impossible. . . . To make a long story short, vast sums of money, including almost three billion which Tiberius Caesar had amassed, were squandered by him in less than a year.

38.   Having thus impoverished himself, from necessity he turned his attention to pillage through a complicated and cunningly devised system of false accusations, auction sales, and taxes. . . . A well-known incident is that of the senator Aponius Saturninus; he dozed on one of the benches, and as Caligula warned the auctioneer not to overlook the noble gentleman who kept nodding to him, the bidding was not stopped until thirteen gladiators were knocked down to the unconscious sleeper at nine million sesterces.

40.   He had the publicans collect new and unprecedented taxes, and then to avoid their commission, he used the centurions and tribunes of the praetorian guard. There were no goods or services on which he did not impose some form of tariff. He fixed a tax on all food sold in the city; and established a two and one-half percent tax on all lawsuits and legal

transactions. Porters paid an eighth of their daily wages, and prostitutes paid each day the price of one trick. (Even if prostitutes and pimps retired from the trade, they still had to pay this daily tax!)

41.   ... To leave no kind of plunder untried, he opened a brothel in his palace, setting apart a number of rooms and furnishing them to suit the grandeur of the place, where matrons and freeborn youths should stand exposed. Then he sent his pages to the public squares to invite young men and old to enjoy themselves, lending money on interest to those who came and having clerks inscribe them as contributors to Caesar's income. He even cheated at dice to increase his revenues. ...

42.   When his daughter was born, he complained that it added the cost of fatherhood to that of government and he took up contributions for the girl's support and dowry. He proclaimed that he would receive New Year's gifts, and on January 1 he sat in the entrance to the Palace to grab the coins which people of all classes showered in his hands and lap. Finally, seized with a mania for touching money, he would pile up gold pieces in some open place, walk over them barefoot, and roll around in them.

43.   Caligula had but one experience with military affairs or war, and then on a sudden impulse ... someone reminded him that he needed recruits for his body-guard and he was seized with the idea of an expedition to Germany. So without delay he assembled legions and auxiliaries from all over, conscripting troops and collecting unprecedented amounts of military supplies.

45.   Since there seemed little chance of action, he had a few Germans of his body-guard hidden across the Rhine and after lunch excited scouts reported that the enemy was close at hand. [He galloped off and claimed a victory.] Another time he took some German hostages from a school where they were learning Latin and secretly sent them on ahead of him; then he rushed from a banquet and pursued them with the cavalry as if they were runaways, caught them, and brought them back in chains, grossly exaggerating this play-acting.

46.   Finally, as if he intended to bring the war to an end, he drew up a line of battle on the shore of the English Channel, arranging his artillery; and when no one could imagine what he was going to do, he suddenly bade the soldiers to gather shells and fill their helmets and the folds of their gowns, calling them "spoils from the Ocean, due to the Capitol and Palatine." As a monument of his victory he erected a lofty tower, from which fires were to shine at night to guide the course of ships. Then promising the soldiers a gratuity of a hundred denarii each, as if this was unprecedented generosity, he said, "Go happy; go rich."

47.   For his triumph he chose a few barbarian captives and deserters and added the tallest Gauls who were "worthy of a triumph" as well as some of their chiefs. They had to dye their hair red and to let it grow long, but also to learn some German words and take German names for his triumphal procession. He also had the triremes used in the Channel hauled overland to Rome and he wrote to his agents to prepare the most lavish triumph at the least possible cost, taking whoever's property was necessary.

49.   When senatorial envoys came to ask him to return quickly, he roared, "I will come, and this will be with me," slapping the sword which he wore at his side. He also proclaimed that he was returning only to those who desired his presence—the equestrian order and the people—and he would no longer be fellow-citizen nor a prince to the Senate. He even forbade any senators to meet him. Then postponing his triumph, he entered the city on his birthday to an ovation. Within four months he perished, committing terrible outrages and planning still greater ones. For he had made up his mind to move to Antium, and later to Alexandria, after first slaying the noblest members of the two orders. Lest anyone doubt this, I should say that two notebooks entitled "The Sword" and "The Dagger" were found among his private papers, and both contained the names of those whom he had decided to execute. There was also a large cabinet full of all kinds of poisons, which they say were later thrown into the sea by Claudius and so infected it as to kill the fish, which were thrown up onto the shore by the tide.

50. Caligula was very tall and extremely pale, with an unshapely body, a very thin neck and legs. His eyes and temples were sunken, his forehead broad and grim, his hair thin and entirely gone on the top of his head, though his body was hairy. For this reason it was a capital offence to look down on him as he passed by or to mention a goat. While his face was naturally forbidding and ugly, he purposely made it even more savage, practicing all kinds of terrible and fearsome expressions before a mirror. He was sick both in body and mind. As a boy he had epilepsy and, though he became more resistant, yet at times he was hardly able to walk, to stand up, to collect his thoughts, or to hold up his head. He himself realized he had mental problems, and at times thought of going into retirement and clearing his brain. It is thought that his wife Caesonia gave him an aphrodisiac, which however had the effect of driving him mad. He was especially troubled by insomnia; he never rested more than three hours at night, and even for that length of time he did not sleep quietly, but was terrified by strange visions, for example once dreaming that the spirit of the Ocean talked with him. Therefore weary of lying in bed wide awake during the greater part of the night, he would now sit upon his couch, and now wander through the long colonnades, crying out from time to time for daylight and longing for its coming.

51. I think his mental weakness produced two contradictory faults in the same person, extreme assurance and, on the other hand, excessive timidity. This man utterly despised the gods, and yet at the slightest thunder and lightning shut his eyes, muffled up his head, and if it increased, leaped from his bed and hid under it.

53. Though no student of literature, Caligula was interested in oratory, and he was quick to speak and quite eloquent, especially if he had occasion to prosecute anyone. For when he was angry, words flowed easily and he became so excited that he could hardly stand still and his voice carried a great distance. . . .

54. Moreover he devoted himself with much enthusiasm to many other arts, appearing as a Thracian gladiator, as a charioteer, and even as a singer and dancer, fighting with the weapons of actual warfare, and driving in regional circuses. He could get so carried away by his interest in singing and dancing that even at the public performances he could not refrain from singing along with the tragic actor as he delivered his lines, or from openly imitating his gestures by way of praise or correction. Indeed, on the day when he was slain he seems to have ordered an all-night festival just so he could take advantage of the freedom of the occasion to make his first appearance on the stage. Sometimes he danced at night, and once he summoned three ex-consuls to the Palace at midnight, and as they sat terrified on a stage, he appeared dressed in an ankle-length tunic to dance to flute music and he then disappeared. And yet, as varied as were his accomplishments, the man could not swim.

55. Toward those whom he loved his affection became madness. He used to kiss Mnester, an actor of pantomimes, even in the theatre, and if anyone made even the slightest sound while his favorite was dancing, he had him dragged from his seat and scourged him with his own hand. . . . He was so passionately devoted to the green faction of charioteers that he constantly dined and spent the night in their stable, and in one of his revels with them he gave the driver Eutychus two million sesterces in gifts. He used to send soldiers on the day before the games to order silence in the neighborhood, to prevent the horse Incitatus from being disturbed. Besides a stall of marble, a manger of ivory, purple blankets and a collar of precious stones, he even gave this horse a house, a troop of slaves and furniture, for the more elegant entertainment of the guests invited in his name. It is also said that he planned to make him consul.

56. During this frantic and riotous career several considered assassinating him. But after one or two conspiracies had been detected and the rest were still waiting for an opportunity, two men made common cause and succeeded, with the connivance of his most influential freedmen and the officers of the praetorian guard. . . . They had decided to kill him when he left the Palatine games at noon. Cassius Chaerea, a praetorian tribune, demanded the principal part, for Caligula used to call him effeminate though he was getting on in years.

When he asked for the password the emperor would give him "Priapus" or "Venus," and when Chaerea had occasion to thank him for anything, he would hold out his middle finger to kiss, wiggling it in an obscene fashion.

57.   Caligula's murder was foretold by many omens. The statue of Jupiter at Olympia, which he had ordered to be taken to pieces and moved to Rome, suddenly uttered such a peal of laughter that the scaffolding collapsed and the workmen took to their heels . . . . The soothsayer Sulla, when the emperor asked him about his horoscope, declared that inevitable death was close at hand. The Oracle of Fortune at Antium warned him to beware of Cassius, and he accordingly ordered the death of Cassius Longinus, who was at the time proconsul of Asia, forgetting that the family name of Chaerea was Cassius.

58.   On January 24 just after noon Caligula hesitated whether or not to get up for luncheon, since he still felt queasy from overeating the day before, but his friends finally persuaded him to come out. In the covered passage through which he had to pass, some boys of good birth, who had been summoned from Asia to appear on the stage, were rehearsing their parts, and he stopped to watch and encourage them. . . . From this point there are two versions of the story: some say that as he was talking with the boys, Chaerea came up behind, and gave him a deep cut in the neck, having first cried, "Take that," and that then the tribune Cornelius Sabinus faced Caligula [and] stabbed him in the breast. Others say that Sabinus, after getting rid of the crowd through centurions who were in the plot, asked for the password, as soldiers do, and that when the emperor gave him "Jupiter," he cried "So be it," and as Caligula looked around, he split his jawbone with a blow of his sword. As he lay upon the ground writhing and calling out that he was still alive, the others stabbed him thirty times with the cry, "Strike again." Some even stabbed him in the genitals. The emperor's bearers ran to his aid with their poles as did his German bodyguards who slew several assassins, as well as some innocent senators.

59.   He lived twenty-nine years and ruled three years, ten months and eight days. His body was secretly taken to the Lamian gardens where it was partly burned on a hastily erected pyre and buried beneath a light covering of turf; later his sisters on their return from exile dug it up, cremated it, and consigned it to the tomb. Until then the caretakers of the gardens were disturbed by ghosts, and terrible spirits appeared every night in the house where he was killed, until at last it was destroyed by fire. With him died his wife Caesonia, stabbed by a centurion, while his daughter's brains were dashed out against a wall.

60.   The terror of those times can be seen in the reluctance to believe that he was dead. Many thought that Caligula himself had made up and circulated the report, to find out how men really felt towards him.

A Jewish View of Caligula

Josephus

Josephus was particularly interested in Caligula for his treatment of the Jews: both his reception of the famous Alexandrian embassy to him (whose leader Philo has recorded how the emperor ran from them in the imperial palace), and his desire to have his statue erected in the Temple in Jerusalem. That account has been printed in Chapter Seven above. Here the Jewish historian provides his analysis of Caligula's madness as well as an overall assessment of his character and achievements.

1.   Gaius not only exhibited the madness of his insolence in relation to the Jews who dwelt in Jerusalem and throughout Judaea, but he also sent it forth to spread over every land and sea which was subject to the Romans, and infected the empire with countless ills, such as had never before been chronicled in history. Rome above all felt the horror of his actions, since he gave it no more privilege than other cities, but harried the citizens, especially the senators and those who were of the patrician class or had special honours because of distinguished ancestors. He also devised countless attacks upon the equites, as they were called. The standing and financial influence of this group gave them equal status with the senators in the eyes of the city because it was from their ranks that the senate was recruited. He deprived the equites of their privileges and expelled them from Rome or put them to death and robbed them of their wealth; for it was usually as a pretext for confiscating their property that he had them slain. He would also have deified himself and demanded from his subjects honours that were no longer such as may be rendered to a man. When he visited the Temple of Jupiter which they call the Capitol and which is first in honour among their temples, he had the audacity to address Jupiter as brother. His other actions too did not fall short of madness. For instance, it was insufferable, he thought, to cross the bay from the city of Dicaearchia in Campania to Misenum, another maritime city, in a trireme. Then, too, he considered it his privilege as lord of the sea to require the same service from the sea as he received from the land. So the thirty furlongs of sea from headland to headland were connected by pontoons, which cut off the whole bay, and over this bridge he drove in his chariot. That way of travelling, said he, befitted his godhead. Of the Greek temples he left none unpillaged, giving orders that paintings and sculptures and all other statues and dedicatory offerings with which they were furnished should be brought to him; for it was not right, he said, that beautiful objects should stand anywhere but in the most beautiful place, and that was the city of Rome. With the spoils which he brought from Greece, he adorned his palace and gardens and all his residences throughout the land of Italy. He even dared to give orders to transport to Rome the "Zeus" that was worshipped by the Greeks at Olympia and was therefore called Olympian, a work of the artist Phidias of Athens. He did not, however, carry out this intention, for the chief technicians reported to Memmius Regulus, who had the assignment of moving the Zeus, that the work would be ruined if it were moved. It is said that Memmius postponed removing the statue not only for this reason but because of certain portents that were too serious to be discredited. He sent Gaius a letter reporting these matters and explaining his failure to carry out his orders. In consequence, he risked being executed, but he was saved by the death of Gaius which intervened.

2.   So far did Gaius' frenzy go, that when a daughter was born to him he actually carried her to the Capitol and deposited her on the knees of the statue, remarking that the child belonged to both him and Zeus and that he had appointed two fathers for her, but left open the question which of the two was the greater. Such was the behaviour that the world had to put up with. He

also permitted servants to bring accusations against their masters on whatever charges they pleased. Anything that was reported was bound to have serious consequences, because most of the charges were brought for his gratification or at his suggestion. Thus Polydeuces, the slave of Claudius, dared to bring an accusation against Claudius, and Gaius was tolerant enough to attend court when a capital charge was brought against his own uncle, expecting to receive authority to put him to death. He was, however, disappointed. As he had made all of the inhabited world over which he ruled a prey to informers and their evil work and had raised high the power of slaves over their masters, conspiracies were now commonly formed against him. Some of the conspirators were angry and sought vengeance for the wrongs they had endured, others counted on doing away with the creature before they fell foul of him and suffered disaster. Therefore, since his death not only was of great importance in the interest of all men's laws and the safeguarding of them, but our own nation was brought to the very verge of ruin and would have been destroyed but for his sudden death, I am resolved to give an exact account of everything that happened. I have another particular motive in that the story provides good evidence of God's power. It will comfort those who are in unhappy circumstances, and will teach a lesson in sobriety to those who think that good fortune is eternal and do not know that it ends in catastrophe unless it goes hand in hand with virtue. . . . [After his account of the conspiracies and murder of Gaius, Josephus moves on to an assessment of his character and achievement.]

5.   Such was the end of Gaius after he had been emperor of the Romans for four years lacking four months. Even before he succeeded to office he was a sinister character who had reached the peak of perversity, a slave to pleasure, a lover of slander, a man dismayed by danger and consequently most bloodthirsty against those of whom he was not afraid. He was greedy of power with one object only, to treat abusively or to bestow senseless largess where it least behooved him, one who obtained his revenue by means of slaughter and injustice. It was his object to be and to be thought stronger than religion or the law, but he had no strength to resist the flatteries of the mob, and regarded as virtuous achievement everything that the law condemns as disgraceful and on which it imposes a penalty. He was unmindful of friendship, however close it was and however great the occasion for it, and he would inflict punishment for the slightest matter on any at whom he became enraged. Everything that went with virtue he regarded as hostile; if he took a fancy to anything he tolerated no opposition to any command that he gave. Hence he even had sexual intercourse with his own sister: this conduct was the source from which the citizens' hatred of him grew fiercer and fiercer. For such a deed, which for ages past had not been recorded, drew them to incredulity and hatred of the doer. No great work, not even a palace, can be cited as constructed by him for the benefit either of his contemporaries or of posterity, excepting the harbour which he planned near Rhegium and Sicily for the reception of the grain transports from Egypt. This was, admittedly, a very great work, and of the greatest utility to seafarers. It was not finished, however, but was left half-completed owing to the laggard way in which he dealt with the task. This is explained by his great interest in useless objects, and by his squandering money on pleasures that would benefit no one but himself; and thus he suffered the gradual loss of any ambition for achievements that would have been without question greater. He was, moreover, a first-rate orator, deeply versed in the Greek and Latin languages. He knew how to reply impromptu to speeches which others had composed after long preparation, and to show himself instantly more persuasive on the subject than anyone else, even where the greatest matters were debated. All this resulted from a natural aptitude for such things and from his adding to that aptitude the practice of taking elaborate pains to strengthen it. For, being the grandson of the brother of Tiberius, whom he succeeded, he was under a great compulsion to apply himself to education, because Tiberius himself also had conspicuously succeeded in attaining the

highest place in it. Gaius followed him in his attachment to such noble pursuits, yielding to the injunctions of a man who was both his kinsman and his commander-in-chief. Thus he came to stand highest among the citizens of his time. For all that, the advantages obtained from education could not withstand the corruption wrought upon him by his rise to power; so hard to achieve, it seems, is the virtue of moderation for those who find it easy to take action for which they need account to no one. At the outset, owing to education and a reputation for a zeal for the higher pursuits, he took some pains to cultivate the friendship of men who were in every respect worthy of regard; but in the end, because of his surpassing brutality, their former loyalty was discarded; when hatred had grown in its place, they aimed at him the plot that cost him his life.

The Character of Gaius

J. P. V. D. Balsdon

The late Dacre Balsdon of Exeter College, Oxford, wrote in 1934 an apologia for Caligula. He did not justify the cruelty of the emperor, but he pointed out the exaggeration and bias of our sources and examined his behavior within the context of the times. He also praised certain administrative achievements and tried to provide rational (though hypothetical) explanations for some of Caligula's stranger exploits, such as the bridge of boats on the bay of Naples. This chapter provides his overall assessment of the personality of Caligula, in which he argues against the ancient view that the emperor was insane.

The appearance of Gaius, according to his biographer in antiquity, was remarkable, and far from handsome. He was very tall, large bodied but, like his father, too thin in the legs. He had a broad forehead and deeply set eyes; his hair was thin and, though he was not thirty years old when he died, he was already bald on the top of his head.... Coins, however, do not tally with this description; they portray a fierce, but not altogether displeasing, face. His portrait in stone cannot be identified with certainty. It has been suggested that the usual 'Caligula type' is really the representation of Gaius, son of M. Agrippa, and that two busts of attractive appearance, one in Venice and the other, discovered in the Alban lake, now in New York, are the true portraits of the Emperor Gaius. It is, of course, possible that his appearance changed somewhat after his serious illness at the end of A.D. 37.

He was a cultured man, and had received a good education, largely, no doubt, during his early twenties when he was living under the eyes of Tiberius on Capreae. In literature as in all else he was a fearless critic and his views are interesting and heterodox. Neither of the great Augustan exponents of Roman pride in her glorious past, neither Livy nor Virgil, was favoured with his capricious favour. He declared that Virgil was a man of no genius and of little learning, and that Livy was long-winded and careless. Concerning Homer he appears to have observed that Plato was the only man who had treated him properly, when he expelled him from his ideal state. Gaius stated that he would like to do the same himself. His criticism of Homer may well have been the same as that of Plato; he perhaps objected to the picture of the gods which was given by the epic poets. Varro had observed, and Q. Mucius Scaevola also, in the later days of the Republic, that there were three different accounts of the gods and three different theologies: those of the poet, the state, and the man in the street. Gaius, with his dislike of humbug of all kinds, perhaps thought it bad that a false picture of the gods should win general approval. Yet the criticism of Homer came from a man who evidently knew the poems well and quoted from the *Iliad* (with approval, on secular subjects) on more than one occasion. . . .

While residence on Capreae may have contributed much to his education, the strongest formative influences, as far as his character and beliefs were concerned, had already been exerted and had already done their work. Philo showed penetrating insight in his imaginary account of the antagonism of Gaius later to the advice of Macro. Macro was a commoner, while Gaius himself had from the cradle been surrounded by relations who were of the blood of princes. Of these his mother Agrippina was the most forceful, the woman who had impertinently reminded Tiberius on one occasion that 'she was the true image of Augustus, and born of heavenly blood'. With stories of wrongs, some real, the majority imaginary, that she had received from Tiberius and from Tiberius' mother, Julia Augusta, she made her son 'an enemy of the whole Claudian house.' He honoured those whom his mother taught him to honour, Germanicus his father, and Augustus his great-grandfather. Julia Augusta he hated, and he spoke scornfully of her ancestry—exhibiting in the process a carelessness in verifying historical facts such as he had criticized in Livy—and he is said to have felt shame on account of his descent from the commoner M. Agrippa; though inscriptional evidence shows that, at any rate in the early days of his government, he did not hesitate to advertise his shame.

Residence in the household of Antonia, while it did not create in him any different feelings towards the Claudii, gave him a fresh outlook on his own ancestry. He was reminded that Antony was his grandfather no less than Augustus. In many of his qualities he resembled Antony; indeed one modern scholar finds common elements in their oratorical styles. From Antonia, whom Gaius liked, he heard stories of her father, of a new, an attractive, Antony, of an eastern policy which, when explained by his daughter, instead of through the travesty which Octavian had once allowed to be put into circulation, had much to commend it. And in her house he met eastern princes, who, like himself,

had the blood of Antony in their veins. As Emperor Gaius brought the memory of Antony once more into honour. He curtailed celebrations of the anniversary of the Battle of Actium. Claudius, his successor, went farther in allowing honour to be done to Antony's memory, announcing once in an edict that he was the more anxious that his father's birthday should be celebrated because it was also the birthday of Antony.

It is not easy to distinguish the traits of character which Gaius inherited in the blood from those which he borrowed from the times. His imperiousness was no doubt inherited from his mother; his aestheticism may have come to him from his father and have descended through the family to his nephew Nero later. In his amours, like his sisters and his nephew later, he showed himself a true descendant of Julia and of Augustus and of a family which most aptly claimed Venus for its patron goddess. But little good is done by seeking after inherited qualities in his character. In his personal life he simply displayed in exaggerated form those weaknesses which were characteristic of the age in which he lived; he was prodigal, immoral, pleasure-loving, and cruel.

Of his private extravagances the authorities tell many stories; how he liked to dress in garments of silk studded with precious stones; how he dissolved pearls in vinegar, and then drank them; how he wore pearls on his shoes; how he bathed in perfumed oils. There are many stories too about gold. . . . He gave golden loaves of bread to his guests and golden barley to his horse. He built galleys, 'with ten men to an oar, with sterns set with gems, particoloured sails, huge spacious baths, colonnades and banquet halls, and even a great variety of vines and fruit trees,' and in these galleys he coasted along the shores of Campania. It would be a mistake to consider that this shining example of wasteful expenditure was the only extravagant man of his age. The elder Pliny mentions the freaks of Gaius in this respect among those of other men, and it is to be noticed that such insanities as the golden loaves and the golden barley find no place in his list. The stories clearly grew in the telling. The golden barley, for example, was not known to Suetonius; that corroborative detail is added by Cassius Dio or his source. No trace survives of the Campanian galleys, so curiously anticipatory of the modern luxury liner, but they differed little, in all probability, from those stationary galleys two of whose wrecks have recently been extracted from Lake Nemi. The skeletons of these boats, in size, respectively, 218 and 234 feet long and 65 and 78 feet wide, give little clue to their former magnificence. The Nemi barges appear to have resembled modern house-boats; their original use is uncertain, though the discoveries indicate that one may have been used in connexion with the cult of Diana. Because of the appearance of Gaius' name upon the lead water-pipes of the barges, it has been commonly assumed that they were built during his principate. Difficulties arise, however, from the experts' dating of the tile stamps and it has been suggested that the barges were built as late as the time of Vespasian (existing water-pipes of Gaius' date being called into service), or even, because of discoveries under the second barge, the principate of Trajan. It is possible that this commonly quoted instance of Gaius' extravagance must be discredited.

In his amours Gaius was immoral, if he is judged by the standards of modern respectability, and, even by the standards of his own times, if the stories of Suetonius and Cassius Dio are true, he was not above reproach. Yet the only fact which is not open to question is that he was four times married, three times in the short period of his rule. His first wife died in childbirth, his third was divorced probably because of the suspicion that she was barren, his fourth was pregnant when he married her. This last marriage was thoroughly successful; Caesonia was loyal and devoted to her husband until his death and her own. This rapid succession of marriages was not abnormal. Claudius was married four times, though not in so short a period of time. Octavian married three times during the years 43–38 B.C., and Livia was pregnant already by her former husband when Octavian married her. We must remember too the depleted condition of the Julian family at the time of Gaius' accession. He was desperately anxious to have a son of his own for his successor.

Gaius is further accused of the most gross seduction of other men's wives, of incest, and of unnatural affections. We must admit that there is not often smoke without fire, and that Gaius was certainly not a model of self-restraint any more than was any other of the Emperors from Julius Caesar to Nero; for against all of them one or other of these charges of immorality is brought. But, unless we are prepared to believe in the absolute truth of the charges which are brought by Suetonius against the moral life of the veteran Tiberius, we ought not to accept blindly all that the biographer tells us of the private life of his young successor. In particular the charge of incest appears to be without foundation. Seneca, who uses every stick that he can lay hands on, in order to beat the memory of his unsympathetic critic, says little of his sexual improprieties. Philo tells us little more than that the belief was current in his lifetime that he had seduced Ennia, the wife of Macro.

Gaius delighted himself excessively in the pleasures and entertainments of the times, and was, as we have seen, a most liberal purveyor of entertainment himself. He interested himself personally in the performers, and in associating himself with this disreputable class of persons—like Claudius and Nero after him—he shocked the respectable prejudices of the conservative members of the upper classes. Tiberius had never so demeaned himself at Rome. But now his successor was seen frequently with actors and charioteers, and known to be on familiar terms with Mnester and Apelles, the actors. In horse-racing he was a keen supporter of the Greens, dined often at their 'Jockey Club,',and once gave the driver Eutychus two million sesterces as a going-away present after dinner.

No less intense was his enthusiasm for gladiatorial and wild beast shows. He abused the populace if ever their interest appeared to flag; yet he abused the knights because their enthusiasm exceeded his own. He drew back the awnings when the sun was hottest and appears to have devised many refinements of torture. Yet some of his recorded eccentricities have little in them that is extraordinary. On one occasion five

Retiarii, marched against five Secutores, hit on an ingenious device for ensuring their lives. They submitted without a struggle. Then, when their death was commanded, one (or all) of them attacked and slew their unsuspecting victors. Gaius regretted this act as a most cruel murder and declared himself shocked that the audience could bear to witness it. He was criticizing the audience for not protesting against a piece of 'foul play.' Nor need he be condemned for brightening the performance by the occasional introduction of a comic turn, the matching of 'worthless and decrepit gladiators against mangey wild beasts.'

There is no suggestion in our authorities that Gaius was an habitual drunkard. It is therefore improbable that, as a modern historian has conjectured, his eccentric acts and sayings are to be explained by the fact that he was intoxicated at the time.

It was the belief of many of his contemporaries and the conviction of succeeding generations that Gaius was mentally unbalanced. Philo, Josephus, and Cassius Dio, in one way or another, speak of his 'mania,' though Josephus believed that this mania was able at times to be discarded. Seneca asserts that the pallor of his face was evidence of 'insania,' and Tacitus speaks of him as being 'impetuously minded'—'commotus ingenio'—and refers to his 'turbata mens,' as he refers in another place to the 'imminuta mens' of Claudius. These are occasional references, and nowhere is the theory propounded or developed that he was simply a madman. He certainly suffered, like Julius Caesar, from epileptic fits, but the great popularity which he won in the city of Rome in the first few months of his government, following the general approval of his succession, cannot be explained unless he was then a perfectly normal and attractive young man.

Now just as Cassius Dio begins his account of Tiberius' principate with a superb description of the fatal weakness of Tiberius, his duplicity, so at the beginning of his account of Gaius he outlines the chief weakness of Gaius, self-contradiction and inconsistency. At first he was an ultra democrat; later the epitome of autocracy; he seized on women and then spurned them; he

honoured his relations, then murdered Antonia; he abused Tiberius, and later praised him; he first forbade, then encouraged, the worship of himself.

Suetonius again stresses the contradiction in his character. It was Suetonius' rule to give first some account of the ancestry of his subject and afterwards to mention in succession his good points and his bad. In the case of Gaius the transition from good to bad is more strongly marked than in any other of the lives. 'So much,' he observes, 'for the Princeps; now for the monster.' 'Hactenus quasi de principe, reliqua ut de monstro narranda sunt.'

Philo appears at first sight to supply the clue. He believes that the serious illness which Gaius suffered at the end of A.D. 37 left its mark upon his character, and that, although he recovered from it, he was afterwards a moral wreck and a cruel tyrant. The silence of all our other authorities prevents us from accepting this most convenient theory. So patent a fact as the complete change of an Emperor's character after serious illness must have been mentioned over and over again, because it explains so neatly the reason for which Rome, which was in transports of joy over his accession in A.D. 37, should have felt little sorrow for his death four years later. No other writer gives Philo his support. Josephus declares that Gaius ruled well for two years, dating the change in his character to A.D. 38 or 39.

An even later date for his 'madness' is found in a 'belief' which Suetonius does not hesitate to recall, that Caesonia gave her husband a love-philtre, which had the effect of sending him mad. But in this event the 'madness' cannot have developed until late in A.D. 39. In the case of the contradictory qualities mentioned by Suetonius and by Cassius Dio, it is impossible to consider that there was any date at which Gaius changed his character, for one of the 'autocratic' acts recorded by Cassius Dio, the acceptance by Gaius of all the imperial titles in a single day, occurred within the first month of his government, while one of the acts for which Suetonius commends the Emperor, the release of the freedwoman Quintilia, was performed late in the year A.D. 40.

That Gaius changed the character of his government, chiefly his attitude to the Senate, in A.D. 39 is certain. He was then for the first time conscious that his life was in danger from plots. It was then too that he began rather late to show proper respect for the memory of Tiberius. From that date onwards he was frightened of assassination, and fear breeds cruelty. Indeed the facts that are recorded make it clear that he changed considerably in the course of this year, but not that he became insane, or indeed that he became really different from his earlier self. He merely developed certain undeveloped (and unpleasant) traits in his own character. His contemporaries naturally hated to make the admission that after Tiberius' death they had imagined, without any basis for their imagination, that Gaius was the paragon that they wanted him to be. He had then, though the public did not yet know it, what he rightly considered to be his most individual quality, . . . his shameless impudence. This quality was not entirely bad, for on its good side it amounted to frank outspokenness and dislike of sham and concealment. Unlike Tiberius, Gaius made no attempt ever to conceal his real feelings. His acts too were his own; there is no suggestion in his case, as there was in the case of Tiberius and Claudius, of ministers who sheltered themselves behind the Emperor, or behind whom the Emperor sheltered.

This open expression of Gaius' feeling was often undignified, for instance in the case of his exuberant behaviour and excited outbursts at the games; often it won ridicule for him and sympathy for his victims, as, for example, when he made Agrippina carry the ashes of her paramour from Germany to Rome, or (if the story is true) when he insulted his troops with the command to pick up shells. Again, after Drusilla's death he exhibited his grief with considerable loss to his personal dignity.

His indiscretions were the more serious because they were not easily forgotten. He had a sharp and a cruel tongue, penetrating insight into other people's weaknesses, and genius in summing them up in a startling phrase. A prisoner once begged him that he might be put to death. 'Are you alive now?' was his reply—

'nunc enim vivis?' The Jews were told that he thought them 'less knaves than fools'. Julia Augusta was described as a 'Ulysses in petticoats'—'Ulixen stolatum'; Silanus, a rich and stupid man, was 'a golden sheep.'

He reminded his grandmother that he had absolute and unqualified power. An occasional interlude in his amours was filled with the observation, 'To think that, when I give the word, off comes this pretty head. ' It is said that when the consuls once inquired why he smiled they received, to their surprise, a similar answer.

It is probable that many of his sayings were remembered and repeated in a context that was later invented to suit them, and that many of the stories of his outrages have been invented in this way. He may well have said that he would like to have an opportunity of showing real generosity, such as Tiberius had shown after the disaster to the grand stand at the show at Fidenae, and this may be the foundation of the declaration of Suetonius that

'he even used openly to deplore the state of his times, because they had been marked by no public disasters, saying that the rule of Augustus had been made famous by the Varus massacre and that of Tiberius by the collapse of the amphitheatre at Fidenae, while his own was threatened with oblivion because of its prosperity; and every now and then he wished for the destruction of his armies, for famine, pestilence, fires, or a great earthquake.' (Suetonius, *Gaius*, 31, tr. Rolfe.)

There was, after all, nothing outrageous in such an observation. The younger Pliny in his Panegyric of Trajan unashamedly gave thanks for the occurrence of a famine in Egypt, because it proved the excellence of the Roman corn supply. Further, in the case of the only comparable disaster, the fire of the Aemiliana of Rome in October A.D. 38, we know that Gaius gave assistance to the sufferers. It is probable too that on some occasion when the mob was tiresome—perhaps when it protested against the new taxes in A.D. 40—he did say that it was possible to deal with a troublesome individual by cutting off his head, but that unfortunately you could not do the same to a mob, and that he then said, 'it is a pity that they haven't a single neck.' This story has probably been improved in the telling, until the Emperor is said to have addressed this observation to the people, and to have made 'Oderint, dum metuant' ['Let them hate, as long as they fear'] a favourite saying. It is probable too that he did on some occasion come in from the courts either to Caesonia, who had been resting, or to some friends at the gambling table, and remark that he had spent a far more profitable afternoon than they had done. The fact that we have two editions of the story shows that it gained in the telling. Suetonius gives the following account:

'and (as he was one who in no wise could abide any little delay) he condemned upon a time, by virtue of one definitive sentence, above forty persons, liable to judgement for sundry and divers crimes; making his boast withal unto his wife Caesonia, newly wakened out of her sleep, what a deal he had done while she took her noon's repose.'

Cassius Dio has heard a far better story:

'at another time he was playing at dice (in Gaul), and finding that he had no money, he called for the census lists of the Gauls and ordered the wealthiest of them to be put to death; then, returning to his fellow-gamesters, he said: 'Here you are playing for a few Denarii, while I have taken in a good hundred and fifty millions.'

Again, it was probably the accident of baldheaded men standing at either end of a file of prisoners, and not mere capricious selection, which led him to order execution 'a calvo ad calvum'—from baldhead to baldhead.

Nor is it likely that the magnificent stories about his favourite horse, Incitatus, rest on a large foundation of truth. Suetonius is cautious in his version. There is a story, he observes, that Gaius intended to make him consul. Once again the story is much improved in Cassius Dio's telling.

'He even promised to appoint (his horse) consul, a promise that he would certainly have carried out if he had lived longer.'

Gaius had more serious failings than any other of the Julio-Claudian emperors, with the possible exception of Nero, but madness was not one of them. He came to power with no experience and with unbounded conceit. He was greeted with extravagant adulation by all classes at Rome, and his head was turned. Contempt for the insincerity of the Senate and the discovery of plots against his life turned him into a cruel tyrant in his dealings with the senatorial class at Rome.

Outside that class his death was received with resignation. It evoked no widespread grief, nor, on the other hand, did it rouse the bloodthirsty exultation which in the city of Rome had followed the news of Tiberius' death. The Jews were delighted, imagining in their folly that the danger of an unfriendly Roman government had disappeared forever. For the Senate at Rome joy was no sooner felt than it was swallowed up in the sorrow of Claudius' accession. The German armies, remembering their bitter insults from Gaius, were doubtless satisfied with his murder, and at Hofheim, as we have seen, some of them satisfied their feelings by defacing his image on their coins. For the rest, the soldiers had a magnificent donative in view—the second in four years. Provincial governors and municipal magistrates duly gave orders for the effacing of Gaius' name upon inscriptions; in one case at least it was simply replaced by the name of Claudius. The new Emperor was old enough to understand the value of civility and affability and wise enough to continue the increase in centralization of government, and the imperial projects that had been conceived by Gaius. He never won the affection of the senatorial class, among whom he wrought far greater havoc by execution than Gaius had had time to do. There was no suggestion after his death, as there had been after the death of Gaius, that his memory should be damned. This time the upper classes kept their exultation to themselves and with Claudius' successor, a youth younger than Gaius had been at his accession, they voted him 'heavenly honours.' They subsequently amused themselves at Seneca's satiric representation of the new god's translation, not to Heaven, but to Hell, where he was claimed, and adjudged, a slave of the nephew who had once threatened to duck him—to be handed by that nephew to Aeacus, and by Aeacus to his freedman. The senators were learning painfully that they could not safely hope to do more than get their own back on an Emperor in a satire after he was dead. Their historians had even better opportunity—and they took it.

The Emperor Caligula: A Re-evaluation

Arther Ferrill

Professor Arther Ferrill of the University of Washington, in an essay written for this volume, provides us with a preview of his forthcoming biography of Caligula. The essay reacts against Balsdon and other recent historians who have tried to show that Caligula was sane, albeit eccentric, and that there was a certain consistency in his policies. Ferrill prefers to accept the ancient judgments on "Caligula the Monster" as essentially justified and suggests that the popular view of the mad Caligula is perhaps more convincing than the scholarly rationalizations.

There is a twist on Lord Acton's famous observation that goes "Power corrupts, and absolute power is even nicer." Inevitably the Roman Emperor Caligula comes to mind, since he did seem to enjoy his power so much, even though he was in many ways a tortured, tormented ruler. After the death of the hated Tiberius, Romans looked forward to the reign of the new, youthful prince of the Julio-Claudian line, son of the popular general, Germanicus. But Caligula proved in the end to be more than a disappointment—his reign was an unmitigated catastrophe, a disaster that was salvaged only by the timely assassination of the immature leader before he had reached the age of thirty.

There have been many popular treatments of Caligula in the twentieth century, including one in the movie, *The Robe*, as well as a pornographic movie made by the publisher of *Penthouse* magazine. And few viewers of the teleplay, *I, Claudius*, based on Robert Graves' novel, will ever forget the wonderful portrayal of the mad emperor by John Hurt. Although popular versions of Caligula's reign vary tremendously in their historical accuracy, they generally all present the Roman emperor as demented and cruel. For the most part, as we shall see, this popular view of Caligula is actually sounder than the ones advanced by twentieth-century scholars, who have offered rationalizing explanations of the mad ruler's behavior.

The most famous of modern, scholarly works on Caligula is J. P. V. D. Balsdon's book, *The Emperor Gaius*. First published more than fifty years ago in 1934, the same year as *I,* *Claudius*, it is a skillful defense of Caligula. Balsdon argues with all the rhetorical devices of an Oxford Don that the emperor, though a disastrous ruler, was not as bad as the ancients believed, and that many of the charges made against him were made also against other emperors, some of whom are considered to have been relatively good. Balsdon simply rejects as fabrications the most extreme stories about Caligula, such as incest with his sisters. In the end Balsdon pronounced Caligula sane. Two biographies by French authors have treated Caligula with compassion, and a friend of Freud, Hanns Sachs, has written a psychobiography that tends to give a semblance of rationality to the madman.

We cannot, however, be misled by these modern, scholarly arguments. Caligula was crazy, and any attempt to diagnose his illness is bound to fail, since there is so little evidence that is clinically useful by twentieth-century standards. But the antics of an Idi Amin or an Emperor Bokassa in the last two decades are nothing in comparison with the more than three years of unrestrained rule by the great-grandson of Augustus, a young man who ruled over all the world. Naturally not everyone in the Roman Empire tasted the emperor's cruelty. Those who were closest to him felt it most. Generally Roman subjects in the capital rather than in the provinces, aristocrats in the Senate rather than commoners in the streets, primarily suffered from Caligula's tyranny. But towards the end of the reign even relations with the plebs deteriorated, and according to Suetonius, Caligula wished that "the Roman people had but one neck."

Caligula was born on August 31, A.D. 12 at Antium in Italy. The emperor Augustus was still alive, although he would die two years later. At the time there was no reason to believe that the infant boy would ever be emperor, since there were elder brothers in line ahead of him. He was, nevertheless, a prince, son of the great Germanicus, who was next after Tiberius in the line of succession. Caligula's mother, the strong-willed and outspoken Agrippina, was the daughter of Julia and Marcus Agrippa and the granddaughter of Augustus himself. On his father's side Caligula traced his ancestry back to Mark Antony, since Germanicus' mother, Antonia, was the daughter of the great Triumvir and of Octavia, Augustus' sister.

At birth Caligula's name was Gaius Julius Caesar Germanicus, but at the age of two or three he was given the nickname "Caligula" by troops under his father's command in the camps in Germany. The little boy had been dressed up in military uniform and wore the *caliga*, the half boot. Caligula simply means "Little Boots," a name that the emperor grew to dislike. Some modern scholars have insisted on calling him the Emperor Gaius, but "Caligula" has remained far more popular.

When Germanicus was transferred to the east early in Tiberius' reign, Agrippina and Caligula went with him. There, in A.D. 19, at Antioch in Syria, when Caligula was only seven years old, the still youthful Germanicus died under mysterious circumstances, and poisoning was suspected. In fact, Agrippina accused Piso, Governor of Syria, of the act and claimed that he had done it on Tiberius' orders. In the teleplay, *I, Claudius*, Caligula is implicated in the death of his father, but there is no evidence for that other than the fact that later in life Caligula revealed an expertise in poisons and even wrote a treatise on them.

After the return to Rome, Caligula lived with his mother (A.D. 20–28). This was the period of the ascendancy of Sejanus, Tiberius' Pretorian Prefect, a dangerous time for any member of the imperial family. Caligula's mother was banished in 28, and then he lived with Livia. Upon her death in 29, he moved in with his grandmother, Antonia, after giving Livia's funeral oration, though he had not liked the emperor's mother. Antonia was different. The future emperor savored his stay with her and enjoyed the company of some of her other friends, particularly the Jewish prince, Agrippa. While living with Antonia, Caligula's eldest brother, Nero, died in exile, a victim of Sejanus' ambition. Later Tiberius called Caligula to the imperial island retreat at Capri (A.D. 32–37). The young prince's mother and sole surviving brother, Drusus, both died in A.D. 33. It must have been difficult for Caligula, who later showed that he loved the members of his family deeply, to pretend, as he had to do in Tiberius' presence, to be unaffected by what had happened to them.

Tiberius had given Caligula almost no experience in public life. The young man had served as priest in 31 and as quaestor in 33, but otherwise had enjoyed no official offices. Sejanus, who fell in 31, had done his work well. In the last years of Tiberius there were almost no surviving male heirs. Claudius was considered an embarrassment to the family. Finally in A.D. 35 Tiberius drew up a will in which he named Caligula and Tiberius Gemellus, the emperor's young grandson, as his joint heirs. But when Tiberius died in 37, the Pretorian Prefect, Macro, supported Caligula for the purple, and the Senate declared the emperor's will invalid so that the popular son of Germanicus would not have to share the throne. It is not likely, despite ancient rumors to the contrary, that Caligula had a hand in Tiberius' death. Seneca, who hated Caligula, later wrote that Tiberius had died a natural death.

Although crowds gathered in the streets urging the new regime to throw Tiberius' body into the Tiber, Caligula insisted on a decent funeral. In other respects, however, he showed a desire to separate himself from the earlier reign and spoke critically of Tiberius. To great rejoicing the twenty-five-year-old emperor declared his desire to cooperate with the Senate, recalled all exiles from banishment, and personally sailed to the islands of Pontia and Pandateria and brought back the ashes of his brother and mother to the Mausoleum of Augustus. The urns and inscriptions still survive. He publicly burned all incriminating documents connected with their cases. He made his grandmother Antonia and his three sisters, Julia Agrippina, Julia Drusilla, and Julia Livilla, honorary Vestal Virgins, and Antonia was named Augusta, an honor previously accorded only to Livia. In a great show of magnanimity, Caligula adopted Tiberius Gemellus and allowed his uncle Claudius to hold a consulship. Censorship was relaxed, and previously banished works were allowed to circulate. The plebs were kept happy with lavish games financed with the vast treasury surplus left behind by the parsimonious Tiberius. Large amounts of money were paid out as gifts or bonuses to the 200,000 Romans who received free grain.

The first few months of the new reign were among the happiest in Roman history, but in October of 37 the emperor fell ill and nearly died. Philo Judaeus later said that this illness had turned the emperor's mind, and some modern historians believe that Caligula suffered a nervous breakdown. Others have suggested hyperthyroidism, acute encephalitis or simply an unknown serious illness. Nor is there universal agreement that the disease of 37 was the decisive turning point in Caligula's life and reign. No ancient author except Philo says so, yet many ancient authors, including Josephus, Dio Cassius, Seneca, Tacitus and Suetonius, regarded Caligula as insane. Josephus specifically attributes the beginning of evil in Caligula's reign to the year 39, but the other authors imply that he had been unbalanced throughout, going back even into the reign of Tiberius. The latter, in my view, is the most likely explanation. Accession to the imperial throne merely provided a greater stage for madness, opening opportunities after the death of Tiberius that had been closed before. That it took a few months for the main lines of the new emperor's personality to show clearly is hardly surprising.

It is difficult to know exactly how to interpret many of the stories told in antiquity about Caligula. Taken one at a time they seem incredible. He is supposed to have had incestuous relations with all three of his sisters and to have been deeply in love with one of them, Drusilla. Certain it is that when that favorite sister died in

38 Caligula gave her a funeral more magnificent than Livia's, almost equal to Augustus'. A period of public mourning was proclaimed for the whole empire that lasted several months, and it was enforced so severely that, according to Dio Cassius, a man was put to death for selling hot water which would have been used for mixing with wine, since public drinking was forbidden during the period of mourning. Several months after Drusilla died Caligula was still in severe grief, and he finally proclaimed her a goddess when a senator was found who testified that he saw her ascending to heaven. Records of the Arval Brethren that survive today testify to the official consecration. Drusilla's statue was dedicated in the temple of Venus, and there were many other honors including construction of a special temple devoted solely to her. Balsdon doubts the stories of incest, but Caligula's reaction to the death of his sister has convinced others of their credibility.

We are also told that he took the wives of prominent dinner guests into another room, forced them to have sexual relations with him, and then returned to talk about their skill in love-making in front of their husbands. He once invited a father to dinner immediately after the son's execution and made the poor man laugh and joke throughout the meal. An equestrian who was about to be thrown to the wild beasts shouted that he was innocent. Caligula had him brought back, cut out his tongue, and led off again for punishment. Probably the most famous story about Caligula is that he intended to make his favorite horse, Incitatus, a consul and was prevented from doing so only by his timely assassination. There are many other similar anecdotes, and no single one of them is necessarily true, but taken together they constitute a considerable indictment against the emperor.

As time went by, Caligula's relations with the Senate grew worse, and in 39 they broke down completely. Even earlier, in 38 before the death of Drusilla, he had executed Macro and Tiberius Gemellus. Then in 39 the emperor became a staunch defender of the memory of Tiberius, and before the senators he gave a strong speech excoriating them for their behavior under his predecessor. The following day they met and passed a resolution calling for an annual sacrifice to the Clemency of Caligula because he had not put them to death.

It was immediately after this incident that Caligula ordered the bay from Puteoli to Baiae, near Naples, bridged by boats. A road similar to the Appian Way was constructed over anchored merchant ships, a distance of more than three Roman miles. For two days he rode back and forth over the road wearing the breastplate of Alexander the Great as well as a cloak of gold and an oak leaf crown. Some believed that the emperor did this to inspire fear in the Germans and Britons, and Balsdon has suggested that it was done to impress Parthian hostages who were present. Equally plausible, however, is that it was done capriciously to surpass the deeds of Xerxes or because an astrologer had once said that Caligula was less likely to be emperor than he was to "drive his horses across the bay of Baiae."

Then in the autumn of A.D. 39 Caligula departed Rome for campaigns in Germany and Britain. He returned to the capital a miserable and ridiculous failure in the summer of 40. Although the testimony of antiquity is unanimous on this point, some modern scholars have attempted to show that the emperor was more successful, or at least more reasonable, than Suetonius, Dio Cassius and Tacitus believed. The ancients said that the campaign was a spur-of-the-moment idea, motivated by a desire for raising money and getting new recruits for the imperial bodyguard. A vast force—some 200,000 men—was assembled in Gaul. Caligula's pace was erratic; it was sometimes so fast that the Guards could not keep up, and at other times so leisurely that he travelled in a litter borne by eight bearers and forced the inhabitants of towns, as the imperial entourage approached, to sweep the roads and sprinkle them with water to control the dust.

In the German "campaign" Caligula advanced with the army across the Rhine, organized a mock battle against his own German bodyguard, claimed a great victory, and reprimanded the Senate and People for living a life of luxury at Rome while he was exposed to the dangers of war. Then he withdrew, having done more damage to his subjects and soldiers, according to Suetonius and Dio Cassius, than he had to the Germans.

The British "expedition" was even more absurd. Having assembled his army on the Channel, the emperor departed in a trireme, returned to shore, mounted a high tower, and ordered his troops to start picking up shells as plunder from the sea to display in his triumph. Before this so-called invasion Caligula had already been hailed as "Britannicus" in anticipation of a great conquest. After paying the troops a victory bonus, he then ordered his army to be decimated, but when mutiny broke out, he rushed back to Rome to celebrate a triumph. He chose some of the tallest Gauls from the Roman province, had them dye their hair red, take German names, and march as apparent captives. Finally, he accused the Senate of trying to thwart his celebration and cancelled the whole thing.

Balsdon and others have offered several rationalizing explanations of these two sorry affairs—that the expedition into Germany was simply a training maneuver; that the Roman army mutinied rather than cross the Channel; that ancient authors misunderstood technical military terminology, confusing the word for shell with the same word for a certain kind of military equipment; that there were not enough ships for the invasion; that Caligula did not want to get too far away from the Senate; and that the invasion of Britain was also simply a mock maneuver for training. Skillful interpretation of the ancient authors permits some reconstruction and modification of what they tell us, but there is no evidence at all for these modern revisions. They are based on the conviction that ancient authors are incredible, but it is not really incredible that Caligula was merely insane. One need not look for a deeper explanation.

One especially significant event occurred while the emperor was in Gaul. He detected a major conspiracy led by Gnaeus Cornelius Lentulus Gaetulicus, who had been the Roman governor of Upper Germany for nearly ten years. Gaetulicus had somehow managed to involve Caligula's two surviving sisters, Agrippina and Livilla, and Drusilla's former husband, Aemilius

Lepidus, in the plan to murder the emperor and replace him with Lepidus. Several other senators in Rome were apparently implicated. Caligula struck fast. Gaetulicus and Lepidus were executed, and Agrippina and Livilla were banished. The property of the two sisters was put up for auction in Lyons in Gaul, where it fetched a great deal of money. This apparently real threat served to make the emperor even more unsure of himself, frightened, and therefore more tyrannical, than he had been before.

Although Caligula returned to the vicinity of Rome in May of 40, he did not actually enter the city but went instead down to the area around Naples. He spent the entire summer there, perhaps afraid of his opponents in Rome. It was probably at this time that he began openly to proclaim his own divinity and ordered that his statue be placed in the temple at Jerusalem. Disturbances broke out in Alexandria when Greeks in that city demanded that statues of the emperor be placed in the Jewish synagogues. The Jews of Alexandria sent an embassy to Caligula under the theologian Philo, who, we are told, had to chase the emperor from room to room only to hear him observe that people who "think me no god are more unfortunate than criminal." Agrippa used his influence with the emperor to persuade him to rescind the order for Jerusalem, but Caligula later changed his mind. If Caligula had not been assassinated, there would almost certainly have been rebellion in Palestine.

In the meantime, in Campania and later in Rome, the emperor cavorted around in the costumes of various gods. First he impersonated some of the minor gods, but soon he moved on to major Olympians: Ares, Hermes and Apollo. It is Caligula's identification with Jupiter, however, that is especially significant. We are told that he wanted to remove the famous statue of Zeus in Olympia from its temple and bring it to Rome, where he intended to replace the head with his own. According to Suetonius and Dio, the statue laughed. In some of our sources Caligula is depicted as Jupiter's equal and also as his rival, so it was not always simply a matter of identification with the great god. On one occasion Caligula asked the famous actor Apelles who was greater, Jupiter or the emperor. On the other hand, Dio Cassius reports that Caligula was so closely identified with Jupiter that the name even appeared in official documents. In the last few months of A.D. 40 he actually established a formal cult to himself as a god, complete with a temple on the Palatine, priests and priestesses.

He did not finally return to Rome itself until August 31, A.D. 40. He had less than five months to live, but much happened in the capital at this time. There were several conspiracies and murders. A reign of terror and of madness horrified the senatorial aristocracy, and even the plebs began to be disenchanted with their high-spending, fun-loving ruler. For one thing, he had run out of money, and to fill his coffers he resorted to confiscation and fiscal abuse. He voided the wills of all who had "intended" to name him heir but had failed to do so. To people who loudly proclaimed that they had made him heir he sent presents of poisoned food. He condemned many to death in order to confiscate their estates, since the property of convicted criminals reverted to the imperial treasury. He personally conducted auctions in which he forced bidders to offer fantastic prices. One senator who dozed and nodded his head at such an auction woke up to find that he had bought thirteen gladiators at a price of 90,000 pieces of gold. According to one report, the emperor actually opened his own brothel. Ancient authors say that Caligula had a special fondness for actors, charioteers and gladiators and spent huge amounts on games and the theaters. He also forced other Romans to pay for the games and spectacles.

The return to Rome at the end of the year 40 was, according to the emperor, only for the equestrians and the plebs and definitely not for the senators, with whom Caligula declared open war. Seneca claims that he considered killing them all. In fact there were conspiracies and executions, and members of the Senate were required to prostrate themselves before their ruler. Inevitably, under the circumstances, there was a final conspiracy, a successful one that ended the regime. At least some of the conspirators were ideologically motivated, believing that liberty was at issue, but many simply hated the monster emperor. One of the leaders was the eminent senator Lucius Annius Vinicianus, who had formerly been consul and was an associate of the late conspirator, Aemilius Lepidus. A Pretorian Prefect, Marcus Arrecinus Clemens, and one of the emperor's freedmen, Callistus, were also involved. Several tribunes of the Pretorian Guard were especially enthusiastic conspirators, and one of them, Cassius Chaerea, was actually zealous. Caligula had teased him often because of his reputation as a womanizer by giving him as password for the day such words as "Priapus" or "Venus." This made Chaerea a laughing-stock, and he hated the emperor for it. The password for the conspiracy was "Liberty."

The opportunity came on the day of January 24, A.D. 41 Caligula appeared in the theater for the last day of the Palatine Games, and the conspirators were going to strike him down at lunch. When the lunchbreak came, however, the emperor did not want to leave, since he was sick from having eaten too much the night before. But he was finally persuaded by friends to go with along a covered walk, where he noticed some boys rehearsing the Trojan war dance. At that point Cassius Chaerea hit him with his sword. As Caligula fell he was stabbed by others, and his wife, Caesonia, was also killed. A young daughter, Julia Drusilla, was picked up by her feet and her head was smashed against a wall. The German bodyguard appeared on the scene, but it was too late to save the emperor's life. A tyrant, one of the most notorious in the history of the western world, had been slain.

It is difficult to assess his reign, which was probably more colorful than significant. Caligula did not rule long enough, as Nero did later, to generate severe strains in the structure of the Roman Empire. There was no civil war after his death, and the greatest trouble spot, in Palestine, was pacified after the assassination removed the problem that had been brewing in Jerusalem. The work of Augustus and Tiberius had been good enough to permit the Empire to survive even the reign of a madman, who fortunately ruled for less than four years. Much later another crazed ruler, Commodus (180–192), would do drastic damage to the state, but

he ruled for more than a decade before he was strangled in his bath. One of the reasons that twentieth-century scholars have tried so hard to discredit the tradition about Caligula in the ancient sources is that he seems to have left no permanent legacy of destruction and damage in his passing. One could argue that he thoroughly demoralized the senatorial aristocracy and left it a helpless victim to the whims of Claudius and Nero, but that raises issues difficult to address in this essay.

In my view Caligula had no consistent foreign policy or provincial policy or fiscal policy or policy of any kind. Although there are relatively long chapters or sections of chapters in Balsdon's book and the two books by French biographers on Caligula's "policy" in various governmental areas, close examination will reveal inconsistency and simple maladministration. One example is that he transferred the elections from the Senate back to the People and then later from the People back to the Senate again. His attitude towards the Senate was hardly predictable and changed drastically, to put it mildly, on several occasions during his reign. Even his attitude towards his own deification was not always entirely clear. He seems to have indulged himself shamelessly when he was angry enough, or drunk enough, or giddy enough to do so. Then he would have moments of sobriety and responsibility, moments which he could not maintain for extended periods of time.

Caligula was a monster, as Suetonius claimed. It certainly was not entirely his fault. His mother had undoubtedly poisoned his mind, and Tiberius did almost nothing to prepare the young man for assumption of imperial power. A twenty-five-year-old, suddenly placed in control of the world, whose father had died when he was only seven, whose mother had railed against the reigning emperor (a member of the family), and who was eventually banished and killed herself, whose brothers were murdered, who had to pretend that he lived in a reasonable world and that he was not bothered by what had happened to him, who was then fawned over and courted by every miscreant in Rome, might in fact find it difficult to offer firm, balanced and judicious leadership in the world's greatest empire.

Claudius is depicted on a large silver cistophorus (a triple denarius) issued in Asia about A.D. 41–42. The obverse of this Greek-style coin contains an expressive imperial portrait, while the reverse depicts a temple of Roma and Augustus with statues of Roma and Claudius.

X

Claudius The Fool?

INTRODUCTION
Ronald Mellor

Tiberius Claudius Nero, whom we know as the emperor Claudius, was for long regarded as an embarrassment to the imperial family and was kept out of public view as much as possible. The son of Livia's son Drusus and Antonia, and thus the brother of the popular Germanicus, Claudius had contracted a childhood disease (perhaps infantile paralysis) which left him with a limp, a stutter and a certain vagueness—enough to cause his mother and grandmother to regard him as feeble-minded. Young Claudius pursued historical research and remained far in the background during the reigns of Augustus and his uncle Tiberius (when Sejanus persecuted the family of his brother, Germanicus), but his malicious nephew Caligula brought him into public life by making him consul and butt of his practical jokes.

Various sources report that at the assassination of Caligula in A.D. 41, the terrified Claudius was forced by the praetorians, or persuaded by his friend Herod Agrippa, to mount the imperial throne. But these hostile sources cannot conceal that Claudius soon took firm command, not only reversing the outrages of Caligula but establishing new foreign and domestic policies that show him to be one of the most innovative of Roman emperors. While in the shadows, Claudius must have thought (or at least fantasized) long and hard about issues of policy and the administrative machinery necessary to implement a new agenda.

This seemingly naive and pedantic scholar had a desire, even an ambition, to rule well. The Suetonian anecdotes emphasize his woolly-mindedness and impetuosity, but both these historical texts and especially the documents from his reign demonstrate a common-sense approach to problems. For example, the anecdotes mock his time spent in the law courts, yet there is ample evidence of a great deal of salutary and humane legislation from their reign, such as the restrictions on the inhumane treatment of slaves and laws to protect the dowries of women and free widows from the tutelage of their male relations. Claudius likewise engaged in a range of building projects and public works. The most famous was the new port at Ostia to facilitate the importation of vast quantities of grain, but there were also canals, supply depots, Tiber embankments and aqueducts to improve life in the imperial capital.

Claudius promoted a policy of Romanization with grants of citizenship to loyal peoples as well as the establishment of colonies for veterans. But one of his most famous policy initiatives was his proposal to admit Gauls into the Roman Senate. The emperor's speech is exceptionally well documented: it is reported by Tacitus and a large portion of it also survives inscribed on a bronze tablet from Lyons. Tacitus' version—rewritten as we would expect in an ancient historian—is more elegant, and the inscription's whiff of pedantry in its wordy historical digression provides a genuine glimpse of the emperor's personality. Despite senatorial opposition, he admitted Gallic senators, and thus began the important process of admission of distinguished Roman citizens from around the Empire into a Senate which included Gauls, Greeks, Spaniards and Africans as well as Italians. His vision of Rome and its imperial future was broader than the jealous aristocratic senators who opposed him. Within a century emperors themselves would come from Spain and Gaul.

Augustus began his reign with conquests and grand imperial ambitions, but the defeat of Varus in Germany gave rise to a policy of retrenchment, which Tiberius followed. Caligula promised new conquests, but it was the improbable Claudius who returned to the expansionistic policy of Julius Caesar and the early years of Augustus. He chose his generals well, and his conquest of Britain stands as Rome's greatest conquest in the first century A.D.—to be surpassed only by Trajan's conquest of Dacia (Romania) at the beginning of the second century. Mauretania (in North Africa), Lycia (in Turkey), Thrace (in northern Greece and Bulgaria), and Judaea all became Roman provinces under Claudius, and Greek cities along the Black Sea looked to Rome's armies to protect them from the barbarians to the north. Claudius saw that earlier Romanization was having an effect and his grants of citizenship, his admission of the Gauls into the Senate, and his extensive road building program formed part of the consolidation of Romanized areas. Yet his replacement of client kings by direct Roman rule and his aggressive and successful military campaigns demonstrate that the ambitious leader judged that Rome was now prepared once again to extend its frontiers.

Claudius also revitalized the administration of Rome's vast empire. He created the administrative mechanism which we will examine in some detail in Chapter 11. Augustus had followed the example of Republican magistrates, and he administered the Empire on the model of a household. Claudius continued to rely on freedmen and slaves, but he promoted his freedmen to positions of recognized authority as the heads of major administrative departments (finance, petitions, etc.). Senators enormously resented the fact that Greek freedmen publicly exercised great power, just as American senators today resent the power of minor White House functionaries. Yet these freedmen were usually highly competent, and one, Narcissus, skillfully protected the emperor from Messalina's conspiracy. The documentary evidence and legislation of this reign show intelligence, compassion, and administrative expertise. The bureaucracy functioned remarkably well: Claudius and his freedmen must be given the credit.

After Claudius' death, a biting satire appeared bearing the title The Transformation of Claudius into a Pumpkin. *It is a parody of the apotheosis by which dead Roman emperors were proclaimed to have become gods. The satire is attributed to the philosopher Seneca, friend of Claudius' wife Agrippina and tutor of her son Nero, and later still a suicide in Nero's terror. Seneca portrays Claudius as unwilling to rest until he had granted Roman citizenship to all barbarians, and Claudius survives in the underworld as a clerk to one of the judges in Hades. Here we see Claudius satirized for his generosity with citizenship (which should not be overestimated) and concern with administration: both contemptible in the eyes of the senatorial elite. Claudius hardly had the supposed "republican" attitudes which were attributed to his father, Drusus, or his brother, Germanicus; of course, they never came to power. But he tried to work with the Senate and transformed the unpredictable lunacy of Caligula into a benevolent despotism. No one should doubt that Claudius the stutterer was, by modern standards, a despot. But his intelligence and his basic compassion impelled him to use his autocratic power for the good of the entire Empire. And for that, and for his use of efficient Greek freedmen, and for his limp and stutter and pedantic manner, neither Seneca nor Suetonius nor Tacitus could forgive him. Only in our own century have his real virtues been recognized and praised.*

Life of Claudius

Suetonius

Suetonius' life of Claudius provides the traditional senatorial picture of the emperor as a slobbering, stammering fool, much under the influence of his wives and freedmen. From his mother Antonia's and grandmother Livia's antipathy to Augustus' concern, expressed in letters to Livia, we find the imperial family struggling to deal with an embarrassment. Suetonius' account of his accession is the least flattering to Claudius: he was hiding behind curtains in the palace and was carried—terrified—to the praetorian camp, where he allowed himself to be proclaimed emperor.

But Suetonius had the widespread ancient prejudice against physical disability: it was a curse of the gods and most likely an indication of a defect of character or intelligence. And the biographer's interest is in the disgraceful anecdote, which made his Caligula biography longer (despite his brief reign) than that of Claudius. Yet the biography provides the raw material for a much more positive assessment of Claudius. His erratic behavior never obscures the good nature that made him popular with the equestrians and the masses, and there are many examples of his kindness, sense of humor and humanitarian concerns. When Suetonius says "Claudius' sole campaign was of no great importance," it is with surprise that we read that he refers to the swift and effective invasion and conquest of Britain—a prime example of the denigration of a great achievement.

It is Suetonius who provides details of Claudius' writings: his lengthy Etruscan and Carthaginian histories as well as his history of the Civil Wars. But the most tantalizing allusion is to the eight books of an autobiography "criticizable for a lack of taste" which inspired the poet and novelist Robert Graves to write his I, Claudius and Claudius the God.

---

1. The father of Claudius Caesar, Drusus, and praetor, led the army in Raetia and, later, in Germany. . . . For these exploits he received the honor of an ovation with the triumphal regalia . . . but died in his summer camp. . . . The Senate voted . . . the surname Germanicus for himself and his descendants. . . . He often pursued the leaders of the Germans all over the field at great personal risk; and he made no secret of his intention of restoring the old Republic when he came to power. It is because of this, I think, that some writers allege that he was an object of suspicion to Augustus; that the emperor recalled him from his province, and when he did not obey at once, poisoned him. I think I should mention this, though I do not think it true or even probable; for in fact Augustus loved him so dearly while he lived that he always called him joint-heir along with his grandsons, as he once declared in the Senate; and when he was dead, he praised him warmly before the people, praying the gods to make these young Caesars like Drusus, and to grant him, when his time came, as glorious a death as they had given that hero. And not content with carving a laudatory inscription on his tomb in verses of his own composition, Augustus also wrote a memoir of his life in prose.

Drusus had several children by the younger Antonia, but was survived by only three, Germanicus, Livilla, and Claudius.

2. Claudius was born at Lyons on August 1, 10 B.C. . . . and he received the name of Tiberius Claudius Drusus. . . . He lost his father when he was still an infant, and throughout almost the whole course of his childhood and youth he suffered so severely from recurring illness that the vigor of both his mind and his body was dulled, and even when he reached the proper age he was not thought capable of any public or private business. . . . It was also because of his weak health that contrary to all precedent he sat muffled in a cloak when he

presided at the gladiatorial games which he and his brother gave in honor of their father; and when he came of age and took the toga of manhood he was taken in a litter to the Capitol about midnight without the usual escort.

3. ... His mother Antonia often called him "a monster of a man, not finished by Mother Nature"; and if she accused anyone of stupidity, she said that he was "a bigger fool than my son Claudius." His grandmother Livia Augusta always treated him with the utmost contempt, very rarely speaking to him; and when she admonished him, she did so in short, harsh letters, or through messengers. When his sister Livilla heard that he would one day be emperor, she openly and loudly prayed that the Roman people might be spared so cruel and undeserved a fortune. Finally to make clear what his great-uncle Augustus thought of him, I append extracts from his own letters:

4. "My dear Livia: I have talked with Tiberius, as you requested, with regard to what is to be done with your grandson Claudius at the festival of Mars. Now we are both agreed that we must decide once for all what we plan to do about him. For if he is sound and "all there," why should he not be given the same public offices which his brother has held? But if we realize that he lacks soundness of body and mind, we must not allow the public (which enjoys laughing at such things) the chance of ridiculing both him and us. Surely we shall always be in trouble, if we worry every time and do not decide in advance whether he can hold public offices or not. But to turn to your immediate request, I do not object to his having charge of the banquet of the priests at the festival if he will allow himself to be advised by his cousin Silvanus, so as not to do anything to make himself conspicuous or ridiculous. But I don't want him to watch the games in the Circus from the Imperial box for he will be exposed to full view. ... You have my view, my dear Livia, that I want to decide something once for all about the whole matter, to save us from constantly wavering between hope and despair. ..."

Again in another letter:

"I certainly shall invite young Claudius to dinner every day during your absence, to keep him from dining alone with his friends Sulpicius and Athenodorus. I do wish that he would choose more prudently someone to imitate in movements, posture, and gait. The poor fellow is unlucky; for in important matters, where his mind does not wander, the nobility of his character is apparent enough."

Also in a third letter:

"My dear Livia: I am astonished that your grandson Claudius could please me with his oratory. How anyone so inarticulate in conversation can speak so clearly in public is quite beyond me."

There is no doubt at all what Augustus later decided, since he gave Claudius no office other than the augural priesthood, and he only named him an heir in the third degree, among those who were all but strangers. ... Claudius received a legacy of only eight hundred thousand sesterces.

5. His uncle Tiberius gave him the consular regalia, when he asked for office; but when he urgently requested the actual position, Tiberius sarcastically declined. ... So Claudius finally abandoned hope of a public position and loafed in the obscurity of his house and gardens in the suburbs, or sometimes at his villa in Campania. Moreover his association with ruffians brought criticism for drunkenness and gambling, as well as for stupidity. Yet, despite his conduct, he never lacked attention from distinguished individuals or respect from the public.

6. The equestrian order twice chose him as their patron, to head a deputation on their behalf: once when they asked for the privilege of carrying the body of Augustus to Rome on their shoulders, and again when they offered them their congratulations on the downfall of Sejanus. They even used to rise when he appeared at the public shows and take off their cloaks as a mark of honor. The Senate too voted that he be made a special member of the priests of Augustus, who were usually chosen by lot; when he later lost his house by fire, that it should be rebuilt at the public expense. ... Yet when Tiberius died, he named Claudius only among his heirs in the third degree, although he gave him in addition a legacy of about two million sesterces, and expressly commended him besides to the armies and to the Senate and people of Rome.

7. It was only under his nephew Caligula, who early in his reign tried to gain popularity by every device, that Claudius at last began his official career, holding the consulship for two months as the emperor's colleague. And when he entered the Forum for the first time with the rods of office, an eagle that was flying by landed on his shoulder. . . . Several times he presided at the shows in place of Gaius, and was greeted by the people with "Success to the emperor's uncle!" and now with "All hail to the brother of Germanicus!"

8. But all this did not save him from constant insults; for if he came to dinner a little late, he could only find a place after making the rounds of the dining-room. Whenever he dozed after dinner, which was a habit of his, he was pelted with the pits of olives and dates, and sometimes he was awakened by the jesters with a whip in pretended sport. They also put slippers on his hands as he lay snoring, so that when he was suddenly aroused he might rub his eyes with them.

9. But he was also exposed to real dangers. He was almost deposed from his consulship, because he had been slow in arranging for statues of Nero and Drusus, the emperor's brothers. . . . When a conspiracy was detected and suppressed and he was sent to Germany as one of the envoys to congratulate the emperor, he was really in peril of his life, since Gaius raged and fumed because his uncle had been sent to him, as if he were a child in need of a guardian. Some say he was so angry that Claudius was even thrown fully-clothed into the Rhine. . . .

10. Having spent most of his life under such conditions, Claudius became emperor in his fiftieth year by a remarkable stroke of fortune. When the assassins of Caligula told the courtiers to disperse, pretending that the emperor wished to be alone, Claudius withdrew with the rest and, a little later, in great terror at hearing the news of the murder, he hid on a balcony among the curtains which hung before the door. As he cowered there, a prowling soldier saw his feet, and intending to ask who he was, pulled him out and recognized him; and when Claudius grasped his knees in terror, the soldier hailed him as emperor. Then he took him to his comrades, who were still confused and angry. They placed him in a litter . . . and bore him to the praetorian camp in a state of despair and terror, while the crowd that saw him pitied him, as an innocent man who was being hurried off to execution. Inside the wall, he spent the night among the sentries without much hope, since the consuls, Senate and the city cohorts had taken possession of the Forum and the Capitol, and were resolved on restoring public liberty. When Claudius was summoned to the Senate by the tribunes to give his advice on the situation, he sent word that he was detained "by force." But the next day, since the Senate dallied due to the squabbling of various factions and the crowd standing about called for the one ruler to be Claudius, he allowed the armed soldiers to swear allegiance to him, and promised each man fifteen thousand sesterces. He became the first of the Caesars to resort to bribery to secure the fidelity of the troops.

11. As soon as his power was established, Claudius considered it vital to obliterate all memory of the two days when men had thought of changing the form of government. Accordingly he decreed that all that had been done and said during that period should be pardoned and forever forgotten; he kept his word too, save only that a few of the tribunes and centurions who had conspired against Gaius were put to death, both to make an example of them and because he knew that they had also demanded his own death. Then turning to the duties of family loyalty, he adopted as his most sacred and frequent oath "By Augustus." He had divine honors voted his grandmother Livia and a chariot for her image drawn by elephants in the procession at the Circus . . . and he took every opportunity of honoring his brother Germanicus. . . .

12. But Claudius was modest and unassuming in accepting excessive honors, refraining from taking the forename Imperator, and celebrating the betrothal of his daughter and the birthday of a grandson with merely private ceremonies. He recalled no exiles except with the approval of the Senate. He asked permission to bring the praetorian prefect and tribunes into the Senate with him . . . and when magistrates gave games,

he stood with the rest of the audience and showed his respect for them by shouting and applause.

He thus won so much love and devotion in a short time, that when it was reported that he had been waylaid and killed on a journey to Ostia, the people were horrified and cursed the soldiers as traitors and the Senate as murderers, until finally witnesses were brought forward to assure the people that Claudius was safe and on his way back to the city.

15. In court he behaved strangely: he was sometimes careful and shrewd, sometimes hasty and inconsiderate, occasionally silly and crazy. In revising the jury-list he disqualified a man who had not mentioned that he was exempt because of the number of his children, on the ground that he had an excessive passion for jury-duty. . . . In a case about disputed citizenship the lawyers were wrangling as to whether the defendant ought to make his appearance in the toga or in a Greek mantle, and the emperor, with the idea of showing absolute impartiality, made him change his garb several times, according as he was accused or defended. In one case he is credited with having rendered the following decision, which he had actually written out beforehand: "I decide in favor of those who have told the truth." He thus brought himself into widespread contempt. . . . I might add that a nasty Greek lawyer let slip this remark in a hot debate: "You are both an old man and a fool. . . ."

17. His single military campaign was of little importance. Though the Senate voted him the triumphal regalia, Claudius thought this beneath his dignity. He desired the glory of a real triumph and he chose Britain as the best place for gaining it—a land that no one had invaded since Julius Caesar. . . .He made the journey from Marseilles all the way to the Channel by land, and without any battle or bloodshed received the submission of a part of the island, returned to Rome within six months after leaving the city, and celebrated a triumph of great splendor. . . .

18. He always gave scrupulous attention to the care of the city and the supply of grain. On the occasion of a stubborn fire in the Aemilian district he remained in the Campus Martius for two nights, and when the soldiers and his own slaves could not extinguish it, he summoned the commons from all parts of the city and with bags full of money he paid each man on the spot a suitable reward for his assistance. When there was a scarcity of grain due to lengthy droughts, he was once stopped in the middle of the Forum by a mob and so pelted with abuse and at the same time with pieces of bread, that he was barely able to make his escape to the Palace by a back door; and after this experience he resorted to every possible means to bring grain to Rome, even in the winter season. To the merchants he held out the certainty of profit by assuming the expense of any loss that they might suffer from storms, and offered to those who would build merchant ships large bounties. . . .

20. His public works were important rather than numerous; they included an aqueduct begun by Gaius, the draining of the Fucine Lake and the construction of the harbor at Ostia. . . . He constructed the harbor at Ostia by building curving breakwaters to the right and left, while before the entrance he placed a mole in deep water. To give this mole a firmer foundation, he first sank the ship in which the great obelisk had been brought from Egypt, and then securing it by piles, built upon it a very lofty tower after the model of the lighthouse at Alexandria, to be lighted at night and guide the course of ships. . . .

25. . . . When certain men were abandoning their sick slaves to avoid providing medical aid, Claudius decreed that all such slaves were free and that, if they recovered, they should not return to the control of their masters; and if anyone killed a sick slave, he was liable to the charge of murder. . . . He expelled the Jews from Rome, since they constantly caused disturbances at the instigation of Chrestus [i.e. Christ]. . . . He utterly abolished the cruel and inhuman religion of the Druids in Gaul, which Augustus had merely prohibited to Roman citizens. On the other hand he attempted to transfer the Eleusinian rites from Attica to Rome, and had the temple of Venus Erycina in Sicily, which had fallen to ruin through age, restored at the expense of the treasury of the

Roman people. . . . But these and other acts, and in fact almost the whole conduct of his reign, were dictated not so much by his own judgment as that of his wives and freedmen, since he nearly always acted in accordance with their interests and desires.

26. He was betrothed twice at an early age [but neither marriage took place]. He then married Plautia Urgulanilla, and later Aelia Paetina. He divorced both these, Paetina for trivial offenses, but Urgulanilla because of scandalous lewdness and the suspicion of murder. Then he married Valeria Messalina, but when he learned that besides other wicked deeds she had actually married Gaius Silius, and that a formal contract had been signed in the presence of witnesses, he put her to death and declared before the praetorian guard that as his marriages did not turn out well, he would remain a widower, and if he did not keep his word, they should kill him. Yet he could not refrain from at once planning another match . . . and his affections were ensnared by the wiles of Agrippina, daughter of his brother Germanicus, aided by a niece's opportunity to kiss and fondle her uncle. . . . He induced some senators to propose that he be compelled to marry Agrippina, on the ground that it was for the interest of the State; also that others be allowed to contract similar marriages, which up to that time had been regarded as incestuous. And he married her with hardly a single day's delay. . . .

27. He had children by three of his wives: by Urgulanilla, Drusus and Claudia; by Paetina, Antonia; by Messalina, Octavia and a son, at first called Germanicus and later Britannicus. He lost Drusus just before he came to manhood, for he choked on a pear which he playfully tossed in the air and caught in his open mouth. . . . Claudia was the offspring of his freedman Boter, . . . and he ordered her to be cast out naked at her mother's door and disowned. He gave Antonia in marriage to Gnaeus Pompeius Magnus, and later to Faustus Sulla, both young men of high birth, and Octavia to his stepson Nero, after she had previously been betrothed to Silanus. . . . When Britannicus was still very small, Claudius would often take him in his arms and commend him to the assembled soldiers, and to the people at the games, holding him in his lap or in his outstretched hands, and he would wish him happy auspices, joined by the applauding throng. Of his sons-in-law he adopted Nero; Pompeius and Silanus he not only declined to adopt, but he even put to death.

28. Of his freedmen he had high regard for Polybius, his literary adviser, who often walked between the two consuls. But most of all he was devoted to his secretary Narcissus and his treasurer Pallas, and he gladly allowed them to be honored in addition by a decree of the Senate, not only with immense gifts, but even with the insignia of quaestors and praetors. Besides this he permitted them to amass such wealth by corruption, that when he once complained of the low state of his funds, the witty answer was made that he would have enough to spare, if he were in partnership with his two freedmen.

29. Wholly under the control of these freedmen and of his wives, he played the part of a servant, not of a prince, lavishing honors, the command of armies, pardons or punishments, according to their interests or whims, quite unaware what he was doing. Not to go into details about less important matters, . . . he put to death his father-in-law Appius Silanus and the two Julias, daughters of Drusus and Germanicus, on unsupported charges and gave them no opportunity for defense. . . . He inflicted the death penalty on thirty-five senators and more than three hundred Roman knights with such easy indifference, that when a centurion in reporting the death of an ex-consul said that his order had been carried out, he replied that he had given no order; but he nevertheless approved the act, since his freedmen declared that the soldiers had done their duty in hastening to avenge their emperor without instructions. But it is beyond all belief, that at the marriage which Messalina had contracted with her paramour Silius he signed the contract for the dowry with his own hand, being induced to do so on the ground that the marriage was a feigned one, designed to turn upon another a danger which was inferred

from certain portents to threaten "Messalina's husband." . . .

30. He possessed majesty and dignity of appearance, but only when he was standing still or sitting in repose. He was tall but not slender, with an attractive face, becoming white hair, and a full neck. But when he walked, his weak knees gave way under him and he had many disagreeable traits both in his lighter moments and when he was engaged in business; his laughter was unseemly and his anger still more disgusting, for he would foam at the mouth and trickle at the nose. He stammered besides and his head was very shaky at all times, but especially when he made the least exertion.

31. Though previously his health was bad, it was excellent while he was emperor except for attacks of pain in the stomach, which he said all but drove him to suicide.

32. He gave frequent and grand dinner parties, as a rule in spacious places, where six hundred guests were often entertained at one time. . . .When a guest was suspected of having stolen a golden bowl the day before, he invited him again the next day, but set before him an earthenware cup. . . .

34. That he was of a cruel and bloodthirsty disposition was shown in matters great and small. He always exacted examination by torture and the punishment of parricides at once and in his presence. . . . At any gladiatorial show, he gave orders that even those who fell accidentally should be slain, in particular the net-fighters, so that he could watch their faces as they died. When a pair of gladiators had fallen by mutually inflicted wounds, he at once had some little knives made from their swords for his use. . . .

35. But he was most notorious for his timidity and suspicion. Though he made a display of simplicity in the early days of his reign, he never went to a banquet without being surrounded by guards with lances and having his soldiers wait upon him in place of the servants; and he never visited a man who was ill without having the patient's room examined beforehand and his pillows and bed-clothing felt over and shaken out. Afterwards he even subjected those who came to pay their morning calls to search, sparing

none the strictest examination. He only reluctantly gave up having women and young boys and girls thus grossly mishandled, and the cases for pens were even taken from every scribe. . . .

36. He was so terror-stricken by unfounded reports of conspiracies that he tried to abdicate. When a man with a dagger was caught near him as he was sacrificing, he summoned the Senate in haste by criers and tearfully bewailed his lot, saying that there was no safety for him anywhere; and for a long time he would not appear in public. His ardent love for Messalina too was cooled, not so much by her unseemly conduct, as through fear of danger, since he believed that her paramour Silius aspired to the throne. On that occasion he made a shameful and cowardly flight to the praetorian camp, doing nothing all the way but ask whether his throne was secure.

37. No suspicion was too trivial, nor the inspirer of it too insignificant, to drive him on to precaution and vengeance, once a slight uneasiness entered his mind. One of two parties to a lawsuit, when he made his morning call, took Claudius aside, and said that he had dreamed that he was murdered by someone; then a little later pretending to recognize the assassin, he pointed out his opponent, as he was handing in his petition. The latter was immediately seized, as if caught red-handed, and hurried off to execution. . . .

38. . . . He did not even keep quiet about his own stupidity, but he said he had feigned it under Caligula and that he owed his life and throne to it. But he convinced no one, and a book was soon published entitled *The Fool's Accession* which argued that no one feigned folly.

39. Men have marvelled at his absent-mindedness and short-sightedness. After he had executed Messalina, he asked at the table why the empress did not come. He caused many of those whom he had condemned to death to be summoned the very next day to consult with him or game with him, and sent a messenger to upbraid them for sleepy-heads when they delayed to appear. When he was planning his unlawful marriage with Agrippina, in every speech that he made he constantly called her his daughter and foster-child, born and brought up

in his arms. Just before his adoption of Nero, as if it were not bad enough to adopt a stepson when he had a grownup son of his own, he publicly declared more than once that no one had ever been adopted into the Claudian family.

40. In fact every day, he would make such remarks as these: "What! do you take me for a fool?". . .

41. In his youth he began to write a history with the encouragement of Livy. But when he gave his first reading to a large audience, he had difficulty in finishing, since he more than once threw cold water on his own performance. For at the beginning of the reading a fat man raised a laugh by breaking his bench, and even after the disturbance was quieted, Claudius kept recalling the incident and breaking into guffaws. Even while he was emperor he wrote a good deal and gave constant recitals through a professional reader. He began his history with the death of the dictator Caesar, but passed to a later period and took a fresh start at the end of the civil war, realizing that he would not be allowed to give a frank or true account of the earlier times, since he was often taken to task both by his mother and his grandmother. He left two books of the earlier history, but forty-one of the later. He also composed an autobiography in eight books, lacking rather in good taste than in style. . . .

42. He also studied Greek eagerly, taking every occasion to declare his regard for the superiority of that language . . . . He even wrote historical works in Greek, twenty books of Etruscan history and eight of Carthaginian. Because of these works there was added to the old library at Alexandria a new wing called "Claudian," and in the one his Etruscan history should be read each year from beginning to end, and in the other his Carthaginian, by various readers in turn, in the manner of public recitations.

43. Towards the end of his life he was clearly sorry that he had married Agrippina and adopted Nero; . . . he declared that it had been his destiny to have wives who were all "unchaste, but not unchastened;" and shortly afterwards meeting Britannicus, he hugged him close and urged him to grow up and receive from his father an account of all that he had done, adding in Greek, "He who dealt the wound will heal it." . . .

44. Not long afterwards he made his will and sealed it with the seals of all the magistrates. . . . Most believe that Claudius was poisoned, but when and by whom is disputed. Some say that it was his taster, the eunuch Halotus; . . . others say that at a family dinner Agrippina served poison to him with her own hand in mushrooms, a dish of which he was extravagantly fond. Reports also differ as to what followed. Many say that as soon as he swallowed the poison he became speechless, and after suffering excruciating pain all night, died just before dawn. Some say that he first fell into a stupor, then vomited up the whole contents of his overloaded stomach, and was given a second dose, perhaps in a gruel, under pretence that he must be refreshed with food after his exhaustion. . . .

45. Claudius' death was kept quiet until all the arrangements were made for the succession. Accordingly vows were offered for his safety, as if he were still ill, and the farce was kept up by bringing in comic actors, under pretence that he had asked to be entertained in that way. He died on October 13, A.D. 54 in his sixty-fourth year and the fourteenth of his reign. He was buried with regal pomp and enrolled among the gods, an honor neglected and finally annulled by Nero, but later restored to him by Vespasian.

46. The principal omens of his death were the following: the rise of a comet; the striking of his father Drusus's tomb by lightning; and the fact that many magistrates of all ranks had died that same year. There are besides some indications that he himself was not unaware of his approaching end, and that he made no secret of it; for when he was appointing the consuls, he made no appointment beyond the month when he died, and on his last appearance in the Senate, after earnestly exhorting his children to harmony, he begged the members to watch over the tender years of both; and in his sitting on the tribunal he declared more than once that he had reached the end of a mortal career, although all who heard him prayed "May the gods forbid."

The Accession of Claudius

Josephus

Josephus provides two quite different accounts of the accession of Claudius, and both are different from that of Suetonius. In the earlier account in the Jewish War, *Claudius seems to be very much in control and uses his childhood friend Herod Agrippa as a messenger. Twenty years later, in the* Jewish Antiquities, *a more nationalistic version surfaces: here Herod Agrippa advises Claudius as well as the Senate and acts as a negotiator between the factions, while Claudius cowers in the praetorian camp. The people wished to avoid a return to civil war, while the senators wished him not to seize power but to receive it from the Senate. The innovation of Josephus was the important role of the Jewish king Agrippa as an advisor to his childhood friend Claudius. This version, which contains embellishments that had circulated in Jewish circles, is not mentioned by Suetonius. In it Agrippa urged Claudius to deal reasonably with the senators despite their initial opposition to him and is generally depicted as being the prudent, experienced advisor of the neophyte emperor.*

The Jewish War

As it happened that Agrippa was then on a visit to Rome, the Senate sent and invited him to discuss the situation with them, and at the same time Claudius summoned him to his camp to assist him as occasion arose. Realizing that he was virtually Caesar already Agrippa went to Claudius, who dispatched him as ambassador to the Senate to explain his intentions. In the first place his hand had been forced by the soldiers, but he felt that to disregard their enthusiasm would be unfair, and to disregard his own future most unsafe; for the fact that he had been summoned to the Imperial Throne placed him in great danger. He added that he would carry on the government like a good popular leader, not like a dictator; for he was satisfied with the honour of the imperial title, and on every matter at issue he would follow the wishes of the people. Indeed, if he had not been a moderate man by inclination, he would have had a sufficient inducement to self-restraint in Gaius' death.

This message was delivered by Agrippa. The Senate answered that they relied on the army and on wise counsels and would not voluntarily submit to slavery. When Claudius heard this answer, he sent Agrippa back to inform them that he would never consent to betray those who had given him unanimous support, and must therefore fight, though most unwillingly, against those who should have been his best friends. However, they must choose a battlefield outside the City; for it would be sacrilege if by their folly they polluted their ancestral shrines with the blood of their countrymen. This message Agrippa conveyed to the Senate.

Meanwhile one of the soldiers with the Senate drew his sword and cried: 'Look here, you fellows; why should we think of killing our friends and attacking men just like ourselves who happen to be with Claudius? We have an emperor with nothing against him, and the closest ties with those we are proposing to march against.' With these words he strode through the middle of the Senate with his entire unit behind him. Left in the lurch the patricians immediately panicked; and as they could find no means of escape they went the way of the soldiers and hurried off to join Claudius. But before the walls they were met by the naked swords of those who had been quicker than they to back the winning side; and the men who led the way might have been in danger before Claudius was aware of the soldiers' violent intentions, had not Agrippa run to him and shown him how dangerous the situation was, pointing out that, unless he restrained the violence of his men who were furious with the patricians, he would lose the very people who could make his reign glorious, and find himself ruler of a desert.

When Claudius heard this, he put a stop to the violent behaviour of the soldiery and received the Senate into the camp, making them welcome and then immediately going out with them to present to God thankofferings for his accession. On Agrippa he at once bestowed the entire kingdom of his forbears, adding the outer districts given by Augustus to Herod. . . .

Jewish Antiquities

By this time, more of the bodyguard were collected around Gratus, and when they saw Claudius being hurried along, apparently being dragged off to punishment, they greeted with black looks the penalization of such a man. For he had all his life avoided meddling in public affairs and had also experienced no small share of danger under Gaius' rule; and some of them urged that his case should be put before the consuls. As more of the soldiers gathered, the crowd began to take flight, but Claudius had no means of proceeding onward owing to his physical weakness; for, when he was seized, even his litter-bearers took to their heels to save themselves, despairing of their master's life. But when they had come to the open area of the Palatine . . . and were just reaching the Treasury, there was a far larger concourse of soldiers, who were overjoyed at the sight of Claudius and who were determined to proclaim him emperor because of the popularity of his brother Germanicus, who had left behind him an immense reputation among all who had known him. They reflected on the rapacity of the powerful members of the senate, and what errors the senate had committed when it was in power before. Moreover, they took into account the impracticability of having the senate handle affairs, and also considered that if the government again passed into the hands of a single ruler they would take a risk upon themselves since one individual would have gained the throne for himself, whereas it was possible for Claudius to receive it by their motion and support. And Claudius

would then show his appreciation by an honorarium adequate to such a service.

They expounded their views to one another, pondered them in their own minds, and reported them to each group as it came in. Then, on hearing the report, welcomed the summons to action. They closed their ranks about Claudius, wheeled around and proceeded towards the camp, taking his litter on their shoulders in order that there might be no drag on their speed. The will of the people and that of the senators were at variance. The latter were eager to regain their former prestige and earnestly aspired, since after long years they now had the chance, to escape a slavery brought upon them by the insolence of the tyrants. The people, on the other hand, were jealous of the senate, recognizing in the emperors a curb upon the senate's encroachments and a refuge for themselves. They rejoiced in the seizure of Claudius, and supposed that his securing the throne would avert from them any civil strife such as had occurred in Pompey's day. The senate, having learned that Claudius had been brought into the camp by the soldiers, sent some of their men of superior character to impress on him that he must not take forcible action to put himself on the throne. On the contrary, they said, he should yield to the senate, submitting, as a single individual, to so large a number of men, and allowing the law to provide for the organization of the commonwealth. He should remember what injuries former tyrants had inflicted on the state and what perils he, along with themselves, had undergone at the hands of Gaius. Since he detested the cruelty of tyranny when insolently practised by others, he should not voluntarily take rash action and indulge in a burst of violence against his fatherland. If he complied and showed that his former good conduct in avoiding trouble could be trusted to continue, he would obtain honours, which would be voted him by free citizens; for if he did his part in yielding to the law, he would gain plaudits for virtuous conduct whether as subject or as ruler. If, however, he was reckless and had learnt no wisdom from the death of Gaius, they certainly would not permit him to act thus; for they were supported by a large part of the army and were well supplied with arms and had a host of slaves to use them. Hope and Fortune, they remarked, were a large asset; and the gods seconded the efforts of those alone who strove to win without sacrificing moral and spiritual values, namely, those who fought for the freedom of their country.

Claudius . . . had recovered from his fear . . . both because of the bold action of the soldiers and because of the advice of King Agrippa not to let slip through his hands such an office which had come unsought. . . . On hearing of the kidnapping of Claudius by the soldiers, Agrippa forced his way to him; and finding him perplexed and on the point of yielding to the senate, he stirred him up and bade him make a bid for the empire. After these words to Claudius Agrippa returned home. On being summoned by the senate, he annointed his head with unguents as if he had arrived from a banquet that had just broken up, appeared before them and asked the senators what Claudius had done. They told him the state of affairs and asked him in return what he thought of the whole situation. He declared that he was ready to die for the honour of the senate, but bade them consider what was expedient and to set aside all personal predilections. For, he noted, those who made a bid to rule the state needed arms and soldiers for their defence, lest on taking a stand unprepared they should find that this was their fatal mistake. The senate replied that they were well supplied with arms and would contribute money, that they had something of an army standing by them, and that they would whip more troops into shape by liberating slaves. "May you succeed, senators," said Agrippa in reply, "in doing what you desire, but I must speak without shilly-shallying because my speech has a bearing on your security. You know, of course, that the army that will fight for Claudius has been long trained to bear arms, while ours will be a motley rabble consisting of men who have unexpectedly been released from slavery and who are consequently hard to control. We shall fight against experts, having brought into play men who do not even know how to draw their swords.

Therefore my judgement is to send a deputation to Claudius to persuade him to lay down his office; and I am ready to act as ambassador."

2. So he spoke, and on their agreeing to his proposal he was dispatched with others. He thereupon recounted to Claudius in private the confusion of the senate and advised him to reply rather imperiously, speaking with the dignity of one in authority. Claudius accordingly replied that he did not wonder that the senate was not pleased at the prospect of submitting to authority because they had been oppressed by the brutality of those who had previously held the imperial office. But he promised to behave with such propriety that they would taste for themselves the savour of an era of fair dealing; that only nominally would the government be his, that in reality it would be thrown open to all in common. Seeing that he had passed through many vicissitudes of fortune before their eyes, they would do well not to distrust him. The envoys, conciliated by the words that they heard, were ushered out. Claudius assembled and addressed the army, binding them by oath that they would remain loyal to him. He presented the praetorian guard with five thousand drachmas apiece and their officers with a proportionate sum and promised similar amounts to the armies wherever they were.

3. The consuls then called together the senate in the Temple of Jupiter Victor while it was still night. Some of the senators who were in hiding in the city hesitated when they heard the summons; others had departed to their private estates, foreseeing how it would all come out. These latter despaired of liberty and deemed it far better to live out their lives free from the perils of servitude and with leisure from toil than to maintain the dignity of their fathers and have no assurance of surviving. Nevertheless, one hundred—no more—assembled; and, as they were deliberating about the matter in hand, suddenly a shout arose from the soldiers who had stood by them, bidding the senate choose an emperor and not to ruin the empire by entrusting it to a multitude of rulers . . . . There would have been a massacre second to none had those who coveted the empire been allowed to range

themselves against Claudius. Above all, there were gladiators—and their number was considerable—and the soldiers of the night watch in the city and all the rowers of the fleet who were streaming into the camp. And so of those who were candidates for the office, some withdrew in order to spare the city, others out of fear for themselves. . . .

5.   Such was the situation in the senate. Meanwhile, from all quarters men came hurrying towards the camp to pay their respects. One of the two consuls, Quintus Pomponius, was especially guilty in the eyes of the troops for summoning the senate in the cause of liberty.

Drawing swords they rushed at him and would have murdered him had not Claudius intervened. Having rescued the consul from peril, Claudius took his seat beside him, but he did not receive the rest of the senators who accompanied Quintus with like honour. Some of them even received blows from the soldiers, who repulsed their attempts to get an audience with him . . . . King Agrippa then approached Claudius, and besought him to take a kinder attitude to the senators; for if any harm came to the senate, he would have no other subjects over whom to rule. Claudius agreed and summoned the senate to the Palatine.

Claudius and His Wives

Tacitus

These excerpts from Tacitus' Annals concentrate on Claudius' ill-fated marriages to Messalina and Agrippina. The story of Messalina almost defies belief. Promiscuity and cruelty were hardly unknown in royal palaces, but Messalina's public marriage to her lover while the emperor was briefly out of town is extraordinary: it cannot be explained except as a plot to seize the throne. Claudius was protected by his freedman Narcissus, who discredited Messalina, rallied the guard, and ensured that the empress was executed before the doting Claudius repented.

The foolish emperor's fourth and final marriage was to his niece Agrippina the younger—daughter of Germanicus and Agrippina and sister of Caligula. Her single-minded desire to place her son Nero on the imperial throne dominated the last five years of the reign. Tacitus often reported Tiberius' crimes through suggestion and innuendo, but here he is remarkably direct: Agrippina arranged for Claudius to be poisoned by his own food-taster and finished off by his doctor. Here again the historian's graphic powers of description demonstrate why he has been called "the greatest painter of antiquity."

And now ended Claudius' ignorance of his own domestic affairs. Now he was, ineluctably, to discover and punish his wife's excesses (as a preliminary to coveting an incestuous substitute). Messalina's adultery was going so smoothly that she was drifting, through boredom, into unfamiliar vices. But now fate seemed to have unhinged Gaius Silius; or perhaps he felt that impending perils could only be met by perilous action. He urged that concealment should be dropped. 'We do not have to wait until the emperor dies of old age!' he told her. 'Besides, only innocent people can afford long-term plans. Flagrant guilt needs daring. And we have accomplices who share our danger. I am without wife or child. I am ready to marry, and to adopt Britannicus. Your power will remain undiminished. Peace of mind will only be yours if we can forestall Claudius. He is slow to discover deception—but quick to anger.'

Messalina was unenthusiastic. It was not that she loved her husband. But she feared that Silius, once supreme, might despise his mistress, and see the crime prompted by an emergency in its true colours. However, the idea of being called his wife appealed to her owing to its sheer outrageousness—a sensualist's ultimate satisfaction. So, waiting only until Claudius had left to sacrifice at Ostia, she celebrated a formal marriage with Silius.

It will seem fantastic, I know, that in a city where nothing escapes notice or comment, any human beings could have felt themselves so secure. Much more so that, on an appointed day and before invited signatories, a consul designate and the emperor's wife should have been joined together in formal marriage—'for the purpose of rearing children'; that she should have listened to the diviners' words, assumed the wedding-veil, sacrificed to the gods; that the pair should have taken their places at a banquet, embraced, and finally spent the night as man and wife. But I am not inventing marvels. What I have told, and shall tell, is the truth. Older men heard and recorded it.

The imperial household shuddered—especially those in power, with everything to fear from a new emperor. There were secret conferences. Then indignation was unconcealed. 'While a ballet-dancing actor violated the emperor's bedroom,' they said, 'it was humiliating enough. Yet it did not threaten Claudius' life. Here, on the other hand, is a young, handsome, intelligent nobleman, consul-to-be—but with a loftier destiny in mind. For where such a marriage will lead is clear enough.' When they thought of Claudius' sluggish uxoriousness, and the many assassinations ordered by Messalina, they were terrified. Yet the emperor's very pliability gave them hope. If they could convince him of the enormity of the outrage, Messalina might be condemned and eliminated without trial. But everything, they felt, turned on this—would Claudius give her a hearing? Could they actually shut his ears against her confession?

Callistus, Narcissus, and Pallas—now basking in the warmest favour—conferred. They discussed whether, pretending ignorance of everything else, they could secretly frighten Messalina out of her affair with Silius. But this scheme was abandoned by Pallas and Callistus as too dangerous for themselves. Pallas' motive was cowardice. Callistus had learnt from his experience dating from the previous reign that power was better safeguarded by diplomatic than by vigorous methods. Narcissus, however, persevered in taking action—with this new feature: she was to be denounced without forewarning of charge or accuser. Narcissus watched for an opening. Then, as Claudius prolonged his stay at Ostia, he induced the emperor's two favourite mistresses to act as informers. They were persuaded by gifts, promises, and assurances of the increased influence that Messalina's downfall would bring them.

One of the women, Calpurnia, secured a private interview with Claudius. Throwing herself at his feet, she cried that Messalina had married Silius—in the same breath asking the other girl, Cleopatra (who was standing by ready), for corroboration; which she provided. Then Calpurnia urged that Narcissus should be summoned. 'I must excuse my earlier silences,' said Narcissus, 'about Vettius Valens, Plautius Lateranus, and the like—and now, too, I do not propose to complain of her adulteries, much less impel you to demand back from Silius your mansion, slaves, and other imperial perquisites. *But do you know you are divorced?* Nation, senate, and army have witnessed her wedding to Silius. Act promptly, or her new husband controls Rome!'

Claudius summoned his closest friends. First he interrogated Gaius Turranius, controller of the corn supply, then Lusius Geta, commander of the Guard. They confirmed the story. The rest of the emperor's entourage loudly insisted that he must visit the camp and secure the Guard—safety must come before vengeance. Claudius, it is said, was panic-stricken. 'Am I still emperor?' he kept on asking. 'Is Silius still a private citizen?'

Meanwhile, Messalina was indulging in unprecedented extravagances. It was full autumn; and she was performing in her grounds a mimic grape-harvest. Presses were working, vats overflowing, surrounded by women capering in skins like sacrificing or frenzied Maenads. She herself, hair streaming, brandished a Baccic wand. Beside her stood Silius in ivy-wreath and buskins, rolling his head, while the disreputable chorus yelled round him. . . .

Rumours and messengers now came pouring in. They revealed that Claudius knew all, and was on his way, determined for revenge. So the couple separated, Messalina to the Gardens of Lucullus, Silius—to disguise his alarm—to business in the Main Square. The others too melted away in every direction. But they were pounced on and arrested separately by staff-officers of the Guard, in the streets or in hiding-places. Messalina was too shaken by the catastrophe to plan. But she instantly decided on the course that had often saved her—to meet her husband and let him see her.

She also sent word that Britannicus and Octavia should go and seek their father's embraces. She herself begged the senior priestess of Vesta, Vibidia, to obtain the ear of the emperor as Chief Priest and urge pardon. Meanwhile, with only three companions—so rapidly was she deserted—she walked from end to end of the city. Then she started along the Ostia road—in a cart used for removing garden refuse. People did not pity her, for they were horrified by her appalling crimes.

On Claudius' side there was just as much agitation. Lusius Geta, the Guard commander, followed his own caprices, regardless of right and wrong. No one trusted him. So Narcissus, supported by others as afraid as he was, asserted that there was only one hope of saving the emperor's life: the transference of the Guard, for that one day, to the command of an ex-slave—himself; for he offered himself as commander. Then, afraid that Claudius, during the return journey to Rome, might have his mind changed by his companions Lucius Vitellius and Gaius Caecina Largus, Narcissus asked for a place in the same carriage, and sat with them.

Claudius, it was widely said afterwards, contradicted himself incessantly, veering from invective against Messalina's misconduct to reminiscences of their marriage and their children's infancy. . . .

Now Messalina came into view. She cried and cried that Claudius must listen to the mother of Octavia and Britannicus. Narcissus shouted her down with the story of Silius and the wedding, simultaneously distracting the emperor's gaze with a document listing her immoralities. Soon afterwards, near the city, the two children were brought forward. Narcissus ordered their removal. . . .

Claudius remained strangely silent. Lucius Vitellius looked unaware of the proceedings. The ex-slave, Narcissus, took charge. He ordered the adulterer's home to be opened and the emperor to be taken there. First, in the forecourt, Narcissus pointed out a statue of Silius' condemned father, placed there contrary to senatorial decree. Then he pointed to the heirlooms of Nero's and Drususes' that had come to the house among the wages of sin. This angered the emperor; he became threatening. Narcissus conducted him to the camp. There, after a preliminary statement by the ex-slave, Claudius addressed the assembled Guard—briefly, for he could hardly express his indignation (just though it was) for shame.

The Guardsmen shouted repeatedly for the offenders to be named and punished. Silius was brought on to the platform. Without attempting defence or postponement, he asked for a quick death. Certain distinguished gentlemen outside the senate showed equal courage. They too desired a speedy end. . . .

Only Mnester caused hesitation. Tearing his clothes, he entreated Claudius to look at his whip-marks and remember the words with which the emperor had placed him under Messalina's orders. Others, he urged, had sinned for money or ambition, he from compulsion—and if Silius had become emperor he, Mnester, would have been the first to die. Claudius had an indulgent nature and this moved him. But the other ex-slaves prevailed upon the emperor not, after executing so many distinguished men, to spare a ballet-dancer—when crimes were so grave it was irrelevant whether they were voluntary or enforced. . . .

Meanwhile at the Gardens of Lucullus Messalina was fighting for her life. She composed an appeal. Its terms were hopeful and even at times indignant, so shameless was her insolence to the very end. Indeed, if Narcissus had not speedily caused her death, the fatal blow would have rebounded on her accuser. For Claudius, home again, soothed and a little intoxicated after an early dinner, ordered 'the poor woman' (that is said to have been his phrase) to appear on the next day to defend herself. This was noted. His anger was clearly cooling, his love returning. Further delay risked that the approaching night would revive memories of conjugal pleasures.

So Narcissus hurried away. Ostensibly on the emperor's instruction, he ordered a colonel of the Guard, attended by staff-officers, to kill Messalina. An ex-slave was sent to prevent her escape and see that the order was carried out. Hastening to the Gardens ahead of the others, he found Messalina prostrate on the ground, with her mother Domitia Lepida sitting beside her. While her daughter was in power they had quarrelled. But in her extremity, Lepida was overcome by pity. She urged Messalina to await the executioner. 'Your life is finished,' she said. 'It only remains to die honourably.' But in that lust-ridden heart decency did not exist. Messalina was still uselessly weeping and moaning when the men violently broke down the door. The officer stood there, silently. The ex-slave, with a slave's foulness of tongue, insulted her. Then, for the first time, Messalina saw her position. Terrified, she took a dagger and put it to her throat and then her breast—but could not do it. The officer ran her through. The body was left with her mother. Claudius was still at table when news came that Messalina had died; whether by her own hand or another's was unspecified. Claudius did not inquire. He called for more wine, and went on with his party as usual.

On the days that followed, the emperor gave no sign of hatred, satisfaction, anger, distress, or any other human feeling—even when he saw the accusers exulting, and his children mourning. His forgetfulness was helped by the Senate, which decreed that Messalina's name and statues should be removed from all public and private sites. It also awarded Narcissus an honorary quaestorship. . . .

The vengeance on Messalina was just. But it had terrible consequences.

Messalina's death convulsed the imperial household. Claudius was impatient of celibacy and easily controlled by his wives, and the ex-slaves quarreled about who should choose his next one. Rivalry among the women was equally fierce. Each cited her own high birth, beauty, and wealth as qualifications for this exalted marriage. The chief competitors were Lollia Paulina, daughter of an ex-consul, and Germanicus' daughter Agrippina. Their backers were Callistus and Pallas respectively. Narcissus supported Aelia Paetina. The emperor continually changed his mind according to whatever advice he had heard last.

Finally, he summoned the disputants to a meeting and requested them to give reasoned opinions . . . . Pallas, proposing Agrippina, emphasized that the son whom she would bring with her was Germanicus' grandson, eminently deserving of imperial rank: let the emperor ally himself with a noble race and unite two branches of the Claudian house, rather than allow this lady of proved capacity for childbearing, still young, to transfer the glorious name of the Caesars to another family.

These arguments prevailed. Agrippina's seductiveness was a help. Visiting her uncle frequently—ostensibly as a close relation—she tempted him into giving her the preference and into treating her, in anticipation, as his wife. Once sure of her marriage, she enlarged her ambitions and schemed for her son Lucius Domituis Ahenobarbus, the future Nero, to be wedded to the emperor's daughter Octavia . . . .

With an emperor whose likes and dislikes were all suggested and dictated to him, anything seemed possible. . . .

Next year, rumour strongly predicted Claudius' marriage to Agrippina; so did their illicit intercourse. But they did not yet dare to celebrate the wedding. For marriage with a niece was unprecedented—indeed it was incestuous, and disregard of this might, it was feared, cause national disaster. . . . [Lucius Vitellius asked Claudius if he would yield to a request of the Senate and, when the emperor agreed, Lucius argued the case for the marriage in the Senate.]

At this, some senators ran out of the house enthusiastically clamouring that if Claudius hesitated they would use constraint. A throng of passers-by cried that the Roman public were similarly minded. Claudius delayed no longer. . . .

From this moment the country was transformed. Complete obedience was accorded to a woman—and not a woman like Messalina who toyed with national affairs to satisfy her appetites. This was a rigorous, almost masculine, despotism. In public, Agrippina was austere and often arrogant. Her private life was chaste—unless power was to be gained. Her passion to acquire money was unbounded. She wanted it as a stepping-stone to supremacy.

. . . Agrippina, however, was anxious not to be credited with bad actions only. So she now secured the recall of Lucius Annaeus Seneca from exile and his appointment to a praetorship. She judged that owing to his literary eminence this would be popular. She also had designs on him as a distinguished tutor for her young son Nero. Seneca's advice could serve their plans for supremacy; and he was believed to be devoted to her—in gratitude for her favours—but hostile to Claudius whose unfairness he resented.

It was now decided to act without further delay. A consul-designate was induced by lavish promises to propose a petition to Claudius, begging him to betroth Octavia to Nero—an arrangement compatible with their ages and likely to lead to higher things. The arguments used closely resembled those recently employed by Lucius Vitellius. The engagement took place.

In addition to their previous relationship Nero was now Claudius' future son-in-law. By his mother's efforts—and the intrigues of Messalina's accusers, who feared vengeance from her son—he was becoming the rival of Britannicus. . . .

. . . In the following year the adoption of Nero was hurried forward. Pallas, pledged to Agrippina as organizer of her marriage and subsequently her lover, took the initiative. He pressed Claudius to consider the national interests, and furnish the boy Britannicus with a protector: 'Just as the divine Augustus, though supported by grandsons, advanced his stepsons, and Tiberius, with children of his own, adopted Germanicus; so Claudius too ought to provide himself with a young future partner in his labours.' The emperor was convinced. Reproducing the ex-slave's arguments to the Senate, he promoted Nero above his own son, who was three years younger.

Thanks were voted to the emperor. More remarkable was the compliment that the young man received: legal adoption into the Claudian family with the name of Nero. Agrippina was honoured with the title of Augusta. After these developments no one was hard-hearted enough not to feel distressed at Britannicus' fate. Gradually deprived even of his slaves' services, Britannicus saw through his step-mother's hypocrisy and treated her untimely attentions cynically. He is said to have been intelligent. This may be true. But it is a reputation which was never tested, and perhaps he only owes it to sympathy with his perils. . . .

Narcissus' suspicions of Agrippina continually grew deeper. 'Whether Britannicus or Nero come to the throne,' he was said to have told his friends, 'my destruction is inevitable. But Claudius has been so good to me that I would give my life to help him. The criminal intentions for which Messalina, with Gaius Silius, was condemned are present in Agrippina. With Britannicus as his successor the emperor has nothing to fear. But the intrigues of his stepmother in Nero's interests are fatal to the imperial house—more ruinous than if I had said nothing about her predecessor's unfaithfulness. And here too there is unfaithfulness.

Agrippina's lover is Pallas. *That* is the final proof that, to imperial ambition, she sacrifices everything—decency, honour, chastity.'

Talking like this, Narcissus would embrace Britannicus and pray he would soon be a man. With hands outstretched—now to the boy, now to heaven—he besought that Britannicus might grow up and cast out his father's enemies—and even avenge his mother's murderers. Then Narcissus' anxieties caused his health to fail. He retired to Sinuessa, to recover his strength in its mild climate and health-giving waters.

Agrippina had long decided on murder. Now she saw her opportunity. Her agents were ready. But she wanted advice about poisons. A sudden, drastic effect would give her away. A gradual, wasting recipe might make Claudius, faced with death, love his son again. What was needed was something subtle that would upset the emperor's faculties but produce a deferred fatal effect. An expert in such matters was selected—a woman called Locusta, recently sentenced for poisoning but with a long career of imperial service ahead of her. By her talents, a preparation was supplied. It was administered by a eunuch who habitually served the emperor and tasted his food.

Later, the whole story became known. Contemporary writers stated that the poison was sprinkled on a particularly succulent mushroom. But because Claudius was torpid—or drunk—its effect was not at first apparent; and an evacuation of his bowels seemed to have saved him. Agrippina was horrified. But when the ultimate stakes are so alarmingly large, immediate disrepute is brushed aside. She had already secured the complicity of the emperor's doctor Xenophon; and now she called him in. The story is that, while pretending to help Claudius to vomit, he put a feather dipped in a quick poison down his throat. Xenophon knew that major crimes, though hazardous to undertake, are profitable to achieve.

The Senate was summoned. Consuls and priests offered prayers for the emperor's safety. But meanwhile his already lifeless body was being wrapped in blankets and poultices. Moreover, the appropriate steps were being taken to secure Nero's accession. First

Agrippina, with heart-broken demeanour, held Britannicus to her as though to draw comfort from him. He was the very image of his father, she declared. By various devices she prevented him from leaving his room, and likewise detained his sisters, Claudia Antonia and Octavia. Blocking every approach with guards, Agrippina issued frequent encouraging announcements about the emperor's health, to maintain the army's morale and await the propitious moment forecast by the astrologers.

At last, at midday on October the thirteenth, the palace gates were suddenly thrown open. Attended by Sextus Afranius Burrus, commander of the Guard, out came Nero to the battalion which, in accordance with regulations, was on duty. At a word from its commander, he was cheered and put in a litter.

Some of the men are said to have looked round hesitantly and asked where Britannicus was. However, as no counter-suggestion was made, they accepted the choice offered them. Nero was then conducted into the Guards' camp. There, after saying a few words appropriate to the occasion—and promising gifts on the generous standard set by his father—he was hailed as emperor. The army's decision was followed by senatorial decrees. The provinces, too, showed no hesitation.

Claudius was voted divine honours, and his funeral was modelled on that of the divine Augustus—Agrippina imitating the grandeur of her great-grandmother Livia, the first Augusta. But Claudius' will was not read, in case his preference of stepson to son should create a public impression of unfairness and injustice.

Letter to the Alexandrians

Claudius

During the reign of Caligula there had been conflict between the Greek and Jewish communities in Alexandria, which had erupted into rioting at his death. Both groups sent embassies to Claudius to press their cases soon after his accession, and this letter, which was set up in Alexandria, is Claudius' reply. The emperor seems annoyed with both groups. He orders the Greeks to respect the long established religious freedom of the Jews, and he reconfirms their rights in this regard. But he also commands the Jews to cease agitating for additional political rights and not to bring additional Jews into the city from Palestine or other parts of Egypt. These strictures, taken together with Claudius' polite refusal of temples or priesthoods in his honor, show a sensible, fair-minded approach to volatile issues. And we should remember that this is direct evidence of imperial policy—far more reliable than the selective and tendentious accounts by ancient historians. This impressive administrative document shows a central government both informed and concerned about local issues.

Lucius Aemilius Rectus [prefect of Egypt] declares: Since the whole of the city, owing to its numbers, was unable to be present at the reading of the most sacred and most beneficent letter to the city, I have deemed it necessary to display the letter publicly in order that reading it individually you may admire the majesty of our god Caesar and feel gratitude for his good will toward the city. Year 2 of the Emperor Tiberius Claudius Caesar Augustus Germanicus, 14th of New Augustus.

The Emperor Tiberius Claudius Caesar Augustus Germanicus, *pontifex maximus*, holder of the tribunician power, consul designate, to the city of Alexandria, greeting. . . . Your envoys delivered your decree to me and discoursed at length concerning the city, directing my attention to your good will toward us, which from long ago, you may be sure, had been stored up to your advantage in my memory; for you are by nature reverent toward the emperors, as I have come to know well from many things, and in particular you have taken a warm interest—warmly reciprocated—in my house, of which fact (to mention the latest instance, passing over the others) the supreme witness is my brother Germanicus Caesar when he addressed you in franker tones [by word of mouth].

Wherefore I gladly accepted the honors given to me by you, though I am not partial to such things. And first I permit you to keep my birthday as an Augustan day in the manner you have yourselves proposed, and I agree to the erection by you in their several places of the statues of myself and my family; for I see that you were zealous to establish on every side memorials of your reverence for my house. Of the two golden statues, the one made to represent the Claudian Augustan Peace, as my most honored Barbillus suggested and persisted in when I wished to refuse for fear of being thought too offensive, shall be erected at Rome, and the other according to your request shall be carried in procession on my name days in your city; and it shall be accompanied in the procession by a throne, adorned with whatever trappings you wish. It would perhaps be foolish, while accepting such great honors, to refuse the institution of a Claudian tribe and the establishment of sacred groves after the manner of Egypt; wherefore I grant you these requests as well, and if you wish you may also erect the equestrian statues given by Vitrasius Pollio my procurator. As for the erection of the statues in four-horse chariots which you wish to set up to me at the entrances to the country, I consent to let one be placed at the town called Taposiris, in Libya, another at Pharus in Alexandria, and a third at Pelusium in Egypt. But I deprecate the appointment of a high priest for me and the building of temples, for I do not wish to be offensive to my contemporaries, and my opinion is that temples and the like have by all ages been granted as special honors to the gods alone. . . .

As for which party was responsible for the riot and feud (or rather, if the truth must be told, the war) with the Jews, although your envoys, . . . confronting [your opponents] put your case with great zeal, nevertheless I was unwilling to make a strict inquiry, though guarding within me a store of immutable indignation against any who renewed the conflict; and I tell you once for all that unless you put a stop to this ruinous and obstinate enmity against each other, I shall be driven to show what a benevolent emperor can be when turned to righteous indignation. Wherefore once again I conjure you that, on the one hand, the Alexandrians show themselves forbearing and kindly toward the Jews, who for many years have dwelt in the same city, and dishonor none of the rights observed by them in the worship of their god but allow them to observe their customs as in the time of the deified Augustus, which customs I also, after hearing both sides, have confirmed. And, on the other hand, I explicitly order the Jews not to agitate for more privileges than they formerly possessed, and in the future not to send out a separate embassy as if they lived in a separate city—a thing unprecedented—and not to force their way into gymnasiarchic or cosmetic games, while enjoying their own privileges and sharing a great abundance of advantages in a city not their own, and not to bring in or admit Jews from Syria or those who sail down from Egypt, a proceeding which will compel me to conceive serious suspicions; otherwise I will by all means proceed against them as fomentors of what is a general plague of the whole world. If, desisting from these courses, you both consent to live with mutual forbearance and kindliness, I on my side will exercise a solicitude of very long standing for the city, as one bound to us by ancestral friendship. I bear witness to my friend Barbillus of the solicitude which he has always shown for you in my presence and of the extreme zeal with which he has now advocated your cause, and likewise to my friend Tiberius Claudius Archibius. Farewell.

The Personality of Claudius

Vincent Scramuzza

Vincent Scramuzza examines the riddle of Claudius: how this sickly youth, apparently dull, deprived of family love and political or military experience, could become a humane and effective administrator and the successful conquerer of Britain. This contradiction cannot be resolved, but there is little doubt that Claudius was the most endearing of the successors of Augustus: free from vanity and self-importance, forgiving, a loyal friend and an administrator wishing to improve the lives of his subjects. Tacitus' indictment of Claudius is political, and Scramuzza argues that what Suetonius takes to be Claudius' foolish behavior in the courts had some justification. And how should we evaluate his alleged dependence on his freedmen if those palace bureaucrats provided efficient administration to this vast Empire? The emperor either set these progressive policies himself, or he was "shrewd enough to select the right advisors."

Claudius, son of Drusus and Antonia, was born August 1, 10 B.C. in Lyons, the capital of Gaul. Drusus was at that time governor of this important province. He was also the ablest general in the service of the Empire, the stepson of Augustus, and a likely heir to the throne. Antonia was a daughter of Mark Antony. The child, who was named Tiberius Claudius Drusus, seemed, then, destined to a glorious career. For a long time, however, that destiny was thwarted. In his infancy and early adolescence the boy was the victim of a disease that not only ravaged his health, but deformed his appearance and retarded the development of his mind until his family feared he would never be fit for public office. Many theories have been advanced regarding Claudius' illness. A recent study diagnoses it as a form of infantile paralysis that is said to be associated with premature birth—a view based on an alleged remark of Claudius' own mother that he "was a monster of a man, not finished but merely begun by nature."

The confused data handed down from antiquity and the limitations of the psycho-medical sciences make it difficult to draw a picture of Claudius at once satisfactory to the historian, the physician, and the psychologist. A conservative reconstruction of the sources suggests that the boy was afflicted with some ailment which, although it did not prevent normal physical growth, kept him in constant ill health and incapacitated him for the activities of his station. At fifteen when he and his older brother Germanicus gave some gladiatorial games in honor of their father who had died in 9 B.C., he came out in public with his head muffled in a cloak as if he had just left the sick room. And when a year or two later he donned the gown of manhood, he was unable to walk to the Capitol for the customary sacrifice, but was carried in a litter in the dead of night and without the usual escort of relatives and friends to wish him good luck.

His malady made him irritable and awkward and acutely conscious of his inferiority to other boys of his age. Thus handicapped, the adolescent was incapable of acting with that dignity expected of a prince of the house of Caesar. Augustus so dreaded that his grandson would make himself ridiculous at social functions that he kept him away from the imperial box in the circus, and on a certain occasion forbade him to preside at a banquet without the escort of a kinsman from whom he should take his cues. The psychological effects of this practical isolation from society cropped out in later years when, sitting on the throne of the Caesars, Claudius felt that no one understood him.

Because his bodily ills did not respond quickly to medical treatment, and his intellect did not develop as rapidly as is the wont of normal children, his elders came to fear that he would remain an invalid and a dullard for life.

Their unwillingness to let him join in ordinary social intercourse gave rise to all sorts of gossip which in turn provoked an unjustifiable resentment against the boy, shared, as tradition has it, even by his mother. As time went on, and his response continued to be negative, their irritation vented itself in open cruelty. Hoping that stern measures might succeed when gentle treatment had failed, his kinsmen placed him, so we are told, under the guardianship of a muleteer. But blows could not cure the luckless boy.

We know of no portrait of Claudius in this early period. We may, however, visualize his appearance after looking at the picture Suetonius draws of him in his mature age.

He possessed majesty and dignity of appearance, but only when he was standing still or sitting, and especially when he was lying down; for he was tall but not slender, with an attractive face, becoming white hair, and a full neck. But when he walked, his weak knees gave way under him, and he had many disagreeable traits both in his lighter moments and when he was engaged in business; his laughter was unseemly and his anger still more disgusting, for he would foam at the mouth and trickle at the nose; he stammered besides and his head was very shaky at all times, but especially when he made the least exertion. Though previously his health was bad, it was excellent while he was Emperor except for attacks of heartburn, which he said all but drove him to suicide.

We may take it for granted that these symptoms were present, and indeed in an aggravated form, in the adolescent.

When the young man reached the age at which he ought to begin his public career, he was still so much of an invalid that his kinsmen were asking themselves whether it would be wise to let him appear in public at all even as a private citizen. This we gather from a question of his grandmother, Livia, to Augustus. Weary of their perennial indecision, the Emperor replied that it was time to stop reopening Claudius' problem every new moon. "I desire," he wrote, "that something be decided once for all about the whole matter, to save us from constantly wavering between hope and fear." Yet at the moment he was writing this, Augustus could not make up his mind whether or not the boy would

be permanently "defective in soundness of body and mind."

The fact that Augustus thought it necessary to speak in these terms suggests a division of counsel in the imperial family. One group doubtless held that the boy must always be kept in isolation. The other thought that he was not so hopeless as to be definitely barred from the magisterial career. This group probably took into account an increasing evidence the youth was giving of intellectual curiosity and a passion for the study of history. He grew so proficient in this field that finally they commissioned Livy to tutor him. Claudius was developing unsuspected abilities. Augustus himself was impressed by this promising turn. "Confound me, dear Livia," he wrote at another time, "if I am not surprised that your grandson Tiberius could please me with his declaiming. How in the world anyone who is so unclear in his conversation can speak with clearness and propriety when he declaims, is more than I can see." Augustus was impressed by another characteristic of his grandson. This again from another letter to Livia: "The poor fellow is unlucky; for in important matters, where his mind does not wander, the nobility of his character is apparent enough." But the Emperor never reversed his belief that Claudius was unfit for the *cursus honorum.* . . .

When, on the threshold of manhood, Claudius' gradual improvement was giving hopes of a complete recovery, there developed one of those unfortunate situations which frequently cause elders to mistake the intellectual integrity of the young for perversity or downright degeneracy. He had made such progress in his studies that Livy encouraged him to write a *History of the Civil War from the Death of Julius Caesar.* We may surmise the spirit of this work. It would seem that when the sensitive youth felt the ill-concealed hostility of his kinsmen, he sought comfort in the memory of his famous father. Drusus was probably not so great a man as tradition represents him, but there is no doubt that he was regarded as a national hero. It was natural for the lad Claudius, rebuffed on every side, to imagine that his kinsmen would have been more kind if his father were alive. This pathetic situation led him to a more intense reverence for his father and the things his father thought or did. Drusus had professed devotion to the Republic. It was said that he had contemplated the issuance of an appeal to Augustus to restore the old régime. Claudius must have written his history with almost instinctive republican bias if both Antonia and Livia, his mother and grandmother, objected to the "freedom and truth" with which he narrated the death agony of the Republic. This view is confirmed by the young man's admiration for Cicero whom his grandfathers, Antony and Octavian, had put to death. It was not politic to mention him in public when Claudius was in his teens. The boy's appraisement of the orator may be gauged from the fact that he wrote a little later a *Defense of Cicero against Asinius Gallus*. His courage in taking a position at variance with the trend of the age and the prejudice of the dynasty must have seemed nothing short of mental aberration to his kinsfolk, especially Livia and Antonia. The moment the young man cast doubts upon the legitimacy of the Principate, the imperial family abandoned whatever hope they had had of making him respectable. It was clear to them that as soon as he overcame an old fault, he fell prey to some new one. Every unorthodox word of his, every awkward gesture which ordinarily might have escaped attention, was now looked upon as fresh evidence that he was incurable. . . .

Excluded by sickness from the military career that had brought fame to his father and brother, he sought excitement in gladiatorial combats. He was the first to arrive at the games and the last to leave. It is said that the sight of blood exhilarated him and caused him to order, when he was Emperor, the despatch even of those combatants who fell accidentally in the arena. It is said also that he made a practice of extracting confession by torture, enjoyed the sight of an execution, and took a morbid interest in watching the faces of dying gladiators. He has been charged with sending thirty-five senators and two or three hundred knights to their doom, but in view of the discrepancy in the transmission of these figures, it

would seem best to judge him chiefly on the evidence of those executions which are recorded individually. However, when we recall the numerous plots to assassinate him we may well believe that he struck back, and sometimes savagely.

Reverence for his family did not prevent him from mixing with scapegraces of the aristocracy and with individuals socially his inferior. Augustus was annoyed by the company he kept. When Tiberius, some time later, refused him a magistracy, he felt this humiliation so deeply that for a time he solaced himself in drunkenness and gambling and the renewed intimacy of disreputable friends. He must have been unable to resist their influence if he put his signature as a witness to a forged will.

The literary sources fail to explain how Claudius, in his boyhood rarely allowed from the nursery, deprived in his youth of the association of his equals, and looked upon when adult as a failure, developed as it were overnight into an efficient administrator. The fact is that when he was offered the Empire, he showed capacity to rule. He forgot and forgave whatever wrongs and injuries he had received in private life, was free from vanity, and although he represented the majesty of Rome and must therefore be clothed in all the honors and prerogatives of his office, he tried to be moderate in this respect. He did not allow the Senate to confer upon him the title Father of the Senate, nor did he assume, after his triumph over Britain, the surname Britannicus. He conferred honors upon his deceased kinsmen out of a sense of reverence, but discouraged marks of distinction for himself and kept his family, even Messalina, in the background. The grant of a special position to the Emperor's consort appears only after his marriage with Agrippina. It would be interesting to know whether the woman's overpowering ambition was the sole reason. The fact that she was of the blood of Augustus and the issue of Germanicus was bound to make a difference. He rewarded liberally all who served him in war or peace, freely acknowledging the debt he owed his friends, even going so far as to support for the quaestorship a certain man for no other reason than that his grandfather had once given him, when ill, a cup of water.

He not only had a remarkable knowledge of the problems of government, but he brought a new sense of responsibility to the throne and a strong conviction that the welfare of the people was dependent upon the policies of the *Princeps*. He stands out as a humane ruler. He did of course strengthen the State, enlarging its rights and defining them in favor of imperial centralization; but he was nevertheless conscious that among the duties of the State towards the individual there was that of protecting the weaker members of society, women, minors, slaves, and provincials. This was a constant preoccupation with him, whether he laid down policies as a ruler, or sat as a judge in the law courts, or acted in the ordinary course of administration.

A glance at his social legislation will illustrate this claim. To protect women from putting their dowry in jeopardy, he forbade them to stand surety not only for their husbands, as ordained by Augustus, but for any person. While protecting their property, he gave them a larger degree of freedom and dignity. Even when *sui iuris*, women had been under the tutelage of their agnates; Claudius did away with this legal disability inherited from a former age when they were regarded as socially and spiritually inferior. He was the first Emperor to rule that a mother could be the natural heir of the estate of her sons and daughters who died intestate. . . . He tried to prevent the exploitation of minors by unscrupulous usurers who were wont to loan them money with payment at their fathers' death. . . . [He protected a son's property in] case his father's property was sequestered by the courts, and would not permit men to bequeath their property to the Emperor if they had living relatives. Masters who, to escape further responsibility abandoned sick and aged slaves, were enjoined from claiming further ownership over them; and if they killed infirm slaves, they were henceforth adjudged guilty of murder. . . .

This liberalism towards those members of society most in need of protection, mild enough in itself, is the more remarkable in view of the fact that Claudius was a conservative by instinct. As a conservative, he remained in general faithful to the ideals and interests of his class. . . .

His ability to win the affection of the common people deserves notice. When a false rumor was circulated that he had been murdered, the mob staged a riot. Since there is no indication that he purchased the popular favor by corrupt methods as did Gaius and Nero, we may perhaps assume that the man in the street looked upon him as a beneficent prince.

As Emperor he displayed prodigious industry. He would begin to work about midnight, and his days were packed full with business. He sat long with his counsellors, rarely missed a meeting of the Senate, presided from early morning to late evening at the tribunal, went from court to court and from bureau to bureau, checking the conduct of officials, and attended to innumerable details, even drafting his own speeches and official papers.

Claudius' achievements in the art of government cannot be ascribed to a sudden awakening of his mind. They can be accounted for only as the result of long preparation in that period of his life which Tacitus characterizes as politically barren. We may put the problem in another way. The literary sources have concentrated upon one aspect of the youth of Claudius, emphasizing his faults. There was no doubt a basis for some of the tales about him, but the legend grew out of all proportion to the facts. The other aspect, the growth of that capacity for serious work and sustained endeavor which had earlier surprised Augustus, the struggle of the young man with himself, the will to overcome his infirmities, and the effort to discipline his mind were ignored.

As a youth Claudius would leave the dinner table to dash off to a lecture. He had purpose and consistency in his studies, was capable of independent thought, and would stop writing on an attractive subject rather than garble it to suit his imperial kinsmen. He became a man of letters and a historian of some ability. Suetonius regards him as a writer of poor taste, but the more fastidious Tacitus states that he could both think straight and express his thoughts with grace.

In addition to the works that have already been mentioned, Claudius wrote *From the End of the Civil War*, in forty-one books, a treatise *On the Latin Alphabet*, an *Etruscan History* in twenty books, and a *Carthaginian History* in eight. He found time to study and write even in the palace, "and gave constant recitals through a professional reader." It was probably at this period that he wrote his *Autobiography* in eight books. He availed himself of his influence as Emperor to carry out the reform of the alphabet which, as shown by his treatise, had long been a subject of study with him. He gave practical encouragement to letters, building and endowing an addition to the Museum in Alexandria, named henceforth the Claudian Institute, and keeping in constant touch with writers and scientists. Whatever scientific information he obtained from his legates and procurators and from the intelligence department of the army, he systematically incorporated in his works.

Pertinent to our problem is also the evidence that Claudius' interest in the study of history was more than academic. While to all appearances he was wasting his time, he was equipping himself for the task of governing in case he should ever be called to the throne. In one of his speeches he reveals a lofty conception of the spirit of the Roman constitution and a knowledge of the methods of its growth. He shows in another document that he had an elastic view of the law and knew when to subordinate the claims of an arid legalism to those of reason and equity. Other documents prove that he was a good diplomat and that while still in private life he was attentively following the course of contemporary politics and storing up information about men and problems. It may perhaps have been due to his interest in the political problems of the day that Tiberius began to consider him as possible imperial timber.

Not that these observations solve the riddle of Claudius' personality. The riddle is still there: untrained and deemed unfit for the throne, he gave the Empire an efficient and enlightened rule. The mistakes of his administration do not materially alter this appraisal. Tradition has suppressed the data necessary for the complete solution of this problem. Worse still it has twisted the evidence. The picture it gives of the youth of Claudius is incomplete. Probably it is also false.

Claudius' sudden translation from obscurity to the most exalted position on earth caused a wag to exclaim that one must be born a king or a fool. . . . The new Emperor did not possess the majestic bearing of an Augustus or a Tiberius, nor the youthful charm of Gaius. He remained always the scholar, not different in the palace from what he had been in his study. He never posed and never acted as if he held the world in his hands. What men saw in him was a good-natured prince, ill at ease in his sudden splendor. The senatorial aristocracy was shocked by his awkward manners. They could not understand how a man without experience in practical politics could ever govern with wisdom. Unwilling to give him credit for a certain nobility of ideas, they riveted their eyes on his faults, his homely humor, his coarse simplicity, and above all his irrepressible habit of mixing the serious with the facetious and rambling, even while addressing the Senate, from official business to irrelevant personal matters. The elder statesmen smiled at this naive Emperor who thought he could restore religion and improve morals by legislation, or cure graft by denouncing evil doers.

The charge of stupidity recurrent in the literary sources is traceable in large part to political bias. True, as a boy Claudius was thought to be wanting in judgment, and even his mother considered him a little fool. Strangely enough, he himself must have been trying to live up to this unenviable reputation if it be true that he feigned stupidity as a means of self-preservation. Here then was ample ground for the charge. It would be a mistake, however, to give Seneca and Tacitus full credence when they too accuse Claudius of stupidity, for their motivation was essentially political. Their indictment narrows down to two counts: first, that Claudius was led like a puppet by his wives and freedmen; second, that he was incapable of assessing the worth of testimony introduced in court but would condemn a party to a suit without giving it a hearing. That is, he heard the plaintiff alone or the defendant alone, and forthwith rendered judgment. Seneca adds a touch of humor when he says that sometimes he heard neither party. We shall deal with the first count later. Let us examine at this point the charges concerning his judicial idiosyncrasies.

The circumstances were as follows. Litigation over trivialities had become so common and had so cluttered the courts that drastic measures were needed to relieve the situation. Claudius sought his remedy in the principle that, if one of the parties to a suit did not appear at the trial, the judges would decide in favor of the party present. Far from being an innovation, the practice of condemning *in absentia* was as old as the Twelve Tables and remained in vigor throughout the republican era. Claudius' successors retained it. Nero himself, hostile though he was to his stepfather, adopted it, and the Justinian Code recognized it as a fundamental principle in court procedure. The courts of our modern states do likewise in certain kinds of litigation. An official speech by Claudius, of which we shall have more to say, throws light on this subject. The Emperor complains that when the courts recessed for the summer holiday, a great number of suits, mostly of a trivial nature, was left pending. This nuisance caused defendants no small amount of inconvenience since they could not leave the city while under indictment, whereas their accusers might travel freely. Claudius did away with this invidious inequality by obliging the plaintiff also to remain in the city during the summer recess.

Suetonius and Cassius Dio see another sign of stupidity in Claudius' alleged practice of sentencing people to death on the sole evidence of the accuser's dream that they harbored criminal designs against the Princeps. But Suetonius speaks of two cases only: that of Gaius Appius Silanus, Messalina's stepfather, and another where he does not take the trouble of naming either the accuser or the accused. As far as Suetonius is concerned, Silanus' case is the more important; yet he records it only as rumor. If we turn to Cassius Dio, we run into more mystery, for according to him Silanus owed his death to Messalina, angered by his refusal to lie with her, and to the freedman Narcissus "who had been

alienated by this slight shown to her." Dio continued that, correct as Silanus had been in his public and private life, no criminal charge could be found against him. Nothing daunted, Messalina and Narcissus concocted the fable that they both had dreamed that he was planning to kill the Emperor.

The sources charge Claudius with cowardice, and the charge would seem valid in view of his lack of training for the battles of public life. Dio relates that Messalina and the freedmen could extort from him any concession by the simple trick of conjuring up before his eyes imaginary dangers. Scribonianus thought he could frighten him into abdicating merely by sending him a threatening letter. Suetonius illustrates Claudius' cowardice with the story that he used to exclaim "every day, and almost every hour and minute, 'Scold me, but hands off,'" but whether this refers to Claudius as a boy or as Emperor, Suetonius does not disclose. Moreover, what Suetonius characterizes as fear Dio regards as prudence. Certain protective measures were imperative in the overcharged atmosphere of the earlier years of Claudius' reign. Such was his absence from the Curia in the first month he was Emperor when the passions aroused by the Senate's failure to restore the Republic were still hot. And such were the precautionary steps he took when appearing out of doors and when accepting dinner invitations, the practice of having every caller searched for concealed weapons, and the order forbidding soldiers to enter the house of a senator. Augustus and Tiberius had found it necessary to take precautions. If Claudius made the protection of the Princeps' person a regular and elaborate system, there was need for it. Several conspiracies had been formed against each of his predecessors; Gaius had fallen victim to one such plot, and no less than six attempts were made against Claudius himself. He was also aware that the Senate's hatred of him was deeper than against his predecessors for the very good reason that he had shattered forever its dream of regaining power. He had acquired a good knowledge of senatorial intrigue in those years when, writing with a freedom that irked his elders, he very likely found encouragement in the aristocratic families opposed to the Principate. Their resentment against the *Princeps* he could not easily forget.

There is another aspect to this question. Claudius gave evidence of fearlessness where other men might have hesitated. In the first hours of his reign, he resisted single-handed the Senate's determination to damn the memory of Gaius. He challenged public opinion in Italy when he decided to confer the honor of senatorial membership upon provincials. Despite the unwillingness of his immediate predecessors to undertake foreign wars lest the legions raise the victorious general to the throne, he entrusted to others the conquest of Britain. He undertook a gigantic project, the building of the port of Ostia, although engineers warned him that the cost would be prohibitive. He must have been endowed with a certain strength of character if despite his bodily ills he could, as a youngster, apply himself to serious study, and in his later years lead an extraordinarily busy life while pain "all but drove him to suicide." He was able to maintain his poise at the approach of danger and distinguish between real plots and those organized by cranks. After one of the numerous attempts on his life he asked the Senate to pass new laws to protect his person. His critics took no notice that he went after this objective in constitutional ways instead of resorting to that type of self-help common among tyrants. They saw only a ruler ignominiously imploring help.

Tradition pictures Claudius as a man who had no independence of mind but did the bidding of others. Under tutelage until well past his minority, it no doubt became a habit with him to depend on others, constantly seek their advice, and defer to their judgment. As Emperor he had more counsellors and surrounded himself with more *amici* than his predecessors. His elders had so emphasized his misfortunes that he must have been overconscious of his limitations. Even when he sat on the mightiest throne on earth, he customarily assumed towards his peers a humble, almost apologetic, attitude. Yet he

was capable of challenging their opinions. We shall see that he could throw off his baggage of erudition, and that when it came to choosing between alternatives, he usually chose one that increased administrative efficiency or was in step with the progressive ideas of the age. Indeed, all evidence points to the conclusion that he either was capable of independent thought or shrewd enough to select the right advisors.

This brings us to the problem of his alleged dependence upon freedman. He made these freedmen secretaries of state, and collectively they formed a cabinet which had no place in the constitution, yet held real power. No wonder that the Senate, a committee of which had previously been the official advisor of the Princeps, saw in the palace council a powerful rival. This was reason enough for representing the freedmen as a pack of malefactors, occupied in intrigue and plunder, and their master as a half-wit, incapable of opposing or even perceiving their greed. Dio's statement that his disreputable public acts were not his, but those of his slaves and wives, equivalent as it is to saying that these helpers were evil, explains nothing. The truth is that Claudius' contemporaries were unable to account for the conflict in his administration. That such a conflict existed is evident, but it was less in Claudius himself than in the society in which he lived and the system to which he fell heir. At his accession the old republican ideal was making its last stand against one-man rule. Although conservative by instinct and attached to the tradition of the Republic, Claudius was drawn by the demands of the Empire to take steps contributing to the further disintegration of the Republic. But this antinomy was not of his making; its seed had been planted by Augustus when he placed himself above the Republic though still dressed in republican robes. It was humanly impossible to maintain the balance struck by Augustus. To preserve the Principate, his successors, barring none, had often to act contrary to their own predilections, thereby incurring the charge of hypocrisy, inconsistency, stupidity, or depravity.

Claudius' Policy of Centralization

Arnoldo Momigliano

The late Arnoldo Momigliano of London, Pisa and Chicago championed the revisionist view of Claudius as an excellent and humane administrator about the same time that Robert Graves incorporated similar themes in his historical novels. Momigliano shows that, for all his talk about collaboration with the Senate and his early popularity with the equestrians, he centralized his administration in the hands of his household freedmen and depended for political support on the praetorians and the army. The conquests of Britain and Mauretania were pursued at least partly to reinforce Claudius' popularity with the imperial troops.

Momigliano also examines Claudius' policies of centralization and Romanization. He attempted to extend to provinces the rights formerly reserved to Italy, but he expected genuine Romanization to occur. Gauls were brought into the Senate; citizenship was given to municipalities; and a system of roads reinforced commercial as well as political ties. Claudius was concerned about his Empire and wished to govern it well, and the documentary evidence records that he was rather good at it.

Claudius' predecessors had no executive machinery at their disposal except in the administration of the provinces. In Rome they affected their purposes either by legislating themselves or by prompting the Senate or the Comitia to legislate: they did not possess any real executive staff of their own. Claudius was the first Emperor to organize a secretariat. He increased the number of the private secretaries already, no doubt, possessed by his predecessors, allotted a clearly defined task to each, and established a special office for each department of administration. Though no formal or legal innovation was made, in practice the imperial court for the first time became the executive headquarters of the administration. The Emperor entrusted his most confidential tasks, not to senators or Equites, either as a class or as individuals, but to members of his own household—to slaves or freedmen. It was the imperial chancery that issued orders and received appeals. The effect of this was to secure the Emperor's independence of both the Senate and the Equestrian Order; to extend and intensify his authority in the provinces, a natural result of the establishment of a strong central organization, which always influences the efficiency of the outlying parts; to establish, in particular, a general control over the procurators in the senatorial provinces, whose duty was in theory to look after imperial property, and in fact to keep a watch upon the senatorial administration; and finally to enable the Emperor to enter more fully into all problems, both political and more especially judicial. The changes carried out by Claudius in the other departments of administration all depend logically upon this reform, which also accounts for that unusual judicial activity which the ancient world regarded as one of his eccentricities, but which is in truth one of the many aspects of his policy of centralization. This reform assumes an even graver significance when we observe that it caused the chief offices in the State to fall to men who stood entirely outside Roman tradition, who represented only the interests of the Princeps, and who regarded those interests mainly from the standpoint of their own private advantage. The whole 'Italic' basis of the Empire, and not merely the ruling class of a particular age, had begun to collapse; and although the freedmen, with their varied origin, introduced a certain cosmopolitanism, this did not amount even to a rough representation of provincial interests; for, being freedmen, these imperial ministers had no real roots in the countries from which they came. In his desire to oppose the Roman aristocracy

Claudius undesignedly took a long step towards estranging the government from the life of the Empire, with the ultimate result of making the channels of communication between the government and its subjects ever more difficult and indirect. A new governing class was arising. The first of the two main justifications for Augustus' compromise with the old governing classes—that they were irreplaceable—was losing its force. The second was the value of the Roman tradition of which these classes were the guardians. Claudius believed that this justification still held good; yet it was the cause of his vacillation between the old order and the new.

The officials of the imperial chancery were Narcissus, the private secretary (*ab epistulis*); Pallas, agent for the *patrimonium* (*a rationibus*); Callistus, a kind of Minister of Grace and Justice (*a libellis*), *whose duty it was to investigate all petitions and perhaps also to look after the judicial inquiries of the Emperor* (*cognitiones*); Polybius, the Emperor's adviser on artistic and literary questions and perhaps on questions of religious policy (*a studiis*). Their importance has led ancients and moderns alike to suppose that the government must have fallen entirely into their hands. The baselessness of this supposition is obvious; the fact that Claudius was the organizer of this ministry is proof enough that his personality dominated it.

The Senate, already shorn of authority by this move, was rendered helpless by all other possible means. It was terrorized, thirty or thirty-five of its members being condemned to death according to our authorities; and new senators were brought in to alter its character. In 47-8 Claudius revived the censorship for the regular eighteen months, after it had been in abeyance for sixty-eight years, and took office himself with L. Vitellius; undoubtedly one of his main reasons was that he could thus carry out . . . a partial reconstitution of the Senate. . . .

To sum up: Claudius brought about a change both of the tone and of the personnel of the Senate, ruthlessly crushing men who were hostile to him and replacing them by his supporters. He centralized the administration in the hands of a group of freedmen belonging to his own household. He destroyed the independence of the [Treasury], leaving it to grow both politically and economically more and more insignificant; and he tried to diminish the importance of the senatorial element in the army. None of the Emperors who had gone before him, not even the orientalizing absolutist Gaius, had dared to make such an assault on the authority of the Senate. Yet the assault was made by a man who seems honestly to have desired the senators to co-operate with him against themselves . . . .

. . . The result was that, in spite of superficial appearances to the contrary, Claudius could not found his régime upon the support either of the Senate or of the Equites—broadly speaking, of what we usually call the Italian upper middle class. Though the Roman populace was friendly, the true source of effective support was the army. Claudius never forgot that he owed his throne to the Praetorians: indeed, he acknowledged the fact on two well-known coins. . . , with designs showing respectively the Praetorian camp and the Emperor holding out his hand to a Praetorian. He was, as we know, the first Emperor to establish the custom of making the Praetorians a present when they proclaimed him imperator, and this present came to be repeated annually. A more difficult problem was that of maintaining the loyalty of the rest of the army which did not know him personally. It is clear that he was helped by the tradition, still not seriously shaken, of loyalty to the Julian house, and also by the distribution of the army in separate groups, which made it hopeless for any one commander to draw a majority of the whole army to his allegiance, as the events of 68-9 were to prove. Once the dynasty was gone, no general found himself able to gain the acceptance of the Empire as a whole, and each had to attempt the overthrow of his opponents by force of arms. Claudius was skillful enough, however, to win the prestige of a victorious general during the first years of his reign, mainly through the conquest of Mauretania and Britain; and there is no doubt that this prestige very definitely helped to reinforce the army's attachment to him, the more so since his campaigns were undertaken not out of mere passion for military adventure but in response to the vital needs of the Empire. . . .

The first signs of Claudius' strong centralizing policy showed themselves in his organization of the provinces. Despite superficial appearances to the contrary, he disregarded the privileges of Rome and Italy, and set himself to achieve uniformity and equal status for the provinces, and to do away with their inferiority to Italy. This reversal of the Augustan conception, still fundamentally a conception of Italy as mistress of the Empire, was at once the consequence and the justification of Claudius' struggle against the senatorial and equestrian aristocracy to bring the Empire under the single control of the Emperor—its consequence, because the Emperor was forced to appeal to the provinces in order to make head against the privileged classes and to check the predominance of the Italian nucleus in the army; its justification, because equality of status for the provinces was the normal goal of an ideal of right that by erecting a sounder and juster system of civic relations transcended the barriers between conquerors and conquered. And it must not be forgotten that once the monarch has made his appearance, even if only unwillingly and by implication as in the case of Claudius, every distinction between governing and governed races must eventually vanish; for both will be reduced to the common level of the subject. The essential nature of monarchy had always produced the same result, whether in the Persian Empire or in the Empire of Alexander. Only we must not expect to find a vast revolution when we examine Claudius' slow, cautious, but still resolute work of reform.

Claudius' contemporaries knew what he was aiming at. Seneca defined his ultimate goal in a famous phrase: ["He was determined to see all Greeks, Gauls, Spaniards, and Britons wearing the toga."] His provisions in respect of the Gallic senators and his edicts of religious toleration towards the Jews have already been mentioned; they were measures intended, from very different points of view, to enable provincials to share on equal terms in the common life and work of the Empire. Certain of Claudius' other measures, at first sight more purely material in character, are perhaps still more significant, as showing how in the economic or the political sphere the ideal of unification was realized in practice. Claudius was a great builder of roads; and the political as well as commercial and military importance of roads for the unity of the Empire is a commonplace. . . .

Claudius' achievement is characterized throughout by a spirit of justice blended with conciliation and good sense, but conservatism always exerted a restraining influence. His feeling for justice can be traced all through his minor legislation, though this need not be closely analysed in search for any deeper meaning than it carries on its face. These are the routine measures of administration which any ruler could take, whether he were Claudius or Gaius, granted a certain administrative tradition; yet even in small matters of this kind a certain direction is observable, certain features of Claudius' personality take concrete shape. The tendency to uphold the Republican social structure which was seen in Claudius' religious restoration reappears here in statements and reminders of the juridical principles that govern the institution of the family. . . .

A true definition of that spirit [of equity] was given in Claudius' own day by a zealous official, Fabius Persicus, proconsul of Asia, even if his words are as flat as the restatement of another's policy is bound to be:

'But I think it better to adhere to this opinion, following the example of the most powerful and just Lord [Claudius], who, receiving the whole race of men into his personal care, has been pleased to include this also among his first and universally acceptable benevolences, that every man shall receive his own.'

In his courtier-like phraseology Fabius Persicus defined the new imperial outlook, which tried, even if it sometimes failed, to dispense justice based on humanity to all subjects of the Empire; whereas the ethic of Republican Rome had secured freedom for the few at the cost of oppressing the majority. The attempt to impose the new ideal, taken over unchanged from Hellenistic sovereigns, upon the ideal of loyalty to the strict Roman tradition, which meant inequality for the provinces, was the most characteristic sign of what we have continually described as the inherent contradiction in Claudius. While he could not envisage an Empire that did not rest upon Roman *virtus* and on the classes which seemed to embody it, he more or less deliberately provided it with a new and incongruous foundation which brought with it new men. The scholar's habit of observing how new institutions are imposed upon old, while ignoring the process of conflict that frequently ensues between the two, prevented Claudius from recognizing in practical politics the opposition that existed between the Imperial world-city and the institutions of Republican Rome. It was an opposition inherent in the Augustan system. Constitutionally unable to see this opposition as a problem demanding to be solved, Claudius perpetuated it and rendered it still more bitter than before.

The Good and Evil of Claudius' Reign

M. P. Charlesworth

The late M. P. Charlesworth of Cambridge University here weighs the pros and cons of the reign of Claudius. The senatorial historians criticize his surrender to his wives, concubines and freedmen, but the actual documents from the period give a distinctive and consistent portrait of the emperor. These edicts and letters show a slightly pedantic, well-informed and humane administrator attempting to impose far-reaching, progressive policies on a sprawling Empire.

[After Claudius' death] there were many [in the provinces] to remember him gratefully, in Rome fewer, yet in spite of the executions that stained his Principate he was the first of the successors of Augustus to be given the honour of deification. The really unpopular parts of his rule are easily discerned from Nero's opening programme to the Senate: what men had objected to was Claudius' absorption in the courts, the abuse of trials, the power of the freedmen, and the gradual encroachment upon the rights of the Senate; all this the young ruler promised he would renounce.

It was the Senate in fact which most had felt itself in danger from Claudius, but what that meant must be carefully defined. Claudius had no idea of dispossessing the Senate or of antiquating it, like Gaius; his historical sense was too keen. But he did intend the Senate to take its duties seriously and to share his views as to the responsibilities of a ruling class. Some were prepared to co-operate with him—there was no lack of willing governors for the provinces—but if they were not they must make room for those whom the Princeps knew to be more able or more conscientious or better fitted. On some of the Senate's functions in Italy he undoubtedly did encroach, but the great bulk of its duties was left unharmed, and he did all he could to safeguard its prestige and high position and to recall the more inert to a realization of these. 'If these proposals,' he said, in recommending some judicial reforms, 'are approved by you, show your assent at once plainly and sincerely. If, however, you do not approve them then find some other remedies, but here in this temple now, or if you wish to take a longer time for consideration, take it, so long as you recollect that wherever you meet you should produce an opinion of your own. For it is extremely unfitting, Conscript Fathers, to the high dignity of this order that at this meeting one man only, the consul designate, should make a speech (and that copied exactly from the proposal of the consuls), while the rest utter one word only, 'Agreed,' and then after leaving the House remark 'There, we've given our opinion.' This was the lesson that Claudius would have the Senate learn, but earnest though he was he could impart it with a touch of humour that lightened it, and these are not the words of a master who holds the whip-hand, but of one reasoning with equals.

Indeed, as senators these nobles had nothing to fear from Claudius; what was dangerous was to be rich or popular with the army or a descendant of the divine Augustus. Riches attracted the greed and envy of the freedmen or wives of Claudius; and if in addition the victim possessed a famous name, or the loyalty of the legions, or claimed descent from Augustus, then the simplest way to incriminate him was to suggest that he was a conspirator or possible rebel and have the case heard in secrecy. There was little likelihood of pardon from an emperor whose timidity or superstition was only too easily excited, who was well aware of his own bodily infirmities and remembered that his predecessor had been assassinated. But this does not prove that the Senate was useless or abject: there were no heroics because there was no call for them; there was plenty of honest discussion. Nor was it as servile as is sometimes supposed. Even in the days when Agrippina's power was high she could not save one of her agents . . . from ignominious expulsion. The Senate could still be a partner as Augustus had wished.

But though Claudius could look to the Senate to supply him with governors and generals . . . and confidential advisers such as L. Vitellius (in whose charge he left the empire during his journey to and from Britain), for his personal assistants he turned mostly to the equites. Though there were incompetents, a man such as L. Julius Vestinus, who carried out important duties with skill and tact, could win his praise as an 'ornament of the equestrian order,' and into this order he was ready to promote freedmen of tried merit or centurions of good service. . . . On this order a *princeps* was bound to rely ultimately for the bulk of his higher civil servants, and a generation later we find Vitellius choosing his chief secretaries from it rather than from the unpopular freedmen. And there is evidence that Claudius was prepared to bestow knighthood and important office upon Greeks or Jews or men of non-Roman extraction from the Eastern provinces. . . . For the equestrian order therefore privileges were carefully guarded, and in his censorship, . . . Claudius punished with enslavement some four hundred men who had usurped these privileges.

Such was his attitude to the two great orders of Roman society. . . . His treatment of the provinces arose out of no mere amiability but from a very real sense of the continuity of the Roman historical process, a process that owed its impulse to the wise admission of precedent. . . . He used the past not as so many do as a contrast or as an object to the future but as a justification and encouragement for still bolder measures.

Were this the whole story Claudius would unhesitatingly be entitled to a place among the greater rulers of Rome, but it is not. Inevitably, with the new efficient secretariat and with increased centralization, the Principate began to draw near to the outward form of a monarchy; the princeps and his family were becoming a royal family, raised above the citizens and protected by bodyguards, his house a palace with courtiers, ceremonials and intrigues. The wife of the princeps begins to assume an importance that would have scandalized Augustus or Tiberius: magistrates celebrated the birthday of Messalina and offered vows for her, and at the British triumph she was allowed to follow her husband's chariot in a *carpentum*, a carriage reserved for Vestal Virgins and priests on solemn occasions. Agrippina was still more exalted; men had spoken jeeringly of Messalina as a queen, but she nearly turned the gibe into earnest; at public spectacles, even at military parades, she would appear gorgeously robed by the side of Claudius, . . . the title *Augusta* was conferred upon her in 50, and Colonia Agrippinensis (Cologne) was named in her honour. The Princeps Iuventutis, Nero, like some young Hellenistic prince, was given the head of the Alexandrian Museum, Chaeremon the Stoic, for his tutor in Greek, and the most famous literary man of his day, Seneca, for his instructor in things Roman.

Nor was this all. While this development was contrary to Roman tradition and sentiment and to Augustus' intentions, there were men happy enough to forward a process which proved profitable to themselves. While smaller fry . . . grew rich on accusations, greater men such as Seneca or Vitellius adapted themselves to furthering their rulers' purposes. When Messalina coveted the gardens of Valerius Asiaticus it was on Vitellius' eloquence that she relied to secure condemnation, and when Agrippina wished to break the betrothal between Junius

Silanus and Octavia—so that she could be married to Nero—who but the faithful Vitellius could be found to inform Claudius of the distressing rumour that Silanus had committed incest with his sister? . . . Thanks to such courtiers and their fellows the language of a divine monarchy was beginning to make headway and phrases Tiberius had deprecated were now freely applied. Men could speak of the majesty of the ruler, of Claudius' sacred hands or sacred duties; Scribonius Largus writes openly of 'our god Caesar.' The fulsome tone of the *senatus consultum* passed in honour of Pallas . . . reveals to what a depth flattery of the freedman could sink. For these court officials, despised and hated, were also to be feared and propitiated and liked to abase the pride of a Roman: 'I have seen,' writes Seneca, 'the former master of Callistus stand before his door and be refused admittance while others passed in,' and Seneca himself from his exile in Corsica courted the goodwill of Polybius in language that pains his admirers.

But the most serious evil of Claudius' Principate was the power that he unwittingly surrendered to his wives and freedmen of enriching themselves by the sale of offices, immunities or grants of citizenship, or by the more brutal methods of confiscation and murder; the number of the victims, senators and knights, dwelt long in the memory of the Roman nobility. Our sources depict, therefore, an emperor weak, absent-minded, and deaf, prematurely aged through a long series of illnesses and by bouts of self-indulgence and gluttony, falling more and more under the domination of wills stronger than his own—a picture which the history of his last three or four years at home and abroad tends to confirm. It is true, but it is not the whole truth. Here as always the difference between Rome and the provinces must be borne in mind. In the edicts and letters that have survived we can judge for ourselves another aspect of Claudius, and the judgment must be favourable. Apart altogether from their content, the importance of which has been discussed above, in every one of them—whether he is counselling the Jews to show for other's religion something of the respect he does for theirs, or reminding senators what is due from their position, or confirming the disputed rights of the Anauni, even if it is merely a plain letter of acknowledgment to the guild of Dionysiac artists in Miletus—there is always present something strongly individual, revealing a nature sometimes pedantic or digressive, but kindly and understanding, not lacking in sense of humour, eager to promote order and justice, and genuinely anxious for the well-being of the ruled. His readiness to grant citizenship, to bring provincials into the Senate, and to found colonies, smacks of Caesar rather than of Augustus, but two generations had passed since the battle of Actium and he could attempt things that Augustus dared not. The good that he did endured and developed into the heritage of the empire, the evil was soon forgotten with Nero and civil wars following, the grotesque figure no longer seen. This was the ruler whom Agrippina killed to set her son upon the throne, herself to fall among his early victims.

The obverse of this Tiberian brass *sestertius* contains the large letters SC which indicate that the coinage was issued by the Senate (*Senatus consulto*). Though the Julio-Claudian emperors kept all gold and silver coinage under their direct control, senatorial mints continued to issue brass and copper coins.

XI

Foreigners, Freedmen, Senators & Slaves: The Imperial Court

INTRODUCTION
Ronald Mellor

The first century of imperial rule saw the growth and elaboration of a system of government which reached from the imperial palace to the most remote provinces of a vast empire. Roman republican magistrates had conducted state business with their personal slaves and freedmen as if they were administering their personal estates or their household finances. Augustus continued this practice, and the army of imperial slaves and freedmen, familia Caesaris, *dominated the clerical and financial posts in the imperial administration. And yet the public image of imperial administration included imperial relatives, senators, equestrians and foreign princes who held positions of genuine authority as generals, provincial governors, prefects and client kings. All these groups centered on the imperial court where together with countless hangers-on like poets, astrologers and actors they competed ruthlessly for the emperor's attention, favor and even love.*

The aristocratic elite had for centuries been suspicious and even contemptuous of foreigners— and into the first century B.C. even residents of Italians cities were regarded as foreigners. These non-Romans had fought for hundreds of years beside the Roman legions to conquer Rome's empire but even their acquisition of Roman citizenship in 88 B.C. did not bring them respect and political influence. Augustus, however, relied on such Italian confidants as his general Agrippa and his close advisor Maecenas—sprung from an ancient Etruscan family and the patron of the dazzling collection of "Italian" writers who adorned the Augustan court: Virgil, Horace, Livy, and Propertius.

Augustus also drew heavily on the commercial elite from Italian cities to provide political support and administrative service. These "new men" became equestrians or were even enrolled in the Senate where they replaced the declining Roman aristocracy. And it was on these senators that the Julio-Claudian emperors relied to lead their armies where arrogant and proud aristocrats with distinguished forebears might be far too dangerous. In the most sensitive posts (praetorian prefect; prefect of Egypt) the emperors preferred lower status equestrians, who would presumably have no ambitions of their own. Of course they did and, despite Tacitus' snobbish mockery of Sejanus' Italian background, those ambitions carried them quite far. The Julio-Claudians were succeeded in

A.D. 69 by the soldier-emperor Vespasian (A.D. 69-79), whose father's service had brought him into the Senate despite his modest Italian ancestry. Vespasian's unpretentious manners offended aristocratic senators, but such snobbish scruples did not impede the march of Romans of Italian origin into the highest positions of the state.

The imperial court also abounded with slaves, freedmen and even princes from much further afield than Italy. We might only mention Augustus' Greek physician Musa, Tiberius' Greek friend and astrologer Thrasyllus (whose grandson later became a consul), Claudius' childhood playmate the Jewish prince Herod Agrippa, Caligula's lover the actor Mnester, and Claudius' senior freedmen Pallas and Narcissus, who amassed the greatest fortunes in the Empire. Freedmen and slaves were bound to their masters by ties of loyalty, and their ambitions were tied more than those of senators or even family members to those of their master. The desertion of Claudius by Pallas (after his seduction by Agrippina) is a rare exception; even the most monstrous emperors were loyally served to the end by loyal slaves.

The diverse groups that constituted the imperial court were in theory bound by their loyalty to the emperor. Unlike modern states in which a citizen's loyalty is to the constitution, or flag, or office, in imperial Rome loyalty was personal, and it was a personal oath that all Roman soldiers swore annually to the emperor. For centuries Roman society had been based upon personal ties— marriage, patronage, friendship (amicitia)—and the emperor and the imperial court must be seen as an extension of traditional Roman social relations. The personal nature of the early Roman Empire is its fundamental characteristic: loyalty, administration, bureaucracy and the succession can only be understood in personal terms. Augustus, Claudius and later Hadrian all made important contributions to the establishment of a state machinery, but personal relationships continued to form the basis of the government of the Roman Empire.

Snobbery Begins at Rome

J. P. V. D. Balsdon

The late Dacre Balsdon of Exeter College, Oxford, here examines the varieties of snobbery to be found at Rome: Patrician vs. plebeian; Roman, Italian or provincial; rich vs. poor; free vs. freedmen. Foreigners were literally beyond the pale. The transition from Republic to Empire may have changed the form of snobbery—there were fewer aristocrats and fewer still patricians—but Roman haughtiness towards outsiders remained until the end of the Empire and, some might argue, to the present day.

Roman society was built on the idea of deference (*obsequium*) in the family as in the State. Whatever their age, sons and daughters owed deference to their father, who had the sanction of power over them (*patria potestas*); their wholehearted and sincere submission was an exaltation of (*obsequium*); it was *pietas*. Freedmen and clients owed deference to their patrons. More than deference, the soldier owed unquestioning obedience to his officers, citizens to the magistrates of the State. In a class-ridden society all owed deference to those above them. Any other behaviour was contumacious, *contumacia*.

At the top were senators, 'Right Honourables,' *viri clarissimi*, as they were eventually to be called. . . .

The bluer a man's blood, the better—membership of a patrician rather than of a plebeian family. His ancestry was unassailable if the founder of his family had come over with the Conqueror (Aeneas), if he had Trojan roots. . . .

Better still, after the aristocratic family-tree-culture of the second century B.C., many aristocrats could assert divine ancestry. 'My aunt Julia,' as Julius Caesar said at her funeral, 'was on her father's side (my own family) descended from Venus'. . . . At human level, a man should have consuls among his ancestry and so, in Roman language, belong to the nobility, be *nobilis*.

The rest of the world was not allowed to forget a man's distinguished ancestry. There was the picture gallery, the *tablinum*, off the hall of a distinguished man's Roman house with the family tree on the wall and the death-masks of his ancestors, all of which were paraded at the public funeral of a member of the family, at first of male members and later even of female. . . .

All this background the 'new man,' the 'man with no father' (like Cicero or, later, Augustus' friend and adviser M. Agrippa) lacked, and he was not allowed to forget the fact. There were no traditions in his own family: how could he make a good senator?

To attack an aristocrat on the ground of his ancestry was to attack him on a very sensitive spot. But, if enough research was done on his mother's side of the family, this was sometimes possible. . . .

Antony discovered (or invented) a maternal great-grandfather for Octavian, a man who was African, ran a scent shop and then was a baker at Aricia in Italy. . . . Nearer reality, Piso, the *bete noire* of Germanicus, is said to have despised the emperor Tiberius' children as being lower in the social scale than himself because of their partly equestrian blood (Atticus having been their great-grandfather).

The emperor Gaius was so much repelled by the thought of Agrippa as an ancestor that he preferred to believe that his mother was born out of wedlock, from Augustus' incest with his daughter Julia.

The 'new man' came from a family which had never taken any part, or any outstanding part, in Roman politics; even though it might be old, respected and wealthy, it was described by the aristocrat as 'sordid, contemptible and obscure.' But when the aristocrat declared that the new man lacked *virtus*, he exposed himself to attack because one of the most irritating qualities of the *parvenu*—like the elder Cato, Marius and Cicero—was that he was always comparing his own *virtus* with the *virtus* of the aristocrat's remote ancestors and contrasting it with the aristocrats' own degeneracy.

So with a certain bravado the 'new man,' launched successfully on a public career or having achieved a measure of political success, could boast about his newness, particularly in public speeches, because the Roman public naturally approved of a self-made man, in his origins one of themselves. Velleius Paterculus, who was such a man, gave examples of such success, using the (when he wrote, triumphant) career of Sejanus as a peg to hang them on. He wrote with attractive modesty: 'an ordinary man like myself.' But more often success went to the new man's head. A *parvenu* of very different temperament from Velleius Paterculus, the historian Tacitus, a man who achieved the greatest success in his public career, was a social snob of the first order; he could compete with the aristocrats on their own ground. . . .

The freedman's relationship to his patron will have differed in different circumstances, sometimes close and friendly as between Cicero and Tiro, . . . sometimes unfriendly, with the patron wondering whether to invoke his legal right to insist on his freedman's removing himself to the distance of a hundred miles from Rome. All turned on the freedman's continuing usefulness to his patron, and on his deference (*obsequium*), which a cynic might have pronounced to be the only virtue that a freedman could possess. Once a slave, always a slave. When a slave was freed, he was released into a hostile world. If he asserted himself, he was 'uppish' in the eyes of his betters—arrogant, contumacious. Cicero was horrified by the airs which his brother's freedman Statius gave himself, and in the Empire there was worse to come when freedmen were admitted to the knighthood by emperors, given honorary magisterial insignia, when they made fortunes which put them in the top millionaire bracket and were even praised publicly, as Pallas was praised by Claudius, before the Senate; the disgrace of it all was enough after half a century to make the younger Pliny blush. There was the awful story of the bounder Callistus, sold in a job lot as an unsatisfactory slave by his master, then emerging as a powerful imperial minister and banning his former master from his receptions.

Freedmen should clearly be left to enjoy their own society, as they did very happily in Trimalchio's circle of friends at Puteoli, a society reproduced with nice but by no means cruel mockery by Petronius, men and women who judged life by purely materialistic standards which some might say were refreshingly modern.

People were respectable or common, *honesti* or *vulgares*, generally a matter of birth. . . . 'Drink up,' says Trimalchio in Petronius' *Satyricon*; 'my guests yesterday were more classy (*honestiores*), and I gave them less good wine than this.' The young roue Encolpius struggled to avoid making a gaffe when he dined with Trimalchio; he wanted to show that he was accustomed to dining in respectable company, '*inter honestos*' . . .

There were a number of ways in which men might earn the disdain of their self-styled betters: by the clothes which they wore, by the kind of Latin that they spoke—uncertain aspirates, an Italian or provincial accent or vocabulary— or by their comic foreign sounding names, evidence, it was to be assumed, of slave origin or slave parentage.

In the judgment of smart Roman society, people sank in the social scale, the further they lived from Rome. A Roman municipal bigwig might be . . . a man of standing at home, but he was something of a rustic, unfamiliar with the modes of the capital. Or if he adopted those modes, it was just as bad. Sejanus' seduction of the princess Julia Livilla made Tacitus shudder; he was not an *adulter* merely, but a *municipalis adulter*. Worse still was a *provincialis*, a Roman from the provinces, whether he was the descendant of a family which had emigrated from Rome or Italy or a man of barbarian stock who had received or inherited Roman citizenship. . . .

'I was born a provincial and an equestrian and have risen to be one of the top people of the State,' Seneca told Nero, and that was why he had the political enemies that he had.

Successive admissions of Gauls to the Senate caused a series of nightmares to the best Romans. Cicero and his contemporaries were horrified by Julius Caesar's new Gallic senators who came, in the main, from south of the Alps. Nearly a century later the senators whom Claudius consulted were shocked by his proposal to introduce senators from northern Gaul. Was it not enough that Gauls from north Italy had battered their way into the Senate already? . . .

Yet these were Tacitus' own people, for as likely as not he came from southern Gaul. So he dropped the Roman aristocratic mask for once and reflected on the revivifying effect of the new blood transfusions, under the Flavians, of Italian townsmen, even provincials, into the Senate: Tacitus himself and others like him, good men and rich, no doubt (as the emperor Claudius would have said approvingly), but men who retained a peasant mentality, careful with their money and reluctant to squander it.

At the bottom of the social scale, below even the provincial, was the *rusticus*, the country bumpkin whom, universally, the city dweller despised. 'Uncultured rustic clots like you,' Apuleius shouted at his prosecutor; . . . 'Were such people men, or were they animals?' Cicero asked.

Beyond the frontiers were foreigners, objects of scorn. Whatever Tacitus might choose to write in his *Germania* in praise of the great blonde-haired palefaces beyond the Rhine, they were men who wilted in normal Mediterranean conditions, unable to face the sun, drinking too much and going flabby. Orientals were softies (as, within the empire, were Greeks). Foreigners tended to be governed by kings, and a Roman senator, a *vir clarissimus*, betrayed his Roman dignity if he did not address a king as his inferior: . . . Popillius Laenas putting Antiochus Epiphanes in his place, drawing a ring round him in the sand and telling him not to step out of it until he had returned a proper answer.

Poverty was reprehensible if reprehensibly incurred, by dissipated living. . . . Senators whose fortunes fell below the million mark (the lowest sum to qualify for membership of the Senate) were to be commended if they retired gracefully from the Senate of their own accord with as little fuss as possible. On the other hand, if they belonged to old families and had children to guarantee the continuance of those families, they should automatically be placed on public assistance, subsidized from the emperor's private purse.

In the schoolboy's rhetorical exercises, interestingly, no social barrier seems to have existed between rich and poor. 'A pauper and a rich man were friends'; this is a not uncommon background to a rhetorical problem in that world of educational fantasy. Or, if the rich man and the pauper were enemies, their sons were friends.

For a professional philosopher it was wrong not to be poor; how indeed, it was asked, could Seneca be a philosopher and a millionaire in one? Were not the heroes of early Roman history advertisements for the virtue of poverty? Poverty existed in terms of material wealth, and who was the real pauper? The man who was never satisfied with what he had, but aspired to greater wealth still, the *avarus*. So philosophers argued. . . .

The question 'What does your father do for a living?' could hardly arise in correct circles, because in correct circles his living came respectably enough, from the slave-labour on his estates, which he farmed, as likely as not, by bailiffs, and from rented property, even including brothels. Cicero's disparagement in the *De officiis* of all occupations which enabled men to live, to say nothing of living well, is notorious. . . . There were grades in disrepute, with tax collectors, brothel-keepers, actors and slave-dealers at the bottom. . . . Dio Chrysostom disparaged occupations which were unhealthy, inactive and sedentary, luxury occupations which pandered to the rich, beauty parlour attendants, interior decorators, actors, musicians, auctioneers, shyster lawyers and brothel-keepers. . . .

The attitude of high-class gentry to money lending was not altogether inconsistent. Much depended on the part of the world in which your operations were conducted. Big lending operations in the provinces, even if they broke the law, could be countenanced. . . . And Seneca is said to have had great sums of money out on loan in Britain. Nearer home, in Rome and Italy, you must not be a professional moneylender; he was the man whose occupation was not *honestum*, respectable, in the eyes of the elder Cato. On the other hand, short-term lending and borrowing among friends was perfectly in order; it was the kind of thing that Atticus was arranging every day for his respectable acquaintances. If it was not for the existence of banks, people would be doing the same thing today as, indeed, they did between a hundred and two hundred years ago.

Cicero made an exception for the professions of architects, doctors and teachers. These were suitable occupations for 'men of that class,' for freedmen, in fact.

Men 'not of that class,' the gentry, if their wealth vanished, had no option but to try to bamboozle a moneylender, to sponge on relatives or friends (even on the Emperor, if they were lucky), to become gladiators, if they were young enough, or, if all else failed, to commit suicide. At a distance from Rome, however, they might be driven to earn money, if the alternative was starvation. After he had left Domitian's Rome in a huff, Florus set up as a schoolmaster at Tarraco in Spain. 'What a terrible shame,' his friends from Baetica said; 'how do you put up with sitting in school and teaching boys?' Florus answered that it had been hard at first, but that he had become a dedicated teacher. And there were men in exile who had no option but to earn a living.

It is a striking fact that there was so little change in outlook through the centuries. One might have expected that with the expansion of the senatorial class to include, eventually to consist predominantly of, Italians and then provincials, depreciation of Italians and of provincials would cease. But that was not the case, for the city of Rome never ceased to be the social centre of the Roman universe, and those who came from outside caught its infection. Snobbery always began at Rome. Horace was a freedman's son; Juvenal was an Italian; Martial and Tacitus were provincials of no particularly eminent extraction. Yet all of them express contemporary upper-class Roman senatorial snobbery. Listen to Tacitus on the debate after the fall of Sejanus. Stern proposals were made by men with great names, a Scipio, a Silanus, a Cassius. Then Togonius Gallus spoke to the same effect, 'pushfully associating his own undistinguished name with the names of the great.'

We have Ammianus Marcellinus' description of the top Roman senatorial society which he found in the fourth century A.D. Rich, narrow-minded, uncultured and conceited, its members looked down their noses at an outsider, even a respectable outsider like Ammianus. 'There are people who, with empty bombast, treat anything born outside the city as simple dirt.'

Herod Agrippa

Thomas Africa

Professor Thomas Africa of SUNY Binghamton traces in this essay the colorful career of Herod Agrippa. This grandson of Herod the Great was raised among the imperial children in Rome and progressed from poverty to riches, from Tiberius' prison to the dining table of Caligula and Claudius. He won popularity with his Jewish subjects by opposing the installation of Caligula's state in the Temple and by persecuting the Christians as heretics. He was even said by Josephus to have negotiated the accession of Claudius to the imperial throne. Agrippa was a skillful politician who did much for his people. His premature death in A.D. 44 prompted direct Roman rule of his kingdom and led to the calamitous Jewish revolt of 66.

Though Herod was hardly a "typical" foreigner at the imperial court, he is one of the many hostages and exiles from various kingdoms (such as Parthia and Armenia) with whom the Roman imperial family formed personal and political ties before sending them home to rule their own people. Herod's divided loyalties were a product of the conflict of values that such rootlessness entailed.

Filled with improbable reversals of fortune, the career of Herod Agrippa had all the elements of cheap melodrama. However, the substance of his amazing story is corroborated by contemporary writers and well told by the Jewish historian Josephus, who relied on good Roman sources as well as the testimony of Herod Agrippa's children. Like Herod the Great, Herod Agrippa was a crafty opportunist who made the most of his luck. Like the emperor Tiberius, the Jewish prince tasted the dregs of failure and despair but finally emerged triumphant over all odds. Neither a saint nor a statesman, Herod Agrippa did well by the Jews, for he was a remarkable man and played a decisive role in the accession of the emperor Claudius. Though his luck was phenomenal, chance only dealt him the cards—Herod Agrippa knew how to play them.

If Antipas was an old fox, Herod Agrippa began as one of the little foxes who spoil the vines. Born in 10 B.C., Herod Agrippa was named after Marcus Agrippa, the right hand man of Augustus. His mother Berenice had many friends at Rome and was particularly close to Germanicus' mother Antonia. Agrippa's father Aristobulus was a son of Herod the Great but had been executed by the Judean despot. As a boy Agrippa was brought to Rome by his mother, whose patroness Antonia was also a widow and had borne a son in 10 B.C., Claudius. Both boys would one day wear crowns, but no one suspected it, least of all Claudius, who was shy and sickly. A lively and attractive youth, Agrippa grew up as a companion of Drusus, the son of Tiberius. While Berenice was alive, the young Jewish prince lived within his means, but after her death he entertained lavishly and scattered bribes among influential freedmen who had high posts at court. Though the frugal Tiberius disapproved of his extravagance, Agrippa considered the expenses a political investment which might win him a client kingdom in the East. The ambitious young Jew went deeper in debt, but his plans were upset in 23 when Sejanus poisoned Drusus. The old emperor could not bear to be reminded of Drusus, and Agrippa was no longer welcome at court. Hounded by creditors, Agrippa fled from Rome to Palestine, where he hid in the bleak desert of Idumea. Living in poverty in an old watchtower with his loyal wife Kypros, Agrippa was a failure at forty and seriously considered suicide.

Like Agrippa, Kypros was a descendant of Herod the Great, but she was made of sterner stuff than her husband and more than once would save his career. Rousing Agrippa from despair, Kypros wrote to his sister Herodias in Galilee. Her husband Antipas was not only Agrippa's brother-in-law but also his uncle, and the tetrarch took a malicious pleasure in rescuing Agrippa from destitution. Herodias' brother was given a minor post as market inspector at Tiberias. At Antipas' court, Agrippa was a poor relation, and the tetrarch enjoyed reminding him that he was dependent on charity. Unable to bear Antipas' sarcasm any longer, Agrippa fled to his old friend, the Roman governor of Syria who preceded Vitellius. However, Agrippa did not enjoy Roman patronage for long, because he tried to peddle his influence with the governor and was asked to leave. In desperation, the adventurer decided to gamble on a trip to Rome, where he might recoup his fortunes. Again deep in debt, he scraped up travel expenses and escaped from Palestine barely ahead of his creditors. At Alexandria Agrippa tried to raise more funds but was considered a bad risk. However, Kypros persuaded a rich Jew to provide Agrippa with ready cash and a bank draft for Italy. While Kypros and their children returned to Palestine, Agrippa sailed on to Rome and an uncertain future.

Arriving in Italy, Agrippa found Tiberius in good humor and was invited to join the circle on Capri. However, reports soon arrived with details of Agrippa's debts and flight from the East, and the emperor forbade him to appear at court until he was solvent. Undaunted, the Jewish prince turned to his mother's old friend Antonia and borrowed the necessary funds. At last in Tiberius' favor, Agrippa managed to become the tutor of the emperor's grandson Gemellus, who was one of Tiberius' two heirs. The other heir was the adult son of Germanicus, Gaius "Caligula," whom Antonia had rescued from the clutches of Sejanus a few years earlier. Realizing that Caligula's prospects were brighter, Agrippa neglected Gemellus and paid court to the older prince. Borrowing again, the wily opportunist paid off his debts to Antonia and made costly presents to Caligula. In his eagerness to flatter the prince, Agrippa carelessly told him that he wished Tiberius were dead and Caligula on the throne. The unwise remark was overheard by a servant who was soon after accused of theft by Agrippa. Fearing that the imprisoned servant might betray his secret, Agrippa asked his patroness Antonia to persuade Tiberius to hold a quick trial. However, the emperor had already been informed of the servant's charges against Agrippa and delayed the hearing as long as possible. When the case was finally brought to trial, the thief blurted out that Agrippa was a traitor who had wished for the emperor's death. Rather amused by the whole affair, the sardonic Tiberius ordered the arrest of Agrippa, and the Jewish prince was led off to prison. Though Antonia bribed his jailers to treat him gently, Agrippa was kept in chains and pondered the malign fate which had brought him to such a plight after so much effort.

According to Josephus, one of Agrippa's fellow prisoners was a German chieftain who had prophetic gifts. During an exercise period Agrippa was strolling in the prison yard and idly leaned against a tree in which an owl was perched. Suddenly the German seer introduced himself to the melancholy prince and assured him in broken Latin that his fortunes would soon change and he would be free again. With a somber tone, the prophet added that the next time Agrippa would see the owl, he would die within five days. Unknown to Agrippa his deliverance was at hand, for Tiberius died in

37 and was succeeded by Caligula. The new emperor quickly freed his old friend and presented him with golden chains to commemorate his brief incarceration. Caligula also invested Agrippa with the title of king and the domains of the tetrarch Phillip, who had died a few years before. Out of the depths, Agrippa had risen again to new heights. . . .

En route to take possession of his kingdom in northern Palestine, Agrippa had stopped at Alexandria to show off his new grandeur in a city which had last seen him as a fleeing debtor. His timing was inopportune, for the metropolis was torn by religious strife between pagans and Jews. Alexandria had a huge Jewish population, and ethnic rivalries had troubled the city ever since the quarrels between Cleopatra and Herod the Great. While the Alexandrian Jews were loyal supporters of Rome, Egyptian nationalists resented Roman rule and relieved their frustrations in outbursts of anti-Semitism. When Agrippa staged an ostentatious parade through Alexandria, the Egyptians retaliated with a mock procession featuring a king of fools. The Jewish philosopher Philo described the episode:

There was a gentle madman called Carabas who . . . wandered through the streets day and night, stark naked regardless of the weather, and teased by idle children. . . . Now, the mob dragged this wretched creature to the public gymnasium and stood him on a platform where he could be seen by all. They made a crown of papyrus-leaf and put it on his head and threw a rug over his body as a robe. For a scepter, somebody gave him a piece of papyrus-stalk which had been picked up in the street. Thus, Carabas received the insignia of royalty and was decked out as a king. Like comic actors in a pantomime, some young men formed mock bodyguard and stood about him with rods like pikes and then other people approached him. While some pretended to do him homage, others played that they were laying a case before him, and others acted as though they had come to consult him on state affairs. The crowd stood around in a circle and shouted the strange cry, "Maran!" which is the Syrian word for "Lord." They knew that Agrippa was a Syrian by race and that his kingdom was a part of Syria.

In many respects, the mocking of Carabas resembled the recent treatment of Jesus at Jerusalem. Whatever religious significance the episode in Alexandria may have had, the Egyptians were primarily interested in displaying their contempt for Agrippa, who beat a hasty retreat from the troubled city. As disorder swept Alexandria, the Roman governor Flaccus permitted the nationalists to convert the Jewish quarter into a ghetto and conduct pogroms elsewhere in the city. Hoping to please Caligula, the Egyptians forcibly installed portraits of the emperor and other images in many synagogues. Meanwhile, Agrippa complained to Caligula about the troubles in Alexandria and the emperor ordered the removal from office and subsequent execution of Flaccus. In order to recover their lost privileges, the Jews of Alexandria sent an embassy headed by Philo to plead their case before Caligula. However, the erratic emperor kept the envoys cooling their heels in Italy. . . .

When the emperor had proclaimed his divinity, the pagan residents of a coastal town in Palestine honored the new god with a small altar, which their Jewish neighbors quickly demolished. Learning of the insult, Caligula decided to meet the issue of Judaic privileges head on. Perhaps influenced by anti-Semitic advisers, the emperor ordered that a gold-plated statue of himself as Jupiter be placed in the Temple at Jerusalem. To the Jews, such a sacrilege would be the "abomination of desolation," which apocalyptic writers warned would take place in the days preceding the coming of the Messiah. The governor of Syria, Petronius, realized that the statue would unleash a religious war of vast proportions, and tried to dissuade the emperor. Since Caligula was adamant, Petronius delayed the completion of the statue and told the emperor that the artists needed more time. When Caligula had ordered the statue, Agrippa had been traveling to Rome and did not learn the news until the emperor casually told him that his image would soon stand in the Temple. Seeing his new kingdom swept away in a holy war, Agrippa fainted and was in a coma for two days. When he recovered, the king tried desperately to change the mind of the arbitrary emperor.

Posing as a pious Jew, Agrippa drafted a memorandum to his friend Caligula. The philosopher Philo of Alexandria has preserved the substance and tone of Agrippa's letter:

All people regard the customs of their own country as excellent, even if in reality they are not, because they judge them with feelings of affection rather than with their reason. I was born, as you know, a Jew. Jerusalem is my home where stands the holy Temple of the Most High God. My grandfathers and ancestors were kings. Most of them were appointed High Priests. . . . Since my heritage is such a nation and city and Temple, I appeal to you on behalf of them all—on behalf of my nation . . . seeing that its attitude to all your family has been one of reverence and piety. . . . The Jews proclaim their reverence in the resolutions of their inmost souls rather than by word of mouth; they are people who do not merely say that they are Caesar's friends, but really are his friends. . . . I myself am one of the people who recognize that they have a lord and master but who are counted among his friends. In rank few are above me. In loyalty I am second to none—I will not go so far as to say that I stand first. Therefore, on the strength of my birth and the multitude of the kindnesses with which you have enriched me, I too might have made bold to ask for my native city, if not Roman citizenship, at least freedom or exemption from taxation. . . . Instead I make a very trifling request, a favor which it will cost you nothing to give, but which will be of greatest value for my city to receive. For what greater blessing could your subjects receive than the good will of their Princeps?

After recounting the favors which Augustus and Tiberius had extended toward Judaism and the Temple, Agrippa reminded Caligula of their own long friendship:

When you have granted me favors beyond my needs, my lord, do not take from me the necessities of life; and when you have brought me into the most brilliant light do not cast me back afresh into the deepest darkness. But I relinquish those splendors; I do not object to returning to my former condition; I give up everything in exchange for one thing, the preservation of our native traditions unchanged. Otherwise, what would be my reputation among my

fellow Jews or among all the gentiles? Of necessity I should be regarded as one of two things—either as a traitor to my people or as one who had forfeited your friendship. What greater evil could there be than these? For if I continue to be numbered among your friends, I shall have a reputation for treachery, unless my homeland is kept safe from all evil and the Temple is kept inviolate, since you great men protect the interests of your friends and of people who have taken refuge in the manifestations of your imperial power. If, however, any hostility lurks in your heart, do not imprison me, as Tiberius did, but destroy my anticipation of a second imprisonment by ordering me to be got rid of at once. For what good would it be to me to live, when my only hope of deliverance lay in your good will?

Responding to Agrippa's frankness and their bond of friendship, Caligula relented and ordered Petronius to abandon the Temple project. However, according to Josephus, the emperor promised his friend Agrippa an unspecified favor at a banquet, and the king quickly asked Caligula not to place his statue in the Temple. Though entertaining, Josephus' story is too similar to the tale of the trick which Herodias played on Antipas, and Philo's account that Caligula was persuaded by Agrippa's letter is far more plausible. According to Philo, the erratic emperor again changed his mind and planned to personally install his image in the Temple. Though the death of Caligula soon solved the problem, the Jews would always remember that, whatever his motives, Agrippa had risked his life to save the Temple from violation.

In 41 Caligula was assassinated by a group of men whom he had driven from exasperation to blind hatred. Government officials had deplored his extravagant spending and senators had lived in fear of their lives. . . . The Praetorian guards sent a detachment to rescue Claudius and conveyed him to the safety of the Praetorian barracks.

Meanwhile, the Senate was in turmoil over the selection of a successor for Caligula. Not accustomed to making decisions of such magnitude, a few senators spoke wildly of restoring the Republic. The problem had already been settled by the Praetorians who hailed Claudius as emperor and gambled that the legions would support their choice because he was the brother of the popular Germanicus. Since Claudius needed the formal approval of the Senate, Herod Agrippa offered to serve as a neutral negotiator between the proposed emperor and the senators. However, Claudius was the son of Agrippa's late patroness Antonia, and the Herodian king secretly favored him in the haggling with the Senate. While he assured the senators that the accession of Claudius was both desirable and inevitable, Agrippa advised Claudius to guarantee consular elections to the Senate. Pleased by the gesture, the senators acclaimed Claudius as emperor. The adroit schemer, Herod Agrippa, had played the game of power politics at the highest level. . . .

The realistic Claudius carefully paid his political debts. The Praetorian guards received cash bonuses and Calistus was given a high administrative post. The emperor also rewarded the freedman Pallas, who had loyally served Antonia. To discourage future regicides, the emperor executed Chaerea, who had killed Caligula but had also opposed the elevation of Claudius. Toward his friend Agrippa, Claudius was particularly generous and enlarged Agrippa's kingdom to include Judea and the rest of the former domain of Herod the Great. Without war and by his wits alone, Agrippa was now as powerful a king as his ruthless grandfather had been.

In Palestine, Agrippa was enormously popular. Freed from direct Roman rule, the Jews idolized Agrippa for opposing Caligula's statue and restoring the Herodian kingdom. Aware of the tense religious situation in Palestine, Agrippa carefully displayed a new-found piety, resided at Jerusalem, and participated in religious ceremonies. To appease orthodox bigots, the king persecuted the followers of Jesus as heretics. While Peter narrowly escaped death at the hands of Agrippa, the king executed James, the brother of John. Like Herod the Great, Agrippa was a dedicated builder and began construction of the Third Wall at Jerusalem. The wall was not completed because Agrippa either ran out of funds or was afraid of the Roman governor of Syria, who had become suspicious over the new fortifications. To display his present success at the scene of a prior humiliation, Agrippa held a conference with neighboring client kings at Tiberias. However, the governor of Syria suspected that an alliance of buffer states was in the making, and he advised the visiting kings to return to their homes. The prudent monarchs promptly departed and left Agrippa frustrated and furious.

Although he ostentatiously played the role of King of the Jews, Agrippa was more at ease with his pagan subjects. He built extensively at the resort city of Beirut and provided its residents with elaborate shows and games. In one spectacular show, 1,400 gladiators died to amuse the Jewish king and his pagan subjects. Bored with the righteous sermonizing of priests and rabbis, Agrippa paid frequent visits to Caesarea, the former Roman capital of Palestine. There in 44, death came unexpectedly to the fifty-four-year-old Agrippa, who had appeared before his admirers dressed in a glittering cloth of silver. When the pagan crowds hailed him as a god, the Jewish king smiled good-naturedly and made no protest. Glancing up, he noticed an owl perched on an awning and was immediately seized with abdominal pains. Convinced that the bird was a messenger of death, Agrippa languished in his palace at Caesarea and died on the fifth day. Both Christians and Jews attributed his sudden death to divine punishment for accepting worship as a god. Perhaps religious guilt contributed to Agrippa's rapid demise when the chance appearance of an owl recalled the chilling prophesy which the German seer had made years before.

The death of Herod Agrippa was a disaster for the Jews of Palestine. Since his son Agrippa II was only a child, an orderly transfer of power could not take place in the new kingdom. With the diplomatic Agrippa gone, the conflict between Jews and pagans erupted in bloody riots throughout Palestine. To restore order, the emperor Claudius made Palestine a Roman province again and gave Agrippa II a tiny state east of Galilee. For two decades frustrated Jewish nationalists would endure inept Roman governors, until the great revolt which ended in the sack of Jerusalem in A.D. 70. Had Herod Agrippa lived long enough to consolidate his makeshift kingdom and train his son for the exercise of power, Judea might have flourished as a loyal client state, and history would not have witnessed the suppression of the Jewish nation. Though he never achieved the stature of a statesman, Agrippa had kept the peace in Palestine, but death prevented him from making Israel a lasting state. However, Herod Agrippa was poorly equipped to be a Messiah, for the only role which he really knew was that of an agile schemer who triumphed over all obstacles with bluff and luck.

Slavery

P. A. Brunt

Professor Peter Brunt of Oxford University here sketches the legal status of slaves in ancient Rome and some ways in which the Romans employed their slaves. Brunt discusses both the cruelty and humanity in treatment of slaves by their Roman masters, and he further raises the important question of the relative efficiency of slave labor. He does not believe that slave labor was intrinsically inefficient nor that it should be seen as a cause of Rome's decline.

The importance of slavery in Roman society [is evident]. As in all other ancient lands it was an institution of immemorial antiquity, which no one ever proposed to abolish. Greeks who were accustomed to question everything had challenged its legitimacy and evoked a powerful defence from Aristotle; the slave was in his view a man who had only enough rationality to understand and obey orders, and it was as much in his own interest as the master's that he should be subject to rational government. (Slightly modified, this argument is familiar today from the writings of imperialist apologists.) But this controversy was in the realm of theory. Even when slaves rebelled, they did not object to slavery as such: they merely wanted to be free themselves. A Roman jurist said that by natural law all men are born free, but he hastened to add that slavery existed by the law of nations. The Stoics, who were influential at Rome, taught that all men were brothers, including slaves; but in their philosophy man's welfare is purely spiritual, and material conditions irrelevant to it; true misery lies in being a slave to one's own passions, and legal servitude does not stop a man from being master of himself in the moral sense. The Christian attitude was much the same. Slaves, according to Paul, are not to worry about the condition in which they were called; and he did not recommend Philemon to liberate Onesimus. Hence it is no surprise that when Christianity became the official religion, the Church did not advocate abolition: on the contrary, it acquired slaves of its own. In the breakup of the Empire slavery gradually dwindled, for reasons that are not clear; but as great numbers of free men were reduced to serfdom, from which it was often harder to escape, the net gain to human freedom was not large.

The children of slave mothers were born slaves, but free men could be made slaves by capture in war, by piracy and by kidnaping. Legally a Roman citizen or a free subject of Rome could not be reduced to servitude within Rome's jurisdiction, but this rule may have been often evaded; in particular, exposure of freeborn infants was not forbidden until Christian times, and when such foundlings were reared as slaves, there would seldom have been evidence of their original status. In primitive Rome, a poor community, there can have been few slaves, but there was a vast influx as a result of Rome's wars of conquest from the middle of the third century

B.C. In one campaign in 167 B.C. the Romans are said to have made 50,000 slaves in Epirus. Trade across the frontiers always swelled the numbers, and so did piracy by sea and brigandage by land until the time of Augustus. In the heyday of piracy the mart at Delos was reputed to be capable of handling 20,000 in a single day. Never before had slaves been so cheap and plentiful as in Cicero's Italy, and nowhere else in the Empire did the economy become so dependent on slave labour. A comparison may be drawn with the Old South in the United States. There, in 1850, only eleven owners had more than five hundred slaves apiece. But in Nero's reign one senator had four hundred serving him in his own townhouse and how many more working in the fields to support this establishment of unproductive mouths? Augustus thought it necessary to forbid owners to manumit more than a hundred by testament. It can be conjectured that in his time there were three slaves for every five free men in Italy.

The slaves were of all nations, including Celts and Germans from the north and Asiatics from the east; many, born in slavery or illegally enslaved, came from Italy or the provinces. These were not only sturdy labourers for the fields or mines, but craftsmen or men with professional talents who brought new skills to Italy. Shrewd owners trained slave boys to be secretaries, accountants and doctors. It was such trained scribes in Atticus' publishing house who copied the works of Cicero. The master and preceptor of a young mathematical genius records with sorrow his death at the age of twelve. The fine pottery of Arretium was made by slaves. Hundreds of epitaphs prove that in such industries as the making of lamps, pipes, and glassware eighty per cent of the workmen were of servile stock; the same is true of goldsmiths and jewelers. Most of these men died as freedmen; they had been presumably employed in the same way as slaves, but manumission was the normal reward for their services.

In Roman law the slave was a chattel. Varro classifies the equipment of the farm as articulate, inarticulate and mute, that is to say, the slaves, the cattle and the ploughs. The slave can be bought, sold or hired out, mated or not (the Elder Cato allowed no women to his farm-hands), fed, clothed and in general punished at the master's will. All that he earns is legally for the master's account. The child of the slave mother is the master's property.

From the first, however, the law was not consistent, and could not be. It had to take account of the slave's humanity, if only in the interests of the free citizens themselves. He might commit a crime; the state would then punish him and more severely than if he were free. He might witness a crime and then he should give evidence. The slave might denounce a plot against the State, and then the State would free him. Moreover the law provided formal procedures under which the master himself might manumit his slave. Manumission is always a concomitant of slavery, but under Roman law, unlike Greek, the freedman of a Roman citizen became a citizen himself, if he was emancipated by the proper formalities.

The interests of the master too required him to care for the slave's welfare. He had to be fed and clothed even when the free poor went hungry and naked. The harsh Cato recommends for farm-hands about as much wheat as the soldier got, with a little wine, oil, olives or pickled fish and salt; they should have shoes and a tunic and cloak every other year; blankets may be made of the discarded clothes. The master was for long empowered to put his slave to death, but only a very capricious owner would destroy his property without strong cause. He could have him flogged, but Varro, for one, preferred verbal rebukes if they were equally effective. Rewards often served the master's interest better than punishments. He might pay his slave a wage or set him up in business and let him retain part of the earnings. The money or other property he then acquired, though legally his master's, was in practice treated as his own (peculum); it might even include other slaves. With his savings he could buy his freedom, "defrauding his belly," as Seneca puts it. But freedom often came as a gift. Owners, especially if they died without natural heirs, were particularly ready to emancipate slaves by their wills; this gave them posthumous acclaim for generosity. But manumission in the owner's lifetime was also frequent—astonishingly at first sight, but it is not hard to explain. Freedom was the greatest spur to good work, and probably no other incentive sufficed for slaves employed in skilled work and trusted posts. Moreover the former owner now became the patron of his old slave and retained a right to respect and services of many kinds; he might actually impose on the freedman the obligation to work for him without pay to an extent limited only by the provision that he must either maintain him or allow him enough time to maintain himself. We do not know how usual this practice was; certainly it was not universal, for many freedmen became rich.

Of course kindly, humane feelings and the philosophic doctrine that a master was custodian of his slave's welfare often fortified the self-interest which by itself dictated good treatment of the slave and even his emancipation. But the chief beneficiaries from all these motives were the skilled slaves and the domestics whose duties brought them into close contact with the masters. Farmworkers on distant estates did not benefit; they were often chained together in work or sleep, and Pliny calls them men without hope. Even the farm manager was normally a slave, not a freedman.

Jefferson, writing from experience, declared that:

the whole commerce between master and slave is a perpetual exercise of the most boisterous passions, the most unremitting despotism on the one part and degrading submission on the other.

How far was this true in Rome? We can not generalize either from instances of kind and friendly relations or from recorded atrocities. But Seneca says that masters notorious for cruelty were pointed at in the streets, and the development of the law, which is apt to lag behind the best opinion of its day rather than lead it, is significant. From the first century A.D. for instance it was murder for a master to kill his slave without cause, and a slave who was starved or subjected to savagery and debauchery could take asylum at one of the Emperor's statues and had a right to be sold

to another master. It is not likely that the protection of the law was very efficacious, any more than in the Old South, where masters accused of slave-murder were always acquitted by their peers. The Christian Emperor, Constantine, moreover, ruled that where a master was charged with murdering his slave, it had to be proved that he intended to kill him; it was not enough if he died under a flogging. But the provisions of the law do at least reveal the moral climate of opinion.

Humanity was not indeed the only reason for protecting slaves against the cruelty of individual masters. Antoninus Pius declared that such protection was in the interest of masters and designed to prevent uprisings. Centuries before, the philosopher-historian Posidonius had pointed out that ill treatment of some slaves had been the cause of the great revolt which desolated Sicily from 134 to 132 B.C. This was not the last slave revolt. In the seventies before Christ, slaves led by Spartacus devastated many parts of Italy and routed Roman armies. The Principate was better able to keep order, but the sense of insecurity persisted. *Quot servi tot hostes* "Every slave is an enemy" was a Roman proverb. Slaves were always running away, and the murder of masters was a constant danger. Under a savage Augustan enactment, which gave rise to much case law, when a master was murdered, all of his slaves "under the same roof" were to be executed; if not accomplices, they were at least guilty of not preventing his death. One slave girl pleaded that the assassin of her mistress had terrified her into silence; Hadrian ruled that she must die, for it was her duty to cry out at the cost of her own life. Still, harsh repression was at least accompanied by some attempts to curb the excesses of masters.

For many who could attain freedom slavery was not a hopeless lot. Petronius depicts a Sicilian who sold himself into slavery (illegally) because he preferred the chance of becoming a Roman citizen to remaining a provincial taxpayer. The freedman could more easily be integrated into society because there was no colour prejudice; there were seldom marked differences of skin to give rise to it. His rights were indeed limited; he could not serve in the army, nor hold state or municipal offices, and he might have onerous obligations to his patron. But if he had economic independence and some little talent and enterprise, he might grow wealthy. His political disabilities, like those imposed in later times on Jews or Quakers, channeled his energies into business, where freedmen were often dominant. They might be assisted by their patron, like the freedman of an Augustan nobleman who managed all of his business affairs and received from him ample gifts for himself, a dowry for his daughter and a commission in the army for his son. Another freedman of this time boasted in his will that he left 4,116 slaves, 3,600 pairs of oxen and 257,000 head of other cattle. Petronius' Trimalchio, whose estates in Italy stretched from sea to sea, is no mere figment of a novelist. These are extreme examples, but many other freedman secured a modest competence, and were able to advance their children, who suffered no legal disabilities, further in the social scale. The poet Horace was the son of a freedman who could give him the education of a gentleman and help to make him the court laureate, and Horace was not ashamed to recall his origin. In Nero's time it could be alleged that most senators had servile blood in their veins and a century later, Marcus Helvius Pertinax, the son of a freedman, rose by military and administrative capacity so high that in 193 he was proclaimed Emperor.

The most favored of slaves and freedmen were the Emperor's, who were employed in the Imperial administration. Under Tiberius a slave who was paymaster in Gaul took sixteen of his own slaves with him on a visit to Rome; of these two were needed to keep his plate. Claudius' freedmen secretaries are said to have been the wealthiest men of their day and the real rulers of the Empire; the brother of one was that Felix who governed Judea in Paul's day and married a descendant of Cleopatra. In some later reigns, chamberlains, often eunuchs, who had the Emperor's private ear, were to exercise power no less great.

The enormous importance of slavery in the economy of ancient Italy raises a large historical question. Obviously if the technical advances of even the early modern period of European history had been anticipated in the Graeco-Roman world, the Empire must have been too strong for the barbarians, whose invasions were at least the proximate cause and the necessary condition for its disruption. Can the extensive use of slavery be held responsible for technological backwardness and economic stagnation?

It has been argued that because slave labour was abundant and cheap the ancient world had no incentive to technological invention and that slavery so far abased the dignity of labour that the best minds turned away in disgust from everything connected with manual tasks; hence the backwardness of the Greeks and Romans in all scientific investigations which, unlike mathematics, demanded any approach other than that of abstract thinking. At the same time, to quote Cairnes' famous judgment on American slavery, slave labour "is given reluctantly; it is unskillful; it is wanting in versatility"; it must therefore be assumed that it was inefficient.

Even on these premises slavery cannot have been a prime cause of Rome's decline. After Augustus the Empire drew its strength increasingly and in the end exclusively from the provinces, where slavery was not predominant, as it was in Italy. Not only did the provinces furnish soldiers; some of them, notably Gaul and Egypt, were economically more prosperous, and it is certain of Egypt and probably of Gaul that slavery there was on a small scale. Yet these regions were no more inventive or progressive than Italy. We must therefore look elsewhere for reasons that will explain scientific or technological stagnation. Some have already been given; and we must add that progress was to depend on the formulation of fertile scientific hypotheses or on crucial inventions like optical glass; it is perhaps no more easy to understand why these happen in one age and not in another than to account for the flowering of poetical genius.

And was slave labour so inefficient? Roman experts on agriculture assumed that, on good land and adequately supervised, it brought in higher profits than free labour. We lack ancient evidence to test this assumption, and modern analogies yield no clear conclusion; the latest analyses of the economy of the Old South seem to show that its backwardness compared with the North cannot be certainly ascribed to slavery. In trade and industry the slaves were skilled workers spurred on by the hope of freedom; they are actually credited with minor inventions (like American negro slaves) and, if other factors had permitted mechanization, they were clearly capable of minding machines; indeed negroes too were used successfully in factories, although they were at a lower culture level and lacked such strong incentives. (Similarly in the last world war German productivity actually increased with the extended use of what was in all but name slave labour.) However cheap Roman slaves were, and we do not know just how cheap, the owners still had no motive to be indifferent to devices that might have increased their output.

It is thus on moral rather than on economic grounds that Roman slavery merits opprobrium. And many Roman slaves were no worse off than the mass of the peasantry who, though free in name, found it hard to assert their rights or defend their interests and never lived far from starvation. In a pre-industrial and poor society, of course, the poverty of the masses is the price to be paid if even a few are to enjoy leisure and civilization and the opportunity of promoting further progress. But in the Roman world such inevitable inequality was carried too far, further, for instance, than in democratic Greek communities. Hence, in the first century B.C. agrarian discontent in Italy helped to bring the Republic down, and in and after the third century A.D. the peasantry, unconscious of the benefits that accrued even to them from the Roman peace, often showed themselves indifferent and sometimes hostile to an empire in which the interests of the wealthy, *beati possidentes*, were always preponderant. This was no doubt one reason why despite its immensely superior resources, the Empire succumbed to the inroads of barbarians.

The Emperor's Men:
Senators, Equestrians, Freedmen and Slaves

Richard Saller

Professor Richard Saller of the University of Chicago in this new essay describes the administrative machinery of the early Roman Empire. He emphasizes the lack of a genuine state bureaucracy, as the emperors merely continued and expanded the system of personal, household administration that Roman magistrates had used under the Republic. Though Saller describes the role of the various orders in imperial government, he also warns against exaggerating the expansion of the bureaucracy under the Julio-Claudian emperors.

The Romans controlled one of the most extensive and stable empires in history, but the size of their governing apparatus was not commensurate with the dimensions of that empire. A rudimentary organization of officialdom sufficed for a government whose concerns were limited to essentials. The basic goals of the imperial government were twofold: the maintenance of law and order, and the collection of taxes. Taxes were needed to pay government officials and the army and to provide spectacles, buildings and handouts of food or cash in the capital city. To meet these very limited objectives the early emperors took the Republican system of senatorial administration and expanded it, creating more positions for senators, and also employing for the first time in governmental posts non-elective officials: men from the equestrian order, or lesser aristocracy, and more controversially, slaves and freedmen from their own household.

The history of the early empire is often represented as one of bureaucratization, as a development from "personal monarchy" to a "bureaucratic monarchy." This view, however, is largely the result of the nature of the very limited evidence. Our predominantly aristocratic literary sources were not much interested in the day to day functioning of government, so historians have been left to rely on the evidence of inscriptions, which often provide no more than the title of posts without indicating what the official did or how he reached the position. Modern historians have tended to fill in the large gaps in our knowledge with anachronistic assumptions about how governments work, based on their own modern experiences.

The increasing size of Roman government must be put into perspective, and anachronism avoided. Expansion in the number of posts and diversification in the social background of officials do not in themselves entail a more rationalized or truly bureaucratic administrative system. The functions of government remained essentially the same under the early emperors, who brought in no sweeping social and economic reforms and were not interested in interfering to any substantial degree in the lives of their subjects. No regulation of the economy was attempted, no elaborate fiscal policy, no standardization of the system of taxation, which continued to vary from region to region in accordance with what the Romans had found when they conquered.

Given their limited aims, the early emperors had no need for a major new bureaucratic organization. Even with the growing numbers of officials, the emperors had a central government numbered only in the few thousands to govern an empire of more than 50,000,000. If anything, the Roman empire remained under-governed. The government was unbureaucratic in terms of procedures as well: the operation of patronage rather than the application of formal criteria and rules determined the admission and promotion of elite administrators, who were not and never became "professionals" in the sense that we associate with civil servants today.

Rome's empire consisted of several dozen provinces in the Julio-Claudian era (the number increasing from reign to reign). These were governed by a thin spread of imperial officials in a partially modified version of the Republican system. Under the Republic all provinces had been governed by proconsuls, chosen by lot in the senate from ex-praetors and ex-consuls and aided by a retinue of friends, relatives and household dependents. Under Augustus proconsuls lost their monopoly over provincial governorships. It was vital for the emperor to maintain control over the provinces where the major armies were stationed, and he did so by personally appointing legates from among trusted senators to govern the provinces and command the armies of Spain, Gaul and Syria.

Among the provinces still governed by proconsuls selected in the senate, the wealthiest and most prestigious were Asia and Africa, the former encompassing much of western Turkey and the latter extending from modern day Libya to eastern Algeria. Each proconsul was assigned a junior senatorial official, a quaestor, and took with him an advisory panel of friends and a small staff of minor functionaries of low rank. The main civilian duties of the proconsul were the dispensation of justice and the oversight of finances. Upon entering the province, he announced the guidelines of his administration with an edict. Much of his one-year term was spent traveling around the province to major cities called assize centers, for the purpose of hearing legal cases and monitoring the activities of the municipal government elite in an effort to suppress financial mismanagement and corruption. The proconsul did not have the time or staff to keep a close, continuous watch over municipal administration. His intervention must to some extent have depended on what was brought to his attention and by whom, with the result that municipal notables with influential connections could manipulate gubernatorial actions to their benefit in political struggles with other locals. The provincial finances were also formally the proconsul's responsibility, but in fact were in the hands of the quaestor. This junior senator saw to the collection of the provincial land tax, the main source of revenue, which was gathered for the imperial government by the cities from individuals in their territories.

In the provinces under the emperor's control, the same basic duties had to be carried out, along with command of the legions. Since the emperor was technically the governor of these provinces, the organization of personnel was somewhat different, though they were no more numerous. For the major provinces (except Egypt), the emperor appointed a legate from among senior senators to govern in his stead. Responsibility for finances fell to a personal agent of the emperor, a procurator.

Egypt, regarded as the emperor's personal domain, and minor provinces such as Judaea were governed by equestrians like Pontius Pilate, chosen by the emperor. It was in the equestrian administration that the greatest changes took place: not only growth, but also unification of disparate elements into a single hierarchy. In the minor provinces the governors initially were chosen from among army officers and consequently had a military title (prefect) and predominantly military duties. Their appointment and their brief testifies to the determination of the emperors to bring to heel hitherto unsubjugated peoples within their empire (as in the Alps, central Sardinia or Judaea). The replacement from the reign of Claudius of prefect by procurator, a civilian title, was meant to signify the success (sometimes more apparent than real, as in Judaea) of the pacification process in these areas. Secondly, emperors appointed equestrians and sometimes freedmen with the title of procurator of Augustus as their financial agents, with the task of managing the vast imperial properties. Thirdly, procurators appear in the provinces as tax officials, collecting dues, the inheritance tax and other indirect taxes. In this capacity they gradually replaced the notorious private tax collectors, the publicani, on whom the Republican government had relied for gathering revenues. This change may well have resulted in better provincial government, since emperors had some incentive to control abuses of their own officials, but the improvement should not be exaggerated: Josephus' description of the early procurators of Judaea shows that emperors could not closely monitor or control the behavior of their agents.

Equestrians also filled an important function in the imperial army as senior officers. Some 360 posts were available: prefectures of cohorts, military tribunates and prefectures of the cavalry units. The holding of one or more of these appointments, termed the *equestrian militiae* by Tiberius' reign, was usually the springboard into the higher posts of the civilian administration. Among the administrative reforms for which Claudius was remembered was a change in the sequence of the three militiae held in the ordinary course of an equestrian's career. For many men their equestrian career went no further than the basic starting point in military service.

Though the emperors' impact on the quality of provincial administration is unclear, they undoubtedly brought improved administration to the city of Rome, simply by introducing some continuing governmental services where little had previously existed. By the end of the reign of Augustus there existed for the first time a "police force" (under the senatorial urban prefect), a fire department (under the equestrian *praefectus vigilum*), and continuous management of the grain supply (under the equestrian *praefectus annonae*). During the Julio-Claudian era another equestrian official, the praetorian prefect, came to be recognized as senior and most powerful in the equestrian hierarchy. His command of the emperor's elite bodyguard, the Praetorian Guard, and his proximity to the emperor offered the prefect enormous potential to build a power base. Tiberius' praetorian prefect Sejanus beyond all others recognized this and tried to exploit his office to manipulate imperial power to his own ends. His temporary success is described by a client, Marcus Terentius, in the pages of Tacitus' *Annals* (6.8): "His kinsfolk and connections were loaded with honors; intimacy with Sejanus was in every case a powerful recommendation to the emperor's friendship. Those, on the contrary, whom he hated, had to struggle with danger and humiliation." That a mere equestrian should reach such heights enraged senators who blackened his memory after his fall. As a precaution against such abuse of power, two praetorian prefects were usually appointed as a check on one another.

The central financial administration in Rome emerged from two quite different bases, senatorial administration of the public treasuries and servile management of the emperor's huge fortune within his own household. The main treasury, the aerarium, into which provincial taxes flowed, was headed by a pair of senatorial prefects, chosen by the emperor. Similar officials were appointed to head the military treasury (aerarium militare) created by Augustus to provide benefits for veterans on retirement. These senatorial officials held office for only a few years. The true financial expertise lay with the freedman and slave accountants in the emperor's household. During the Republic senators and other wealthy men relied on their servile dependents to manage their estates and keep their books, so it was natural for Augustus to draw on his household for his accountants. The chief accountant came to be known as the secretary a rationibus. Only gradually did it become clear that this was a position of such intimacy with the emperor and hence potential power that it was unsuitable for an ambitious freedman like Pallas. Only after the demise of the Julio-Claudians was this office recognized as an official one outside the emperor's household, to be held by a Roman of higher standing, a senior equestrian.

The last element of the administration for consideration comprises the emperor, his advisers and personal staff. The emperor was ultimately responsible for policy decisions (concerning, for example, foreign policy, war, or changes in the administrative system) and the appointment of imperial officials, but in reaching his decisions he took advice from those around him. The good emperor, in the eyes of the aristocracy, found his advisers in his consilium, a group of leading senatorial and equestrian friends. This council also advised the emperor in his legal capacities as a judge both of appeals and as a formulator of new laws. The emperor was also surrounded by freedman assistants to help in replying to letters (the secretary ab epistulis) and to petitions from his subjects (the secretary a libellis). When an emperor like Claudius allowed himself to be greatly influenced by freedman secretaries and the women of his household, he aroused the anger of senators who regarded Pallas, Narcissus and Callistus as unworthy advisers and resented their positions as power brokers. This resentment is reflected in the ancient accounts of Claudius' reign which have far more to say about the abuses of his freedmen than about Claudius' administrative accomplishments. The influence of imperial freedmen and slaves diminished but did not disappear after the Julio-Claudian emperors. Their power was a natural result of their access to the emperor while helping him carry out routine duties, such as receiving reports from provincial officials and writing replies, and responding to petitions for favors or justice from cities and individual subjects. The potential power of the freedmen and slaves was, however, limited by the fact that the emperor seems to have dealt with many letters and petitions personally; hence the flow of information to the emperor was usually not as closely controlled by staff as in modern bureaucracies.

How did this system of administration develop during the early Principate? The basic elements can be found in the reign of Augustus: the appointment of senators by the emperor to new administrative posts, the employment of equestrians and freedmen as imperial officials and agents, and the use of the imperial household as the supporting staff. The new senatorial posts were fitted into the already existing framework of magistracies to form an enlarged career structure: the praetorship might lead to a minor governorship, legionary command, or an administrative post in Rome, and the consulship to the governorship of a major province; the prefect of the city of Rome was chosen from among senators who had been honored with a second consulship. The position of senators remained fairly stable during our period; the only significant change was accomplished by the first emperors, the separation of proconsulships from army commands. It should be stressed that despite the common assumption that the emperor used his lesser officials to offset the power of the senatorial order, senators remained in command of all the empire's legions outside Egypt throughout our period. The development of the equestrian administrative posts took place at the expense of the emperors' freedmen, not senators. During the first century the disparate equestrian positions were gradually organized into a standard career hierarchy, so that an equestrian would go through a sequence of militiae before appointment to a series of graded procuratorships, to be capped off for the fortunate few by appointment to the great prefectures (the night police, the corn supply, the governorship of Egypt, and the command of the Praetorian Guard, in ascending order). This hierarchy of office was only beginning to emerge by the end of the Julio-Claudian dynasty.

Similarly, a clearly defined hierarchy of posts can be discerned among the freedmen and slaves in the emperor's household. A slave on the clerical staff could reasonably hope to be manumitted around the age of 30, and then promoted to a higher post (e.g., as *tabularius* or recordkeeper) and finally to a freedman procuratorship. Imperial freedmen and slaves continued through the Principate to provide the backbone of the administrative system. Unlike most senators and equestrians, they were lifetime administrators, able to provide continuity and expertise in government.

For an understanding of how this administrative organization worked and where power lay, it is important to know how the office-holders were appointed. Of course, the emperor made all of the above-mentioned appointments except to the proconsulships and quaestorships, but it must be asked how he made his decisions. This is an important question because it shapes our view of how bureaucratic the administration became in the early Principate.

Numerous historians have taken the position that bureaucratic rules came to regulate appointments and promotions to the point where the process became nearly automatic, leaving the emperor little discretion. According to this view, Claudius, influenced by his patronage-wielding freedmen and wives, was an aberration. But this is to misunderstand the nature of the senatorial hostility toward Claudius. The system of appointment was never so automatic that patronage could be eliminated in the selection and promotion of officials. Our literary sources quite openly speak of the exercise of influence to reach high office in positive terms. The senatorial complaint against Claudius was that he permitted the wrong people, people of inferior rank, to influence him in his appointments.

In regard to promotions and in other respects, the administration of the Principate represents an advance in organization over the Republic, but the advance should not be exaggerated. The administration at top levels remained amateurish: senators and equestrians spent only part of their working lives in office; they received no special training for their duties; and in the course of their careers they did not develop specialist expertise. If there were any administrative "professionals," they were the emperor's freedmen and slaves. Furthermore, though the administration grew, it remained relatively tiny, with a few hundred senatorial and equestrian officials governing scores of millions. The number was small enough to make unnecessary the development of a hierarchy of responsibility: by and large, each senatorial and equestrian official was responsible directly to the emperor. The organizational chart, had there been one, would not have been a pyramid, but a circle of dots linked to the emperor at the center. All this is perhaps not surprising in view of the limited aims of the government. It did not require an apparatus to keep track of each individual subject. Rather, it could rely on the network of cities to siphon off taxes and to do much of the work of maintaining order. Only in the later empire did the goals of government grow more ambitious, requiring a larger and more highly organized staff.

Senatorial Aristocracy Under the Emperors

Keith Hopkins

Keith Hopkins once taught sociology at the London School of Economics and is now Professor of Ancient History at Cambridge University. This dual background can be seen in this essay, which differentiates between competing groups in the senatorial aristocracy. Those with noble ancestry were distrusted as possible contenders for the imperial throne, and they were thus kept far from the important provincial commands and the armies. The emperors entrusted the armies to a second group of senators: loyal followers without a sufficiently distinguished lineage to pose any threat to the throne. The emperors successfully played off these groups against each other until the powers of the collective Senate were negligible.

It was the breaks with the Republican practice which most enhanced emperors' power. First, emperors cut off senators' access to a popular electorate. This restricted the arena of their political campaigns, and so limited their chances of getting broad political support. Secondly, emperors themselves appointed commanders of legions and governors of provinces in which legions were stationed. This control over appointments separated traditional marks of high status, such as the praetorship or consulship, from the effective exercise of political power in the provinces. The traditional marks of high status became only a necessary, and were no longer a sufficient, condition of wielding political power. This bifurcation of power and status enabled emperors to establish a second arena for competition among senators, but outside the senate: namely competition for posts in the imperial service. From among the competitors, emperors could then choose as generals in the provinces, men whose activities they knew about from their performance in several posts over more than a decade. This supervision of provincial governors' power was patently crucial for the survival of the Principate as a political system; in the late Republic, governors' capacity to construct power-bases with their armies in the provinces had precipitated the disintegration of the Republican political structure.

The separation of high status and political power also tempts us, at the risk of considerable simplification, to identify two sets within the senatorial elite. These are the 'grand set' and the 'power set.' The first set comprises the most noble, those who were closest in status to the emperors and were his most obvious rivals. Among these, patricians, as we have already noted, were normally as a privilege given fast promotion from quaestorship to consulship; they were thereby precluded from the military experience which was normally a necessary condition for the governorship of the provinces in which legions were stationed. Other aristocrats, sons of consuls but not necessarily of patrician status, may also have been passed over and not chosen as imperial provincial governors. They were kept away from military power. Some of them probably comforted themselves with social influence and with an extravagant social life in the city of Rome, which both expressed and enhanced their status. Indeed some members of this grand set may not have been in the senate at all. They remained members of the grand set by virtue of their inherited wealth and social status; they did not follow their fathers into political office. Their existence follows logically from the evidence on differential rates of succession which we presented earlier. The grand set thus spread beyond the senatorial elite. Other members of the grand set retreated into philosophy which either elevated the ideal of Liberty or scorned the slavishness of political ambition. Many might not have wanted to serve as governor in a distant province with a bad climate. As one late orator declared of early imperial times: 'The hard work of military service was rejected by all the nobles as sordid and ungentlemanly.'

In this grand set, patricians and nobles of Republican lineage (such as Licinius Crassus, Pompeius Magnus and Calpurnius Piso) were the prime targets of early emperors' persecutions. They were attacked partly because they were so rich and their property was worth confiscating, and partly because they did plot against the emperors, sometimes preemptively. In the second century A.D., confiscation and persecution was less pervasive. Some holders of the ordinary consulship, with their relatively high rate of succession between generations, can be identified as members of the grand set. For example, the Brutii Praesentes produced six *ordinary* consuls in just over a century. . . ; but only the first of these is known to have governed a military province. Such men may have had influence as friends, dinner companions or advisers of emperors, and their prestige and marriage connections extended to the imperial family itself (a daughter of a Bruttius Praesens married the emperor Commodus), but their social status was not matched by the exercise of effective power in administrative positions, and certainly not in the frontier regions of the empire. It is for these reasons that we call this set, the grand set.

Our second set, the power set, embraces senators who governed the major military provinces. These men competed for success and fame mostly by serving the emperor for long years as commanders of legions and as governors of frontier provinces. They were the men to whom the emperors delegated most power and these were the men who in a crisis of succession led rebellious armies against unpopular monarchs and against each other. Only a few of these men had consular or even apparently senatorial fathers; for example, of all known consular legates (i.e. governors of important imperial provinces) from the period A.D. 96-138, five out of six did not have a consular father. Most must have come from families new to the political elite, and were descended from rich and respectable Italian or provincial gentry. Only a few are known to have been fast social risers, who made their way up from less respectable social milieux by personal prowess usually through military service. For example, Curtius Rufus, reportedly the son of a gladiator, was appointed governor of Upper Germany under Claudius, and the future emperor Pertinax was said to be the son of an ex-slave timber merchant.

The grand set and the power set are analytically distinct; but in practice there may have been some overlap between them. Ties of patronage and intermarriage doubtless linked individual members, while some powerful governors, having skillfully increased their fortunes in the provinces, returned to the city of Rome to live in ostentatious luxury as members of the grand set. It seems likely that many sons of consuls in the power set were elevated to the grand set, either inside or outside the senate; other sons dropped out of the metropolitan elite altogether. These are the implications of the evidence . . . on succession rates. Few sons of suffect consuls had successful careers in provincial administration. And sons of ordinary consuls, if they entered politics, tended to have brilliant rather than powerful careers; they rarely finished as suffect consuls, in contrast to Republican practice, in which sons of consuls quite often finished their careers as praetors. . . .

By establishing different though linked ladders for promotion to honours (praetor, consul) and to offices (governor, legate), the emperors also created, consciously or unconsciously, a system which prevented the formation of a powerful hereditary elite. Circulation in the elite was enlivened by three complementary techniques: (1) the promotion of outsiders to positions of power; (2) the expectation of ostentatious expenditure by aristocrats, supplemented by occasional confiscations; (3) the elevation of sons of the politically successful to positions of higher status without power, in which aristocrats had to maintain their status by competitive ostentation without recompense from public office. Unlike the old British system of offices, for example, Roman imperial politics offered almost no offices of profit at court in the metropolis. To be sure, some of the emperors' favorites were richly rewarded; but there was no regular system of supporting aristocrats at court out of state funds.

Staying at court in Rome cost money. In order to make large fortunes, or even in some cases in order to support their extravagance, ambitious senators had to go away from the capital to govern provinces, and make money there. Even then, they ran the risk of being prosecuted by outraged provincials or by political rivals in Rome. The inability or reluctance of many nobles and other senators to serve for long periods in the provinces must have drained the family wealth, and even endangered some families' social standing. In effect, by leading a life of ostentatious luxury in Rome, aristocrats were colluding in their own social suicide. Some could avoid falling out of the political elite only by securing imperial favour and generosity, or by securing a large inheritance from a distant relative or from a friend without heirs, or by marriage to an heiress, or by skillful management of their estates. But a change of ruler cut old lines of patronage and favour; exceptional wealth tempted attacks and confiscation; and parsimony, if they tried that, lowered their social prestige. In some cases, restricted fertility by chance or design concentrated resources in the hands of a single surviving heir or heiress; but in other cases, restricted fertility endangered the biological survival of the family. Some senators could choose between political activity or withdrawal, between relatively high or low fertility. But each course of action involved risk. And the overall effect was that vacancies were continually left free in the senate for outsiders. Our main point here is that the Roman aristocracy under the emperors never banded together effectively to minimize the risks to their individual or collective status. That was both symptom and cause of the weakness of the senatorial aristocracy during the Principate.

Social Relations

Peter Garnsey and Richard Saller

In this excerpt from their new book on the Roman Empire, Peter Garnsey of Cambridge and Richard Saller analyze the web of personal relationships in imperial Rome. Relations between patrons and clients, gifts and obligations between friends, and the importance of family and status all derive from the traditional social relations in the Roman Republic. But all were transformed in a new political structure in which the emperor was patron of the entire Empire.

The place of a Roman in society was a function of his position in the social hierarchy, membership of a family, and involvement in a web of personal relationships extending out from the household. Romans were obligated to and could expect support from their families, kinsmen and dependents both inside and outside the household, and friends, patrons, proteges and clients. In the eyes of Seneca, whose longest moral essay was devoted to the subject, the exchange of favours and services (*beneficia*) which underlay these relationships 'most especially binds together human society.' Seneca's emphasis on reciprocal exchange is justifiable on several grounds: it eased tensions and conflicts provoked by divisions and inequalities; and it provided many of the services for which today we turn to impersonal governmental or private institutions.

Honour, Status and the Reciprocity Ethic

Despite the general comment about human society quoted above, Seneca's *On Benefits* is not a work of sociology or anthropology, but an ethical treatise about how men ought to conduct themselves in the giving and receiving of favours and services. His central premise is that a man in receipt of a favour owes his benefactor gratitude and a return in kind. Of the man who neglects this ethical precept, Seneca wrote: 'Homicides, tyrants, traitors there always will be; but worse than all these is the crime of ingratitude.' A century earlier Cicero expressed the same view: 'To fail to repay [a favour] is not permitted to a good

man.' The ideal benefactor was supposed to act without thought of what was due to him, but this was unrealistic. It was understood by both the author of the *Handbook on Canvassing* attributed to Q. Cicero and by Tacitus in his *Dialogue on the Orators* that the orator and politician would succeed by distributing benefits that would subsequently be reciprocated. Consequently, Seneca could use the metaphor of treasure for benefits that could be recalled in time of the benefactor's need, and the language of debt and repayment regularly appeared in discussions of exchange between friends or patrons and clients.

Just as a loan created a relationship between creditor and debtor, so a favour or service gave rise to a social relationship between Romans. Because benefaction and requital were matters of honour, the dynamics of the exchange partially determined the relative social standing of the men involved. Very little pretence was made about egalitarianism in friendships. A man might have 'superior friends,' 'equal friends,' 'lesser friends' and humble 'clients,' and the categorization of others into one or another of these depended on their resources. Those who could exchange comparable benefits were friends of equal social standing, whilst most stood higher or lower in the hierarchy by virtue of their capacity to provide superior or inferior services in return. Some Romans tried to conceal the favours done for them precisely to avoid the implication of social inferiority arising from the fact that they had to turn to someone else for help. The proper conduct of a recipient was to acknowledge and advertise his benefactor's generosity and power.

The Emperor as Patron

Augustus sought to establish his legitimacy not only by restoring the social order, but also by demonstrating his own supremacy in it through the traditional modes of patronage and beneficence. Much of the *Res Gestae*, his own account of his reign, was an elaboration of the staggering scale of his benefits and services to the Roman people (15-18). In Pliny's *Panegyric* (e.g., 2, 21), the ideology of the good emperor was one not so much of an efficient administrator as of a paternal protector and benefactor. Since subjects could not repay imperial benefactions in kind, the reciprocity ethic dictated that they make a return in the form of deference, respect and loyalty. Consequently, as Seneca pointed out, the emperor who played the role of great patron well had no need of guards because he was 'protected by his benefits.' (*Clem.* 1.13.5)

The emperor distributed his benefits individually to those who had access to him and, more broadly, to favoured groups, notably the Roman plebs and the army. Proximity to the emperor opened up to a privileged circle, including friends of high rank, relatives, and servile members of his household, a wide range of benefits from offices and honours to financial assistance to citizenship and the right of tapping the water supply. The norms guiding the distribution of these goods and services were openly particularistic, in contrast to the universalistic rules associated with modern bureaucracies. They were treated as personal favours granted to the loyal, not as governmental services and positions to be distributed on the basis of impersonal competition and universally available to all qualified citizens or subjects. In return, devoted service and gratitude were expected, one manifestation of which was the naming of the emperor in the will. T. Marius Urbinas caused a scandal by failing to acknowledge Augustus' generosity to himself in this way (Valerius Maximus 7.8.6). From more conscientious friends and clients Augustus received 1.4 billion sesterces in bequests over the last twenty years of his reign (Suetonius, *Aug.* 101).

The emperor also took on the role of benefactor of the plebs, in the cause of order and the security of his regime. Augustus' interest in the tribunate, the prerogatives of which he gradually assumed between 36 and 23 B.C., is to be explained in these terms. The appeal of the tribune lay in its historic role as the champion of the common people. More important, Augustus saw to the material needs of the masses by tending to their supply of food, water and housing, by providing public shows and by occasional distributions of considerable sums of money to all male citizens of the city. The sums cited in *Res Gestae* were the equivalent of at least several months' rent for the poor (15). Whatever their feelings about these handouts, later emperors felt compelled to continue in this role. Though the plebs lost all semblance of constitutional power with the transfer of elections to the senate in A.D. 14, they still possessed means of making their discontent known and the emperor's position awkward, whether through protests at public spectacles or riots in the streets.

Emperors did not and could not monopolize patronage. They did not attempt to be universal patrons to all their subjects, since universality would have undermined the incentive for personal gratitude on the part of the subjects. Far from contemplating the suppression of the patronal networks of the aristocratic houses in Rome, emperors positively encouraged them by providing some of the resources that helped aristocratic patrons like Pliny to reward their clients. The letters of Pliny show Trajan granting offices and citizenship at Pliny's request, thus bolstering Pliny's status as an effective mediator. The successful emperors were the ones who kept the imperial aristocrats content by allowing them to maintain their exalted social status, and that implied a willingness to permit the great houses to display their patron influence in the traditional way.

Patrons and Clients

Tacitus in writing of the 'part of the populace . . . attached to the great houses' (*Hist.* 1.4.)

attests the patronal ties linking aristocrats and members of the lower classes in the city of Rome. The *salutatio* and other Republican customs characteristic of patronage continued throughout the Principate, though with a different complexion. After A.D. 14 the relationship could no longer revolve around the electoral process. In the *Handbook on Canvassing* (11) it was stressed that a Republican candidate for high office had to make every effort to win followers of all ranks, even to the extent of lowering himself by mixing with and flattering members of the lower classes who would ordinarily be beneath his dignity. In the imperial era the impotence of the popular assemblies deprived the ordinary people of their political leverage and, with it, the incentive for aristocrats to treat their humble clients with a modicum of respect.

Nevertheless, some *quid pro quo* was still possible and provided the basis for patronal exchange. Clients could contribute to their patron's social status by forming crowds at his door for the morning *salutatio* (Tacitus, *Ann.* 3.55) or by accompanying him on his rounds of public business during the day and applauding his speeches in court. In return, they could expect handouts of food or *sportulae* (small sums of money, customarily about six sesterces in Martial's day) and sometimes an invitation to dinner. Martial lists attendance on a patron as one way that an immigrant to the city of Rome might hope to support himself, though he warns that the *sportulae* were not enough to live on. They must have been just one of the possible supplements to the grain dole (*Epig.* 3.7 and 8.42). These epigrams were written after the inauguration of Vespasian, whose more austere habits were supposed to have set an example for a retreat from the lavish clienteles of the Julio-Claudian era (Tacitus, *Ann.* 3.55). Martial's verses and other evidence, however, leave no doubt that the salutatio and other patronal customs continued to characterize life in Rome throughout the Principate.

Patron-client bonds extended out from Rome to the provinces. Like the emperor, governors and other officials representing his power had a patronal role. In a speech before a

governor of Africa Proconsularis, Apuleius claimed that provincials esteemed governors for the benefits they conferred (*Flor.* 9). This is corroborated by a number of north African inscriptions dedicated by provincials to governors as their 'patrons.' In their official capacities governors could help provincials secure citizenship, offices and honours from Rome, and they could also make administrative and legal decisions in their favour. The public dedications to governor 'patrons' from lawyers (*advocati*) may strike the modern reader as an ominous sign of corruption, but in fact highlight the differences between ancient and modern ideologies of administration (e.g., *CIL* VIII.2734, 2743, 2393). Governors also received from grateful provincials, gifts (or, differently interpreted, bribes) and support in case of a prosecution for maladministration after the governor's term of office. For his part in discouraging a prosecution against a senatorial ex-governor of Gaul, T. Sennius Sollemnis received from the former governor a tribunate on his staff in Britain (salary paid in gold), several luxury garments, a sealskin and jewelry (*CIL* XIII.3162). The advertisement of all these details on a public monument demonstrates that the exercise of patronage in government was not considered dishonourable or corrupt.

As the provincialization of the Roman aristocracy progressed in the late first and second centuries, a steadily increasing number of provincials had fellow townsmen well placed in Rome to serve as patronal mediators between themselves and the Roman rulers. This gave them alternative means of access to the benefits distributed from Rome, and also a means of influencing the administrators sent out to rule them. No longer were they governed by foreign conquerors, but by friends of friends. The increasing integration into the patronal networks centred on Rome was naturally most advantageous to the well-connected—that is, the local elites. The plight of the tenants on the imperial estates of the saltus Brutus illustrates how the patronal links between local magnates and imperial officials could result in collusion whereby the former drew on the force of the latter to reinforce their own ability to exploit the humiliores.

Patrons and Proteges

The relationship between patron and protege, or superior and inferior friends, falls between that of friendship on equal terms and that of patron and humble client. Because the label *cliens* was regarded as demeaning, considerate patrons generally avoided using it in references to their junior or less powerful friends. Since the extant Latin literature was written largely by the 'superior friends,' the word *cliens* rarely appears in descriptions of proteges, with the consequence that some historians have argued that the Romans did not consider these relationships to be patronal nor should we analyze them as such. But if we define patronage as 'a reciprocal exchange relationship between men of unequal status and resources,' then bonds between patrons and proteges clearly qualify. Further, the contrary argument minimizing the dependence of 'lesser friends' on their 'superiors' goes astray by taking the polite language of the superiors at face value. Young and ambitious men behaved in ways typical of *clientes* in their search for powerful supporters: Plutarch refers to aristocrats in search of high office as those who 'grow old haunting the doors of other men's houses,' a reference to attendance at morning *salutationes* (*Mor.* 814D). Finally, the argument from the absence of the particular words *patronus* and *cliens* in descriptions of these relationships fails to take account of all the evidence. While courteous patrons generally did not wish to highlight the inferior social position of their protege by calling them *clientes*, the latter did use *patronus* in dedications to their benefactors. For example, C. Bivius Maximus, starting out in his equestrian career, honoured his *patronus*, the senior equestrian governor of Numidia, L. Titinius Clodianus, for his support in securing office (*Ann. Epigr.* 1917-18, 85).

The question of how to categorize these relationships is more than a quibble over words, insofar as it draws attention to the issue of whether they were characterized by the dependence and deference associated with patronage. Pliny's relationship with his supporter, the senior senator Corellius Rufus, suggests that they were. Corellius Rufus paid Pliny the compliment of treating him as an equal, but his behaviour was taken as complimentary only because they were not equal (*Ep.* 4.17.4). Pliny shows a deferential attitude in seeking and following the advice of his supporter on nearly every issue (*Ep.* 9.13.6). In their unequal exchange Corellius provided support that Pliny, as a new man, depended on for advancement in his career, while Pliny displayed respect, extended his patron's influence after the completion of the latter's career by acting on his advice, and finally provided help for Corellius' family after his death (*Ep.* 4.17.4-7). The quasi-paternal quality of these friendships stands out in Pliny's description of his own protege, who used him as a model, accompanied him on his daily business and even assumed the toga with the broad stripe (*latus clavus*) in his house (*Ep.* 8.23.2, 6.6.5f.).

Several features of imperial society gave this type of patronage a special importance in the Principate. Patronal support was essential in the recruitment of the imperial elite, because no bureaucratic mechanisms were developed to supply the next generation of aristocratic officials. The emperor's role in making these appointments is often emphasized, but in the absence of training schools or application procedures the emperor had to appoint those brought to his attention by senior friends like Corellius Rufus. The mediators who supported the careers of young senators and equestrians were generally patrons rather than fathers, because most young aspirants were from new families and only a small fraction of those in the early stages of their careers (perhaps a fifth of thirty-year-olds) had a living father on account of the relatively late age at marriage for men. Thus, the imperial elite was renewed, and the new families from across the empire were introduced to traditional Roman ways, in large part through the patron-protege bonds.

The exchange between patron and protege extended beyond the political sphere. Pliny's letters show him offering lesser friends support in a legal matter related to an inheritance (*Ep.* 6.8), a gift of 300,000 sesterces (*Ep.* 1.19) and other financial favors. The smaller resources of these proteges normally precluded a comparable return—that is what made them 'inferior friends'—but they could honour their patron with gratitude and, more concretely, with bequests after their death.

The literary talents of some proteges gave a few of these relationships a cultural dimension. While some authors and poets of the Principate were men of substantial means and high rank, others hoped to support themselves by writing for patrons. In return for the fame that would accrue to the patron of a successful author, the latter might hope that his patron would draw attention to his work and improve his material position with gifts ranging from an estate and an apartment in the city to an official salaried appointment, money, clothing and food. Many writers were disappointed by lack of generosity and others had no need of it, but that should not obscure the fact that important literary figures from Virgil to Martial did receive significant material support from patrons, such as Maecenas, Seneca and C. Calpurnius Piso, who viewed themselves as supporters of literature.

Friends

Roman philosophers placed great value on friendship, stressing that ideal friends should share common interests and values without thought of self-interest. Though the philosophers eschewed material advantage as a motive for friendship, for other Romans (and indeed for the philosophers in their more pragmatic moments) the exchange of services was a foundation for friendship (Fronto, Ad M. Caesarem 1.3.4f.). The exchange between friends of comparable social standing and resources had a different character from those described above. Though neither party was in a permanent position of superiority, one or the other might be better placed at a particular time to confer a favour.

The glittering prizes of later Republican senatorial politics were no longer available, yet support in the competition for magistracies and other posts before the emperor and in senatorial elections remained essential. Governors had staff offices to bestow not only on their own 'lesser friends,' but also on those of their peers. Pliny introduced a request that his friend Priscus confer such a post on a protege of his with the comment that Priscus had had time to reward his own friends and should now be prepared to spread his favours more widely (Ep. 2.13.2). . . .

The benefits exchanged in friendship resemble those given between patrons and protege, but the tone of friendship on an equal footing is different. Pliny's relationships with men like Priscus were characterized by courteous cooperation. Behind the facade of cooperation lay competition: if a friend failed to make a return of the same order, he risked slipping into the position of a 'lesser friend' and losing honour in the process. In contrast, Pliny's relationship with Corellius was not competitive, because genuine equality was not possible. Corellius was the backer, and the roles were not reversible. Pliny eventually surpassed his supporter, but his success as a new man was not a foregone conclusion, and he needed whatever help he could get from senior senators like Corellius and Verginius Rufus.

The personal exchange relationships described above effectively mitigated cross-order conflict and tension, the importance of which has often been exaggerated. Specifically, the old view that emperors preferred as administrators equestrians, who were directly dependent on them for offices and honours, rather than senators, who were potential competitors for power, is no longer tenable. Many senators were as dependent on imperial favour as equestrians, many equestrians were more directly tied to the senatorial mediators who won them offices and honours than to the emperor, and senators and equestrians were generally integrated through kinship, friendship and patronage into a single social network. Consequently, equestrians as a group were not noticeably more loyal than senators.

An instantly recognizable Nero is depicted on a large brass sestertius issued in commemoration of the emperor's restoration of the city after the great fire of A.D. 64.

XII

Nero And The Fall of The Julio-Claudian Dynasty

INTRODUCTION
Ronald Mellor

The fifth Roman emperor was born in A.D. 37 to Domitius Ahenobarbus and the younger Agrippina, great-granddaughter of Augustus and sister of Caligula. Upon his mother's marriage to the emperor Claudius, young Domitius was adopted into the imperial family as Nero Claudius Drusus and was known to all as Nero. When Claudius died in 54, his son Britannicus left Nero alone on the imperial throne. But the boy was not without advisors: the praetorian prefect Burrus and the philosopher Seneca prudently guided the boy in his initial speech which displayed an Augustan moderation. Nero confirmed senatorial rights and refused excessive titles of honors during the quinquennium Neronis—the successful first five years of the reign applauded in antiquity as a golden age.

But his mother Agrippina had not poisoned Claudius in order to be neglected and ignored. She encouraged Nero's autocratic tendencies and paid the price when he had her murdered in 59. Despite palace intrigues, Seneca and Burrus had administered the Empire well and attended to the economic well-being of the provinces, but the death of Burrus in 62 brought the withdrawal of Seneca from public life. The odious and sycophantic Tigellinus became praetorian prefect and treason trials reminiscent of Tiberus' reign began. Nero's wife (and Claudius' daughter) Octavia was first exiled and later killed. Nero's reign of terror had begun.

On July 18, A.D. 64, a fire broke out which raged across Rome for a week and destroyed large sections of the city. Despite later rumors that during the fire Nero played the lyre (not the anachronistic fiddle) and sang his poem on the burning of Troy, the emperor is unlikely to have been responsible for setting the fire and he actually seems to have led the fight to halt its spread. But, with the damage done, he sought a scapegoat in the new and widely distrusted Jewish sect called "Christian," and Christian tradition attributes the deaths of St. Peter and St. Paul to these Neronian persecutions. As part of the rebuilding of the city, Nero constructed in its center a vast palace—the "Golden House"—with parks, lakes, and a 120-foot statue of the emperor, colossus, whence the great amphitheater later built on the site took its name. The Golden House and the reconstruction of the city were financed by taxes as well as by forced contributions and proved to be a dangerous drain on the resources of the Empire.

Nero's artistic inclinations were genuine, and the surviving fragments of his poetry are at least competent. But his desire for applause led him to make public appearances which shocked the Roman elite (as Caligula had done) and when he toured the Greek festivals in 67, they were outraged. He may have won 1,808 gold crowns from the delighted Greeks, but the more sober Romans were disgusted. In A.D. 65 a major conspiracy had been uncovered (supported by one of the praetorian prefects) and dozens of senators were executed. Nero's old tutor Seneca was forced to commit suicide, and other Stoic philosophers who preached against tyranny were killed or exiled. Tacitus tells the story of the suicide of the courtier Petronius, author of the hilarious Satyricon and known as the arbiter of good taste at the imperial court, who left in his will to be read by Nero a detailed description of the emperor's disgusting, and supposedly secret, vices. Petronius must have seen it as his last joke.

Nero's declining authority in Rome was reflected in the provinces. Boudicca's revolt in Britain, a revolt in Judaea and a mismanaged policy on the eastern frontier caused anxiety among the troops. Nero had forced one of his greatest generals, Corbulo, to commit suicide, and other generals were looking for an opportunity to protect themselves by striking first. Julius Vindex, a romanized Gaul who served as governor in Gaul, rose in revolt, but the nationalist undertone of the rebellion kept the Rhine armies loyal and the revolt was soon put down. The armies of Spain, however, proclaimed their distingushed governor Galba as emperor, and Nero's support collapsed even among the praetorians. On June 9, A.D 68. Nero ran on a sword held by a faithful slave, and died at the age of thirty. He was little mourned in Rome but in the Greek world the name of Nero was revered and decades later men who claimed to be Nero attracted popular support. At his death Nero lamented, "How great an artist dies in me." He may have been right, but he was playing the wrong role in the wrong play.

Nero's Crimes: Matricide and Arson

Tacitus *Annals*

In the first excerpt from the Annals, *Tacitus provides a dramatic account of Nero's murder of his mother Agrippina; the first failed attempt brings a certain black humor to the horror of matricide.*

The second passage records the terrible fire that swept Rome in A.D. 64 during which Nero is rumored to have sung with his lyre of the burning of Troy. Tacitus does not take a firm stand on whether the fire began by accident or from arson, but his account gives little credit to the emperor. Nero embarked on the construction of an immense palace—the "Golden House"—in the center of the city, and he also launched the first great persecution of the Christians as he sought scapegoats for the fire.

Book 13

Finally, however, he concluded that wherever Agrippina was she was intolerable. He decided to kill her. His only doubt was whether to employ poison, or the dagger, or violence of some other kind. Poison was the first choice. But a death at the emperor's table would not look fortuitous after Britannicus had died there. Yet her criminal conscience kept her so alert for plots that it seemed impracticable to corrupt her household. Moreover, she had strengthened her physical resistance by a preventive course of antidotes. No one could think of a way of stabbing her without detection. And there was another danger: that the selected assassin might shrink from carrying out his dreadful orders.

However, a scheme was put forward by Anicetus, an ex-slave who commanded the fleet at Misenum. In Nero's boyhood Anicetus had been his tutor; he and Agrippina hated each other. A ship could be made, he now said, with a section which would come loose at sea and hurl Agrippina into the water without warning. Nothing is so productive of surprises as the sea, remarked Anicetus; if a shipwreck did away with her, who could be so unreasonable as to blame a human agency instead of wind and water? Besides, when she was dead the emperor could allot her a temple and altars and the other public tokens of filial duty.

This ingenious plan found favour. The time of year, too, was suitable, since Nero habitually attended the festival of Minerva at Baiae. Now he enticed his mother there. 'Parents' tempers must be borne!' he kept announcing. 'One must humour their feelings.' This was to create the general impression that they were friends again, and to produce the same effect on Agrippina. For women are naturally inclined to believe welcome news.

As she arrived from Antium, Nero met her at the shore. After welcoming her with outstretched hands and embraces, he conducted her to Bauli, a mansion on the bay between Cape Misenum and the waters of Baiae. Some ships were standing there. One, more sumptuous than the rest, was evidently another compliment to his mother, who had formerly been accustomed to travel in warships manned by the imperial navy. Then she was invited out to dinner. The crime was to take place on the ship under cover of darkness. But an informer, it was said, gave the plot away; Agrippina could not decide whether to believe the story, and preferred a sedan-chair as her conveyance to Baiae.

There her alarm was relieved by Nero's attentions. He received her kindly, and gave her the place of honour next to himself. The party went on for a long time. They talked about various things; Nero was boyish and intimate— or confidentially serious. When she left, he saw her off, gazing into her eyes and clinging to her.

This may have been a final piece of shamming— or perhaps even Nero's brutal heart was affected by his last sight of his mother, going to her death.

But heaven seemed determined to reveal the crime. For it was a quiet, star-lit night and the sea was calm. The ship began to go on its way. Agrippina was attended by two of her friends. One of them, Crepereius Gallus, stood near the tiller. The other, Acerronia, leant over the feet of her resting mistress, happily talking about Nero's remorseful behaviour and his mother's re-established influence. Then came the signal. Under the pressure of heavy lead weights, the roof fell in. Crepereius was crushed, and died instantly. Agrippina and Acerronia were saved by the raised sides of their couch, which happened to be strong enough to resist the pressure. Moreover, the ship held together.

In the general confusion, those in the conspiracy were hampered by the many who were not. But then some of the oarsmen had the idea of throwing their weight to one side, to capsize the ship. However, they took too long to concert this improvised plan, and meanwhile others brought weight to bear in the opposite direction. This provided the opportunity to make a gentler descent into the water. Acerronia ill-advisedly started crying out, 'I am Agrippina! Help, help the emperor's mother.' She was struck dead by blows from poles and oars and whatever ship's gear happened to be available. Agrippina herself kept quiet and avoided recognition. Though she was hurt—she had a wound in the shoulder— she swam until she came to some sailing-boats. They brought her to the Lucrine lake, from which she was taken home. . . .

To Nero, awaiting news that the crime was done, came word that she had escaped with a slight wound—after hazards which left no doubt of their instigator's identity. Half-dead with fear, he insisted she might arrive at any moment. 'She may arm her slaves! She may whip up the army, or gain access to the senate or Assembly, and incriminate me for wrecking and wounding her and killing her friends! What can I do to save myself?' Could Burrus and Seneca help? Whether they were in the plot is uncertain. But they were immediately awakened and summoned.

For a long time neither spoke. They did not want to dissuade and be rejected. They may have felt matters had gone so far that Nero had to strike before Agrippina, or die. Finally Seneca ventured so far as to turn to Burrus and ask if the troops should be ordered to kill her. He replied that the Guard were devoted to the whole imperial house and to Germanicus' memory; they would commit no violence against his offspring. Anicetus, he said, must make good his promise. Anicetus unhesitatingly claimed the direction of the crime. Hearing him Nero cried that this was the first day of his reign—and the magnificent gift came from a former slave! 'Go quickly!' he said 'And take men who obey orders scrupulously!'

Agrippina's messenger arrived. When Nero was told, he took the initiative, and staged a fictitious incrimination. While Agerinus delivered his message, Nero dropped a sword at the man's feet and had him arrested as if caught red-handed. Then he could pretend that his mother had plotted against the emperor's life, been detected, and—in shame—committed suicide.

Meanwhile Agrippina's perilous adventure had become known. It was believed to be accidental. As soon as people heard of it they ran to the beach, and climbed on to the embankment, or fishing-boats nearby. Others waded out as far as they could, or waved their arms. The whole shore echoed with wails and prayers and the din of all manner of inquiries and ignorant answers. Huge crowds gathered with lights. When she was known to be safe, they prepared to make a show of rejoicing.

But a menacing armed column arrived and dispersed them. Anicetus surrounded her house and broke in. Arresting every slave in his path, he came to her bedroom door. Here stood a few servants—the rest had been frightened away by the invasion. In her dimly lit room a single maid waited with her. Agrippina's alarm had increased as nobody, not even Agerinus, came from her son. If things had been well there would not be this terribly ominous isolation, then this sudden uproar. Her maid vanished. 'Are you leaving me, too?' called Agrippina. Then she saw Anicetus. Behind him were a naval captain and lieutenant. 'If you have come to visit me', she said, 'you can report that I am better. But if you are assassins, I know my son is not responsible. He did not order his mother's death.' The murderers closed round her bed. First the captain hit her on the head with a truncheon. Then as the lieutenant was drawing his sword to finish her off, she cried out: 'Strike here!'—pointing to her womb. Blow after blow fell, and she died. . . .

This was the end which Agrippina had anticipated for years. The prospect had not daunted her. When she asked astrologers about Nero, they had answered that he would become emperor but kill his mother. Her reply was, 'Let him kill me—provided he becomes emperor.' But Nero only understood the horror of his crime when it was done. For the rest of the night, witless and speechless, he alternately lay paralyzed and leapt to his feet in terror—waiting for the dawn which he thought would be his last. Hope began to return to him when at Burrus' suggestion the colonels and captains of the Guard came and cringed to him, with congratulatory handclasps for his escape from the unexpected menace of his mother's evil activities. . . .

Nero's insincerity took a different form. He adopted a gloomy demeanour, as though sorry to be safe and mourning for his parent's death. But the features of the countryside are less adaptable than those of men; and Nero's gaze could not escape the dreadful view of that sea and shore. Besides, the coast echoed (it was said) with trumpet blasts from the neighbouring hills—and wails from his mother's grave. So Nero departed to Naples.

He wrote the senate a letter. Its gist was that Agerinus, a confidential ex-slave of Agrippina, had been caught with a sword, about to murder him, and that she, conscious of her guilt as instigator of the crime, had paid the penalty. He added older charges. 'She had wanted to be co-ruler—to receive oaths of allegiance from the Guard, and to subject senate and public to the same humiliation. Disappointed of this, she had hated all of them—army, senate, and people. She had opposed gratuities to soldiers and civilians alike. She had contrived the deaths of distinguished men.' Only with the utmost difficulty, added Nero, had he prevented her from breaking into the senate-house and delivering verdicts to foreign envoys. He also indirectly attacked Claudius' regime, blaming his mother for all its scandals. Her death, he said, was a national blessing. Even the shipwreck he cited as providential. Yet even the greatest fool could not believe that it had been accidental, or that a shipwrecked woman had sent a single armed man to break through the imperial guards and fleets. Here condemnation fell not on Nero, whose monstrous conduct beggared criticism, but on Seneca who had composed his self-incriminating speech. . . .

Nero lingered in the cities of Campania. His return to Rome was a worrying problem. Would the senate be obedient? Would the public cheer him? Every bad character (and no court had ever had so many) reassured him that Agrippina was detested, and that her death had increased his popularity. They urged him to enter boldly and see for himself how he was revered. Preceding him—as they had asked to—they found even greater enthusiasm than they had promised. The people marshalled in their tribes were out to meet him, the senators were in their fine clothes, wives and children drawn up in lines by sex and age. Along his route there were tiers of seats as though for a Triumph. Proud conqueror of a servile nation, Nero proceeded to the Capitol and paid his vows.

Then he plunged into the wildest improprieties, which vestiges of respect for his mother had hitherto not indeed repressed, but impeded.

Book 14

Disaster followed. Whether it was accidental or caused by the emperor's criminal act is uncertain—both versions have supporters. Now started the most terrible and destructive fire which Rome had ever experienced. It began in the Circus, where it adjoins the hills.[1] Breaking out in shops selling inflammable goods, and

fanned by the wind, the conflagration instantly grew and swept the whole length of the Circus. There were no walled mansions or temples, or any other obstructions which could arrest it. First, the fire swept violently over the level spaces. Then it climbed the hills—but returned to ravage the lower ground again. It outstripped every counter-measure. The ancient city's narrow winding streets and irregular blocks encouraged its progress.

Terrified, shrieking women, helpless old and young, people intent on their own safety, people unselfishly supporting invalids or waiting for them, fugitives and lingerers alike—all heightened the confusion. When people looked back, menacing flames sprang up before them or outflanked them. When they escaped to a neighbouring quarter, the fire followed—even districts believed remote proved to be involved. Finally, with no idea where or what to flee, they crowded on to the country roads, or lay in the fields. Some who had lost everything—even their food for the day—could have escaped, but preferred to die. So did others, who had failed to rescue their loved ones. Nobody dared fight the flames. Attempts to do so were prevented by menacing gangs. Torches, too, were openly thrown in, by men crying that they acted under orders. Perhaps they had received orders. Or they may just have wanted to plunder unhampered.

Nero was at Antium. He only returned to the city when the fire was approaching the mansion he had built to link the Gardens of Maecenas to the Palatine. The flames could not be prevented from overwhelming the whole of the Palatine, including his palace. Nevertheless, for the relief of the homeless, fugitive masses he threw open the Field of Mars, including Agrippa's public buildings, and even his own Gardens. Nero also constructed emergency accommodation for the destitute multitude. Food was brought from Ostia and neighbouring towns, and the price of corn was cut. Yet these measures, for all their popular character, earned no gratitude. For a rumour had spread, that while the city was burning, Nero had gone to his

---

1 The Palatine and Caelian.

private stage and, comparing modern calamities with ancient, had sung of the destruction of Troy. . . .

Of Rome's fourteen districts only four remained intact. Three were levelled to the ground. The other seven were reduced to a few scorched and mangled ruins. To count the mansions, blocks, and temples destroyed would be difficult. They included shrines of remote antiquity, the precious spoils of countless victories, Greek artistic masterpieces, and authentic records of old Roman genius. All the splendour of the rebuilt city did not prevent the older generation from remembering these irreplaceable objects. . . .

But Nero profited by his country's ruin to build a new palace. Its wonders were not so much customary and commonplace luxuries like gold and jewels, but lawns and lakes and faked rusticity—woods here, open spaces and views there. With their cunning, impudent artificialities, Nero's architects and contractors outbid Nature. . . .

Next came attempts to appease heaven. After consultation of the Sibylline books, prayers were addressed to Vulcan, Ceres, and Prosperpina. Juno, too, was propitiated. But neither human resources, nor imperial munificence, nor appeasement of the gods,

eliminated sinister suspicions that the fire had been instigated. To suppress this rumour, Nero fabricated scapegoats—and punished with every refinement the notoriously depraved Christians (as they were popularly called). Their originator, Christ, had been executed in Tiberius' reign by the governor of Judaea, Pontius Pilatus. But in spite of this temporary setback the deadly superstition had broken out afresh, not only in Judaea (where the mischief had started) but even in Rome. All degraded and shameful practices collect and flourish in the capital.

First, Nero had self-acknowledged Christians arrested. Then, on their information, large numbers of others were condemned—not so much for the incendiarism as for their anti-social tendencies. Their deaths were made farcical. Dressed in wild animals' skins, they were torn to pieces by dogs, or crucified, or made into torches to be ignited after dark as substitutes for daylight. Nero provided his Gardens for the spectacle, and exhibited displays in the Circus, at which he mingled with the crowd—or stood in a chariot, dressed as a charioteer. Despite their guilt as Christians, and the ruthless punishment it deserved, the victims were pitied. For it was felt that they were being sacrificed to one man's brutality rather than to the national interest.

Life of Nero

Suetonius

Suetonius' life of Nero is a catalogue of cruelty and eccentricity. In the following selections we follow Nero as he tours his Greek subjects, singing at the great festivals and being showered with wreaths and prizes. After the murder of his mother he is surely a monster, but a pathetic monster as he seeks reassurance far and wide. He neglected the army and, even more, alienated them with his antics until he was forced to commit suicide in another tragicomic episode.

6. Nero was born on December 15, A.D. 37. Many people at once made many direful predictions from his horoscope, and a remark of his father Domitius was also regarded as an omen; for while receiving the congratulations of his friends, he said that "nothing that was not abominable and a public danger could be born of Agrippina and himself. ". . .

At the age of three he lost his father and inherited a third of his estate; but he did not receive it, since his co-heir Caligula seized everything and banished his sister Agrippina. Nero was brought up in modest circumstances in the house of his aunt Lepida under two tutors, a dancer and a barber. But when Claudius became emperor, Nero not only recovered his father's property, but was also enriched by an inheritance from his stepfather, Passienus Crispus. When his mother was recalled from exile, he enjoyed the benefits of her influence. . . .

7.   While he was still a young boy he performed with great success in the Troy game in the Circus. When he was eleven Claudius adopted him and named Seneca as his tutor. There is a story that on the next night Seneca dreamed that he was teaching Caligula, and Nero soon proved the dream prophetic by showing his innate cruelty. [He intrigued against his stepbrother Britannicus, and testified against his aunt Lepida.]

8.   When the death of Claudius was made public, Nero, who was seventeen years old, appeared to the palace guard between the sixth and seventh hour, since the omens were bad earlier in the day. Acclaimed as emperor on the steps of the Palace, he was carried in a litter to the praetorian camp, where he spoke briefly to the soldiers. He then went to the Senate, where he remained until evening, refusing only one of the honors that were voted to him, the title of Father of his Country, and that because of his youth.

9.   Beginning with a display of filial piety, Nero gave Claudius a magnificent funeral, spoke his eulogy, and proclaimed him a god. He paid the highest honors to the memory of his father Domitius and allowed his mother to manage all his public and private business. On the first day of his rule he gave to the palace guard the password "The Best of Mothers," and later he often rode with her through the streets in her litter.

10. To show his good intentions, he declared that he would rule according to the principles of Augustus, and he took every opportunity to be generous and merciful, or even to be congenial. He either abolished or reduced the heavier taxes. . . . He gave the people four hundred sesterces each, and granted to distinguished but impoverished senators an annual salary up to five hundred thousand sesterces; and to the praetorian guard he gave a free monthly allowance of grain. When he had to sign the usual death warrant for a condemned man, he said: "How I wish I had never learned to write."

He greeted men of all classes casually and from memory. When the senate gave thanks to him, he replied, "When I shall have deserved it." He even allowed the common people to watch him exercising in the Campus, and often declaimed in public. He read his poems too, both at home and in the theater as well, so greatly to the delight of all that a thanksgiving was voted because of his recital, while parts of his poems were inscribed in gold letters and dedicated to Jupiter of the Capitol. . . .

16. . . . During his reign many abuses were severely punished and new laws were enacted: to limit private expenditures; to replace public banquets with a simple distribution of grain; to restrict the sale of cooked food in the taverns to greens and beans, whereas before every sort of dainty was on sale. Nero punished the Christians, men who believed a new and mischievous superstition; and he put an end to the diversions of the chariot drivers, who had long claimed the right of ranging at large and amusing themselves by cheating and robbing the people. He banned the pantomime actors and their partisans from the city. . . .

19. . . . I have brought together these acts of his, some innocent, while others deserve some praise, to separate them from his shameful and criminal deeds, of which I shall proceed now to give an account.

22.   [Nero wished to sing in Rome, and he did so at festivals and when the crowd demanded.] . . . Not content with performing at Rome, he went to Greece [to perform in all the festivals.] . . .

23. He ordered that even those festivals that were held at long intervals all should be celebrated in a single year, so that some had to be repeated, and he even introduced a new musical competition into the Olympic games. To avoid being distracted while busy with these contests, he replied to his freedman Helius, who reminded him that business required his presence at Rome: "However much you may wish that I should return quickly, you ought rather to counsel me to stay so that I may return worthy of Nero."

While he was singing no one was allowed to leave the theatre even for the most urgent reasons. And so there are stories of women giving birth there, while many who were worn out with listening and applauding, secretly leaped over the back wall, since the entrance was closed, or feigned death and were carried out as if for burial. The trepidation and anxiety with which he took part in the contests, his keen rivalry of his opponents and his awe of the judges, can hardly be believed. He was usually respectful and charming to his rivals as though they were his equals, but he slandered them behind their backs, and sometimes even abused them to their faces, and bribed those who were particularly good. He would begin by addressing the judges in the most deferential terms, saying that he had done all that he could, but the issue was in the hands of Fortune; but since they were men of wisdom and experience, they should exclude the element of chance. . . .

24. To obliterate the memory of all other victors in the games, their statues and busts were all torn down by his order, dragged off with hooks, and cast into latrines. He also drove a chariot in many places, at Olympia even a ten-horse team, although in one of his own poems he had critcized Mithridates for just that thing. But after he had been thrown from the car and put back in it, he was unable to hold out and gave up before the end of the course; but he received the crown just the same. On his departure he presented the entire province with freedom and at the same time gave the judges Roman citizenship and a large sum of money. These favors he announced in person on the day of the Isthmian Games, standing in the middle of the stadium.

25. Returning from Greece, . . . he rode at Rome in the chariot which Augustus had used in his triumphs in days gone by, and wore a purple robe and a Greek cloak adorned with stars of gold, bearing on his head the Olympic crown and in his right hand the Pythian, while the rest were carried before him with inscriptions telling where he had won them and against what competitors, and giving the titles of the songs or the subject of the plays. His cart was followed by his claque as by the escort of a triumphal procession, who shouted that they were the attendants of Augustus and the soldiers of his triumph. . . . All along the route victims

were slain, the streets were sprinkled from time to time with perfume, while birds, ribbons, and sweets were showered upon him. He placed the sacred crowns in his bed-chambers around his couches, as well as statues representing him in the guise of a lyre-player; and he had a coin too struck with the same image. So far from letting up on the practice of his art after this, he never addressed the soldiers except by letter or in a speech delivered by another, to save his voice; and he never did anything for amusement or in earnest without an elocutionist by his side, to warn him to spare his vocal organs and hold a handkerchief to his mouth. To many men he offered his friendship or announced his hostility, according as they had applauded him lavishly or grudgingly. . . .

27. His vices gradually grew stronger, and he dropped jesting and pretense as he openly broke out into worse crime. He prolonged his revels from midday to midnight, often livening himself by a warm plunge, or, in summer, into water cooled with snow. Sometimes he drained the artificial lake in the Campus Martius or the Circus, and banqueted there waited on by harlots and dancing girls from all over the city. Whenever he drifted down the Tiber to Ostia, or sailed about the Gulf of Baiae, brothels were set up along the shore, where noble-women played the part of madams and solicited his business. He also demanded dinners from his friends, one of whom spent four million sesterces for a banquet at which turbans were distributed. . . .

28. Besides abusing freeborn boys and seducing married women, he debauched the vestal virgin Rubria. The freedwoman Acte he all but made his lawful wife, after bribing some ex-consuls to perjure themselves by swearing that she was of royal birth. He castrated the boy Sporus and actually tried to make a woman of him; and he married him with all the usual ceremonies, including a dowry and a bridal veil, took him to his house attended by a great throng, and treated him as his wife. And the witty jest that someone made is still current, that it would have been well for the world if Nero's father Domitius had that kind of wife. He decked out Sporus with the finery of the empresses and rode in a litter . . . fondly kissing him from time to time. It

was notorious that he even desired illicit relations with his own mother, and was kept from it by her enemies, who feared that such a relationship might give that insolent woman too great influence, and he even added to his concubines a courtesan who was said to look very like Agrippina. Some say that he did commit incest with his mother whenever he rode in a litter with her, which was betrayed by the stains on his clothing.

30. He thought that there was no other way of enjoying riches than by wild extravagance, declaring that only misers kept track of what they spent, while true gentlemen spent recklessly. He admired his uncle Caligula for having run through in a short time the vast wealth which Tiberius had left him. . . .

31. He was especially wasteful in building. He made a palace extending all the way from the Palatine to the Equiline, which he first called the House of Passage, but when it was burned shortly after its completion and rebuilt, the Golden House. These details will give an idea of its size and splendor: its entrance hall was large enough to contain a colossal statue of the emperor a hundred and twenty feet high, and it had a triple colonnade a mile long; an enormous pool, more like a lake, surrounded with buildings to represent cities, besides tracts of country, varied by tilled fields, vineyards, pastures and woods, with great numbers of wild and domestic animals. In the rest of the house all parts were overlaid with gold and adorned with gems and mother-of-pearl. There were dining rooms with fretted ceilings of ivory, whose panels could rain down flowers and were fitted with pipes for sprinkling the guests with perfumes. The main banquet hall was round and constantly revolved day and night, like the heavens. He had baths supplied with sea water and sulphur water. When the palace was finished and he dedicated it, he said that he was at last beginning to live like a human being. . . .

32. He soon was bankrupt and so impoverished that he was obliged to postpone the soldiers' pay and the veterans' rewards, and he then turned to false accusations and robbery. A new law stated that five-sixths of the property of deceased freedmen should be made over to the emperor, if they bore the name of any family with which he himself was connected without justification; further, that the estates of those who were ungrateful to their emperor should belong to the privy purse, and that the advocates who had written or dictated such wills should not go unpunished. Finally, that any word or deed on which an informer could base an action should be liable to the law against lese-majesty. He demanded the return of the rewards which he had given in recognition of the prizes conferred on him by any city in any competition. Having forbidden the use of amethystine or Tyrian purple dyes, he secretly sent a man to sell a few ounces on a market day and then closed the shops of all the dealers. It is even said that when he saw a matron in the audience at one of his recitals clad in the forbidden color he pointed her out to his agents, who dragged her out and stripped her on the spot, not only of her garment, but also of her property. He never appointed anyone to an office without adding: "You know what my needs are," and "Let us see to it that no one possess anything." At last he stripped many temples of their gifts and melted down the statues of gold and silver. . . .

33. He began his murderous career with Claudius, for even if he was not the instigator of the emperor's death, he at least knew about it, as he openly admitted; for he used afterwards to laud mushrooms, through which poison was administered to Claudius, as "the food of the gods," as the Greek proverb has it. At any rate, after Claudius's death he vented on him every kind of insult, charging him both of folly and of cruelty; . . . and he ignored many of his decrees and acts as the work of a madman and an idiot. . . .

[Nero had his stepbrother Britannicus poisoned and finally had his mother Agrippina killed as well. He exiled and later executed his wife Octavia and, after he married his beloved Poppaea, he even kicked her to death while she was pregnant. Nero drove his tutor Seneca to suicide, poisoned Burrus, and killed many other senators after conspiracies were uncovered.]

39. But he showed no greater mercy to the people or the walls of his capital. When someone quoted the Greek verse: "When I am dead, be earth consumed by fire," Nero answered

"Nay, rather while I live," and his action was wholly in accord. For feigning disgust at the ugliness of the old buildings and the narrow, crooked streets, he set fire to the city so openly that several ex-consuls did not dare to interfere with his men though they caught them with firebrands on their estates. The emperor particularly desired the site of some granaries near the Golden House, but since they had stone walls, they were first demolished by engines of war and then set on fire. For six days and seven nights destruction raged, while the people took shelter in the tombs. Nero's men burned a large number of tenements, mansions of great Romans of the past, still adorned with trophies of victory, and temples of the gods dating back to the monarchy and to the Punic and Gallic wars—in fact, every important monument that had survived from antiquity. Viewing the conflagration from the tower of Maecenas and exulting in "the beauty of the flames," he sang the whole of the "Fall of Troy," in his regular stage costume. . . .

. . . Gibes and lampoons were posted or circulated both in Greek and Latin, for example the following:

"Nero, Orestes, Alcmeon their mothers slew."

"Who can deny our Nero descends from Aeneas' great line? One carried off his mother; the other one carried his sire."

40. After the world had put up with such a ruler for nearly fourteen years, it finally got rid of him. The Gauls began under the lead of Julius Vindex, who then served as propraetor. . . . The emperor learned at Naples of the uprising of the Gallic provinces, and received the news with calmness and indifference. . . .

42. But having learned that Galba and the Spanish legions had also revolted, he fainted and lay for a long time insensible, without a word and all but dead. When he came to himself, he rent his robe and beat his brow, declaring that it was all over with him; and when his old nurse tried to comfort him by reminding him that similar evils had befallen other princes before him, he declared that unlike all others he was suffering the unheard of and unparalleled fate of losing the supreme power while he still

lived. Nevertheless he did not abandon nor amend his slothful and luxurious habits. . . .

43. At the very beginning of the revolt it is believed that he made terrible, but characteristic, plans: to recall and execute the commanders of the armies and the governors of the provinces, on the ground that they were all united in a conspiracy against him; to massacre all the exiles everywhere and all men of Gallic birth in the city: the former, to prevent them from joining the rebels; the latter, as sharing and abetting the designs of their countrymen; to turn over the Gallic provinces to his armies to ravage; to poison the entire senate at banquets; to set fire to the city, first letting the wild beasts loose, that it might be harder for the people to protect themselves. But he abandoned these plans, not from any scruples as because he knew he could not carry them out before he had to take the field. . . . Having assumed the consulship, he declared as he was leaving the dining room after a banquet, leaning on the shoulders of his comrades, that immediately on setting foot in the province he would go before the soldiers unarmed and do nothing but weep; and having thus led the rebels to change their purpose, he would next day rejoice among his rejoicing subjects and sing paeans of victory, which he ought at that very moment to be composing.

45. Nero aroused general resentment by profiteering in grain which was then very expensive. . . . He had thus aroused the hatred of all, and was subjected to every form of insult. On the neck of his statue a sack was tied and with it the words: "I have done what I could, but you have earned the sack." People wrote on the columns that his crowing had roused the cocks—Galli means both "cocks" and Gauls. . . .

47. When word came that the other armies had revolted, he tore to pieces the dispatches which were handed to him at dinner, tipped over the table, and dashed to the ground two favorite drinking cups with scenes from Homer's poems. Then taking some poison from Locusta and putting it into a golden box, he went to the Servilian gardens, where he tried to induce the tribunes and centurions of the Guard to accompany him to his flight, first sending his most

trustworthy freedmen to Ostia, to get a fleet ready. Some praetorians gave evasive answers and others openly refused, and one even quoted Virgil: "Is it such a terrible thing to die?"

Undecided, Nero thought about throwing himself on the mercy of the Parthians or of Galba, or to appear to the people on the rostra, begging pathetically for pardon for his past offenses; and if he could not soften their hearts, to entreat them at least to allow him the prefecture of Egypt. Afterwards a speech composed for this purpose was found in his writing desk; but it is thought that he did not dare to deliver it for fear of being torn to pieces before he could reach the Forum. Procrastinating until the following day, he awoke at midnight and found that his military guard of soldiers had left. He called for his friends and went to their rooms but found they had fled and, returning to his own chamber, he discovered even the valets had fled, taking with them even the bed linen and the box of poison. Then he at once called for the gladiator Spiculus or any other executioner at whose hand he might find death, and when no one appeared, he cried "Have I then neither friend nor foe?" and ran out as if to throw himself into the Tiber.

48. Changing his mind again, he looked for some quiet spot where he could collect his thoughts; and when his freedmen Phaon offered his own suburban villa four miles away, just as he was, barefooted and in his tunic, he put on a faded cloak, covered his head, and holding a handkerchief before his face, mounted a horse with only four attendants, one of whom was Sporus. At once he was startled by a shock of earthquake and a flash of lightning full in his face, and he heard the shouts of the soldiers from the camp hard by, as they prophesied destruction for him and success for Galba. He also heard one of the wayfarers whom he met say: "These men are after Nero," and another ask: "Is there anything new in the city about Nero?" Then his horse took fright at the smell of a corpse lying near the road, his face was exposed, and a retired soldier of the Guard recognised him and saluted him. When they came to a path leading to the villa, they turned the horses loose and he made his way amid brambles along a path

through a thicket of reeds to the back wall of the house, with great difficulty and only when a robe was thrown down for him to walk on. Phaon urged him to hide for a time in a sandpit. Nero said that he would not go under ground while still alive, and after waiting until a secret entrance into the villa could be made, he scooped up in his hand some water to drink from a pool close by, saying: "This is Nero's distilled water." Then, as his cloak had been torn by the thorns, he pulled out the twigs which had pierced it, and crawling on all fours through a narrow passage that had been dug, he entered the villa and lay down in the first room on a common mattress covered by an old cloak. Though hungry and thirsty, he refused some coarse bread but drank a little lukewarm water.

49. At last, while his companions all urged him to try to save himself from the indignities that threatened him, he ordered them to dig a grave suitable for his own body, to collect any bits of marble that could be found, and at the same time to bring water and wood for presently disposing of his body. As each of these things was done, he wept and said again and again: "What a great artist the world is losing!" While he hesitated, a courier brought a letter to Phaon. Nero took it and read that he had been declared a public enemy by the senate, and that they would punish him in the ancient fashion. When he asked what kind of punishment that was, he learned that the criminal was stripped, fastened by the neck in a fork and then beaten to death with rods. In mortal terror he seized two daggers which he had brought with him, but after testing the point of each, he put them down and said that his last hour had not yet come. Then he begged Sporus to begin to lament, and also asked another to set him example by committing suicide. Then he bermoaned his own cowardice: "To live is a scandal and shame—this does not become Nero, does not become him—one should be resolute at such times—come, rouse thyself!" And now the horsemen were near who had orders to take him off alive. When he heard them, he quoted Homer: "Hark, now I hear the gallop of swift-footed horses." He drove a dagger into his throat,

aided by his private secretary Epaphroditus. He was nearly dead when a centurion rushed in, and as he placed a cloak to the wound, pretending that he had come to aid him, Nero merely gasped: "Too late!" and "This is fidelity!" With these words he was gone, with eyes so set and staring from their sockets that all who saw him shuddered with horror. He had made his companions promise to let no one have his head, but to contrive in some way that he be buried unmutilated. And this was granted by Icelus, Galba's freedman, who had just been freed from prison to which he had been consigned at the news of the revolt. . . .

52.   When a boy he took up almost all the liberal arts; but his mother turned him from philosophy, warning him that it was a drawback to one who was going to rule, while Seneca kept him from reading the early orators, to make his admiration for his teacher endure the longer. Turning therefore to poetry, he wrote verses with eagerness and without labor, and did not, as some think, publish the work of others as his own. There have come into my hands notebooks and papers with some well-known verses of his, written in his own hand so that it is perfectly evident that they were not copied or taken down from dictation, but with erasures and corrections exactly as one writes when thinking and creating. . . .

53.   But above all he was carried away by a craze for popularity and he was jealous of all who in any way stirred the feeling of the mob. . . .

55.   He had an irrational longing for immortality and undying fame, so that he changed well-known names as when he called the month of April Neroneus and intended to name Rome Neropolis.

57.   He died at the age of thirty-two, and such was the public rejoicing that the people put on liberty-caps and ran all over the city. Yet for a long time some decorated his tomb with spring and summer flowers, put his statues on the rostra, and published his edicts, as if he were still alive and would shortly return to punish his enemies. When Vologaesus, king of the Parthians, sent envoys to the senate to renew his alliance, he earnestly begged that the senators honor the memory of Nero. In fact, twenty years later, when I was a young man, a mysterious person appeared, who claimed that he was Nero, and the name was still in such favor with the Parthians that they supported him vigorously and surrendered him with great reluctance.

Nero and the Senate

B. H. Warmington

Professor B. H. Warmington of the University of Bristol has written a general treatment in which he attempts to differentiate the colorful stories that grew up around the figure of Nero (even in antiquity) from what cam be known with any degree of certainty about his life and reign. In this chapter Warmington first traces the relations between Nero's predecessors and the Senate and examines the role of Seneca and Burrus in the effective government of the Empire in the early years of Nero's reign. These two sensible provincials presided over conservative policies that produced a harmonious relationship between the emperor and the Senate while they remained in power until 62, which Tacitus saw as the turning point of the reign.

Over eighty years had passed since the day in January 27 B.C. when C. Julius Caesar Octavianus laid down the extraordinary powers by which he had been ruling the Roman world and, to use his own words, 'transferred the Republic from (my) own power to that of the Senate and the People of Rome' (*Res Gestae*). The constitutional devices through which, now under the name of Caesar Augustus, he not only retained but extended his personal power need not be detailed here. They were so ingenious and so effective that formal changes under later emperors during nearly two centuries were unimportant. They enjoyed from the beginning of their principates the powers which Augtustus accumulated over a period of time—in particular proconsular power over the largest and militarily the most important provinces, tribunician power, and the chief priesthood. The division of the Roman Empire between so-called imperial provinces whose governors (of senatorial rank in most cases, with a few provinces allotted to men of equestrian rank) were appointed directly by the emperor, and senatorial provinces whose proconsuls were chosen by lot from senior ex-magistrates, continued, but the distinction became increasingly formal. By the time of Nero all the legions and almost all auxiliary units were in the imperial provinces and in any case all soldiers took their oath of allegiance to the emperor. The latter was entitled to intervene in or legislate for all provinces alike. In Rome itself the ancient magistracies continued, but their activities were increasingly confined to judicial business in the city and in Italy.

The most important developments since Augustus were in the realities of power, not in changes of form. It would certainly be held for a while that traces of true Republicanism survived, especially since Augustus often preferred to use his overwhelming prestige (*auctoritas*) to have his ideas put into effect rather than formally to legislate himself. But the ease with which Rome and Italy accepted an autocracy only faintly disguised is remarkable. The emperor Tiberius is said to have been disgusted at the way in which the Senate, the body which should have manifested the traditions of the Republic, showed itself increasingly servile, and the theme is a constant one in Tacitus. The reasons given for this are no doubt correct—the civil wars and disorders of the late Republic were destructive of life and property in Rome and Italy, and were seen to be likely to destroy the Roman Empire itself; only firm control by one man could maintain peace, and so it proved. Over forty years of generally successful rule by Augustus did as much as anything to justify his whole system; when he died there was no one left who could remember from his own experience how the old Republic had actually worked. His concessions to Republican forms were sufficient to win the acquiescence of the upper class in Rome and Italy as a whole, though there were exceptions. This class, through the Senate and equestrian order, provided the traditions and experience in government required by Augustus for the running of the Roman Empire.

There was a price to be paid, and it was not small. The contradiction between the fact of a government monarchical in all but name, and the theory that Republican government, and especially the supremacy of the Senate, survived, led to tensions between some emperors and the upper class which poisoned the atmosphere in Rome and Italy. It was useless for emperors such as Claudius to urge the Senate to behave as a Senate should, while at the same time increasing his own direct control over affairs. This contradiction was the so-called 'lie of the Principate.' Augustus himself possessed or could easily have acquired the powers of emperors later regarded as tyrants; what mattered was the way in which the emperor used his powers. The Augustan principate was generally agreed to represent the standard by which his successors should rule, but this was useless; so much depended on the personal approach rather than forms, that within a generation of his death no one could know what the reality had been. Tiberius tried to follow closely, perhaps too closely, the 'precepts of Augustus,' but he had little gift for the pretences which Augustus had kept up. Gaius in his turn knew of nothing but imperial rule, and saw the possibilities and the pleasures of undisguised absolutism.

The principate of Claudius brought more trouble. The Senate, it might be said, was bound to be in difficulties with a ruler like Gaius whose approach was irresponsible, but Claudius, with an undoubtedly sincere feeling for the spirit and traditions of the Republic, was surely different. Furthermore, the number of noble families whose traditions of active power went back to the Republic was by now negligible; the Senate consisted to a large extent of wealthy Italians who were the first of their families to enter it, or at any rate whose rank went no further back than Augustus. It became plain, however, that the 'new men' recruited generation after generation from the equestrian order into the Senate were liable to feelings of nostalgia for the Republic. Although the great majority willingly acquiesced as individuals in imperial rule, resentment at any real or imagined slight to the Senate's prestige was easily roused. This affected their attitude to Claudius. This emperor, it transpired, in spite of his undistinguished past and the comic way in which he had been thrust

into the imperial position, positively enjoyed the activity of government. He immersed himself in day to day judicial business, very probably to the detriment of larger concerns, and was active in responding to issues raised particularly in the government of the provinces. It was not that he had a vast plan of reforms for the Empire—no Roman statesman except perhaps Julius Caesar ever had—but as problems and requests were presented to him he responded in a way which could generally, though not always, be described as reformist. But the increase in the emperor's activity and his assumption of personal responsibility in fresh fields led to importance being acquired by his personal assistants, at the expense of Senate and knights.

All his predecessors, including Augustus, had had a staff of personal secretaries and assistants drawn, as the custom was in noble Roman houses, from their own slaves or freedmen, many of Greek origin. It is often loosely said that Claudius created a centralized bureaucracy or even a civil service, and ancient sources are unanimous that the freedmen of the emperor vastly increased their power under Claudius. In form he may have done little more than allot clearly defined functions and establish special offices with larger staffs under chief secretaries. We know in particular of his chief private secretary (Narcissus by name), chief accountant (Pallas), judicial secretary (Callistus) and cultural secretary (Polybius). The effect was that what was in law the emperor's private household became in fact the central executive office of a large part of the imperial administration. It was quite clear that important decisions would in practice be made by the imperial freedmen, and that this would increase imperial control over officials of both senatorial and equestrian rank. In one sense the latter had only themselves to blame; till the end of the century it was considered socially unacceptable for men of free birth to hold such secretarial positions, however responsible.

Tradition was unanimous that Claudius was dominated by his wives and freedmen, but this has been disputed by modern writers. The envy and resentment of the senatorial and equestrian orders at the power and wealth of a socially despised group is manifest. Yet it is notable that although the importance of the freedman element in the administration continued to the end of the century, no other emperor is portrayed like Claudius. Many freedmen of importance are known by name from the principate of Nero, and their influence is on specific occasions attested; for example, Polyclitus, sent to Britain to settle a dispute between governor and procurator, and Helius, left in charge at Rome when Nero visited Greece. Yet for all the hostility shown to Nero, it is not alleged that he was dominated by them. The fact seems to be that Pallas, Narcissus and the rest really did enjoy more power, and acquire more wealth, than any other freedmen known to us. This may not show that Claudius was dominated by them, but does indicate that he listened to their advice as often as to his senatorial councillors, and turned a blind eye to their spoils of office. There was perhaps a vicious circle here. Claudius, unsuccessful in obtaining the co-operation of the upper classes yet determined to increase his personal role, turned to his household officials, which only aroused more resentment. There is a useful analogy with certain medieval rulers whose difficulties with their feudal subjects were often attributed to the influence of unworthy favourites. To deny the power and influence of the freedmen would be to fall unconsciously into the same error as Claudius' detractors, that freedmen were the wrong sort of people to advise an emperor. No doubt their profits were enormous, but profits (in moderation, it was hoped), were expected from all posts in the administration. They certainly worked harder and were more professional than the senatorial, if not the equestrian, officials, with their amateurism and tradition of dignified leisure; and it may be supposed, though it cannot be proved, that the complaints and requests of provincial communities would be not less favourably received by them than by men of the Roman and Italian upper class, still frequently indifferent to the claims of the subjects of the Empire.

Many senators and knights had lost their lives under Claudius both as victims of intrigues at court and as the result of tensions between the emperor and the two orders. It could be hoped that the young Nero, only seventeen on his accession, would follow a different path, whether as a result of his own personality and upbringing or, in view of his own inexperience, a willingness to be guided by advisers sympathetic to the ideas of the Senate. His tutor Seneca hoped that his book *On Clemency*, which he dedicated to Nero in 55, 'would serve as a mirror in which you may see yourself'. . . .

Seneca is said to have had early forebodings of Nero's cruelty but this was perhaps wisdom after the event. It will be seen that Seneca and his friends had little to complain of for a number of years. Judgement on how far Nero was acting autonomously or under the advice of others during the first part of his principate must be subjective; ancient writers were always ready to see hidden influences at work. Thus, since it was the general view that Nero was vicious and cruel from the start, the relatively good beginning to his principate had to be explained by his lack of interest and by the efforts of his advisers. Dio stated roundly that 'Seneca and Burrus took the government into their own hands and administered affairs in the best and fairest way they could, with the result that they were equally praised by everyone.' His view, or that of his source, was that Nero was basically not interested in public business and preferred to indulge in his private pleasures while allowing the government to be carried on by others. Tacitus is not so direct but is in substance in agreement, and indeed most of the evidence favours this view. Nero was not like his ancestor Augustus, dedicated to the pursuit of supreme power from the age of eighteen. His personal activity in affairs is certainly attested on a number of occasions, and we read of discussions with his advisers, but the fact is that the emperor's direct participation in business could not be reduced below a certain minimum. In particular, judicial business took up much time, appointments to high positions needed care, as did the military problems of the time, and there were always documents for signature. Within these activities, there was scope for the well attested examples of Nero's extravagant and unrealistic ideas, sometimes of a sentimental kind, which, however, he was willing to be talked out of. Nevertheless, it is clear that Nero's concern with public business was spasmodic, and that Seneca and Burrus were the men largely responsible for the day to day running of affairs for some eight years. . . .

Seneca wrote the speech which Nero delivered at Claudius' funeral, and speeches on later occasions as well. The funeral speech was laudatory and unimportant; that delivered by Nero in the Senate House on the same day gave the aspirations of the new government. Nero promised to govern according to the principles of Augustus, and rejected practices which had caused resentment under Claudius—the emperor's sitting in judgement in private, the corruption of his court and the identification of his household with public administration. The privileges of the Senate and its competence in Italy and the senatorial provinces were assured. . . .

Government according to the precepts of Augustus meant in practice government which respected as far as possible the pretensions of the Senate, and for some eight years this was what was provided under the influence of Seneca. Conciliatory gestures were numerous. Nero refused the title *Pater Patriae* (Father of his Country), though he then accepted it in 56. He asked the Senate to decree a statue in honour of his father Domitius, and consular insignia for the man who had acted his guardian on the death of Passienus Crispus, but refused statues in silver and gold for himself. Domitius was honoured in subsequent years, though he did not appear in Nero's official nomenclature. Senatorial flattery in a proposal that the calendar year should begin in December (Nero's birthday month) was rejected. In the face of Agrippina's opposition, the obligation laid by Claudius on quaestors designate to put on gladiatorial shows was removed; it had been a heavy burden on poorer entrants on a senatorial career. Following the practice of former emperors, Nero subsidized members of noble families who had become poor to save them the disgrace of losing senatorial rank, and in 55 excused his colleague in the consulship

that year from the annual oath taken by all magistrates to observe the emperors' enactments. . . .

The men who composed the imperial government mattered at least as much as the ideas which animated it. The political history of the Republic had lately been that of its ruling class, and since the system of Augustus preserved the hierarchic structure of society, while making the constant renewal from below of the senatorial and equestrian orders an easier and less turbulent process than in the late Republic, analysis of its membership has much to teach us of the inner history of the principate. Struggle for power continued, with family influences, intrigue and bribery all being weapons as before. The favour of the emperor, however, became of decisive importance as a man advanced in his senatorial career; although the semblance of election by his peers lasted up to the praetorship, it is clear that the consulship and the more important governorships were by imperial choice. Historians of the Roman Empire have devoted much attention to changes in the type of person predominant in the administration, and especially to the stages by which one province after another began to be represented in it. The gradual enlargement of the Roman ruling class to include Italians, then men from Spain and southern Gaul followed by other western provinces and finally the east, was a most important historical phenomenon, though it is by no means so certain that each stage was particularly noticeable at the time, and the references to it are few. The absorption of the provincials into the senatorial (and for that matter the equestrian) order was at a modest pace; in the Julio-Claudian era consuls from Italy still outnumbered those from the provinces by more than ten to one. This would indicate why Tacitus, who was undoubtedly interested in changes in the governing class and—himself a 'new man'—sensitive about social origins, was not obsessed by them. At a cool look, once the descendants of the Republican nobility had been reduced to a negligible proportion, the Senate of one generation was remarkably similar to that of another. Naturally when provincials reached a position of power they used their influence to support their own friends and relations, strictly in accordance with social custom which laid a heavy obligation on a great man to support anyone who had a claim on him, as the letters of the younger Pliny make so clear.

Thus the fact that two men of provincial origin presided for eight years over a government, the tone of which was thoroughly conservative, was no paradox, nor was the mixture of persons advanced to the consulship or to high commands at all unusual. . . .

The record of senatorial and other governmental measures that can be dated comes almost to an end in 62, the year in which Burrus died and Seneca withdrew from public life. The reasons for the lack of information after this point are obscure but even after 62 there was no immediate breach with the Senate, though the conduct of public business was carried on in a different manner and other advisers were influential. Down to 62, the policy of working in harmony with the Senate had been scrupulously followed. There had been no private, or for that matter public, trials in which members of the senatorial and equestrian orders were victimized; the influence of the emperor's household on affairs had been limited, at any rate after the dismissal of Pallas in 55; the government had shown itself excessively deferential to the prejudices of the uppper class, without, however, giving in to its extreme demands in social legislation. It was as a result of the harmony between the Senate and Nero and his advisers that during much of his principate our sources find little to complain of except Nero's crimes and follies in private life; and it was the same harmony that enabled the Senate to overlook them.

The Courtier Seneca

Thomas Africa

Professor Thomas Africa of the State University of New York at Binghamton is well known for his psychohistorical treatment of prominent Romans. In this essay he sees contradictions between the high moral standards of Seneca as a philosopher and the greed and opportunism of Seneca's actions as tutor and advisor to Nero. Though Africa argues that the hypocrisy of a man does not necessarily negate the value of his philosophy, he finds it instructive to examime the conflicts between abstract moral values and the corruption engendered by the immense power of a friend of the emperor.

Other scholars have shown more compassion for Seneca's predicament. He was recalled from exile to serve as Nero's tutor, amd some see him as a moderating force on the unstable young prince until his ally Burrus was murdered and the corrupt Tigellinus became praetorian prefect. The argument that an official or soldier serving under an evil or insane or incompetent leader has merely tried to make the best of a bad situation has been recited across the centuries. There is no simple solution: Seneca may indeed bear moral responsibility as Nero's tutor and advisor, but he may also have delayed that monster's cruelties.

As a philosopher, Seneca was an attractive exponent of Stoicism. While too many Stoics were stiff-necked and self-righteous, Roman Stoicism was flexible and eclectic. For Stoics, the world was controlled by Divine Providence, the ways of which were often hidden to man but were considered to be good and just. Not a sparrow fell without divine approval, and men were expected to faithfully execute the roles to which Providence had assigned them. In practice, the doctrines of duty and submission were endorsements of the established order—hence the popularity of Stoicism in Rome. Though moralists sensed a danger in fatalistic approval of the status quo, redress was left to Providence which was responsible when rulers abused their authority. According to Seneca, awareness of sin was a sinner's worst punishment. Though he often criticized contemporary luxury, the Spanish Stoic conceded that young people were more moral in his era than in the Rome of Cicero and Caesar. Respectful toward rival philosophies, Seneca admired the saintly Epicurus whose views were anathema to most Stoics. Like many Romans, Seneca loathed the senseless brutality and bloodshed of the gladiatorial games. He had a high regard for women and praised conjugal fidelity, but the philosopher had difficulty following his own precept.

In Roman society slavery was a running sore which no one was willing to cauterize. However, responsible Romans treated their slaves with consideration and criticized cruel owners who abused bondmen. In the Senate and salons of Rome, severity and liberality toward slaves were hotly debated. It is to his credit that Seneca was on the side of sanity:

I am glad to learn, through those who come from you, that you live on friendly terms with your slaves. This befits a sensible and well-educated man like yourself. "They are slaves," people declare. Nay, rather they are men. "Slaves!" No, comrades. "Slaves!" No, they are unpretentious friends. "Slaves!" No, they are our fellow-slaves, if one reflects that Fortune has equal rights over slaves and free men alike. That is why I smile at those who think it degrading for a man to dine with his slave. . . . Finally, the saying . . . becomes current: "As many enemies as you have slaves." They are not enemies when we acquire them—we make them enemies. . . .

The syndrome of slavery contained glaring contradictions which were obvious to all Romans but disturbing to only a few. Like Shakespeare's Shylock—"Hath not a Jew eyes? . . . When you prick us, do we not bleed?"— Seneca protested against the false distinctions which society made between men:

Kindly remember that he whom you call your slave sprang from the same stock, is smiled upon by the same skies, and on equal terms with yourself, breathes, lives, and dies. It is just as possible for you to see in him a free-born man as for him to see in you a slave. . . . Despise, then, if you dare, those to whose estate you may at any time descend, even when you are despising them. I do not wish to involve myself in too large a question and to discuss the treatment of slaves, towards whom we Romans are excessively haughty, cruel and insulting. But this is the kernel of my advice: Treat your inferiors as you would be treated by your betters. And as often as you reflect how much power you have over a slave, remember that your master has just as much power over you. "But I have no master," you say. You are still young; perhaps you will have one. Do you not know at what age Hecuba entered captivity, or Croesus, or the mother of Darius, or Plato, or Diogenes?

From bitter experience, Seneca knew that free men were often slaves in reality, particularly when they served a despot. Behind his reflections on slavery lay Seneca's deep belief in the brotherhood of man and the overriding importance of the human mind:

Let us grasp the idea that there are two commonwealths—the one a vast and truly common state, which embraces alike gods and men, in which we look neither to this corner of earth nor to that but measure the bounds of our citizenship by the path of the sun; the other, the one to which we have been assigned by the accident of birth. This will be the commonwealth of the Athenians or of the Carthaginians or of any other city that belongs, not to all, but to some particular race of men. Some yield service to both commonwealths at the same time—to the greater and to the lesser—some only to the lesser, some only to the greater. This greater commonwealth we are able to serve even in leisure—nay, I am inclined to think, even better in leisure—so that we may inquire what virtue is, and whether it is one or many; whether it is nature or art that makes men good; whether this world, which embraces seas and lands and the things that are contained in the sea and land, is a solitary creation or whether God has strewn about many systems of the same sort; . . . what God is—whether he idly gazes upon his work or directs it; whether he encompasses it without, or pervades the whole of it; whether the world is eternal or is to be counted among the things that perish and are born only for a time. And what service does he who ponders these things render unto God? He keeps the mighty works of God from being without a witness!

Centuries later, the Christian philosopher Augustine would be impressed by Seneca's dichotomy between the all-important City of God and the trivial City of Man. . . .

The life of Seneca was more than a moral parable, for his rise to power reflected the increasing importance of provincials at Rome. Seneca came from the province of Spain. . . . The political abilities of provincials could not be denied, and the emperor Claudius was particularly anxious to broaden the base of the Roman ruling class. The emperor himself had been born at Lyons and admitted Gallic aristocrats into the Senate. . . . As a politician, he [thought] that provincial leaders would bring wealth as well as stability to Rome. The future proved the wisdom of his views.

Though not the first provincial to prosper at Rome, Lucius Annaeus Seneca rose higher than most in the world of politics. Born at Cordova in 4 B.C., he was one of three sons of Seneca the rhetorician. An old-fashioned man, the elder Seneca disapproved of his wife educating herself and complained when his sons, Lucius, Gallio, and Mela, took up the study of philosophy. . . . Mela's son Lucan would be a successful poet and write a melodramatic epic on the Civil Wars. As a child, Lucius Seneca was raised by his aunt in Rome. Throughout his life he suffered from a variety of ailments, including asthma which he described as "practicing how to die." Sickly and scrawny, young Seneca once contemplated suicide but decided that the shock would be too great for his father. Plagued with a delicate stomach, Seneca criticizied people who ate foods which he could not enjoy—shellfish, mushrooms, and rich sauces. Briefly attracted to Pythagoreanism, he became a vegetarian, but when his father protested that only subversive cranks abstained from meat, Seneca gave up his diet. Tormented by claustrophobia and other morbid fears, Seneca was highly neurotic and prone to hypochondria. Like Augustus, he was a chronic invalid who lived to a ripe old

age. Grumbling about his poor health, Seneca would be seventy years old when Nero forced him to commit suicide.

At Rome, Seneca had begun his career as an orator and held his first political office under Tiberius in 33. However, the emperor Caligula disliked Seneca and sneered that his speeches were only "copy-book exercises" and "sand without lime." According to gossip, the tyrant planned to execute Seneca, but a court lady persuaded Caligula that the orator would soon die of consumption. Giving up oratory as too dangerous, Seneca devoted himself to writing essays and tragedies. Filled with descriptions of horror and agony, his dramas would later inspire the Elizabethan Tragedy of Blood. However, unlike *"The Duchess of Malfi"* and *"Titus Andronicus,"* the plays of Seneca were designed for recitation only and were not performed on a stage. In 41, under the emperor Claudius, a real tragedy befell Seneca. To advance his career, the Spaniard became too friendly with Claudius' nieces, Julia and Agrippina the Younger, who enjoyed the emperor's favor. However, Claudius' beautiful wife Messallina was jealous of Julia and soon arranged her downfall and death. The fall of Julia was disastrous for Seneca, who was exiled to Corsica on a charge of adultery with the princess.

On the dismal island of Corsica, Seneca spent eight years in boredom and despair. To console his mother Helvia, the philosopher wrote brave sentiments:

How little it is that we have lost! Wherever we betake ourselves, two things that are most admirable will go with us—universal Nature and our own virtue. . . . Eager, therefore, and erect, let us hasten with dauntless step wherever circumstance directs, let us traverse any lands whatsoever. Inside the world there can be found no place of exile, for nothing that is inside the world is foreign to mankind.

Despite his noble words, Seneca found exile unendurable and wrote cringing appeals to Claudius' freedman Polybius, lauding the merits of the emperor and his henchmen. Nevertheless, his pleas for mercy went unheeded and Seneca found himself a middle-aged failure expecting to die in exile.

Unknown to Seneca, events in Rome would soon bring about a change in his fortune. . . . [Messallina was executed and Claudius married Agrippina.] The new empress planned that Claudius would be succeeded by her son Nero, whose dead father Ahenobarbus had been an incompetent brute from an illustrious family. Remembering her old friend Seneca, Agrippina brought the philosopher back from exile and appointed him Nero's tutor. Though he gave the boy an excellent education, Seneca still found time for court intrigue. By 52 his brother Gallio was a governor in Greece and on one occasion listened with indifference to a complaint against Paul.

Though Claudius was fond of his son Brittannicus, Agrippina persuaded the emperor to adopt Nero as his heir. To insure harmony in the imperial family, Nero was married to his stepsister Octavia. The empress gained further strength when her friend, Sextus Afranius Burrus, became Praetorian prefect. A battle-scarred officer from Gaul, Burrus won the respect of the Praetorian guards and had many friends in the army high command. When Claudius tired of his wife's nagging demands and began to favor Britannicus, Agrippina formed a cabal with Seneca and Burrus to remove the emperor. Agrippina served Claudius a dish of poisoned mushrooms, but the emperor vomited the potion and had to be dispatched with an enema of deadly colocynth. Nero easily succeeded to the throne, and Rome was in the hands of Agrippina and her clique. Though the new regime deified Claudius, Seneca wrote a vicious lampoon on the late emperor, who had exiled him to Corsica. Disparaging Claudius' achievements and mocking his apotheosis through colocynth, Seneca's "*Apocolocyntosis*" showed that the Stoic philosopher could be petty and vengeful.

In 54 the Roman throne was held by a polite, handsome adolescent who had blond hair and blue eyes. Trained by Seneca to appreciate Greek literature, Nero had a good voice and was fond of the theater. Though he was only seventeen years old, the new ruler could rely on his shrewd mother, his wise tutor, and the loyal prefect of the Praetorians. Seneca composed Nero's inaugural address, which promised a reign of moderation and clemency on the Augustan mode. When Burrus presented him with his first order of execution, the young emperor sighed that he wished he had never learned how to write. However, his mother was not so squeamish. On the grounds that he had plundered the treasury, Agrippina deposed her old enemy Narcissus and demanded his death. All of Claudius' freedmen had enriched themselves at public expense, but the emperor had ignored their graft because the efficiency of his aides had more than compensated for their peculations. Not satisfied with the death of Narcissus, Agrippina planned to purge others at the court. But the dowager empress ran into unexpected opposition from Seneca and Burrus, as Tacitus reports:

These two men, with a unanimity rare among partners in power, were, by different methods, equally influential. Burrus' influence lay in soldierly efficiency and seriousness of character, Seneca's in amiable high principles and his tuition of Nero in public speaking. They collaborated in controlling the emperor's perilous adolescence; their policy was to direct his deviations from virtue into licensed indulgences. Against Agrippina's violence inflamed by all the passions of ill-gotten tyranny, they united.

At first, Agrippina had the support of Pallas, but the wily freedman soon realized that power had shifted to the opposition. Having amassed a huge fortune, Pallas retired to private life and escaped the fierce struggle in the palace. To keep Nero distracted, Seneca provided the young emperor with a beautiful slave girl, Acte, who could not hope to be more than a mistress. Delighted with Acte, Nero ignored his wife Octavia, whose humiliation was ridiculed by the court. Thwarted at every turn, Agrippina raged at Seneca and Burrus and tried to play Britannicus against Nero. In her fury, she threatened to appeal to the Praetorian guards: "Let them listen to Germanicus' daughter pitted against the men who claim to rule the whole human race—the cripple Burrus with his maimed hand, and Seneca the deportee with the professorial voice." In 55 Nero had Britannicus poisoned and hinted that his mother would suffer the same fate if she did not retire from politics.

Though Nero had shown a capacity for violence, Seneca and Burrus believed that they could still control the young emperor. While they managed the government, Nero spent his time with Acte, composed poetry, and sang in the theater. Old-fashioned Romans disapproved of actors, but Nero yearned for acclaim and his performances amused the mob. Under Seneca's administration, the empire ran smoothly and considerable profits went into the pocket of the Spanish prime minister. Though his writings deplored avarice and high interest rates, Seneca had a flair for finance as did his brother Mela. Like most Roman officials, the prime minister peddled political influence and dabbled in various enterprises. Near Rome he purchased vineyards at high prices and sold them at a profit. "What branch of learning," a critic snorted, "what philosophical school won Seneca 300,000,000 sesterces during four years of imperial friendship? In Rome, he entices into his snares the childless and their legacies. His huge rates of interest suck Italy and the provinces dry." According to his enemies, Seneca forced loans on British tribes and brought on a rebellion when he called in the debts. In 58 Nero considered abolishing indirect taxes for Seneca had managed the imperial budget with great skill. Though the tax reform did not take place, the Roman empire was never run so well as during the first five years of Nero's reign. At least, such was the verdict of the Spanish emperor Trajan on the period when the Spaniard Seneca dominated Nero. . . .

To keep pace with the young emperor, Seneca had to be both agile and wary. When Nero fell in love with the haughty and beautiful Poppaea Sabina, Seneca suggested that her husband Otho would be happier as governor of Lusitania. The emperor agreed and Otho departed for his distant post, leaving Poppaea behind in Rome. Nero's running quarrel with his mother was not resolved as amiably, for Agrippina now posed as the champion of his neglected wife Octavia. Despite the efforts of Seneca and Burrus to restrain him, the emperor had Agrippina murdered in 59. Though her death was no loss to Rome, Nero

was guilty of matricide. To soothe public opinion, Seneca composed a defense of the crime which Nero delivered before the Senate. However, Seneca was criticized in many quarters as an apologist for murder. After Agrippina's death, her guilt-ridden son sought distraction in dissolute amusements, but the extent of his misbehavior was exaggerated by salacious gossip. Physically, the dissipated ruler became fat and flabby. Though he indulged in private orgies, Nero still bored the court with his musical recitals, and more than one politician ruined his career by falling asleep while the emperor was performing. The major flaw in Nero was a growing taste for blood, which Seneca had failed to curb. The emperor readily purged senators whose loyalty was in doubt. In 62 the stalwart Burrus died, supposedly poisoned by Nero, and was succeeded as Praetorian prefect by the vicious Ofonius Tigellinus, who encouraged the emperor to more crimes. Without Burrus, Seneca was defenseless and isolated. Claiming that illness and old age incapacitated him from further service to the state, Seneca presented most of his wealth to Nero and retired to private life. The emperor politely accepted Seneca's resignation and took up more pressing matters, the divorce and murder of Octavia and a quick marriage to Poppaea. After the great fire of 64, Nero rebuilt the burned areas of Rome with wide streets, stone buildings, and mandatory cisterns for fire-fighting. However, his cruel treatment of the Christians, whom he blamed for the fire, offended public opinion in the capital.

In retirement, Seneca returned to intellectual pursuits and wrote a moralistic handbook on natural history. On scientific matters, Seneca was often inaccurate, for he relied on research assistants who were not always competent. Like many moderns, he believed in scientific progress: "The people of the coming generation will know much that we do not know; much is reserved for ages which will have forgotten our names. The world is a tiny thing, except that it contains questions enough for all the world." Fretting in retirement, Seneca could not overcome his desire to meddle in politics:

Although people may often have thought that I sought seclusion because I was disgusted with politics and regretted my hapless and thankless position, yet, in the retreat to which apprehension and weariness have driven me, my ambition sometimes develops afresh. For it is not because my ambition was rooted out that it has abated, but because it was wearied or perhaps even put out of temper by the failure of its plans.

Fearing that the erratic Nero might poison him, Seneca confined his diet to fresh fruit and spring water.

By 65 Nero's purges of suspected senators had spread fear among the Roman aristocracy. A makeshift conspiracy was formed to replace Nero with an incompetent noble, C. Calpurnius Piso, but the plot was betrayed and the emperor executed everyone suspected of complicity. Apparently, Seneca had given moral support to the Piso clique, for Nero ordered his former tutor to commit suicide. True to form, Seneca posed before his friends as a Roman Socrates and told them to remember his splendid life of virtue. The historian Tacitus dismissed the public scene as humbug and described Seneca's final hours with vivid reality.

Seneca embraced his wife and, with a tenderness very different from his philosophical imperturbability, entreated her to moderate and set a term to her grief and take just consolation in her bereavement from contemplating his well-spent life. Nevertheless, she insisted on dying with him and demanded the executioner's stroke. Seneca did not oppose her brave decision. Indeed, loving her wholeheartedly he was reluctant to leave her for ill-treatment. "Solace in life was what I commended to you" he said "but you prefer death and glory." I will not grudge your setting so fine an example. We can die with equal fortitude. But yours will be the nobler end." Then, each with one incision of the blade, he and his wife cut their arms. But Seneca's aged body, lean from austere living, released the blood too slowly. So he also severed the veins in his ankles and behind his knees. Exhausted by severe pain, he was afraid of weakening his wife's endurance by betraying his agony—or of losing his own self-possession at the sight of her sufferings. So he asked her to go into another room. But even in his last moments, his

eloquence remained. Summoning secretaries, he dictated a dissertation. . . .

However, his brave wife Paulina was not allowed to share death with her martyred husband:

Nero did not dislike Paulina personally. In order, therefore, to avoid increasing his ill repute for cruelty, he ordered her suicide to be averted. So, on instructions from the soldiers, slaves and ex-slaves bandaged her arms and stopped the bleeding. She may have been unconscious. . . . She lived on for a few years, honorably loyal to her husband's memory, with pallid features and limbs which showed how much vital blood she had lost. Meanwhile, Seneca's death was slow and lingering. Poison such as was formerly used to execute criminals at Athens had long been prepared; Seneca now entreated his well-tried doctor, who was also an old friend, to supply it. But when it came, Seneca drank it without effect. For his limbs were already cold and numbed against the poison's action. Finally he was placed in a bath of warm water. He sprinkled a little of it on the attendant slaves, commenting that this was his libation to Jupiter. Then he was carried into a vapor-bath where he suffocated. His cremation was without ceremony, in accordance with his own instructions about his death—written at the height of his wealth and power.

After a life of sham and compromise, Seneca died well. However, his nephew Lucan, who too had been involved in the Piso affair, met death with dishonor, for he denounced his innocent mother in hopes of winning Nero's pardon. Lucan's father Mela had avoided active politics but also perished in the Piso debacle, and even Gallio was dragged down in the purges. After years of success and wealth, the Seneca brothers died by violence far from Spain.

Except for its sensational aspects, Seneca's career was representative of a major development in Roman history, the prominence of provincials in the intellectual and political life of the capital. However, the personal life of Seneca was a moral tragedy of noble words mocked by ignoble deeds. While Stoics were often prigs, they were not supposed to be scheming opportunists, as was Seneca. Nietzche called him the "toreador of virtue" and Seneca received similar criticism in his own lifetime.

With his usual frankness, Seneca anticipated the charges which posterity would level against him:

If, therefore, any of those who bark against philosophy, should ask the usual thing: "Why then do you talk so much more bravely than you live? Why do you speak humbly in the presence of a superior and deem money a necessary equipment, and why are you moved by a loss, and why do you shed tears on hearing of the death of your wife or a friend, and why do you have regard for your reputation and let slander affect you? Why do you till broader acres than your natural need requires? Why do your dinners not conform to your own teaching? Why do you have such elegant furniture? Why is the wine that is drunk at your table older than you are yourself? Why this show of an aviary? Why do you plant trees that will supply nothing but shade? Why does your wife wear in her ears the revenue of a rich house? Why are your young slaves dressed in costly stuffs? Why is it an art to attend at your table and instead of the plate being set out carelessly and as you please, why is there expertness of service, and why to carve your meat is there a professional?" Add, too if you like: "Why do you have domains across the sea? Why more than you have seen? And shame to you!— you are either so careless that you do not know your handful of slaves by sight, or so pampered that you have more than your memory can recall to your knowledge!" Later I shall outdo your reproaches and bestow on myself more blame than you think of; for the moment I shall make this reply: "I am not a wise man nor—to feed your malevolence!—shall I ever be. And so require not from me that I should be equal to the best, but that I should be better than the wicked. It is enough for me if every day I reduce the number of my vices, and blame my mistakes."

Unfortunately, Seneca's apology was incomplete and lame.

The Spanish Stoic cannot be blamed for turning out a bad pupil in Nero, for Socrates failed with Alcibiades and Aristotle had questionable success with Alexander. However, Seneca set Nero an excellent example of duplicity and self-interest and encouraged the vices of the young ruler in order to keep power in his own hands. To advance his career, Seneca had committed adultery with Julia and condoned the murder of Claudius. It was an easy step to pander to Nero and justify the death of Agrippina. An attentive pupil, Nero became an intellectual dabbler and a completely immoral man. Compromise was the least of Seneca's sins, and many of his deeds were motivated solely by a blind will to power. Since few moral problems are simple choices between right and wrong, the moral flexibility of Seneca was preferable to the doctrinaire fanaticism of a Calvin or a Robespierre. Nevertheless, a man cannot put on and take off morality as he would a coat. A Christian contemporary of Seneca realized that words without works are hollow: "So with faith; if it does not lead to action, it is in itself a lifeless thing." Centuries earlier, Socrates had demonstrated that morality was not a matter of eloquent words but of difficult actions.

Conspiracy Against Nero

Miriam Griffin

In this essay on the senatorial conspiracy against Nero, Miriam Griffin of Oxford examines the reasons for the political opposition that resulted in the plot in 65 to put the senator Piso on the imperial throne. Nero's increasingly outrageous behavior, senatorial insecurity and, finally, the great fire of 64, produced a far-ranging conspiracy which included senators, equestrians and officers in the praetorian guard. The guilty and innocent were punished in the aftermath, but it was only later in 65, after the death of Poppaea, that Nero and his henchmen began widespread prosecutions for treason—neither justified nor indiscriminate, but motivated by the desire for confiscations to rescue the faltering imperial treasury.

That Nero escaped more and more into a world of fantasy from the time of the second Neronia [Festival of Nero] is a conclusion difficult to resist, even allowing for malicious distortion in our sources. There had always been a tendency for the theatre to invade his life, as when a collapsible boat used on stage showed him how to murder his mother or when a podium reminiscent of architectonic state decor was used to adorn a nymphaeum of his first palace. Insulated from facts by flatterers, more and more convinced of his musical talents, Nero made of the trip to Greece a physical demonstration of his mental withdrawal from the tensions and compromises demanded by political life in Rome. From his belief in real competition, which led him to fear his judges and bribe or slander his rivals, to his neglect of Helius' warnings about disaffection at home, a crescendo of illusion was rising to a climax in his paralysis after news came of Vindex' rebellion, his subsequent address to his body of advisors on the subject of water-organs, and his final panic after the defeat of the rebel.

In order to understand the form that political opposition to Nero eventually assumed and the nature of his reaction, we must return to the point when his performance as Princeps ceased to attract applause.

One of the leaders of the conspiracy that was hatched early in 65 reproached him with these crimes: the murder of his mother in 59 and of his wife in 62, his performance as a charioteer and actor, and the burning of Rome in 64. According to Dio, the conspirators could no longer endure Nero's shamelessness, licentiousness and cruelty. The last vice had been demonstrated much earlier, while the first example of open sexual depravity had come in 64 when Nero celebrated his marriage to the freedman Pythagoras at a public banquet. His shamelessness had not yet emerged: Nero was still sensitive and responsive to public opinion. He had not yet performed publicly at Rome but had chosen for his debut in 64 a Greek city where Romans traditionally relaxed their standards. Even when he arranged for the prosecution in his absence of D. Junius Silanus Torquatus, on a charge of harboring imperial ambitions, he was careful to say that he would have exercised clemency had the accused not forestalled condemnation by suicide. He was still concerned to justify his sexual excesses on the ground that no man was chaste or pure, and even as late as 66 he was shocked to discover that his activities were known to Petronius. His behaviour after the Fire of 64 showed clearly how eager he was to dispel the rumour of imperial arson. Even after the conspiracy of 65 he was concerned to present proofs of its existence to the Senate and to counter the suspicion that he was punishing innocent men out of envy and fear of their distinction.

Even if not dead to shame, however, Nero had by 65 given alarming indications that his tendency to fear and insecurity, especially when aggravated by disapproval, could lead to the total disappearance of his earlier *clementia* and *civilitis*. The murder of his mother had filled him with deep feelings of guilt that never left him.

According to Suetonius, he believed he was haunted by her ghost and by the avenging Furies. The truth of the story is suggested by his failure, when in Greece, to visit either Athens, which had harboured the Furies, or Eleusis, where a herald ordered the godless and wicked away before the performance of the Mysteries. Just after his mother's death, when the soldiers, the Senate and the people were all acquiescing in the official version that the Emperor had been saved from a plot against his life, Nero had his first encounter with the displeasure of P. Clodius Thrasea Paetus, a senator of considerable moral influence with a numerous band of loyal associates.

Thrasea was the first senator in his family, but he had married the daughter and assumed the cognomen of Caecina Paetus who, as governor of Dalmatia, had led an armed rebellion against Claudius. Consul in 56, thereafter governor of a province, he had respected Nero's efforts in the early years to encourage senatorial initiative and free speech: he had participated even in minor senatorial debates and assisted provincials in the prosecution of a corrupt governor. But the servile conduct of the Senate after Agrippina's murder was too much for him: he made a dignified exit from the House, and later in the year, at the Juvenalia, he showed his disapproval of the performances given by the Emperor and his own peers. Then in 62 he cunningly thwarted Nero and demonstrated his power to carry the Senate with him, at the trial of Antistius Sosianus for treason. But Nero was still on amicable terms with him at the end of that year.

The first open sign of his irritation with Thrasea came after Poppaea gave birth to a daughter in January of 63. Nero was elated, for the birth gave him a daughter to use in dynastic marriages and, more important, hopes of an heir that would more than compensate for the divorce of Octavia in consolidating his position on the throne. The Senate was invited en masse to Antium, but Thrasea was asked not to attend. When the infant died within four months Nero's grief was as intemperate as his joy had been. He no doubt grieved for the damage to his political prospects as well as for his personal loss,

and, regretting his earlier display of pique, he was reconciled with Thrasea. For Nero, Thrasea Paetus represented those who were hardest to please among the senators, and 'EX S C' on his gold and silver coins still advertised his intention to please.

The disappointment of his hopes for the succession revived fears that his mother had implanted in him years before. It was now that he reverted to her remedies and disposed of the prominent descendant of Augustus, whose brothers, Lucius and Marcus Junius Silanus, had been among her victims. He was now afraid to leave Rome and offered the plebs a grand public banquet to underline his message that it was concern for them that had led him to abandon his travelling plans.

Then came the Fire—a disaster for Rome and for the Emperor, whose relations with his subjects were becoming precarious. The rumours of his responsibility showed him, once and for all, how fragile was the popularity of a ruler. The long-term consequences of the Fire—loss of property and financial exactions by the government—aggravated the hostility of the upper orders in Rome and was eventually to turn the most powerful and prosperous of the provincials against the Emperor.

The first plot to overthrow Nero, however, seems to have been planned without any connivance from governors, armies or subjects outside Rome. Like Caesar's assassins, like the murderers of Gaius, those who conspired to kill Nero on 19 April 65 had made no contact with sympathetic generals, though they clearly expected the armies to welcome, or at least accept, the deed. Our only reliable account of the Pisonian conspiracy comes from Tacitus who had read the reports of at least two historians contemporary with the events and knew what some of the participants said when they returned to Rome from banishment.

The cast of characters included senators, *equites*, praetorian tribunes, centurions and eventually one of the Prefects. The list resembles closely that of the assassins of Gaius in January 41, except that no imperial freedmen are named. The plan was modelled closely on the murder of Caesar: the senator Plautius

Lateranus, who had earlier enjoyed Nero's clemency was to present a petition to the Emperor and, by grasping his knees, prevent him from avoiding the daggers of the others. Lateranus had signified his intention to present the petition in advance, if one can connect with this episode an anecdote recounted by the philosopher Epictetus: when asked by Epaphroditus, Nero's secretary in charge of petitions, what the cause of his confrontation with the Emperor was, Lateranus replied, 'If I wish to discuss it, I will do so with your master.' In all three plots, some participated out of patriotism, others out of pique, and the various conspirators reacted to various wrongs. Lateranus, a patriot according to Tacitus, is made to allude, in Epictetus' story, to the resurgence of the power of the freedmen; the freedwoman Epicharis was to adduce, in addition to Nero's crimes, the fact that the Senate had no power; the praetorian officers stressed Nero's domestic murders, public performances and attempt to destroy the capital.

The plot to kill Gaius had succeeded, but many of Piso's allies, who had been at the theatre, or at least in Rome, on that day, were keenly aware of the weaknesses of planning that had nearly led to chaos and disaster. Gaius' assassins, like Caesar's, had made no plans for government after the tyrant was dead. Even in 44 B.C. it had been rash to assume that the machinery of the Republic would automatically resume operation; in A.D. 41 it was a monstrous folly. There had been a prolonged struggle between the ringleaders of the conspiracy, acting in concert with the Senate, and the urban troops who finally prevailed, but not before leading senators had started bidding for the throne in an unseemly competition.

In 65 the plan provided for the replacement of the dead Nero by C. Calpurnius Piso, a descendant of the Republican nobility who enjoyed widespread popularity. He himself had been in exile when Gaius was killed, but he was well aware of the possibility of rival candidates. Tacitus notes that he feared the ambitions of L. Junius Silanus, and that M. Julius Vestinus Atticus, the consul, was not informed of the plot lest he favour a return to

the Republic or give his support to another candidate. (In 41 the consul had made a lengthy speech celebrating the restoration of the Republic while Claudius was already being hailed Emperor in the praetorian camp.) Piso refused to have the murder carried out at his villa at Baiae, ostensibly because it would taint him with sacrilegious disregard of the duties of hospitality and remind men that the Emperor trusted him as a friend. It would also have allowed others to take control of the situation in Rome—his real motive, according to Tacitus.

Nero was to be attacked when attending chariot races at the Circus Maximus, just as Gaius had been killed on his way to a theatrical performance. Access to the Emperor at such a time was easy and Nero's movements would be restricted by the crowds. The lesson about securing the allegiance of the Praetorian Guard as a whole had been learned: no Claudius was to be found by the soldiers behind a curtain and spirited off to the camp. Piso himself, right after the murder in the Circus Maximus, was to be escorted from the temple of Ceres nearby to the praetorian camp by Faenius Rufus and other officers.

There had been some delay and hesitation, but Tacitus states firmly that the whole conspiracy was both conceived and hatched in 65, though he mentions a report that the praetorian tribune Subrius Flavus had been tempted to kill Nero earlier during a stage performance or in the confusion of the Fire the year before. Why 65? If Tacitus is right to name praetorian officers among the initiators of the scheme, it seems remarkable that they waited so long after Nero had murdered his mother. Yet until 62 her two former protégés, Burrus and Faenius Rufus, Prefects in succession, had been able to control what resentment there was among the praetorians. After that Faenius steadily lost influence with Nero as the other Prefect Tigellinus ingratiated himself. Then there were fresh insults to the traditional sentiments of the Guard, as when a detachment accompanied Nero to Naples in 64 and watched him sing in public. Again, with regard to the senatorial ringleaders, Lucan may only have been banned from writing and publishing his poetry in 64, while the poem in which Nero offended Afranius Quintianus may have been of recent composition.

When the consuls took office in 65 the immediate future held the second Neronia at which Nero clearly intended to perform. Another consideration may have been the fact that Poppaea was pregnant again, if the fact was known. For the birth of an heir, now a distinct possibility, would certainly encourage Nero to throw off what inhibitions remained, and would also cause complications for any later assassination: not even the most vehement enemies of Gaius can have been pleased to see his infant daughter murdered in 41. But if Poppaea's son was to be spared, it would be better to have Nero's successor safely installed before its birth.

In the event the scheme was a dismal failure. It foundered on the disloyalty of a freedman of the senator Flavius Scaevinus, who reported his patron's suspicious preparations to the Emperor; it was finally wrecked by the indecision of Piso, who immediately lost heart and could not be persuaded to appeal to the praetorians and people and seize the city. Abject confessions and dishonourable accusations followed, and Nero learned with growing alarm what numbers were involved. The disloyalty of the praetorian officers was particularly distressing: Nero could only trust new or recent recruits to deliver the death order to Piso, and, after the revelations and punishments, he felt it necessary to buy the loyalty of the Guard with a handsome donative and a free corn allowance. In addition to the tribune Subrius Flavus and the centurion Sulpicius Asper, who were guilty and suffered execution, four praetorian tribunes were dismissed. Two other tribunes were spared for co-operating in the punishment of their fellow conspirators, but killed themselves.

According to Tacitus, many innocent men were punished on inadequate evidence: some, like Vestinus Atticus, Seneca and Rufrius Crispinus, because Nero had personal reasons for hating them; others because they were falsely accused by conspirators trying to help themselves by giving information. Yet Nero had powerful support in uncovering the plot: the consular Petronius Turpilianus, the praetor-designate Cocceius Nerva, the loyal Prefect Tigellinus and the imperial freedman Epaphroditus all received honours befitting a military victory. Although the Emperor treated the exposure and punishment of the conspirators as a serious war, he still retained his balance: some of the accused were pardoned, others ignored. The Senate felt confident enough to stop the malicious prosecution of Seneca's brother Gallio by one of its members, and Nero refused a temple to himself, an unprecedented honour for the living Emperor at Rome.

It was only later in 65, after the death of Poppaea and her unborn child, that the unprovoked persecution of influential senators on treason charges began in earnest. . . .

Tacitus detects financial motives behind some of the political convictions that followed Poppaea's death later in the year. Moreover, while Seneca had already been forbidden to change his will which was doubtless favourable to Nero, it was in 66 that the condemned were advised to make the Emperor or Tigellinus a part heir in order to save the rest of the estate for their families.

Poppaea's extravagant funeral must have added to the state deficit: she was not cremated as was customary but embalmed, and her public obsequies involved the burning of quantities of oriental spice. There is no reason to doubt that Nero's personal grief was intense, despite the widespread belief that her miscarriage and death were caused by a kick from her angry spouse. Not only was she given divine honours: Nero demonstrated his sexual dependence on her by having Sporus, a young freedman who resembled her, castrated and using him as a substitute, even going through a marriage ceremony later on the Greek tour. In the eulogy he pronounced at her funeral, however, Nero lamented not only her beauty but the fact that she had once given him a child. The loss of his second child and possible heir must have contributed greatly to his grief: it also explains why he was to marry again within a year. But for the moment he was consoling himself in Naples, from which letters were sent to the Senate ordering prosecutions for treason.

The Fall of Nero

B. H. Warmington

Professor Warmington here concludes his treatment of Nero with an account of the causes of Nero's fall: not only his frivolity and cruelty, but the severe financial exactions and his neglect of the armies. Frightened and confused, Nero died at the age of thirty and left a legacy of civil war, hatred and even adulation. He remained admired and loved in the Greek-speaking world where "false Neros" appeared to the acclaim of the masses. But the emperor died, hated by the Jews and Christians whom he persecuted, and in their traditions he is depicted as a monster: Satan or Antichrist. The glittering extravagance of Nero's court was scorned and satirized by moralizing writers of a later age, when emperors—Vespasian, Trajan and Marcus Aurelius—ruled the empire with frugality and seriousness: traditional Roman virtues, now ignored in the capital, but still cultivated and revered in Italian towns and in the provinces.

I t was not so much the cruelty as the frivolity and ineptitude of Nero which led to his downfall. At the best of times cruelty is a relative term; for example, as understood by the Romans, it did not include the savage penalties of the cross, the beasts and the fire inflicted on criminal slaves and non-citizens. Emperors were charged with cruelty who were ruthless in the removal of members of their family and men whom they regarded as potential rivals, and also for sadistic enjoyment of the physical and mental sufferings of their victims. Nero could be accused on the former count; the latter played little part in the tradition, and Nero generally adhered to the convention which allowed a senator to commit suicide rather than suffer the indignity of execution.

It is not surprising that the personality and interests of Nero, so different from those of other emperors, were displayed in many an anecdote. Suetonius has a large number and they were doubtless in the sources used by Tacitus and Dio as well, though the former only retells a few. Most of them centered on his musical and theatrical pursuits and his sexual life, his wives, mistresses and eunuchs. It is often said that in this respect the historians merely provided what their readership required, but the notion that the private indulgences of even approved figures such as Augustus or Trajan should be concealed from posterity was alien to the Romans. The licence of autocratic power was

enjoyed by the emperors as by the rulers of seventeenth- and eighteenth-century Europe if not indeed of later times as well. It must be admitted, however, that Neroniana lost little in the telling, and were not difficult to manufacture. This applies even to quoted remarks of the emperor, although *ipissima verba* [the very words] are generally supposed to resist the ravages of time better than anecdotes.

For example, it was said that he looked at his mother's corpse and said, "I did not know that I had such a beautiful mother." (Tacitus doubts this); that when the head of Rubellius Plautus was brought to him he remarked, "I did not know he had such a big nose," and that when he saw the head of Faustus Sulla he laughed at its premature baldness. It may be suspected that these came from the biographies of his victims and served to illustrate the theme of Nero as a callous tyrant. Another example concerned the fire of Rome. Someone quoted a well known line from a Greek poet: "When I am dead, may the earth be consumed with fire," to which Nero replied, "No, when I am alive," and set about his activities as an incendiary. Quite apart from the responsibility for the fire, faith in the attribution of the remark is weakened by the fact that the quotation is attributed also to Tiberius, in a fit of gloomy misanthropy. Perhaps those to do with his art are the most likely to be true; before he finally ventured to appear in public he quoted the Greek proverb, "No one has any regard for music they have not heard," and when dining in public at Naples addressed the bystanders, "When I have had a drink I'll give you a rousing song." A celebrated remark referred to what he would do if he lost the Empire: "My art will support me." His last words show him obsessed to the end by his theatrical mania.

For an emperor to survive the alienation of the upper class was difficult; Domitian failed, like Nero and Gaius, though he lasted longer. Nero had little compensating strength; he was popular among the proletariat of Rome, but this body counted for more when it was hostile than when it was favourable to an emperor; his popularity in the Greek world, though real, was likewise of little practical value. In his later years, financial pressure on the provincials was doubtless considerable, and we hear of the unpopularity of his taxes and of his procurators in connection with the movement of Vindex and Galba, but there was no general hostility on which these two could rely. In general, provincials were powerless to do anything other than obey the wielders of power, legitimate or usurpatory. They were not disloyal to Rome, but did not, or could not, show much effective enthusiasm for a particular ruler.

Nero's neglect of the army also played its part, but it should not be exaggerated. He is said to have allowed the pay of the soldiers and the provision for dischaged veterans to get into arrears. If widespread, this would have been very serious, but it is only reported by Suetonius who notoriously generalized from individual instances. On the whole, there is little evidence that Nero was not popular among the soldiers, and some units (e.g. XIV Gemina) are known to have been enthusiastic for him. In fact, the notion that the legionaries, as opposed to their officers, frequently played a part in the rise and fall of emperors is illusory for this period. The legionaries of the army on the Rhine were admittedly enthusiastic for Vitellius, but the movements of 69 were all plotted and inspired by provincial governors, commanders of legions and the legionary tribunes and centurions. On the other hand, Nero's failure ever to visit an army was important in a negative sense. It made

things worse in the crisis as he simply had no idea how to act; if he had acquired a military reputation, or even some prestige, like Claudius, there might never have been a venture like that of Vindex.

One of the cherished beliefs of Roman moralists was that the country towns of Italy preserved the sober and respectable habits which had once characterized the citizens of Rome but which had now died out in the city. Tacitus saw an example in the decline of Nero's authority. The repetition of Neronia in 65 was popular with the city masses. But, says Tacitus, "those who had come on official or private business from distant country towns in Italy where the strictness of ancient manners was retained, and from distant provinces, without experience of such decadence, could not bear the sight of an emperor on the stage." The participation of such men in the Pisonian conspiracy and in the later opposition gives some support to Tacitus' view.

The first day of a new principate is the best, it was said, and there is no reason to doubt that at the fall of Nero there was enthusiasm in Rome among wider sections of the people than the Senate, but it was not universal. Tacitus differentiates:

The senators were happy and at once used their new freedom of speech the more freely since they had an emperor who was still absent; the most important of the knights were next to the senators in feeling satisfaction; the respectable part of the people, attached to the powerful families, and the clients and freedmen of the condemned and exiled, were full of hope. But the base plebs, addicted to the circus and the theatre, and the worst of the slaves, and those who had wasted their money and were maintained by the emperor, to his own disgrace, were resentful and open to rumour. The praetorians, long accustomed to their oath to the Caesars had been led to depose Nero by diplomacy and pressure rather than their own wish. . . . (Histories I, 4-5.)

Some of his freedmen were killed, mostly by mob violence, but the number was perhaps not large. Only one senator, Petronius Turpilianus, was killed for his association with Nero, and his death made Galba unpopular. In 69 and 70 some of the delators were prosecuted, but with little success. The same phenomenon is observable after the death of Domitian; it was considered bad form to rake over the past once a detested emperor was dead.

But it was not long before some regret for Nero was felt. In Rome his tomb was honoured with flowers for many years, from time to time his images were displayed, and edicts circulated in his name as if he were about to return. In 69 Otho found it worthwhile to try to win some popularity in the city by claiming to follow in Nero's footsteps after the gloomy and disappointing Galba; among other things he thought of marrying Statilia Messalina. Vitellius also tried to gain credit from his former close association with Nero. But it was in the East that the memory of Nero remained vivid. To the Greeks in Greece itself and no doubt also to educated Greeks everywhere, the "liberation" of Achaea was important not only because it was symbolic of the concern of the first philhellene emperor and because it appealed to the nostalgic pride of the educated classes, but precisely because it lasted such a short time, being rescinded by Vespasian; they never had much chance to complain about its lack of reality. So Plutarch was able to regard it as Nero's one good deed that "he freed the race of men that is the best and most dear to the gods of all the subjects of the Empire"; Pausanias somewhat later agreed and in the third century Philostratus, who also had high praise for the projected canal through the Corinthian isthmus.

More than this, the obscure circumstances of his death provoked many rumours, and the belief grew up in the East that he was still alive. Dio Chrysostom wrote (under Trajan) that "even now all long for him to be alive; indeed, many actually think he is still alive." No less than three pretenders to the name of Nero appeared before the end of the century. The first, in 69, a slave or freedman, gathered some deserters and seized the Aegean island of Cythnos, killing the merchants there and arming the slaves. He was soon put down, but Tacitus says that Achaea and Asia were terrified, no doubt by the servile nature of the movement and the prospect of civil war. Under Titus another appeared, again similar in appearance and musical accomplishments to the dead emperor. He attracted a number of followers in Asia Minor and finally crossed the Euphrates into Parthian territory where his identity was soon discovered, though not before the Parthians had made some threatening gestures to restore him. Finally an impostor appeared in 88 who also fled to Parthia; it was with some difficulty that the Parthians were prevailed upon to hand him over. Their attitude was significant; they cherished the memory of Nero, and rightly in view of the Armenian settlement which was in their favour. They were, however, determined to maintain peace with the succeeding dynasty, and did not indulge in more than token gestures when the pretenders appeared.

Belief in the return of Nero entered still more humble circles, but with different implications. The Jews, embittered by the destruction of their country and the centre of their religion, continued to hope for divine vengeance on the Roman Empire, and from time to time prophecies of this, related to contemporary events, circulated among them. One such foretold that at the time of the eruption of Vesuvius (79), "the exiled man of Rome, lifting a mighty sword, will cross the Euphrates [from Parthia] with many tens of thousands." This no doubt refers to the pretender under Titus; the Jews hoped against all experience for Parthian support. The belief also existed among the early Christians, for whom Nero was known as the first persecutor; he appears in apocalyptic writings as the precursor of Antichrist at the end of the world.

A famous passage in Tacitus, one of the few in which he speaks directly, makes a favourable comparison between his own age and the past. He believed there had been an important change in the whole tone of Roman society in his own lifetime. Ostentatious luxury, which had run riot for a century since the victory of Augustus at Actium, had declined after the death of Nero. (Tacitus clearly thought that Augustus' measures to improve Roman society had had little effect.) The change was partly due to the liquidation of the richest nobles, which induced prudence in the rest. But, at the same time:

Numerous self-made men admitted into the Senate from Italian towns and even from the provinces brought frugal domestic habits, and, though by luck or hard work many of them became rich later, they did not change their ideas. No one did more to promote simplicity than Vespasian, with his old-fashioned way of life; for deference to the emperor and the wish to imitate him were more effective than legal penalties, and threats. It may, however, be the case that not only the seasons of the year but everything, including social change, moves in cycles. Not that earlier times were better than ours in every way—our own age has produced moral and intellectual achievements for our descendants to copy. (Annals III, 55.)

This naturally applied primarily to the upper class in Rome and Italy.

A notable example of the new type of senator (which included Tacitus himself, was his friend the younger Pliny. The latter's correspondence, which contains some indications of the wholesome life of the towns of his beloved northern Italy and hints of disapproval of individuals of the Neronian era, reveals the unostentatious way of life and sensible and well meaning attitudes of himself and many contemporaries. Again, when the satirist Juvenal was seeking examples of sophisticated vice, he turned back naturally to the age of Nero. . . .

There can be little doubt that Tacitus was correct in his belief in a change and in the reasons for it. Vespasian's abandonment of the Golden House, the most notorious example of Neronian extravagance, symbolized the whole process. The standards set by the emperors were important, and those who followed the short-lived emperors of 69 all came from precisely the circles praised by Tacitus— Vespasian from Italy, Trajan, Hadrian and Marcus Aurelius from Spain and Antoninus from Gaul. Perhaps Titus had a different outlook from his father, but Domitian paraded a severe morality. The emperors from Vespasian to Marcus were in some ways all in the same mould, unlike the Julio-Claudian successors of Augustus, all markedly individual. The death of Nero brought to an end a dynasty which had links of blood and attitude with the great noble houses of the Republican era; now there were hardly any left, and those unimportant. The success of the new emperors depended much more on their abilities and conscientiousness. Although the monarchic character of the principate became ever more pronounced, no other dynasty achieved the prestige, or lasted half as long, as the Julio-Claudian.

Suggestions for Further Reading

General Books

Cambridge Ancient History. vol. X 44 B.C.–A.D. 70. Cambridge: Cambridge University Press, 1934.

The *Cambridge Ancient History* remains the most comprehensive treatment of the ancient world, though its scholarship is quite outdated. Each chapter is written by a different author, and some, by such scholars as Syme, Momigliano and Nock, have stood the test of time well. A new edition has been announced.

Garzetti, Albino. From *Tiberius to the Antoines*. London: Methuen, 1974.

Large-scale textbook treatment of the first two centuries of the Roman Empire. Garzetti includes over two hundred pages of detailed "Critical Notes" which discuss both sources and modern interpretations of historical problems.

Grant, Michael and Rachel Kitzinger. *Civilization of the Ancient Mediterranean: Greece and Rome*. Three volumes. New York: Scribners, 1988.

These volumes contain one hundred essays in which leading scholars provide up-to-date surveys of important topics in ancient civilization. Some relevant topics are Roman Class Structures (Saller), Slavery (Wiedemann), Ruler Worship (Fears), Roman Games (Humphrey), Women in Rome (Dickison), Roman Marriage (Treggiari), Roman Historiography (Mellor).

Lewis, Naphtali and Meyer Reinhold. *Roman Civilization*. vol. II "The Empire." New York: Harper and Row, 1966.

This remains the most comprehensive sourcebook on the Roman Empire. It contains translations (with helpful comments) of hundreds of inscriptions, papyri and literary texts arranged by topic (e.g. taxation; imperial cult; oaths of allegiance).

Oxford Classical Dictionary. 2nd ed. Oxford: Oxford University Press, 1978.

The standard reference book for names and constitutional terms (e.g., *imperium; proconsul*) in the ancient world.

Scullard, H. H. *From the Gracci to Nero*. New York: Barnes & Noble, 1982.

For thirty years this often-revised book has remained the most reliable brief survey of the late Republic and the Julio-Claudian era. The book is clearly organized and the extensive notes have assisted a generation of students in preparing term papers.

Starr, Chester. *Civilization and the Caesars*. New York: Oxford University Press, 1965.

This engaging survey of the Empire avoids the factual detail of a textbook and concentrates on the intellectual and cultural milieu in which the political events unfold.

Wells, Colin. *The Roman Empire*. London: Fontana Books, 1984.

This recent interpretative survey of the Roman Empire is particularly strong in discussing sources and archaeological evidence for developments in the provinces and the army. An extended critical bibliography for further reading.

Chapter I The Rise of the Julio-Claudians

Beard, Mary and Michael Crawford. *Rome in the Late Republic*. Ithaca, N.Y.: Cornell University Press, 1985.

This remarkable book consists of a series of stimulating essays that survey the main problems of late Republican history in fewer than one hundred pages. An exciting and intelligent antidote for those who prefer ideas to an encyclopedic collection of facts.

Brunt, P. A. *Social Conflicts in the Roman Republic*. New York: W. W. Norton, 1971.

This brief text provides a clear treatment of the social and economic conflicts which led to the fall of the Roman Republic.

Gruen, Erich S. *The Last Generation of the Roman Republic*. Berkeley: University of California Press, 1974.

A detailed, comprehensive examination of politics in the age of Cicero and Caesar.

Gelzer, Matthias. *Caesar, Politician and Statesman*. Cambridge, Mass.: Harvard University Press, 1968.

A readable reliable biography of Julius Caesar by the great German historian of late Republican Rome.

Plutarch. *Fall of the Roman Republic*. New York: Penguin Books, 1972.

Plutarch's lives of Crassus, Pompey, Caesar and Cicero bring alive the ruthless ambition of Roman politicians of the first century B.C.

Syme, Ronald. *The Roman Revolution*. Oxford: Oxford University Press, 1939.

Sir Ronald Syme has given us the greatest modern work on the fall of the Roman Republic. He begins from the First Triumvirate in 60 B.C. and covers the Civil Wars and the reign of Augustus. The book is not easy for the beginner, but Syme's brilliant analysis of the personalities and ideas of the period make it indispensable.

Chapter II   Augustus: The Republic Restored and Chapter III   Augustus: The New Regime

Earl, Donald. *The Age of Augustus*. London: Elek Books, 1968.

A useful book which combines excellent illustrations with readable essays on important topics (religion; army; etc). This is perhaps the best general introduction to the politics and culture of the Augustan Age.

Jones, A. H. M. *Augustus*. New York: W. W. Norton, 1970.

A brief paperback survey which focuses on the political and administrative achievements of Augustus.

Millar, Fergus and Eric Segal. *Caesar Augustus: Seven Aspects*. Oxford: Oxford University Press, 1984.

This collection of essays is based on a colloquium organized to celebrate the eightieth birthday of Sir Ronald Syme. It includes important historical essays by Zvi Yavetz, Millar, Claude Nicolet, Werber Eck, and Glen Bowersock, as well as a fascinating historical chapter by Emilio Gabba.

Syme, Ronald. *The Roman Revolution*. Oxford: Oxford University Press, 1939.

Though not a biography of Augustus, Sir Ronald's brilliant study remains the most penetrating analysis of the emperor's climb to power and his construction of a new regime.

"Roman Empire Anniversary Issue," *Thought* 55 (1980) New York: Fordham University Press.

This special issue contains interesting articles on historical aspects of the reign of Augustus by David Stockton, Thomas Mitchell, Meyer Reinhold, Henry Boren, and J. Rufus Fears.

Wirszubski, C. *Libertas as a Political Idea at Rome During the Late Republic and Early Empire*. Cambridge: Cambridge University Press, 1960.

A provocative monograph in which Wirszubski argues that *libertas* did exist in the Augustan principate. Though there was obvious potential for tyranny, Wirszubski maintains that Augustus was not a despot.

Yavetz, Zvi. *Plebs and Princeps*. Oxford: Oxford University Press, 1969.

This book examines the ways in which the Julio-Claudian emperors relied upon the Roman masses for political support.

Chapter IV   The Armies and the Provinces

Grant, Michael. *The Army of the Caesars*. New York: Scribners, 1974.

A popular and readable narrative of Roman military history beginning with the civil wars of the late Republic.

Keppie, Lawrence. *The Making of the Roman Army*. London: Batsford, 1984.

An up-to-date chronological account of the development of the imperial army which includes discussions of the command structure, auxiliaries and military organization.

Luttwak, Edward N. *The Grand Strategy of the Roman Empire*. Baltimore: The Johns Hopkins University Press, 1976.

Luttwak is a distinguished strategic analyst who has held high positions in the Pentagon. This book attempts to reconstruct the strategy of Roman imperial defense by examining frontier policy, military deployment and the use of client kingdoms.

Millar, Fergus. *The Roman Empire and its Neighbors.* 2nd ed. London: Duckworth, 1981.

An excellent survey of the government and administration of the Empire, its cities and provinces, and such neighboring peoples as the Dacians, Germans and Parthians.

Watson, G. R. *The Roman Soldier.* Ithaca, N.Y.: Cornell University Press, 1969.

This book examines aspects of the lives of Roman soldiers: e.g., religion, marriage and the conditions of service.

Webster, Graham. *The Roman Imperial Army.* 2nd ed. New York: Barnes & Noble, 1979.

Webster's book remains the standard general book on the Roman army. It is not a chronological history, but it describes recruitment, organization, strategy, equipment, camps and forts of the army.

Chapter V   Women and the Family in Imperial Rome

Balsdon, J. P. V. D. *Roman Women.* Rev. ed. London: Bodley Head, 1974.

A pleasant, general book on Roman women, but one which preceded the extensive research in this area during the last two decades.

Gardner, Jane F. *Women in Roman Law and Society.* Bloomington: Indiana University Press, 1986.

Gardner examines the legal position of Roman women with chapters on such topics as marriage, dowry, children, divorce, inheritance, and emancipation. Good recent bibliography.

Lefkowitz, Mary and Maureen Fant (eds.) *Women's Life in Greece and Rome.* Baltimore: The Johns Hopkins University Press, 1982.

A reader of ancient sources on women.

Pomeroy, Sarah. *Goddesses, Whores, Wives and Slaves: Women in Classical Antiquity.* New York: Schocken Books, 1975.

Pomeroy's book was the first feminist overview of women in Greece and Rome using both historical and literary evidence. Though it concentrates on Greek women, it provides useful chapters on the Roman world.

Rawson, Beryl, ed. *The Family in Ancient Rome.* Ithaca, N.Y.: Cornell University Press, 1986.

A collection of essays incorporating the latest research on Roman family life. The long introductory essay by Rawson is especially useful.

Chapter VI   The Reign of Tiberius

Levick, Barbara. *Tiberius the Politician.* London: Thames and Hudson, 1976.

A thoughtful and readable biography that concentrates on the political aims and family interests of Tiberius.

Marsh, Frank B. *The Reign of Tiberius.* Oxford: Oxford University Press, 1931.

An early attempt to rescue the reputation of Tiberius from his ancient detractors. The first chapter provides an excellent survey of the literary sources for the reign of Tiberius.

Seager, Robin. *Tiberius.* Berkeley: University of California Press, 1972.

This enjoyable biography of Tiberius attributes the emperor's cruelty and despotism to a continual fear for his own life.

Syme, Ronald. *Tacitus.* 2 vols. Oxford: Oxford University Press, 1958.

This immensely learned work (with ninety-five appendices) is not for the novice, but Syme's interpretation of Tacitus is closely tied to that historian's treatment of Tiberius.

Chapter VII   Emperors as Gods: The Transformation of Roman Religion

Chadwick, Henry. *The Early Church.* New York: Penguin Books, 1967.

This first volume of *The Pelican History of the Church* provides a general treatment of Christianity through its first four centuries. Chadwick is one of the leading scholars of early Christianity.

Liebeschuetz, H. H. W. G. *Continuity and Change in Roman Religion.* Oxford: Oxford University Press, 1979.

A scholarly account of the changes which transformed Roman religion in the early Roman Empire.

Ogilvie, R. M. *The Romans and Their Gods in the Age of Augustus*. New York: W. W. Norton, 1969.

A readable survey of Roman religion in the Augustan age.

Price, Simon. *Ritual and Power: The Roman Imperial Cult in Asia Minor*. Cambridge: Cambridge University Press, 1984.

A stimulating examination of the Roman imperial cult in the context of anthropological theory and comparative religious material.

Schurer, Emil. *The History of the Jewish People in the Age of Jesus Christ (175 B.C.-A.D. 135)*. Revised edition by G. Vermes and F. Millar. Vols. 1–3. Edinburgh: T.&T. Clark, 1973/1986.

This careful revision of a standard reference book will be too detailed for beginners, but it contains a wealth of information and careful references to the sources. It remains the most important book on the Jews in the Roman period.

Smallwood, E. Mary. *The Jews Under Roman Rule from Pompey to Diocletian*. Leyden: Brill, 1981.

A comprehensive survey which is more readable than Schurer.

Taylor, Lily Ross. *The Divinity of the Roman Emperor*. Middletown, Conn.: American Philological Association Monographs, 1931.

The classic treatment of the ruler cult in the Roman Empire. Though much new evidence has been discovered since 1931, Taylor remains the only general treatment of the subject in English.

Wardman, Alan. *Religion and Statecraft Among the Romans*. London: Granada, 1982.

A survey of the interaction between religion and politics at Rome.

Wilken, R. L. *The Christians as the Romans Saw Them*. New Haven: Yale University Press, 1984.

A recent treatment of the pagan view of the early Christians.

Chapter VIII   Bread and Circuses: The Politics of Entertainment

Arnott, Peter. *The Ancient Greek and Roman Theatre*. New York: Random House, 1971.

An overview of Greek and Roman drama.

Balsdon, J. P. V. D. *Life and Leisure in Ancient Rome*. New York: McGraw Hill, 1969.

An entertaining survey of the pleasures and duties of the Romans.

Cameron, Alan. *Circus Factions: Blues and Greens at Rome and Byzantium*. Oxford: Oxford University Press, 1976.

An examination of the public demonstrations by the supporters of various circus factions and a fascinating discussion of the political context of the games.

Carcopino, Jerome. *Daily Life in Ancient Rome*. New Haven: Yale University Press, 1940.

A survey of how the Romans lived their day-to-day lives. While Carcopino's attitudes on social relations and family life are now out of date, his discussions of food, houses, and the daily routine remain useful.

Christ, Karl. *The Romans: An Introduction to Their History and Civilization*. Berkeley: University of California Press, 1983.

A recent text which provides a convenient overview of Roman civilization.

Friedlander, Ludwig. *Roman Life and Manners Under the Early Empire*. New York: Routledge & Kegan Paul, 1968 (reprint of the 1908 edition). Volume 2.

Pages 1-130 deal with Roman Spectacles. Though written over eighty years ago, Friedlander remains a comprehensive and readable account of aspects of Roman society: spectacles, banquets; funerals, etc. He fully recounts the relevant anecdotes from the ancient literary sources, but he tends to avoid any interpretation. For sociological, economic or political explanations of these cultural manifestations, we must turn to more recent authors.

Grant, Michael. *Gladiators*. London: Wiedenfeld & Nicholson, 1967.

A brief account of Roman gladiators suitable for the beginning reader. As always with Grant, well-written and enjoyable.

Rickman, Geoffrey. *The Corn Supply of Ancient Rome.* Oxford: Oxford University Press, 1980.

The most complete scholarly treatment of the logistics of supplying adequate food to the million inhabitants of Rome.

Shelton, Jo-Ann. *As the Romans Did: A Sourcebook in Roman Social History.* New York: Oxford University Press, 1988.

A new collection of ancient source materials in clear, lively translations: personal letters, tombstones, poetry, philosophical texts, and graffiti. The useful notes make this an excellent reader for courses in Roman civilization.

Chapter IX   Caligula and the Politics of Madness

Ferrill, Arther. *The Emperor Caligula.* London: Thames and Hudson, 1991.

Ferrill's forthcoming book on Caligula will be the first biography of this emperor in English in a half century.

Balsdon. J. P. V. D. *The Emperor Gaius.* Oxford: Oxford University Press, 1934.

A fascinating attempt to provide reasonable explanations for the bizarre behavior of Caligula. Balsdon's book serves as an apologia for the emperor—an interesting historical exercise, but finally unconvincing.

For additional discussions of Caligula and bibliography on his reign, cf. Garzetto, Scullard and the *Cambridge Ancient History* (all listed under General Books).

Chapter X   Claudius the Fool?

Momigliano, Arnaldo. *Claudius, The Emperor and His Achievement.* Oxford: Oxford University Press, 1934.

A brief but pathbreaking study, in which Momigliano rejected the unfavorable interpretations of Suetonius and Tacitus and created a more positive picture of Claudius and his reign.

Scramuzza, Vincent. *The Emperor Claudius.* Cambridge, Mass.: Harvard University Press, 1940.

A more detailed favorable biography of Claudius.

For additional discussions of Claudius and bibliography on his reign, cf. Garzetti, Scullard and the *Cambridge Ancient History* (all listed under General Books).

Chapter XI   Foreigners, Freedmen, Senators and Slaves: The Imperial Court

Bradley, Keith. *Slaves and Masters in the Roman Empire: A Study in Social Control.* New York: Oxford University Press, 1987.

A fine general treatment of slavery in the Roman Empire.

Duff, A. M. *Freedmen in the Early Roman Empire.* Oxford: Oxford University Press, 1928.

The classic treatment of the class that staffed the imperial administrative apparatus.

Garnsey, Peter and Richard Saller. *The Roman Empire: Economy, Society and Culture.* Berkeley: University of California Press, 1987.

The latest account of society and the economy in the Roman Empire. The book, by two of the leading young social historians of Rome, provides an analytical discussion of problems rather than a narrative history. Chapters on the social hierarchy, the family, and social relations provide an excellent overview of the main issues. This book, which is aimed at undergraduates, contains an extensive current bibliography.

Millar, Fergus. *The Emperor in the Roman World (31 B.C.–A.D. 337).* Ithaca, N.Y.: Cornell University Press, 1977.

This book discusses the entire administrative apparatus as well as the emperor's place in it. It is packed with detail and not suitable for beginners. They might refer to the chapter on the administration in Millar's *The Roman Empire and its Neighbors*, listed in Chapter IV.

Chapter XII   Nero and the Fall of the Julio-Claudian Dynasty

Grant, Michael. *Nero.* London: Wiedenfeld & Nicholson, 1970.

A readable, well-illustrated popular treatment of Nero.

Griffin, Miriam. *Nero The End of a Dynasty*. New Haven: Yale University Press, 1984.

An incisive, recent study of Nero, his values and the cultural ambiance of his reign. The best current book on the emperor.

Henderson, G. W. *The Life and Principate of the Emperor Nero* . London: Methuen, 1905.

The classic (and very detailed) treatment of Nero which should almost be regarded as a reference work.

Warmington, B. H. *Nero: Reality and Legend*. New York: W. W. Norton, 1969.

A brief, reliable discussion of Nero and his court.

Copyrights and Acknowledgments

Chapter I

"Life of Augustus" by Suetonius. Freely adapted from Suetonius *Lives of the Caesars* trans. by J. C. Rolfe, Loeb Classical Library, Harvard University Press (1913). Reprinted with the permission of Harvard University Press.

Chapter II

"The Death of Augustus" by Tacitus. From *The Annals of Imperial Rome* 1, 1-10, trans. by Michael Grant. London: Penguin Classics, 1956, 1959, 1971© Michael Grant Publications Ltd., 1956, 1959, 1971. Reproduced by permission of Penguin Books Ltd.

The Res Gestae (Achievements of Augustus) by Augustus Caesar. Trans. by Frederick Shipley, Loeb Classical Library, Harvard University Press (1924). Reprinted with the permission of Harvard University Press.

"The Augustan Settlement" by Dio Cassius. From *Roman History* (vol. 6) 53, 11-33 (excerpts), trans. by E. Cary, Loeb Classical Library, Harvard University Press (1917). Reprinted with the permission of Harvard University Press.

"The Shield of Aeneas" by Virgil. From *The Aeneid of Virgil* 676-731, trans. by Allen Mandelbaum, University of California Press, © 1971 Allen Mandelbaum. Reprinted with the permission of Bantam Doubleday Dell Publishing Group, Inc.

"The Cleopatra Ode" by Horace. From *Horace: The Complete Odes and Epodes*, 1, 37, trans. by W. G. Shepherd (London: Penguin Classics, 1983), © W. G. Shepherd, 1983. Reproduced by permission of Penguin Books Ltd.

"Paean to Augustus" by Ovid. From *Ovid: Metamorphoses*, 15, 750 ff., trans. by Mary M. Innes (London: Penguin Classics, 1955), © Mary M. Innes, 1955. Reproduced by permission of Penguin Books Ltd.

"The Republic Restored" by Donald Earl. From *The Age of Augustus* pp. 55-71. London: Elek Books, ©

1968 Paul Elek Productions Ltd. Reprinted with the permission of Grafton Books.

"Peace and the Princeps" by Sir Ronald Syme. From *The Roman Revolution* pp. 509/524. © 1939 Delegates of the Oxford University Press. Reprinted by permission of Oxford University Press.

"Augustus and the Succession" by Ralph Galucci. Original essay.

Chapter III

"Augustus: The New Regime" by Ronald Mellor. Original essay.

"Roman Judgments on Augustus" by Velleius Paterculus. From *Compendium of Roman History* 2, 89, trans. by Frederick Shipley, Loeb Classical Library, Harvard University Press (1924). Reprinted with the permission of Harvard University Press.

Natural History by Pliny the Elder, 7, 147-150, trans. by H. Rackham, Loeb Classical Library, Harvard University Press (1942). Reprinted with the permission of Harvard University Press.

De Legatio ad Gaium by Philo, 143-151, trans. by E. Mary Smallwood. Leyden: E. J. Brill. © 1970 E. J. Brill. Reprinted with permission.

"On Mercy" by Seneca. From *Moral Essays* vol. 1, 1, 9-11, by J. Basore, Loeb Classical Library, Harvard University Press (1928). Reprinted with the permission of Harvard University Press.

"War and Peace in the Age of Augustus" by Erich S. Gruen. From *The Age of Augustus*, ed. Rolf Winkes. © 1986 Art and Archaeology Publications, College Erasme, Louvain-la-Neuve, Belgium. Reprinted with the permission of Rolf Winkes.

"Modes of Propaganda" by Chester Starr. From *Civilization and the Caesars* pp. 45-49. © 1965 Oxford University Press. Reprinted with the permission of Cornell University Press.

"Augustus' Conception of Himself" by Meyer Reinhold. From *Thought* 55, 36-50. ©1980 Fordham University Press. Reprinted with permission.

"Augustus in the View of History" by David Stockton. From *Thought* 55, 12-17. © 1980 Fordham University Press. Reprinted with permission.

Chapter IV

"Mutiny" by Tacitus. From *The Annals of Imperial Rome* 1, 17-29, trans. by Michael Grant, (London: Penguin Books, 1956, 1959, 1971), © Michael Grant Publications Ltd., 1956, 1959, 1971. Reproduced by permission of Penguin Books Ltd.

"The Roman Army" by Josephus. From *Jewish War* 3, 5, 71-107, trans. by H. St. John Thackeray, Loeb Classical Library, Harvard University Press (1928). Reprinted with permission.

"The Empire and the Army" by Donald Earl. From *The Age of Augustus* pp. 134-147; 163-165. London: Elek Books, © 1968 Paul Elek Productions Ltd. Reprinted with the permission of Grafton Books.

"The Julio-Claudian System" by Edward Luttwak. From *The Grand Strategy of the Roman Empire* pp. 13-50. © 1976 The Johns Hopkins University Press. Reprinted with permission.

"The Praetorian Guard" by Michael Grant. Excerpts from *The Army of the Caesars*. © 1974 Michael Grant Publications, Ltd. Reprinted with the permission of Charles Scribner's Sons, an imprint of Macmillan Publishing Company, and for Canadian rights, with the permission of George Weidenfeld & Nicolson Limited.

"The Army in Peacetime" by Graham Webster. From *The Roman Imperial Army* pp. 273-280. London: A. & C. Black. 2nd edition © 1979 Graham Webster. Permission granted by Barnes & Noble Books, Totowa, N. J.

Chapter V

"Letters on the Virtues of Roman Women" by Pliny the Younger. From *The Letters of the Younger Pliny*, 3, 16; 4, 19; 5, 16. Trans. by Betty Radice (Penguin Classics, 1963, 1969), © Betty Radice, 1963, 1969, Reproduced by permission of Penguin Books Ltd.

"Perspectives on Roman Women" by Judith P. Hallett. Original essay. "Divorce and Adultery" by Beryl Rawson. From *The Family in Ancient Rome* pp. 32-37. London: Croom Helm. © 1986 Beryl Rawson. Reprinted with permission.

"The Roman Matron" by Sarah Pomeroy. From *Goddesses, Whores, Wives and Slaves: Women in Classical Antiquity* pp. 164-172. New York: Schocken Books. © 1975 Sarah B. Pomeroy. Reprinted with the permission of Random House, Inc.

"Livia" by J. P. V. D. Balsdon. From *Roman Women: Their History and Habits* pp. 90-95. London: The Bodley Head. © 1962 J. P. V. D. Balsdon. Reprinted with the permission of the Bodley Head.

Chapter VI

"The Reign of Tiberius" by Tacitus. From *The Annals of Imperial Rome* trans. by Michael Grant (London: Penguin Classics, 1956, 1959, 1971), © Michael Grant Publications Ltd., 1956, 1959, 1971. Reproduced by permission of Penguin Books Ltd.

"Life of Tiberius" by Suetonius. Freely adapted from *Lives of the Caesars* trans. by J. C. Rolfe, Loeb Classical Library, Harvard University Press (1913). Reprinted with permission.

"In Praise of Tiberius and Sejanus" by Velleius Paterculus. From *Compendium of Roman History* 2, 71-72, 76-78, trans. by Frederick Shipley, Loeb Classical Library, Harvard University Press (1924). Reprinted with permission.

"The Psychology of Tiberius" by Gregorio Maranon. From *Tiberius: A Study in Resentment*, trans. by W. B. Wells, pp. 183-186; 199-201; 211-215. London: Hollis and Carter (1956). Reprinted with the permission of the Bodley Head on behalf of Hollis and Carter.

"The Politician Sejanus" by Thomas Africa. From *Rome of the Caesars* pp. 22-41. © 1965 John Wiley and Sons. Reprinted with the permission of Thomas Africa.

"Judgment on Tiberius" by Robin Seager. From *Tiberius* pp. 247-250. Berkeley: University of California Press. © 1972 Robin Seager. Reprinted with permission.

Chapter VII

"The Deification of Augustus" by Dio Cassius. From *Roman History* (vol. 7) 56, 46, trans. by E. Cary, Loeb Classical Library, Harvard University Press (1924). Reprinted with permission.

"The Personality of Claudius" by Vincent Scramuzza. From *The Emperor Claudius* pp. 35-50. © 1940 President and Fellows of Harvard University. Reprinted with permission.

"Claudius' Policy of Centralization" by Arnaldo Momigliano. From *Claudius, The Emperor and His Achievement* pp. 39-71, trans. by W. D. Howarth (1934). © 1934 Oxford University Press. Reprinted by permission of Oxford University Press.

"The Good and Evil of Claudius' Reign" by M. P. Charlesworth. From *Cambridge Ancient History* X (1934) 697-701. Reprinted with the permission of the Cambridge University Press.

Chapter XI

"Snobbery Begins at Rome" by J. P. V. D. Balsdon. From *Romans and Aliens* pp. 18-29. Chapel Hill: University of North Carolina Press. © Estate of J. P. V. D. Balsdon. Reprinted by permission of the University of North Carolina Press.

"Herod Agrippa" by Thomas Africa. From *Rome of the Caesars* pp. 42-61. © 1965 John Wiley and Sons. Reprinted with the permission of Thomas Africa.

"Slavery" by P. A. Brunt. From *The Romans* ed. by J. P. V. D. Balsdon pp. 182-191. © 1969 C. A. Watts & Co. Ltd. Reprinted with permission.

"The Emperor's Men: Senators, Equestrians, Freedmen and Slaves" by Richard Saller. Original essay.

"Senatorial Aristocracy Under the Emperors" by Keith Hopkins. From *Death and Renewal* pp. 171-175. Cambridge University Press. © 1983 Keith Hopkins. Reprinted with permission.

"Social Relations" by Peter Garnsey and Richard Saller. From *The Roman Empire: Economy, Society and Culture* pp. 148-159. Berkeley: University of California Press. © 1987 Peter Garnsey and Richard Saller. Reprinted with permission.

Chapter XII

"Nero's Crimes: Matricide and Arson" by Tacitus. From Tacitus: *The Annals of Imperial Rome* trans. by Michael Grant (London: Penguin Classics, 1956, 1959, 1971), © Michael Grant Publications Ltd. 1956, 1959, 1971. Reproduced by permission of Penguin Books Ltd.

"Life of Nero" by Suetonius. Freely adapted from *Lives of the Caesars* trans. by J. C. Rolfe, Loeb Classical Library, Harvard University Press (1913). Reprinted with permission.

"Nero and the Senate" by B. H. Warmington. From *Nero: Reality and Legend* pp. 21-28; 32-34; 39-42. London: Chatto & Windus. © 1969 B. H. Warmington. Reprinted with permission.

"The Courtier Seneca" by Thomas Africa. From *Rome of the Caesars* pp. 83-100. © 1965 John Wiley and Sons. Reprinted with permission of Thomas Africa.

"Conspiracy Against Nero" by Miriam Griffin. From *Nero The End of a Dynasty* (New Haven, 1984) pp. 164-169. New Haven: Yale University Press. © 1984 Miriam Griffin. Reprinted with permission.

"The Fall of Nero" by B. H. Warmington. From *Nero: Reality and Legend* pp. 163-170. London: Chatto & Windus. © 1969 B. H. Warmington. Reprinted with permission.

Illustration Acknowledgments

Frontispiece

Augustus of Prima Porta. Vatican Museum.

Photo by permission of Bildarchiv Foto, Marburg, and Art Resource, New York.

Chapter Illustrations

I am very grateful to Numismatic Fine Arts (NFA), Los Angeles, California, for photographs of coins in their collection, and to Dr. Jane Cody and Tory Fleming of NFA for their kind asssistance.

I   M. Crawsford *Roman Republican Coinage* 480, 3. Photo by NFA.

II   *Coins of the Roman Empire in the British Museum* Augustus 625. Photo by NFA.

III   *British Museum Coins Galatia, Cappadocia and Syria* p. 167, 135. Photo by NFA.

IV   *Coins of the Roman Empire in the British Museum* Augustus 624. Photo by NFA.

V   *Coins of the Roman Empire in the British Museum* Tiberius 82. Photo by NFA.

VI   *Coins of the Roman Empire in the British Museum* Tiberius 85. Photo by NFA.

VII   *Coins of the Roman Empire in the British Museum* Nero 180. Photo by NFA.

VIII   Photo by NFA.

IX   *Coins of the Roman Empire in the British Museum* Caligula 58. Photo by NFA.

X   *Coins of the Roman Empire in the British Museum* Claudius 228. Photo by NFA.

XI   *Coins of the Roman Empire in the British Museum* Tiberius 70. Photo by NFA.

XII   *Coins of the Roman Empire in the British Museum* Nero 180. Photo by NFA.